# THE ATLANTIC PROVINCES IN CONFEDERATION

# The Atlantic Provinces in Confederation

EDITED BY E.R. FORBES AND D.A. MUISE

L.D. McCANN, Cartographer
BILL PARENTEAU, Picture Editor

UNIVERSITY OF TORONTO PRESS
Toronto Buffalo London
and
ACADIENSIS PRESS
Fredericton

© University of Toronto Press Incorporated 1993
Toronto Buffalo London
Printed in Canada

ISBN 0-8020-5886-8 (cloth)
ISBN 0-8020-6817-0 (paper)

Printed on acid-free paper

**Canadian Cataloguing in Publication Data**

Main entry under title:

The Atlantic Provinces in Confederation

Includes bibliographical references and index.
ISBN 0-8020-5886-8 (bound) ISBN 0-8020-6817-0 (pbk.)

1. Atlantic Provinces – History.   2. Maritime
Provinces – History – 1867–.   3. Newfoundland –
History – 1949–.   I. Forbes, Ernest R., 1940–.
II. Muise, D.A. (Delphin Andrew), 1941–.

FC2012.A86 1993        971.5        C92-095005-1
F1035.8.A86 1993

This book was developed with the aid of grants from the Council of
Maritime Premiers and the Canadian Studies Directorate of the
Department of the Secretary of State and was published with the help of a
grant from the publications program of the Social Science Federation of
Canada, using funds provided by the Social Sciences and Humanities
Research Council of Canada. Acadiensis Press is also pleased to
acknowledge the support of the University of New Brunswick and the
Canada Council.

# Contents

# Figures

Most of the maps and diagrams produced in this book are based on original, primary research. Materials were compiled from a variety of manuscript sources housed in provincial and national archives in Halifax, Fredericton, and Ottawa. Information from government documents, especially from Statistics Canada publications, were also used. Several of the maps were adapted from *The Historical Atlas of Canada*, vol. 3, edited by D. Kerr and D. Holdsworth, and published by the University of Toronto Press. The Press graciously consented to the republication here of figures 6 (in part), 11, and 12. Ralph Kruger of the University of Waterloo provided some regional development information for Figure 13.

# Preface

The absence of a publicly accessible history of Atlantic Canada's experience within Confederation has been strongly felt for some time. Part of the predicament one faces in capturing it lies with the region's fragmented political structure and the uneven understanding of its various components. Moreover, the field was late in developing, remaining for most of the century outside the research interests of Canadian historians. The provincial histories available deal only briefly or in some specialized fashion with the post-Confederation period. This collaborative project is intended to give the public access to the scholarly research on the region, research that has flourished during the past two decades, while advancing that scholarship through synthesis, new information, and fresh interpretations.[1]

Fragmentation versus integration, plenty versus scarcity, centre versus periphery, and other models inform the analysis, which addresses fundamental questions faced by Atlantic Canadians. While the authors span the ideological spectrum from liberals to neo-marxians, all are fervently committed to furthering the understanding of the regional experience. In writing this synthesis, they have attempted more than a popularization of economic and political history; they offer as well an integrated and original analysis of the region's social and cultural experience and the responses to the forces of modernization that have transformed virtually every aspect of daily life.

The book is more, too, than a history of relations between provincial and national governments or an account of the sayings and doings of the wealthy and powerful in the region. Here ordinary people – workers, women, and ethnic and other groups – take centre stage. Their experience reveals much of the strength and resilience of Atlantic Canadians as they struggled to overcome the problems and share in the benefits of life in the Canadian community. The book also reveals something of their frustration at the limitations of life on the periphery of a much larger community's vision.

The study is produced by thirteen academics, each of whom has previously pioneered some major aspect of the region's history. Though the scholars accepted responsibility for individual decades, they were not required to write to a particular formula. All were free to highlight those developments of their decade that they believed to be most important, using the approaches and methods they deemed most appropriate. The result is variety in both focus and method, a rich tapestry in which individual chapters often emphasize and explore different aspects of the political, business, class, cultural, and gendered dimensions of the region's history, presented against the backdrop of its relations with the rest of Canada.

Despite the authors' different emphases and perspectives, the reader will find the work unified by a number of recurring themes. One of the most prominent of these is the commitment of Maritimers and, later, Atlantic Canadians to the dream of a nation extending from sea to sea and to the realization of Confederation's promise of sustained development and equal opportunity. Persistent supporters of national integration, Maritime leaders sought for their people the full benefits of national participation. There was also a strong tradition of political protest in the region. A close examination of this tradition over several decades reveals, however, that the protests were primarily expressions of frustration at the perceived exclusion of the region from the full benefits of national union. Most protesters wanted more fully in, rather than out of, Confederation.

The volume is divided into four thirty-year phases in the region's history, with each part highlighting slightly different themes. The first three decades after Confederation emphasized institutional consolidation and political integration, which set new terms for development as well as spelling out the limits of provincial action. From the 1890s through to the close of the First World War, the region responded to the opportunities offered by national expansion by developing a new industrial capacity. The third phase (1920–50) witnessed the breakdown of this new economy and the emergence of decline and marginalization as the dominant motifs. The final stage (1950–80) – with four rather than three provincial players, following Newfoundland's entry into Confederation in 1949 – featured vigorous efforts to overcome regional disparity and underdevelopment.

A problem in planning this book was how to integrate Newfoundland into the narrative. Today the community of interest among the four Atlantic provinces – at least in their relations with central metropolises and the federal government – is well recognized. All have large trade

View from the periphery. Cartoonist Robert Chambers referred to the delay in the advent of television in the Atlantic Provinces in 1950s, but the theme invoked was by this time a very familiar one.

deficits with central Canada that they finance through their international trade surpluses and the flow of transfer payments from the federal government. For most of the period of this history, however, Newfoundland was not part of Confederation; its perspective and that of Canada's three Maritime provinces diverged sharply after the latter entered the union. Since Newfoundland's entry into Confederation in 1949, areas of shared interest have re-emerged and continue to develop, but the process is a slow one. The distinctiveness of its traditions should not be underestimated. Thus, the volume includes a special chapter on Newfoundland's experience between 1867 and 1949. Only in the chapter on the 1860s and in those on the decades after 1949 has the Newfoundland experience been integrated with that of the remainder of the region.

This book could not have happened without the help of more people than one could readily mention here. Virgil Duff, then of Macmillan of Canada, first charged the two editors to produce a regional history. They in turn spread the responsibility among others in the field. Phillip Buckner organized the conference for the initial integration of chapters. Critics included David Bell, Gwen Davies, Ron Labelle, Ken MacKinnon, Ian Robertson, W.Y. Smith, Janet Toole, and Murray Young – several of whom later supplied formal critiques on later drafts of the manuscript. Individual authors drew financial support for their research from their universities and such granting agencies as the Social Sciences and Humanities Research Council of Canada (SSHRCC). Meanwhile they received the customary high level of service from archives and libraries within the region and at Ottawa. The SSHRCC, *Acadiensis*, and the University of New Brunswick funded the initial conference. More than twenty-five individuals wrote to the Council of Maritime Premiers in support of our request for a grant to aid in the preparation of our manuscript. The council came through with a generous grant, which was then matched with funds from the Canadian Studies Directorate of the federal department of the secretary of state. Maps for the project were funded in part by the Centre for Canadian Studies at Mount Allison University and drafted by Cartographic Services, Department of Geography, at the University of Alberta. At the University of Toronto Press, Gerry Hallowell provided constant support. Margaret Allen's careful copy-editing saved us all from innumerable errors. To all those who donated time and other assistance in support of this volume, the authors wish to express their sincere gratitude.

# THE ATLANTIC PROVINCES IN CONFEDERATION

# *Prologue*
## The Atlantic Colonies
## before Confederation

Diversity and fragmentation characterized the geography of Nova Scotia, New Brunswick, Prince Edward Island, and Newfoundland. Their best farming lands were concentrated in Nova Scotia's Annapolis Valley, New Brunswick's Saint John River Valley, and most of Prince Edward Island. Except for margins bordering rivers and lakes, the rest of the region held mostly poor soil, at least in terms of its capacity to support the wheat-based agriculture that Europeans hoped to establish in North America. The region's quite variable climate featured shorter growing seasons than the more continental areas of North America, a factor that reduced agricultural possibilities still further. Nevertheless, a majority of the region's early settlers – outside Newfoundland at least – made their livelihoods as farmers. From the earliest times, agriculture was supplemented by a rich fishery, and by the early nineteenth century the region's forests would be brought into play as a third major resource.[1] Unlike the fur trade, which depended on the labour of Native peoples, fishing and forestry attracted large numbers of European workers to harvest and process resources for export, thus encouraging colonization.

The first peoples in the Atlantic region, however, were probably the Micmacs, a migratory people who for several hundred years before arrival of the Europeans in the sixteenth century were established at the most advantageous spots throughout much of Nova Scotia, Prince Edward Island, and New Brunswick; Micmac territory included parts of western Newfoundland, as well. They pursued both the coastal and riverine fisheries and hunted game throughout the interior of the region. The Saint John River and its tributaries were home to the Maliseet, another Algonkian people who, though they differed in language from their Micmac cousins, shared with them a common material culture and world view. By the early nineteenth century, the Beothuks, Newfoundland's major aboriginal group, had been eliminated through the combined pressure of economic competition, disease, and violence; in the

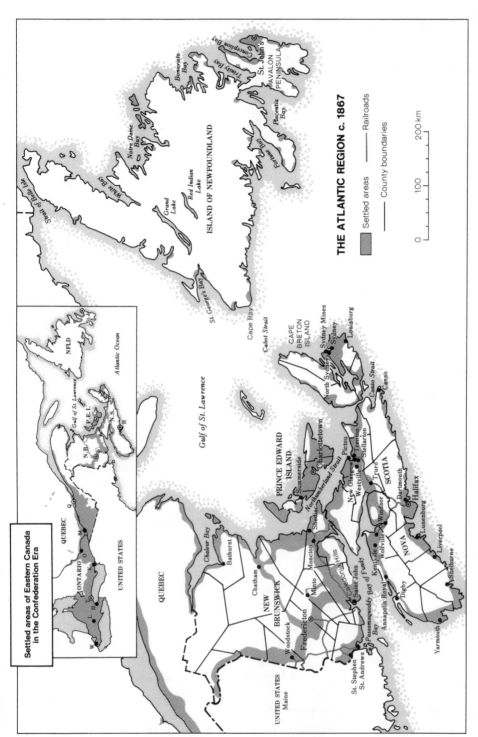

Figure 1 The Atlantic Canada region at the time of Confederation

Maritimes the Maliseet and Micmac were pushed to the margins of society, increasingly confined to reserved lands where they became charges upon the dominant community. Natives, by and large, had co-operated with European settlers, who had responded to their openness by gobbling up available land and resources with utter disregard for their rights – usually with disastrous results for the 'People of the Dawn,' as Natives characterized themselves.[2]

Early in the seventeenth century a small group of French immigrants – the Acadians – became the first permanent European settlers in what would become Nova Scotia. As agents of French imperial policy designed to claim the territory for France, they represented the first wave to introduce European notions of land ownership and national sovereignty, thereby challenging the existing Native world view regarding the disposition of land and resources. The Acadians gradually developed a series of self-sufficient agricultural communities along the Bay of Fundy, where the fertile marshes and high tides ensured healthy grain surpluses to trade for New England manufactures. In 1713, at the conclusion of one of the succession of wars between Britain and France, mainland Acadia passed permanently under British control. A half-century later during the final stages of that struggle, which by then was for control of the entire continent, the Acadian settlers professed their neutrality and refused to take up arms against France. In 1755, following a decade of turmoil, they were brutally expelled from their Fundyside communities, a dislocation from which they would be slow to recover. Following the cessation of hostilities, some made their way back to the region, but they found their lands taken up by newcomers and were forced to retreat to more marginal areas, such as Digby County in Nova Scotia or New Brunswick's northeastern shore.[3]

The Acadians' farms had been occupied by several thousand New England 'Planters,' who brought their experience in fishing, lumbering, and trading, as well as an enthusiasm for dissenting Protestant religion. They also brought a century and more of the colonial experience of self-government, which they demanded be delivered to the colony they were helping to form. Attracted as well by the inshore fishery, many New Englanders established new communities, among them Yarmouth and Liverpool, on Nova Scotia's 'South Shore.' Halifax had been founded there more than a decade before, in 1749, to counter French military strength at Louisbourg. A few years later, Lunenburg was established to the south-west of Halifax by several hundred German-speaking Protestants.[4]

In the American Revolutionary War (1775–83) Nova Scotia's 'Yankees,' who might have been expected to sympathize with their rebellious American brethren, were cowed by the strength of Britain's naval fortress at Halifax. The rebels' success in the older colonies brought about 30,000 refugee Loyalists to Nova Scotia, more than doubling the colony's population. About 3,000 of these were Black colonists – slaves or ex-slaves who had achieved their freedom by fighting on the British side. In seeking compensation for the losses incurred by their support of the British cause, the Loyalists demanded land grants and preference in the filling of colonial offices. They secured a division of the larger colony of Nova Scotia by the separation of New Brunswick, which became a Loyalist preserve. Cape Breton was also set aside as a Loyalist enclave at this time, though it was later (1820) restored to Nova Scotia. The Loyalists' conspicuous support for the Crown would guarantee them a dominant role in regional politics for some time to come.[5]

Other major waves of settlers to the Maritime colonies came from Scotland and Ireland. Most, starting with the Scots who arrived at Pictou before the American Revolution in 1774, settled along the shores of the Gulf of St Lawrence, including much of Prince Edward Island and Cape Breton. The area also became a magnet to recently disbanded soldiers who had fought in the American Revolution or the Napoleonic Wars. Presbyterians settled in Pictou and north along the shoreline; Roman Catholics established themselves near Antigonish and spread eastward towards Cape Breton. This pattern of establishing communities according to ethnic or religious adherence was continued over the next half-century as new waves of Scottish settlement filled in the area.[6] Meanwhile, New Brunswick received a larger proportion of the Protestant and Irish Catholics, with the latter forming substantial communities in Halifax and Saint John.

Prince Edward Island, which was separated from Nova Scotia in 1769, evolved as a distinctly different experiment in colonial development after British administrators were convinced to attempt a 'proprietorial' system of land ownership. In 1767 the island had been surveyed into sixty-eight lots, which were granted to proprietors on condition that they bring out Protestant settlers and pay taxes (quit rents) to maintain the government.[7] This system, which was intended to replicate the stratified social structure of rural Britain, ended up rewarding a small number of court favourites and speculators with large and potentially profitable land grants in America. Unfortunately for the Island, this anachronism stuck. Loyalists, Scots, Irish, and Acadians who made their way there found it impossible to gain title to lands they often worked hard to improve. Proprietors' failure to pay required taxes or bring out sufficient immigrants gave settlers a rationale to demand 'escheat,' a legal process through which unimproved land could be returned to the Crown, presumably to be placed under control of local people. British officials sympathized with both the proprietors and the clique that controlled local government. The latter were so concerned to get lands for themselves that they failed to resolve the issue, which came to dominate Island affairs for the next hundred years.[8]

Newfoundland, reaching much farther out into the Atlantic than the other colonies, was at once the newest and oldest of Britain's North American colonies. Adventurers from Britain and France had attempted colonies there throughout the seventeenth century, but it never really escaped description as a wharf for the thousands of fishermen who came each spring from west country British ports or from the west of France to exploit the rich cod fishery. The European countries discouraged settlement in order to restrict the fishery to a transoceanic trade and reserve its benefits for themselves. Nevertheless, English and Irish immigrants slowly settled along the southeastern coasts, spreading in time around the whole island and into southern Labrador. Government was sparse and distant, the British authorities being unwilling to provide more administration than was necessary for what was supposed to be a migratory fishery, and the merchants unwilling to pay for it. By 1815, the migratory fishery had been replaced by a resident fishery, however, and St John's had emerged as a busy entrepôt and a naval base of some significance.[9] Constitutional change followed hesitantly, and in response to increasing pressure from St John's. In 1817, the governor was instructed to remain at his post all year; in 1824, Newfoundland received Crown colony status; and in 1832 representative government. As elsewhere in British North America, power ultimately rested with a relatively small group of officials and merchants, whose power was not effectively challenged until the arrival of responsible government in the mid-1850s. Even then, Newfoundlanders' ability to plan for their future was to some extent limited by French fishing rights on the west coast and the northern peninsula, deriving from the Treaty of Utrecht (1713), which in other respects recognized British sovereignty over the island.[10]

All four colonies enjoyed constitutions similar to a British model; each had a governor, guided in his actions by a series of letters and instructions from the Colonial Office. They were to be assisted by executive councils appointed to advise and to administer the various departments. Each colony as well had two legislative bodies; one (the legislative council) was appointed by the British government, on the recommendation of the governor. Legislative assemblies were elected in a rough replication of Britain's House of Commons. This constitutional establishment, designed in the late eighteenth century, was intended to keep colonies in a state of political equilibrium and avoid those 'excesses of democracy' that many felt had been responsible for the American Revolution. Political life in the Atlantic colonies evolved around interactions among these institutions, which came to represent the interests of different groups. In all colonies contests for influence and patronage were complicated by the tendency of governors, who were usually in a colony for only a few years, to depend on the support of the office-holding élites with which they socialized. When these councillors and officials used their positions to advance their own interests, the basis for clashes within the assemblies was laid. Generally, councillors became associated with the Conservative Party, known colloquially as the 'Tories.' Assemblymen who opposed them took on the name of 'Reformers' and evolved into the Liberal Party.

Lord Durham's pivotal 1839 report on the rebellions in Upper and Lower Canada focused attention on the need for constitutional change in the Atlantic colonies as well. His solution to conflict between elected assemblies and appointed councils, which he saw as the nub of colonial political disputes, was to extend a fuller version of British constitutional practice to the colonies. The colonial governors, he argued, like the monarch back home, should be required to choose executive counsellors from the group or party holding a majority in the elected assembly. He was responding to a position being advanced by 'Reform' politicians throughout the colonies, who characterized themselves as representatives of the 'common people.' If councils were unable to sustain support from a majority of assemblymen, reformers argued, they should be forced to resign in favour of a new set who could. In this way governments would be made more 'responsible' through their elected representatives. This demand for 'responsible government' animated reformers across the colonies through the 1840s; it was introduced to Nova Scotia and New Brunswick in 1848; and to Prince Edward Island and Newfoundland a few years later.[11]

Limited self-government coincided with the arrival of profound changes in the economic organization of the Empire. Spearheaded by the demands of a rising middle class in Britain's manufacturing cities, a campaign for free trade swept away the protective tariffs under which colonial staples like fish, wheat, and timber had enjoyed privileged access to British markets. This created a profound panic among merchants who had risen to prominence on the basis of such access, especially in New Brunswick where the removal of timber duties seemed to portend disaster. In 1854, however, the local panic was eased in part when British negotiators secured greater access to American markets for colonial staples through a reciprocal free-trade treaty that included timber, coal, fish, and farm products. Reciprocity, the Crimean War and, in the early 1860s, the American Civil War all contributed to an inflationary spiral that bestowed a period of prosperity on the colonies. A key ingredient of this transition was the emergence of a powerful locally based merchant marine that carried regional produce and also made regionally based shippers a force to be reckoned with in the large international carrying trade of the time.[12] Later generations would look back upon this era as the region's 'golden age.'

Though they had few direct connections with each other, the four Atlantic colonies shared institutional perspectives derived from their ties to Britain. Particularism was reinforced by years of separate existence, as well as by the conflicting interests of political leaders unable to agree on social and economic policies. Each colony was poised between the limits of a colonial past and the independence accompanying the newly won freedom and maturity under responsible government. At the same time, fluctuating prices for fish and timber on international markets exposed the weakness of continued dependence on such fragile realities for regional prosperity.[13]

Through the 1850s the burning issue in Nova Scotia and New Brunswick became railway development. After failing to agree on distribution of the costs of constructing the Intercolonial line to link them with Canada, the two colonies had embarked on their own more limited railways, linking Halifax with Truro and Windsor and Saint John with Moncton and Shediac. There also emerged a cadre of politicians who had not experienced the struggle over responsible government and who were prepared to look to the future with the interests of their colonies to the fore. They began to lead political discussions into new paths – paths that came to include new schemes for economic development, railway expansion, and intercolonial union.

PART ONE
CONSOLIDATING THE UNION, 1867–1890

# CHAPTER ONE

# The 1860s
## Forging the Bonds of Union

Analyses of Atlantic Canada's experience of Confederation often emphasize dislocations within the regional community after 1867. These visions of Confederation's consequences in terms of underdevelopment and regional disparity also inform discussions of events surrounding the achievement of union in the 1860s. On the surface, a reluctant group of disparate and fragmented Atlantic colonies were hustled into an unequal union with Canada for which they were not prepared. By some accounts, they were pushed into it by anxious colonial administrators, ambitious Canadian politicians searching for solutions to their internal problems, and concern about the increasing bellicosity of the United States, which had just emerged from its civil war and was nursing a grudge against Britain for having supported the rebellious South. Yet, whatever the external inducements or pressures, collusion by local politicians was a precondition for Confederation's first stages.[1]

The emergence of a new middle class, composed of locally born leaders prepared to make the colonies the main focus of their political and social endeavours, was the most important factor in the success of union in Nova Scotia and New Brunswick. This group, which had come to dominate political and economic life in those colonies, still occasionally represented British mercantile interests in the older style of paternalistic politics. More frequently, though, they were advocates for local community interests. This meant that their perspective on the potentials and promises of their colonies was vastly different from that of the older politicians of the pre-1850s era for whom the emphasis was on the exploitation of local resources in order to maximize profit for faraway investors. In such colonies an older perspective was often represented by merchants who had profited most from the staples trade and feared any disruption to their freedom to extract profit from the exchange of goods.

In Nova Scotia and New Brunswick, Joseph Howe and Charles Fisher, victors in the struggle for responsible government, pushed their colonies to accept public construction of railways as an instrument of development. They and their supporters were prepared to increase public debt in the hope of stimulating new resource development and of opening new areas for settlement. They were fearful of the consequences of continued dependence on resource extraction and wanted to expand the economic and social opportunities within their provinces. Behind this strategy was the idea that improvements to landward transportation were a necessity if isolated communities were to be linked into a network of economic interaction. These ideas were very much part of an international preoccupation with the transforming potential of steam technology. There was, however, basic disagreement over government's role in such endeavours.[2]

In Prince Edward Island and Newfoundland, where the vexing land questions took centre stage, railways were hardly an issue. In Prince Edward Island, the British refused to interfere with the rights of the (often absentee) landowners, in spite of repeated attempts by colonial legislators to find some resolution to what they saw as a debilitating brake on the Island's potential for 'development.' In Newfoundland, where the 'French Shore' comprised almost a third of the coastline and restricted access to some of the most productive fisheries, several attempts by the local legislature to limit these privileges were blocked by British officials determined to avoid any confrontation with their French allies.

So, in spite of disparities in terms of potential development strategies, considerable argument was occurring over the future of the colonies. Before discussing the working through of those vital debates, we must turn briefly to the social and economic background of the Atlantic colonies on the eve of Confederation.[3]

PEOPLE AND PLACES OF THE ATLANTIC COLONIES

Atlantic colonists remained largely rural in orientation at mid-century, their populations thinly stretched the better to exploit the narrow bands of seaward and landward resources bordering the coastal areas and great rivers. Out of a total population of less than a million in 1861, slightly more than a third lived in Nova Scotia and about a quarter in New Brunswick; Newfoundland held about 140,000 and Prince Edward Island approximately 80,000. By 1871 combined populations had increased to more than a million, with roughly the same proportions (see Graph 1). The vast majority were native born, of British stock, and about evenly split among English, Irish, and Scottish, though the proportions of each fluctuated from province to province. Most of those claiming

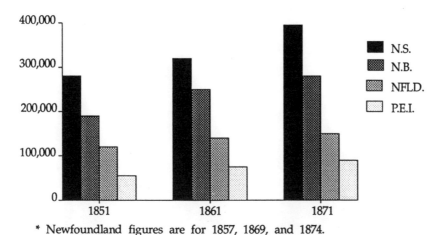

* Newfoundland figures are for 1857, 1869, and 1874.

Graph 1 Population growth in the Atlantic colonies, 1851–1871

English ancestry in the southern halves of Nova Scotia and New Brunswick were in fact descended from Americans who had settled there almost a century earlier. New Brunswick's large Irish minority had resulted from a large-scale immigration associated with that province's active timber trade during the 1830s and 1840s. The numerous Scots in the northern sectors of Nova Scotia and on Prince Edward Island had arrived mostly before the 1840s. Newfoundland's population was overwhelmingly English and Irish in origin, descendants of migrants who had come there over the years to exploit the island's large fishing industry (see Graph 2).

By mid-century, all three Maritime colonies had significant Acadian minorities, people who had either escaped the expulsion or had returned to their homelands following the cessation of hostilities between France and Britain a century earlier. They tended to be located in isolated pockets in southern and northern Nova Scotia, in northern Prince Edward Island and, in their greatest numbers, along the north shore of New Brunswick. Roman Catholic in religion, they had remained outside the mainstream of the predominantly Protestant and British political and cultural life of the colonies. In the 1860s a transformation, brought about by a church-centred 'Renaissance,' resulted in the founding of a French-language newspaper and a series of church appointments that gave Acadians more control over their religious and cultural institutions. This transformation would soon lead to a more active defence of their political and social rights within the various provinces.[4]

Neither Halifax nor Saint John, the region's two major cities, had yet surpassed thirty thousand people; and hardly any other town in the region had more than a couple of thousand inhabitants. St John's, New-

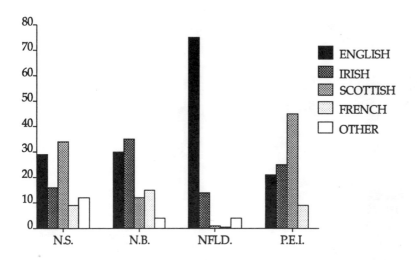

Graph 2  Ethnic origins of Atlantic colonists, 1861 (Newfoundland, 1874)

foundland's most significant town, with about fifteen thousand people, directed the bulk of the colony's overseas export trade in fish, but most actual production was carried out by migratory workers and occurred in tiny villages nestled in harbours and bays along the south and east coasts or far away on the Labrador coast. Though much of the fish never even passed through the capital, virtually the whole process was controlled by the small number of merchants there. Charlottetown, reflecting Prince Edward Island's relative underdevelopment, was little more than a large village of a few thousand. So the urban face of the region was hardly very developed; and there was still little to connect communities to one another, apart from the drive of merchants in the entrepôts to maximize the profits from the exploitation of resources. Still, the embryo of an urban system was forming as the profits from the carrying trade based on locally built, manned, and operated sailing ships were invested in the communities to produce necessary institutions and local services. Yarmouth and Pictou, at opposite ends of mainland Nova Scotia, were among the most developed communities in this regard. By mid-century both were moving beyond the fixation with staples extraction to more diverse economies and greater control over their local affairs. Within all these towns distinctions between those who had wealth and those who did not were becoming more palpable, creating the seeds of class-based frictions that would blossom decades later.[5]

The larger towns had comparatively diverse ethnic and religious populations, while smaller towns and rural areas tended to be fairly homogeneous. Roman Catholics were the largest single group in all four colonies – as they were in most of the larger towns – though significant

William Hall, a Nova Scotian, was awarded the Victoria Cross for heroism during the Indian Mutiny. The first soldier outside Britain to receive the award, he is commemorated by this sculpture exhibited at the Black Cultural Centre in Cherry Brook, just outside Dartmouth.

divisions existed among French, Irish, and Scots, with the Irish hierarchy taking precedence in most political interventions. The largest Protestant sects were the Presbyterians, Baptists, and Methodists. The Anglicans, though the smallest Protestant group in the Maritimes, included an élite who were thought to exercise an influence out of proportion to their numbers. Part of that image was a consequence of Britain's earlier insistence on the role of the Anglican church in the constitutional establishment of the various colonies, and the public support given to the church's expansion. In Newfoundland, by contrast, Anglicans were the largest Protestant denomination, the Methodists making up the second group. Religion may have been the most important determinant of social and cultural norms within the colonies. It marked the significant passages in an individual's life, from baptism to marriage to death, as well as providing the bulk of social services that today are associated with the state. At mid-century, as colonists began to struggle with the limits of and potential for self-government, disagreement erupted over how far the state could go in taking over responsibilities long seen to have been part of the churches' role. The relationship of religion to politics was problematic; reflecting the deep-seated community basis of life in the nineteenth century. Advocacy of fundamental political and religious freedoms was a preoccupation of dissenting Protestant religions, such as the Baptists and Methodists, who demanded the separation of church and state and called for non-denominational schooling for all. Over the course of the 1850s, as an offshoot of a Protestant revival, the practice

The Halifax Public Market, c. 1860. Urban markets provided the opportunity for the sale of handicrafts by people who lived on the fringe of larger towns.

of giving privileges to Roman Catholics and Anglicans in the form of public support for church-run education began to be questioned. Generally, Anglicans and Catholics were seen to be supporters of the more conservative political agendas of the Tory Party, while dissenting Protestants were more likely to support the Liberals. But there were so many exceptions to this pattern that it would be foolhardy to make any definitive statements, except to say that religious questions were central issues in the public life of the colonies.[6]

### DEPENDENT ECONOMIES AND INDEPENDENT WORKERS

Across the entire region, the economy was dominated by merchants who specialized in marketing the region's timber, fish, and agricultural staples throughout expanding North Atlantic markets. These staples generally required little investment in fixed capital, save for extensive shipping, with the producing communities remaining separate 'resource enclaves.' Through their ownership of large ocean-going vessels, merchants were able to control producers' access to markets abroad, collaborating with each other in price fixing as well. Involvement in the

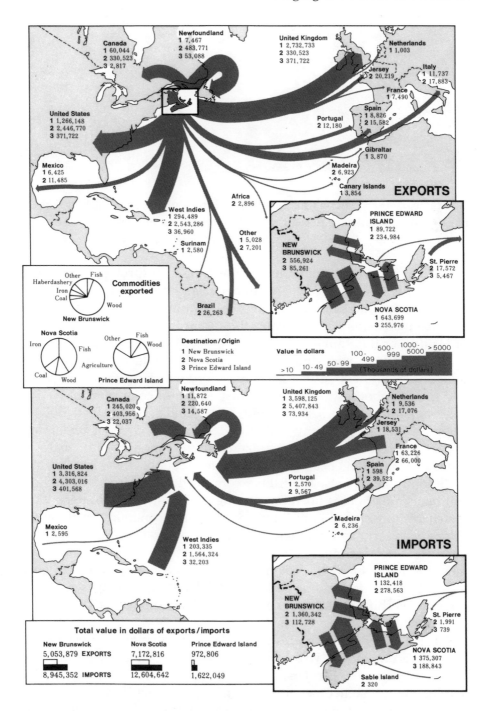

Figure 2  The Maritimes in the North Atlantic economy, 1864

Cod table, c. 1875. Though men usually did most of the actual fishing, pre-paring fish for market required the work of all family members.

same markets overseas often linked them together through their British sponsors, whose collusion with imperial authorities allowed them to control the political life of the colonies. The most prominent of these regional merchants – men such as the Cunard brothers or Enos Collins of Halifax, or the Rankine and Gilmore families, who controlled much of the Saint John and Miramichi rivers' timber industries on behalf of their British partners – used their connections with large overseas trading and financial houses to dictate the disposition of colonial assets.[7]

Economically as well as socially, Newfoundland remained isolated from the other three Atlantic colonies. Its singular economic orientation around the cod fishery was augmented by its rich harvest of seals, an industry whose larger capital requirements brought even closer control by St John's merchants. The fishery continued to be dominated by English mercantile houses operating through resident agents or dependent merchants, positioned in St John's or at smaller communities along the colony's eastern and southern coasts. St John's merchants jealously guarded their near-monopoly control over a trade that was one of the most profitable in all the colonies during good times, even though it was subject to drastic fluctuations caused by bad fishing seasons or tumultuous shifts in the very competitive international markets for cod overseas.[8]

Outside larger urban centres a 'truck' system dominated most aspects of staple economies. It was a complex system, operating with little exchange of currency. Farmers, fishermen, and lumber producers traded surplus output, sometimes in the form of their own labour power, in exchange for credit at merchants' stores. This credit was, in turn, used to acquire sugar or flour as well as necessary fishing gear, axes, or other equipment. These were mostly metal goods of one form or another that the settlers were unable to fabricate for themselves, though increasingly such implements began to be made in the larger colonial towns. Merchants maximized profit by paying as little as possible for fish or timber and charging as much as they could for imported goods. They seldom absolutely controlled this process, for they in turn were part of another chain of dependency stretching across the Atlantic to the heart of the imperial trading system. Success for merchants and producers alike depended on quality of product and skill at gauging markets; these were often quite problematic given the long delays that could be encountered in preparing and transporting goods in advance of their sale.[9]

Seasonal work by settlers away from farms or villages was directed by merchants who needed their casual labour – sometimes along with that of their horses or oxen – to produce timber or fish for market. Younger men, in fact, might often work at several jobs on a seasonal basis as they sought the sort of financial independence that would permit them to set up their own households. While begun as a temporary expedient to accumulate the funds necessary to establish farms or fishing stations of their own, this 'occupational plurality' often became a permanent feature of many regional workers' experience. Woods work, an exclusively male preserve, was often pursued by farmers and others in search of employment during the winter months. In early spring, however, when the winter's harvest was floated down snow-swollen spring rivers, logging work could, if stretched too far into spring, compromise the planting of new crops. In spite of negative commentaries on the impact of woods work on farming, the two generally complemented one another. There was also a tendency for poorer farmers, generally those who had arrived later, to barter their labour to their more affluent neighbours for surplus output.[10]

Wherever fishing was conducted from small boats near to the shore, the unit of production was the family, whose head owned or mortgaged both boat and equipment and whose male and female members caught, cured, and prepared fish for sale to merchants who would in turn sell it on international markets.[11] The annual round was adjusted to migrations of different marketable species – cod in spring and autumn, mackerel in the summer, and seals in early spring. Workers generally spent the winters repairing gear or in woods work that supported the subsistence basis of their small communities. Fishermen, like farmers and timbermen, required extensions of credit to function. Such situations created one-sided dependencies, where arbitrary price settings or highly idiosyncratic judgments regarding the quality and value of catches could spell the difference between bare survival and some sort of prosperity for the supposedly independent fishermen. In practice unhappy producers' only recourse was to remove themselves from the community. There were seldom competing merchants in the isolated fishing or farm villages; and producers remained unable to co-operate in marketing their own catches because of their lack of access to the ships that were necessary to carry produce to foreign markets. Constant indebtedness was commonplace enough to make the lives of most fishermen and farmers more precarious than they would have liked.[12]

Prior to mid-century, opportunities for regular paid work in towns were intermittent for all but the most skilled, who were often self-employed artisans. Port towns needed large labour pools when fish or timber had to be loaded, but there was constant conflict over how much shore labour was to be performed by sailors and how much by gangs of shore-based workers.[13] Public construction provided only occasional employment before railway building began in the 1850s; there were few of the massive public-works projects of the sort initiated by canal building in Canada. The constant rebuilding of the Halifax citadel along with other harbour defence works throughout the region created some jobs; but much of that work was contracted to skilled masons brought out specially for the job, or was done by soldiers as part of their daily round of work at the site. Halifax and Saint John grew appreciably during the 1850s and early 1860s, with the construction of churches, banks, and commercial buildings, as well as a number of government structures, such as Halifax's new Rockport Prison, and the Asylum for the Insane in Saint John. While this activity brought hundreds of new skilled workers to those port cities, finding steady work remained a problem for the mass of the working classes.[14]

Only when workers were concentrated for protracted periods or if their skills were in high demand could they demand higher wages or other improvements in the conditions of their labour. Sailing vessels, which were still manned largely by local labour prior to Confederation, bound thousands of young men in paternalistic relationships in a pre-industrial setting aboard ships captained by men from their own communities. At sea, work patterns were dictated by traditions inhibiting any worker action against the iron rule of 'Bluenose' captains. Yet early employment at sea introduced many a young Maritimer to his first experience of working for wages and conditioned many to expect more on their return to land. When such expectations were not met, the result was often migration out of the home community or even from the region.[15] Coal mining, begun haphazardly in Pictou and Cape Breton counties in Nova Scotia in the early part of the century, took off after 1827 when the British-based General Mining Association (GMA) imported experienced British mine engineers and miners and large doses of new technology and cash to sink deep mines. With a monopoly over the province's mineral resources and the promise of expanding markets in the United States, the comany was hopeful of making the coal mines

Saint John waterfront, c. 1860. Saint John's busy docks were controlled by powerful merchants, who directed much of New Brunswick's political and economic life as well.

a paying proposition. The miners were used to the piece-work practices typical of independent commodity production. They also brought long-established traditions of collective solidarity in the management of their workplaces, insisting on their exclusive right to cut coal below ground. Though able to defend their interests in times of high demand, they could not control access to the pits by hordes of unskilled labourers during periods of expansion, or after 1858, when the GMA lost its monopoly and the mines increased dramatically in numbers. Overall, miner solidarity, reinforced by a common British background and an interdependence that came from a sometimes brutal living and working experience, was unique to the region.[16]

Ship building was the most significant and widespread manufacturing industry in the region throughout the century. It required large numbers of highly skilled men, but their work tended to be seasonal and widely dispersed through the region. Centres like Saint John, where up to 50 per cent of tonnage produced in the region was finished and registered, developed a large and multi-skilled work-force. For all that, however,

Launching the *Maggie Chapman*, Dorchester, N.B., 1868. Completion of a large vessel, which could take up to a year to build, usually prompted a celebration by entire communities.

ship work remained a highly transient profession, with large numbers of workers moving in and out of a given shipyard over the course of a year. The scarcity of certain types of workers, such as riggers and caulkers, and the high demand for their services at key times of the year led to some collective bargaining, but no permanent or sustained labour organizations emerged. It was in fact more common for vessels to be manufactured as a community effort in smaller towns, where seasonal workers would be directed by a small number of master builders, with the ships moved for final finishing to larger yards of the sort available in Saint John or Halifax. By mid-century the practice of building ships primarily for foreign buyers was giving way to construction for local ownership.[17]

Across the broad spectrum of the work world, there was very little labour organization. In fact, labour unions as such were outlawed by statute until a decade after Confederation. If, periodically, workers defended their work practices or demanded increases in their wages through

Corpus Christi celebrations, Kingsclear, N.B., 1887. Each June, New Brunswick's Maliseet Indians held a formal meeting near Fredericton. There, Native people from widely scattered settlements exchanged information, had their children baptized, formalized weddings, and generally renewed their sense of community.

stoppages or confrontations, as in the case of the shipwrights and caulkers at Saint John or the coal miners of Cape Breton in 1864, they as often as not met brutal repression from troops called in to protect the capitalists' property; this was particularly true in coal mining.[18] If there was a scarcity of labour unions in the sense in which we know them today, class distinctions were nevertheless firmly entrenched. On the surface, however, there existed few barriers to upward mobility, except for the racial and ethnic discrimination against the Black, Native, and Acadian populations. It also became increasingly difficult for more recent arrivals to achieve the personal independence that immigration to America held out to them. Among the British element, the Irish were particularly disadvantaged, partly because of their later arrival and partly because of their Roman Catholic religion.[19]

Gender divisions were another source of inequality, one that bisected all social classes. Women were denied the vote in most instances, were legally wards of their fathers or husbands and, except for widows in special circumstances, could not control their own property. Men and women followed separate work patterns; women spun and wove cloth in rural areas, helped to cure fish during the busy season, and did all the day to day activities necessary to the success of farms throughout the region. They had few opportunities for employment outside their own homes, save as domestic servants in the houses of more well-to-do people, and that only before marriage or in the event of a breakdown of the family through the death of the husband.[20] Robert Sedgewick, a Presbyterian minister, articulated the prevailing ideology that woman's place was in the home in an address (later published as a pamphlet) at Halifax in 1856. He argued that women should concentrate on providing a nurturing and uplifting influence on their children and husbands, and that all society would benefit from their doing so. In his view, women had no place in politics, the law courts, factories, mines, fisheries, or the timber trade.[21]

Sedgewick allowed one exception only. Woman's sphere could include social-reform activities such as fighting for temperance or for the closure of brothels. At mid-century women were still on the fringes of these great reform movements, though they would come to occupy a more central place in succeeding decades. This 'cult of domesticity' was not without its challengers, such as the anonymous Halifax woman who, in another pamphlet, called for equal rights for women in higher education, an appeal that received a favourable response from the Methodist conference, which voted for a women's college at Mount Allison.[22] The more common early feminist approach accepted the doctrine of separate spheres, while working to expand women's public role and influence in the name of good works and reform.[23]

The burgeoning economy of the 1850s and 1860s demanded all the human resources available, but the staples trades that were the backbone of regional productivity were notoriously fickle; a year of plenty was all too likely to be followed by a year of want. The middle classes were cushioned against these fluctuations by their wealth. On the other hand, marginal agricultural areas were unable to provide sufficient land for the next generation, and a demographic quandary loomed. As emigration to the United States increasingly became the outlet of choice for the excess populations during periods of economic downturn, politicians began to wonder about the future of their communities. Unless there was some change in the economic structure to provide more jobs, a serious crisis was inevitable.[24]

TOWARDS A CLIMATE OF REFORM

In the early 1860s reform-minded politicians worried over the potential economic disruption should the United States withdraw from the Re-

ciprocity Treaty. Termination of the treaty became a very strong possibility once the Civil War confirmed the power of the North, with its
protectionist orientation. The colonies and Britain began to consider
alternative political alignments. Britain hoped that some form of political
union of the colonies would allow it to reduce its liabilities for governing
them while retaining their involvement within the imperial economy.
The advocates of union seemed determined to infuse their communities
with new purpose. Little distress had accompanied implementation of
responsible government in the Atlantic colonies, which is not to say
there was not considerable disagreement over political alternatives. For
some political leaders, union emerged as a way of achieving certain
objectives, such as the Intercolonial Railway, that had proved impossible
under separate and dependent status. For the two Canadas a federal
type of union, which could separate the two warring colonies, offered
an escape from their political impasse; such a union would also further
economic progress, hitherto blocked by French-Canadian solidarity. A
federal union would thus overcome a major constitutional barrier to
economic progress.[25]

Britain's outlook towards its colonies was transformed by its support
of railway development. Gradually, the Colonial Office came to agree
with Britain's capitalist class, which had come to view the colonies in
North America primarily as consumers of capital and technology rather
than as suppliers of raw materials. The closed mercantilist system of the
early Empire was dismantled as 'free trade' lessened Britain's dependence on colonies as safe sources of raw materials. Railways were an
expensive proposition for Nova Scotia and New Brunswick; in acquiring
the long-term debts that such investment entailed the colonies became
more and more like Canada in requiring steadily increasing taxation to
fund their new liabilities. A new dependence on British banks gradually
forced consideration of political action in light of this need.[26]

So long as the sale of timber, fish, and agricultural staples had determined the region's ideological perspective, few had challenged the
certainties of continuing to export resources in exchange for manufactured goods. The emergence of another vision, one promoting a more
diverse economy, was tied to the construction of railways and other
improvements. Optimism was tempered by a fear of the consequences
of inaction; to avoid collapse from the carrying charges on their bonds,
railway builders needed continuous expansion or the delicate mechanisms of borrowing in anticipation of growing revenues. Failure to meet
revenue needs had by 1860 forced modest increases in *ad valorem* tariffs
in both Nova Scotia and New Brunswick. Because of reciprocity, the
new taxes were levied almost exclusively on manufactured goods, thereby
giving a slight incentive to locally based producers of consumer goods.

New ideas about the state's role in transforming the life of communities were first tested in such areas as education and temperance. While most people concurred that a literate and temperate community was a laudable objective, agreement was harder to reach about who could best implement universal programs, what levels of compulsion were appropriate, and how such programs should be funded. Together these issues tested the limits of a colonial government's capacity to tax and to impose responsibilities and liabilities across the community. Ethnic and religious diversity further complicated the task of legislation in such sensitive areas. Beliefs about the rights of individuals to choose the form of their children's education or to produce and consume intoxicating liquor without interference from outside authority were deeply ingrained and strongly held. State intervention in such matters struck at the vaunted 'individualism' that was supposed to characterize colonial communities and reflected the preoccupations of a primarily urban governing élite concerned about the social problems they were encountering in the towns. Churches, which had acted as educators and moral arbiters over the previous century, became active in politics, heightening Protestant-Catholic tensions.[27]

In education, all three Maritime provinces would arrive at systems featuring compulsory local taxation for provincially administered common schools, with mandatory attendance at younger ages. They also found compromises that allowed publicly supported Catholic schools where numbers and interest warranted, though considerable disagreement occurred over the extent of support, as well as the degree of freedom local authorities would have to disburse funds levied at the local level for education. While Prince Edward Island introduced a form of compulsory education in 1851, it was less successfully applied than the legislation indicated.[28] Nova Scotia implemented a more demanding system in 1864 and 1865, following a decade of furious debate between various Catholic and Protestant activists over a common curriculum for such schools and the nature and form of any religious instruction that might occur there. New Brunswick's implementation of its comparable system did not occur until the 1870s. The delay was due to problems related to rights for Catholics in Saint John and along the north shore.[29] In Newfoundland, an inadequate government education grant was split proportionately between the Roman Catholic and the Protestant denominations. During the 1860s, a campaign by Anglicans for their own separate schools was temporarily suspended. Outside major centres the rate of illiteracy was very high, though starting to decline.[30]

Temperance was probably as important a social issue at mid-century as education. Alcohol abuse was rightly seen as a key cause of the social dislocation, that became more apparent with the growth of towns and cities. The middle classes across all four colonies attacked the 'drink problem' vigorously, though traditional mercantile élites were opposed to any interference with the established trade with the West Indies – a trade still grounded to some extent in the demand for rum. As with the schools question, the right of the state to regulate individual social activity was at issue. It was one thing for people voluntarily to limit their drinking by taking temperance pledges; it was quite another for a government to intervene either to prohibit drink altogether, to regulate people's access through the licensing of places where liquor could be consumed, or to tax liquor with special vigour. The temperance movement became a social crusade that directly affected political development. In the process, all leaders were compelled to take a stand on the responsibility of governments to intervene in the social realm. Full prohibition was achieved for only a short while in New Brunswick under Leonard Tilley's guidance. It was less successful elsewhere; but the issues that it raised would reverberate through regional politics for generations to come.[31] Education and temperance crusades reflected a revolution in middle-class expectations that colonists identified with a government revolution sweeping the Atlantic world. As 'social reform' became the dominant ideology of the era, it absorbed politicians who, no matter what their political persuasions, saw in it the opportunity to challenge entrenched interests.

The feebleness of the Atlantic colonies' political ties with each other and with Canada inhibited movement towards political realignment. In 1863, plans to strengthen links to Canada by building the Intercolonial Railway fell prey to rancorous negotiations and came to nothing. Trade with Canada made up less than 5 per cent of the region's total exports and imports, and Canada's political instability and continuing French-English tension was a source of anxiety and scepticism. But politicians of the new generation, typified by Charles Tupper and Leonard Tilley, were increasingly finding common ground with each other and their Canadian counterparts and turning away from the older notions of particularism that had soured earlier discussions. Urged on by London officials and bankers, they came together several times through the early 1860s to discuss railways; but they always seemed to end up focusing on the possibilities for founding a transcontinental nation. For the longest time the building of a railway connecting the colonies had been seen as the essential precondition for union; now union was becoming the precondition for railway consolidation and expansion.[32]

THE POLITICS OF UNION

Charles Tupper, a former Conservative premier of Nova Scotia, had been out of office for almost two years when he advocated uniting the

Charles Tupper and Leonard Tilley

three Maritime colonies at a speech in Saint John in the fall of 1861; he would return to office two years later. In asserting the inevitability of some form of broad colonial union, he voiced a commonly held view among middle-class politicians of the region that the future had to be different from the past if society was to advance. Only such a larger union, he argued, could save the colonies from the social and economic decline that would follow on the ending of free trade with the United States. He emphasized the immediate benefits that an intercolonial railway would bring to the region; it would, for example, enable Halifax and Saint John to become entrepôts for landlocked St Lawrence cities during the long winter. Like most politicians of his era who addressed the question, he did not consider Newfoundland as a potential partner in any such union, though he was prepared to project the absorption of the far off North-west and creation of a transcontinental nation on the American pattern as the logical outcome of such an initiative.[33] Neither Tupper nor Adams G. Archibald, his reform counterpart in Nova Scotia, nor Leonard Tilley, the perennial premier of New Brunswick – who had invited Tupper to speak in Saint John, had experienced directly the struggles over responsible government in their provinces. Like their fellow 'fathers of Confederation' all three were in their forties and had risen to prominence as colonial governments extended their reach into new areas of the social and economic lives of their communities. Archibald and Tupper, from Truro and Amherst, respectively, represented communities that were becoming more attuned to a new economy, one that was increasingly being shaped by the interests of coal mines and railroads. For his part, Tilley was a druggist and real estate speculator from Saint John. Tupper was a medical doctor; Archibald, a lawyer. In fact, all three speculated actively in properties bordering coal deposits and proposed rail routes. Typical as well of this group were Charlotte-town lawyers James C. and William H. Pope of Prince Edward Island's Conservative Party. Members of an important Conservative family, they had entered politics in the fifties determined to advance the affairs of their community by working within the political structure to resolve the troublesome land question. All of them, along with their counterparts from Canada, would play important roles in the Confederation drama that was about to be enacted.[34]

In the Atlantic colonies, political parties, on the surface at least, mir-rored Liberal/Reform versus Tory/Conservative divisions similar to those in Britain. While political labels had become fixed during the struggle over responsible government, they became less precise following 1850. Reformers generally advocated more open access by communities to government decisions about community resources and positioned them-selves as opponents to entrenched élites, which they identified with the Tory Party. By and large, Conservatives tended to regard the support of individual property interests as a basic function of government; but they were caught by their earlier defence of entrenched privilege during the struggle over responsible government. In reality, there were few clean-cut divisions. Instead, politics was characterized by rather loose coalitions made up of individualistic politicians pursuing the interests of either their constituents or the powerful within society. Party for-mation lagged, particularly in New Brunswick, where the broad coalition led by Tilley promised all things to all people and managed to hold together in spite of pervasive ethnic and religious tensions. Prince Ed-ward Island and Newfoundland were different, partly because they were slower to attain self-government, partly because of the singular nature of their economic conditions. Political parties in these colonies were more unified on the central questions of land or fisheries reform, respectively. So long as entrenched landowners or fish barons remained at the centre of their political discussions, they had little need to concern themselves with futuristic economic or political strategies.[35]

Tupper's victory in the election of 1863 was based on his promises to build railway extensions to Pictou and Annapolis, to establish a free and compulsory school system supported by local taxation, and to or-ganize a conference to discuss Maritime union. His union proposal was viewed by his opponents as a ruse to draw attention away from the tax implications of his educational reforms and his railway-building pro-gram. In the face of New Brunswick and Prince Edward Island indif-ference, it remained an unfulfilled element in an aggressive enunciation of the middle-class belief in reform. New Brunswick, urged on by Lieu-tenant-Governor A.H. Gordon, consented to attend any meeting that was convened but expressed little enthusiasm; its political agenda was dominated by debates over supposed corruption in the Tilley government. Prince Edward Island's government, led by J.C. Pope, was preoccupied with the attempts of the 'Tenant League' to end the worst abuses of the landholding system using mainly passive but sometimes active resistance; at times the mood in the P.E.I. countryside bordered on insurrection.[36] Pope, with support from all factions on the Island, refused to attend any meeting unless the land question was given priority. Thus, despite general recognition that such a union might ennoble colonial politics by opening the door for new economic initiatives, it continued as an unlikely possibility through the summer of 1864. In Newfoundland no attention whatsoever was paid to union during this early stage of the political restructuring of the Maritime community.[37]

Just as hope of convening a meeting of Maritime governments to discuss union appeared dead, Canada reached the end of its constitutional tether. Over the previous decade ministry after ministry had failed to hold power in the tendentious legislative union of Upper and Lower Canada (later Ontario and Quebec). A 'Great Coalition' of John A. Macdonald's Conservatives and George Brown's Reformers proposed a federal union of all the colonies as a solution to the impasse. This prompted a tour of Nova Scotia and New Brunswick in July 1864 by a delegation of Canadian legislators and newspapermen, one of the most ambitious public-relations endeavours in the history of the colonies. It was led by the ebullient Montreal Irishman Thomas D'Arcy McGee, who waxed eloquent on the need for a 'new nationality' in the Maritimes to match the emergence of a similar sentiment in Canada. He convinced the government in Quebec that only a little pressure from London was needed to force a conference to which they would be invited. A flurry of telegrams and arm-twisting prompted Prince Edward Island and New Brunswick to endorse the idea; the Island government insisted that the conference be held at Charlottetown, and the date was set for mid-September.[38]

At Charlottetown, on the first day of the meeting, Tupper's original proposal for a legislative union of the three Maritime colonies was shelved, and the Canadians were invited to present their ideas for a broader federation. They argued for a strong central government to integrate and defend colonial economies against the threat of American protectionism. To encourage development, John A. Macdonald and his associates proposed an immediate start on the long-sought Intercolonial Railway. For the New Brunswick and Nova Scotia delegates, this laid to rest the protracted tension over earlier failures on that score. It did little, however, to convince Islanders that union would produce any immediate benefits. Any significant constitutional change for them would have to

Fathers of Confederation, Charlottetown, 1864. This famous photo testifies to the overwhelming male dominance in nineteenth-century politics. Women were present at social occasions in Charlottetown and Quebec, but negotiation was an all-male affair.

include attention to the specific problem of absentee landowners. Most landlords were unwilling to allow piecemeal sale of their properties. The government would have to acquire the lands *en masse* in order to sell them to the tenants, but lacked the money to do so. What Islanders wanted was a promise of sufficient funds to allow them to buy out the landlords, a question that was left open for the time being.[39]

Charlottetown really only prepared the ground for further discussions; delegates left after a week to tour Halifax and Saint John before formally reconvening at Quebec a month later, in October 1864. The initiative obviously lay with the Canadians, who, after Charlottetown, set the time and agenda for all meetings. In fact, they even sent the government steamer *Queen Victoria* to pick up delegates at Pictou, Charlottetown, and Shediac for the discussions at Quebec. There the foundations for the new Canadian nation were laid out pretty much as they had been outlined by the delegates to Charlottetown. There was much debate about the distribution of powers within a federation; the American Civil War, which was being fought over 'states' rights.' was fresh in the delegates' minds. How much power to turn over to the new national government and how much to retain in the hands of the provinces was the central issue to be decided. The New Brunswick and Nova Scotia delegates argued repeatedly that such a union's basic purpose was to consolidate and expand the economic basis of the colonies. While legislative union was the preferred choice of politicians used to British traditions of indivisible sovereignty, the Maritimers became convinced that devolution of critical cultural issues along with natural resources to provincial jurisdiction was the only way to secure Quebec's approval of the union.

The resolutions that were agreed to in the end called for the major powers associated with nation making to be transferred to the proposed federal jurisdiction, leaving the newly created provincial level with more limited areas of activity such as education and local affairs. Such a distribution of powers also helped to ensure the individual identity of various provinces, an arrangement that Maritimers hoped would be to their advantage as well. Several of the Maritime delegates opposed the proposals for regionally balanced representation in a Senate, however; many thought this provision insufficient to protect local interests at the national level. All present knew that Maritime representatives would be engulfed in a House of Commons selected on the basis of 'representation by population,' a demand of the Ontario delegates. In effect the Quebec Resolutions did not so much create a federation as consolidate the activities of a number of separate colonial entities and invent a new level of government to carry out functions and deal with issues that the new central government preferred to avoid.[40]

At both Charlottetown and Quebec, the Nova Scotia, New Brunswick, and Prince Edward Island delegations participated actively. Nova Scotia and New Brunswick found the terms equitable (these included transfer of railway and other debts and assets from the colonies to the national government) and endorsed them as presented by the Canadians. The Prince Edward Island delegation was more divided at Quebec than any other. Edward Palmer, the Conservative leader in the Legislative Council, denounced the terms as inadequate to deal with the land question. George Coles, leader of the opposition in the Assembly, focused on the limited representation Island interests would have in a federal parliament, where their numbers would be tiny. Widespread opposition to resolutions regarding representation by population, distribution of powers, and financial terms made it problematic for Premier John H. Gray and Provincial Secretary W.H. Pope to speak with much authority for the Island as a whole. With virtually no public debt and few sources of income aside from a small tariff on imported goods, Islanders seemed to have little to gain from union unless the conference addressed the

Ice boats in Northumberland Strait, c. 1910. Effective winter communication with the mainland was a critical demand for Prince Edward Islanders in all negotiations about union. Before Confederation, Islanders were dependent on small boats fitted with iron runners, such as the above, to ferry passengers, freight, and mail to the Island.

issue of absentee landholders by making some provision for a fund to assist in acquiring unimproved lands. In the *bonhomie* of Charlottetown, Canada's delegates had hinted that an interest-free loan to facilitate the purchase of existing lands might be considered once a new government was created. At Quebec, Island delegates introduced resolutions calling for a loan of $800,000, but the Canadians refused. Nor would they yield to Island delegates' requests to strengthen the relatively weak P.E.I. representation in the proposed houses of parliament. With only four senators and six MPs, Prince Edward Island would stand little chance of moving its concerns on to any national agenda once union was accomplished. After a long series of procedural and substantial setbacks, the Island delegates, in spite of ample personal enthusiasm for union, could commit themselves only to placing the issue before their legislature on their return.[41]

Newfoundland, reflecting its remoteness, had not even been invited to Charlottetown. Two delegates, Conservative Deputy Premier F.B.T.

Carter and the Liberal leader of the opposition, Ambrose Shea, went to Quebec as observers but participated in few of the discussions. During the last stages of the conference they were invited to take part as full delegates, though there is little evidence that they voted. Provision was made for Newfoundland representation in the House of Commons and the Senate in the event that the colony was interested, but there was little enthusiasm for the idea back home. A few politicians, including Premier Hugh Hoyles and Governor Musgrave, expressed sympathy with and interest in the possibilities offered by union, but St John's-based merchants quickly pointed out that no union could improve fish catches, which had been disastrous the previous year; nor could it effect the price. More likely, in their view, it would result in increased taxation of Newfoundlanders to support endeavours in far-off parts of the new Dominion.[42]

Following the Quebec meetings, delegates embarked on a sight-seeing tour to Montreal, Toronto, Ottawa, and Niagara Falls, a visit punctuated by several festive dinners and widespread public celebration. During this tour, the basic outlines of the proposed union were made public, and delegates were given a chance to expound on the new 'nationality' they had set in motion. Then delegates returned to their respective colonies later in the autumn with the so-called Quebec Resolutions ready for submission to their legislatures. Prince Edward Islanders debated the union question at public meetings in halls and schoolhouses across the Island, as well as in their legislature. In the end, union was emphatically rejected, mostly because of the failure of the Quebec Conference proposals to safeguard the Island's specific concerns. Newfoundland, following widespread opposition to the terms proposed in the resolutions, did not even submit them to the legislature at this stage.[43] In Nova Scotia an accepted practice was for delegates to intercolonial conferences to report on their deliberations before a public forum on their return. Late in December, Adams G. Archibald and Jonathan McCully, reform leaders in the assembly and the council, respectively, joined Tupper in introducing the Quebec Resolutions to a packed meeting at Halifax. There was little debate at this stage, perhaps because of the subject's importance, perhaps to give delegates a chance to explain the terms without interruption. A second meeting was called for the following week to give those who might oppose union an opportunity to voice any concerns. There prominent Halifax merchants William Stairs and Patrick Power expressed disquiet over the fate of regional economic interests under such a union, arguing that integration with the Canadian economy was at least as likely to be unfairly competitive as it was to be complementary, as claimed by the delegates. Others concentrated on the scheme's financial terms, which gave provinces so little means to carry out their many responsibilities. Still others mirrored the concerns of Prince Edward Islanders about the need to protect the interests of a smaller province in a federal rather than a legislative union where the Canadians would inevitably dominate any House of Commons selected on the basis of representation by population. The possible submergence of Nova Scotia's specific provincial identity within Confederation was brought forward as another serious problem. The meeting commenced a long and bitter debate over union's consequences for the region.[44]

In New Brunswick, partly by an accident of timing, the 'Quebec scheme' was judged at the polls by the electorate – a contingency that Leonard Tilley would have preferred to avoid. But with the assembly's term scheduled to expire in the spring of 1865 and his government dependent on a fragile coalition, Tilley hesitated to raise the issue in the legislature. After canvassing of the province through December and January, he decided to proceed with a general election – announced at the end of January to be held through February. As the euphoria generated at Charlottetown and Quebec subsided, the realities of the proposed union came to be viewed within the context of the local and particular focus of provincial politics. In New Brunswick opposition emerged not only to the terms agreed to at Quebec, but to the very idea of union. Tilley emphasized union's potential to foster economic development, ignoring its failure to deliver the Intercolonial Railway terminus to Saint John. He lost the election and his own seat in Saint John to a loose alliance of oppositionists led by maverick MLA Albert Smith, mostly as a result of bad strategies and a powerful coalition of those opposed to the transfer of control over local affairs to Ottawa.[45] Smith won partly by coaxing to the surface long-standing Irish and Acadian fears of Protestant discrimination. His campaign was fuelled in Saint John by those convinced that the proposed union could never secure their ambition to become entrepôt of the new nation. As in Nova Scotia, there was also anxiety about the nature of the relationship with Canada.

With New Brunswick out of the chase following Tilley's electoral defeat, Tupper could only wait on events, probably not such a bad thing given the powerful cabal of Halifax and outport merchants organizing to oppose Confederation. Opposition from entrenched Halifax and Saint John merchants was predictable. They reacted instinctively against radical changes to a world they were used to managing in their own interest. In doing so, they characterized union's advocates as recent arrivals with little real economic experience or understanding of what was best for the colonies. Merchants also used control over the regional press to belittle the views of new middle-class representatives who threatened their political and economic hegemony. Support for union from British officials surprised them by its intensity and determination. British pressure became so strong in fact that it became impossible for any colonial oligarchy to resist it for long. Meanwhile, the Canadians went on with their debate and approved union by a substantial margin.

A powerful alliance of British, Canadian, and local interests favouring union set out to turn the tide in New Brunswick. There, Lieutenant-Governor A.H. Gordon refused to co-operate with Smith's shaky government. As it turned out, Smith's loose alliance of anti-Confederationists was even more fragile than Tilley's coalition of unionists had been earlier. They were individualists who found it difficult enough to agree among themselves. With large railway debentures falling due, extra strains were placed upon them, and they soon fell prey to imperial machinations. They had proposed a Western Extension railway to connect Saint John to the American network to the south. Relations between Britain and the States were still strained by the Civil War, however, and Britain continued to refuse to guarantee the bonds needed to raise funds for Western Extension, thus effectively freezing the Smith government out of the London money market.[46]

The threat of invasion by the Fenians – disaffected American Irish anxious to influence affairs in Ireland by annoying Britain in North America – offered the opportunity to raise imperial defence to a central place in the campaign for Confederation. Early in 1866, Lieutenant-Governor Gordon accepted Smith's resignation, thereby forcing a second election. A revitalized Tilley fought a hard campaign on the promise of renegotiating the terms of union with other colonies. In the midst of the campaign, Britain called out the militia against phantom Fenian invaders, thereby convincing the still-Loyalist-dominated colony that continued opposition to union was frowned upon by the Empire. Important, too, were the Canadians' large financial contributions to Tilley's campaign chest. In the final analysis, though, the tide was probably turned by Roman Catholic clergymen throughout the province. Although they had previously opposed union out of fear of losing their control over religious education, they were eventually induced by Archbishop T.L. Connolly of Halifax to support union out of fear that Catholics might be branded disloyal to the Crown.[47]

In Nova Scotia, with only a year to go before his own mandate expired, Tupper seized the opportunity provided by Tilley's victory to introduce a resolution authorizing Nova Scotia's participation in a new conference, this time to be held in London under the protective wing of imperial officials. The resolution, passed in the dying hours of the legislative session in March, caught the anti-Confederates off guard. If rewards to members who reversed their previous opposition to union to support Tupper's resolution are indicative, his actions were carefully calculated to ensure its passage.[48] This initiative provoked a public outpouring of indignation, which, fortunately for Tupper, took place after a new delegation was on its way to London. A stanza of a contemporary bit of political doggerel captures some of this sentiment:

O that by inspiration's light
I could illume that fateful night
Lift up the veil that all might see
That dark deed of inequity,
By which our Nova Scotia braves
Were sold to Canada as slaves.[49]

Joseph Howe's leading role in opposing union in Nova Scotia has been controversial. During his long political career he had from time to time emphasized the expanded role that intercolonial co-operation would give to local politicians and called for a broader imperial union as part of a restructuring of the Empire.[50] Following his defeat by the Conservatives in the 1863 general election, he had been appointed a British commissioner to oversee American fishermen in the Gulf of St Lawrence fishery under the terms of the Reciprocity Treaty. Thus, he was unavailable to serve on delegations to either Charlottetown or Quebec. In fact, by that point his political career seemed largely behind him; he was, after all, past sixty and had spent the better part of forty years in the public eye. When opposition to the Quebec Resolutions surfaced in 1865 he maintained public silence, ostensibly because of his imperial appointment. Privately, however, he supported the 'anti' position in 1865 with his anonymous series of newspaper articles – 'The Botheration Letters' – in which he pilloried the 'Quebec scheme' with his well-known sarcastic wit.

When an 'Anti-Confederation League' was formed to oppose Tupper's new conference initiative in the spring of 1866, Howe was persuaded to return from a short sojourn in New York to serve as the league's secretary and mouthpiece. Over the ensuing summer a number of petitions were gathered from throughout the province, and a committee was formed to go to England. By summer's end they had several thousand signatures and an ample war chest made up of generous donations from the province's wealthiest merchants.[51] In London, Howe presented the petitions as evidence that Tupper's lame-duck government did not represent the electorate's views. He hounded Tupper with more public letters, with appearances before bureaucrats in the Colonial Office, and with lobbying efforts before parliamentarians. Unfortunately, Howe's expectations regarding Britain's sense of fair play and liberal ideals was sorely misplaced. After only cursory debates, in which MPs and Lords displayed little or no knowledge of colonial affairs, the British North

America (BNA) Act passed with hardly a whisper of disagreement. The terms of the act were little changed from those agreed to at Quebec. Some recognition that the responsibilities being left to the provinces might prove more onerous than had been acknowledged at Quebec was reflected in improved financial terms for New Brunswick. Tilley and Tupper both insisted that a provision for construction of the Intercolonial Railway be added to the clauses of union, thereby ensuring that the line would be undertaken immediately and completed in good time. A new clause provided additional protection for the educational rights of religious minorities, something insisted upon by both Maritime and Quebec bishops.

When delegates returned home in the spring of 1867, Tupper's government narrowly withstood a non-confidence motion in the assembly based on the supposedly new terms. Tilley did not even introduce the terms into the legislature, but began immediately to prepare for the upcoming elections.[52] Canada's birthday on July first met with a mixed reception in Nova Scotia, where anti-Confederation parades featuring the burning of effigies of Tupper and other Confederationists were staged in Halifax and several provincial towns. The ceremony was dampened as union's outspoken opponents threatened further struggle to overthrow the 'scheme' they were coming to revile. Disillusioned though they were by their London experience, the 'antis' were reluctant to give up the fight. On returning from London, Howe made a series of speeches calling upon Nova Scotians to use the upcoming elections to make clear their opposition to Confederation. Once it was clear that there would be little or no support from New Brunswick, the Anti-Confederation League, patriotically renamed the Nova Scotia Party, began organizing for the upcoming election by nominating candidates in every constituency for both federal and provincial houses. The new Conservative government in Ottawa, formed under the direction of John A. Macdonald and George-Etienne Cartier, included Leonard Tilley as minister of customs. Tupper, who had withdrawn his claim to a cabinet seat in favour of Thomas Kenny of Halifax in order to maintain the ethno-religious balances needed to form the first cabinet, called upon his friends in Ottawa to delay the election as long as possible. By the time Nova Scotians finally went to the polls in mid-September, elections had already taken place in every other province. The new government's success was assured no matter how Nova Scotians voted. Led by Howe, the Nova Scotia Party focused its emotionally charged opposition on the manner in which Tupper's government had usurped the colony's right to political self-determination. They also attacked the joining of a Maritime economy to Canada's larger continental one, stressing that their province's staples-oriented regional economy would suffer in competition with Canada and that infant regional manufacturing industries would soon be swamped. Unionists, for their part, continued to stress imperial imperatives that made a separate existence difficult, at the same time defending the legitimacy of the means undertaken to carry the union. The assurance that the railway would remedy the economic woes of the province was central to their promise of future economic development. In the bitter campaign that followed, Howe's earlier support of union was brought up in an attempt to embarrass the antis. Tupper's supporters, particularly Jonathan McCully, delighted in quoting Howe to himself, pointing out the inconsistency of his opposition to union when he had so publicly endorsed it earlier. In rebuttal, Howe protested that it was one thing to favour the idea of union, which virtually everyone did, and quite another to support a federation imposed upon his beloved province by such nefarious means. The antis surprised even themselves by winning eighteen of nineteen seats for the federal House of Commons and thirty-four of thirty-six seats in the provincial assembly, as well as garnering two thirds of all votes cast in an election where there were several acclamations. The lone Unionist survivor in the federal contest was Tupper, who carried his home riding of Cumberland County by less than a hundred votes. Howe himself was elected for Hants County.[53]

### CORRALLING CONFEDERATION'S OPPONENTS

The election campaign had provided Nova Scotians with a cathartic outlet for their frustration over the manner of Confederation's passage. Howe, staunchly loyal to Britain in spite of his bitter experience in London, continued to hope that, once British officials were fully aware of the depth of Nova Scotians' opposition to the union, the province would be released from its new 'bondage.' When all the newly elected antis met in early October to decide future strategy, federal MPs decided to attend the first sitting of the House of Commons scheduled for later that month. There they introduced a resolution demanding Nova Scotia's release from union. Following a brief debate, the motion was defeated by the large government majority. A few Ontario and Quebec reformers sympathized with some of the Nova Scotia MPs' viewpoints regarding provincial rights, but refused to support their resolution. New Brunswick MPs, who might have offered some sort of bridge between the warring factions, remained silent, except for Tilley, who called upon the 'antis' to abandon their opposition.[54]

On returning to Halifax, the antis, led mostly by the provincial government, organized a second delegation to London. Howe was joined this time by William Annand, proprietor of the Halifax *Morning Chronicle*

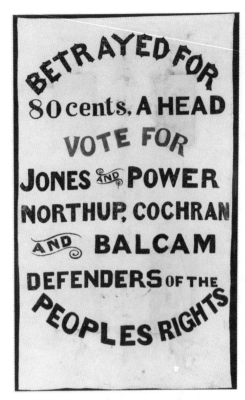

Nova Scotia 'Betrayed.' Hung across one of Halifax's main thoroughfares during the election campaign of 1867, this crude banner captured the anti-Confederates' emotional message.

and premier of Nova Scotia's first post-Confederation government. In London they made the rounds of government and parliamentary offices, presenting yet another set of petitions and an assembly resolution demanding Nova Scotia's immediate release from Confederation. British officials, however, declared the province legally bound by the union, and referred delegates to officials in Ottawa for any re-examination of their status. Behind the public drama of these discussions another scenario was played out as Charles Tupper, now a non-official representative of the Canadian government, dogged Howe's every step. He responded to every public letter, visited the same officials and members of Parliament and insisted on the rightness of Confederation's cause at every turn. Just as the delegation was set to return home, Howe and Tupper were brought together for private conversations at the residence of the colonial secretary, the duke of Buckingham, where Tupper appears to have convinced Howe of the hopelessness of further opposition. He had been authorized to promise Howe a renegotiation of some of the financial terms of the British North America Act that affected Nova Scotia, on the condition that Howe cease his opposition and join the government.[55] Back in Halifax, Howe and Annand reported once again to Nova

Scotia Party MPs and MLAs on their failure to make any headway with British officialdom. Annand, leader of a government dedicated to seeking repeal at any cost, supported a further effort to release the province from union, while Howe counselled caution. At Tupper's and Tilley's prompting, John A. Macdonald sent emissaries to Halifax to discuss the elements of new financial terms with Howe. They were careful not to engage in negotiations with the provincial government, a strategy that provoked great bitterness in Annand, who felt he had been frozen out of the negotiations.[56] Finally, Macdonald himself arrived in Halifax to offer Howe a cabinet post, control over provincial patronage, and revision of the BNA Act's financial terms for Nova Scotia. This would form the basis for what would become known as 'better terms,' which in fact offered little more than a temporary relief from the financial strait-jacket of a system of subsidies that left smaller provinces unable to maintain previous levels of service without additional taxation or borrowing. Alarmed by the flirtation of the anti government with ideas of independence or some form of annexation by the United States, in September Howe announced his support for 'better terms'; he was backed by a majority of the more moderate 'anti' MPs.[57]

Later that autumn, following meetings at Portland, Maine, with Finance Minister John Rose, Howe agreed to the final offer of better terms and the antis were effectively split between the provincial and federal wings. The terms of the final offer amounted to an additional subsidy of about $80,000 per year for a ten-year period and additional compensation for the transfer of some public buildings that had been built during the years just prior to Confederation. Howe and Hugh MacDonald of Antigonish accepted cabinet posts, eventually bringing the majority of the federal antis into line with him. Hard-liners Frank Killam of Yarmouth and J.W. Carmichael of Pictou, who reflected more traditional mercantile opposition to union, soon made common cause with the emerging Reform opposition, which coalesced behind the leadership of Ontario Reformer Alexander Mackenzie. Howe's acceptance of a cabinet post made a by-election necessary; it was held later that winter, and all the federal government influence available was needed to ensure Howe's return. The provincial government, angry that Ottawa had negotiated solely with Howe, opposed him fiercely at every turn. He carried Hants by a very narrow margin, and the bitter fight broke his health.[58]

Nova Scotia's anti-Confederation crusade was more than a temporary diversion along Canada's certain road to success. The movement emerged from a debate that had convulsed the entire Atlantic region for a decade, and union continued to be the central issue facing Atlantic Canadians for generations to come. Personal determination, powerful outside support, and sheer good fortune had enabled Tupper and Tilley to guide their provinces into Confederation. Their promises of development through the encouragement of railways and of industrial expansion through participation in the larger national economic unit raised expectations that were difficult to fulfil, given the fragmented nature and disparate interests of the new nation. For their part the antis, whether in Nova Scotia where the drama was played out, or in the other provinces, viewed the demise of reciprocity less as a harbinger of future policies than as an aberration, to be corrected once Americans became persuaded of the error of their protectionist ways. The antis freely predicted that some form of reciprocity would return, if the region could remain free of interference from Canadians, who were viewed as supporters of the reviled protectionist policies of the Americans. The anti-Confederationists' exaggerated view of the value placed by Americans on access to the inshore fishery convinced them that the United States would eventually come round. Their anger over lost independence, outrage at being 'railroaded' into union, and broader concerns over the future of their economy combined to create a tradition of suspicion and hostility towards union that would infuse regional politics for some time. That hostility could be deflected only by a focus on the promised delivery of services from Ottawa.

One side-effect of the manner in which Nova Scotia had been pacified was a deliberate weakening of the provincial government. By ignoring it completely in the negotiations over better terms, John A. Macdonald gave force to his view that the provincial governments were little more than glorified municipal governments. After sending a last delegation to London in 1869, Annand abandoned opposition, though he would continue to oppose the federal government in concert with the rump of the federal antis aligned with the Grit and Rouge coalition that was emerging in Canada.[59] In order to defuse opposition to Confederation, Tupper, Howe, and Tilley together demanded that Ottawa deal sensitively with regional issues. Priority was given to construction of the Intercolonial Railway with Ottawa absorbing the existing New Brunswick and Nova Scotia lines, along with the debts incurred in their construction. A new line was constructed, running from Rivière du Loup in Quebec along New Brunswick's north shore and linking up with existing lines to Halifax and Saint John. It would be owned and operated as a public utility, much as Canada's canals had been a generation earlier. Completed in 1876, the Intercolonial's headquarters at Moncton would provide concrete evidence of the government's intention to integrate the regional economy with that of the new Dominion.[60] In 1870, Howe and Tupper persuaded reluctant Ontario and Quebec colleagues to accept a modest tariff of fifty cents per ton on coal to encourage the consumption of Nova Scotia coal in central Canada, though the tariff would be removed before the next general election. In addition, tariffs were drawn back on materials imported for use in ship construction, a direct response to shipbuilders' claims that such tariffs impeded their productivity.[61] These and other actions, such as local harbour improvements, were designed to allay fears that the federal government was too removed from the local scene to meet the region's requirements for government services.

The decision by Ottawa to defend Canadians' exclusive rights to their inshore fishery was the government's most important step in demonstrating that it was equipped and willing to look after regional interests. A licensing arrangement limiting American access to inshore waters had been put in place just prior to Confederation and was rigorously enforced by the new Canadian government, at Tupper's urging. The objective was to force the Americans to the bargaining table on the fishery, in hopes of securing an arrangement as close to the terms of the original Reciprocity Treaty as possible.[62] The Treaty of Washington (1871), which settled a broad range of issues outstanding between Britain and the United States as a result of the Civil War, would resolve the fishery question, for the time being at least, in a manner agreeable to Nova Scotians. While Macdonald's dream of a broad free-trade agreement proved impossible, he did secure access for the fishermen of the Maritimes to U.S. territorial waters, the free exchange of fish products between both nations for a ten year period, and compensation for the excess value of the Canadian over the American fishery to be settled by an independent board. John A. Macdonald, who represented Canada on the commission, was ably prompted by Tupper in a long sequence of letters that placed Maritimers' interests in the foreground. The negotiations were made difficult by Britain's determination to avoid confronting the Americans on any issue of significance. While the political fallout was substantial in other parts of the Dominion over the failure to gain concessions on such matters as claims related to the Fenian raids, the Treaty of Washington was soon heralded throughout Nova Scotia and New Brunswick as a foundation for a prosperous economy and a harbinger of Ottawa's capacity to serve regional interests. The federal election the following year would confirm the government's success locally, as it won resoundingly in both provinces.[63] Prince Edward Island and Newfoundland remained aloof from these negotiations. From their withdrawal at Quebec until 1871, Prince Edward Islanders built railways and accumulated debts at rates comparable to those of Nova Scotia and New Brunswick in the 1850s. Some of these debts were acquired in the purchase of lands from absentee landlords, thereby furthering resolution of the land problem. The debts, encouraged at every turn by the British, would soon leave Islanders little choice but to reconsider their position on union. Furthermore, the Island government still needed British co-operation in expropriating the properties of absentee landholders. On Canada's counsel, the imperial government resisted all attempts to re-negotiate some sort of favourable trade arrangement with the United States on behalf of the Island government. New Brunswick and Nova Scotia federal politicians pressed Ottawa for additional concessions to assist in negotiations with the Islanders. Eventually talks began, but they would not be completed until 1873.[64] Newfoundlanders followed events on the mainland with interest, as they continued to debate the merits of joining the new dominion. They had been promised an election on the issue by the Conservative government led, from 1865, by Frederic Carter, and knew that the question would be decided in 1869. Though the Colonial office made it quite clear that Newfoundland's joining Canada would be the preferred result, it exerted no direct pressure. In the event, an anti-Confederate party representing an unlikely alliance of merchants and Roman Catholic Liberals won an overwhelming victory over Carter's Confederates. It would be many years before the colony voted on the issue again.[65]

CONCLUSION: TOWARDS A REGIONAL CONSCIOUSNESS

The political and constitutional development of the Atlantic colonies had been defined by the achievement of responsible government. Up to the middle of the century, mercantile capitalism had focused the colonial economies on the exploitation of staples. As the colonies became integrated with a broader North Atlantic community over the next two decades, however, their economies and societies matured. A new middle class emerged to give new direction to the politics of all colonies in the region, though this new group enjoyed more success in Nova Scotia and New Brunswick than in Prince Edward Island or Newfoundland. Its members associated economic development with a more diverse econ-omy that placed more priority on the manufacturing sector, and they invoked the new power of the government to intervene in the economic affairs of the colonies. Vigorous debates ensued; at the centre was the railway, the engine of change that promised to reshape the community.

Escape from dependence on the export of staples required new de-velopment capital, or redeployment of local capital into new endeavours. Encouragement for manufacturing became tied to a political strategy of amalgamation with similarly directed groups of Canadian leaders. Nova Scotia's coal mines, a critical source of energy for the new economic thrust, provided the inspiration for these new ambitions. But the wide-spread movement of capital towards such industrial pursuits was also occurring across the entire region, particularly in Saint John and Halifax, where capital was available to support manufacturing. As Maritimers entered their Canadian century, further changes began to flow from the new nationality that was being created. For better or worse, Confederation directed the region onto new paths. Yet Maritimers had no more control over the direction those paths would take than they had had when British interests so decisively guided them during their British century.

# CHAPTER TWO

# The 1870s
## Political Integration

Maritimers entered the 1870s resentful at the way in which Confederation had been imposed upon the region. Most historians have simply attributed Maritime discontent to continuing hostility to Confederation and dismissed the malaise expressed during the 1870s as mere nostalgia for a golden age that had never existed. But the majority of Maritimers had never opposed the idea of Confederation, only the unpalatable terms imposed upon the region at the Quebec Conference, and what they sought was not separation but accommodation within the union.[1] At the federal level the desire for better terms led to gradual integration into the federal party system and an attempt to ensure that national policies had a Maritime dimension; at the provincial level it meant a continuing effort to gain for the provincial legislatures the financial resources that would enable them to carry out their constitutional responsibilities and to develop provincial programs that would meet the needs of their constituents.

The resentment Maritimers felt was compounded in Nova Scotia by the undemocratic way in which the province had been coerced into Confederation. Partly because of the willingness of Sir John A. Macdonald, advised by Charles Tupper from outside the cabinet, to negotiate better terms and partly because of the growing recognition of the futility of further agitation, the repeal movement collapsed in 1869. Out of despair a small number of the most bitter opponents of Confederation talked of annexation to the United States, but there was little support for the idea. In New Brunswick it could not be claimed that the province had been coerced into union, since the issue of Confederation had been put to the people. Not one of the fifteen members returned in 1867 had been elected on a repeal platform,[2] although the majority of the New Brunswickers opposed the decision to build the Intercolonial Railway along the north shore, protested against the tariff increases of 1867 and 1870, and demanded 'better terms' comparable to those granted to Nova

Scotia. A few disgruntled New Brunswickers also advocated annexation, but when an annexation bill was introduced into the New Brunswick assembly in 1869, no one supported it and it was not permitted to remain on the books.[3] Like the Nova Scotians, most New Brunswickers accepted Confederation as a *fait accompli* and, also like the Nova Scotians, they increasingly recognized that they could achieve better terms only by integrating into the federal political system.

Part of the reason for the continuing Maritime discontent was that New Brunswick and Nova Scotia were seriously underrepresented in the federal bureaucracy. The new civil service was little more than the bureaucracy of the old United Province of Canada writ large and, except in departments headed by Maritimers, the positions were filled almost entirely by Canadians. The limited success of government candidates in Nova Scotia and New Brunswick in the first federal election, compounded by P.E.I.'s decision to stay out, had also left the region weakly represented in the cabinet, particularly since Macdonald naturally tended to rely on men with whom he had previously worked. Maritimers received four of the thirteen seats in the first cabinet but only Samuel Leonard Tilley and Peter Mitchell received important ministries. Even Tilley, who was generally conceded to be the ablest of the Maritime ministers, admitted to Macdonald that there was a 'general' impression that he had 'no influence with the government' and that he had 'not been able to give much visible evidence that such is not the case.'[4]

The entry of Howe into the cabinet in 1869 did little to alter Maritime weakness in the government, since Howe was largely a spent force. The successful wooing of the Nova Scotia anti-Confederates did, however, begin to change the balance of power in the Commons. By the end of 1869 the government could usually count on the support of the majority of the Nova Scotia members, and a place was found for Tupper, who entered the cabinet as president of the privy council in 1870. Tupper was determined to demonstrate that Ottawa could look after the interests of the Maritimes, and he directed a stream of appropriations to the region, including a subsidy for steamship communication between Nova Scotia and Prince Edward Island and harbour improvements for Saint John and a variety of smaller ports. In 1870 he helped to persuade the cabinet, over the opposition of a number of Ontario members, to introduce a fifty-cent duty on coal, although it was abolished the following year.[5] Both Tupper, who acted as Macdonald's personal physician, and Tilley, who frequently took charge of the cabinet during Macdonald's absences, increased in stature during this period and began to exercise greater influence over the policies of the government.

Initially the negotiations that led to the Treaty of Washington in 1871 slowed down the integration of the Maritime members into the governing party. Macdonald was legitimately suspected of being willing to sacrifice Maritime interests for the sake of gaining a settlement more acceptable to central Canada.[6] In the end he failed to persuade the Americans to renew reciprocity and was forced to grant access to the inshore fisheries in return for free entry to the American market for Canadian fish and financial compensation for the fisheries. The *Acadian Recorder* described the settlement as a 'disgrace and humiliation,' while the *Newcastle Advocate* reflected a widespread Maritime belief when it declared; 'In the matter of the fisheries we have been sold, and basely sold.'[7] But the opposition to the treaty receded as Maritime Canadians found a wider market for their fish in the United States. In the vote over the treaty only two of the Nova Scotia members opposed acceptance, and even a majority of the New Brunswick members, who remained angry that the Americans had been given the right to use the Saint John River, grudgingly voted for it.[8] Like the Nova Scotians, New Brunswickers were, however, impressed by the conciliatory attitude of the Macdonald government during the early 1870s. The Saint John *Daily Telegraph* even proclaimed that 'The Dominion Government has made some mistakes in the past, but as far as New Brunswick is concerned, they have been condoned and rectified to a large degree.'[9]

The gradual reconciliation of the Maritime members was reflected in the election of 1872. Although there was continuing confusion over party affiliation during the election, fifteen of the twenty-one Nova Scotia members and half of the sixteen New Brunswickers consistently supported the government during the first session of Parliament. Initially, a substantial majority of the Maritime members voted against the motion calling for a committee of investigation into the CPR contract. But there remained considerable discontent with the western orientation of the government and a feeling that vast expenditures on public works like the CPR must be counterbalanced by expenditures in the east. During the CPR negotiations Howe threatened resignation, and he only stayed in the cabinet in return for increased expenditures in Nova Scotia on wharves, public buildings, and bridges and the promise of the Baie de Verte canal and the extension of the provincial railway system. Howe's days in the cabinet were numbered, however, and on 7 May 1873 he resigned to become lieutenant-governor of Nova Scotia. He died a month after assuming office. With Howe's departure and because a number of the key members of the cabinet from Ontario had lost their seats in the election of 1872, the Maritimers began to move up the cabinet ladder. Tilley became minister of finance, and Tupper replaced him as minister of customs and also became minister of national revenue. Because of George-Etienne Cartier's disabling illness, Tupper rose to be the second man within the ministry. The influence of the Maritimers within the

Governor General Dufferin visits Charlottetown. After finally accepting
Ottawa's terms for union in 1873, Prince Edward Islanders responded
enthusiastically to a touring Lord Dufferin.

government was also enhanced during the Pacific Scandal, which tarnished the reputation of a number of the central Canadians. Unfortunately for the Maritime ministers, the scandal also led to the government's
defeat.

One of the last acts of the Macdonald government was the successful
wooing of Prince Edward Island. In both Island and Canadian historiography, a tradition of Island 'exceptionalism' has developed that explains the Island's opposition to Confederation as rooted in its intense
parochialism.[10] Yet the depth of Island opposition to Confederation is
open to question. Although the colony's government rejected a set of
marginally improved terms in 1869, the Island was gradually drawn
within the Canadian orbit. Even before joining Confederation it was
placed under the jurisdiction of the governor general of Canada, and in
1871 it decided to adopt the Canadian decimal system of coinage.[11] It
also had little option but to follow Canadian policy in regulating its
inshore fisheries.

A variety of internal factors explain the Island's decision to enter
Confederation in 1873. Pressure from the British government intensified
the feeling that Confederation would have to come in time. The un-

willingness of the American government to renegotiate reciprocity cast a pall over the economic future of the Island. The agitation by the Tenant League pushed the local élite towards abolition with a greater sense of urgency, and it was clear that, without Canadian financial support, there could be no resolution of the land question. The local government also embarked upon an overly ambitious program of railway building.[12] Undoubtedly the financial crisis generated by the railway debt explains the timing of Confederation, but the debate in 1870, when the legislature rejected the Dominion government's 1869 terms, nevertheless, revealed that the number of MLAs willing to accept Confederation if the terms were fair was growing steadily.[13] In 1870 James Pope formed the first of a series of Conservative governments that would dominate provincial politics for two decades. Local issues – particularly the Conservatives' abandonment of their traditional hostility to the demise of the leasehold system and their ability to reach a compromise with the colony's Catholics on the subject of denominational schools – were responsible for the realignment that took place in Island politics after 1870. This realignment brought to office a government dominated by pro-Confederates and committed to railway development.[14] In the provincial election of 1872 Pope and his supporters were defeated, and Robert Haythorne became premier. The new government did not reverse the railway policy of its predecessor, however, and by the end of 1872 it was so deeply in debt that it decided to reopen negotiations with the Dominion.

Fortunately for the pro-Confederates the federal government proved more sympathetic to the Island's plight than it had in the past. Haythorne and David Laird travelled to Ottawa and returned with an offer that they placed before the electorate in March 1873. Partly because he demanded even better terms and partly because of support from Catholics who believed that only a Conservative government would ever give financial support to Catholic schools, Pope was returned to power and another round of negotiations ensued. The result was that the Island ended up with much of what it had demanded at Quebec City in 1864. The federal government assumed the province's railway debt, increased its debt allowance, gave it a special subsidy in consideration of its lack of Crown lands, and loaned it $800,000 to purchase the estates of the landowners. The Island also received the guarantee of continuous communications with the mainland and, because of an increase in the size of the House of Commons following the census of 1871, it was given the sixth MP it had been denied at the Quebec Conference. Even so, Haythorne was perhaps making a virtue of necessity when he attributed the change of opinion in 1873 to the fact that the terms of union offered by Canada were for the first time 'advantageous and just' to P.E.I.[15]

The six P.E.I. members arrived in Ottawa just in time to participate in the death throes of the Macdonald administration. So evenly matched were the supporters and opponents of the government that the Islanders, according to Sir Richard Cartwright, 'held the balance of power,' when David Laird led four of the six into opposition on the CPR issue. The defection of the majority of the rest of the Maritime MPs sealed the fate of the government. It also forced the Maritimers into an uneasy alliance with the Liberal Party, which was dominated by the Ontario Grits who had repeatedly showed themselves unsympathetic to Maritime needs. In 1869 the Liberals had opposed both harbour improvements for Maritime ports and the subsidy for steam communication to P.E.I., as well as the better-terms settlement made with Nova Scotia.[16] When Nova Scotians had lobbied for a tariff on coal the Grits had resisted it, even though it was balanced by increased protection for grain. The opposition of the Grits was viewed by most Maritimers as 'the worst form of central Canadian narrow-mindedness.'[17] During the 1872 session the Grit opposition continued its policy of niggardly criticism of expenditures in the Maritimes, including such small items as a government subsidy for a steamship service between Halifax and Saint John and the construction of a pier in Digby. Yet the Liberal leadership was annoyed when the Maritimes did not return a solid phalanx of Liberals to the House of Commons in the election of 1872 and angry over the initial refusal of the Maritime members to defeat the government. When Alexander Mackenzie was chosen as the first leader of the party in 1872, the Maritime members played no part in his selection; and in 1873 Mackenzie wrote to remind a Maritimer that, 'In Ontario and Quebec we can carry all before us and N.S. and N.B. should understand that the country cannot be governed by the smaller Provinces combining against the two larger.'[18] After Mackenzie's appointment as leader of the Liberal Party, the most prominent New Brunswick opponent of Confederation, Albert J. Smith, announced his support for Macdonald.[19] Smith also led the exodus over the Pacific Scandal, however, and he joined the government formed by Mackenzie in 1873.

The election of 1874 saw the first truly national campaign in Canada. In Nova Scotia nineteen of the twenty-one members elected were pledged to support the Mackenzie government, even though a number of them were men who had previously supported Macdonald. In New Brunswick most of the members who had sat in the previous house were re-elected, but now twelve were classed as Liberals. On P.E.I. the government swept all six seats. Although not all of those elected as government supporters were well integrated into the Liberal Party and there would be defections, the Maritimes were central to the Liberal victory, since Mackenzie barely carried Quebec. Yet the Maritimes remained weakly represented in the cabinet. Of the Maritime ministers Mackenzie seems to have had respect only for Smith, the minister of marine and fisheries, who frequently served as leader of the government during the Prime Minister's absences.[20] Smith was able to secure a number of benefits for his constituency, including the decision to locate the Maritime penitentiary in Dorchester and to ensure that a branch line of the Intercolonial was built to Dorchester Island. He also successfully defended Maritime interests before the Halifax Fisheries Commission of 1877 and, as a result, became the first New Brunswicker to receive a knighthood. Mackenzie had less respect for David Laird.[21] In 1876 Laird was shunted off to become governor of the Northwest Territories in order to make room for David Mills, a much respected Ontario politician, who wrote to praise Mackenzie for abandoning the 'vicious' system of 'provincial representation in the Government.'[22] When the Islanders complained of their exclusion from the corridors of power, Mackenzie simply pointed to the fact that Ontario had a population of one and a half million and the Maritimes, including P.E.I., only three-quarters of a million. Yet, while this argument might appear 'not unreasonable' to Mackenzie,[23] it did not seem so to the Islanders.

Despite the need to maintain a strong Maritime base in order to overcome his party's weakness in Quebec, Mackenzie remained stubbornly unsympathetic to Maritime concerns. 'It seems that the smaller the province the more trouble it will be,' he wrote to Lord Dufferin in 1874. 'Half my time is taken up with this question of patronage in N. Scotia and Prince Edward Island. My life has become a torment to me about it. I am not troubled anywhere else.'[24] Certainly Mackenzie, as minister of public works, was deluged with requests for harbour improvements; but he never seems to have grasped that harbours were as critical to many Maritime communities as roads and railways were to the towns and villages of central Canada, nor that the weakness of municipal governments and the lack of resources in the Maritimes made the region more dependent on federal support. In the budget of 1874 the government included a series of nuisance taxes on specialized tools used only in the shipbuilding industry, taxes that were criticized by Conservatives as a regional levy, intended to fall only on the Maritimes. A few weeks after introducing the tax the cabinet removed them from the budget, but the damage had already been done.[25] Mackenzie tried to repair his image by allotting $500,000 for the Baie de Verte canal and included $1 million in the estimates for the following year, but in 1875 the Nova Scotia members suggested that the money would be better spent on Nova Scotia's railways. A commission, appointed to assess the commercial feasibility of the canal, recommended against proceeding, and in March 1876 Mackenzie announced the government's decision to abandon the project. The *Moncton Times* angrily declared that 'The Grit idea that one County in Ontario is more important than the whole of the Maritime Provinces, has shaped ... the policy of the Government with regard to the Lower Provinces ...'[26] On some issues the Maritime Liberals did exert considerable influence. During 1875 and 1876 they pressured Mackenzie not to rush ahead with the CPR and in 1876 the Nova Scotians helped to block any substantial increase in the tariff.[27] Their influence brought few positive benefits to the region, however. On 30 January 1878, the *New Brunswick Reporter* proclaimed: 'The Maritime Provinces have been so neglectfully treated during the past five or six years that they seem to have been almost blotted from the map of Canada.' This was undoubtedly an exaggeration, but one that was widely believed throughout the region.

The Liberals went into the election of 1878 resigned to defeat in Quebec but hoping to hold their support elsewhere, despite the persistence of the trade depression of the 1870s and the appeal of the Conservatives' National Policy. In fact, they were routed in Prince Edward Island and Nova Scotia and barely held their existing seats in New Brunswick. Part of the credit for the substantial Conservative victory must be given to the indefatigable efforts of Tupper and Tilley at strengthening Conservative prospects in the region. Untarnished by the CPR scandal, Tupper continued to play a leading role in defining government strategy in the House of Commons and became a close confidant of Macdonald. In Nova Scotia he organized the Liberal-Conservative Association, the first extra-parliamentary association in the province since the Anti-Confederation League and a model for similar organizations in other parts of the country. Tilley theoretically retreated to the non-partisan position of lieutenant-governor of his native province after 1873, but he corresponded regularly with Macdonald and devoted much of his time to party business. Both Tilley and Tupper played key roles in formulating the National Policy of tariff protection that became the basis of the Conservative Party's platform after 1876. They were not merely adhering to a policy created in Ontario and Quebec but were instrumental in advocating and in defining the nature of that policy. Although the protective impulse was weaker in the Maritimes than in central Canada, it was growing in strength in the urban centres of Halifax and Saint John, where the Conservatives did well.[28] As the Prince Edward Island result would indicate, however, protection was not the sole issue in the election and the general perception of Liberal indifference to Maritime concerns undoubtedly contributed to the substantial swing to the Conservatives.

In the ministry formed in 1878 the Maritimers received their reward. Tilley became minister of finance and receiver general; Tupper minister of public works and in 1879 the first minister of railways. There has probably not been a cabinet since Confederation in which Maritimers held so many key portfolios. Tilley and Tupper, in particular, were responsible for dealing with two of the most controversial policies of the government, the introduction of the protective tariff and the completion of the CPR. In implementing these policies both men showed not only that they possessed a national vision but also that they were sensitive to Maritime interests. Thus Tilley responded to the desire of Maritimers for a tariff on items such as coal and sugar that were critical to the regional economy,[29] while Tupper responded to the equally legitimate concern of the Maritimers that at least a portion of the vast sums of money being spent on railways should be directed to meeting their regional needs. One also has the impression that Maritimers began to receive a larger share of government patronage than in the past. The concern of the Maritime constituencies with patronage has been seen by some scholars as reaffirming the parochialism of the inhabitants and their somewhat limited horizons. Yet it was central Canadians who had established the rules of the game.[30] To a considerable extent Maritimers were engaged in a catching-up operation, and it is unlikely that they were able to approach anything like proportional representation in the Ottawa bureaucracy during this decade. Even at the constituency level they were demanding only equality of treatment with the Canadians, who rigidly insisted that only Canadians be appointed to federal positions in central-Canadian ridings and who tended to view positions in Ottawa as belonging to them. Tilley and Tupper and the other Maritime ministers had little choice but to follow the Canadian example, although they claimed to find the Canadian obsession with patronage distasteful.[31]

If Maritime politicians were successful in exercising greater influence at the federal level, their provincial counterparts had much more limited success in winning the kind of power and resources they required. The anti-Confederate ministry in Nova Scotia, initially united by little more than the insistence on repeal, was gradually transformed into a Liberal government and, like the federal Liberals, went down to defeat in 1878 when Simon Hughes Holmes formed the first Conservative government since Confederation. In New Brunswick party lines remained less clearly drawn; regardless of party affiliation, however, all the governments of both provinces found themselves in desperate financial straits in the 1870s. By 1874 Nova Scotia was spending $755,000 per annum instead of the $371,000 upon which Tupper, in preparing the financial settlement of 1867, had predicted the province could manage. At the London Conference, New Brunswick and Nova Scotia had received transitional subsidies[32] and the better-terms deal of 1869 led to a further $83,000 per annum for Nova Scotia for ten years, but the additional funds only temporarily prevented the deficit from getting out of control. New Brunswick was in even more desperate financial straits by the early 1870s. When the province sent a delegation to Ottawa in the fall of 1871, it aroused the ire of the Ontario members, and the Toronto *Globe* carried a strong editorial against the corrupt 'parish politics' of New Brunswick.[33] While the New Brunswick government remained optimistic that its claim for better terms would be sympathetically viewed in Ottawa, the debate over separate schools dashed the province's hopes, since the Quebec MPs sought to tie better financial terms to better terms for the Catholics of New Brunswick.[34] Thanks to Tilley, New Brunswick was given $58,000 per annum in 1873 as compensation for allowing American lumber to flow out of Saint John free of duty, in accordance with the provisions of the Treaty of Washington.[35] This grant became particularly important after 1877 when the province's ten-year transitional subsidy of $63,000 came to an end. But it still left New Brunswick in much the same position as Nova Scotia, with inadequate resources to embark upon a much-needed program of railway extension or to establish adequate educational institutions.

With its small population and lack of Crown lands, Prince Edward Island had even bleaker prospects. On the surface the financial terms offered by the Dominion in 1873 were exceedingly generous, but the amounts the Island received were too small to sustain an adequate level of provincial services. The first provincial government gave priority to dealing with the land question, but its first land bill, passed in 1873, was disallowed because it failed to provide an adequate means of appeal against the amount of compensation given to the landlords. An amended Land Purchase Bill was passed in 1874, and the province began the process of expropriating the estates of landlords whose holdings exceeded five hundred acres. The money from the resale of the land to the tenants was simply incorporated into general revenues rather than used to repay the federal loan, with the result that until the 1950s the Island was still paying interest on the loan to the federal government. In fact, the rigid system of financing introduced in 1873 left the provincial government with wholly inadequate means of meeting its responsibilities, particularly after its expenditures were dramatically increased with the introduction of a system of free schools and as the subsidies from the debt allowance declined. To meet this crisis the government sharply increased taxes in 1877 and introduced a one-dollar poll tax. The opposition bitterly attacked the burden placed on the tenant farmers trying to purchase the estates they worked and denounced the bill as 'class legislation.' During 1877, 'indignation' meetings were held throughout the province. So long as the central issue in Island politics was the creation of free, non-sectarian schools, the government of Louis Henry

Davies, a coalition of Protestants from both parties, held together. Once that issue was resolved, however, the members of the coalition began to revert to their former partisan allegiances, and in September 1878 four of the five Conservative members of the cabinet resigned. The Davies government promised a program of retrenchment to remove the need for higher taxation, but on 6 March 1879 it was defeated by nineteen to ten and W.W. Sullivan, the Island's first Roman Catholic Premier, formed a Conservative administration. After an election in which Sullivan assured Protestant voters that he would not tamper with the nonsectarian school system and campaigned on a program of retrenchment, he introduced bills cutting the salaries of MLAs, reducing the cost of the small civil service, abandoning the secret ballot to save the money spent on registration and administration, amalgamating Prince of Wales College and the Provincial Normal School, and abolishing the Legislative Council. Although the Sullivan government became the first administration since Confederation to balance the provincial budget, these draconian measures did nothing to resolve the financial crisis, and during the 1880s P.E.I. would be faced with a chronic deficit, which it could only meet by appeals to Ottawa. It also bitterly protested the federal government's failure to provide the 'continuous communication' with the mainland promised at the time of Confederation and vainly demanded a share of the Halifax Fishery Award of 1877, since the principle of compensation had been agreed to before P.E.I. had become a part of Canada.[36]

Some contemporary central-Canadian Liberals and later historians have tended 'to see something derogatory and even shameful about the insistent claims of the provinces for revisions of the subsidy arrangements.'[37] Yet, as Wilfrid Eggleston pointed out many years ago, the source of the problem lay in the 'faulty and unfortunate' financial settlement made at the time of Confederation, one that 'confined certain provinces within a strait-jacket while allowing other provinces with more ample resources to expand in a natural fashion.'[38] It is, of course, possible that some reductions could have been made in provincial expenditures, but the two big items in all the provincial budgets were education and transportation, both essential services. Other than federal grants, the sources of revenue available to the provinces, such as various forms of licences, were extremely limited, and the Maritime provinces did not possess the resource base of central Canada. Indeed, the fiscal needs of the Maritime governments and their limited options had serious long-term consequences. The royalties from coal and timber were so essential to the provincial governments that they encouraged rapid resource depletion. Although their dependence on these revenues promoted a much greater degree of government involvement in the development of provincial resources than in Ontario, it was interference primarily for the purpose of ensuring a steady flow of royalty income rather than proper resource utilization. As the *Halifax Chronicle* correctly declared, 'Confederation is a system under which the rich upper provinces are growing richer and the poor lower provinces poorer every year.'[39]

The provinces could have resorted to direct taxation to solve their financial problems, but this was not a realistic option. The provinces had been left with the authority to impose direct taxes on the assumption that they would establish municipal institutions with the power to levy direct taxes, such as already existed in Ontario and Quebec. In fact, there was no great enthusiasm for such institutions in the Maritimes. P.E.I. was too compact to need municipal institutions outside of Charlottetown and Summerside, which were incorporated in 1855 and 1875. In New Brunswick and Nova Scotia, the counties had been given the right in the 1850s to establish elected county governments to replace the older and clumsy quarter-sessions system, but only a handful of counties had taken advantage of the permissive legislation in New Brunswick and none at all in Nova Scotia. None the less, in order to force the counties to assume the financial burden for the maintenance of roads and bridges, in 1877 in New Brunswick and in 1879 in Nova Scotia the provincial governments rammed bills through the provincial legislatures providing for compulsory incorporation.[40] These county incorporation acts remained the framework of municipal government in the rural areas until the mid-twentieth century. As urban areas expanded in size in the 1870s, particularly along the railway lines, a growing number of towns were also incorporated during the decade, a sign of the increasing continental integration that was taking place even before the industrial boom generated by the National Policy.

The economic depression of the 1870s, which coincided with Mackenzie's years in office, created immense hardship throughout the region and both delayed and accelerated the process of continental integration. The vast majority of Maritimers continued to live in rural communities, and their livelihood depended on the production of raw materials. Although agricultural production would decline markedly in economic significance during the latter part of the nineteenth century, it was still the single most important economic activity in the region. In Nova Scotia it was worth more than the combined value of the fishing, shipping, and coal industries, and in New Brunswick it probably exceeded the value of lumbering. Much of the farming was subsistence, carried on by part-time farmers who combined it with fishing, lumbering, mining, or even local craft manufacture. Yet there were significant pre-industrial markets for agriculture in the region and many prosperous agricultural communities. Indeed, Maritime farmers seem to have weathered the

Taking out the pine, 1868. New Brunswick's timber industry peaked during the 1870s. Employing a large seasonal work-force, it depended upon stands of virgin timber, which, though still available, were becoming less easily accessible.

depression of the 1870s and the beginnings of continental integration rather better than most sectors of the economy. Wheat farming, for which the climate was not especially suited, was gradually abandoned, but both the livestock and dairying industries expanded and, by the end of the decade, Maritime farmers had begun to turn to apples, seed potatoes, and fox farming for cash crops. Mixed farming gave way to more specialized production.

The other resource-based industries of the region felt the impact of the depression later than the agricultural communities, and until the mid-1870s the demand for Maritime exports remained comparatively strong. The lumber industry, in particular, reached new heights in the early 1870s, until the depressed condition of the British market brought to an abrupt halt in 1875 the previously rapid growth of the industry and led to a decline that would continue for the rest of the century.[41] The fishing industry, which was particularly important in Nova Scotia, fared somewhat better, but it too underwent a transition during the 1870s, as production of dried cod declined in significance, while lobsters and oysters and the canning of salmon and sardines increased. The coal mines of the region, however, languished after the ending of reciprocity, with the exception of the Springhill mine, whose coal fuelled the Intercolonial Railway and was primarily produced for consumption within the region.

Over the long term, all the resource industries would recover, but not the wooden shipping and shipbuilding industries, which entered a prolonged and irreversible decline. The increasing deployment of the iron hull and the steam engine and the shrinking British market for wooden ships destroyed the long-term viability of the shipbuilding industry, and the collapse of that trade in the mid-1870s led large numbers of carpenters and other skilled labourers to seek alternative employment, frequently in the United States where there was a growing demand for their skills in the rapidly growing urban centres of New England. For many Maritime communities the emigration of these skilled and comparatively highly paid labourers was a serious loss.

Closely linked to the timber trade and the shipbuilding industry was the related activity of shipowning. Initially many Maritime shipowners were short-time or part-time owners who sold their vessels in Britain,[42] but by the 1870s Maritime-owned ships were to be found on almost all the international trading routes. By 1878, at its peak, the Canadian fleet was, albeit briefly, the fourth-largest merchant marine in the world, and 72 per cent of the tonnage was registered along the Atlantic coast.[43] But the era of the wooden ships was passing, and they were increasingly confined to the coastal trade, the fisheries, and the more marginal oceanic trades. It may be too simple to explain the decline of the shipping industry 'simply by reference to the technological transition from sail to steam and from wood to iron,' particularly since it remained profitable to operate wooden ships for several decades after the 1870s.[44] But since the Maritime shipowners were rational men, it is hardly surprising that they were increasingly sceptical of tying their futures to an industry that did represent an outmoded technology – 'a thing of the past' as one veteran shipbuilder referred to sailing ships in 1875.[45] Although shipowning could still generate short-term opportunities and profits, many shipowners began to diversify their investments into other economic activities. Indeed, the high level of ownership during the 1870s was artificially induced by the limited alternatives available to investors during the recession, and in the 1880s, when given the option of profitable landward investments, Maritime merchants would run their seaward investments down. Only around the Great Lakes was the demand for shipping large enough to justify the substantial investment that steamships required, and Maritimers turned not to steamships as an alternative but to domestic manufacturing.

Even at its peak, the shipping (as opposed to the shipbuilding) industry

Shipbuilding crew, Scots Bay, N.S., 1871. Workers started young, as can be seen from the group of boys in this photo. They learned their trades working beside their fathers and older brothers.

never employed more than a relatively small percentage of the labour force, and it generated a limited amount of capital flow into the region. In 1870 mariners accounted for only 2.4 per cent of New Brunswick's and 6.6 per cent of Nova Scotia's labour force, and it is apparent from the treatment of 'Jack in port' that going to sea was not necessarily considered a desirable career option for young Maritimers.[46] In fact, most Maritimers in the 1870s, as their fathers and forefathers had done, looked to the land to provide them with their means of subsistence, and even the vast majority of those who did look to the sea for a livelihood were land-based, inshore fishermen. In a few of the coastal communities with no hinterland and limited agricultural or industrial potential – Yarmouth and Liverpool are obvious examples – the call of the sea may have been stronger than the appeal of the land, but they were the exceptions rather than the general rule. For most Maritimers the real transition after Confederation was from a staples economy, based upon the export of unprocessed or slightly processed raw materials to metropolitan centres across the Atlantic, to a more diversified economy with a significant manufacturing component and continental integration.

Until the end of the 1870s the movement in this direction was slight. A handful of small industrial firms were established; but they lacked a large regional market and sufficient capitalization, and many did not survive the depression of the 1870s. In fact, the most substantial growth came from the influx of funds for the building of the Intercolonial. For strategic reasons the Intercolonial ran through the lightly populated north shore of New Brunswick, but those cities fortunate enough to be located in its path benefited substantially. Moncton, which became the headquarters for the railway, grew particularly rapidly, and Moncton time, the basis of the ICR's timetable, became the standard for the whole region. By 1881, 12.7 per cent of Moncton's 5,032 inhabitants worked for the Intercolonial, and the city had pinned its hopes for future growth on closer integration through the National Policy with national markets.[47] The ICR also stimulated the development of manufacturing in Halifax; but Halifax was not well located to engage in staple processing, the major industrial activity in most mid-nineteenth century cities, and it remained essentially an entrepôt town, a role strengthened after the completion of the ICR.[48]

Saint John was a different story. Having entered the 1870s as the largest urban centre in the region and one of the most dynamic in British North America, it was the only urban centre in the country to shrink in size during the decade. Yet as a case study, Saint John shows how nonsensical it is to assign the decline of the region to entrepreneurial failure. The business community of Saint John had limited control over the economic destiny of the city. From its foundation Saint John's prosperity had been intimately tied to the British market, first for timber and increasingly for timber products, particularly wooden ships. By 1870 the city 'was becoming less a hinterland extension of Liverpool and more the centre of its own metropolitan system,'[49] but timber for the British market remained the most significant export that flowed from the port. Reflecting this dependence on the timber trade, the city possessed the largest fleet of wooden ships of any port in British North America, and its vessels were significantly larger. Shipbuilding accounted for 20 per cent of the value of goods produced in the city and employed 15 to 20 per cent of the work-force.[50] Strategically located at the mouth of the major river system in the Maritimes, Saint John controlled the province's banking and financial institutions, accounted for half the province's manufacturing output, and employed half its artisans. A variety of factors explain the city's rapid decline after Confederation. Pre-eminent among them was the collapse of the timber trade and of the market for wooden ships. During the 1870s the tonnage of ships built in the city declined dramatically, and the city's merchants were forced to retain ownership of an increasing proportion of the ships and to operate them in the international carrying trades. The impact of the collapse was both aggravated and mitigated by the Great Fire of 20 June 1877, which left 15,000 homeless and destroyed 1,612 houses and ten miles of street, with estimated losses of $27 million. This devastation undoubtedly con-

The Saint John fire, 1877. Destroying virtually the entire business district, the fire added to the problems of a city already hit by depression and a declining shipbuilding industry.

stituted a severe drain on the capital and human resources of Saint John, although it also led to a substantial influx of federal funds to rebuild the city. For a time the out-migration of large numbers of carpenters, masons, and builders was delayed by the artificial demand for their services. It is easy, however, to overemphasize both the positive and negative implications of the Great Fire. The real challenge that faced Saint John in the 1870s was to adjust to the declining significance of the British market and to carve out a new role for itself as part of a continental transportation system.

Because of its location and the decision to build the Intercolonial along the northern route, the city started at a disadvantage. But the leading commercial interests in the city did not give up hope. In the summer of 1869 the eighty-nine-mile New Brunswick section of the proposed European and North American railway – the Western Extension – was completed, and by 1871 Maine had built its part of the line from Bangor to the New Brunswick border. When it became apparent that the Americans would not renew reciprocity and that the anticipated business from the Western Extension was unlikely to materialize, Saint John turned to a national strategy and sought a larger share of Canada's continental trade. In 1871 the federal government agreed to subsidize two steamship lines to Saint John, one of which linked the city to Windsor and the other to Halifax.[51] The local merchant community eagerly pushed for an extension of the ICR, which finally arrived in Saint John in 1876. The city also sought to improve its harbour facilities. Part of the price that had to be paid for this strategy was the transfer of a portion of the city's charter-granted waterfront to the federal government. By 1879 the fortunes of the port 'had been entrusted to Ottawa.'[52]

As part of this continentalist strategy there was growing pressure from at least a minority in Saint John for the protection of local industry. In 1871 the per-capita output of New Brunswick ($59.80) was closer to Ontario's ($69.60) and Quebec's ($62.00) than to Nova Scotia's ($30.70), and more than half of New Brunswick's industrial output of $8.3 million was produced in and around Saint John. Although the largest components in this output were sawmill products and wooden ships, 'virtually every industry that had been given even a modest degree of protection in the previous generation flourished. The manufacture of foundry products, footwear, and clothing all exceeded shipbuilding in value, while furniture and carriage making, boiler, saw and file manufacturing, tin and sheet-iron output, and leather making all played significant roles in the local economy.'[53] The clothing trades were particularly important, employing 1,033 people, 828 of them women, in 1871. Virtually all this industrial production was for local consumption and, while the completion of the ICR opened up the region to competition from central Canada, it also encouraged the development of foundries and machine shops. In 1875 the Harris Works in Saint John was awarded a contract of $300,000 to build cars and trucks for the Intercolonial, and by the 1880s it had emerged as one of the most extensive car works in the country.[54]

Many Saint John businessmen believed Saint John would benefit from and could successfully compete within a national policy of tariff protection: 'the time will come when St. John will be the greatest manufacturing city in Canada,' predicted a youthful James Hannay in 1875.[55] But greater investment in regional industry was hindered by several factors. One was the mercantile – and essentially *rentier* – outlook of the local business communities. In the 1870s Saint John investors were responsible for the development of the coal resources at Springhill, but they were motivated by short-term commercial considerations and would sell out to Montreal interests in the 1880s at a time when the mine was earning a steady profit. Indeed, even during the 1870s, shareholders were earning at least 5 and frequently closer to 10 per cent. These were reasonable profits, but they were not high when compared to the returns generated in the shipping industry, where most of the investments of the 1870s seem to have been concentrated. The merchant capitalists of

The Intercolonial, 1876. Maritimers welcomed completion of the Intercolonial Railway from Lévis, Quebec, to Halifax as part of the Confederation agreement. They expected the railway, like the canals on the St Lawrence, to serve regional interests without necessarily earning a profit.

Saint John were thus motivated by 'a strategy of minimal capital investment and maximum dividend levels' and not by a long-term 'strategy of industrialization.'[56] The mercantile orientation of such men, who viewed the coalfields as simply another form of real estate to be sold to the highest bidder, meant that they overlooked the significant industrial potential of an area like Springhill.

Many smaller towns suffering from the recession of the 1870s sought salvation in the development of railways. There was nothing distinctive and nothing trivial in the obsession of every small town to be on a railway line, for the location of the railway was a crucial factor in deciding the town's future. Indeed, enthusiasm for the Intercolonial had persuaded many Maritimers of the economic benefit of Confederation. The Intercolonial has traditionally received a bad press, partly because for many years it was the only major Canadian railway system operated by the state and came to symbolize government corruption and waste. Undeniably the railway never ran at a profit and was thus unattractive to private investors. Indeed, it is hard to see how it could have been run at a profit since, primarily for strategic reasons, it was forced to follow a circuitous route via the sparsely populated north shore of New Brunswick. Since it passed through eighteen constituencies in the Maritimes and Quebec, the services of contractors, suppliers, and labourers were used by the government to reward its supporters. Yet it is easy to exaggerate the significance of political interference. The managers of the Intercolonial were prepared to distribute positions on the basis of patronage, but only to those who were qualified to hold them. Purchase contracts were usually given to the lowest bidder, and the ICR spent less on wages and material per train than did the CPR and only very slightly more than the Grand Trunk. By the standards of the day the ICR was 'a comparatively efficient railway.'[57] Although Alexander Mackenzie insisted that the ICR must be run as a commercial enterprise, Tupper, the minister of railways after 1878, allowed it to run at a slight annual deficit and to set fares on the 'value of service' principle, which kept the rates on goods flowing west low to encourage the development of industries within the region.[58]

Industrialization was hindered, however, by the depression, which greatly handicapped the comparatively small financial institutions of the region. There was an expansion in banking facilities after Confederation, and many of the new institutions were prepared to invest in industrial projects within the region. But the resources of the Maritime banks were extremely limited, and the depression destroyed the viability of a number of banks and reduced the effectiveness of the rest.[59] Despite the depression, however, considerable industrial growth did take place in the urban centres of the region. In places it rivalled that of central Canada, but it was unequally distributed and, overall, the Maritimes lagged behind in manufacturing output in the 1870s, as they had in the two previous decades, particularly in the area of non-durable goods industries (such as brewing, flour milling, and woollens).[60] Moreover, many Maritime industries began to feel the impact of central-Canadian competition. Partly as a response to growing American penetration of the Canadian market, central-Canadian manufacturers sought to dominate the national market, and swarms of salesmen travelled from the larger central-

International Coal Company shipping pier, Sydney, 1871. Coal companies'
access to outside markets was improved when new piers such as this one
permitted them to load directly onto waiting ships.

Canadian industrial firms to sell their products in the Maritimes. But
integration moved slowly so long as the Canadian market was open to
external firms, and Maritimers continued to import manufactured goods.
As the recession deepened, a growing number of businessmen began to
consider seriously the option of protection for Canadian industry. The
protective impulse was obviously strongest in the industrial heartland
of central Canada, but there were sympathetic Maritimers among the
membership of the Saint John and Halifax manufacturers' associations
and the Nova Scotian Association for the Encouragement of Industrial
Interests.

  Protection was also not without appeal to the large number of workers
who lost their jobs during the depression. The widespread distress led
to a substantial out-migration of the carpenters and other skilled workmen who had relied on the shipbuilding industry for employment, while
the collapse of the lumber industry forced many loggers to move south.
As the market for agricultural goods dried up, many farmers had to turn
from commercial to subsistence farming at a time when they could no
longer rely upon part-time employment in the timber industry, and their

sons and daughters were compelled to move to the United States to supplement the family income. Population growth rates slowed to 14 per cent for Nova Scotia, 12 per cent for New Brunswick, and 16 per cent for P.E.I., so that even some of the natural increase was lost. Except for Halifax and a few sparsely settled areas in northern New Brunswick, every county experienced net out-migration.[61] The migration was partly a rural-to-urban movement, and the proportion of people living in urban areas in the mainland provinces grew from 8 to 28 per cent. But for many Maritimers the ultimate destination was the booming New England states, and pull factors seem to have been at least as important as push factors in accounting for the outpouring.[62] Since the Irish and the Scots left in larger numbers than other ethnic groups, the Maritimes became more English and more French. The young were overrepresented among the migrants, with the result that the population became older. Single women also migrated in large numbers, attracted by the lure of domestic and factory work in the booming cities of New England. The full impact of the 'great exodus' would not be felt until the 1880s, but even in the 1870s there was widespread concern over the implications of a population decline.

The depression of the 1870s and the movement towards industrialization had a particularly significant impact upon the older artisanal culture. The collapse of the shipbuilding industry, which had always been dominated by small units of production and a series of traditional crafts, such as riggers, spar-makers, sail-makers, caulkers, and shipwrights, meant that such crafts were overrepresented in the exodus. Although the small workshop organized on craft lines continued to dominate the manufacturing sector, during the 1870s the region's urban economies became increasingly industrial and the scale of production of many factories increased dramatically. By 1875 Saint John's 10 foundries employed on average 43 men and its 614 manufacturing establishments 9,531 operatives. The size of the wage bill for such establishments doubled between 1870 and 1875. Indeed, the post-1875 depression intensified the trend by bankrupting marginal producers and forcing many small firms out of business.[63] With the decline of the traditional crafts and the consolidation of capital, class conflict became increasingly pronounced and strikes became more frequent. Unionization proceeded as the economic crisis deepened after 1873, although many of these craft unions did not survive the depressed conditions of the decade.[64] Few of the craft unions of this period had any connection with international unions, although the Knights of St Crispin began to organize Maritime shoemakers and the International Typographical Union expanded from its Montreal headquarters into the region.

The largest and most active labour organization in the Maritimes was the Ship Labourers' Benevolent Association of Saint John, which had more than a thousand members in the 1870s. In the midst of the depression, Saint John experienced its most important strike of the century when the ship labourers struck in 1875.[65] But the most serious labour unrest occurred in the coalfields of Nova Scotia. Strikes by colliers over wages had never been uncommon, but the introduction of American managers and the depressed market for coal in the 1870s led to bitter confrontations. In 1873 the government of Nova Scotia introduced a comprehensive bill to regulate mining. The bill gave even fewer rights to miners than the British statute on which it was modelled. Moreover, although it restricted the employment of boys under ten years, it only limited those under twelve to sixty hours per week, compared to the British limitation of thirty-six hours.[66] During the depressed conditions in the industry after 1873, the miners, like the ship labourers, were forced to accept wage reductions and, after a massive and unsuccessful strike in 1876, many unemployed Cape Breton miners were forced to migrate to Springhill. Only at Springhill were the miners able to resist pay reductions by establishing the Provincial Miners' Association in 1879, renamed the Provincial Workmen's Association in 1880.[67]

Symbolic also of the beginnings of the transition to industrial society was the collapse of the mechanics' institutes, founded in the second quarter of the nineteenth century to encourage education among the producing classes. Although frequently these organizations were dominated by members of the mercantile or professional élite, artisans played a key part in their activities until the early 1870s, when fees began to rise. By 1880 only the Saint John Mechanics' Institute survived, and it had become an anachronism, sustained as much by its rental income as by its attraction to mechanics.[68] It is difficult not to see this development as inevitable. The institutes were introduced into the region at a time when there seemed to be a considerable overlap in the interests of the artisans and the mercantile and professional élites. Both groups subscribed to an ideology that emphasized liberal political values, self-improvement, and a community of interest in pursuing economic growth. As class divisions became more pronounced the mechanics' institutes lost their essential *raison d'être*. Their educational function was rapidly usurped by the state and by the creation of public libraries. A series of more specialized organizations, such as the Nova Scotia Institute of Science (1863), the New Brunswick Natural History Society (1864), the New Brunswick Historical Society, and the Nova Scotia Historical Society (1878), assumed responsibility for promoting various kinds of scholarly inquiry. The new organizations were more exclusive in their membership. The historical societies, in particular, were small and unrepresentative bodies, drawn largely from the ranks of the older colonial

Baseball on the commons, 1878. Hockey, football, and baseball replaced cricket as the region integrated with the broader North American culture. Here two Halifax teams, the Resolutes and the Athletics, square off before a substantial crowd.

élites; some of their members opposed Confederation, and they saw in the historical societies a vehicle for establishing respect for a way of life that was threatened by the coming of industrial society. But it is misleading to think that such men were the authentic voice of the region and that their vision of a past 'golden age' was widely shared. Indeed, the younger generation of intellectuals, like Charles G.D. Roberts and Bliss Carman, looked forward, not backward, and sought to carve out national reputations for themselves.

Much of the anguish of the older élites was due to their increasing irrelevancy. The rapid expansion of scientific and professional associations, first at the provincial and then at the national level, was one sign of the specialization required in late-nineteenth-century society. In 1872, at the urging of the Nova Scotia Medical Society, the provincial legislature passed an 'Act to Regulate the Qualifications of Practitioners in Medicine and Surgery,' which established a provincial medical board to control entry into the profession. New Brunswick followed suit in 1874.[69] As industrialization took hold in the late nineteenth century, businessmen, labourers, and professionals were all affected by the 'protective

Bliss Carman (left) and Charles G.D. Roberts (right)

impulse' and began to organize along occupational rather than community lines, a process encouraged by the establishment of national associations in the latter part of the century.

The strongest of these national organizations were undoubtedly those associated with the temperance movement. The Sons of Temperance, the Good Templars, the United Temperance Association, and, after 1875, the Women's Christian Temperance Union all spread rapidly through the region. A New Brunswick delegation was present at the founding of the Dominion Alliance for the Total Suppression of the Liquor Traffic in 1876 and the Maritime legislatures and MPs strongly supported the passage of the Canada Temperance Act (or Scott Act), which became law on 8 May 1878. The first place in the Dominion to vote for prohibition was Fredericton, where the law went into force on 1 May 1879. Within a few years, virtually every county in the Maritimes had opted for the suppression of the liquor traffic, either by holding plebiscites under the Scott Act or by municipal ordinance. Even Saint John nearly fell under the control of the temperance forces. Only in Halifax did the supporters of 'demon rum' remain in control.[70]

The strength of the temperance campaign was in part a reflection of the strength of evangelical Protestantism in this period. As in Ontario, the middle decades of the nineteenth century had seen the rapid ex-

Saint John police court, c. 1876. The abuse of liquor was considered a problem; after each weekend, municipal courts were busy with drunkards and
other petty offenders.

pansion of four well-organized Protestant churches, the Presbyterians,
Anglicans, Methodists, and Baptists. By the post-Confederation period
the historic rivalry among these denominations had considerably fallen
off, and they were becoming part of what has been described as an
'omnibus Protestantism denomination,' based upon a broad religious
consensus.[71] By the 1870s all four churches had come to accept the need
for a separation of church and state, incorporation, an educated and paid
ministry, Sabbath schools, missionary work, interdenominationalism and
presbyterian-style ordinations. They joined in an informal alliance committed to introduce non-sectarian religious instruction into the schools,
prevent the growth of Catholicism, uphold the sanctity of the sabbath,
and encourage the spread of temperance. Although the Allinite tradition,
which promoted a less formal, less structured form of worship, lay participation and control, and radical enthusiasm, remained strong in the
Annapolis Valley of Nova Scotia and along the Saint John Valley of
New Brunswick, particularly among Free Will Baptists, even the latter
gradually underwent 'the transition from an Allinite "sectarian" to an
evangelical "church" outlook' during the late nineteenth century.[72] Con-

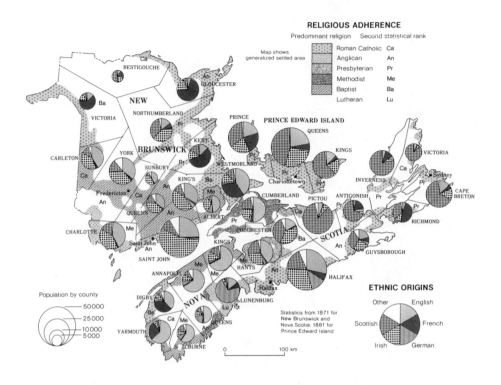

Figure 3 Cultural hearth areas: the religious and ethnic character of the Maritimes, 1871

federation accelerated this process because it led to the Canadianization of all the Maritime churches, as they were integrated into national organizations, beginning in 1874 when the Eastern British American Conference united with the Canadian Conference to form the Methodist Church of Canada.

The Baptist and Methodist churches both experienced major revivals and particularly rapid growth and led the way in raising funds and volunteers for overseas missions. They also led the way in accepting a wider sphere for women. Minnie De Wolfe, a Baptist from Truro, organized the first women's missionary society in the region and became the first unmarried woman missionary from any church in Canada.[73] Both the Baptists at Wolfville and the Methodists at Sackville had established academies for women in the 1850s and 1860s and, partly as a response to financial pressures to expand enrolments, the small, Methodist-controlled Mount Allison University admitted women to its regular programs in 1872. In 1875 a Mount Allison student, Grace Annie Lock-

Hannah Maria Norris, Baptist missionary from Canso, N.S. Denied financing from traditional sources for a career in Burma, Norris found support through pioneering in 1870 the organization of women's missionary societies. Such societies not only founded missions but became a means of education and building confidence for Canadian women.

hart, became the first woman to be awarded a bachelor's degree at any institution in the British Empire.

Inevitably, evangelical Protestantism came into conflict with an increasingly well-organized and determined Catholic hierarchy over the crucial issue of education. What most Protestants wanted was a system of publicly supported schools in which religion would be taught on a theoretically non-sectarian basis. For Catholics non-sectarianism was a smoke-screen designed to hide the reality of Protestant evangelism, and they demanded that the principle of compulsory assessment be accompanied by a recognition of the right of Catholics to their own publicly funded separate schools. At the London Conference in 1866, the Catholic bishops of the Maritimes had sought to have the protection afforded to Canadian Catholics extended to their Maritime brethren as a reward for the hierarchy's decision to support Confederation. Their failure led to a bitter conflict in the post-Confederation period.

That conflict was least bitter in Nova Scotia where Catholics formed only 26 per cent of the population. Here the basic outline of the school system had been created by the Free School Act of 1864, which abolished both French and Gaelic schools and placed the province's non-sectarian schools under the control of a superintendent of education who reported to the cabinet acting as a council of education. In 1865 the Tupper government amended the bill to make public assessment for education compulsory. The Catholics of Nova Scotia under the leadership of Archbishop Thomas Connolly continued to press for separate schools, and it was partly because of Catholic pressure that the first superintendent of education, Theodore Harding Rand, an outspoken defender of non-sectarian schools, was dismissed in 1870. The provincial government was not prepared to support separate schools, but it defused much of the resentment by allowing local school trustees to rent Roman Catholic schools in which Catholics were taught by Catholic teachers and religious instruction was allowed after hours.[74] On Prince Edward Island, where Catholics formed 42 per cent of the population, a similar compromise was reached. To pacify the Protestant majority, the 1873 and 1877 schools acts established a non-sectarian system, with Bible reading as part of the morning exercises. In practice, however, Catholic schools were allowed to operate in communities with a Catholic majority.[75]

In New Brunswick, where Roman Catholics formed 33 per cent of the population, the conflict over separate schools was less easily resolved. Under the provincial schools act of 1858 Catholic schools had not only been permitted but had flourished. In 1871 the government of George E. King pushed through the legislature a bill similar to the Nova Scotia act. But a compromise along the lines worked out in Nova Scotia was rejected by the cabinet, which published a series of regulations that effectively prohibited Catholic priests and nuns from serving as teachers and thus prevented Catholic schools from operating as non-sectarian schools. The Catholics appealed first to the courts, which eventually upheld the constitutionality of the 1871 Common Schools Act, and then to the federal government. Under intense pressure from Tilley, who threatened to resign if Ottawa disallowed the act, Macdonald refused to intervene on the grounds that education was a provincial responsibility. When Catholics in New Brunswick refused to pay assessments for public schools, they were prosecuted for non-payment. In 1873 the New Brunswick assessment legislation was ruled unconstitutional on technical grounds, and the New Brunswick legislature moved to close the loopholes in the act. Once again the issue of disallowance was debated in the House of Commons, and once again the federal government refused to use disallowance. To Macdonald's embarrassment, however, a motion for disallowance was carried with the support of half the French-Canadian Conservatives. Macdonald shuffled responsibility to the imperial government, which advised the governor-general to assent to the assessment act and so affirmed the principle of provincial responsibility.

Faced with the obstinacy of the New Brunswick government, the bishops of the Maritimes circulated a pastoral letter insisting that, 'As Catholics we form nearly one half of the population of Canada, and we have, therefore, an undoubted right to obtain in the Maritime Provinces what the Catholic majority accorded long ago to the Protestant minority of the Province of Quebec ...' New Brunswick Protestants viewed the bishops' intervention as an attempt to bring about 'the utter subversion and ruin of the Free School System' and, in the election of 1874, the King government swept to victory. Only five supporters of separate schools were returned, all of them in counties in the north with Acadian majorities, and 73 per cent of all the votes cast were in favour of candidates who supported the 1871 schools act.[76]

In the fall of 1874 the New Brunswick government began to move against those refusing to pay school taxes. Cows, stoves, the books of various priests, and, in Saint John, the horses and carriage of Bishop Sweeney were seized and sold for taxes due on Roman Catholic school properties. In Caraquet, a small group of English-speaking Protestants used the refusal of Catholics to pay their rates as an excuse for overturning the parish elections and put into power parish officers committed to enforcing the payment of the schools tax. In a county that was overwhelmingly French and Catholic this provocation unleashed a storm of indignation and a series of protests, dubbed 'riots' by the authorities. On 'bloody Wednesday,' 27 January 1875, one constable and one rioter were accidentally killed during a clash. Nine Acadians were accused of murder. The first of the Acadians put on trial, Joseph Chiasson, was found guilty, but the Supreme Court eventually quashed the conviction because of various errors committed during the trial, and all the defendants were released. In the aftermath of the Caraquet riots the Roman Catholic members of the legislature and the New Brunswick hierarchy finally arrived at a compromise. According to the agreement of 1875, Roman Catholic children would be grouped in the same schools and taught by members of Catholic religious orders, would read texts from which passages offensive to Catholics had been removed, and would receive religious instruction after hours. Somewhat reluctantly, since the compromise fell far short of the equality they had sought, the bishops of New Brunswick advised Catholics to cease their opposition to the act.[77]

The compromise of 1875 fell even shorter in meeting the aspirations of the French-speaking population of New Brunswick. The proportion of Acadians rose from 15.7 per cent to 17.6 per cent of the population during the 1870s. The majority of Acadians continued to live along the north shore in small, relatively self-sufficient communities. The women supplied the domestic labour, spinning and weaving at home, preserving and preparing food, and caring for large numbers of children, since the Acadians continued to have fertility rates far above the national average. Acadian men earned their livelihood by combining seasonal work in the fisheries or the timber industry with part-time subsistence agriculture. The phenomenal growth of the lobster industry in the latter part of the 1870s did, however, bring revolutionary changes to many fishing com-

The Caraquet Riot, 1875. A clash between special constables and a small group of militant Acadians left two dead and encouraged both government and church leaders to compromise on the regulations accompanying New Brunswick's Common Schools Act.

munities in New Brunswick and saw for the first time hundreds of Acadian women in wage-earning positions in the lobster factories.[78] The Acadians did not emigrate in anything like the same numbers as anglophone New Brunswickers in the 1870s and 1880s, but began to establish new communities in the interior of the province and to swell the urban proletariat of Moncton. An Acadian nationalist movement also began to take shape in this period. Acadian nationalism had been given impetus by the publication of Longfellow's *Evangeline* in French in 1865. In a way never intended by Longfellow, the poem entered the Acadian consciousness and served as an effective symbol for the cultural revival of suffering *Acadie*.[79] But the Acadian renaissance also reflected the ambitions of the newly emergent Acadian élite, many of them graduates of St Joseph's College, which reopened at Memramcook in 1864 and was given a university charter by the New Brunswick government in 1868.[80] Although housed in a small and unimpressive wooden building, described by one of the students as 'Notre pauvre wigwam,'[81] it became the training ground for the children of the Acadian élite – as well as many Irish Roman Catholics, since the school was conducted on bilingual principles. Some of its graduates, like François-Xavier Cormier, became priests; others, like Pierre-Armand Landry and Pascal Poirier, politicians; still others became merchants and businessmen. The first generation of Acadian graduates entered public life during the debate over the New Brunswick Common Schools Act. Landry, in particular, was an outspoken critic of the act and assisted in the defence of the Caraquet rioters. Tying himself to the Conservative Party, which was more sympathetic to Catholic demands both federally and provincially, he was invited to join the Conservative administration formed in 1878 as commissioner of public works and so became the first Acadian cabinet minister in the province's history. As commissioner of public works he sought to include Acadians in the distribution of provincial patronage, and he appealed for more federal appointments on the grounds that 'the French-Acadians of the Maritimes are not recognized by existing institutions in a fair proportion ...'[82]

New Brunswick Acadians had limited success in securing recognition of their needs. In 1870 the New Brunswick government translated the debates of the legislature into French; but soon, citing the high costs, it abandoned this policy, and virtually all government activities were carried on solely in English until the 1960s. Most levels of the education system were also unilingual and English. In the other Maritime provinces, which had even smaller francophone minorities, the pattern was similar. Prior to 1877 the choice of courses and texts on P.E.I. had been decided at the local level, but thereafter the rules were tightened and all textbooks had to be in English except for one reading text. In 1864, Nova Scotia, which had formerly allowed the use of Gaelic and French in the schools, imposed a standard English curriculum. In New Brunswick, a series of bilingual texts with the French version on one side and the English on the other were approved in 1875, but no provision was made for the training of Acadian school teachers, who had to attend the wholly English Normal School in Fredericton. After 1878 the government established a program to assist francophone students in completing the anglophone course, but few students enrolled and it would be abandoned in 1884.[83] Fortunately for the Acadian community, French students were prepared in both languages at the various convents established by the Sisters of Charity, the Sisters of Nôtre Dame, and the Religious Hospitallers between 1872 and 1880. The convents, many of them staffed initially by nuns from Quebec, helped not only to preserve the French language but also to interest francophone students in their own culture.[84] The women's religious orders were also responsible for the establishment of the first francophone hospitals in the region. Although the Maritime hierarchy, composed of Irish and Scottish bishops, gave tacit approval to the establishment of French institutions, the Acadian leadership and the growing number of Acadian-born priests felt that the hierarchy's support for the French language was lukewarm and began to push for greater Acadian representation in the higher ranks of the church.

The Acadians fared better than many other minorities in the aftermath of Confederation. It is impossible to know whether the region's Native peoples welcomed the transfer to Ottawa of responsibility for their affairs. In the event, the new regime proved little different from the old, and most Maritime Natives continued to eke out a marginal living in squalid, semi-permanent villages. Although Joseph Howe, when secretary of state, managed to increase the annual grant voted for Indian affairs in the Maritimes, the amount was still grossly inadequate. Ironically, Howe was also persuaded to copy the system of fixed reserves that had been developed in the United Province of Canada – a system that made little sense in a region where the Native peoples lived in small and scattered bands. The federal Indian department assumed that, as in Canada, the Native peoples would eventually achieve financial self-sufficiency by selling some of their land and investing the income. But the Maritime Native peoples had no reserves of any value, and without special grants they could never develop a viable economy. The assumption that the Ontario system could be made to work in the Maritimes was both 'unwarranted and dangerous,' and it doomed the Native peoples of the region to continued marginality.[85]

For most Maritimers, however, the 1870s was a decade of integration. Although they had entered Confederation sullen and angry at the terms of union that had been imposed upon them, by the end of the decade their anger had been considerably dissipated. Maritime politicians had carved out an important role for themselves at the federal level and were able to ensure that Maritime interests were no longer ignored in the making of federal policies and the distribution of federal patronage. The provincial governments in the region were less successful in pressing their financial demands upon Ottawa, and it is hardly surprising that in the 1880s they would join with the other provincial governments in pushing for increased revenues and larger constitutional powers. Only a small and unrepresentative minority sought separation from Canada, however. A whole host of trade, religious, and professional associations, unions, and other organizations had begun to form bonds across the nation. Most of these organizations reflected central-Canadian goals and priorities, but never exclusively so. Among the older, pre-industrial élites there remained a hard core of dedicated anti-Confederates, but they spoke for the past, not the future. Most Maritimers approached that future hopefully. As industrial exhibitions held at Saint John and Halifax at the turn of the decade showed clearly, most Maritimers still believed that there was a future for them in an emerging industrial nation.

# CHAPTER THREE

# The 1880s
## Paradoxes of Progress

Paradox is the stuff of history and of no decade is this truer than the 1880s in the Maritimes. These were the years when the Maritimes enjoyed the highest rate of industrial expansion in Canada but suffered the highest rate of out-migration. As some communities experienced population growth rates of over 50 per cent, so others declined in population. Throughout the Maritimes land transportation continued to be subsidized by the state, whereas oceanic transportation, the long-time speciality of the region, was allowed to languish. The value of deposits added by Maritimers to their savings accounts in local chartered banks exceeded the value of new loans that the banks were willing to make to local enterprises. One year nationalistic fervour found expression in Nova Scotia with the raising of a battalion to fight the North-West Rebellion; the next an outburst of anti-Confederate sentiment was manifested in the election of a repeal government. Social reformers who evinced enthusiasm for combatting the exploitation of children and women by their employers decided that the home was an easier target than the capitalist workplace and contented themselves with measures for protecting children and women against abuse by their kinfolk. While efforts were made to extend the benefits of higher education to women, racially segregated schools of inferior quality were steadfastly upheld. The total effect of such paradoxes was to produce uneven development, the sacrifice of local interests to 'national' interests, renewed dissatisfaction with federal policies, increasing tensions between capital and labour, and the reinforcement of social inequalities. These themes emerge in an examination of the nature of economic growth, the quality of life, and the character of regional consciousness.

### THE NATURE OF ECONOMIC GROWTH

During the 1880s relatively little growth occurred in the resource-based industries – agriculture, fishing, and timber – or in shipping, and even coal production enjoyed only a modest increase. Timber processing remained the employer of the largest industrial work-force, but in New Brunswick profitability in the timber industry fluctuated greatly. New ventures entailed risks even for well-established timber producers. These were lean years, for example, for the new woods operation of the lumber business of George Burchill and Sons in Northumberland County.[1] More important than staple production was the emergence of new, or, where they already existed, enlarged manufacturing establishments producing goods for a national market. The rate of industrial expansion in the Maritimes outstripped that of central Canada by 15 per cent, with the manufacturing sector increasing from 37 per cent of the region's value of production in 1880 to 48 per cent in 1890. The expansion was most noticeable in the production of cotton cloth, refined sugars, rope and twine, glass, and iron and steel.[2]

The hothouse industrial growth of the eighties resulted largely from a national policy of tariff protection promoted by Canadian businessmen, a policy that encouraged local manufacturing by making foreign imports prohibitively expensive.[3] The accompanying increase in the cost of living was the price that Canadians were required to pay in order to foster industrialization and avoid underdevelopment. For most of the eighties, the National Policy, inaugurated in 1879, was nurtured by two finance ministers from the Maritimes, fathers of Confederation Sir Leonard Tilley (until 1885) and Sir Charles Tupper (1887–8). With regional politicians at the peak of their influence in Ottawa, we might assume that the policy would be designed to work in the best interests of Maritimers. Unfortunately, the blossoming of secondary manufacturing was totally piecemeal and haphazard. It was based on the traditions of the shipping industry involving independent, community-based, family-oriented enterprises and lacked the strength and resilience needed to withstand the centralizing, monopolistic tendencies of industrial capitalism that favoured the heartland cities of Montreal and Toronto. Moreover, too many separate communities in the Maritimes competed for the same type of industry with scant regard for the need to identify and secure consumer demand, operating capital, and industrial expertise. As for the national market in which Maritime manufactures were intended to compete, it was not possible to predict the extent to which the flow of goods from east to west would be swamped by a veritable flood in the opposite direction from central Canada. Protection from foreigners did not compensate for a lack of protection from 'Upper Canadians.'

The unsophisticated level of the institutions of finance capital in the region made matters worse. Maritime enterprises were dependent in the 1880s on loans from chartered banks, not only for start-up capital, but for the funds to maintain operations. This was a costly mode of financing that put a strain on the fragile community banks. Moreover, with few exceptions, the individuals who entered the industrial fray in the 1880s had never seen the inside of a large factory and knew nothing about the complicated machinery and production techniques involved; such knowledge was essential for developing a competitive edge in a highly volatile market. Neophyte industrialists could hardly be expected to improve existing means of production or invent new ones without trained technicians and managers. To meet the short-term necessity they imported the required expertise from more advanced industrial countries; for the longer term they needed local facilities for technical education at the very least. Yet during a decade when the expansion and diversification of education was impressive in the fields of art, music, agriculture, and law, virtually nothing was done to encourage the technical sciences, apart from science summer schools for teachers and the first mining schools.[4] As if problems arising from such basic oversights were not enough, in the mid-1880s international factors and Canadian overproduction brought on an economic recession. This undermined much of the local potential and sent producers and investors alike scurrying outside the region to find both better management for local industries and safer opportunities for the investment of Maritimers' money.

An instructive illustration of the flawed consumer-oriented industrial strategy of the 1880s is provided by the resort to cotton textile manufacturing by seven communities in New Brunswick and Nova Scotia. The cotton industry was, to a greater extent perhaps than any other, a child of the National Policy. A successful industry in the northern United States (to say nothing of Britain), which had hitherto supplied Canadian markets, cotton seemed a natural choice for the new industrialists of the east. With the exception of William Parks's New Brunswick Cotton Mill established at Saint John in 1861, all the Maritime cotton mills went into operation between 1882 and 1885. The two major industrial centres of the region, Halifax and Saint John, were joined in the cotton venture by Moncton, a bustling railway town; Milltown, a declining lumber community near St Stephen; Windsor and Yarmouth, shipping communities of the golden age in the process of reorientating themselves towards landward industries; and Marysville near Fredericton, the personal creation and fiefdom of the legendary lumber baron Alexander Gibson. Also producing cotton textiles were fifteen mills located in Ontario and Quebec. This multiplicity of factories caused an undue degree of duplication, which, in the absence of regional marketing strategies, soon precipitated a crisis for the fledgling mills of the Maritimes. By the mid-1880s, with a slowdown in the economy, the Canadian cotton industry was seriously ailing; the Saint John Cotton Mill closed down completely for two years until it was absorbed by the Parks company. By the end of the decade Maritime cotton was ripe for a takeover by

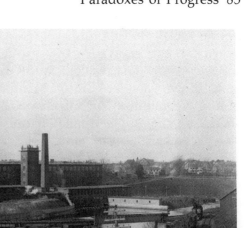

St Croix cotton mill, St Stephen, N.B., c. 1900. Massive new brick and stone factories housed both water- and steam-powered machinery imported mostly from the United States. Such machines came to characterize the industrial transformation of the region.

outside interests. The survival of all the cotton factories can be attributed to political expediency rather than economic stability; but the cotton industry tied up capital that might have been used for more viable local projects.

The nature of the problems that beset the Maritime cotton industry can be exemplified by the experience of the St Croix cotton mill in Milltown.[5] Launched by businessmen of the St Stephen, Milltown, and Calais (Maine) area, the mill was originally envisaged as the nucleus for an industrial city on the St Croix River. Forced by the large scale of the undertaking to look beyond the St Croix communities for investors, the mill fulfilled the expectations of the National Policy planners by securing foreign backing, primarily from New England textile manufacturers and Rhode Island banks. The mill was also managed by Americans, thereby compensating for the lack of local expertise. Labour had to be imported until enough local hands could be trained. Like the other Canadian cotton mills, the St Croix mill, which produced coloured rather than grey cloth, was soon adversely affected by the general over-production, a development that resulted in the formation, at the initiative of Montreal, of the Canadian Cotton Manufacturers' Association in 1883. The aim of the voluntary organization was to control production and prices in all Canadian mills. It failed because some of the mills, including the one in St Croix, refused to be governed by its regulations. More serious for cotton mills in general and the St Croix mill in particular was the failure of the cotton marketing company Morrice and Sons of Montreal, which had been a major source of operating capital. Because of its deep indebtedness, the St Croix mill was placed under trusteeship in 1883 and allowed to continue production only under trustee-dictated conditions. Even then, an attempt at diversification into different types of cloth led to an unacceptable surplus. Management responded by cutting the work-force by one-third, shortly after the mill hands had struck successfully to protest a wage reduction and increased pressures for better productivity.

The impact of the depression of the mid-1880s was serious enough not only to hurt the livelihoods of the employees but also to force the St Croix mill into the Dominion Cotton Manufacturers' Association, which replaced the earlier organization in 1886. The St Croix mill, however, proved to be a renegade member, breaking from the coloured-cotton section of the association in 1888, a move that damaged both the association and the mill, which once more fell badly into debt. But like the other mills, the one at St Croix survived by becoming part of the Montreal-controlled Canadian Coloured Cotton Company in 1892, a parallel organization to the Dominion Cotton Mills Company, which was for producers of grey cotton. Within a decade the St Croix mill had been transformed from a local enterprise warmly welcomed by the inhabitants to an externally owned institution unresponsive to the needs of the population. In the process, the community rallied to support the mill workers in their quarrels with capital, but the largest National Policy industry in the area became the employer providing the lowest-paid industrial jobs in Charlotte County.

Given the low wages in the cotton industry, a supply of cheap labour was essential. The employees were drawn in large numbers from the ranks of women and children, not from a male work-force with serviceable labour traditions. In Saint John, where 115 women employed in the cotton industry appear in the census of 1891, the typical operative was in her late teens or early twenties and worked in the two Parks mills at one of more than a dozen different tasks, none of which was supervisory in nature. Half the women lived with their parents and another third with widowed or single mothers, or, in a few cases, with widowed fathers. The large size of many of their families, or, in the case of viduity, the precarious circumstances of the family, suggest that their wages were needed to keep the household together. Forty-seven per cent of the seventy-three households containing female cotton workers comprised families with four or more children, and the daughters at work in the factory were usually the eldest girls. Half the female cotton workers had sisters in the same industry, and about one-sixth shared their factory experiences with their brothers. Most of the fathers of cotton girls had labouring jobs, but only a small fraction worked in the cotton factories themselves. Since most of the operatives were native-born at this date, only 14 per cent of the women were lodgers and half of these shared their lodgings with their mothers. Few young mothers worked in the mill. Most were fully occupied in reproductive labour at home with large families to feed and clothe.

In Halifax, with its one cotton factory, eighty-six female cotton operatives were recorded in the 1891 census. The average age as well as the median was eighteen, with the range from thirteen to forty-two years. These employees lived in households clustered in working-class Ward 5 or near the factory in Ward 6, and were drawn from backgrounds similar to those of the Saint John workers. Family necessity emerges from the data as an even more critical consideration in Halifax than in Saint John. Sixty-four per cent of the fifty-six households in which female cotton workers lived comprised families with four or more children, and indeed thirty households, amounting to 54 per cent, contained six or more children. Teen-age daughters were therefore under urgent pressure to get out and work in order to contribute to the family income. Households were headed most commonly by an unskilled labourer or a widow. The only alternatives to the factory were the poorly paid needle trades or round-the-clock household service.[6]

Not that factory work was an unmitigated blessing: several witnesses before the federal Royal Commission on the Relations of Capital and Labour explained in Halifax in 1888 that a female cotton worker was hard pressed to pay board at commercial rates out of her scanty wages, let alone support any dependants. And yet, on wages of between three and four dollars a week – one-third to one-half those earned by men in comparable positions – some experienced mill hands managed to pay board of two dollars a week and feed their children. Girls beginning at the mills earned little more than one dollar for a week of sixty or sixty-five hours. When work was slack, because of either over-production or a shortage of materials, the management put the workers on piece-work rates. Ostensibly these netted a larger income when the mill was running at full tilt, but they were less satisfactory than daily wages when there was a lack of work. In Halifax the women were transferred to piece-

Cotton-mill workers, Yarmouth, N.S., c. 1900. Sharp divisions of labour encouraged large-scale employment of women and children for the first time in wage-paying jobs. Despite the long hours, factory work was more attractive than domestic service.

work in the late 1880s with no intimation of the rate until they collected their fortnightly pay packets. Wages were low, the hours of repetitive and boring work were long, and working conditions were poor – suffocating heat and dust, endless standing, and draconian discipline, with fines for lateness and spoiled work. And yet many of the women who testified before the Labour Commission had been employed for years in the same grinding, unrewarding routine.[7]

Since wages in the cotton industry were low, what made the employment attractive to young women? It offered the first work that working-class women experienced outside the home, either their own or someone else's. The setting itself was therefore a liberation from the domestic routine that would shape most of their lives. The work was also confined to specific hours of the day and, since it was reliant on machinery, the women did not have to take any of it home with them. Despite long hours, factory workers appreciated the predictable, strictly limited nature of the work. Another feature of factory work that attracted girls away from domestic service was the camaraderie it afforded. Instead of being isolated and lonely in a stranger's house, cotton operatives, tobacco and candy makers, and seamstresses enjoyed the companionship of other young people and drew strength from shared experiences. As workers outside the home, they elicited the interest and sometimes the sympathy of the public far more readily than their sisters in the scullery, who were too precious a commodity to their middle-class employers to arouse a concern for their working conditions.

Apart from secondary manufacturing, coal mining was the only other sector of the regional economy to increase in percentage value of production during the 1880s. It was subject to the same kind of growing control by Montreal interests. Confined to Nova Scotia, the most impressive performance in the decade was that of the Springhill mine, the coal from which found a major market in supplying the recently completed Intercolonial Railway. The Springhill mine provided steady work for 13 per cent of the province's coal miners in 1881. Mining was the most gruelling and dangerous work on land for male workers. Like factory workers, they often began work by the time they were ten years old. The playfulness and lack of concentration of juveniles made them more susceptible to accidents than mature workers. Despite their vulnerability, the proportion of boys employed in Nova Scotia's coal mines increased during the 1880s. Mine managers wanted them for the cheapness of their labour and the usefulness of their small size for some of the underground jobs. Their wages of sixty-five cents a day were low for a miner but higher than those of the average female cotton worker. The tasks of driver and trapper that they usually performed were important enough to give the boys a certain degree of independence and bargaining power. They did not fit the stereotype of docile children overwhelmed by harsh conditions; rather, their brazenness resulted in boys' strikes in all three coalfields of Cumberland, Pictou, and Cape Breton counties in the 1880s.[8]

As the Nova Scotia coalfields were the only eastern-Canadian source of coal, owners set their sights on capturing the domestic market. They soon found that the degree of protection afforded their coal, amounting to only fifty to sixty cents a ton, was not enough to enable them to compete with the American product for the central-Canadian market. Nova Scotia coal was seldom sold west of Montreal, except as fuel to heat the Parliament Buildings in Ottawa. Although the insufficient quantity produced was blamed rather than the quality of the bituminous coal, the federal government decided to allow the import of American anthracite coal duty free in 1887 in order to build up a central-Canadian steel industry. To add insult to injury, this industry would ultimately grow at the expense of the older, Nova Scotia steel industry that was being developed in the 1880s by the Nova Scotia Steel Company in Pictou County.

Coal's importance to the economy as well as to the working class of

Nova Scotia cannot be assessed only in terms of its 3 to 4 per cent share of the total regional value of production. The provincial government was coming to rely increasingly on coal royalties, which would constitute the single largest source of provincial revenue by the beginning of the twentieth century. Moreover, colliers achieved a remarkable range of legislative reforms in the 1880s, largely through the effectiveness of their union, the Provincial Workmen's Association (PWA). Founded, like the National Policy in 1879, it has often been compared to the Knights of Labour, an international industrial union of the 1880s and 1890s that made little headway in the Maritimes.

Certainly the most noteworthy aspect of the coal industry in the 1880s was the growth and power of the PWA. Drawing on Scottish traditions of the independent collier, the union, under the leadership of Robert Drummond, spread throughout the Nova Scotia coalfields and into a number of manufacturing establishments. Although total membership in locals of international unions was larger, the PWA dominated the labour scene, securing legislation and winning strikes at a time when the rights of workers were exceedingly fragile. The successful emphasis on safety regulations in the early 1880s gave way in the second half of the decade to legislation to provide for miners' education and the certification of supervisory staff; to extend the franchise to miners who lived in company houses; and, in 1888, to introduce Canada's first compulsory arbitration measure. 'In five years, the PWA won a string of political victories – the most impressive series of reforms wrung by a Canadian trade union from a nineteenth-century government.'[9] These victories were secured through an alliance with the Liberal Party, especially under W.S. Fielding, who became premier in 1884 and who understood the vital role of coal in the provincial economy. The political leverage gained by the industry brought the benefits of protective and ameliorative legislation but did not ensure the miners unimpeded progress in their labour battles. Like the cotton workers and other wage labourers, the miners suffered from the mid-1880s recession, which cut into their pay packets as the price of coal slumped. Strikes were frequent throughout the decade at various mines, the most widespread one occurring in Pictou in the winter of 1886–7 when a threatened 20-per-cent wage reduction precipitated the largest Canadian strike of the late nineteenth century. Nor was legislation on paper any guarantee of implementation in the workplace. The inadequacy of the arbitration procedures, for example, was apparent as early as 1890, when management failed to submit a major strike at Springhill to arbitration. The miners won the strike, but the shortcomings of alliances with middle-class politicians stood revealed.

Besides manufacturing and coal mining, other areas of production

Provincial Workmen's Association badge. This badge, depicting both the tools of the coal miner's trade and his search for respectability, typified the philosophy of working men during a period when unions were as much benefit societies as bargaining agents.

showed no overall regional growth during the 1880s. This does not mean of course that stagnation was universal or that new initiatives were unknown. In the case of farmers, who still comprised the largest occupational group, greater specialization and organization were the response to the crippling problems of marketing and competition. Aided by steam transportation, Nova Scotia apples found an outlet in Britain, and Prince Edward Island butter and cheese supplied mainland markets. The number of farms continued to increase during the decade, reaching an all-time census high in 1891, but the productivity of the farms was considerably lower than in central Canada.[10]

As usual, the fisheries were affected capriciously by the complications of diplomacy. Beginning in 1882, the federal government poured into the Maritime fishing industry $150,000 worth of bounties, available annually from the Halifax Award of 1877. In 1885 the Americans refused to renew the Treaty of Washington's fishery clauses, which had been in effect since 1873, and the major continuing benefit of which had been the free entry of Canadian fish to American markets. Instead, the Convention of 1818, 'a fossil treaty,' again applied.[11] The markets for Maritime fish were now jeopardized and the advantages of supplying American fishing vessels removed. After several years of uncertainty, a meeting of the Joint High Commission in Washington in 1887 proposed that American fishermen be excluded from Canada's inshore waters (i.e., its three-mile limit) but allowed commercial privileges in Maritime ports in return for the free entry of Canadian fresh fish to the American market. Until the decision could be ratified, an interim arrangement went into effect whereby Americans could use Canadian ports on payment of a licence fee. Since the U.S. Senate refused in 1888 to ratify the accord, the temporary expedient remained in being until the early twentieth century. The loss of the free American market would have been a greater blow to local fishermen but for the increased demand for fresh fish and lobster that Maritimers were able to supply.[12]

Specialization by fishermen to meet changing tastes did not mean that earlier sea products were abandoned. The older traditions of the cod fishery were still preserved in Lunenburg, a county isolated from the manufacturing and railway construction of the National Policy. Devoid of new industrial alternatives, Lunenburgers concentrated more and more of their resources in the schooner fishery, continuing to build wooden vessels and to market their produce abroad. The self-contained nature of the fishery preserved its viability. For the rest of the century ample scope remained for selling a low-grade dried-cod product in the Caribbean, especially to the richer Spanish-speaking islands. Even so, the fishing industry remained a precarious way of making a living.[13]

The bias of the Maritime economy towards a national market and the stagnation in the traditional staple-based industries were accompanied, in the 1880s, by a continued emphasis on improving land transportation and, except for intraregional commmunication, a failure to exploit opportunities for water transportation. Railway fever dominated political life in the 1880s in the Maritimes as elsewhere in Canada. But Maritimers were sceptical about the benefits that federal railway policy were likely to contribute to regional development. True, the federal government allocated millions of dollars in railway subsidies for a variety of branch lines in the region. As a result, railway mileage in New Brunswick increased by 50 per cent between 1880 and 1890. Not all the subsidies were well conceived, however. One dismal failure, perhaps the greatest folly of the period, was the Chignecto Marine Transport Railway designed to transport vessels across the Isthmus of Chignecto. This totally unrealistic railway 'diverted resources from more useful projects, and so may have actually contributed to the decline of the Maritime economy.'[14]

One of the subsidiary plans associated with the ship railway concerned the construction of a line from Amherst to Cape Tormentine to service the passenger and freight trade of Prince Edward Island. Sackville businessmen were opposed to this proposal, advocating instead a line from Sackville to the Cape to enable them to reap the benefits of the lucrative trade envisaged for the line. The community elected the president of the company, Josiah Wood, to Parliament as their Tory MP. On Cumberland MP Tupper's resignation as minister of railways, Wood succeeded in obtaining the standard government subsidy of $3,200 a mile for his railway. This deliberately engineered conflict of interest was typical of the way in which things were done in the 1880s: 'Political power was necessary to secure subsidies and stave off rival lines.'[15]

Maritime enthusiasm for federal railway policies was considerably undermined in the early 1880s when government support of the Canadian Pacific Railway, then under construction, appeared to favour American rather than Canadian ports as the eastern termini. The major urban centres and the merchants of the region expressed deep concern about the winter-port issue, which was the crux of the matter. Despite the pains taken by the federal government to ensure an all-Canadian route to the west coast, the promotion of such a route to the Atlantic coast was regarded by some politicians as an undue interference with the rights of businessmen to get their products shipped in the most expeditious way. The Intercolonial Railway did not seem a viable alternative because of the time-consuming circuitous route it followed through Canadian territory. The danger was that Halifax and Saint John would be rejected in favour of Portland, Maine. Fortunately, Maritime representatives had enough political clout in Ottawa to guarantee that

*Northern Light* in the ice, 1881. With winter ferry service across the Northumberland Strait erratic at best, Islanders repeatedly invoked the clause promising 'continuous communication' that had been a condition of their entry into Confederation.

additional loans to the CPR were conditional on the construction of a short line from Montreal to Saint John as part of the CPR network. The Short Line was completed in 1889.

The region's islands had their own quarrels with railway policy. For most of the eighties Cape Breton was without a railway, but its politicians pressed successfully for the completion of an eastern extension. Prince Edward Island needed connections to the ferry ports. The branch line on the Island to Cape Traverse was finished in 1884, but, as one Charlottetown newpaper reasoned, without the line between Cape Tormentine and the ICR mainline, 'to expect much improvement in our winter service is as hopeless as to expect a man to walk well with one stilt.'[16] For this reason, Islanders supported the intentions of the Sackville-based New Brunswick and Prince Edward Railway Company and benefited from the completion of that line in 1886.

Prince Edward Island's greatest transportation concern of the decade was ferry service across the Strait of Northumberland, something for which the federal government was also responsible but typically neglected because of its enthusiasm for steel rails over steel ships. The failure to live up to a Confederation promise to establish continuous steamer commmunication across the strait preoccupied public attention on the Island in the eighties. In winter the carriage of mail and passengers was haphazard, the movement of freight and produce virtually impossible. The government in Ottawa had tacitly acknowledged its responsibility in 1876 when it had put the secondhand, wooden St Lawrence River steamer *Northern Light* on the route. In the eighties the vessel was almost constantly in need of repairs and could not withstand the winter ice. For the winter months, therefore, Islanders were dependent on little boats hauled across the ice and sailed through the open patches of water over the nine miles between the capes. The dangers of this primitive mode of transportation were graphically portrayed in 1885 when three boats encountered a fierce snowstorm that forced passengers and crew to camp out overnight on the ice without provisions and with only the boats and mail to use as fuel. The hapless travellers' sufferings from frost-bite received wide publicity and, as a result of the ordeal, national attention was finally focused on the problem. The local government appealed to the British government to make the federal authorities live up to their promises, a move that further befogged the issue with unduly optimistic discussions and surveys regarding the feasibility of a submarine rail tunnel to connect the Island to the mainland. This scheme was quietly shelved in 1888 after a new steel steamer, the *Stanley*, replaced the derelict *Northern Light* and in its first winter season of 1888–9 made an impressive seventy-nine round-trip crossings of the strait, compared to only twenty-one by the *Northern Light* during the previous winter.[17]

The federal government's procrastination over steamer communication to the Island was paralleled by its failure to subsidize a fast transatlantic steamer mail service for the Maritimers. This regional demand for steamers does not mean that the sailing vessel had disappeared from the assets of local merchants. Shipowners continued in the 1880s to squeeze the last drop of profitability out of their wooden vessels by making greater demands on their masters, who in turn worked the crews even harder. By these means owners were able to compensate for the decline in freight rates and for the second-class treatment accorded to sailing vessels in port and make it worth their while to retain their existing vessels until they wore out. They seldom replaced their old ones with new wooden ones, however, a trend that hastened the decline of shipbuilding. Nor did they replace the wooden vessels with steel ships in the absence of the government encouragement and support needed to foster a shipping industry. As a result, the tonnage in service in the 1880s declined in all the ports of registry but Windsor, a late bloomer in the shipping industry. Undoubtedly Maritime shipowners would have pressed harder for a national navigation policy if they had not been tempted to withdraw their investments from vessels and put them instead into the new landward industries fostered by the National Policy.[18]

The momentous changes of the 1880s, fostered by the National Policy and shaped by the fluctuations of the business cycle, especially the deep trough of the mid-1880s, were accompanied by the loss to the region of both human and capital resources. The realization that local opportunities were not attractive enough to encourage young people to seek their livings in the region grew alarmingly in the 1880s as the 'exodus' became a cause for anxiety. Although Canadian society as a whole was extremely mobile in the nineteenth century, the significant feature of the 1880s was that out-migration from the Maritimes surpassed that from the rest of Canada for the first time. The exodus had become a regional rather than a national phenomenon. The Maritimes lost 12.5 per cent of their population, with Cumberland County, home of industrial Amherst and Canada's most productive coal mine, the only county to avoid what has been called 'epidemic' out-migration.[19] Because of increasing emigration and minimal immigration, the growth rate of the population stagnated, and some communities experienced absolute decline. Between 1881 and 1891 Nova Scotia's population grew by only 2 per cent, Prince Edward Island's by 0.18 per cent, and New Brunswick's by 0.09 per cent, whereas Ontario's grew by 10 per cent. While some of the decline occurred in communities formerly tied to the seaward economy, agricultural counties also lost population, especially those in the Saint John River Valley. Even the city of Saint John, which shared in the industrialization of the region, was sufficiently tied to shipping, shipbuilding, and the ailing timber trade to experience a fall in population from 41,000 to 39,000.[20]

On the other hand, some of the railway, industrial, and industrial-resource communities enjoyed an extremely high rate of population growth. The population of Moncton increased by 74 per cent, of Amherst by 66.3 per cent, and of Stellarton by 50.7 per cent. The urbanization of the region occurred at an unprecedented rate in the 1880s, but the highest growth rates were seldom maintained into a second decade. Only four of seventeen urban communities in Nova Scotia with population increases of 10 per cent or more in the 1880s were able to maintain a comparable or better growth rate in the 1890s.[21] Because of the attraction of manufacturing centres stimulated by the National Policy, out-migration normally proceeded in two stages – from rural community to urban-industrial centre within the region, and then from the urban centre to a destination outside the region. Observers in Saint John in the late 1880s still spoke of the exodus as a seasonal movement, and indeed there were reasons why both workers and students might at first leave only temporarily for a seasonal job or a term at university. But a sojourn often became a permanent change of residence. In New Brunswick, with a population of 321,233 in 1881, 44,000 people emigrated between 1881 and 1891. The migrants were three times as likely to go to the United States as to other parts of Canada. Unique documents exist to chart the exodus from the village of Canning in Kings County, Nova Scotia. There the out-migration peaked between 1884 and 1888, and most of the migrants were young and single and went to New England. Arguably, the inability of the region to retain its talented young people, at a period of considerable shift in the nature of the economy, weakened its ability to compete in the national market and withstand the centrifugal pressures from central Canada. The exodus of the last quarter of the nineteenth century may have resulted in the decapitation of Maritime society.[22]

As with population, so with capital. The 1880s witnessed a significant surge in the capital outflow from the region. The tendency of local banks, for example, to invest in safer prospects outside the Maritimes was stimulated when the failure of many local businesses in the depressions of the 1870s and 1880s jeopardized the banks' accounts. In some cases the economic problems led to the collapse of the banks themselves. The Bank of Prince Edward Island, which had by 1880 invested in a wide range of enterprises throughout the Island, including shipping, starch factories, and lobster canneries, suspended operations in 1881. The unluckiest of the three Island banks, it was liquidated between 1882 and 1887. The other two suffered from a declining confidence among depositors after that failure, and one of them, the Union Bank, was forced to amalgamate in 1883 with the Bank of Nova Scotia. Island investors displayed their unease by placing their deposits in the government savings banks, a regional trend; Island banks revealed their unease over local economic conditions by investing outside the local communities. The Union Bank, for example, before its absorption into the Bank of Nova Scotia, loaned $1.55 to local enterprises for every $1.00 deposited; thereafter it loaned only 78 cents locally for every dollar deposited.[23] In Saint John, the Merchants' Bank failed in 1887, and even a bank with an expanding branch system like the Bank of Nova Scotia was shaken by the business failures of many of its customers in the early 1880s and consequently adopted more rigorous rules relating to local loans. Its search for safe investments meant that a diversified industrial town like Amherst was well supported, as was New Glasgow, home of Nova Scotia's emergent heavy industrial complex, but they were the exceptions. By the late 1880s the extensive branch system had become a vehicle for garnering local investment, not for sponsoring local industry.

The reluctance of the Bank of Nova Scotia to loan the deposits of Maritimers to Maritime industries was illustrated between 1886 and 1888 by the growth in deposits by $1.2 million, whereas loans made locally increased by only $200,000. Like the young emigrants, the region's bank managers opted for better opportunities outside the Maritimes.[24]

During this decade of uneven and intermittent economic development, the political behaviour of the male electorate reflected both regional pessimism and national optimism. The two federal elections in 1882 and 1887 were, on the whole, enthusiastic endorsements of the National Policy of the Conservative government, with both Nova Scotia and New Brunswick returning a majority of Conservative MPs. On the other hand, Prince Edward Island, the province most excluded from the policy of industrialization, returned a majority of Liberals. At the provincial level, dissatisfaction with the economy and with federal policies was more clearly manifested. Nova Scotians turned out the Conservatives in 1882 and endorsed the Liberals again in 1886. Premier W.S. Fielding capitalized on the secessionist tradition in Nova Scotia by advocating repeal of the union. Prince Edward Island experienced ten years of Conservative rule under Premier W.W. Sullivan, who was dedicated to convincing the federal government that better terms were essential to Island loyalty. In New Brunswick, a loose alliance of all the political interests in the legislature was formed. Dominated by a Liberal Party that coalesced only in 1886 under Premier A.G. Blair, the coalition opted for parish-pump politics.

The deep-set divisions of opinion over the impact of the National Policy and the anxiety over federal-provincial relations were nowhere more clearly illustrated than in Nova Scotia. The province remained split, much as it had been at the time of Confederation, between those areas that welcomed the industrial growth stimulated by protectionism – the northern and eastern portions of the province – and those that believed in the economic doctrine of free trade, particularly as it had been practised with the United States during the halcyon days of the reciprocity treaty of 1854–66. Confined largely to the south coast and the valley, these were also the areas that had profited from the shipping economy, a dying golden age to its proponents and dependants. The depression of the mid-1880s, which adversely affected markets for fish, lumber, and agricultural produce and undermined the shipping industry, together with the troubled circumstances of the new consumer industries, created a profound discontent. This was exploited by W.S. Fielding, a man for whom political expediency was everything. When he won the 1886 provincial election, ostensibly on a secessionist ticket, he conceived of a renewed attempt to promote Maritime union as the best way of convincing the British government to repeal the act of Confederation.

In this he met with indifferent responses from the governments of the other Maritime provinces.

Historians have long speculated over the degree of seriousness in Fielding's secessionist proposal. His bluff was never called, however, because he delayed action for eight months, pending the outcome of the federal election in early 1887. At that time, in the wake of Conservative spending and promises, repeal was repudiated by an electorate that gave only seven of the twenty-one seats to the Liberals at the national level. The Fielding Liberals then chose instead to campaign for reciprocity and provincial rights. In his call for a freer trading policy with the United States, Fielding was joined by his New Brunswick counterpart and by the federal Liberals, out of power throughout the 1880s and therefore in a position to be antipathetical to the National Policy. Premier Blair of New Brunswick also participated with Fielding in the first interprovincial conference, held in Quebec in 1887. Since the resolutions emanating from that essentially Liberal conference were not endorsed by the Tory legislative councils of the provinces, this first concerted demonstration of interprovincial co-operation was significant only as a portent of things to come.[25]

In the meantime, W.W. Sullivan's administration in Prince Edward Island was characterized by an itemized agenda of retrenchment during his years in office from 1879 to 1889. He pressed the federal government for greater financial assistance and fulfilment of neglected Confederation promises. In his own legislature he resorted to such reactionary but allegedly cost-cutting measures as the abolition of the secret ballot, reinstatement of statutory labour on the roads, and reduction of MLAS' salaries and the number of civil servants. His attempt at balancing the budget succeeded only once after he repealed the reviled direct taxation introduced by his predecessor in 1877. He had therefore to resort to expensive government borrowing to keep his administration afloat.[26]

One economy measure that Sullivan failed to implement was the elimination of the Legislative Council. In this ambition he was joined by A.G. Blair in New Brunswick, whose major achievement in his ten years as premier (1882–92) was the abolition of the second chamber. Political corruption was rife in New Brunswick in the 1880s; election after election was challenged for irregulaties, and the search for constituency favours dominated political life. The emergence of a strong premier in Blair, one capable of satisfying various economic, ethnic, and geographical interest groups, was to be an enduring feature of New Brunswick politics. But effective and popular leadership provided no substitute for the financial well-being that eluded each of the three Maritime provinces in the 1880s.[27]

### THE QUALITY OF LIFE

Beyond the public sphere of economic and political life, the family remained the focus of everyday existence in the Maritimes in the 1880s. The quality of Maritimers' lives depended on a number of variables: social status, gender, ethnicity and race, place of residence, and cultural traits.

Social status was partly a question of social class, but it was also a matter of luck. The early death of a father-provider could plunge a well-supported, middle-class family into ruin, affecting a whole generation of that family. A poor but bright lad from a large family might, with encouragement from his teachers and parents, pull himself up by his bootstraps and achieve a comfortable middle-class existence in adulthood. Since social status was not necessarily fixed by inheritance, both upward and downward mobility were widely prevalent. To illustrate this, let us compare the careers of two men, Thomas Norbury and John Naylor, who came from similar backgrounds but ended up in quite different circumstances.

Thomas Norbury arrived in Halifax in 1868 as a sergeant in the British army. He purchased his discharge and entered civilian life as a tavern-keeper in the upper streets, the area east of Citadel Hill where much of the carousing, drinking, and *demi-monde* activity occurred. Tavern keeping was not necessarily lacking in respectability. Some Haligonians used it as an entré to prestigious positions in the drink trade or other commercial pursuits more acceptable to a society suffused with temperance sentiment. Unfortunately, this was not the case with Norbury, who was inclined to drink too much of the profits. He also broke the licensing laws and appeared frequently in court and in jail. By 1876 he had left tavern life and married a Halifax County woman. They produced two children. Mrs Norbury alternated domestic service with prostitution, and Norbury became a confirmed drunkard, working on the wharves as a labourer. His unreliability as a provider and his wife's irregular habits meant that the children were neglected, a circumstance that brought Norbury into contact with John Naylor in 1883.

Naylor was also an Englishman, having settled in Halifax some seven years later than Norbury. He came from a rank-and-file army family background. Like Norbury, he ventured into small-scale business pursuits. He was, however, a strong advocate of temperance, and thus his social contacts differed from those of Norbury. As a real-estate agent, Naylor got to know the upper streets from a different perspective than that of the erstwhile tavernkeeper. One of Naylor's major interests was animals. Unlike Norbury, whose only concern with animals was as a scavenger employed for several years before his death to remove dead animals from the streets, Naylor was keen to protect animals and dispose of old and injured ones humanely. He was appointed secretary and agent of the Nova Scotia Society for the Prevention of Cruelty to Animals (SPCA), which was established in Halifax in 1876. Naylor stalked the province, responding to reports of cases of cruelty. When he realized the extent of similar cruelty to humans, especially women and children, he promoted the expansion of the organization to a general anti-cruelty society, the first in Canada. Like most social workers of the day, Naylor was backed by a prestigious board of directors drawn from the ranks of the local élite. In his capacity as agent for the Society for the Prevention of Cruelty (SPC) that replaced the SPCA, Naylor prosecuted the Norburys in 1883 for child neglect and in 1887, three years after legislation was passed empowering the society to remove children from their parents, arranged for the Norbury children to be institutionalized.

The SPC established a number of branch societies in Nova Scotia, and the New Brunswick SPCA, concerned in these years with cruelty to animals only, was organized in 1881 in Saint John. While the anti-cruelty societies did not direct their attention to the lower classes alone, the vast majority of both human and animal cases involved the poor and disadvantaged. The cross-class intervention brought together the Norburys and the Naylors of the period, the rough and the respectable.[28]

A second variable determining the quality of life was gender. Little girls might experience a similar life to their brothers until puberty, but thereafter the expectations of society and family were different for each. While a boy might have some choices about his life's work, a girl was expected to leave her dependence on her father's household to become a wife and mother in her husband's home. Until 1884 married women in Nova Scotia were legally unable to own their own property. The 1880s not only removed that particular hurdle to a degree of independence, but also provided new opportunites for breaking out of the traditional mould for both working-class women and those born in more comfortable circumstances. The former had a wider range of employment to pursue in the interval between childhood and marriage: in factories, as we have seen; in teaching, if their families allowed them to stay in school long enough to qualify; in nursing; in the new white-collar jobs as store clerks and telephone operators. Some might even escape matrimony altogether. The opportunities in Catholic religious orders also increased with the expansion of separate schools, hospitals, and special-care homes.

One significant improvement in the status of women resulted from opportunities for higher education, especially for the daughters of business, professional, and landowning fathers. Although convent schools and private academies had been available for some time, the universities finally threw open their doors in the 1880s. Of the degree-granting institutions in the region, only Mount Allison had admitted women before 1880. Now Acadia, Dalhousie, and New Brunswick followed suit. The women best placed to take advantage of the opportunities were those who resided in the college towns, but attendance was by no means confined to them. Rural women from modest homes were enabled to attend Dalhousie in the 1880s through the generosity of the university's expatriate benefactor, New York millionaire-publisher George Munro, who, in good Scottish democratic fashion, did not confine his scholarships to men.[29]

Most university women became teachers. Their rate of singlehood was much higher than that among non-university women. Some of the spinsters were career women; others were the genteel daughters of well-to-do families who devoted their lives to their parents and siblings. Many joined the exodus, either temporarily or permanently. Given the high degree of mobility and the close ties between the Maritimes and the northern United States, women sought in American institutions training that they were unable to undertake at home, such as doctoral studies, or, until 1888, medicine. Eliza Ritchie, a Dalhousie graduate of 1887, was the first Maritime woman to acquire a doctorate when she graduated from Cornell in 1889. After a brief career as a university professor in Massachusetts, she returned to her native Halifax to play a prominent role in the women's movement of the early twentieth century. Maria Angwin, a graduate of the Wesleyan Ladies' Academy at Sackville, studied for her MD degree at the Women's Medical College of the New York Infirmary for Women and Children and in 1884 became the first woman licensed to practise medicine in Nova Scotia.[30]

Activist middle-class women, both single and married, continued the practice, already well established by the 1880s, of compensating for their lack of civil rights and political power by participating in voluntary associations concerned with the welfare of women and children. Their philanthropy and campaigning included the provision of clothing for poor families, housing for cotton mill workers, and seats for dry-goods-store clerks. Through such efforts 'ladies of leisure' were brought into contact with lower-class women. One cross-class undertaking was the Haven, established in Saint John in 1887. It grew out of city mission work and a community of interest between the male Evangelical Alliance and the Women's Christian Temperance Union. Originally intended as a home for prostitutes, the Haven took on a wider role as the women's executive assumed more and more of the control of the operation. The Haven began to take in abandoned children, women devastated by such disasters as the Springhill mine explosion of 1891, and ex-prisoners, as the organizers developed a special interest in prison-gate work. The

Eliza Ritchie

experience that women derived from their voluntary activities of the 1880s, including the management of the Haven, would crystallize in the demand for the franchise in the 1890s, though limited voting in municipal elections began in the late 1880s.[31]

A third variable influencing the quality of life for Maritimers was ethnicity or race. Fairly equal opportunities were available to the white English speakers who comprised the majority of the population. The Acadian and Black minorities were not so fortunate.

The Acadians were one of the few ethnic groups to be threatened but not weakened by out-migration. As a result of three factors – their reluctance to leave the Acadian enclaves of the region, the determination of Acadian priests to promote rural Acadian life, and natural increase – their percentage of the population rose. The largest concentration of Acadians was in New Brunswick where, with only two exceptions, the counties that grew between 1881 and 1891 were those in which Acadians predominated or constituted a significant minority.

Population expansion coincided with a resurgence of group consciousness, known as the Acadian Renaissance, which helped to enhance the Acadian identity. Fundamental to the Acadian awakening were education and leadership, the one essential for the creation of the other. By the 1880s educated, secular leaders, such as Pascal Poirier in New Brunswick and Joseph-Octave Arsenault in Prince Edward Island, were ready to define Acadian goals. To promote the Acadian identity, newspapers were established in Bathurst in 1885 and Weymouth in 1887. It was also in the 1880s that the Acadians held their first two national conventions – in New Brunswick in 1881 and in Prince Edward Island in 1884, followed by a third in Nova Scotia in 1890. There the Acadians adopted special symbols of identity to accentuate their distinctiveness not only as French-speaking Catholics but as francophones independent of Quebec influences. These included a flag – the French revolutionary tricolour, sporting a gold star on the blue background – an anthem set to a hymn tune venerating the virgin Mary, a motto ('L'union fait la force'), and a national holiday, the Feast of the Assumption on 15 August.

Many problems remained for the Acadian community, providing the substantive agendas for the conventions and gaining attention in the popular press. Issues included the poor quality of French-language instruction, the dangers of assimilation, especially in Nova Scotia and Prince Edward Island, the threat that emigration posed for the future, and the limited opportunities available to the vast majority of Acadians in the rural resource sectors of farming, fishing, and lumbering. As primary producers living in the marginal areas of the region, they were often poor. As Catholics they were not accorded equal rights with their Irish co-religionists. Indeed in 1882, the Collège Saint-Louis in Kent County, founded in 1874 by Father Marcel-François Richard, was closed by the bishop of Chatham because it was too explicitly Acadian.[32]

While Acadians wanted to be equal but separate, Black Maritimers aspired to be equal and integrated. Except for the urban areas, Blacks lived in highly segregated communities, as they had done since the Loyalist immigration. In the cities, however, they had become integrated with the lower order of whites by mid-century. In the poor and rough areas of Halifax, Black and white citizens lived cheek by jowl, often intermarried, ran small businesses – legal and illicit – and engaged in a

ACADIAN EXPANSION 1871-1971

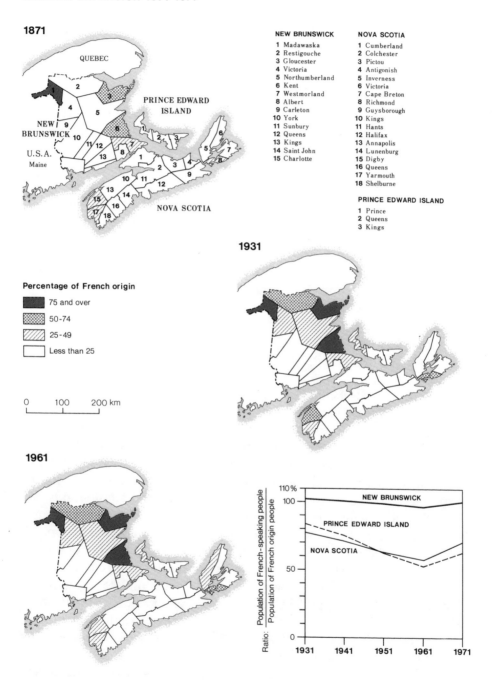

| NEW BRUNSWICK | NOVA SCOTIA |
|---|---|
| 1 Madawaska | 1 Cumberland |
| 2 Restigouche | 2 Colchester |
| 3 Gloucester | 3 Pictou |
| 4 Victoria | 4 Antigonish |
| 5 Northumberland | 5 Inverness |
| 6 Kent | 6 Victoria |
| 7 Westmorland | 7 Cape Breton |
| 8 Albert | 8 Richmond |
| 9 Carleton | 9 Guysborough |
| 10 York | 10 Kings |
| 11 Sunbury | 11 Hants |
| 12 Queens | 12 Halifax |
| 13 Kings | 13 Annapolis |
| 14 Saint John | 14 Lunenburg |
| 15 Charlotte | 15 Digby |
| | 16 Queens |
| | 17 Yarmouth |
| | 18 Shelburne |

PRINCE EDWARD ISLAND
1 Prince
2 Queens
3 Kings

Percentage of French origin

- 75 and over
- 50-74
- 25-49
- Less than 25

0    100    200 km

Figure 4  A century of Acadian expansion: territorial growth and French-language retention, 1871-1971

range of occupations at the bottom of the socio-economic ladder. Black children attended the oldest public schools in the heart of the city, but the school board also extended support to schools for Blacks located in Zion Church in the working-class district north of the Citadel and in Africville, the semi-rural Black ghetto on the northern fringes of the peninsula. By 1876 Black Haligonians found that the predominantly white schools were, with school board encouragement, starting to exclude them; by the early 1880s they were confined almost exclusively to three inferior schools for Black children in wards 5 and 6. Thoroughly dissatisfied, the parents began to agitate for integration to provide the quality of education their children needed, including access to the higher grades unavailable in their own schools. The matter came to a head in 1883 when Henry Russell complained to the school board that he had to send his sixteen-year-old daughter Blanche to the United States for education at a cost of two hundred dollars a year because she was denied admission to both the girls' secondary schools in her neighbourhood. A protracted controversy ensued entailing petitions, letters, public meetings, school-board and city-council deliberations, debates in both houses of the legislature, and widespread publicity throughout Canada. Saint John Blacks met to urge their brethren to keep up the struggle 'until the narrow prejudice of a bygone age shall be compelled to give place to a more ennobling and elevating spirit characteristic of British justice and fair play.'[33]

In response the Halifax city council resorted to enlightened rhetoric, proclaiming that 'colored citizens having equal rights as voters have also equal rights in educational privileges.'[34] The school board translated these high-sounding sentiments into a policy of graded but segregated elementary schools for Black children with an emphasis on vocational training, admission to classes in white schools for the tiny minority they expected to pass the grade seven examinations, and admission to high school on the same terms as whites for those who passed the entrance examinations. In 1884 the provincial legislators took a different approach but one that had the same effect. They supported the legality of separate schools but insisted that Black children must be allowed to attend a school in the city ward in which they lived. By the mid-1880s, therefore, Blacks were still trapped in separate elementary schools that whites claimed to be so greatly improved 'as to entirely allay their ambition to mix in the white schools.'[35] Black pupils had access to the higher grades in the hitherto all-white schools, though in 1884, when Blanche Russell was finally admitted to Brunswick Street girls' school, white parents petitioned to have this 'obstacle' to their children's education removed.[36]

Place of residence was another important factor determining the quality of life in the 1880s. Rural areas offered the advantages of neigh-

The Halifax skating rink. Seasonal carnivals were traditional in garrison communities. Halifax's exhibition building was one of several to be used for skating balls and, increasingly, for competitive hockey and curling.

bourliness and a sense of community. But, as Andrew Macphail described in *The Master's Wife*, a novel about life in the small community of Orwell in Prince Edward Island, industrialization undermined local self-sufficiency and attracted away the young people. Declining country areas also lacked many of the organized leisure activities and social amenities that increasingly enhanced life in urban areas. The cities provided a number of facilities for sporting activities. In Halifax, for example, a skating rink opened in the Exhibition Building in 1880, and the Wanderers' Amateur Athletic Association Club was organized in 1882 to promote such amateur sports as cricket, football, and hockey. Art exhibitions, concerts and other musical entertainments, and drama were all a regular part of life in Halifax and Saint John. Every town of any reasonable size had a building of one sort or another that could be used for public and private performances. In 1882, when the controversial Oscar Wilde included the Maritimes on his North American lecture tour, he appeared in a variety of lecture halls in Fredericton, Saint John, Amherst, Halifax, Truro, Charlottetown, and Moncton. In the country, on the other hand, a more modest cultural life still centred on the churches and temperance halls.

The cities were also the centres for most hospitals, institutions for children, educational facilities, and public transportation systems, many of which underwent expansion in the 1880s. In Halifax, the Victoria (later Halifax) Infirmary was opened by the Sisters of Charity in 1887, a new wing was added to the Victoria General Hospital, the St Patrick's

Industrial School for Boys was expanded, Dalhousie University moved to a new building in 1887, and the street railway was restored in 1886 after a ten-year hiatus. For the more affluent citizens of Halifax, Saint John, Charlottetown, and some of the new industrial towns, water, sewerage, and electric light made their lives more comfortable. The urban poor, however, were huddled together in substandard housing with no sanitary facilities, privacy, or ventilation to speak of. Epidemics, particularly of smallpox and the killer childhood diseases of diphtheria and whooping cough, stalked the working-class districts with inescapable regularity.

Poverty was not just an urban phenomenon. The chronically poor and helpless were found in every type of community, but the level of public support available for their relief depended on where they lived. An instructive example is provided by two cases in Nova Scotia: the poorhouse in Halifax and the farming-out of paupers in Digby County. Both systems were in the public eye in the 1880s because of a fire that destroyed the poorhouse in Halifax in 1882 and complaints in Digby in 1885 about the quality of the care that was provided for the poor.[37]

The 'poor's asylum' in Halifax was established soon after the initial settlement of the town; almshouses followed in Saint John, Fredericton, Chatham, and Charlottetown in the period between 1800 and 1870. Rural areas were reluctant to maintain poorhouses, and the overseers instead contracted out the care of the poor to local residents known as indemnifiers. In some cases the indemnifiers doled out supplies to families that had fallen on hard times; in other cases they paid keepers to board paupers in their homes, not unlike modern foster-care arrangements. The indemnifiers themselves often acted as keepers. This system provided opportunities for abuse, as no standard of care was enforced and keepers and indemnifiers tried to support the poor at the lowest possible cost and pocketed any savings. Much of the debate over the care of the chronically poor turned on which system – institutional care or private care – was the more humane and economical. Given the contemporary trend towards institutionalization, poorhouses were considered the more progressive approach.

The people in both town and country who found themselves destitute of means and reliant on long-term support in the late nineteenth century included the elderly, the incurably ill and disabled, the feeble-minded, the hopelessly dissipated (usually alcoholics), and, in areas lacking special institutions, pre-adolescent orphans. Others who might seek seasonal or occasional assistance were the unemployed, single or abandoned pregnant women, and working-class people recuperating from illness or injury. The diversification of philanthropic institutions gradually diminished the need for the government to care for those with short-term problems, especially in the urban centres, but the wrecks of humankind, 'the poor' that 'always ye have with you,' required continuous support at public expense if no relatives could be persuaded to do the job. They filled the Halifax poorhouse in the 1880s, and thirty-four of them died unnecessarily in the 1882 fire because the keeper concentrated on fighting the flames rather than rescuing the helpless inmates in the hospital wards on the top floor of the five-storey building. Between 1882 and 1886 the poor were housed in the old Halifax penitentiary buildings, where the facilities included a black hole for Black paupers. Notwithstanding the disaster and the four years of inadequate housing, during which as many as four hundred unfortunates were sometimes packed into space designed for eighty prisoners, the poorhouse provided succour – three meals a day, clean beds, medical treatment, religious services, and visits from every conceivable charitable and church organization. A workhouse component was included in the form of farm labour and various jobs around the building for the able-bodied, though the statistics reveal that there were probably few enough of these. There was of course no drinking, smoking, family life, or intellectual stimulation. Even the poorhouse school was closed by 1885, though this may have been an indication that the institution fortunately no longer catered to children. As well as accommodating city residents, the poorhouse supported transients and people from other parts of the province at the expense of the province and the relevant local authority. Increasingly, however, non-residents were being sent back to their place of settlement.

Until 1880 most of the rural and small-town poor in the Maritimes were looked after in the Digby fashion – that is, farmed out annually to those local residents who would care for them at the lowest bid – a form of 'white slavery' described in T.C. Haliburton's *The Clockmaker* fifty years earlier. Charlotte Hill was one of the Digby paupers. A feeble-minded woman who kept getting pregnant, she was on poor relief for her fifth or sixth pregnancy in 1880 when her keeper, a man known for horse-whipping his charges, throttled her on a country road and set her alight. Joseph Thibeau was hanged for the crime in the Annapolis County jail in 1881. That well-publicized trial aroused unease in a number of quarters about the system of rural poor relief, which made no provision for such extras as doctors' bills and funeral expenses. The motive for Thibeau's murder of Hill might have been his unwillingness, or indeed inability (being a poor man himself), to feed another mouth.

The miserable circumstances in which many of the paupers in Digby were boarded were probably no worse than the normal destitution accepted as a fact of daily life in a poor and declining county with disadvantaged Acadian and Black minorities. In 1885, when several cases of mistreatment of the old, sick, and insane came to light in the same

'Hillfoot Farm,' Aylesford, N.S., 1889

poor-relief district of the county as the Hill murder, a one-man commission of inquiry was appointed by the provincial government to investigate the circumstances. Although the report confirmed that auctions of the poor to the lowest bidder had not occurred for at least a decade, it suggested that the farming out of the poor at the cheapest possible rate was just as bad. These events in Digby hastened the establishment of county homes, beginning with Bridgetown, Annapolis County, in 1882.[38] But vested interests resisted the substitution of 'modern poorhouses' for the contracting-out system. As one Halifax paper noted: 'The indemnifier will not willingly forego his annual gains. The farmer or housekeeper is not willing to begin now to hire servants, seeing that, under the previous system, he or she can have servants from the overseers and be paid for maintaining them.'[39]

Not all the poor assigned to local farmers and tradesmen were residents. Children from industrial Britain were frequently dispatched by various agencies to receiving homes to be placed out as farm hands and servants. Emma Stirling, a pioneer in Scottish day-care and child rescue, embarked on such a venture in 1886 when she bought Hillfoot Farm near Aylesford in the Annapolis Valley. By 1890 several hundred deprived children from Scotland had been settled in the Maritimes under her direction.[40]

A final factor to consider in this assessment of the diversity of experiences that determined the quality of life is that elusive variable, culture. A heterogeneous population produced a heterogeneous culture: varieties of leisure activities, religious practices, and historical traditions that were determined by economic means, needs, and opportunities. Two innovations in the culture of working-class Maritimers in the 1880s will serve as illustrations. One was the introduction of the Salvation Army, the other the abolition of the tavern in Nova Scotia.

The conservatism of the long-standing evangelical churches and the relative ineffectiveness of the indigenous city-mission movement left the way open for the invasion of the Salvation Army as it expanded eastwards from its first foothold in Ontario. The Salvation Army 'opened fire' in both Saint John and Halifax in 1885 and quickly spread to the smaller communities where its mission appealed to the native-born as well as the British-born working class. In particular, the movement attracted the young, the single, the exploited, and women. The occupation of a majority of Salvationist women in the paid work-force of the two cities in 1891 was domestic service, and most of the men were skilled, semi-skilled, and unskilled wage earners.[41]

In the early years the Salvationists were subjected to heckling and abuse, but middle-class admiration soon followed. Christians in the evangelical tradition considered the Salvation Army to be the harbinger of a new spiritual purity; other citizens were inspired by its social work, which began in the Maritimes in 1890. Temperance workers also found allies among the Salvationists, whose crusade against drink they shared. In addition, the organization provided religious and social-service leadership roles for its women that no other Protestant church condoned. Salvationist encouragement of women was ensured by the opening of a female training home in Saint John in 1887.

The arrival of the Salvation Army coincided with continued attempts by authority to suppress plebeian culture, particularly in its more exuberant forms in Halifax where the dance halls on Grafton Street and the taverns throughout the city became the objects of reformist zeal. The keepers of the dance halls voluntarily closed them in 1884 to avoid threatened raids that usually ferreted out illicit drinking and sex. Closure did not last, however. The attack on tavern life was merely another episode in the long temperance struggle to render society dry. The federal Canada Temperance Act of 1878 (the Scott Act) was in operation in most areas of the Maritimes, the major urban centres being the exceptions. There the plebiscites to prohibit the sale of liquor could not be won. When the Nova Scotia legislators passed a liquor licence act to replace the defunct McCarthy Act in 1886, they decided to get rid of the tavern altogether. Described as 'One of the most stringent liquor license laws ever enacted,' the act made it no longer legally possible, beginning in 1887, to drink at a public bar.[42] Liquor was sold in quantities no smaller than one pint to be drunk off the premises. The abolition of the tavern was more theoretical than real, enforcement being what it was. But it did mean that the traditional centre for popular entertainments, in which ordinary people could fraternize and exchange ideas and news, no longer openly existed. For the working people caught in the turmoil of the industrial revolution, the destruction of the tavern and the intrusion of the Salvation Army were dual examples outside the workplace of the control and regimentation that had begun to permeate their lives.

### THE CHARACTER OF REGIONAL CONSCIOUSNESS

The term 'Maritimes' was used by people outside the three provinces to describe the eastern extremities of the Canadian Dominion. It no more reflected a collective sense of identity within the region in the 1880s than it had ever done. There was a certain regional pride that even non-industrial Prince Edward Islanders could feel in the early, heady flash of industrialization, but there were few demonstrable signs of concerted regional behaviour. The idea of Maritime union was given little credence despite the occasional rhetoric of politicians like Fielding and the student orator at the Mount Allison graduation exercises in 1887 who asserted 'that a great saving would be effected by such an union, and said it would be infinitely better if the three provinces were united under one government.'[43] The moulders of public opinion gave precedence to almost any identity other than a regional one, whether it be community, province, nation, continent, or empire.

Consequently, manifestations of interprovincial co-operation were slight, and the provinces' emotional distance from one another was aggravated by community rivalries such as those that divided Saint John and Halifax or Sackville and Amherst. From time to time, however, certain economies of scale could be effected by treating the three provinces as a unit; hence the establishment in 1880 by the federal government of a penitentiary in Dorchester to replace separate provincial ones. Even the provinces themselves were sometimes disposed to economize regionally when it came to supporting helpless minorities, the regional use of the School for the Blind in Halifax (now Sir Frederick Fraser School) being a case in point. Churches and secular organizations, for their part, demonstrated a greater inclination towards interprovincial co-operation. One of the Methodist conferences included both New Brunswick and Prince Edward Island, and the latter province remained part of the Anglican diocese of Nova Scotia. The Women's Christian Temperance Union held Maritime conventions in different towns, the Maritime Provincial Grange met in a variety of locations, and the Acadian

Dorchester Penitentiary, Dorchester, N.B. The federal presence in the region was often expressed architecturally in post offices, customs houses, or railway stations. This federal prison, which reflected prevailing notions of rehabilitation through 'isolation and useful toil,' was one of the largest buildings in the region.

conventions moved from province to province. These peregrinations enabled the leaders of such groups to know the region better and to begin to develop a sense of regional consciousness, though the respective matters of gender, occupation, and ethnicity remained uppermost in their minds. From 1876 to 1881, some co-operation among the regional universities was attempted, with the Nova Scotia government supporting its own denominational colleges, plus Mount Allison in New Brunswick. The experiment of a central examining board in the guise of the University of Halifax came to naught, however.[44] Some of the colleges limped along, and Saint Mary's in Halifax closed temporarily. The desirability of a regional university continued to be acknowledged. The editor of the Saint John *Sun*, a relatively disinterested observer, believed

that the system of higher education prevailing in the Maritime provinces is not the best possible. By a combination of the resources of all the colleges there might be created a university equal to the University of Toronto ... A university formed by the co-operation of all our existing institutions would have great possibilities. It could make for itself a continental reputation and perform magnificent work if the best and most aggressive elements of the present colleges were drawn into it.[45]

Given the absence of regional sentiment, the first loyalty tended to be to province. Most residents would have agreed with the New Brunswick politician who said he was a New Brunswicker first, a Canadian second.[46] Evidence of robust provincial pride surfaced every time a provincial or national exhibition was held or a native son or daughter made the headlines. Maritimers could also exhibit a sense of national achievement. Despite uncertainty about what the CPR would mean for the region, the driving of the last spike in 1885 drew favourable comment. The *Daily Examiner* of Charlottetown considered it 'the most important event of the year for Canada and the British Empire, if not for the world.'[47] The underlying resentment against the devotion of regional resources to the opening of the west did not prevent Haligonians from raising a battalion to fight in the North-West Rebellion in 1885 and, when the soldiers' somewhat less patriotic employers refused to give them back their jobs locally, a volunteer relief fund was raised to tide the heroes over the winter of 1885–6. In fact, however ambivalent the feelings towards Confederation, Maritimers made some of the best nationalists. Fredericton-born poet Charles G.D. Roberts, an influential intellectual and an exemplar of 1880s nationalism, proposed a toast for Dominion Day in 1880:

> Here's to the glory of the land that we name
>   The dear Land of Canada the Free,
> Where our hope is, and our home, and our faith, and our fame, –
>   For Canadians – Canadians are we![48]

Beyond national sentiments, the 1880s saw an upsurge of pride in empire. Maritimers were certainly in the vanguard of enthusiasm for imperial federation and preserving the Anglo-Saxon identity of the English-speaking world. New Brunswickers found the centennial of the coming of the Loyalists to be a serviceable British tradition, which they marked in 1889 with the formation of the New Brunswick Loyalist Society.[49] Celebration of the Golden Jubilee of Queen Victoria in 1887 may have been stimulated by a range of local interests, but the parades, picnics, and competitions that marked the occasion reflected a genuine pride in and sense of belonging to an empire on which the sun never set. More important, the way people celebrated tells us something about their collective perceptions of self. For the upper echelons of urban society, the 1887 jubilee provided an opportunity to erect permanent memorials of benefit to their communities and, in some cases, their region. The promoters of the Victoria School of Art and Design in Halifax (now the Nova Scotia College of Art and Design) considered that both the aesthetic and industrial benefits of the training would foster the interests of the region and would also discourage young people from leaving the Maritimes to train in the United States.

To the Black residents of Saint John, celebration of the jubilee meant a display of patronizing racism on the part of some 'sporting' whites who decided to hold a 'coloured' baby show. Some of the Blacks objected that 'such an exhibition can only tend to excite laughter and ridicule and to degrade the race.' It was only after the most prominent Black leader expressed the opinion that the queen would regard with contempt 'all who dare close the jubilee year of her memorable reign with a most degrading insult to her loyal and respectable colored subjects' that the event was cancelled.[50] Others insulted by the jubilee celebrations were the working classes who, in some of the major centres, were denied the right to participate by organizing trades processions, on the ground that this was not appropriate to the occasion.

The jubilee meant different things to different people. For the mass of the population it meant a summer holiday much like a modern civic holiday, during which sundry spectator events, from boat races to fireworks, were staged. For the region's intellectuals, the jubilee afforded a chance to display their learning, sophistication, and urbanity. The jubilee issue of the *Critic*, a Halifax weekly paper with a regional readership, included a contribution by Bliss Carman, whose verses were 'free from our besetting fault of provincialism,' and an article by Charles G.D. Roberts, who suggested that the flowering of literature and nationalism went hand in hand. Nova Scotia attorney general J.W. Longley endorsed both the causes of Anglo-Saxon superiority and, as a Liberal in politics, free trade between Canada and the United States. For these Maritimers, imperial occasions were chances to define Canadian nationalism and regional economic interests. Editor Frederick Fraser, superintendent of the School for the Blind, was the only contributor with a radical viewpoint. He espoused the opposition of American propagandist Henry George to private landownership. As George wrote in *Progress and Poverty*, private landholding was 'prejudicial to the best interests of society, and utterly opposed to the fundamental principles of equity and justice.'[51]

In their idealization of society, Maritimers looked forward, like Fraser, to significant reforms that would produce social democracy, or backward, like Andrew Macphail, to the mythical self-sufficiency of the rural past. The intellectual responses were reflected, *mutatis mutandis*, at every level of a society challenged in the 1880s by increased urbanization, emigration, industrialization, and class conflict.

PART TWO
TRANSFORMING HORIZONS, 1890–1920

# CHAPTER FOUR

# The 1890s

## Fragmentation and the New Social Order

The Maritimes, like Canada itself, experienced a continuing sense of disunity and fragmentation through the 1890s. The forces of industrialization, urbanization, and immigration, along with ethno-religious tensions, shaped a Canada of strong regional differences. They added complexity to the country: an urban-industrial core in Ontario and Quebec split along cultural lines; and western and eastern hinterlands each depending on different staples and peopled by old and new immigrants. In the Maritimes, the new industrial order reinforced social and economic disparities between Halifax and Saint John and rural communities; between thriving, industrial Cape Breton and stagnating areas of longstanding farming, fishing, and lumbering activity; or between acculturation in cities of British immigrants and cultural survival in the Acadian countryside.

A clearer view of the region's 1890s character – a part of the 'shreds and patches' of Confederation, to use Sir Richard Cartwright's infamous phrase[1] – may be seen through the prism of the 1896 federal election.[2] The election, which swept Laurier and the Liberals to power, was fought largely over the very issues that polarized national and regional viewpoints: the impact of the Conservatives' National Policy; American reciprocity versus British preferential trade; and the divisive Manitoba Schools Question. Divided Maritime interests, in fact, led to varied responses. The industrial towns situated along the Intercolonial Railway favoured retention of the Conservatives' pro-industrial stance. Outport settlements, dependent upon the export trades, swung their support to the reciprocity notions of the Liberals. Ethnic and religious divisions were reflected in reactions to the Manitoba Schools Question. While some Nova Scotians thought it best to downplay the 'picturesque ... grievance of a very small Catholic minority,'[3] New Brunswick's Acadians used the issue to focus attention on the differences in quality of English and French public schools and the appointment of the Catholic bishop.

The 1896 election results showed the Liberals cutting significantly into the Conservatives' 1891 Maritime hegemony (31 of 43 seats), but coming up short of a majority (17 of 39).[4] The election did give the region two powerful cabinet representatives in Ottawa, but the presence of Nova Scotia's W.S. Fielding in Finance and New Brunswick's A.G. Blair in Railways and Canals further divided the region. Fielding's support of American coal and steel interests in Nova Scotia and Blair's pro-Saint John stance on the winter-port issue meant that a unified Maritime response to issues of regional development was not forthcoming. The fight for 'better terms,' the 1890s forerunner of the Maritime Rights movement of the 1920s, would be fought at a restricted, provincial level, and over largely local financial matters.

The claim that fragmentation characterized the Canadian experience in the 1890s requires further comment, particularly because this decade forms part of a critical era in Canadian nation building. True, it was a period of national consolidation in party politics; of a rising sense of national self-awareness in imperial matters; and of geographical integration through railway construction.[5] Cries for repeal aside, Maritimers generally supported the concept of a closer national unity. Maurice Harlow, a young farmer-lumberman-storekeeper from rural North Brookfield, Nova Scotia, viewed attempts at nation building as essential. Writing in his diary in response to the Pacific Scandal, he noted that corruption was evil, but (disagreeing with his Baptist minister) believed that Canada's leaders were correct in building a railway of such gigantic proportions. The nation, according to Harlow, required just such a vision.[6]

The forces shaping Canada and cementing the Canadian federation were not, however, creating a homogeneous, uniform Canada. Herein lies a paradox. The Maritimes were an integral part of the young nation, but the forces of the new industrial order – industrialization, immigration, and urbanization, particularly as they were acted out on the metropolis-hinterland stage – were moulding a strongly fragmented Canada. The nation had yet to coalesce. Industrialization bred competition between regions, producing steel and textiles, winners and losers. Trading ties with foreign markets were often stronger than interprovincial links, and the decline of foreign trade was of more serious consequence for the Maritimes than for other regions during the economic depression of the early 1890s. The surge of new immigrants – 'stalwart peasants in sheepskin coats' – to the prairie West bypassed Atlantic Canada and gave the West issues of ethnic concern that meant little to Maritimers. Cities across Canada looked inward upon themselves to solve pressing problems that only later, after the turn of the century, would draw a progressive, united response through such groups as the Union of Canadian Municipalities. It is to the credit of Canadian federalism that parliamentarians throughout the twentieth century would ultimately strive to repair the shreds and to stitch together the patches of the country; in the 1890s, however, fragmentation was more common than uniformity.

The Maritime provinces in the 1890s comprised a region that was diversified, separated – that is, fragmented – geographically, culturally, economically, and politically. It was structured, it may be argued, more by localism than by regionalism. A rugged, broken coastline; large, uninhabited forest tracts; and scattered patches of usable agricultural land had shaped isolated communities of considerable independence that remained, in the 1890s, weakly connected despite several decades of railway building. Alvaretta Estabrooks, a music teacher from Carleton County, New Brunswick, travelled locally where possible by train to visit friends, relatives and pupils, but a trip to Fredericton, some eighty kilometres away, was rare.[7] Moreover, shipping materials by rail from place to place for manufacturing, or moving finished products to scattered and distant markets, was generally costly and subject to deal making with Intercolonial Railway officials. Despite a modest program of constructing spur lines, such difficulties were not alleviated in the 1890s.[8]

Communities were still marked by their own distinctive cultural traits, even after a century or more of settlement. The Germans of Lunenburg, the Acadians of New Brunswick's north shore, the Irish of the Miramichi, and the Presbyterian and Catholic Scots of Pictou and Antigonish counties, amongst other groups, all bore witness to a region of 'limited identities' where Old World traditions still held fast. While the German and Gaelic languages were not as prominent as earlier, they were still spoken; and many Acadians north of the Miramichi could not speak English, let alone follow the quickness and rhythm of a still-present Irish brogue.[9] Even the churches lacked unity, whether Protestant or Catholic. For example, New Brunswick Baptists were very different from Nova Scotia ones; and, at an even more local level, Halifax Baptists were quite distinct from those found in the Yarmouth region or on the eastern shore. Ethnicity, language, and religion produce a variety of attitudes to industrialization: Calvinistic Scots promoted manufacturing, whereas Catholic Acadians, restrained by the church and fearful of assimilation, held fast to rural ways.[10] Differences ran beyond language and religion to include farming and fishing techniques, furniture making methods, marriage practices, and architectural forms. Consumerism and mass marketing – traits that might uniformly characterize a society – were making inroads (witness the entry of the Eaton's catalogue and a few chain stores to the region by the early 1890s), but the widespread acceptance of these metropolitan traits awaited later decades.

Maritime communities once had shared a common interest in trade

Hibernians at play, Charlottetown, 1894. The Irish were known for their
music and plays, in this case a farce set in Victorian Dublin. Except for
occasional touring troupes, such amateur productions were the only
theatre available to much of society.

through their connections with Britain, the United States, and other
countries in the North Atlantic economy. By the 1890s, however, the
new industrialism had embraced a successful few, failed the poorly en-
dowed, and bluntly ignored many others: busy industrial Amherst; fading Londonderry, 'the iron disappearing from its veins'; and sleepy
Berwick, a stable agricultural and marketing village in the Annapolis
Valley – each felt the direct and indirect impact of industrialization.[11]
Besides further differentiating regional communities along economic lines,
and adding more groups and contrast to their social structures, the new
industrialism split the working class and increased the disparity between
rich and poor. In a pre-industrial, mostly mercantile world, rural Maritimers combined farming and lumbering – and sometimes even fishing
– in a seasonal round of job-shifting, pluralistic work. Industrial town
life, on an upsurge through the 1870s and 1880s, put an end to this
pattern for some. But many more workers, discouraged by the lack of

full employment, either left the region altogether or combined, on a traditional seasonal basis, town and country jobs in a way that held back the formation of a united proletariat.[12] Attempts by unions such as the Provincial Workmen's Association to raise a regional consciousness ended in failure. Local lodges simply could not agree on common unifying issues.[13] Nor did the prosperity earned by select 'captains of industry' and 'merchant princes' bind the threads of an élite together. Competition for scarce resources and limited markets might unite profit-minded entrepreneurs and stockholders within a single community, but regional alliances did not materialize. There was no regional metropolis to unite the regional economy, only limited industrial and financial leadership by Halifax and Saint John. Without shared strategies and metropolitan strength, regional industries in the 1890s fell prey (the cotton-textile industry is a telling example) to territorial incursions and business take-overs by central-Canadian enterprise.

Diversity and separation also revealed themselves strongly in political matters. The three provinces did share a common framework of responsible, representative (dual- or multi-member constituencies), and quasi-party government, but provincial status itself was divisive. Nova Scotia, New Brunswick, and Prince Edward Island were polities unto themselves. This had been confirmed in the 1880s by their failure to join in discussions about Maritime union. Despite the provinces' similarities in economy and society, and their similar causes for complaint – for example, the lack of federal funds for railway construction and steamship subsidies – they did not generally co-operate to solve these problems. A go-it-alone attitude prevailed.[14]

The Liberals dominated the various legislatures through the 1890s, but in each province they struck separate agendas. Personalities, parochial political platforms, and patronage shaped their policies. The electorate sometimes shifted allegiance between provincial and federal elections. Industrial Cape Breton rallied behind the federal Conservatives' protectionist policies of industrialization in both the 1891 and 1896 elections. This same area favoured the provincial Liberals' attempts at expanding the coal trade in the 1890 and 1897 elections, but not that of 1894. Local matters offer an explanation. In 1894, David McKeen, manager of the Dominion Coal Company and a Conservative MP, told Cape Bretoners what they wanted to hear: his company soon would be hiring great numbers of men. As J. Murray Beck has argued, 'it would not be the last time that Cape Bretoners appeared to bite the hand that fed them.'[15]

Political fragmentation was particularly acute in New Brunswick, where localism was the order of the day. Commenting on the 1890 election returns, Premier Blair was struck 'by the remarkable circumstance that in no two constituencies of this province has the government been attacked upon the same ground, or are the people being appealed to sustain the opposition for the same reasons and based upon the same arguments.'[16] In 1895, the *Globe* of Saint John argued that 'local political concerns are not very much hedged by the principles and ideas which control the two great political parties of the country. They are much affected by other motives, such as ... the bestowal of patronage.'[17] Compacts of personalities controlled government. Broad divisions in society could be reconciled in this manner – Protestant and Catholic, anglophone and francophone, Liberal and Conservative, businessman and farmer. All could find a political home and share an affinity. Every interest and every community placed its own concerns first, ahead of a provincial development scheme. Saint John leaders pursued a role as Canada's winter port for their city. Lumbering matters were high on the Miramichi's agenda. Schools were an issue in Bathurst. Heterogeneity rooted in localism thus shaped New Brunswick's political culture.[18]

It did so as well in Prince Edward Island. Local matters constantly conflicted with attempts to implement uniform inshore fishing practices, or educational, roadbuilding, or financial-restraint programs. The dual-constituency framework virtually guaranteed such division. Even in Nova Scotia, the province most responsive to the new industrial order, localism remained the more potent force. For example, there was strong opposition to Premier Fielding's attempts in 1894 to centralize more government functions and spending in Halifax, particularly since these attempted to erode the traditional base of power associated with municipal government.[19]

### THE STAGING OF THE NEW INDUSTRIALISM

Industrialization played a powerful role throughout the 1890s. Maritimers originally had been slow to embrace the new industrialism. In part this attitude was determined by political circumstances, in part by economic realities. Imperial policies and merchant control of pre-Confederation government agendas were stronger than artisanal enthusiasm and limited local markets. But change and acceptance of the new industrialism prevailed as the century unfolded. It was inevitable if for no other reason than that manufacturing could be more profitable than the import-export trades. It was therefore not accidental that coinciding with the decline of the region's shipping industry, there was widespread support for the federal government's National Policy of tariffs, bounties, and other incentives. Implemented between 1879 and 1887, these provisions greatly stimulated industrial development.

Many manufacturing sectors had expanded dramatically in the 1880s.

Merchants and shipping magnates invested heavily in cotton-textile mills, iron and steel plants, and sundry other factories. New technologies were imported, tested, and accepted. Skilled immigrants were recruited for prominent positions in the factories. Rates of employment growth and product output were unprecedented. Towns gathered in rural migrants and built, for the first time, substantial districts of distinctive working-men's cottages. Halifax and Saint John, revelling in new-found roles as industrial centres, ranked as leading Canadian cities.

But these promising gains were replaced in the 1890s by contradictory events – the seeds of eventual despair. Manufacturing output increased by only 4 per cent over the course of this decade, compared to rates in Ontario and Quebec of 21 and 30 per cent, respectively.[20] With ten times the population of the Maritimes and with better access to richer and more diversified markets, central Canada had many advantages over the Dominion's weaker, peripheral regions. With such advantages in hand, the business interests of Montreal and Toronto swept through the Maritimes, collecting majority interests in the cotton, glass, cordage, and several other industries.[21] Compensating for these take-overs, or at least making them seem less worrisome (because most of the factories taken over still turned out products through the 1890s), was the considerable expansion of the coal and steel industries. Coal production in Nova Scotia increased from 2,181,000 to 3,624,000 tons between 1890 and 1900.[22] Production in a closely related industry, pig-iron manufacturing, shot up fivefold through the decade, to a total of some 151,000 tons in 1901.[23] The seeds of this expansion, however, were not deeply planted in the region's soil: foreign capital, Newfoundland iron ore, or the carrying capacity of Norwegian time-charters could be transplanted, so to speak, as they eventually were, to other areas of more profitable growth.

Thus, the new industrialism yielded both positive and negative results through the 1890s. The way in which the Nova Scotia Steel and Coal Company (Scotia) developed illustrates both, as well as the fragility (in the long term) of the region's industrial structure. Scotia was founded in New Glasgow in 1872 as the Hope Iron Works when two Pictou County tradesmen of Scottish descent, Graham Fraser and George Forrest McKay, formed a partnership to produce marine and railway forgings. The growing demand for forgings encouraged the formation of a new enterprise in 1874, the Nova Scotia Forge Company. This new firm prospered to such an extent that it shifted some operations to neighbouring Trenton in 1878 and then, in 1882, with the support of local, mainly merchant-provided capital, created the separate Nova Scotia Steel Company. Under the protection of the National Policy's tariffs, both the forge and the steel operations prospered, and in 1889 they merged to become the Scotia Steel and Forge Company. The amalgamation was

logical. It not only achieved greater efficiency in management and production, but also took advantage of the two firms' complementary operations and location.[24]

More than this, the company's growth and restructuring demonstrated
the capability of Maritime enterprise. Pictou County, thoroughly Scottish
and Presbyterian in character, possessed coal and iron-ore resources; its
entrepreneurs and politicians had helped to shape the National Policy
of industrial development; and the local community, braced by strong
family and kinship ties and belief in Calvinistic principles ('faith without
works is dead'),[25] raised the essential capital. In fact, Scotia was Canada's
leading producer of iron and steel products. Nevertheless, there were
weaknesses in its operations. It still did not produce its own pig iron.
In 1890, nearly 90 per cent of Canadian output came from Londonderry,
located some 150 kilometres west of New Glasgow. Despite its relative
importance, the Londonderry Iron Company was plagued by high production and transportation costs, iron ore that was difficult to mine, and
an inconsistent supply of good quality coke. These were problems that
not even its new Montreal owners could overcome. Scotia did not compete directly with Londonderry at this time, nor could it use Londonderry's pig iron in its steel furnaces. The chemical make-up of the ore
prohibited such a link. Scotia relied instead on British imports; but the
duty on pig iron was rising – a trend that Scotia's politically minded
directors, including John F. Stairs of Halifax, were powerless to reverse.
Clearly, Maritime industry was vulnerable to external conditions.

Such problems could at least be met throughout the 1890s, and often
in a spectacular way. In 1891, now forced to look beyond the local
community for its capital, Scotia's capitalists developed a separate enterprise, the New Glasgow Iron, Coal and Railway Company. Aiding in
the venture were Halifax financier J. Walter Allison and industrialist
Stairs. A blast furnace was 'blown in' at Ferrona in 1892. Despite shaky
markets and low prices, Scotia used newly won tariffs and bounties and
a price-fixing agreement with the Londonderry people both to meet its
own needs and to capture Ontario and Quebec customers. Buoyed by
success, Scotia's directors created the Nova Scotia Steel Company in
1895 through a merger of Nova Scotia Steel and Forge and New Glasgow
Iron, Coal and Railway. No sooner was it formed than Scotia experienced
a temporary crisis when, in 1896, severely depressed prices and reduced
bounties caused financial losses, forcing the reduction of wages and
salaries for all workmen and officials. A more serious problem, and one
that would eventually force Scotia to pursue a fragmented pattern of
operations, was the poor quality of Pictou County's iron ore and coking
coal. To solve these matters, Scotia won access to rich deposits of red

haematite at Wabana on Bell Island, Newfoundland, and purchased the coal properties of the General Mining Association near Sydney Mines, Cape Breton. The high costs and inconvenience of transporting these materials to Pictou County, however, eventually forced Scotia to abandon its Ferrona blast furnace in favour of an integrated iron and steel complex at Sydney Mines. Operational in 1905, it was reportedly the most efficient and technically advanced in Canada. Along the way, the company was reorganized in 1901 as the Nova Scotia Steel and Coal Company, with capital assets of $14 million.

The company had grown spectacularly through the 1890s, as Scotia spawned a sizable metal-working complex in Pictou County, stimulated the growth of several towns (notably New Glasgow, Trenton, Wabana, and Sydney Mines), innovated with new technologies, and demonstrated an ability to adjust rapidly to changing forms of capitalism (family, industrial, managerial). In short, at the close of the decade, it was one of Canada's leading industrial enterprises. Even so, a careful observer might have noted some telling signs marking the fragility of Scotia's structure: the uneconomical dispersal of its metallurgical operations; a growing dependency upon the staple trades (iron ore, coal) to balance manufacturing losses; an inability to sway government industrial policies, particularly after the Liberals gained power in 1896; and an increasing need for metropolitan-based capital, a need that would eventually lead to a take-over by American interests in 1917.

For other sectors of the manufacturing economy, the metropolitan stage held little room for Maritime manoeuvring. Local entrepreneurs were forced to the sidelines. The cotton-textile industry fully illustrates the changing scene and the actions of Montreal's metropolitan directives.[26] Except for the Parks firm in Saint John, the cotton-textile factories established in Halifax, Windsor, and Yarmouth, Nova Scotia, and in Milltown, Marysville, and Moncton, New Brunswick, had followed hard on the heels of the National Policy incentives. Each enterprise was a community venture, the product of local merchant and industrialist enthusiasm. Each used similar sources of cotton. Each advertised for skilled English and New England supervisory personnel and weavers, but characteristically employed Maritime families for unskilled tasks. And each relied on imported technology. When misfortune befell the industry, however, there was no regional leadership capable of beating back outside intrusions or solving regional problems. Despite a substantial outlay of capital, initial returns on investment were minimal. Output far exceeded domestic demand, glutting the market. Voluntary attempts through the mid-1880s to regulate the production, pricing, and marketing of cotton textiles brought little success. Nor did a more formal

Marysville, on the Nashwaak River near Fredericton, c. 1885. 'Boss' Gibson typified the transition of regional entrepreneurs from a dependence on externally marketed staples, such as timber, to manufactures sold in the protected market of the National Policy. Gibson's cotton mill (here seen on the right in the background) was also typical in its eventual subordination to external metropolitan control.

agreement signed with Quebec and Ontario companies in 1886. Neither Halifax nor Saint John possessed the business acumen or financial resources to salvage industrial disorder.

Instead, an act of external metropolitan dominance resolved the crisis. The directive took the form of corporate monopoly. The Dominion Cotton Mills Company, capitalized in 1890 at $5 million with headquarters in Montreal, was organized by A.F. Gault and David Morrice 'to bring all of the grey cotton producers under the control of a single directorate.'[27] In January of 1891, mills in Halifax, Windsor, and Moncton relinquished control in return for cash and bonds in the new company. In Saint John, the reportedly collusive alliance there of Dominion Cotton and the Bank of Montreal failed to win ownership of the long-established Parks Mills. The bank's demand for immediate payment for all outstanding debts was rejected by the courts, foiling the take-over. To bring other Maritime firms under control, Gault and Morrice organized the

Clayton and Sons clothing factory, Halifax, c. 1900. The electric bell attached to the post in the foreground was used to signal the start and completion of each work day, as well as the infrequent breaks in the long days worked.

Canadian Coloured Cotton Company, a co-directive to the Dominion Cotton Mills, in 1891. The St Croix Mill at Milltown accepted the new directorship in 1892, while Alexander Gibson's enterprise at Marysville took on associate status, retaining a separate corporate structure, but agreeing to market its entire output through the new consolidation.

This scene of merger and take-over activity also characterized other mass-consumption industries, notably the sugar, cordage, and glass sectors. All were industries of considerable recent growth and expansion that ultimately failed in their attempts to compete with metropolitan interests. Unlike the cotton-textile example, however, the business consequences associated with these consolidations were not as destructive for the region. Returns on original investments were more equitable, Maritimers remained in management and directorship positions and, except for the glass industry, production was maintained through the 1890s.

Nevertheless, loss of ownership to metropolitan interests did not bode well for the region, because it appeared that only smaller-scaled manufactories, servicing mainly local markets, could remain under the control of regional entrepreneurs. This was true of companies that produced such diverse goods as boots and shoes, cigarettes or cigars, carriages, agricultural implements, pianos, stoves, confectionery, clothing, books, and beverages. The main threat, however, was looming off-stage in the form of mass-production and mass-marketing techniques that included both wholesaling and retailing these goods through branch business outlets. There were at least 264 branch businesses in 1891, 416 in 1901. There would be nearly 1,000 by 1921. Together with the catalogue sales of Eaton's, the goods sold in this mass manner began to slow significantly the expansion of Maritime firms that manufactured consumer products. Clearly, the force of metropolitan influences was felt in many ways.[28]

Metropolitanism loomed large as well in the regional coal industry. More than any other enterprise, coal was the pivotal factor in both the region's industrial development and its integration within the national economy. Concentrated in Nova Scotia, the industry was initially encumbered by the London-based General Mining Association's monopoly on mineral rights. Although this monopoly was unwillingly relinquished in 1858, and despite a flurry of local investment spurred by reciprocity (1854–1866) and protective tariffs (after 1879), coal production again came into the hands of external capitalists. Montreal interests were most prominent during the 1880s in the mainland coalfields, notably at Springhill and in Pictou County. On Cape Breton Island, however, the formation of the Dominion Coal Company in 1893, led by Boston's Henry Whitney, was the principal evidence of continental interest in Nova Scotia's industrial revolution. It is also a powerful example of the blending of politics and business in the age of the gilded entrepreneur.[29]

Whitney's interest in Cape Breton coal for use in his various gas, light, and tram companies in the Boston area coincided with Premier W.S. Fielding's need to raise provincial revenues to maintain credit and to meet increased expenditures. The two men were brought together through mutual friends as a result of Fielding's announcement in mid-February 1892 that the coal royalty would be raised from seven and a half to ten cents per ton. This proposal not only brought stormy complaints from existing coal operators, but also piqued Henry Whitney: an unstable investment climate was a curse on his projected plans. J.A. Grant, a contractor and Whitney's close business associate, had met Fielding through Liberal lawyer B.F. Pearson. Pearson and Grant had worked together on the development of the People's Heat and Light Company of Halifax. Shortly after the royalty announcement, Grant informed Fielding that Whitney would like to talk to him. The outcome of the confidential April meetings between the gilded-age entrepreneur and the progressive premier was two significant amendments to the mines and minerals bill, then under debate. Passing with minimal discussion, the first ensured that the royalty of ten cents per ton could not be increased before 1906 and that a maximum rate of twelve and a half cents could not be altered before 1926. The second guaranteed that a new lease with new conditions could be authorized at any time.

Fielding's program of industrial development for the coalfields was focused, seemingly, on the achievement of progress through foreign investment. 'It was particularly desirable,' he argued, 'that influential capitalists in the United States should be induced to make investments in our coal mining operations.'[30] Moreover, Fielding supported consolidation as a means of ensuring successful development. Whitney was able to sign an initial lease with an unprecedented ninety-nine-year term, renewable for an additional twenty years, at a fixed royalty rate of twelve and a half cents per ton. This royalty fee was higher than that paid by other operators, but the lease also applied to all unassigned or existing coal properties that the Whitney syndicate might subsequently acquire. Such favourable terms, by eliminating competition, virtually ensured monopolistic control of the Sydney coalfield.

To guide Dominion Coal's development, Whitney put together a board of directors in 1893 that represented an alliance of New England, Montreal, and Nova Scotia capitalists. As David Frank has argued, this event 'marked the integration of the coal industry in Cape Breton into a metropolitan network of financial control.'[31] Whitney, of course, wanted cheap coal for his gas manufacturing and other operations. Other board members, echoing Fielding's statement that nature intended the shipment of large quantities of coal to the United States, held hopes of rekindling New England links, so prominent during the mid-century reciprocity era. The more realistic Montreal people were interested in capturing the expanding St Lawrence urban-industrial market.

While Dominion Coal's production did climb from some 826,000 tons in 1893 to more than 2.5 million tons by 1901 (better than 60 per cent of Nova Scotia's total output), the company's mining operations through the 1890s were marked by inefficiency, waste, and extravagance – all, according to one critic, the result of 'utter ignorance and incompetency.'[32] These poor management practices did not result from the failure of the New England market. Loss of this market was caused by restrictive American tariffs and anti-pollution measures; but it was more than compensated for by the growth of the St Lawrence trade, and by a 50 per cent reduction in the coal royalty won by Whitney in 1899 from the Liberal government, now headed by George Murray. This particular concession was linked to Whitney's creation, in the same year, of the Dominion Iron and Steel Company, which was designed to use much of Dominion Coal's output. (Indeed, in 1913 alone, the steel plant would

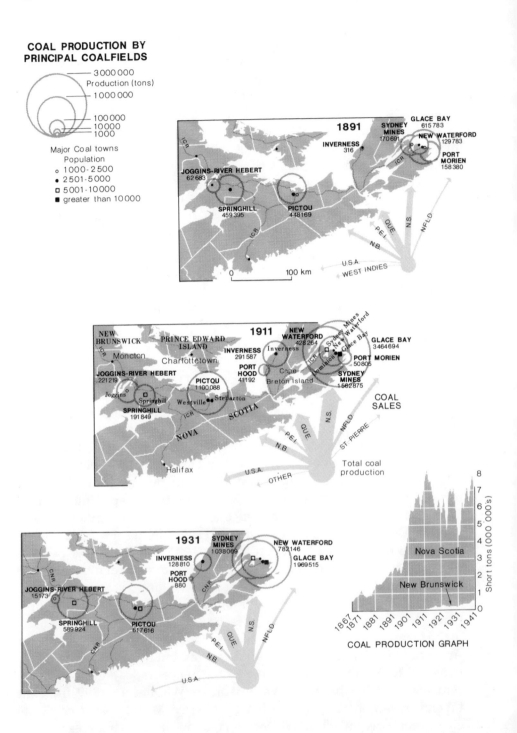

Figure 5 Coal production and urban population growth in the principal coalfields of Nova Scotia, 1891–1931

consume nearly 1.4 million tons of coal, more than half the total coal sales in Nova Scotia.) The steel company's establishment was again aided by Fielding, now in Ottawa but still a Whitney supporter, who managed to persuade a reluctant Laurier government to extend the federal bounty on iron and steel from 1902 to 1907, although on a depreciating or sliding scale.

The mistakes and poor performance of Dominion Coal can be blamed, first, on the inexperience of the company's board of directors (few of the individuals, including Whitney himself, had much experience in either mining or international finance); and second, on Whitney's short-sighted vision of sustained industrial development. The promotion of stocks for quick and easy financial gain appeared to take precedence over long-term development. Of course there were few regulations in place to monitor such schemes. Nor had the provincial government much experience in devising an industrial strategy that might compensate for mismanagement in the private sector. In the climate of continuous difficulties, Henry Whitney retreated from Cape Breton in 1901, relinquishing control of both the coal and steel concerns to central-Canadian interests headed by James Ross.

Schemes of coal and iron and steel development also surfaced in New Brunswick during the 1890s, but only the prospective production of coal was realistic. Government-commissioned surveys claimed in 1893 that upwards of 150 million tons of coal lay buried at Grand Lake. Unlike its Nova Scotia counterpart, the Liberal administration of Andrew Blair offered few substantial inducements to encourage the exploitation of this resource, hoping that worthy entrepreneurs would supply their own capital and work within the context of existing mining regulations. Instead, only small-scale-operators and speculators came and went. Their production was sporadic, averaging about 6,000 tons annually through the 1890s. The reasons for limited development are clear. Besides the poor quality of Grand Lake coal, which had a high sulphur and ash content and was found in thin seams, there was no railroad to carry the resource to major industrial and domestic markets in Saint John, Fredericton, and Moncton. When a rail line to Minto, the principal mining site, was finally completed by 1905, this government-sponsored link was so tainted in scandal that in 1908 the Liberal government would finally be brought down by the 'Central Railway Mystery.'[33]

The new industrialism also reached into the more traditional staple industries of the Maritimes. Changing technologies, advances in transportation facilities, new corporate structures, marketing strategies – the agents of late-nineteenth century industrial capitalism – affected the forest, fishing, and even agricultural sectors. They did so despite the rather limited advance in the gross value of production in these indus-

Boiestown shingle mill, c. 1900. Specialized mills dotted the countryside, and woodworking factories were a feature in most towns. Barrels of water positioned along the roof line served as primitive fire extinguishers.

tries. Between 1890 and 1900, forest output rose marginally from $16.2 to $17.2 million, fishing increased by $5 million to total $20.3 million, and agriculture, showing the greatest advance, jumped from $40.2 to $58.8 million.[34] These modest gains lagged behind those of Canada as whole, largely because traditional external markets for Maritime products did not expand.

But these remarks must be qualified by the varied regional response to changes in the staple industries, changes that were adding further grist to the fragmentation mill. Diversity increased in agriculture, for the 1890s mark a pivotal point in farm-specialization trends.[35] Farming areas that surrounded the growing industrial towns prospered most by increasing their production of milk, eggs, butter, meat, and cereals. Farm incomes rose, as did the value of farm property. This contrasted sharply with the 1890s decline of marginal farms, their soils depleted, in upland areas such as Cape Breton, Colchester, and Cumberland counties in Nova Scotia, or Albert and Westmorland counties in New Brunswick. Other areas became identified with a particular crop. The orchard industry made a substantial advance in the Annapolis Valley. Here the annual production of apples between 1890 and 1899 doubled to more than 1.1 million bushels. Potato production remained most prominent in Prince Edward Island and the upper Saint John River Valley. Dairy belts formed in the immediate hinterlands of Halifax and Saint John, notably around Truro and in the Sussex district. Linked by railroads, these areas attracted new creameries and butter and cheese factories. Unlike parts of Ontario, however, a specialized export market for dairy products never materialized. Products moved short distances across the region, with some butter and cheese going to Newfoundland outports, but, except in the case of apples, the substantial British market remained virtually untapped. In fact, the region became more susceptible through the 1890s to increased food imports from Ontario (grains), the United States (flour), and even South America (canned meat).

Regional agriculture fell victim to external factors in less serious ways. Attempts at specialization and improvement prompted New Brunswick agricultural officials in 1898 to purchase a Jersey bull from Ontario for breeding purposes. The failure of the Ontario bull to perform satisfactorily became a *cause célèbre* in the 1899 provincial election in the Woodstock area. Charles Smith, the farmer-turned-Conservative politician who tended the hapless animal, was ribbed mercilessly by Liberal critics for his poor management. In a staunch but intriguing defence, Mr Smith had declared: 'The bull proved to be no good, but it was not his fault, as both Mr. Saunders and Mr. Dibblee [the government members] knew.'[36] Petty political problems aside, attempts at improvement, such as the further development of an agricultural college at Truro, Nova Scotia, were usually more successful than this particular incident. They were insufficient, however, to overcome the commercial prominence of Ontario or to check the emerging potential of western Canada.

Stability was more notable than change in the forest-products industry, but industrialization made an impact nevertheless. Employment and output were steady in the logging sector, and related sawmilling remained the region's leading manufacturing employer. Newly built and government-supported railways, aided by the introduction of the portable steam sawmill in the late 1880s, pushed the forest frontier further into the interior of northern New Brunswick and the inland hill country of Nova Scotia. In Nova Scotia, a few lumbermen even experimented with private railways. This was true of Emile Stehelin, a French engineer who emigrated to Digby County in 1894. Within a few years, he had built New France, a model industrial village based on modern principles of vertical integration, including logging, sawmilling, and transportation. Like other lumbermen, Stehelin also recognized that success was linked to large-scale timber leases and land ownership.[37] It was also true of Alexander Gibson, of Marysville cotton-textile fame, who owned more than 200,000 acres in the Nashwaak River basin. The New Brunswick

Railway Company cut heavily from its nearly 1.7 million acres of private and Crown lands. Long-term planning and management of such vast New Brunswick tracts was now facilitated by the long-lease system, introduced in 1893, which replaced the yearly renewable system that had encouraged rapid exploitation of Crown lands. Stumpage fees in New Brunswick provided about $40,000 annually – much less than Nova Scotia's coal royalties – and, unlike those coal royalties, proved incapable of reducing provincial debt.[38]

Ownership, location, and market trends in the forest industry were also quite stable. Not far from Stehelin's Digby County operation, the Davison Lumber Company sent logging crews to work on its tracts of some 200,000 acres in Queen's, Lunenburg, and Annapolis counties. It was Nova Scotia's largest landholder and oldest firm. However, deaths in the Davison family during the 1890s prompted a turn-of-the-century sell-out to the American Lumber Company, headed by John Hastings of Michigan. The largest producer in the mid-1890s, however, the T.G. McMullen Company of Colchester County (owner of 150,000 acres and producer of 20 to 26 million board feet annually), was Nova Scotia-owned. The only other significant foreign incursion occurred in the upper Saint John River Valley, where Maine lumbermen continued to play a prominent role, cuttin.; timber for movement to home-based mills under the encouragement of American tariffs on the finished product. Elsewhere, most of the capital invested in the Maritime forest industry remained family-held and community-based. It emanated from a myriad of small settlements where access to water power, as well as to a stream or river suited to the spring log drive, dictated sawmill location. The largest mills, most of which expanded in the 1890s, occupied sites in towns such as Chatham and Newcastle on the Miramichi River, Campbellton and Dalhousie near the Restigouche River, or Liverpool and Bridgewater on Nova Scotia's 'South Shore.' Saint John was the principal sawmilling and export centre. From these places, it was easy to ship ocean-borne lumber to the major British markets. The Miramichi and the South Shore had also attracted the region's earliest sulphite pulp mills, which sold pulp abroad for the first time in the 1890s. Mirroring the fragmented pattern of National Policy industries, the various forest-products centres typically functioned in isolation, catering primarily to overseas markets.[39]

A similar situation held in the fishery, but the pattern of fragmentation was even more acute. Highly volatile export markets – some active one year, but in decline the next; some taking dried cod, others wanting fresh fish (delivered by steamers that plied between Halifax, Saint John, and Boston and by daily trains to Montreal) – were the order of the decade. Fish products totalled nearly a hundred kinds, as did their curing, processing, or handling techniques, making uniform marketing impossible. Nova Scotia led in production, followed by New Brunswick and Prince Edward Island. The coastline of each province was home to hundreds of isolated fishing villages that were slowly feeling the impact of the new industrial order.

The inshore fishery, always uncertain from one year to the next, sustained a livelihood for perhaps one-tenth of the region's population. It was particularly important on Prince Edward Island. Here, the soaring European demand for lobsters caused an industrial revolution of sorts through the 1880s and 1890s. From a limited pack of a few thousand pounds at Confederation, it jumped to the millions. Lobster canneries, which could be crude shanties or well-laid-out premises, were always called factories. Most required little start-up capital. Their seasonal labour force typically drew mainly farm women and children to work for the 'boss,' who might be a neighbouring farmer. But the assault on the lobster created numerous problems: depletion of stocks, poor canning techniques, and factories that were 'mere hovels with inadequate appliances for cleanliness.' Attempts at regulating the length of the season and the size of lobsters kept politicians busy through the 1880s and 1890s, but their policies fell short of an ideal solution because too many fishermen in too many locations provided too many exceptions to a uniform policy. The most serious problem, however, rested in the canning industry where discolouration and spoilage were rampant. To seek solutions, an Islander, Dr Andrew Macphail of McGill University, was appointed in 1897 to investigate. He recommended sterilization of cans, but the problems persisted, and only the introduction of a cannery licensing system early in the twentieth century would bring order to the industry.[40]

The lobster 'problem' did not plague Nova Scotia and New Brunswick to quite the same degree. Here lobster canning often came under the control of large companies, including American firms, which imposed higher and more uniform standards on canning techniques. The largest firm in the 1890s, from neighbouring Maine, was the Portland Packing and Canning Company, which operated canneries throughout the region. Standards were also higher because of the prominence in Nova Scotia of the offshore fishery and the competitiveness associated with this more capital-intensive and technology-adaptive division of the industry. To the extent that marketing standards existed in the offshore fishery, these were more likely to be adopted by the competing inshore fishermen of Nova Scotia than by the isolated Island fishermen.

The offshore fishery, in fact, was quite responsive to new industrial technologies. It still relied on cod as the staple product and depended on external markets, chiefly in the West Indies and the United States

Lobster cannery workers, Murray Harbour, P.E.I., c. 1910. Canneries provided seasonal income for rural people; men did the catching; women most of the packing. Because so much of the product was exported, lobster canneries were among the first food industries to come under health inspection.

but also in Europe and central Canada. To reach these markets, some fish merchants now shipped by steamer or rail and were experimenting with freezing techniques for storing bait and preserving fish. Moreover, a few recognized the benefits of industrial capitalism, at least for its corporate structure and integrating ability. W.C. Smith and Company of Lunenburg, the forerunner of National Sea Products, was incorporated in 1899 to fish, process, and outfit schooners involved in the 'bank' fishery. Lunenburg itself was the home port for the largest fishing fleet in Nova Scotia. Its landward services included shipbuilding and repair facilities, as well as marine insurance and banking businesses. Lunenburg's industrialization, however, was an exception among the scattered, highly independent communities that comprised the fishery. Most still sent fish directly to market by using the schooner fleets of long-established mercantile firms.[41]

### THE SOCIAL ORDER OF TOWN AND COUNTRY

The new industrialism possessed a social component as well. It reshaped people's livelihoods, created new class interests, rekindled tensions between ethno-religious groups, and forced resolution of social issues that now had a distinctly urban focus. In fact, the newly emerging social order imposed by industrialization was strongly influenced by the fragmentation of town and country. Opportunities were better in town for work and success, but social and labour unrest were more prevalent; the countryside offered fewer possibilities, and was the repository of more traditional ways.

Demographically, the differences between town and country widened during the 1890s. At Confederation, about one of every ten Maritimers lived in a place that was urban in size (at least 1,000 people), if not in character. Thirty years later, at the close of the century, the proportion was one in four. The comparable ratio for Canada as a whole in 1901 was one in three. The biggest shift in the urbanization level (from 18.8 to 24.5 per cent) occurred, in fact, in the 1890s. During that decade, while the region's population climbed rather slowly from 880,737 to just 893,953 people and nearly 100,000 Maritimers migrated from the region, the urban total shifted upward from about 165,000 to some 219,000. Not surprisingly, rural-urban migration, rather than natural population increase, accounted for most of this increase. These people were generally younger, better educated, and more highly skilled than their rural counterparts. Despite stability in numbers of people, the Maritimes was very much a society in motion.[42]

The Maritime countryside had always comprised a patchwork quilt of economic activities and ethno-religious groups, but the patches were threaded together weakly. In the 1890s, the most notable change to the quilt occurred in northern New Brunswick, where the Acadian population expanded in numbers and territory across Gloucester, Restigouche, and Victoria counties, reinforcing the area's cultural autonomy. Compared to the out-migration of neighbouring Québécois to the United States at this time, relatively few Acadians relinquished their cultural hearth. It is this factor that best explains how the Acadians increased their share of New Brunswick's population between 1881 and 1901 from 17 to 24 per cent; their expansion was not solely due to their Catholic religiosity and high birth rate. While others left, they were the ones who stayed behind.[43] Elsewhere, the cultural identity and the ethnic composition of the population remained remarkably stable, despite the transiency and mobility that thinned the countryside. The old immigrants of the mercantile era were to be recognized in clusters of Scots in Cape Breton, Antigonish, Pictou, and Colchester counties; the Yankee and Loyalist Baptists of the Annapolis and lower Saint John River valleys; the Irish of coastal Halifax County, the city of Saint John, and the Miramichi basin; or the German Lutherans of Lunenburg County.

Even the new immigration spurred by industrialization did little to loosen the basic form of these and other ethnic enclaves. For the most part, this movement was directed towards the towns and cities that grew

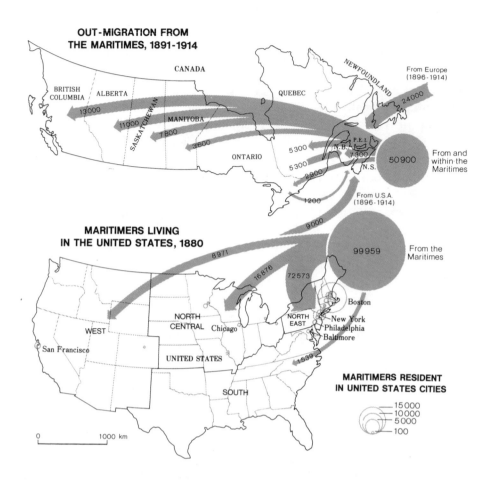

Figure 6 Out-migration from the Maritimes to the United States and Canadian provinces

out of the countryside. More important, and in contrast to other Canadian regions, which experienced a substantial influx of eastern and southern Europeans after the mid-1890s, the Maritime provinces were largely overlooked by late-nineteenth-century immigrants. Many thousands of Europeans first landed in Canada at Halifax or Saint John; for most of them, however, it was only a brief stop en route to central or western Canada. True, skilled English artisans and Irish labourers did stay to work in Halifax and Saint John; Scottish metalworkers, recruited from Glasgow, accepted supervisory positions in Pictou factories; and small groups (a few hundred in each) of Belgian miners and glassworkers, Ukrainian foundry labourers, Italian railroad navvies, and American textile workers – to name several – took up residence in scattered lo-

George Dixon. World featherweight champion throughout the 1890s, George Dixon is remembered as Nova Scotia's outstanding boxer.

cations. For many, however, their sojourn was limited. They quickly left the region when specific contracts were finished, or when the struggling economy offered no alternative employment. Of those immigrants who arrived and stayed for a time in the region between 1891 and 1901 – an estimated 75,000 – only about 17,000 remained at the close of the decade.[44]

A more substantial out-migration was that of the younger sons of farmers with little hope of inheritance, as well as of the daughters of fishermen, lumbermen, or farmers with minimal work or marriage prospects so long as they stayed at home. These and others who left the Maritimes often made temporary moves beforehand – a year or two at sea, a season in the woods, a period in domestic service, or a harvest excursion to western Canada; but the region could not hold them indefinitely. Indeed, marriage and church membership records for the 1890s verify the rural-to-urban movement and out-migration of thousands of Maritimers in search of a better life.[45] Shorter moves tended to be made by the unskilled sons of farmers; longer moves by the more skilled and experienced. Daughters more commonly sought out larger cities, avoiding the limited work opportunities of the smaller communities. Some of these migrants did achieve upward social mobility in the towns, but success and persistence were not the dominant trends. Most seem to have moved on, after only a few years' residence, to areas beyond the Maritimes – New England, the American Midwest, or even British Columbia. In a sense, the Maritime diaspora amplified the internal fragmentation of the region.

Adding complexity to the diversity of the region was the growth of towns. In 1891, there were thirty-seven places of 1,000 or more population scattered across Nova Scotia, New Brunswick, and Prince Edward Island; in 1901, the total was fifty-three. Spurred on by National Policy industries, coal production, or revitalized staple activity, the different towns pursued varied courses of development, with their economic structures differing remarkably in function, scale, and importance. The most successful towns were located along the main line of the Intercolonial Railway. Growth centres in the 1890s included Glace Bay, Sydney Mines, New Glasgow, Stellarton, Amherst, Moncton, and Campbellton. Most towns grew rather modestly, and several actually lost population. The losers included places such as Digby, a long-established Loyalist and fishing community, and the likes of Oxford (lumbering), Westville (coal), or Milltown (cotton textiles). Poor transportation and communication links held them back – weaknesses that are sometimes still apparent today.

To a certain extent, these towns created patches within patches. Town and country could act in harmony with each other when supplying raw materials, recruiting a seasonal labour force, selling goods, or providing essential social services. They might also share the same ethnic fabric. Many elements did not blend, however, particularly those that distinguished the urban and rural classes, or those that affected town and county government. As industrialization gained momentum in the 1890s, the range of social divisions in the towns expanded. Supplementing the earlier prominence of skilled artisans, many more unskilled labourers and semi-skilled operatives now took up positions in, for example, Amherst's boot and shoe factory, Trenton's steelworks, or Truro's woollen mill. Furthermore, while some mercantile families teamed with successful industrialists through marriage to maintain élite status, others did not. Nor did fledgling industrialists necessarily mix with merchants or the expanding professional class. The class structure of the industrial towns thus became more complex and fragmented. In the process, the towns were further separated from the social order of the countryside.

Industrialization forced communities to respond to problems of development, but the very classes it produced frequently blocked the resolution of pressing matters. An illustrative case is the incorporation in 1899 of Newcastle, New Brunswick, and the town's subsequent search for industry.[46] Incorporation had been an option for Maritime communities since the early 1870s, but was only sporadically undertaken. Sometimes a disaster, such as a destructive fire and the consequent need to raise revenues to provide essential services, was the stimulus for seeking official status. This was the case of New Glasgow, Nova Scotia, which took on town status in 1875, the year following a fire that swept through the entire central business area. In New Brunswick, the revised Towns Incorporation Act of 1896 encouraged communities to reconsider the pros and cons of implementing a charter; and a number did so, including Newcastle. The goal of incorporation in this Miramichi community was not easily won. It pitted the long-established patrician class of sawmill owners against a new leadership element, composed largely of merchants but also including a smaller reform group, of which the most prominent was H.H. Stuart, the celebrated teacher, eventual newspaper editor, and advocate of socialism.

By the 1890s, the new industrialism had largely bypassed Newcastle, prompting Stuart to ask: 'Why is it that our town ... is so little different from what it was fifty years ago? Why is it she has made so little progress?'[47] To the merchant and reform groups, town incorporation was viewed as the best means of acquiring greater power for promoting civic improvement and economic rejuvenation through industrial development. Incorporation was especially attractive to these groups because it would remove the town from the administrative control of the county, which was strongly dominated by the patrician sawmillers. Patrician influence was strong enough to squelch a first attempt at incorporation in 1897. It was done by arguing that incorporation would greatly increase taxes. This was a largely specious point, raised in response to the reform group's call for a new water system, but a point that nevertheless united the patricians and the 'poorer souls' of Newcastle to vote down incorporation.

Such arguments were not sufficient, however, when the incorporation issue was again espoused, successfully, in 1899 by the Board of Trade. Following a new tack, the merchants and their allies now insisted that incorporation would give Newcastle a stronger voice when the town negotiated with provincial and federal authorities about such matters as the completion of the Canadian Eastern Railway (which would link Fredericton directly with Newcastle). The costs of incorporation would be minimal. Also, the financing of municipal services could be done on rather favourable terms. Especially significant was the merchants' suc-

Newcastle, N.B., 1878. Newcastle experienced the ups and downs of the conversion from a timber- to a lumber-based economy. The town tried to make steamboats and the Intercolonial Railway drawing cards for the industries it hoped to attract to diversify its economy.

cessful appeal to the working class with a promise to impose a non-resident tax on labour to limit the number of outside workers entering the town.

After incorporation, an uneasy alliance among the millowners, merchants, workingmen, and other classes characterized Newcastle's initial pursuit of progress. Basic services such as water, sewerage, and electric lights were put in place, but the quest for an industrial base to sustain well-being came to naught. The stumbling block was apparently the division of interest between the sawmillers on the one hand, and the promoters and supporters of the potentially rewarding pulp-and-paper industry on the other. To the advocates of progress, it was a logical expansion – perhaps the only sensible one – of Newcastle's dependence on the forests of the Miramichi region; but the patrician sawmillers saw it as change that would create water shortages, take away labour, and cut into the supply of timber. In short, town-granted bonuses would provide preferential treatment for a competitor in all these areas. In time, some small businessmen sided with the millowners, fearing loss of business should a pulp mill, with its fewer employees, force the labour-intensive sawmills to close down. Not even the conciliatory efforts of H.H. Stuart could resolve the division. Stuart suggested that the town receive in stock the value of any financial concessions granted to the proposed pulp-and-paper company, but his compromise position was rejected. As the debate came to a close in the early 1900s, even the working class abandoned its support of the merchants.

The achievement of harmony in a province marked by latent and potentially divisive class, ethnic, and religious fragments did, in some instances, rest ultimately on the very diversity that distinguished the provincial ethos. This paradox is well illustrated in the 1890s by the H.H. Pitts affair. Pitts, a young newspaper editor and sometime independent MLA, was Presbyterian in religion, a federal Conservative in politics, an ardent imperialist, the Grand Worthy Associate of the New Brunswick Sons of Temperance, and an Orangeman to boot. The Pitts affair charged provincial politics with friction throughout the 1890s, pitting Protestants against Catholics, anglophones against Acadians, townspeople against country folk. Its resolution required all the consummate political skills of the Blair and Emmerson administrations.[48]

Herman Pitts, and the people who initially rallied around him, believed fervently in cultural uniformity, and specifically in the development of a homogeneous New Brunswick that was English speaking, Protestant in religious outlook, and morally reformed in character. The actual issue that crystallized the call for cultural uniformity focused on the administration of schools in Bathurst, a small lumbering town with a religiously and ethnically mixed population. Since the heady days of the conflict over the sectarian schools in the early 1870s, governments in power had practised an 'easy going tolerance' to appease the province's diverse fragments. In the field of education, this meant that the Common Schools Act, adopted by the provincial government in 1875, 'legalized within the non-sectarian system of the province, schools of a sectarian bias.'[49] Under this guise, in 1890 Bathurst's Catholic-dominated board of school trustees permitted a hitherto private girls' school at a local convent to enter the public school system and receive financial support. Within a year, Roman Catholic (and mainly Acadian) students were transferred to this school, where they received more than the permitted allotment of religious instruction, further irking the Protestant minority, who were now paying higher school rates.

Gradually, this issue entered the larger political arena, first as a petition to the House of Assembly, then in a Kent County by-election, and finally as a province-wide matter championed by Herman Pitts. For people like Pitts, the pragmatic tolerance of distinguishable differences had gone too far. In his ensuing campaign for cultural uniformity, Pitts forced the people of New Brunswick to reconsider the most basic principles of their society. Throughout the decade, but especially during the provincial and federal elections of 1895 and 1896, voters debated the specific concerns on the Pitts agenda of cultural uniformity: prohibition, women's suffrage, the place of French-language instruction in schools, and, of course, the non-sectarian school question. New Brunswickers favoured prohibition by a four-to-one majority; many supported the right of women to vote; others wanted instruction in French eliminated altogether; and some called for a purely non-sectarian school system. But few, when actually confronted by the ballot, wanted all these things together. Uniformity could not win at the expense of diversity, and in the end 'the politics of accommodation ... defeated and discredited the politics of confrontation.'[50]

Unfortunately, accommodation meant playing into the hands of parochialism and, not infrequently, sweeping divisions temporarily under the table. For example, while Irish and Acadian Catholics did join in expressing their dislike of Herman Pitts by supporting the government, they remained bitterly divided over the issue of appointing a bishop. For the Irish ecclesiastical hierarchy, the English language offered the greatest potential for the expansion of Catholicism; yet such a focus ignored the demographic reality of the province. In the Chatham diocese, for example, Acadians totalled 52,000 of the 65,000 Catholics. In Moncton alone, 7 out of 10 Catholics (1,919 of 2,803) were Acadians. And, despite concerted efforts within the region and appeals to Rome by such Acadian leaders as Pierre-Amand Landry and Pascal Poirier, Acadians were kept from even the lowest ranks of the hierarchy when an Irish priest was appointed, after much debate through the 1890s, as coadjutor to the bishop of Chatham in 1900. Thereafter, Acadian Catholics would fight strenuously, and often bitterly and in public, for their own diocese with its episcopal see in Moncton.[51]

Similar divisions characterized a working class radically altered by the new industrialism. Skilled artisans were particularly affected. While farmers, fishermen, or lumbermen retained varying degrees of independence through the 1890s, the skilled artisan witnessed the further transformation and degradation of craft and self-reliance. Not only was the large and impersonal factory or corporation gaining ground, reducing the importance of well-honed skills, but the chances of personal accommodation within this process were very much weakened. The protests against change increased dramatically in the 1890s. Agitation for improved workers' rights mounted and, when all else failed, strike action was taken to achieve recompense and lost dignity. There were particularly difficult and bitter strikes in the Springhill mines in 1890 and 1897 among coal miners, at Joggins in 1896, on the Saint John docks in 1891, and by the moulders at Fawcetts Foundry in Sackville in 1894.

Fishing boats at Miscou, N.B., c. 1900. Most Acadians continued to live in the countryside, where they depended on seasonally based subsistence activities. The single-sailed 'chaloupes' shown here typified the vessels used in the inshore fishery before gasoline engines.

The disorganization of the labour movement, in fact, points to the further fragmentation within the region's new industrial order. Workers shared the need to organize, whether it be to form a small, local group; to accept affiliation with an international union; or to unite, as did the coal miners and some transportation workers in Nova Scotia, behind the banner of the Provincial Workmen's Association (PWA). All these types participated in strikes; and at this time local revolts were more customary than region-wide action. As Ian McKay argues, these were 'strikes waged by men whose actions had little possible bearing on workers elsewhere in the region.'[52] By contrast, strikes in the twentieth century, particularly those against the coal industry, would greatly affect – even shut down – many linked industries. In the 1890s, however, the labour movement was highly decentralized, and its impact scattered. Nowhere was this more apparent than within the PWA. District subcouncils, such as the radically minded Holdfast Lodge in Joggins, struggled militantly and independently for working-class rights. They despaired over what they considered the political expediency and the corporate pandering of their leader, Robert Drummond. Further, the closing of ranks by labour, government, and big business was not to the liking of the fiercely independent mainland miners. The check-off between miner and employer worked well enough in Cape Breton's large coal companies but did nothing for the security of mainland miners employed by small firms. In short, the PWA 'came to mean very different things in different places.'[53]

Local conditions thus shaped different attitudes. The conditions of the time – notably the recession of the early 1890s – also played a part. In tough times when jobs became scarce, townspeople agitated against their country cousins, and urban-based unions worked hard to keep rural workers at bay. For a period in the summer of 1897, for example, co-operation in the building trades among carpenters, masons, plumbers, and labourers created the Citizens' Protective Association of Halifax to prevent transient labour coming to the city.[54] Further division occurred even within the city when workers argued that differences of skill and therefore remuneration between 'the competent mechanic and ... [the] inferior class of workmen must be recognized.'[55] Such divisions within the labour movement ensured that the experience of the working class in the era of the new industrialism was not a significant force in shaping unity within the Maritimes. Nor could the leading cities, Halifax and Saint John, unify and gain control over the region.

METROPOLITANISM DENIED

The urban characteristics of Saint John and Halifax were markedly different from those of town and countryside. With populations of 39,179 and 38,437, respectively, in 1891, they ranked sixth- and seventh-largest in the nation and housed about one-fifth of their province's population. Not only their size, but also their various social, cultural, and economic traits set them apart within the region. Here could be found the greatest variations in wealth and social prestige; a plurality of ethnic groups and cultural associations; and a variety of businesses. In Halifax, the urbane South End ruled over the working-class North End; Saint John's élite Pleasant Street stood above the tenements fronting the waterfront. Class-divided districts apart, English, Scots, and Irish intermingled freely with each other, as well as with the few immigrants recently arrived from continental Europe. When of the same class, they usually shared the same neighbourhoods. The apparent homogeneity of the British majority was contradicted, however, by the great variety of Protestant religious groups, and by the gulf that still separated pockets of Irish Catholics from others. A degree of accommodation nevertheless existed in Halifax, where Protestants and Catholics, by mutual agreement, al.ernated in the mayoralty seat, occupied the same schoolhouses, and shared the dual constituency in federal elections. In Halifax and to a lesser degree in Saint John, Blacks occupied small but separate districts of poor housing. Architecturally, church spires, symbols of a stable past, were losing pride of place against the skyline to rising temples of commerce and administration, and to factories of industrial diversification. The rapidly changing business districts of these two port cities revealed the scope of this transformation: office blocks were taller, factories bigger, and shipping facilities larger. Electric street cars, introduced by 1896, now gathered workers more quickly from suburban areas.

Despite this evidence of change and apparent regional leadership, decisions were taken in the 1890s that would deny both Saint John and Halifax claim to true metropolitan status. Metropolitan centres attain such prominence by gaining the upper hand and dominating their hinterlands in such key sectors as transportation, commerce, manufacturing, and finance. The Maritime cities lost out on two fronts: they failed to industrialize fully; and they failed to retain control of a once-prominent banking and financial community.

The industrial structure of both cities had expanded under the aegis of the National Policy and certain favourable location factors. Saint John's performance was the more substantial. By 1891, it was a leading Canadian producer of brass, nails, machinery, rope, and lumber – all supportive of and closely tied to New Brunswick's forest-products industry. Sawmilling, the largest employer, depended on the easy movement of logs down the Saint John River. Saint John also manufactured cottons, shoes, tobacco, and, on a much smaller scale, a variety of other products. Accordingly, no other provincial centre acquired such a large industrial proletariat (some 5,700 manufacturing employees in 1901) to add complexity to its social structure. In Halifax and adjacent Dartmouth, the most notable industrial advance had been made in the consumer-products sector, not in the production of staples or of goods essential for the staples trades. These activities remained the prerogative of lesser towns, outport settlements, or external competitors, all of which were located closer to supplies of raw material. Sugar, cotton textiles, clothing, rope, publications and other printed materials, boots and shoes – these were some of the products that the Halifax-Dartmouth area sent to regional and even national markets.[56]

In the 1890s, however, the industrialization of both Saint John and Halifax encountered severe obstacles. The misfortunes of the cotton textile industry, buffeted by over-production, severe national and foreign competition, and poor marketing strategies, have already been mentioned. Other industries suffered from one or a combination of factors:

Halifax Street Railway, 1894. Affordable urban transit encouraged the development of neighbourhoods distant from workplaces. This decade would see the transition from horse cars to electrically powered streetcars.

the financial hardships of world-wide depression; the tyranny of a marginal, peripheral location that added burdensome transportation costs; the limited size of local and regional markets that kept production units small and impeded the development of savings associated with large-scale production; and – not insignificantly from a metropolitan viewpoint – either the take-over of local firms by central-Canadian and foreign corporations, or the central-Canadian and American implant of branch distribution outlets selling a wide variety of manufactured products. Saint John's and Halifax's sugar-refining industry was taken over. The proliferation of branch plants held more lasting implications for the metropolitan ambitions of these two Maritime centres, as well as signalling Toronto's rising influence across the region. Montreal's businessmen were the merger and take-over specialists, whereas in the 1890s, the emerging Ontario metropolis began to set up a Maritime distribution network in various manufacturing sectors, including flour milling and the production of agricultural implements, business machines, home appliances, rubber products, and heavy machinery. Saint John and Halifax manufacturers could not compete with such large-scale enterprise.[57]

The demise of the financial community in both cities by the turn of the twentieth century is a paradox of metropolitan ambitions. At the beginning of the 1890s, both cities had strong financial institutions that dominated banking throughout their respective provinces and elsewhere in the region. Their support of Maritime industrialization, as James Frost has shown, was initially unequivocal, but was severely tested by local industrial failures and the fact that the rewards for investment outside the region were better.[58] As the decade progressed, therefore, the national aspirations of several Halifax institutions, notably the Bank of Nova Scotia and the Merchants' Bank (later the Royal Bank of Canada), led to the eventual withdrawal of their headquarters from the region. The Bank of Nova Scotia's move to Toronto in 1900 was a telling blow. Its Canadian, American, and foreign customers would be better served from that metropolis. Clearly, metropolitan ambitions had taken these banks to the national stage, weakening the stature of both Maritime cities, and hence of the entire region.

If the metropolitan ambitions of Saint John and Halifax were thwarted in the manufacturing and financial sectors, an alternative growth strategy might have been built around the winter ports. Whether to adopt such a strategy was an issue that had been debated since Confederation. It was a plan that depended on the continuation of long-standing import-export activity and that only compounded the increasingly peripheral status of both cities. Securing expanded port facilities, fast mail service, subsidies to steamers, and related benefits required constantly importuning the railway companies, lobbying the federal government, arguing for a subservient association with Montreal, or giving concessions to international shipping agencies.[59] Moreover, each city was entirely self-serving, pointing to a fragmented response in matters of regional economic development. Perhaps because of its better political representation in Ottawa, where Andrew Blair served as minister of railways and canals from 1897 to 1903, Saint John was more successful in realizing its ambitions to become a national port. It also seemed that Saint John's various lobbying groups – particularly the Board of Trade and the Common Council – were more active than their Halifax counterparts.[60] By the close of the decade, Saint John could boast the services of two national railways (the CPR and the ICR), better freight rates than its Maritime competitors, more frequent calls in fast mail service, considerable harbour improvements, and, most important, increased trade. All of this was achieved at the cost of a considerable loss of independence, however, for 'in developing a strategy for securing facilities, the civic and business elite in their negotiations emphasized Saint John's appendage relationship ... [to] Montreal's pivotal position.'[61] Furthermore, when local shipowners and merchant-capitalists did not lead the way, control of the waterfront fell to shippers and the agents for international steamship lines. In the long run, the benefits of seeking national winter-port status in Saint John and Halifax proved largely spurious: the volume of trade did increase, but very little occurred during the winter shipping season. Halifax and Saint John had become mere intermediaries for handling trade in the North Atlantic economy, a role that was hardly the basis for sustained metropolitan growth.

Against these broad changes of declining fortune and status, other events – of a social nature – point to the inability both of Halifax or Saint John to assume the mantle of regional leadership, and of the region as a whole to coalesce. Throughout the 1890s, there were strong cries for various reforms related, however loosely, to the new industrialism: public ownership of utilities, the physical improvement of cities, relief for the urban poor, municipal tax reform, temperance and prohibition, and furtherance of women's rights. Some items on the agenda concerned only particular places; others had a regional audience. None received centralized attention.

The nature of Halifax's response makes the general case. Preaching 'true economy,' the city's mayor, its civic engineer, and most aldermen focused chiefly on debt, the condition of 'dilapidated' streets, and the 'folly ... [of building] sewers too small for the locality,' rather than upon the vexatious issues of housing shortages, slum landlords, or disparities in services.[62] Instead of initiating its own innovative policies, the city often turned for guidance to other metropolises. For example, the system of waterworks was to some extent modelled on those of Boston and Philadelphia; and Reginald Clarke's enlightened scheme for public housing was modelled on British experiments. In a similar way, leading Halifax feminists Eliza Ritchie and Edith Archibald tended to raise issues then in vogue in Boston or Toronto.[63]

Often the issues pursued by women such as Archibald in Halifax or the suffragist Emma Fiske in Saint John exposed the fragmented nature of both urban societies. A women's suffrage bill in 1893 almost slipped through the Nova Scotia legislature, arousing little more fuss than the passage of legislation allowing women the municipal franchise six years earlier in Nova Scotia and the preceding year in New Brunswick. Only by skilful manoeuvring did the attorney general, J.W. Longley, manage to delay and finally kill it near the end of the session. A similar proposal in Fredericton the next year failed by four votes. Soon, however, the lines were more clearly drawn. A Catholic newspaper denounced women's suffrage as a threat to the family, and suffragist and Women's Christian Temperance Union leaders tabled supporting signatures by the tens

Edith Archibald

of thousands. The politicians backed off, and the issue was defeated, if not dead, before the end of the decade. In organizing locals of the new National Council of Women in both Halifax and Saint John in 1894 and in Charlottetown in 1897, local leaders were careful to make clear that theirs was not a suffrage organization but merely a lobby by club women on reform and women's issues.

Similar divisions also marked the long-standing debate over temperance and prohibition. Decidedly different responses sprang from the various religious denominations and different class interests, and from rural and urban areas. Centralizing forces strong enough to bridge the diverse perspectives of the social fragments on these issues would await a later decade.

Despite the Maritimes' fragmentation in the 1890s along class, ethnic, political, and industrial lines, by the close of the century the foundation was already being laid for a later source of unity. Although Laurier's boast that the twentieth century would be Canada's century reflected a prevailing optimism that the country could achieve a stronger identity based upon a new prosperity, the Maritimes had already failed to benefit fully from industrialization. From this failure there was emerging a shared consciousness that would ultimately rally the people to a defence of regional interests. The 1890s were a turning point in the emergence of this consciousness. The transition from a seaward to a landward economy that restructured the social order had both positive and negative consequences in this decade. Advances were made in some sectors to the benefit of a small minority, but the long-term effects were to force the region farther off the metropolitan stage onto the periphery. The ultimate impact of fragmentation was the development of a dependent status. As unity grew, it did so from this marginal perspective, rather than through leadership and innovation. This was the legacy of the 1890s.

# CHAPTER FIVE

# The 1900s
## Industry, Urbanization, and Reform

As the new century opened, the Maritime region was abuzz with talk of war. In Halifax preparations were already underway for the embarkation of a second contingent of some 1,200 men and horses for the South African war. Even the discovery of typhoid fever among the crew of the troop ship *Montezuma* failed to dampen the patriotic spirits of a community that regarded the war as a modern religious crusade to 'ring the death knell of political inequality, of race or creed, or nationality.' The nineteenth century, the Halifax *Herald* noted, began with the French Revolution, that 'sanguinary struggle for the fraternity of men,' and ended with the Boer War, 'the most effectual for his equality.' In between, the American Civil War had buried slavery in the southern States, and a new concern for the less fortunate had resulted in a proliferation of hospitals and various other institutions for the deaf, the blind, the aged, and the orphaned.[1]

This crusading liberalism involved more than the rhetorical musings of imperialists at war. At home it was the rallying cry of a reform battalion that sought to rid modern industrial society of its most obvious abuses. Marrying a faith in the principles of Christian charity and imperial patriotism to the seemingly progressive impact of modern science and technology, these reformers called for a collective assault on sweatshop conditions, slum housing, child labour, unsanitary dwellings and thoroughfares, alcohol and opium addiction, prostitution, crime, and disease. Most believed that religion and science acted inexorably to ensure social improvement. 'All the forces in the world are moving towards the consummation of [the Lord's] work,' said Mrs Dodge, president of the Presbyterian Church Women's Foreign Missionary Society in Halifax. 'All the paraphernalia of modern science are accessories towards this end; telephones, telegraphs, submarine cables, steam, electricity, rapid transit, are all bringing the world nearer to Christ.'[2]

Accompanying this starry-eyed crusade for God, Empire, and the

Volunteers for South Africa. Commemorative arches and flags symbolized the strong attachment still felt by Haligonians for the mother country, Britain. The thirst for adventure and incipient nationalism also played a role in enlistments.

progress of mankind, was a more hard-headed faith in the efficient and 'scientific' administration of the social system – the application of scientific management principles to society in the name of greater efficiency. Largely drawn from the urban middle class, the proponents of a new reform program included journalists, ministers, medical doctors, businessmen, lawyers, feminists, social justice advocates, labour leaders, politicians of both mainstream political parties, and ordinary people across the political and occupational spectrum. Even if they disagreed about what changes were necessary, one can discern the general contours of a progressive impulse that resonated throughout all of North America, most particularly in areas of urban or industrial growth. In general, progressivism called for the peaceful resolution of labour disputes, a 'scientific' approach to the problems of social and moral degeneracy (including marriage control and the science of race improvement), the establishment of an effective public-health system, a more positive or interventionist state, the transcendence of political partisanship and religious sectarianism, and a commitment to various forms of social regeneration, from temperance to child saving to physical culture, recreation, and sport.[3]

Many of those in the vanguard of the reform movement were advocates of the new 'Social Gospel,' which called upon Christians to contribute actively to the task of social improvement. By the end of the nineteenth century, most of the mainstream churches were turning away from an earlier preoccupation with individual sin and personal salvation and embracing a new gospel that stressed the possibility of social regeneration. Protestant theologians of various denominations reinterpreted the scriptures to show Christ as a social reformer and urged their parishioners to follow his example. If this new gospel of reform led to attempts to humanize and Christianize modern capitalistic society it also revealed a waning commitment to traditional theological discourse. As the historian Ramsay Cook has observed, these 'regenerators,' in responding to the challenges of the new biological sciences and contemporary biblical criticism, contributed to the declining importance of the traditional church.[4] Furthermore, as commitment to progressive reform measures united Christians in common cause, the distance between the denominations narrowed. Even the Catholics evolved a reform rationale, as expressed in the 1891 papal encyclical *Rerum Novarum*, which denounced the abuses of unrestrained capitalism but rejected socialism as the solution.

The Protestant application of Christian principles to social reform did not necessarily imply fundamental alterations to the existing system. The large phalanx of 'Social Gospellers,' professionals, volunteer agencies, and reform-minded politicians stopped far short of advocating a radical remodelling of modern society. Instead, the reformers steered a middle course between the advocates of traditional individualism – those who defended *laissez-faire* economics, maintained partisan political loyalties, and adhered to traditional notions of individual salvation – and those on the left, the socialists, labourites, and more radical critics of modern industrial capitalism whose prescriptions for economic democracy struck directly at the distribution of power and ownership within society.[5]

## POLITICS

Despite the growing commitment to progressive reform among their constituents, regional politicians faced serious obstacles in achieving a more interventionist provincial state in matters of social and economic management. Many within the mainstream parties were shielded from

Georgina Pope. Daughter of a prominent Charlottetown family, Georgina Pope led a contingent of nurses to accompany Canadian troops to South Africa. Through such experiences came a heightened awareness of the inequalities faced by women in Maritime society.

popular pressures by a patronage-based and highly partisan political order; and even when politicians were stirred to action on particular issues, financial deficiencies often blocked the way. The three provinces continued to operate under significant fiscal disabilities within the larger Confederation. The financial arrangements of the Confederation settlement had long been a sore spot for Maritimers, and had been a major contributing factor to W.S. Fielding's campaign for repeal of the BNA Act during the 1880s. Not surprisingly, much of the political life of the provinces in these years centred upon the fiscal issue, especially since – unlike more contentious arguments for reform – calls for fiscal relief tended to garner universal support. Furthermore, with Liberal governments in each of the three provinces and at Ottawa, the Maritime provinces in this decade strenuously pressed their case for a revision of the financial terms of Confederation. At the same time they moved cautiously forward into the uncharted waters of social reform.

In Nova Scotia the management of provincial affairs fell to the Liberal government of George H. Murray. An adroit but cautious politician, Murray had become premier of the province in 1896 when W.S. Fielding left provincial politics for a post in the Laurier cabinet. A native of Grand Narrows and well schooled in the province's case for a better deal within Confederation, Murray none the less realized the importance of the National Policy tariff for the continued growth of regional industry, particularly in his native Cape Breton. While calling for increased subsidies and criticizing the diversion of goods destined for overseas markets through Portland, Maine, he offered no radical alternatives.

The Murray government also advanced haltingly into the field of social and economic reform. Espousing a progressive concern for a more scientifically managed social system, Murray's government provided initiatives in agriculture, technical education, public health, and the control of public utilities, and attempted to reduce labour unrest through a mixture of coercion and reform. On the whole, however, Murray entered into the arena of social legislation cautiously, pursuing a course that ultimately served the interests of capital more than those of labour.

Murray's caution stemmed largely from the existence of three divergent groups within the Nova Scotia Liberal Party. One was largely rural. Committed to a *laissez-faire* market-place of freely competing individuals, this group generally distrusted big capital and organized labour and remained hostile to most social-reform initiatives, except for prohibition. Prominent among them was Attorney General James Wilberforce Longley, an advocate of lower tariffs and an unreconstructed opponent of powerful labour unions and female emancipation. A second group coalesced around former premier William Pipes of Amherst, Halifax businessmen David McPherson and George Mitchell, and former mayor of Halifax, Michael Keefe. Members of this group spoke for the business interests of the province and supported reform only when they saw it contributing to a more businesslike administration of provincial affairs. A final group, led by Cape Breton doctor A.S. Kendall, urged a broader commitment to social justice, workers' rights, and public-health reform in response to the unfortunate side-effects of too-rapid industrialization.

Given these divisions it is hardly surprising that Murray proceeded into the realm of social and labour legislation with particular care. His concern was to keep the divergent elements from breaking the party apart. Murray's consensus orientation helped in the long run to encourage political stability in the province; however, it also left unsolved many of the deeper problems inherent in the development of modern industrial capitalism. This was particularly true, as we shall see, of Murray's handling of industrial relations.

New Brunswick's political life at this time remained unsettled. The decade witnessed four different administrations; those of L.J. Tweedie (1900–7); William Pugsley (1907); C.W. Robinson (1907–8); and J. Douglas Hazen (1908–11). The Tweedie government was a continuation of the Liberal coalition once presided over by Andrew G. Blair. Essentially a coalition of competing interests held together by patronage, Tweedie's government was unable to effect much in the way of reform. In a decade characterized by the tendency to place issues of principle and broad significance above local self-interest, it remained for the opposition Conservatives in New Brunswick to take up the cause of reform. They advocated a number of changes directed at controlling the excesses of Tweedie's pork-barrel politics, including the appointment of a provincial auditor, the reduction of legal costs in connection with election trials, and the submission of all government contracts to public tender.

In the election of 1908, J.D. Hazen's Conservative Party swept to power on a progressive reform platform that included a more scientific approach to agriculture, the regulation of public utilities, a more modern public health system, and a more efficient approach to road making and maintenance. Hazen also advocated joint action by the Maritime provinces to defend their interests within Confederation. At a ceremony in Halifax commemorating the 150th anniversary of the Nova Scotia legislature, Hazen warned of 'coming Western influence in the Dominion and the necessity of "United Acadia" standing together to prevent any further decrease in its representation at Ottawa.'[6] This marriage of progressive reform proposals and the defence of regional interests within Confederation became a common formula for political success in all three provinces.

In Prince Edward Island, the Liberal government of Arthur Peters followed a similar course, calling for a greater degree of economic management, a revision of the fiscal arrangement within Confederation, and the fulfilment of the federal government's promises to maintain effective year-round communication between the Island and the mainland. The Peters government encouraged a more scientific system of agriculture, actively supported the province's temperance movement, and worked to make the province more attractive to tourists. Strapped for revenue, the Island considered tourist dollars and the acceptance of its claims for an increased federal subsidy essential prerequisites to future social and economic development.

Of particular concern to the Island province was the unpredictability of steamer service across Northumberland Strait during the winter months. The two steamers, the ss *Stanley* and the ss *Minto*, often were unable to complete the crossing owing to dangerous pack ice. In March 1903, both steamers became stranded in the ice and were threatened with grounding and destruction on the Nova Scotia shore. For weeks the Island's only contact with the mainland was by ice-boat or sled, and crossings were hazardous. Thereafter demands for a tunnel crossing increased, but the Laurier government – balking at the projected cost – responded instead with a new ice-breaking ferry, the *Earl Grey*, which in 1909 replaced the twenty-year-old *Stanley*.[7]

Failure to maintain continuous communication with the mainland, as promised in the province's terms of entry, provided one basis for Peters' demands for subsidy increases. Others relate to the Island's relinquishment of the P.E.I. railway at Confederation, and its difficulties in raising revenue without forest or mineral resources. Hopes for a favourable resolution of the claim rose briefly in 1906, when the financial terms of Confederation became the major item on the agenda of an interprovincial conference. In the general subsidy revision that emerged from the conference, however, the Maritime provinces fared badly. While the governments of British Columbia, Quebec, and Ontario received increases of 121 per cent, 66.1 per cent, and 62.5 per cent respectively, Prince Edward Island's increase was 59.8 per cent, Nova Scotia's 46.7 per cent, and New Brunswick's only 41 per cent. The explanation for this discrimination, James Maxwell has suggested, was that the needs of the Maritimes were so great that provincial leaders grasped 'at any offer of better terms, with little thought of remote consequences.'[8]

Whatever the explanation for the poor bargain made by the Maritime governments at this juncture, it left them weakly situated to pay for reforms. To make matters worse, provincial fiscal problems accompanied a diminished influence in the House of Commons. In the redistributions of 1892 and 1903, the Maritimes lost a total of eight seats. Prince Edward Islanders were particularly incensed with the reduction in their representation to four. At the time of their entry into Confederation their Commons representation had been set at six. Although no guarantee had been written into the terms of entry, Islanders felt that this should be the province's minimum representation. An appeal to the courts by the three provinces failed to secure the desired end, although a subsequent agreement in 1915 made senatorial representation the minimum for a province's representation in the House of Commons.[9]

To compensate for their declining numbers, Maritimers relied heavily on the influence of federal cabinet ministers from the region. In the Laurier cabinet this appeared strong. Their numbers included Frederick W. Borden, minister of militia, William Pugsley, minister of public works, and former provincial premiers W.S. Fielding, minister of finance, and Andrew Blair, minister of railways and canals. Unfortunately, in their haste to establish a larger political base than that provided by the Maritimes alone, the most ambitious ministers often came to serve other masters. Fielding, the old secessionist, became a faithful servant of the national party and gradually emerged as a spokesman for the Montreal business community.[10] On the opposition side, Conservative leader Robert Borden, a Nova Scotia native, also put national concerns before local needs. Indeed, Borden found it convenient to leave the Maritimes to establish his claims to national leadership. First elected to Parliament from Halifax in 1896, Borden gave up his local law practice in 1905, moved to Ottawa, and eventually sat in the House of Commons as a member from Ontario.[11]

Borden was a progressive. His 'Halifax Platform,' unveiled in 1907, four years before he became prime minister, called for an expanded role for the public sector, reform of the civil service to reduce patronage and encourage bureaucratic efficiency, a public utilities commission to regulate railways and telegraph and telephone companies, and a system of free rural mail delivery.[12] Borden was also a nationalist committed to the establishment of a new politics of national unity and social responsibility, and his progressive ideals left him suspicious of regional protest or the promotion of local needs. 'The interest of the East is the interest of the West,' Borden commented in 1911. 'The interest of Nova Scotia is and always must be the interest of British Columbia.'[13] For a region increasingly concerned about its worsening political and economic fortunes, this was by no means helpful advice.

Andrew Blair, on the other hand, remained a staunch defender of the Maritimes, and more particularly of his native New Brunswick. Under his direction as minister of railways the Intercolonial flourished. Deficits were kept to a minimum and cheap and flexible rates were provided for Maritime industry.[14] It was Blair's regional loyalty, or more particularly his defence of the Intercolonial, that resulted in his resignation from his cabinet post in 1903. Blair had been horrified when in the previous year Laurier unveiled plans to extend the transcontinental to Moncton and to have the Grand Trunk – the Intercolonial's traditional rival for winter port traffic – take control of the operation. If having the government assume the heavy costs of construction only to hand it over to the Grand Trunk seemed questionable, Blair regarded the duplication of the Intercolonial's line from Levis to Moncton as little short of insanity. But insanity bred of the optimism of this expansive era was good politics for Laurier. Blair resigned, and the railway scheme went ahead, ironically for a brief period under Fielding as the acting minister.[15]

Laurier's railway policy promised something for everyone. The extension of the National Transcontinental to Moncton was touted as meaning that the eastern port cities of Halifax and Saint John would finally become the outlets for Canada's winter trade, about which there had been much talk at the time of Confederation. With Moncton the official terminus, however, many in Saint John felt that their interests were not fully served. By 1907 that city had begun a determined agitation for the building of a line running from the National Transcontinental at Grand Falls down the river valley to Saint John. Normally an irresistible force in New Brunswick politics, the Saint John influence eventually secured a complex deal in which the province would guarantee the interest on the bonds for construction of the Saint John Valley and Quebec railway. The federal government would pay the cost of three expensive bridges and remit to the province 40 per cent of the gross revenues from the operations of this new section of the National Transcontinental.[16]

The dénouement, which came in the next decade, would be fully as bad as anything Blair had predicted. Canadians wound up with at least one more transcontinental railway than the traffic would sustain. The government's retention of the railways' debt when it took over the bankrupt lines in 1917 saddled the new Canadian National Railways with a burden from which its railways would never escape. The duplication of lines in the east undermined the economic validity of the Intercolonial. Under the pressure of war, the federal government reneged on its promise of bridges to make the Valley Railway part of the National Transcontinental. Without the additional traffic from integration into a trunk line, the Valley Railway and its more than $9 million in bonds remained a revenue-draining burden on the provincial government.[17]

As the Maritime provinces came to recognize the need for more concerted action in defence of regional interests, the idea of a legislative union among them was dusted off once again. Progressive reformers, many of them businessmen, were attracted to the scheme because it seemed to promise more rational and efficient government. The most vocal supporters of the scheme were members of the Maritime Board of Trade, including Nova Scotia senator William Ross, W.G. Fisher of New Brunswick, and Halifax lawyer Reginald Harris. In two articles in the magazine *Acadiensis*, Harris stressed the financial savings implicit in having a single legislature and lieutenant-governor, the benefits of uniform tax and company laws, and the greater political influence a united region would exert at the federal level. The pro-union Saint John *Standard* attributed the scheme's lack of popularity to local selfishness, a more powerful force than the impulse to rationalize regional affairs.[18]

INDUSTRY AND LABOUR

The Maritimes' decline in political influence coincided with a diminished role in their own economy. During the 1880s regional entrepreneurs had invested heavily in textiles, sugar refining, confectionery, foundries, and related enterprises. But these entrepreneurs often lacked the capital necessary to sustain their enterprises through a period of extended depression. The centralization of the Canadian banking system undermined still further the ability of local businessmen, especially those in wholesale or consumer-goods industries, to secure the resources necessary to avoid take-over by outside interests.[19] During the first decade of the twentieth century the take-overs continued, and the number of branch businesses in the Maritimes – many of them Montreal-based – increased by almost half.[20] The region's financial institutions underwent a similar process. After the turn of the century a number of regional banking companies succumbed to the competition from centrally located banks that could offer nation-wide services through their various branches. The Halifax Banking Company was absorbed by the Bank of Commerce in 1903, the People's Bank of Halifax by the Bank of Montreal in 1905, and the Union Bank of Halifax by the Royal Bank in 1910. Only three of the thirteen banks operating in the Maritimes in 1900 remained in 1910. Two of these, the Bank of Nova Scotia and the Royal Bank (until 1904 the Merchants' Bank of Halifax), recognized the need to operate nationally in order to survive, and shifted their head offices to Toronto and Montreal respectively. The third, the Bank of New Brunswick, was absorbed in 1913 by the Bank of Nova Scotia.

The 'nationalization' of the banking system further diminished the control that the region could exert over its future development. As early as the mid-1880s, capital accumulated in the region was being exported to more lucrative fields of investment. This process accelerated over time. Between 1900 and 1910, net transfers of funds from Maritime branches to the head office of the Bank of Nova Scotia alone amounted to more than $4 million. It is impossible to know how much capital was drained from the region in this critical period of industrial expansion and consolidation. Nor can we know whether regional capitalists would have availed themselves of easier access to capital. It can be said, however, that the creation of a national financial market served to build up industry elsewhere using capital accumulated in the Maritimes, and that this threatened the long-term industrial potential of the region.[21]

For most Maritimers, however, continuing economic growth and urban expansion masked the deeper weaknesses of the regional economy. Indeed, while the rural population of the Maritimes declined by a quarter between 1881 and 1911, the urban population of the region doubled in size. Expansion was especially noticeable in a northeastern industrial belt running from Moncton, New Brunswick, to Sydney, Cape Breton. In 'Busy Amherst,' a diversified industrial sector that included textile milling, boot and shoe manufacturing, gas-boiler production, and railway-car construction helped to boost the town's population by 80 per

Dominion Iron and Steel Company plant, Sydney, 1905. Two huge new steel plants were built along the shores of Sydney Harbour between 1900 and 1905. The DISCO plant produced rails, nails, and wire, as well as raw steel for regional industries.

cent between 1901 and 1910. Coal-mining towns such as Westville, Springhill, Inverness, and Glace Bay experienced a similar growth: Westville went from 3,471 to 4,417, Glace Bay from 6,945 to 16,562, and Inverness from 306 to 2,719. Elsewhere the gains were more modest but revealed the continuing urbanization of the region. Moncton, a major distribution centre, grew in population by 25.6 per cent, Halifax by 14.2 per cent, and Saint John by 4.4 per cent.[22]

The rapid urbanization of the period is also reflected in the significant growth of manufacturing and mining output. The value of manufactures in the Maritimes jumped by 94.7 per cent from $46,891,691 in 1900 to $91,364,956 in 1910, while by 1910 the capital invested in Nova Scotia's booming mineral sector reached $28,494,822 or 26.3 per cent of the total for the nation.[23] The opening of the Dominion Iron and Steel Company (DISCO) plant at the beginning of the century contributed significantly to this expansion. A blooming mill was added in 1902, allowing for the production of unfinished forms of steel. By 1905 finishing mills suited to the fabrication of wire rods and steel rails were also completed. With the opening of DISCO, Nova Scotia vaulted into prominence as a steel-producing province. By 1910 the combined output of DISCO at Sydney and the Nova Scotia Steel and Coal Company (Scotia),with operations in Trenton and Sydney Mines, amounted to one-half of the iron and steel production of the entire Dominion.[24]

The expansion of the coal and steel industry changed the face of Cape

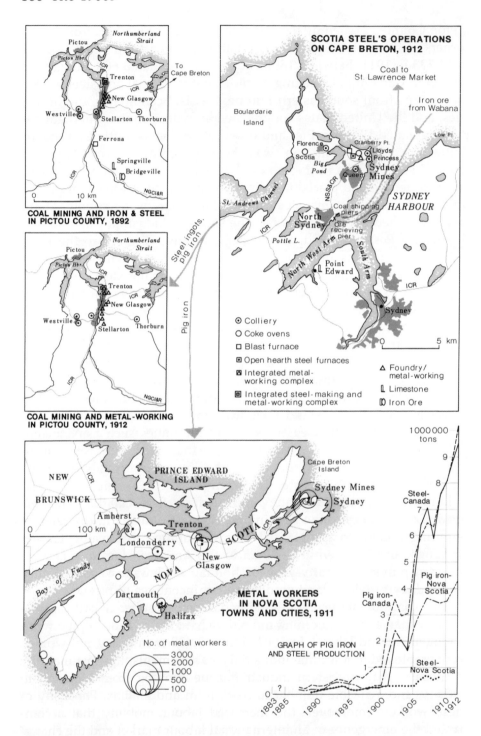

Figure 7 The iron, steel, and metalworking industries of Nova Scotia: selected case studies, c. 1890–1912

Breton County. Fuelled by the rapid immigration of workers from many corners of the globe, Sydney's population jumped from 9,903 in 1901 to 17,723 in 1911. Between 1896 and 1900 more than 3,600 immigrants arrived in Cape Breton seeking employment in its coal and steel works. Immigrants from southeastern Europe, Russia, Scandinavia, the British Isles, and the United States congregated at Sydney in the 'International Pier,' renamed Whitney Pier and often referred to as 'Little Chicago' or 'Little Italy.' Significant, too, was the large influx of Newfoundland workers seeking jobs in the mines.[25] This rapid growth continued into the next decade and placed inordinate demands upon towns for proper housing, sewage systems, electrification, and pure water supply. Many faced wretched living conditions. The slums of industrial Cape Breton, the *Sydney Post* remarked, would be 'a positive disgrace to the most filthy parts of Constantinople.' Nevertheless, beneath these concerns there was an essential optimism; Sydney was a major steel capital and its future looked bright even if rapid industrialization meant temporary social dislocation.[26]

Other towns in the region devised strategies that linked their development to the traditional farm, forest, and fishing economy. At Bridgewater, on the south shore of Nova Scotia, Acadia Gas Engines opened in 1908, turning out engines for new gasoline-powered fishing vessels. Towns such as Newcastle and Edmundston in New Brunswick tried to attract industries that would take advantage of the forest and water-power resources of the region, while communities such as Moncton, Kentville, Truro, and Sussex sought to consolidate their role as distributing centres for agricultural hinterlands. They offered incentives in the form of cheap land, free water, and exemption from municipal taxation to industries that would locate within their borders. Charlottetown offered tax incentives to the Dominion Packing Company in the hope of acquiring a cold-storage plant; Newcastle offered free water, tax exemptions, and an interest-free loan to the Anderson furniture factory; Amherst provided a thirty-year tax holiday to Hewson Woollen Mills; and Sydney provided land grants and tax incentives to DISCO.[27]

The expansion of the region's industrial sector resulted in both a growing industrial labour force and a rapidly changing relationship between management and labour. In 1901 some 33,000 men and 9,500 women were employed in Maritime industrial establishments, the vast majority of these in a northeastern industrial zone running from Moncton to Sydney, and a sizable number in Saint John and Halifax. For many of these workers, moreover, the increased labour mobility that accompanied the emergence of an international labour market and the changing character of the industrial workplace resulted in a sense of class solidarity and a resistance to new forms of managerial discipline. As

Main Street, St Stephen, N.B., c. 1900. Main streets in the region were transformed by industrialization. Electric lights, streetcars, and new fire hydrants coexisted with horse-drawn wagons, unpaved streets, and family-owned shops.

capitalists responded to the extreme competition of the turn-of-the-century merger movement, they resorted to a variety of new techniques that collectively, Ian McKay has called, 'scientific management – a systematic effort to obtain greater productivity from workers by exerting managerial discipline.' McKay suggests that workers' resistance to the resulting loss of personal control in their workplace was an important factor in the 1,986,146 days of work lost through strikes in the Maritimes between 1901 and 1914.[28]

The bitter strikes of these years, fought by coal miners, steelworkers, civic labourers, textile workers, longshoremen, and even such unlikely individuals as paid members of church choirs and professional hockey players, bear witness to the deep class conflict that accompanied the development of modern industrial capitalism. In this setting of sharpening class antagonism, the demand for radical social change increased. The Saint John Fabian Society (1901), with socialist Warren F. Hatheway as its first president, called for public ownership of electric lighting, the

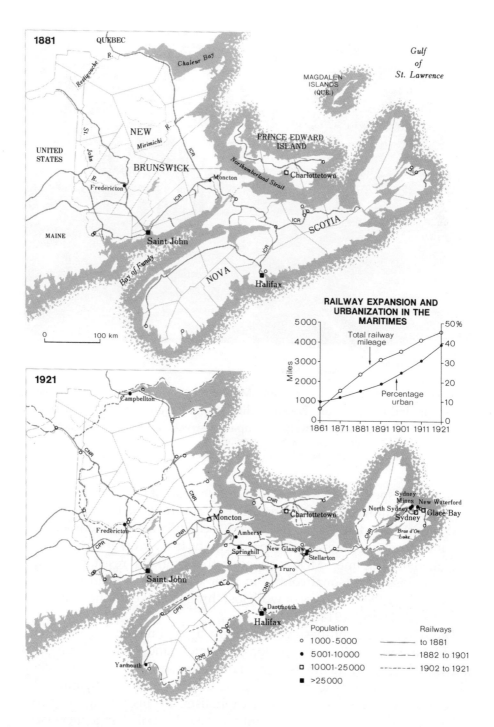

Figure 8 Urban and economic development in the Maritimes, 1861–1921

H.H. Stuart of the Socialist Party of Canada, 1907. A sometime teacher, Social Gospel preacher, and journalist from New Brunswick, Stuart worked to spread the gospels of union organization and socialism throughout the region.

gas and water supply, street railways, telegraph lines, railways, and 'all natural products which from their nature can easily become monopolies.'[29] Radical Social Gospellers and 'civic populists' such as H.H. Stuart, Rabbi Abraham Rabinowitz, and the Rev. A.A. Gandier defended workers' rights, demanded improved housing for working people, advocated producer and consumer co-operatives, and supported the municipal ownership of utilities.[30] In addition, socialist magazines and newspapers, such as *Cotton's Weekly*, *Butler's Journal*, the Moncton *Free Speech*, and the *Western Clarion*, preached a message of radical change to a small but dedicated readership, while socialist organizers such as

Roscoe Fillmore and Wilfrid Gribble worked assiduously in defence of the labouring classes and the dispossessed.[31]

The first decade of the twentieth century also witnessed the growing influence of the trade-union movement. Before the turn of the century the labour movement in Canada, though regional in outlook, had a predisposition towards mass rather than craft trade unionism. In the Maritimes, the Provincial Workmen's Association (PWA) had drawn together coal miners, blacksmiths, printers, plumbers, and other trades into a broad labour coalition. With the growing involvement of the craft-oriented American Federation of Labor in Canadian labour matters, however, there was greater focus on the skill or trade. Beginning in 1901 the AF of L's Canadian organizer, John A. Flett, conducted an organizing drive in the Maritimes that spawned more than two dozen new unions in the three provinces. Flett was particularly successful in New Brunswick, organizing longshoremen, cigar makers, machinists, painters, carpenters, and bartenders.[32]

Even in Prince Edward Island, where industrialization had developed only sporadically, Flett's drive met with considerable success. Assisted by volunteers Harry Corcoran and G.W. Snelgrove, Flett organized carpenters, painters, printers, trackmen, iron workers, and teamsters into locals of international unions. In January 1902, Corcoran and Snelgrove also helped to create a federation of Charlottetown labour unions, with Snelgrove as president. When this local council received AF of L recognition in the following month it included more than 400 active union members.[33]

The organizing efforts of the AF of L in the Maritimes may have led to a growing involvement of the region's working class in the union movement, but they also nourished a rivalry between international trade unions and regional unions such as the PWA. Often erroneously dismissed as a company union, one easily manipulated by the mine operators, the PWA had accomplished much in its first two decades. It had won strikes, influenced the passage of useful labour legislation, and vigorously campaigned against the open shop.[34] After the unsuccessful steelworkers' strike of 1903, however, doubts grew about the ability of the PWA to defend the rights of its members, especially with the expanding power of the Dominion Coal Company, established in Glace Bay in 1893. Thus, when the United Mine Workers of America (UMW) began a drive to organize mine workers in Nova Scotia in 1907, many adherents of the PWA defected and demanded that Dominion Coal recognize the UMW as their legitimate bargaining agent.

When the company refused, the miners struck in July 1909. Battle lines between the company and its workers were quickly drawn. The operators erected houses inside the fences surrounding the collieries for those who wished to continue working and evicted striking miners from company-owned housing. In response, some 2,000 canvas tents went up in Glace Bay to provide shelter for the miners and their families.[35] Dominion Coal was a formidable opponent with the resources necessary to fight a lengthy strike. By 1900 it controlled some 300 square miles of coal lands, containing an estimated 1.4 billion tons of coal, 12 working collieries, 100 miles of railway track, 10,000 employees, and an average annual output of 4 million tons. In addition, general manager G.H. Duggan reported, the company had banked between 100,000 and 150,000 tons of coal. Given these advantages the company's strategy would be brutally simple: starve the miners out.[36]

In order to defeat the strike, Dominion Coal also drew upon the support of the state. Demanding protection of its property and its strike-breakers, the company first asked the mayor of Glace Bay, John C. Douglas, to request a special force of militia for the town. When Douglas refused, the company turned to a more co-operative local magistrate, who issued a request for a force of 508 officers and men from the Halifax garrison.[37] In the end, despite the financial support of the UMW, the strike collapsed and with it the aspirations of UMW supporters in Cape Breton.

Meanwhile, another miners' strike involving 1,700 employees of the Cumberland Railway and Coal Company had broken up in Springhill. This twenty-two-month dispute began in June 1909 after a conciliation board chaired by J.W. Longley failed to resolve the difficulty. The major issues of the strike included the company's demand for a 15 per cent wage reduction and its alteration of traditional measures of productivity in the mines. The miners demanded recognition of the UMW as their bargaining agent, a consistent schedule of wages for all kinds of labour, and a new standard weight for a box of coal.[38] Both sides were prepared for a long and bitter battle. As in Cape Breton, workers were evicted from company homes, a special force of constables and militiamen was enlisted to protect the company's property, and strikers were occasionally arrested for illegal picketing or stealing coal for personal use.[39] For the miners, however, no grievance caused more bitterness than the reliance of the operators on scab labour. When the Dominion Coal Company sent its agent Don Gregor to Springhill to recruit miners for the Cape Breton collieries in August 1909, posters quickly went up warning residents to 'Beware of Scab Labour Agents.' When this failed to intimidate Gregor, a group of between 200 and 300 men arrived at his boarding-house and deposited him on a wagon leaving the community.[40]

These images of class confrontation disappointed progressives convinced that class harmony would grow out of a common commitment to public responsibility on the part of working people and capitalists alike. Particularly embarrassing was the stance of capital in these disputes. Outraged by the behaviour of the mine operators, Halifax newspaper magnate William Dennis attributed the strike at Dominion Coal to 'irresponsible' capitalists who in alliance with a remnant of the PWA enforced an open shop in contravention of the will of the majority. What Dennis failed to note was the extent to which these disputes transcended the activities of individuals. What the strikes of 1909–11 had revealed was the failure of the progressive hope for eradicating class conflict within the existing capitalist system.

Provincial governments answered to the challenge of labour radicalism with progressive programs of their own. In New Brunswick the Tweedie government responded to the demands of various radical organizations for the regulation of child and female labour with the New Brunswick Factory Act of 1905. This act made fourteen the minimum employment age for children in industrial establishments and limited the hours of work for women and children. In the following year the same government passed an act requiring compulsory school attendance for children up to the age of sixteen. No child under sixteen could be employed in any business or industry during school hours without proof of successful completion of the seventh grade. That act also prohibited employment of children under thirteen years of age in any manufacturing, mercantile, or mechanical establishment.

In Nova Scotia the Murray government's approach to the labour crisis included new mine-safety legislation, an old-age pension scheme, and workers' compensation. Legislation passed in 1907 provided for use of safety lamps in mines, and gave employees a say in the choice of a physician. The Nova Scotia Colliery Workers' Provident Society Act created a pension fund for miners based predominantly on worker contributions supplemented by smaller contributions from the government and the mine operators. In 1910 the government introduced a rudimentary workers' compensation bill that made limited compensation available to those employed in firms of ten or more employees and swept away the doctrine of contributory negligence that often allowed employers to escape liability in cases of injury or death to employees.

In general, Murray's approach to the labour crisis was to propose only those reforms that had the blessing of the province's business leadership. This often gave the illusion of reform when in fact little was being done. The striking of the Royal Commission on Hours of Labour in 1908, with David Robb, president of Robb Engineering in Amherst, as chairperson, and Glace Bay labour representative Henry MacDonald and Professor Robert Magill of Dalhousie University as commissioners, is a case in point. Not only would a shorter work day improve the physique, intelligence, and morale of workers, the commissioners noted, but it would encourage more efficient work habits, and reduce time lost to accidents, irregular attendance, drinking, or boredom. A shorter work day would also have 'citizenship benefits,' providing working men with the leisure time to acquire an intelligent grasp of the responsibilities of citizenship and make them 'less prone to the unprincipled agitator and revolutionist.'[41] But, after listening to expressions of alarm from manufacturers that any unilateral adoption of shorter hours would destroy their competitive position nationally, the commissioners recommended against the eight hour day. For the Murray government the commission had served a useful purpose. Merely establishing the commission had demonstrated Murray's interest in reform, while the report itself justified doing nothing.[42]

On issues that had the support of business, the Murray government could be quite innovative. Responding to the lobbying of the Mining Association of Nova Scotia, in 1907 it passed 'the Technical Education Act' which provided for state-funded education of engineers and evening technical classes for working people. Expressing the characteristic progressive faith in science and technology, advocates of technical education argued that a more scientific approach would encourage efficient use of provincial resources, stimulate industrial prosperity, stem the loss of population, and provide working men with the prerequisites for upward mobility. The leading proponent of technical education in Nova Scotia was Frederick H. Sexton, a graduate of the Massachusetts Institute of Technology who had come to the province in 1904 to take up a position at Dalhousie University. In 1907 Sexton assumed the office of 'Director of Technical Education' within the Department of Education. In 1909 the Nova Scotia Technical College opened its doors in Halifax.

The progressive gospel of efficiency that permeated education at all levels also revealed itself in the turn-of-the-century school-consolidation movement. The altered demography of the Maritimes that had accompanied industrialization and urbanization had already had a significant impact upon the ability of various school sections to attract teachers and maintain schools. A.H. MacKay, Nova Scotia's superintendent of public schools, for example, reported in 1907 that the lucrative employment opportunities accompanying Cape Breton's 'good times' resulted both in a diminished supply of teachers and a high incidence of student dropouts. At the same time out-migration from many rural districts made it necessary to close a number of schools. By 1906 some fifty-three schools in Nova Scotia had been consolidated into twenty-two effective school sections.[43]

School consolidation appealed to those progressives who argued for a society run on firm business principles. One of these was Prince Edward Island tobacco magnate Sir William C. MacDonald, who personally funded a pilot program in school consolidation in Middleton, Nova Scotia, and Hillsborough, P.E.I. Superintendent MacKay estimated that MacDonald's contribution to the Middleton school alone for the founding year of 1903 would exceed $30,000. In addition to attracting high-quality teachers, these model schools, introduced through the introduction of 'MacDonald Gardens,' were intended to develop an appreciation of nature that would help to stem the drain of people to urban areas from the countryside.

RURAL LIFE

The shift in population from rural to urban communities between 1901 and 1911 was dramatic. Nova Scotia lost 23,981 rural inhabitants and gained 56,745 urban dwellers. New Brunswick's rural population fell by 1,493, while its urban population increased by 22,262. Prince Edward Island maintained its urban population but lost 9,546 rural dwellers.[44] Still, most Maritimers continued to live in communities of less than 1,000 people, most of them employed in fishing, forestry, or agriculture. Occupational pluralism helped many rural dwellers to maintain their attachment to the land: farmers cut pulpwood, tapped for maple sugar, or built barrels for sale in local markets; fishermen kept gardens and worked in the woods; lumbermen worked in the mills or temporarily on roads or railways.

Discussion of the rural Maritimes at the beginning of the new century, however, does not permit easy generalization. Although the loss of population to urban communities suggests a crisis in the rural economy, pockets of growth and prosperity remained. In the Annapolis Valley of Nova Scotia the apple industry continued to expand and, through the efforts of various marketing co-operatives, further consolidated its presence in the British market.[45] Potato farmers in Carleton County, New Brunswick, were also successful in maintaining access to markets in the United States. On Prince Edward Island, one of only two provinces in Canada to witness increased gross earnings on agricultural investment in 1910 as compared with 1900,[46] farmers continued to market their produce extensively in Cape Breton and Newfoundland.

A widespread feeling remained, however, that the rural economy was in a vulnerable state, and that the fishing, forestry, and agricultural sectors all should be reorganized in line with progressive notions of efficiency and scientific practice. The east-coast fishery exhibited continuing stagnation. Little growth in aggregate annual value had been realized in the previous two decades. Essentially a small-boat operation dependent upon the maintenance of the individual craft skills of inshore fishermen, the fishery lacked both the local capital resources to transform itself or a merchant élite committed to its modernization. To John J. Cowie, author of the chapter on the Atlantic fisheries in *Canada and Its Provinces* (1914), the existing stagnation was 'due to the fact that the fish-trade of the Atlantic Coast has remained largely a salt-fish one.' Cowie saw the future of the industry in an expanded fresh-fish industry. In his mind, the introduction of gas engines – in 1910 more than 2,300 boats in the east-coast fishery were gas powered – and the development of steam trawling were steps in the right direction, even if steam trawlers roused bitter opposition from those engaged in longlining.[47]

To those New Brunswickers interested in the scientific management of the resource sector, lumbering represented the crucial sector of the economy in need of modernization. Logging in New Brunswick was still carried out as it had been for decades. Nevertheless, the increasing distance of the best timber from rivers and streams, the difficulty in attracting woods workers, and competition with southern pine and other imported woods such as Douglas fir led reformers to call for the introduction of machine logging and the building of spur lines to allow for the railway transport of logs to market. In Nova Scotia, where forest resources had been substantially depleted, organizations such as the Western Nova Scotia Lumberman's Association campaigned for the more effective husbanding of forest resources. The Nova Scotia government responded with a forest survey during the summers of 1909 and 1910, the purpose of which was to inventory the province's forest resources with an eye to future management. In 1912 the federal Conservation Commission published the report, but it had little apparent impact.[48]

A more progressive approach to agriculture was the goal of all three Maritime governments at the turn of the century. In Nova Scotia the Murray government undertook a major expansion of the Nova Scotia Agriculture College in Truro (established in the 1880s) and invited students from the whole region. It also encouraged the importation of stock, organized travelling dairy schools, promoted the formation of agricultural and horticultural associations, and developed experimental orchards.

Prince Edward Island established a provincial Department of Agriculture in 1901, used the Government Stock Farm as a model farm, and extended the curriculum of Prince of Wales College to provide courses in nature studies and domestic science. Professor S.J. MacMillan of the college, a particularly vocal exponent of agricultural education, became the first superintendent of the province's Department of Agriculture.[49] In New Brunswick, a provincial Royal Commission on Agriculture (1909) also laid out a progressive blueprint for agricultural reform that included practical education tailored to the needs of farm families, involving courses in nature study, domestic science, animal husbandry, and fruit growing;

The Acadian flag. Semi-annual conventions continued to consolidate symbols of Acadian culture. Acadians' confidence grew as they achieved majority status in northern counties in New Brunswick.

better railway, road, telephone, and rural postal-delivery services; co-operative marketing of poultry and eggs; model farms; the encouragement of agriculture societies; and the promotion of immigration to the region.

Despite such good intentions, the region's rural population continued to decline, and established farmers found it difficult to recruit farm labour as the young people steadily drifted away. In Prince Edward Island the province's population dropped from 103,259 in 1901 to 93,728 in 1911, a decrease of 9.23 per cent. In New Brunswick and Nova Scotia the provincial population increased by 6.27 per cent and 7.14 per cent, respectively, but primarily rural counties such as Annapolis, Antigonish, Colchester, Digby, Guysborough, Hants, Kings, and Richmond in Nova Scotia, and Carleton, Charlotte, York, Kings and Albert counties in New Brunswick all registered declines.[50]

One exception to this trend occurred in counties with a significant Acadian population. In Restigouche, Gloucester, Northumberland, Madawaska, and Victoria counties in New Brunswick, population remained stable and even increased. It is hard to know why this was so. Part of the explanation may lie in the overspill of population into northern New Brunswick from the province of Quebec. In addition, the common practice of combining wood cutting with subsistence agriculture or fishing contributed to a largely self-sufficient rural economy in these areas. Some Acadian farmers even continued to grow wheat for their own use during this decade, despite the availability of wheat from western Canada.[51] Whatever the explanation, by 1910 Acadians made up a quarter of New Brunswickers and two-thirds of the province's Catholic population.[52]

Another explanation for the maintenance of population in these counties may rest with the nationalism of the Acadian élite, who regarded agriculture as the pursuit that would most effectively unite Acadians in defence of their language and culture. This nationalism was manifested in a number of ways. In 1900, the fourth Acadian national convention at Arichat, with Prime Minister Laurier as guest speaker, attracted a large crowd. The common interests of Acadians throughout the Maritimes was also a recurring theme in the columns of the weekly Acadian newspaper L'Evangéline, founded in Digby in 1889 but moved to Moncton in 1905, and in the Société l'Assomption, a co-operative society established in 1903 that subsequently became the Mutual Life Insurance Company, with its head office in Moncton.[53] The nationalist movement also resulted in demands for an Acadian bishop, even if a separate Acadian diocese was required. In 1912, Monseigneur Edouard LeBlanc was appointed bishop of Saint John, and two years later Moncton received its first Acadian parish.[54]

CULTURAL TRENDS

Rapid industrialization and rural depopulation encouraged essentially romantic testimonies to the virtues of small-town and rural life. In literature, Lucy Maud Montgomery's *Anne of Green Gables* (1908) depicted the traditionalism of the church and family in rural Prince Edward Island. Charles G.D. Roberts' *The Heart That Knows* (1906), set in the village of Westcock, New Brunswick, portrayed the simple, idyllic life of a community living in touch with nature and unspoiled by modern industry. This rural romanticism was reiterated in Frederick William Wallace's *Blue Water: A Tale of the Deep Sea Fisherman* (1907). Writing in an age when fishing trawlers and modern processing plants were beginning to transform the Maritime fishery, Wallace painted an idealized picture of the courageous, steadfast, and contented inshore fisherman.

The idealization of rural life found a particularly powerful expression in the Acadian literary romance. Margaret Marshall Saunders' *Rose à Charlitte: An Acadian Romance* (1898) and Charles G.D. Roberts' *By the Marshes of Minas* (1900) catered to a growing interest in the Maritimes by summer visitors from the United States. In fact, the connection between literary and artistic themes and the emergence of the tourist trade is striking. Photographer Amos Lawson Hardy's picturesque views of Grand Pré willows, Fundy tides, and peaceful orchards collected in *The Evangeline Land* (1902) were intended to evoke images of an unspoiled natural paradise that would attract summer visitors to the province. This was the image that the Intercolonial Railway attempted to create in its promotional brochures 'A Week in the Canaan Woods,' 'Tours to Summer Haunts,' and 'Moose of the Miramichi.'[55]

This decade also witnessed a revival of interest in local and regional history. From 1901 to 1908 the quarterly journal *Acadiensis* flourished under the editorship of David Russell Jack, a Saint John native of Scottish Loyalist ancestry with wide-ranging antiquarian and historical interests. Jack's basic objective was to cultivate feelings of a shared historical past to facilitate the creation of a united Acadia. During its eight years of publication, *Acadiensis* received contributions from a number of prominent scholars and writers. One of these was the journalist/historian James Hannay, whose two-volume *History of New Brunswick* (1909) represented the culmination of a lifetime's interest in the history of the region. Another was William F. Ganong, a Saint John native who began teaching botany at Smith College in Massachusetts in 1896, and, as one of the leading natural scientists in North America, sought to demonstrate the relationship between historical evolution and scientific investigation.[56]

Ganong's faith in the relationship between scientific knowledge and progress contrasted sharply with the rural romanticism that characterized much of the region's literature. Most progressives had little time for what they regarded as literary sentimentalism, promoting instead a doctrine of scientific utilitarianism. In Nova Scotia Dr A.H. MacKay argued the case for a scientific library and museum in Halifax because 'science in some form or other lays at the foundation of success of all the industries of the country.'[57] Responding to MacKay's urging, the Nova Scotia government funded a new science library and museum in 1900 under the curatorship of archivist Harry Piers.[58] The New Brunswick government also answered the call for applied science with the establishment of new chairs in chemistry and forestry at the University of New Brunswick.

Attitudes towards modern science and technology were more ambivalent in Prince Edward Island. Convinced that modernization would undermine the Island's distinctiveness and attractiveness to tourists, the

Micmac guides, Yarmouth, N.S. Hunting and fishing were promoted as part of a new focus on American tourism, which offered employment for Native guides.

provincial government passed an act in 1908 prohibiting the use of automobiles in the province. Other expressions of modern technology, however, received little criticism. The Charlottetown *Patriot* reported favourably on the future of air travel, on the organization of the Halifax Aerial Experimental Association in 1906 (which included Alexander Graham Bell and J.A.D. McCurdy in its list of officers), and on the famous flight of McCurdy's *Silver Dart* on a frozen Cape Breton Lake on 7 February 1909. Three years later at the Provincial Exhibition of 1912, the first airplane to test Island skies soared over an enthralled crowd of spectators.[59]

### HEALTH AND RECREATION

In the public-health field, municipal reformers, women's organizations, and health-care professionals all advocated a more comprehensive and scientific approach to disease prevention. In Saint John, Fredericton,

A successful hunt, c. 1890. The species hunted changed about the turn of the century; the moose remained a popular target, the caribou died out in New Brunswick and Nova Scotia, and the white-tailed deer began a more successful penetration of the region. The person on the left was Gabe Atwin, a popular Maliseet guide in the Fredericton area.

Moncton, Charlottetown, and Halifax, public-health reform initiatives were the strongest. Urban sanitary reformers such as Charlottetown's Richard Johnson, Saint John's William Bayard, and Halifax's Alexander Reid worked to ensure pure milk and water supplies, efficient sewage systems, improved health conditions in factories, and a more healthy youth. Johnson carried on a relentless campaign for a more scientific approach to public-health administration after Charlottetown discontinued the collection of mortuary statistics in 1893. In Johnson's view the city's new water and sewer systems left it with nothing to lose and much to gain by statistically demonstrating that 'it is a place of safe and attractive resort for tourists and health seekers.' In 1906 Prince Edward Island passed a Vital Statistics Act, which encouraged a more systematic approach to disease prevention and control; Nova Scotia followed suit two years later.[60]

Other municipalities also were committed to sanitation and the introduction of sewer systems. The annual report of the New Brunswick

The Halifax Business School, c. 1910. Education became a key to employment opportunities. These night-school students were studying book-keeping. The presence of women testifies to their penetration of clerical occupations in this period.

provincial Board of Health for 1909 noted that Moncton, once considered a haunt of typhoid fever, had reduced its disease rate from more than 300 cases annually with from 40 to 50 deaths to only 22 cases and a single death. Fredericton's mortality rate also dropped with the establishment of its sewer system,[61] although the neighbouring county of Sunbury complained bitterly about the city's dumping of more than four tons of excrement daily into the Saint John River.[62]

For a generation concerned about the efficient management of its natural and human resources, the physical and mental health of the community were issues of paramount concern. Middle-class reformers – most of them white, Anglo-Saxon Protestants – were convinced that appropriate social management would protect against a growing physical and moral degeneracy that threatened the well-being of the Empire and resulted in a rising incidence of crime, alcoholism, and insanity. Reformers suggested a number of antidotes to these ills. These included physical training (often with military drill) in the schools, improvement of the sanitary condition of factories, protection of women and children from exploitive labour practices, marriage control (including the steri-

lization of the insane or morally defective), and the restriction of immigration.

Convinced that immigration infected Canada with disease and class
antagonism, Dr Edward Farrell of Dartmouth warned against the importation into Canada of the 'off-scourings of the old world'. Immigrants,
Farrell argued, were usually from the 'lower orders' who carried with
them inherited or epidemic disease and a degraded moral nature derived
from 'inherited tendency and criminal surroundings.'[63] Arguing that
Canada's need was a healthy native stock, MP J.B. Black called from
Windsor for greater state involvement in disease prevention, an end to
child labour, medical inspection in the schools, and a campaign to ensure
pure water and milk.[64] Dr A.B. Atherton of Fredericton called for a better
breeding of the race through preventing the marriage of 'those who are
defective in physical or mental or perhaps even moral qualities' and the
sterilization of 'the insane, the feeble minded, the diseased, and the
chronic criminal.'[65]

This turn-of-the-century preoccupation with physical and moral degeneracy – a preoccupation that has been referred to as the 'dark side
of progress'[66] – encouraged various initiatives directed at bringing about
social regeneration. In addition to the Christian reformism of the Social
Gospel, secular reformers saw physical culture, recreation, and sport as
antidotes to apparent social disintegration. Concerned about the destructive impact of ill-ventilated schoolrooms and workplaces, the lack of
suitable playgrounds, and the deleterious impact of 'over-study' on children's nervous systems, reformers saw sport and athletics as a positive
force for maintaining social well-being and inculcating appropriate
'manly' values such as courage, loyalty, teamwork, friendship, and patriotism. 'There is nothing better than hockey, football, and gymnasium
exercise to nerve a man and give him physical strength in order that he
may be able to use his mind to better advantage,' wrote a student at
Prince of Wales College in March 1903 when calling for gymnasium
drill and improved sport facilities at the school.[67] Other reformers suggested calisthenic exercises for women based upon the 'New Gymnas-
tics' of Dioclesian Lewis in order that their strengthened reproductive
organs would help stem the 'decline of the race.'[68]

But sport could also be a subversive influence. The problem, many
believed was professionalism. With crowds of five thousand not uncommon to watch rowing challenges, track-and-field meets, and baseball
and hockey games, promoters were drawn to sport in search of easy
profit. In turn, the traditional virtues of 'gentlemanly amateurism' were
threatened. When John Mack, the professional athletic trainer of the
Wanderers' Athletic Club in Halifax, visited Saint John in 1901 he tried
to induce the star batters of the Saint John baseball team the Alerts to

break their contracts and join the Halifax Resolutes at salaries 'higher than those offered in the New England League.' To the Saint John *Globe* this was evidence of the growing power of 'the ring of sporting men, whose sole idea is to gamble on it.' The effect of these promoters, the *Globe* continued, was to turn the game 'into a money-making speculation, robbing it of all that is genuine and lowering its standard to that of cock-fighting and professional pugilism.'[69]

Professional baseball had first come to New Brunswick in 1890, followed after the turn of the century by professional circuits in Cape Breton and mainland Nova Scotia.[70] Despite its immense popularity, however, the sport received constant criticism for the unsavoury practices of the professional athlete. The image of the tobacco-chewing, hard-drinking professional who in playing for pay had more loyalty to his pocketbook than to his team contrasted with that of the choir-boy goodness of the young amateur, playing for the love of the game. The real fear was that sport led not to regeneration but to social degeneracy. While sport was sometimes elevating, the *Maritime Merchant* concluded, it more often was demoralizing. 'Some young men are absolutely spoiling their chances of success in life because sport fills such a large space in their minds.'[71] At the same time the managers at Dominion Coal complained of high levels of absenteeism on days when baseball was scheduled before five o'clock.

Hockey seemed less affected by the 'evils' of professionalism if only because of the greater availability of skilled local players and the lesser reliance on imports. Nevertheless, the 'amateur' Nova Scotia Provincial Hockey League, founded in 1903 and whose games by 1905 were 'more discussed by thousands of people than the Russian Japanese War,'[72] routinely paid under-the-table salaries to its players. By the end of the decade it was impossible to maintain that this was amateur hockey, particularly in the wake of a 1908 court case involving the executive of the Fredericton Capitals hockey club, in which all the team's players were revealed to be on salaries that allowed them to live on hockey alone.[73] These revelations prodded officials of the recently organized Maritime Provinces Amateur Athletic Association (MPAAA) to require players to declare themselves once and for all as amateur or professional. Past violations of amateur standing were forgiven, but future violators would be suspended from amateur play without reprieve.[74]

If sport required such scrutiny, so did marriage, sexuality, and childhood. Influenced by Darwinian and Lamarckian notions of evolution and heredity, many turn-of-the-century reformers argued for greater attention by parents to the institution of marriage. W.H. Hattie, medical superintendent of the Nova Scotia Hospital, suggested that the idea that marriages were made in heaven interfered with a more scientific ap-

University of New Brunswick Ladies' Hockey Team, c. 1911. For women prior to the First World War, university was often a social rather than a professional experience. As more women enrolled in universities, they began to engage in such activities as intercollegiate sports, previously an exclusive preserve of male students.

proach to human breeding. 'Marriages may be made in heaven,' Hattie rather tactlessly wrote, 'but most engagements are made in the back parlour, with the gas so low that a fellow doesn't get a square look at what he is taking.'[75] The ordinary stock-breeder, Hattie suggested, showed infinitely more care in raising horses than in siring children.

Concern about racial up-breeding also led to a greater emphasis upon the appropriate socialization of children. Hattie warned that those city-bred children of the poorer classes who suffered from bad hygiene and improper nutrition would make up an increasingly large number of mental and moral defectives. 'Criminality and insanity,' he wrote, 'are bred side by side in the slums of the cities.' The obvious antidote was improved housing for the working classes, demolition of slums, and well-ventilated homes, schools, and factories.[76] For those who could not be 'uplifted' from promiscuity or criminality, 'proper' facilities were necessary in order to segregate them from other children: these included homes for the feeble-minded, industrial or ragged schools for the young offender – such as the Halifax Industrial School founded in 1865 – or 'miscellaneous schools' with special attention to the three Rs for truants.[77]

The desire to create a strong and hardy race free from the degenerative characteristics that could be passed to another generation led progressives to demand the rehabilitation of criminals and the insane in improved penal institutions and asylums. In Halifax, a meeting of the Local Council of Women in March 1903 denounced the practice of placing adults, both sane and insane, in county poor farms and asylums, and called for a home for feeble-minded children.[78] Principal Fearon of the Halifax Institution for the Deaf and Dumb agreed, noting the possibility of helping children whose faculties were underdeveloped and dormant. Dr George Sinclair, the inspector of humane and penal institutions in Nova Scotia, deplored the conditions of the county jails and called for institutions that rehabilitated the criminal. Sinclair also urged the differential treatment of offenders by age, and the development of an effective probation system that would aid the reformed criminal to find employment and earn a livelihood.[79]

The reformers' concern to eliminate diseases such as smallpox, tuberculosis, venereal disease, and alcoholism encouraged a greater concern about public-health matters. Smallpox outbreaks in 1901 and 1903 in Nova Scotia and New Brunswick, and in 1907 in Prince Edward Island, led to demands for more widespread vaccination and for greater provincial control over local health boards. There was considerable resistance to compulsory vaccination, however. In New Brunswick and Nova Scotia anti-vaccinationists were particularly vocal, arguing that compulsory vaccination infringed upon their liberties and increased the likelihood that an individual would contract the disease.[80]

Venereal disease was more insidious than smallpox, and more widespread. Unlike smallpox, the effects of the disease could be hidden. Paul Ehrlich's 'Magic Bullet,' or Salvarsan, offered some relief from syphilis, but in many cases the cure was only partially effective and often suggested to the afflicted that they had been cured when they had not. Gonorrhoea was not yet recognized to be as serious as we now know it to be. Thus, while concerns grew about the rising incidence of venereal disease during this decade, a vigorous campaign against it would await the national concern about the 'inefficiency' of the troops during the First World War.[81]

Of all the diseases to afflict Maritimers in these years none was more deadly or more feared than tuberculosis. The 'white plague,' as it was known, caused more than 2,000 deaths per year in the region. In addition it was costly to society, often striking young people as they were entering their most productive years, and thereby robbing society of their con-tribution. In 1909, S.J. Walker of Truro estimated that tuberculosis cost Maritimers $10.8 million per year.[82] Walker drew attention to the need for proper inspection of milk, medical supervision in the school system, and a program to improve housing for the poor. In order to address these issues, various reform-minded people in the urban areas of the region established voluntary anti-tuberculosis societies to educate the public with respect to the disease and its prevention.[83]

The Nova Scotia government responded to the tuberculosis epidemic by establishing the Provincial Sanatorium in Kentville in 1903. The first of its kind in the country, the sanatorium had limited effectiveness. Its forty beds were far too few to deal with a problem of such magnitude and were generally inaccessible to the working poor amongst whom the disease was most prevalent.[84] Furthermore, in order to demonstrate its effectiveness, administrators at the sanatorium restricted themselves to handling cases in the early stages of the disease. Accordingly, when a deputation of concerned citizens approached New Brunswick premier Douglas Hazen in January 1908 requesting a grant of $30,000 towards the establishment of a sanatorium in the province, they were rebuffed. The experience of Kentville, Hazen argued, was that 'incipient cases did not care to come to the institution and that others came too late.'[85] The real solution lay in a comprehensive attack on poor nutrition, inadequate housing, and the physical debilitation of the working poor. But such a comprehensive assault on the failings of industrial capitalism extended beyond both the fiscal and ideological resources of existing provincial governments.

To progressive reformers, debilitating diseases, including alcoholism, bred social inefficiency. Alcoholism was a special evil, breaking up homes, encouraging crime, and contributing to accidents and absenteeism in the workplace. The federal plebiscite of 1898 had yielded large majorities in support of prohibition in all three Maritime provinces. When the Laurier government refused to act because of the weak support for the movement in Quebec, the traditional temperance forces – now strength-ened by the vigorous Social Gospel element in all the Protestant de-nominations – turned to provincial governments. Prince Edward Island was the first to act, supplementing the local-option provisions of the federal Scott Act (1878) with a provincial prohibition statute in 1900.[86] In Nova Scotia the Dominion Alliance under the leadership of the Rev. H.R. Grant, a Presbyterian clergyman from Trenton, co-ordinated the pressure on an unwilling government, pressure that finally resulted in the passage in 1910 of legislation imposing prohibition on all the prov-ince's municipalities but Halifax.[87] This legislation and the municipal prohibition under the Scott Act, still in place in much of Protestant rural

Beer parlour, Boiestown, N.B., 1912. While beer parlours were illegal through most of the region, enforcement of prohibition usually lagged well behind legislation.

New Brunswick, could not prevent individuals from ordering their liquor by mail from wet areas of the country. 'Bone-dry' prohibition still seemed far in the future. But the progressive forces were clearly on the march and the liquor sellers on the defensive. Symbolic of the reformers' growing prominence was the Protestant denominations' organization of Moral and Social Reform councils in the three provinces near the end of the decade. Their stated goal was the reorganization of society on Christian principles, and prohibition came high on their agenda.

The turn-of-the-century progressive emphasis on efficiency and expert management eventually extended to the political system itself. In New Brunswick, reformers attacked the Liberal government of L.J. Tweedie for its use of patronage, demanding the submission of all government contracts to public tender and the reduction of legal costs for election trials. In Nova Scotia, the province took steps to create non-partisan control over provincial expenditures with the appointment of a provincial auditor, and in 1909 established the Board of Commissioners of Public Utilities to regulate the rates, tolls, or charges levied by utility companies. The impulse towards responsible and expert management also affected municipal politics. Newspapers like the Halifax *Herald* and the Saint John *Standard* assaulted 'ring rule' in civic government and demanded that their cities should be run on strict business principles.

They favoured taking power out of the hands of elected aldermen and placing it in the hands of successful businessmen who would not mix civic business with party politics. In Halifax the eventual result would be establishment of the municipal Board of Control in 1913. In Saint John a similar movement had previously resulted in the establishment of the first commission-style government in Canada.[88]

## WOMEN

Women also demanded political reforms that would enhance their influence. Drawing upon the inspiration provided by suffragists in Britain, women in the Maritimes demanded universal suffrage, citing their superior nurturing instincts and their municipal and provincial housekeeping abilities. Various Local Council of Women (LCW) groups, the franchise department of the Maritime Women's Christian Temperance Union (WCTU), and municipal suffrage associations argued for enfranchisement. In some ways, however, the movement in the Maritimes as in the rest of the country, marked time in this decade. The doctrine of 'separate spheres,' which implied that women had superior domestic abilities and that men were intellectually, commercially, and mechanically superior, undermined the arguments for sexual equality. When a delegation of women, supported by MLA, J.E. Wilson and W.F. Hatheway, approached Premier Hazen in May 1908 demanding the right for women to vote in provincial elections, Hazen responded in predictable fashion. He argued that women 'would get the franchise when they wanted it, but that they were not yet ready to so. The two sexes each had their own functions,' he continued, 'and very many women felt they could do no better work along their own line without being burdened with the public work of the country.'[89]

Aside from suffragism, women were involved in a number of reform ventures, many of which were intended to 'uplift' women of the working class and to educate immigrants in the appropriate values of the Anglo-Saxon middle class. Women's organizations offered cooking schools and sewing classes to working-class wives, took the lead at times in the temperance movement, worried about the plight of the 'feeble minded,' and fought against unsanitary conditions, impure water and milk, and 'microbe-laden dust.'[90] Middle-class women also worried about the 'servant question.' Concerned that the new opportunities for female employment in factory work had diminished the market for domestic servants, they introduced a number of reform initiatives directed at improving the status and efficiency of domestic work. In 1907, for example, the Halifax Local Council of Women unveiled an Official Employment Bureau designed to increase the number of available domestics and operated a School of Domestic Science, which, in addition to the 'attention to detail and neatness taught there, inculcates a moral attitude that must make for integrity.' Other organizations, such as the Women's Christian Association, provided exercise clubs, courses in serving and business principles, and music instruction for working girls who might otherwise descend into prostitution.[91]

For the most part those involved in the women's movement, like Edith Archibald, Agnes Dennis, Eliza Ritchie, and May Sexton in Halifax and Mabel Peters and Emma Fiske in Saint John, were progressives who were committed to ameliorating the abuses of modern industrial society and to securing a more appropriate place for women within the existing system. One result of their efforts was a growing involvement of women in the medical and legal professions. In 1894 Annie Hamilton became the first woman to graduate from Dalhousie Medical School. More than a dozen others would graduate over the next decade.[92] The legal profession was slower to open its doors to women, but in April 1906 Mabel French, a reformer and activist from Saint John, became the first female lawyer in the region.[93] On the whole, however, these achievements fell far short of the objectives of more radical feminists such as Ella Hatheway, who actively promoted the doctrine of equal pay for equal work and denounced woman's 'secondary position in the community, in the church, in the home, everywhere.'[94]

CONCLUSION

For Maritimers the first decade of the new century was one of economic and social transformation, providing challenges and seeming opportunities. When the new century opened, few had realized the serious weaknesses of the region's economy in relation to central Canada, and most were content instead to blame the problems of the region on the apparently unfair financial terms of Confederation or the inappropriate policies of the federal government. At the same time, while the rapid growth of urban centres promised a relatively prosperous future, expansion had created in its wake a number of social problems, from slum conditions to labour unrest and radicalism. Faced with these problems, the region's business, professional, religious, and political élite adhered to a progressive reform program similar to that espoused by turn-of-the-century reformers elsewhere in North America. Emphasizing the virtues of professional management, efficiency, and public responsibility and imbued with the Christian moralism of the Social Gospel, this élite called upon the state, the professional classes, and the church to take a more active role in promoting social well-being and class and gender co-operation. The results of their efforts can be seen in reforms in public health, education, labour-management relations, sport and recreation, public morals, urban politics, and rural life.

Nevertheless, the achievements of these reformers fell far short of the efficient, prosperous, disease- and conflict-free society that they had originally envisaged. Although some advances were made in alleviating social abuses and in modernizing the education and public-health systems, much had been left undone. By the end of the decade, the Maritimes had lost control of their economic future. Ownership of the Maritimes' industrial base had become increasingly alienated from the region. In addition, the bitter strikes at the end of the decade revealed serious deficiencies in the progressive approach to labour-management relations. Accompanying these problems was the waning influence in federal politics, which contributed in turn to the undermining of the regionally oriented Intercolonial Railway. Finally, as industrialization and urbanization continued, the traditional economy of fishing, agriculture, and lumbering remained ill-equipped to meet the challenge of reorganization or modernization.

Despite the optimism of this decade's progressive reform brigades, therefore, the reform movement in the Maritimes bore withered fruit. Constrained by fiscal economy and a declining influence at Ottawa, faced with the gradual erosion of the industrial base that had emerged during the last quarter of the nineteenth century, and unable to escape their own middle-class biases, reformers in these years failed to alter in any fundamental way the class and gender inequalities that pervaded Maritime society. The extent of that failure, and the price it would exact, would become abundantly clear in the decades to follow.

# CHAPTER SIX

# The 1910s
## The Stillborn Triumph of Progressive Reform

In the summer of 1914, Saint John belonged to the social reformers, rioters, and patriots. It was difficult to miss the social reformers that summer, for they were everywhere, reforming everything. In June, the Community Council of Saint John was coming together to promote measures 'on broad lines for the advancement of the welfare of the entire community.' The city's Equal Suffrage Association was planning an educational booth at the Saint John Exhibition to promote the enfranchisement of women. The Anti-Tuberculosis Association was sternly warning Saint Johners that they faced a higher death rate from the disease than citizens of any other North American city north of Baltimore. The Young Men's Christian Association was promoting playgrounds, the federal Commission of Conservation town planning. And pity the person seeking a moment of escape from this earnest reforming world! Turning to her local theatre for a moment's diversion, she might well find, instead, a 'problem play' exploring the complexities of modern life – such as *The Blindness of Virtue* playing at the Opera House, which explored the 'sex question' in 'a delicate and sensible manner.' Turning to her church for a consoling vision of the life hereafter, she might well find instead jarring vistas of the here and now. On one summer Sunday in Saint John in 1914, while one congregation listened to gruesome accounts of child slavery, another was bombarded with revelations of local sweatshop conditions. Even taking a quiet stroll down the city's streets in 1914 did not guarantee one relief from the stresses of modernity: on 23 July, for instance, one might have encountered a crowd of 10,000 angry people, who, in the cause of punishing the anti-labour streetcar company, overturned trolleys, braved a cavalry charge, smashed windows, and vandalized the electrical dynamo, plunging the city into darkness. And how, that month in 1914, on the eve of the Great War, could even the most unregenerate escapist avoid confronting the epochal events of the modern world, when crowds of Saint Johners responded

Saint John Street Railway strike, 1914. Workers sometimes used dramatic means to get their employers' attention. Here a peaceful demonstration turned ugly when the police attempted to disperse the strikers.

with patriotic uproar to martial music pouring from their local theatres and booming in the streets?[1]

Although a well-established tradition of analysis has emphasized the hidebound conservatism of Maritimers, these lively Saint Johners of the 1910s seem surprisingly modern, wrestling – some confusedly, some with the greatest lucidity – with the challenges of urban and industrial life under capitalism. In Saint John in 1914 and more generally in the region throughout the 1910s, progressive zeal and a wave of reforms – female enfranchisement, the prohibition of alcohol, town planning, measures for public health and public housing, technical education, workers' compensation – signalled the triumph of an ambitious agenda. And even more startling, for those who have accepted a stereotype of a region slumbering in its contented conservatism, is the radical post-war working-class revolt, which demanded that a progressive agenda aiming at social transformation itself be transformed to bring power to the dispossessed. Not till the closing months of this storm-tossed decade did it become clear that the industrial structure that supported both the progressive agenda and its radical nemesis was tottering on its cracked foundations. When those foundations finally did crumble, many of the hopes and dreams of both the liberal progressives and the working-class radicals would be buried in the rubble.

Of the approximately 937,965 Maritimers of 1914, few would have foreseen this bleak outcome; few, indeed, would have identified themselves as 'Maritimers,' citizens of a distinctive region of Canada defined by its economic and political dependence. Although its politicians had recently denounced developments that seemed to hurt the Maritimes – in particular the federal government's generous settlement of central-Canadian land claims and the region's declining presence in the House of Commons – neither 'regionalism' as an ideology nor 'region' as an important term had attained the status of common sense. By 1910, control over almost all banks and secondary manufacturing had passed into outside hands, Maritime influence in Ottawa had diminished, and Maritimers by the thousands were leaving for the United States and the West. None of these well-known facts provoked a sustained groundswell of regional protest.[2]

That the Maritimes was a fast-growing part of Canada and the British Empire was instead the common assumption of politics, on both the right and the left. Businessmen might hail bustling cities and smoke-belching chimneys as signs of the virtues of *laissez-faire*, minimal government, and their own rugged individualism; the region's small but sophisticated socialist movement might analyse the same phenomena as harbingers of a planned society run by workers and even urge small businessmen to realize that their days were numbered in an epoch of monopoly capitalism.[3] The centre of political debate was occupied by progressives – including many male trade unionists and middle-class professionals and many male and female volunteers and social activists – who built voluntary organizations designed to pressure the state to reform the evils of a fast-growing capitalism. Some drew upon Edwardian sociology, with its emphasis on the power of the 'environment' to shape 'the individual' and on society as a 'social organism'; many more were inspired by versions of the 'Social Gospel' – a heterogeneous ensemble of doctrines and schemes that sought to fashion a Christian (and mainly Protestant) response to capitalism by emphasizing the this-worldliness of Christ's message. Whether primarily secular or religious in their thought, progressives shared a burning sense of the need to rethink their society's key institutions. They typically wanted to replace an older, chaotic, 'individualist' framework with more efficient and 'collectivist' concepts and strategies. Drawing from a selectively interpreted New Testament, from such thinkers as Spencer, and from the glowing social and technical achievements of Britain and Germany, progressives brought powerful new social metaphors – 'function,' 'organism,' 'efficiency,' and 'environment' – to public discourse.

The typical progressive reformer championed not one but many different reform causes, such as technical education, temperance, juvenile courts, urban reform (through the elevation of disinterested experts), and moral regulation (through the elimination of prostitution, public swearing, and pornography). Progressives inclined to both eclecticism, in the type of authorities they invoked in pursuit of their objectives, and holism, in the all-encompassing inclusiveness of their social vision. In Halifax, such holism found expression in the tightly woven and vibrant progressive network centred on the Halifax Local Council of Women and the Halifax *Herald*, which repeatedly swung into action on questions of enfranchisement, cruelty to women and children, a reformed and more efficient city government, and technical education.[4] Much the same holism was in evidence in New Brunswick in 1911, when the New Brunswick Sons of Temperance proclaimed their support not only for tougher liquor laws, but also for juvenile courts and public playgrounds.[5] Progressivism – this loose network of voluntary movements and visionary intellectuals in search of a reformed, fairer, more Christian and more efficient capitalism – acknowledged few boundaries between economic improvement and moral reform.

Ida Whipple, a seventeen-year-old Saint John resident, caught the spirit of the 1910s in a prize-winning essay on civic improvement. Miss Whipple began with a description of her city's economy, then briskly proceeded to discuss what might seem, at least to non-progressive eyes, to be an odd mix of unconnected topics: the public library, playgrounds, the need for a better patrol wagon on the city streets to curb 'disgraceful scenes,' the chemistry equipment in the local high school, the wonderful advantages of city government under an efficient and expert 'board of control.' Saint John's most burning need, Miss Whipple believed, was the prohibition of the liquor traffic, which kept families poor and uneducated, filled the jails, hospitals, and almshouses, and tended to destroy 'the sturdy type of manhood which the climate of Saint John develops.' Miss Whipple's imagined progressive 'city upon the hill' was harmonious, healthy, liquor-free, Christian, and scientifically planned. Drawing, like most of the region's progressives, on a tame version of the Social Gospel, Miss Whipple discerned an organic connection between the chemistry equipment in the high school and the paddy wagons on the street: both were promising signs of scientific and moral progress for that evolving organism called society.[6]

These were progressive ideas one might have expected in Britain or in the United States: but what were they doing in the 'underdeveloped' Maritimes? A good deal of the answer lies in the peculiar status of the 1910s as the last decade in which the region's economic development seemed assured – and the last decade in which the key question of social and political life was not 'How can we attract capital and make it stay here once we get it?' but 'How can we adjust to this dizzying pace of economic growth and social change?' The gross value of production in the Maritimes, estimated in constant 1935 dollars, rose from $222,291,000 to $236,660,000 from 1910 to 1920, and although output in the forest, mining, and fishing industries declined, manufacturing continued to advance.[7] A sense of rapid economic progress was pervasive. The building of two new transcontinental railways in Canada and the construction of a vital rail line up the Saint John River Valley led to talk of Saint John as the great terminus of three trunk railways. The *Busy East* – the regional business publication whose very name captured the optimism of the day – predicted that even sleepy Woodstock, whose citizens had been contented with an easy existence 'derived from exchanging dollars between themselves,' oblivious to the 'wonderful possibilities for commercial achievement that were lying dormant in their midst,' would be seized by the 'spirit of the age.'[8] In 1913, progressive Maritimers could pride themselves on a threefold increase in coal production since 1900 and a seventeenfold increase in pig-iron output.[9] That the region's growth was dwarfed by that of the Canadian West did not dim the spirits of regional progressives. As they liked to point out, western population growth meant new markets for Maritime entrepreneurs. Describing one prairie town in 1910, the Halifax *Herald* proudly noted all the regional brand names crowding the shop windows: Hartt Shoes, Stanfield's underwear, Fowler's axes, Starr's skates, Ganong's and Moir's chocolates, and McVitties' plumbers' supplies.[10] The 'New Era of Progress,' the 'Brillliant Commercial Future,' cities that promised 'to yet outdo the progressive cities of Canada in enterprise and development'– such were the golden phrases showered by boosters upon Maritime port-redevelopment schemes, mines, mills, and railways. The Halifax *Herald* was not unusual in naming Nova Scotia 'The Province of Prosperity.'[11]

This optimistic period has the melancholy charm of all Indian summers. Boosters ignored the three fatal weaknesses of the Maritime economy. The first and most important was the fact of economic dependence: the leading industries of the Maritimes were owned by external capital and carried out a low level of transformation within the region, conditions that minimized industrial spin-offs and maximized vulnerability to international recessions. Coal and steel, to cite the most glaring example, had been taken over by external corporations whose ever-more-ambitious mergers were driven less by the desire for efficiency than by their promoters' thirst for windfall profits.[12] (The one outstanding exception to this pattern – locally owned Nova Scotia Steel and Coal – was less exceptional than it seemed, since as early as 1910 it was suffering from financial difficulties that would ultimately drive it into the same unsavoury maw of external domination, watered stock, and overvalued assets that had swallowed most of the rest of the industry).[13] A second weakness was that an economy so heavily dependent upon unreconstructed nineteenth-century states – at both the federal and provincial level – was especially vulnerable if state structures or policies were transformed. Much depended on the continuing growth of an already greatly extended Canadian railway system and on the responsiveness of the Intercolonial Railway to regional conditions – both of which were directly subject to political decisions over which Maritimers had little control.[14] A third weakness was the fragmentation of the region and the lack of a large, unified, business class with a strategy for development. In its absence, all three provinces, particularly Nova Scotia, adopted economic policies myopically based on a strategy of pumping royalties out of a diminishing and non-renewable resource base. In short, the path of dependent development followed by the state and by capital in the region had produced the impressive appearance of growth, but not the specialization, technical expertise, corporate structures, capital pools, and long-term planning capacity that were prerequisites to prosperity in the age of corporate capital.

To say anything like this in 1914, however, was to court dismissal as a negative thinker. For many contemporary Maritimers, the three most pressing issues were labour unrest, the restructuring of the state, and the women's question – all of them informed by a vivid sense of a fast-changing, dynamic society.

Events in the workers' movement certainly prompted a sense of accelerating – even uncontrollable – change. In 1913, about 60 per cent of the region's approximately 66,344 industrial workers were concentrated in a northern belt of coal, steel, and railway towns from Moncton to Glace Bay. By 1914, according to conservative official estimates, about 9,342 workers were organized in trade unions (down from about 12,713 in 1911).[15] This workers' movement was both less and more important as a force for social change than these statistics suggest. It was less important because it was divided by province, craft, ideology, and affiliation: the result was a highly fragmented movement that more readily pursued immediate economic objectives than radical visions. (Only coal miners, metal workers, and some longshoremen seemed to be paying much heed to socialists and labourites.) Divided among railway brotherhoods, craft unions affiliated with the American Federation of Labor (AF of L), purely local bodies (the most important of which was the Nova Scotia coal miners' Provincial Workmen's Association [PWA]), unions spoke with many voices – almost all of them white, anglophone, and (outside a few factories, notably in Amherst and Truro) male.[16] The working-class movement was also more important than it seemed at first sight, however, because its presence was concentrated in the industrially strategic coalfields and cities, because many unionists' family members and other members of local communities supported the movement's objectives, and because unions fought in this period with an unprecedented militancy. The colossal coal strikes – one of them twenty-two months long – in Cumberland, Inverness, and Cape Breton counties from 1909 to 1911 for the recognition of the international United Mine Workers of America (UMW) over the local PWA illustrated both labour's weaknesses and its strengths. The coal miners, defeated by the coal companies and by the armed might of the state, failed to win the union most activists had democratically chosen; but the tenacity with which they fought was burned into memory. For the remainder of the decade the state would make far-reaching concessions to the miners in a successful effort to prevent another such confrontation. As a result the coal miners won collective bargaining rights well before most industrial workers in Canada.[17]

Much the same balance – between the general fragmentation of the forces for change on the one hand, and their surprising local strength on the other – must characterize any assessment of political change in the Maritimes on the eve of the war. Although the Conservatives had come to power armed with Robert Borden's Halifax platform, and were thus pledged to make Canadian politics honest, efficient, and business-like, the march towards these goals had barely begun. If the 'Commission of Conservation' – which had the classically progressive mandate of scientifically surveying 'resources' both natural and human – was an interesting experiment in a new politics, it was also a tiny bureaucracy insecurely positioned within a generally hostile or indifferent state.[18]

On the provincial level, there is some sign of political movement, but little indication of the thoroughgoing renovation of politics progressives wanted. Those who wanted a more efficient and systematic state were split among the two traditional parties, which always deplored the stagnation, patronage, and lassitude of governments when out of power and smoothly resumed such traditions when they gained it. None the less, contrary to myth, many Maritimers of the 1910s did not vote automatically as their grandfathers had before them: many began to shift massively from one traditional party to the other, giving elections a lopsided character.

Nova Scotia was the exception to this rule of political landslides. Throughout this decade – indeed, from 1896 to 1923 – the province seemed the very epitome of political immobility and stagnation, under the rule of the Liberals (who still hold the Canadian record for political longevity). At first sight this frozen political conventionalism seems flatly to contradict any emphasis on the conflicts and contradictions of modernity. On closer inspection, however, the Murray regime – the Liberal government throughout the decade – was, in a very peculiar way, unmistakably influenced by progressivism. Murray liked to define his approach as one of safeguarding the 'masses' against the 'classes,' and his strange party attracted both those who approved of (and profited from) its monopoly-generating policies in the economy and labourites looking for a reforming political party. The two sides of Nova Scotia Liberalism came to the fore in 1910. In that year the provincial government created a provincial police force to help undermine the striking coal miners – and a somewhat progressive Workmen's Compensation Act. Juvenile courts, children's aid societies, urban planning, technical education: such reforms, along with an astute cultivation of the labour movement, gave the Murray government a plausible claim to the label 'progressive.' It was typical of the era that the 1911 radical campaign of the Halifax Labour Party (founded in 1908 and incorporating socialists and liberals) won the support of both Halifax daily newspapers, each anxious to establish progressive and 'non-partisan' credentials; it was also typical that John Joy, the labour candidate and leader of the city's longshoremen, was later co-opted by the Liberal government as commissioner of its new Workmen's Compensation Board. There were complicated progressive undercurrents at work beneath the frozen surface of Nova Scotia liberalism.[19]

The same currents were more dramatically evident in the less stable provincial politics of New Brunswick and Prince Edward Island. J.D. Hazen's New Brunswick Conservatives had come to power in 1908 with the backing of the Saint John labour movement. In 1910, his 'non-partisan' administration – it claimed this eminently progressive label by virtue of one lone Liberal renegade in the cabinet – brought in measures providing for a commissioner of labour to try to settle strikes and lock-outs, regulating telephone, electric, and gas-lighting companies, and prohibiting the export of pulpwood from Crown lands (in order to encourage the pulp-and-paper industry). Armed with a manifesto bristling with popular reforms, James Kidd Flemming marched the Conservatives to a record political landslide in 1912, winning forty-six out of forty-eight seats (if one includes two 'Independent Conservatives'). In Prince Edward Island, a Liberal Party that in 1910 had threatened rebellion if Ottawa reduced the Island's representation in the House of Commons was defeated in 1912 by a Conservative Party promising clean, efficient government, aggressive enforcement of liquor legislation, and an improved ferry service.

In contrast to muted structural changes at the provincial level, progressive reform in city politics often meant far-reaching experiments in new state structures. Both Saint John and Halifax introduced new forms of urban government. In 1912, with the support of both the Board of Trade and important labour leaders, Saint John became the first city in Canada to adopt the most drastic model of urban reform: commission government. This model replaced the old system of wards, those havens of bosses and liquor-sellers, with a commission elected by all voters but dominated, at least in theory, by expert civic officials. Halifax preferred the milder medicine of a Board of Control. Here the campaign for municipal reform was championed by the Board of Trade and punctuated by an intensive 'uplift revival' campaign starring the city's leading progressive reformers. This impressive and militant army of reformers also launched a vehement struggle against monopoly control of the streetcar service.[20]

Of course, the case for political discontinuity must not be pressed too far. No electorally successful new party gave progressive currents an independent identity in any provincial legislature. Yet, on balance, one is struck more by the reformist enthusiasm than by the inert passivity of electorates: mainstream parties clearly felt the need to appear to be progressive, even if, on attaining office, they then retreated to the traditions of liberal individualism. By 1914, the progressives who so dominated public discourse in Saint John could be found wherever social and political ideals were at issue, pressing for reforms in civil society and for a more activist, efficient, and 'scientific' government. Many of the most talented and effective of these progressive reformers were middle-class women activists, whose ambivalent and partial triumph was one of the decade's most momentous events. Gender politics, no less than politics in general, provides superficial evidence of traditionalism and subtler evidence of change. The roles of most women were defined by society and by themselves as ones inextricably tied to biological and cultural reproduction; a vast network of laws, traditions, and beliefs defined a woman's place as the home, where under the guidance of her husband she would raise the children. From this perspective, paid employment was at best a necessary evil, an intermission in a woman's true career of domesticity. Women were increasingly diverging from the 'reproductive matrix' that bound them to the home, however. One close analysis of Yarmouth, Amherst, and Sydney Mines shows marked variations in the patterns of paid women's employment: in Yarmouth, where the proportion of women in the work-force rose from 6 per cent in 1881 to 31 per cent in 1921, almost half the work-force of the local sailcloth factory was made up of women; in Amherst, where the work-force reached its peak in 1911, 22 per cent of it was comprised of women, many of them working in the boot-and-shoe factory; in Sydney Mines, where the coal and steel economy provided far fewer opportunities for women's waged labour, women's participation in the paid work-force

(14 per cent in 1921) was lower. Against this mixed evidence of new options open to women must be set facts suggesting their still-inferior status. In these three towns, for example, women's earnings, far below those of men of all ages, tended to rise more gradually than those of men, peaking at about age thirty and declining thereafter; in 1921, the salaries of male teachers in the three towns averaged more than $1,200 per annum, compared to women's mean earnings of $667.[21] A similarly complicated picture emerges from a study of violence against women within the household: it was true that the law was based upon reverence for the reproductive matrix and the husband's superior status, but it was also true that women were increasingly turning to the Nova Scotia Divorce Court to press claims of cruelty against their husbands, and that such cruelty was given more weight as grounds for divorce in this decade than had ever before been the case.[22]

When the contemporary journalists referred to 'women's work' in the region, they generally meant not this invisible experience of hundreds of waged workers but the more conspicuous activities of that minority promoting women's rights. The women's movement defies easy generalizations. In New Brunswick, for example, there were divisions between socialists and non-socialists, militants and non-militants. Local activist Ella Hatheway caught the movement's holistic idealism when she observed the 'growing demand from women that they shall no longer be regarded by men as sex beings, but as human beings; that they shall be recognized, politically and economically, as persons, not as females merely'; the secretary of the New Brunswick branch of the Women's Enfranchisement Association of Canada, founded in 1894 (and after 1910 a branch of the 'Canadian Suffrage Association ') was no less emphatic when, after a visit from the renowned Sylvia Pankhurst of the British Women's Social and Political Union, she expressed qualified approval of Pankhurst's strategy of direct action:

> Lady-like effacement for the sake of party was productive of nothing and the suffragettes so-called have made themselves stepping stones for all women in the world to cross the river of injustice and gain the solid shores of human rights. Let us withhold our judgement upon the window smashers until quiet comes after victory and not condemn what seem rude and mistaken methods to those who have had no experience with old country politics, but remember what these English women are fighting for.[23]

Despite support for suffrage from temperance organizations and some trade unionists, suffrage was repeatedly rebuffed in New Brunswick.

Different strategies prevailed in Nova Scotia, where a cadre of progressive women leaders downplayed suffrage immediately before the war, and concentrated instead on fashioning a formidable, progressive, social-reform network. Anna Leonowens, author and artist; Eliza Ritchie, Ph D, philosopher and academic; May Sexton, a technocrat with a degree from the Massachusetts Institute of Technology; Agnes (Miller) Dennis, wife of the manager-publisher of the Halifax *Herald*; and Edith Archibald, daughter of a British diplomat and wife of the president of the Bank of Nova Scotia: here was the core of a well-connected and well-trained progressive leadership.[24] One 1912 article by Alice Houston in the *Herald* praised the Halifax women's network and its dramatic success in progressive reform: 'Every cause in this city which has as its object pure helpfulness in any of its forms, or "uplift," intellectual, moral, material, owes a large debt to women ...' Who had moved for appointment of an immigration matron? The Local Council of Women. To whom was the opening of the School of Domestic Science due? Who had initiated and advanced the movement for supervised playgrounds? For Women's Welcome Hostel? The Local Council of Women. And beyond the council proper were all the women in its affiliated bodies. Young women at Dalhousie now had their own new residence, and the Halifax Ladies' College had a science laboratory, thanks to women activists. Women's auxiliaries – attached to such organizations as the Young Men's Christian Association, the Church of England Institute, the Society for the Prevention of Cruelty – did much of the hard work; indeed, Houston argued, it was whispered 'that practically all the work of the Nova Scotia Anti-Tuberculosis League is being done by women.' And who could dispute the worth of the Victorian Order of Nurses, whose voluntary service to much of Halifax had made it one of the most appreciated organizations of all? These accomplishments were all the more precious, the author argued, because 'the council is not an organization of clamorous and militant screamers after "rights." It is an organization of balanced, thinking, intelligent, essentially womanly women, who are quite content with conservative methods.'[25] There was clearly a wide diversity of tactics and ideas within women's movements in the region. If they were mainly 'middle-class,' the class position of activists did not mean that the questions they asked were necessarily not radical or 'fundamental' ones, nor that they did not have a significant impact on their working-class sisters. Even when based on 'maternal' premises, which was by no means invariably the case, arguments for women's rights imaginatively redefined the boundaries of the state and civil society in ways that could only undermine liberal individualism. 'Women of Nova Scotia!' Edith Archibald proclaimed in December 1912. 'You stand today in the growing light of the early dawn of the most wondrous epoch that shall ever be.'[26] There spoke a woman who had imbibed, deeply, from the well of progressive optimism.

## WAR AND REFORM

In 1914, a region that workers and employers, radicals and progressives all thought was steadily growing received the summons to war. War fever swept through the region in the closing weeks of July 1914. When the manager of the Imperial Theatre in Saint John announced from the stage that the leaders of Britain's two great political parties had submerged their differences in the interests of the war effort, 'there was a great demonstration of emotion. Many of the audience rose from their seats and cheered until the house re-echoed with their enthusiasm.' In Sydney, on the last evening of that July, when word was spread of the imminent arrival of soldiers from Halifax, 'excitement increased to fever heat,' the street and railway station were crowded with spectators, and a tumultuous welcome was showered upon the force – of just ten men – sent to protect the Marconi station near Glace Bay from the enemy. It showed, said the Halifax *Herald*, that the 'mighty war which threatens' would be of such magnitude that it would be felt even in the cities of Cape Breton, so far from the scene of active hostilities.[27]

The war began as high theatre, as an experience of drama, spectacle, and adventure. On 9 May 1915, people crowded around a Halifax harbour bristling with mines and shimmering beautifully under the searchlights on a distant shore to watch the 26th Nova Scotia Battalion – the first regiment officered and manned by Nova Scotians – depart for France: 'left Halifax about 5 p.m. on board the Cunarder Saxonia,' soldier Frank Ferguson would write in his diary when he left Halifax for the War, nine months later, 'on the greatest adventure of my life.'[28]

The First World War required organization, imagination, and energy, from both those who left for Europe and those who stayed behind. This was not because there were many profound doubts about the justice of the Empire's cause. Apart from a few eccentrics, almost everybody – workers, employers, Acadians, Blacks, Catholics, Protestants, Liberals, Conservatives, men, and women – supported the Empire in its struggle against the Germans. Certainly, in August 1914 there were no important dissenters. Most Maritimers were intensely loyal to a Britain they identified with Christianity, civilization, and progress; for them, loyalty to King and Empire overshadowed loyalty to Canada or to the region. Even native-born socialists attended to the Empire's call: Colin McKay, whose brilliant Marxist analyses had enlivened the *Eastern Labor News*, and who had in 1912 analysed the looming war as the outcome of rich men's greed, could be found penning patriotic thoughts on board a hospital steamship in the English Channel.[29] Initially, the war had apparently accomplished the impossible: it seemed to bring almost everyone together in a common project. Throughout the region, workers and busi-

Elizabeth Hetherington, Fredericton. War tended to relegate women to a supporting role, which many avidly embraced. Hetherington was a member of the Women's Volunteer Reserve Corps, No. 5 Reserve Auxiliary of the New Brunswick Regiment.

nessmen, children and governments made donations to the great cause: these gifts ranged from the grandiose and official (100,000 bushels of oats from Prince Edward Island, $100,000 cash from Nova Scotia, 100,000 bushels of potatoes from New Brunswick) to the poignantly personal (Christmas plum puddings for the troops from the owner of the Halifax Hotel; $9 for the Army Field Kitchen and Ambulance Fund from a patriotic concert staged by young boys in Charlottetown; and more than $80 from young working-class Haligonian girls for a 'North End Machine Gun for the North End Martell Boys').[30] How much of this widespread popular enthusiasm for the war can be explained on economic grounds? Although the Maritimes had not been plunged into a pre-war recession as serious as that faced by the West, the war did bring relief to slack local labour markets and offered businessmen a prospect of continuing prosperity. Unemployment disappeared in some parts of the Maritimes as early as January 1915, and by September industries most directly affected by war production were reporting acute labour shortages. 'Business as usual' – the motto adorning the cover of the *Busy East* in December 1914 – conveyed a reassuring sense, prevalent until 1917, of the war's economic potential. 'We are sorry that Europe is in trouble and in need,' wrote one apologetic booster. 'Our sorrow finds expression in tremendous expenditures and sacrifices. But Europe's need – particularly her need of food – is our profit ...' After a year of war, the *Busy East* was pleased to report that in very many areas of the economy, 'The discovery has been made that it is possible to carry on war and do a profitable business at the same time.'[31]

Initially, wartime did not require a break with the limited liberal state and the free market. Even the essential manufacture of munitions was left in private hands. Four Canadian manufacturers secured all the British shell orders through the good offices of General Sam Hughes, the minister of the militia, and then sublet them to other Canadian manufacturers and to themselves. Competitive tendering was as rare as windfall profits were common. Thomas Cantley of Nova Scotia Steel and Coal, the one Maritimer on the Shell Committee, exemplified the entrepreneurial aggressiveness of these munitions men. In 1914, Cantley transformed his problem-wracked steel company into a pioneer of commercial shell-making, first by adapting to shell manufacture a German hydraulic press designed for other purposes, and second by turning out open-hearth steel of a quality that even the fussy War Office could find acceptable. By January 1916, Scotia was forging more than 300,000 shells a month in its Pictou County factories.[32] Wartime prosperity extended beyond manufacturing: the fisheries were more active than they had been for years; farmers throve on a higher demand for their products and on higher prices; lumbermen exploited new market possibilities, such as supplying British collieries with the pit props they could no longer obtain in Europe. There even seemed to be new hope for wooden shipbuilding.[33]

Yet explaining the remarkable popularity of the war purely on economic grounds is surely too simple. Patriotic fervour transcended calculations of immediate economic advantage. The working-class response to the coming of the war was telling. After the outbreak of war, there were apparently no strikes at all in 1914; there were eleven strikes, none major, in 1915, and just three in 1916. In December 1915, the Department of Labour noted that the industrial situation was more peaceful than at any other time recorded in its files.[34] Times of labour scarcity are classically times of heightened labour activism; this pattern did not hold in the early years of the war. Labour entered the war somewhat weakened by recession, by the defeat of the coal strikes of 1909–11, and by the departure of scores of labour militants for Europe; but the simplest and most plausible explanation for the uncanny labour peace was that most workers did not want to do anything to impede a war effort in

Drill-press operator, Nova Scotia Steel Company, Trenton, N.S., c. 1917. Labour shortages opened opportunities for women in areas previously confined
to men. But women were expected to vacate these jobs for returning soldiers
once the war ended.

which they firmly believed. The many labour militants who had not left
for Europe clearly had both motive and opportunity for a strike wave
that was conspicuous by its absence in 1914–16. Patriotism, albeit for-
tified by prosperity, was the real key to the war's early popularity.

Such class harmony was especially important – and difficult to preserve – in those plants given over to munitions. At Nova Scotia Steel,
older craft patterns of work, already disrupted by new technology, American managers, and European immigrants, were further convulsed by
the new rates and the threatened devaluation of traditional skills entailed
by munitions manufacturing on a large scale. The organization of an
effective Federation of Labour in Pictou County completed the recipe

for an explosion. It came in August 1915. A massive protest by more than 2,000 munitions workers brought production to a halt; yet, despite high emotions, the revolt was over within three days, calmed by the promise of a federal conciliation board. A subsequent strike by machinists worried about the impact of female employment was settled no less quickly. These strikes suggested that Maritime workers were highly circumspect in the early years of the war about taking advantage of the tight labour market. Other strikes suggested even more directly the extent of working-class patriotism. In August 1915, about 1,125 Springhill coal miners demanded the removal of 110 Germans and Austrians from the employ of the Dominion Coal Company. After a five-day strike, these 'enemy aliens' were fitted with special lamps, which, it was hoped, would discourage a 'suicidal fanatic' among them from destroying the mine.[35]

The churches and universities were no less patriotic. Ministers who had spent 1914 denouncing capitalist greed spent 1915 reviling the Kaiser. The Rev. J.J. McCaskill of Saint John, a regular speaker at recruiting rallies, drew (rather selectively) on Ruskin when he praised war as the foundation of all the high virtues and faculties of humanity. H.L. Stewart of Dalhousie quoted (no less selectively) from Nietzsche to convince a Halifax audience of Germany's incurable militarism. Dalhousie's president was thinking of professors like Stewart when, in proudly reporting at the end of 1915 that one out of three of his male students had enlisted, he praised the professors for their success in instilling patriotism in their classes.[36] No less patriotic were students at Acadia University, where of the class of 1918, 'only 4 of the original 29 men remained at graduation time; the rest had enlisted.'[37]

Progressive women joined with workers, ministers, and professors in this war of the imagination. At a women's meeting in Halifax in August 1915, May Sexton, a leading suffrage advocate, ingeniously integrated the principles of the women's movement and those of patriotism by denouncing the German ideal of 'women's sphere' – the kitchen, the nursery, and the church. 'Woe to the feminist movement,' she concluded, 'were the German tyrant to win in this struggle.' In Saint John, according to the secretary of the Saint John Board of Trade, the women were doing 'splendidly': 'They have been nobly standing behind the Patriotic Fund, the Red Cross, the Soldiers' Comforts, the Soldiers' Convalescent Home, and all the other patriotic projects.'[38]

RECRUITING FOR WAR

Recruiting was another sphere in which progressives excelled. Middle-class notables dominated a recruiting system that relied on prominent men for the raising of a battalion. As of June 1916, according to the calculations of the *Canadian Annual Review*, out of 184,706 men between the ages of eighteen and forty-five in the Maritime provinces, 31,061 (16.8 per cent) had enlisted, compared with 23.8 per cent in Ontario and 23.1 per cent in the western provinces. The much lower numbers of recent British immigrants and of males in the right age group accounted for a good deal of this 'enlistment gap.' Nova Scotia, with between 21 and 22 per cent of the appropriate male age group enlisted, came the closest of any of the three provinces to the levels of Ontario and the West. By the last year of the war, approximately 30,500 Nova Scotia men, 37 per cent of the male population between eighteen and forty-five, had enrolled for service, with an additional 7,000 employed in home defence. New Brunswick, on the other hand, lagged behind, and had been (the Halifax *Herald* smugly reported) 'bitterly humiliated' by its failure to fill the 55th New Brunswickers. Strenuous efforts in New Brunswick, although they did not bring the province up to its allotted number, brought an estimated 9,600 new men into the army between 1 November 1915 and 1 November 1916, from mainly English-speaking counties of the Saint John River Valley and the ethnically mixed counties of Westmorland and Restigouche.[39]

There was a peculiar intensity to recruiting in the cities. As early as July 1914, middle-class women vigilantes, enlisted in 'white feather committees,' were pinning the 'white feathers' of cowardice on perceived shirkers. Men who were perceived to be avoiding their duty to the Empire were assailed in the public press:

> Now, then, nine cheers for the Stay-at-Home Ranger!
> Blow the great fish-horn and beat the big pan!
> First in the field that is FARTHEST from the danger,
> TAKE YOUR WHITE-FEATHER PLUME, 'Sweet Little Man.'

As the Halifax *Herald* explained, 'The Duty of Every Nova Scotia Woman, Every Nova Scotia Girl Today Is to See that the Men Folk Fight or Farm: Women Must Show the Way to Loafers, Funkers, and Pink Tea Tango Boys!' Such hard-hitting appeals to a sense of masculine pride were backed up by the most efficient and progressive methods: in Sydney's ward-by-ward canvass in 1915, women recruiters were extensively used to appeal to young unenlisted men.[40] The war of the imagination often worked through the intensification of localist and regional appeals, which were frustrated by the early breaking up of Maritime (particularly Nova Scotia) battalions to reinforce other battalions before they were shipped overseas, and intensified as the ideal of a Highland Brigade of Nova Scotia attained prominence in the local press.[41]

In Saint John, the war proved so hard to sell that the mayor feared for the Loyalist honour of his city and province. In September 1915, fifteen thousand people crowded King's Square; only nine of them enlisted. A second and a third rally proved no more successful, leaving newspapers to wonder why so few 'responded to the call for the defence of the women and children of St. John and the salvation of New Brunswick and of Canada from capture and possession by the Huns.'[42] The 1916 New Brunswick drive was orchestrated by Col. P.A. Guthrie, the special recruiting officer for the Maritime provinces, who, still on crutches from his wartime experience, mobilized war sentiment throughout New Brunswick. He was thought to have organized 225 meetings over two weeks in September 1916, in a campaign heavily reliant upon mass rituals and reinvented traditions:

> Beacon fires were lit in every county, striking posters utilized and the fiery cross of St. Andrews was sent through the country after the old Highland fashion. At each of the fifteen meetings, to be held on a given date, it was hurled by a runner at the foot of the speaker, who picked it up, pausing in his address, and passed it on to another runner who then carried it on to the next shiretown or meeting, and there dropped it again at the feet of the speaker. These fiery torches were carried by automobile, motor cycle, horseback and on foot and a complete circuit of the Province, covering about 1,500 miles, was made.

Saint John's immediate response to this impressive display of pyrotechnics? Four new recruits.[43] In many rural areas enlistment was equally unimpressive. As in Ontario, farmers thought twice about leaving for Europe without firm guarantees that their farms would be tended in their absence.[44]

In the coalfields and environs, by contrast, recruitment campaigns were minimal and popular response overwhelming. As early as August 1915, out of about 13,500 mine workers in Nova Scotia, about 1,751 coal miners had volunteered for active service, an enlistment rate above the provincial average. 'We have lost roughly 1,500 men as a direct result of this war,' a spokesman for the Dominion Coal Company complained in December 1915. The federal government, worried about declining output, was finally forced to curtail the enlistment of the coal miners. Once again, cynical or economistic explanations – which would see the coal miners' enthusiasm for the war as the outcome of their rotten jobs and uncertain employment prospects – are at best very partial ones. Enlisting *en masse* for the war was of a piece with the collective traditions of struggle in the pits; the militia had long been popular with many coal miners. Moreover, economism is confounded by the mining towns' heartfelt *financial* support for the war, which offered no immediate personal gains. In the first year of the war, Springhill sent not only 265 men but money for a machine gun and $1,000 for the Dominion-wide Patriotic Fund. In subsequent years, in Victory Loan campaigns, Springhill's remarkable financial contributions ($100,900 was subscribed in one ten-day period in 1917) were widely hailed. The growing left in the coalfields wisely never adopted an anti-war stance, and some of its leading radicals participated in the rites of patriotism as enthusiastically as everyone else.[45]

MORAL REGULATION

Besides relief work and recruiting, a third facet of progressive war work was the regulation of public morals. Although there were major campaigns against venereal disease and for rational recreation, most progressive energy was poured into the regulation of drinking. The temperance crusade had historical depth (its roots in the region were almost a century old) and social breadth (although centred in the prosperous middle class, its influence had been felt in a variety of working-class movements). In wartime, temperance advocates prospered, because they could make a direct connection between the health of the war effort and the health and sobriety of the well-regulated soldier.[46]

By 1917, a campaign mounted by the New Brunswick branch of the Dominion Temperance Alliance had borne fruit in the province's Prohibition Act, which stipulated that no person (outside the area covered by the more liberal Scott Act) could sell, procure, use, purchase, or transfer any liquor for a financial consideration without a wholesale or retail licence. (Such licences were to be granted only for medical, scientific, sacramental, or industrial purposes.) Moreover, liquor was not to be carried from one part of the province to another. So rigorous was this law that a convention of Maritime Baptists – people not easily impressed by temperance legislation – praised it as 'one of the most comprehensive and drastic prohibitory laws of any Province in the Dominion.' In 1918, Prince Edward Island – which had already won renown when in 1901 it became the first Canadian province to enact prohibition in the twentieth century – brought in a new Prohibition Act, whose 186 clauses and 15 schedules gave the appearance of plugging every conceivable loophole. True progressives, its authors scoured the statute books of North America in a systematic and scientific analysis of liquor regulation elsewhere, and came up with a system that gave the state-appointed inspectors virtually unlimited powers to enforce federal 'bone-dry' prohibition. More difficult problems confronted the prohibitionists of Nova Scotia. Here Halifax remained a wet blot on an otherwise well-regulated moral landscape. Licensed establishments blossomed in the highly militarized city. Outraged Protestant clergymen – who in progressive style undertook their own first-hand survey of Halifax depravity – charged that those sworn to uphold the licensing laws in the city were little better than the Kaiser in viewing their oath of office as a mere 'scrap of paper.' Moral regulation in a city that was at once a port, a garrison, and a naval station, and where the 'upper streets' beneath Citadel Hill had long been crowded with cheap groggeries, brothels, and other disreputable resorts, was not for the faint of heart. Whether the imposition of federal 'bone-dry prohibition' under the War Measures Act in March 1918 or the increasingly punitive enforcement of licensing laws brought the 'upper streets' up to the high standards of Protestant clergymen is open to serious doubt. Still, the effort was made, and page upon page of the local press was filled with shocked exposés of the inter-racial, unregulated, and wholly unrepentant Halifax bar scene.[47]

Whatever the pitfalls on the path to a well-disciplined Halifax, the victory of the federal temperance legislation demonstrated the accelerated pace of progressive reform in wartime. It was an exciting time to be a progressive reformer, and an extraordinary moment for the cadre of Halifax women who had done so much to shape the progressive outlook in Nova Scotia. Agnes Dennis, for example, called a meeting on 5 August, the day after Britain declared war, summoning 'the women of Halifax' to organize; they made the decision to focus their energies on the Red Cross. Through control of this organization, women entered into the direction of significant aspects of the war effort. They coordinated relief for Canadian prisoners of war, ran a factory for the production of hospital clothing and surgical dressings for the wounded, and toured the province to instruct and to inspire. Some of them became major public figures: the war, one historian observes, 'yielded the largest and most cohesive network of women's organizations that the city had ever known.'[48] Women used this cohesion and prominence to push for a wide range of reforms, on the grounds that the war emergency required the most far-reaching examination of social institutions. Their agenda was progressive and technocratic. 'Feeble-minded' children who demoralized the classroom and the orphanage should be segregated; and education, in the view of the 'Press Committee of the Woman's Council,' should be streamlined in the interests of efficiency: perhaps 'a higher education for the FEW who are capable of using it' could be combined with manual training for the rank-and-file, 'so that our children may be more efficient in the occupations they must follow.'[49]

Where progressive women had triumphed, other groups with other causes were less successful. Black Maritimers tried as hard as temperance advocates and progressive women to make the war work for them. Two weeks after the beginning of the war, fifty Black Haligonians declared themselves 'eager to be chosen' for service overseas.[50] Although some Blacks were enlisted in the 106th battalion, the Nova Scotia Rifles, the colour bar was otherwise effective, at the insistence of local recruiters and the authorities in Ottawa. Even when the military finally decided to recruit Blacks, its concession to them was half-hearted: Blacks were segregated in the No.2 Construction Battalion, under the command of white officers; and hence, unlike some Micmacs – who did defy racism by enlisting and fighting with conspicuous courage in Europe[51] – Blacks did not emerge from the First World War with new 'heroes' that a mainly white society would be obliged to recognize. Moreover, although the Construction Battalion might be seen as a partial breakdown of racial barriers, its significance was later downgraded when conscription criminalized Blacks who thought the military's colour line still held firm. Blacks were unable to promote their interests in the war to the same extent as other groups. They undoubtedly shared many of the same progressive ideals. Through their publication, the *Atlantic Advocate*, through the visits of foreign luminaries (including Booker T. Washington), through their campaigns against the showing of the racist film *Birth of a Nation* and for the establishment of their own home for 'coloured' orphans, Blacks demonstrated a new consciousness of their collective identity and a commitment to winning allies within other communities. Yet increasingly their struggles were defensive, as racial disturbances broke out in Glace Bay and Truro, segregated public facilities found respectable defenders, and racist stereotyping increased in the media. The explanation for this disappointing outcome of a decade's energetic Black activism lies both in the depth and power of racism and the difficulty of associating Black issues with the dominant wartime drive for moral regulation.[52]

Until 1917, most Maritimers found the war to be a good and noble cause. They heard about the war through their newspapers and through censored letters from the front. Propaganda abounded. The Halifax journalist Andrew Merkel produced a noteworthy example of the propagandists' art in his book of letters from soldiers in Europe. He included letters from German soldiers that illustrated their spinelessness, fear, and demoralization; there was satisfaction to be gained in noting that the cowards had perished shortly after committing their fears to paper. His selection of letters from Canadians showed them to be, in contrast, essential men: tough, gallant, fearless. 'We knew, or most of us did, at any rate, that we were not going on any picnic and were going to play the game to the finish,' wrote Sapper G.W. Connell of Digby in a letter from England. 'Every fellow here is anxious for the time to come when he will have his little chance to contribute to the store of German sausage meat.'[53]

Two Islanders at the Front. Jack Turner and Lee Allan take a break some-
where in France in 1917. Lee reads the Allied propaganda in the Island
*Patriot* while Jack peruses a comic strip showing the heroics of soldier Jack
Canuck.

### WAR WEARINESS

By degrees, almost imperceptibly, this sense of war as a great imperial
and manly adventure was transformed into a sense of war as a cruel
ordeal. Social harmony turned into social upheaval. A political leadership that had once relied mainly upon consent turned increasingly to
coercion. 'Business as usual' – that confident slogan of 1915 – was undermined by the new closeness of the war, by the failure of politicians
to match a rhetoric of sacrifice with a politics of service, and by the
intense stress of life and work in a wartime society.

The soldiers were the first ones to get the bad news about the war.
Sometimes trained in sword-fighting before their departure, they then
faced an unexpected world of toxic chemicals, trenches, and tanks. Many
of their patriotic illusions rotted, along with their defective boots, in the
mud of the training camp on Salisbury Plain. Even when they were still
in the Maritimes, a veteran remembered, it took soldiers little time to
adopt the adage, 'The only crime in the Army was in getting caught.'

In England, the Maritime soldiers learned unorthodox methods of responding to abysmal conditions. The best way of improving wretched canteen provisions, one group of Nova Scotia soldiers discovered, was to eject the proprietor and set his canteen on fire.[54] Yet it took time for the bad news about the war to reach home. To describe the rough, pragmatic ways men adapted to military training, let alone vividly bring home the meningitis and muddle on Salisbury Plain, was to mock the unquestioned truths of a religion, as poor Horatio C. Crowell of the *Halifax Chronicle* discovered to his cost early in 1915. His generally accurate account of the disastrous disorder of the British training camps provoked debates in the House of Assembly in Halifax and in the House of Commons in Ottawa; Lord Kitchener himself issued an angry denial.[55]

As Maritimers started being killed in large numbers, questioning the purposes of the war or the means by which these were pursued became even more difficult. A note of quiet despair can be heard even in the stilted letters of condolence from the front: 'If only this war would end,' wrote a nurse to the mother of slain Private Arthur Joe Munroe of Bridgewater. 'There won't be a young man left shortly, but it doesn't seem any nearer than it was two years ago ...'[56]

Heightened xenophobia and hysteria were other manifestations of a general war weariness. Rampant hostility to all things German prompted the New Brunswick Historical Society to resolve unanimously that the name of the province be changed to Acadia, given the tainted Germanic origins of 'Brunswick.' Halifax patriots busied themselves in identifying street names with 'Hunnish' origins. The citizens of Lunenburg were placed in a delicate position. Whether 'The men of Lunenburg [were] all strong Germans' who reaped 'the harvest of British waters,' as J.W. Daly, Ph D, urged, or whether they were more properly regarded as loyal 'Hanoverians,' just like the British royal family itself, as their MP, William Duff, argued in reply, were burning questions in 1918.[57]

Even the most committed patriots could scarcely conceal from themselves the sombre futility of the Allied effort during the summer and autumn of 1917. Passchendaele defied optimism. Moreover, the war became, in 1917 and 1918, something the Maritimes – more than any other part of Canada – experienced at first hand. Germans began to destroy the offshore fishing vessels, leaving their crews to brave the Atlantic in lifeboats.[58] The most compelling instance of the horrible new closeness of the war was the Halifax Explosion, which resulted from the collision of the vessels *Imo* and *Mont Blanc* in Halifax harbour on 6 December 1917. This massive disaster destroyed at least 1,963 people, much of the city's north end, and whatever remained of the city's innocent enthusiasm for the war. Whole families were swept away, work-

The Halifax Explosion, 6 December 1917. The explosion, which reduced much of the city's north end to rubble, brought the war home in a way that touched everyone. Hundreds were buried in mass graves.

ers were crushed in demolished factories, and a pitiful procession of refugees straggled out of the ruins of the city. 'And such a procession!' remembered a survivor: 'A trail of blood. Its impression is indelibly stamped on my brain. Men and women, babes in arms, children, young and old, soldiers and smoke blackened sailors, rich and poor, all alike as it will be on that last day, flocked in a seemingly unending humanity. Homes behind them, not knowing what was ahead ...'[59] Had anyone, wondered the notice in the newspaper, seen a 'Boy, age 18 months, fair hair, blue eyes, just been circumcised, four teeth, top and bottom; tucker in bib?' Whatever had become of 'Walsh, Freddie – Two years. Last seen at Armouries. Sister fainted, and boy was taken from her then.' Surely somebody had heard from four-year-old Ruth Moody, with 'brown-grey eyes, light brown hair, inclined to be curly, point broken off one front tooth. Large mole on back'? If you did find her somewhere, perhaps still alive, alone in some ruined building, she might be calling out for Jean and Marion, her sisters, or for her brother, William ...[60]

In the wake of such horror, could one even contemplate a return to 'business as usual'? The hoarding of foodstuffs, condoned when the war began, now became antisocial, as new policies encouraged a collective approach to the control of food supplies. After urging Nova Scotians to curb their supposed Scottish individualism, J.W. Robertson, chairman of the advisory council for food control, brought patriotism down to the micro-level of the body, to the 'regulation of single bites and the prevention of any bit of waste.'[61] Particular attention was paid to flour and bread: under an order-in-council of 15 July 1918, the use of white flour without substitutes was made a violation of the law, and the words 'Victory Bread' were to appear only on bread guaranteed to contain these prescribed substitutes.[62] The Canada Food Board exhorted every Nova Scotia farmer to grow at least one extra acre of cultivated crops, offering in turn to provide easy credit and cheap 'soldiers of the soil' – boy labourers aged fifteen to nineteen.[63]

Demands for a progressive state – one that would enter many social and economic fields for the first time in order to prosecute the war more efficiently and fairly – were further fuelled by inflation and wartime scandals. The workers' movement denounced the high cost of living. In Nova Scotia, a wide spectrum of labour leaders denounced living costs that in 1916 were higher than in any other province east of Manitoba.[64] Wartime scandals also undermined the popularity of a 'voluntarist' war. The charge that boot manufacturers had unloaded defective merchandise on the government could be mitigated – perhaps – by their pleas of inexperience in filling war orders, and of ignorance of European weather conditions. It was far harder to overlook the evidence that sharp-eyed horse traders had sold the government lame, broken horses for military duties – evidence that was unkind to the reputation of the government, the horse traders, and the poor horses alike. Most dismaying of all was New Brunswick's Patriotic Potato Scandal. In 1918, it was established that even the province's generous donation of potatoes to the war effort had been tarnished by the politics of petty embezzlement and partisan kickbacks that had prevailed in the province since 1914; clearly, prominent Tory potato shippers had enriched themselves while organizing the province's patriotic gesture.[65] These problems confirmed many people in their belief that the state should intervene to plan the war effort through the 'conscription of wealth.' The introduction of the business profits tax in 1916 and the income tax in 1917 came partly in response to this popular demand.

Perhaps the most striking provincial example of this new centrality of the state was provided by the 1918 epidemic of Spanish influenza, yet another demoralizing development of the last year of the war. In New Brunswick, the Department of Health, organized just months before, was commanded by Dr William F. Roberts. For Roberts, an advocate of pure milk, regulated theatres and restaurants, women's suffrage, and compulsory vaccinations, a progressive state needed a scientific analysis

William F. Roberts

of the vital characteristics of its population, just as businessmen needed a system of 'cost accounting.' This no-nonsense progressivism spoke perfectly to the era of the First World War. While other Maritime jurisdictions hesitated in the face of the epidemic, Roberts brusquely shut New Brunswick down, prohibiting for more than a month all gatherings of six or more people, and thereby closing schools, churches, theatres, and clubs. In this instance, the progressive state conceptualized civil society as an organism under attack and felt justified in suppressing the rights of the individual in the interests of collective health and order.[66]

The federal Halifax Relief Act and the reconstruction of the ruined city were equally symptomatic of the state's new power. This act gave a federal commission, incorporated with a budget of $20 million, the responsibility of meeting the needs of 6,000 homeless Haligonians. The expropriation of land, the imposition of arbitrary work rules, the complete bypassing of constituted civic authorities, the wielding of an absolute power to grant aid to or withhold it from the victims of the explosion: all these features of the Halifax Relief Commission raised the spectre of authoritarian progressivism.[67] Here was the progressives' 'commission government' writ large! It was one more indication that in trying to preserve the pre-war social system, 'the government of Canada had changed it almost beyond recognition.'[68]

The triumph of progressive reform! Yet a chill, hollow triumph, an 'imposed' and coerced triumph, desolate in the stillborn hour of its birth. For in the closing years of the war, the progressive dream of class harmony had begun to unravel. In October 1918, the federal government brought in an order-in-council forbidding strikes and lockouts for the duration of the war; the penalty for violating the order was military service. In the region, the number of wartime strikes more than doubled from eleven in 1917 to twenty-seven in 1918, and the number of striker-days soared from 12,549 to 84,121. (There would be a further seven strikes in 1918 after the Armistice on 11 November.) That workers would go on strike when the country was fighting a war seemed preposterous to the government and to the daily press. In Halifax, the Liberal *Chronicle* argued that 'the moment when the forces of freedom are locked in a death struggle with the enemy of mankind on the embattled fields of France is not the time for industrial and labor disputes in this country.' The Conservative *Herald* denounced a steelworkers' strike in 1918 because it 'vitally and dangerously affects the power of the resistance which must be presented to the Prussian demon ...[69]

Whatever had happened to the quiet, loyal workers of 1914? Workers had been driven hard; they felt pinched by soaring prices; and they had grown bitterly weary of the war. The federal fuel controller intuited this in 1917, when he came down to Pictou County to persuade striking coal miners to return to work. He told his superiors in Ottawa that he had wasted no time in 'making any oratorical appeals to their patriotism or national duty,' but 'got the discussion upon a business basis.'[70] War weariness seemed to possess the very miners and steelworkers who had earlier been such ardent zealots: in 1918 they revealingly called their numerous little strikes 'holidays,' much to the outrage of the daily press.[71]

NEW LANGUAGES OF CLASS

This novel use of the word 'holiday' was part of the general renovation of the language of class in 1918. Workers and their employers often referred to each other in terms normally reserved for the detested Germans. The Minto coal miners' modest demand that their output be weighed prompted the Saint John *Standard* to speculate that the labour activists were the pawns of 'agencies hostile to all Allied causes.'[72] For their part, steelworkers in Trenton defined as 'enemy aliens' their American business manager and others associated with new, 'scientific' ways of organizing work.[73] A new spirit of class was confirmed by the surprising ease with which the Amalgamated Mine Workers of Nova Scotia (AMW) dislodged the Provincial Workmen's Association as the major trade union of the coalfields. For left-wing and militant miners, who had been defeated in their earlier attempt to replace the PWA with the more radical United Mine Workers of America (UMW), this was a wonderful reversal of fortunes: that which had been impossible in years of intensive, at times violent, struggle from 1907 to 1911 was now quietly conceded. Guided by its dynamic secretary-treasurer, J.B. McLachlan, the AMW soon became in name what it was already in essence: a powerful district (No. 26) of the UMW. The new union resumed the miners' prewar struggles for the eight-hour day, prosecuted those it believed responsible for a disastrous mine explosion in New Waterford in 1917, and won significant wage concessions.[74]

Throughout much of the region, unions raised two pivotal issues: the high cost of living and union recognition. Many workers were falling behind in their struggle to keep up with prices, and many commentators on the new labour unrest felt that inflation was the major driving force.[75] Union recognition, less commonly mentioned, was just as central. Before the end of a strike of plumbers and steamfitters in Saint John in 1917, largely over union recognition and the closed shop, an employer's summer home had been burned down, a man accused of strike-breaking had been killed on the street, and several strikers had been arrested for intimidation. (The city would then face, over the coming years, serious debates over recognition of a police union.) One of the most serious recognition strikes involved Pictonian coal miners. The workers peremptorily declared a 'holiday' and shut down four major pits, evidently in protest against a policy of increased hours. By April 1918, after the management had refused to deal with anything other than tame 'mutuality committees,' the workers, now united in a 'Federation of Labour' representing about 5,000 miners and metal workers, launched a strike. The press was astounded. 'A strike to secure a satisfactory living wage is one thing; a strike to secure recognition of an abstract principle, not vital just now, will be regarded by most people as something entirely different,' remarked the *Amherst Daily News*. Many Maritime workers showed themselves quite willing to resort to direct action in defence of this 'abstract principle' in 1917 and 1918.[76]

The federal government's imposition of military conscription on 18 May 1917 added further fuel to the funeral pyre of wartime harmony by raising the spectre of opposition to the war itself. Quebec excepted, conscription may well have been less favoured in the Maritimes than in any other region of Canada. In the federal election of 1917, which centred on this issue, a majority of civilians in Prince Edward Island and Nova Scotia voted for the mainly anti-conscriptionist Laurier Liberals. The Liberals' weaker showing in New Brunswick was counterbalanced by the concentration of their support on the province's north shore.[77] The *Canadian Annual Review* interpreted the election of ten

Laurier Liberals in the Maritimes simply in terms of the region's traditionalism, even though the defeat of senior pro-conscription 'Unionist' Maritime politicians could hardly be considered a vote for 'tradition.' The Unionists' poor showing in 1917 is more plausibly explained by the lukewarm or even hostile attitudes towards conscription prevalent in the labour movement, among the rural population, and in Acadian areas.

In 1917, the thirty-third annual convention of the Trades and Labor Congress of Canada approved the project of a national 'Labor Party.' In Cape Breton, although Labor Party supporters were highly circumspect about the issue of conscription and the war (about which the party did not speak with one voice), they were still pilloried as disloyal agitators, 'shouting with lusty lungs full with free air, and encouraging with every shout the shackles of Hunnish slavery.' When the labour council in Halifax argued that there should be no conscription unless it was combined with nationalization of food supplies, the conscription of surplus wealth, and comprehensive control by the Dominion of all essential war industries, patriotic writers began to mutter ominously about the precedent of lynching labour agitators in the United States. It was characteristic of the new class polarization that these threats did not silence conscription's critics, or prevent the Labor Party's Cape Breton candidates from polling a very respectable vote.[78]

Some farmers, disillusioned when the Borden government reneged on earlier promises not to conscript their able-bodied sons, mounted a quieter but effective opposition. One historian observes that in southern New Brunswick 'there were significant pockets of anti-conscription sentiment, especially in the rural areas,' and cites a telling statistic: by November 1917, of the 6,250 New Brunswickers called up under the new Military Service Act, 5,500 had applied for exemption. The Berwick Register noted in February 1918 that a search was underway for men from Shubenacadie, Renfrew, Elmsdale, Nine Mile River, Mt Denson, and Walton who had failed to report for duty. In Pictou County, a historian observes, 'youths who had never pulled a cow's teat had themselves classified as farmers by ingenious means – growing potatoes at summer cottages, feeding pigs in the back yards of town houses.' These tactics had worn thin by 1918, with a more stringent and inclusive definition of those to be called up for military service.[79] Some fishermen were no more enthusiastic about conscription. In April 1918, about one-third of the 3,000 Lunenburg County fishermen on the Grand Banks were viewed as potentially 'conscriptable.' When the fleet arrived in Lunenburg, police officers sparked a riot when they began to arrest fishermen, including some clearly ineligible. At least 35 young men were thought to have simply defied the law by refusing to take their registration notices from the post office before they returned to the Grand Banks.[80]

The most visible opponents of conscription were Acadians, although they should by no means be seen as uniformly anti-war. Many Acadians enlisted. The clergy and Acadian newspapers – *Le moniteur acadien* (Conservative) and *L'acadien* (Liberal) – supported the war. According to statistics in the *Canadian Annual Review* in 1916, as many as 1,200 men could be found in such largely Acadian battalions as the 132nd and the 165th, with an estimated further 3,000 scattered among the other battalions of the Maritimes, including 500 in the 10th Prince Edward Island Highlanders.[81] Voluntary enlistment was one thing; compulsory conscription another. Conscription prompted many Acadians to break with a long tradition of circumspect accommodation with the anglophone majority. *L'Evangéline*, the most independent of the Acadian newspapers, came out flatly against fighting in 'foreign wars' in one issue of April 1916, although by the next issue it had reversed its stance: the episode suggested considerable conflict on the issue. Acadians were not less loyal than other Canadians, wrote the worried pro-conscription editor of *Le moniteur acadien*, but like a good many Australians and English-speaking Canadians, they opposed conscription. In 1917, Acadians voted against the Conservative government in New Brunswick, largely because Liberals exploited the conscription issue, and, in defeating a government on the basis of their bloc vote, they raised the fear of 'Acadian domination' in the minds of some New Brunswick anglophones. Even more remarkable as a break with a past tradition of quiet accommodation was the federal election of 1917, in which Acadians throughout all three provinces of the Maritimes voted *en masse* against conscription, even in such ethnically 'mixed' constituencies as Yarmouth-Clare, Cape Breton-Richmond, Inverness, and Cumberland in Nova Scotia, and Westmorland in New Brunswick. However much *Le moniteur acadien* might regard as 'ridicules et déplacés' the emotional outbursts of the *Fredericton Gleaner* or the Saint John *Standard* on the subject of 'Acadian domination,' there could be little doubt that conscription had decisively sharpened perceptions of the cultural and political gap between anglophones and Acadians in the region.[82] Nor was Acadian resistance to conscription confined to the polls. The 'rebellious and defiant attitude of deserters under the Military Service Act at Buctouche and other points in Kent County' led to gun-fights between the police and 'deserters.' By 19 May 1918, one Acadian resister in the area had been seriously wounded by Dominion police officers, and police had apprehended twenty-six others, 'mostly all French Acadians from various points of Kent,' who were taken to Saint John under military escort. Other shooting incidents were reported between resisters and police near Buctouche.[83]

There was not much jubilation when, after more than four years, the war finally ended. Soldiers returning home to Halifax were shocked by the sight of their devastated city. Veterans were both readily offended and prone to collective action. When the Acadia Coal Company evicted from company housing the widow of a soldier killed at the front, outraged veterans threatened to have their legal counsel test the nationality of all officials of the company and demanded the internment of any found to be of enemy extraction. Other veterans complained about perfunctory welcoming ceremonies and the late delivery of back wages. They threatened to mount massive demonstrations. Soon there were riots.[84]

In Sydney, a crowd of returned soldiers and civilians was broken up only after the chief of police warned that 'we will fire on any who attempts [sic] to storm the building and cartridges will not be blanks.' In Halifax on the evening of 25 May 1918, a crowd of thousands broke windows, threw stones at the police, overturned vehicles, and attempted to burn down the city hall by lighting piles of straw stacked up against the building. The most serious rioting took place in Halifax on 18 and 19 February 1919, when soldiers and civilians destroyed stores and restaurants, concentrating their anger on those that were foreign-owned. Dozens were hospitalized, and property damage was estimated at more than $20,000 worth. The sight of rioters wearing soldiers' unmistakable trench caps and overcoats appalled patriotic observers. 'No! No! No! Not the Work of Huns in France and Belgium but the Work of Hoodlums in Halifax,' cried the heart-broken Halifax *Herald*. As it surveyed the aftermath of the February riot, a grand jury reporting to the Nova Scotia Supreme Court drew the general conclusion that social conditions were by now so disturbed that 'a close affiliation should exist between civil and military police, so that by joint prompt action, they could nip in the bud any threatened uprisings.'[85]

Everything seemed to be falling apart. The sky, once alight with patriotic fireworks as Maritimers headed for Europe, glowed with the light from incendiary fires set by rioting soldiers and civilians at the end of a war that had changed the world of 1914 beyond recognition.

RIVAL RECONSTRUCTIONS, 1919–1920

How was this wounded world to be healed? One writer put what appeared to be the two main choices in the form of a little story about a war-weary Halifax soldier, Jones. While on furlough in England, Jones has two dreams about his native city fifteen years in the future. One dream, the author explained, was 'inspiring and full of hope.' In this optimistic dream, Halifax had turned into the progressives' planned Utopia. Everything was in its rational place. The factories (surrounded by workmen's model cottages), the smallpox hospital, and the oil tanks had all been whisked away to tidy, well-planned suburbs. (Even the separate

'African settlement' was to be filed away there.) The other dream of soldier Jones, however, was 'depressing and full of despair.' Jones himself degenerated into a trade-union organizer and strike leader. In this slum-infested Halifax, a 'new war' was starting between the 'capitalists and their discontented and badly housed workers.' Gazing at the pathetic, stunted children of the Halifax slums, Jones (a practical, 'scientific' progressive even in his dreams) remarked, 'What a waste of good material.'[86]

So did one progressive writer imagine the starkly divergent possibilities of 1919: the 'dream' of progressivism overtaken and ruined by the 'nightmare' of class polarization. Underlying both 'dreams' was something so obvious it scarcely needed to be said: that industrial growth would continue. Such confidence was central to the progressive vision and to its increasingly influential radical critics; and in 1919 it still seemed well-founded. Early in that year, Halifax and Sydney were singled out as two exceptions to a national pattern of high unemployment. One merely needed to look at the physical evidence of industrial progress in the transformed waterfront of greater Halifax, with its magnificent Imperial Oil refinery, its ocean terminals, its shipyards – all of them brand new, and the last-named the fulfilment of the highest hopes of turn-of-the-century boosters.[87]

Economic achievements seemed to be fully matched by progressive state initiatives. Critics called the rigorous search-and-seizure provisions of New Brunswick's 1919 prohibition legislation 'un-British,' but prohibition was triumphantly reconfirmed in various provincial referenda in 1920. Radical and labour critics viewed the power of the Halifax Relief Commission with alarm, especially when it seemed to ride roughshod over collective bargaining; but who could reject it entirely when out of the rubble of north-end Halifax emerged the new Hydrostone district, the Dominion's first experiment in public housing, reflecting at least some of the progressive and functionalist ideals of Thomas Adams, the foremost urban visionary of his time in Canada?[88]

If politics was the realm of the possible, 'the possible' in 1919 seemed to include the most imaginative and far-ranging recalculations of the boundaries of civil society and the state. For decades, one of the firmest of those boundaries had separated the 'domestic sphere' reserved for women from the 'political sphere' reserved for men. Now that boundary was eroding. In Nova Scotia, the image of women's initiative after the Explosion, when the burden of organizing civil society, bandaging the wounded, and co-ordinating supplies of food and clothing had been borne by the progressive women's network, silenced even those who had earlier blocked women's suffrage. Legislation in 1918 gave the women of Nova Scotia the franchise, bringing them the same rights recently granted to the women of Ontario, and going beyond Ontario in also giving Nova Scotia women the right to run for public office. The local council promptly launched a registration campaign and declared its intention of educating all women in 'citizenship, education, public health.' 'Now that women have votes it is more necessary than ever before that they should learn more about public affairs, questions of civil as well as national importance,' a supporter declared.[89] (In New Brunswick in 1919, after decades of debating the issue, legislators granted New Brunswick women the vote in provincial elections, although they did not grant women the right to run for public office; Prince Edward Island would follow suit in 1922.) Almost as soon as women won the franchise, there were complaints that they were not using it effectively. Surveying the results of a recent civic vote in Halifax, in which women had apparently cast but one-sixth of the total number of votes, one writer was dismayed to find, 'after the desperate battles that have been fought for so many years by the pioneers of women's interests ... so many of their sisters who have nothing to do but make use of the privileges they have gained by the labour and efforts of the more hardy and enthusiastic of their sex making so little use of the franchise.'[90] The very achievement of the vote may well have weakened the progressive women's alliance that had achieved it, by removing its unifying issue. None the less, the boundaries of so fundamental a category as citizenship had changed; and in this instance civil society would not return to its prewar pattern.

It was this sense of open possibilities that changed the stance of so many workers in the post-war Maritimes. Their response was sometimes a defensive one: when workingmen in Charlottetown and the New Brunswick Federation of Labour defended the worker's traditional right to drink beer, or when the Halifax Trades and Labour Council opposed Daylight Savings Time, the compulsory vaccination of children, and the Halifax Relief Commission's power to fix wages, they were registering defensive opposition to some of the aspects of triumphant progressivism that impinged directly on their interests. Yet on balance the labour movement did not fear this progressive moment, but rather sought to push beyond it, to push for a state responsive to their economic needs. If the state could break with traditional liberalism in so many other areas, why could it not do so with advanced workers' compensation legislation, minimum wages, and countless other labour reforms? It was this question of the state that, when added to the classic ingredients of labour militancy (a tight labour market, inflationary pressures on wages, unresolved struggles over working and living standards), made the post-war labour revolt such a profoundly radical event.

The First World War echoed and re-echoed in this labour revolt. Many workers firmly believed that their labour rights had been etched in stone by the Treaty of Versailles. When machinists in Saint John were locked out in 1920 by their employers and replaced with other workers, their organizer remarked: 'We have given the St. John employers ample time to make up their minds to negotiate ... If they wish to keep on refusing us the rights which are guaranteed by the Peace Treaty, and sealed with the blood of millions of workers, we will see what we can do about it.'[91]

This spirit of discontent was particularly strong in workers who were also veterans. Represented by the Great War Veterans' Association (GWVA), returned soldiers initially demanded such things as new clothes, prompt attention to their discharges, and back pay; they then called for economic security for the widows of the men killed in Europe, and jobs for themselves. The palliatives they were offered – technical education for the shell-shocked, special consideration in housing – only went so far in assuaging the veterans' discontent. They pressed for more, sometimes in close collaboration with the labour movement. And often they pressed for more from within the labour movement, as militants of the labour revolt.

They were not the only new elements contributing to labour insurgency. Labour organizations, and the people who led them, were doing very different things after the war than they had before. Influenced by such figures as the UMW's J.B. McLachlan and the AF of L's C.C. Dane, the one a radical Scot and the other a militant Australian and self-proclaimed 'Bolshevist,' Maritime workers developed their own equable variant of socialist trade unionism. They often poured this heady new wine into musty old craft-union bottles, but nobody who looks closely at the 'districts,' 'councils,' and 'federations of labour' that dotted the post-war region can doubt that these organizations effectively gathered masses of workers together for novel, socially radical purposes. These bodies tended to supplant the older union forms in bargaining with bosses. They were immersed in radical politics: in truth, they were much closer to the spirit of the One Big Union in the West than they were to traditional nineteenth-century craft unionism. In Pictou County, in Amherst, and momentarily in Sydney Mines, 'federations of labour' and not individual craft unions were the principal bargaining bodies for workers; in Halifax, councils of unions in the building trades and shipyards were the agents of collective bargaining; and in the coalfields the massive force of District 26 of the UMW, encompassing more than 13,000 coal workers from Minto to Glace Bay, bore no resemblance to anything seen before in Maritime labour history. Conservative estimates suggest that the labour movement's membership quadrupled (to about 40,000) from 1916 to 1920. In 1919, the Halifax Labour Council, with 8,000 workers, was the fourth-largest local labour council in Canada; only labour councils in Montreal, Toronto, and Quebec City were larger. These movements were young, aggressive, idealistic. Rank-and-file democracy was the norm. Although the Nova Scotia coal miners did not share the 'war born British distrust of accredited union leaders,' one commentator noted, the same rank-and-file spirit was evident in the unions' growing tendency 'to negotiate *en masse* and face to face with employers rather than depend upon the hitherto prevalent system of delegating the whole affair to small groups of union officials.'[92]

The strike wave of 1919–20 was unprecedented in its magnitude, intensity, and objectives. Over 1919 and 1920 there were at least ninety-three strikes accounting for 278,172 striker-days. A number of these strikes were of epic size indeed. The Hants County gypsum strike, the Amherst general strike, and the Halifax construction-trades strike of 1919 all suggested startling parallels with the Winnipeg General Strike. The most unlikely workers seized the day. At Hopewell Hill, New Brunswick, not hitherto notorious as a site of working-class radicalism, a strike-bound employer offered a political explanation of his workers' surprising militancy in 1919: they revolted, he said, 'because the government had given way to similar strikes.' Spontaneous rebellions rocked the little communities of the rural Maritimes. A general strike on the Miramichi started spontaneously at Robinson's Mill in Newcastle on 20 August 1919, when workmen went on strike for the nine-hour day:

> They then proceeded to Chatham Head and were joined by employees of Maloney's and Fraser's mills there and thence to Burchill's, O'Brien's and Sullivan's at Nelson. Returning to Newcastle the employees of the gear works joined the strikers as did also the men loading sleepers for J.F. Kingston. Richard's mill is also down. Sinclair's had already shut down for a picnic. Several hundred men then marched to Buckley's mill at French Fort Cove and thence to the Miramichi Lumber Co. mill at Douglastown, both of which shut down. The union organizer is expected from Chatham this afternoon. Perfect order is prevailing. The longshoremen continue out in sympathy with the millmen.

And so, without union or organizer, inspired by down-to-earth demands for the nine-hour day and a sixty-five-cent hour, 1,500 Miramichi workers had spontaneously mounted a massive general strike, in defiance of decades of rural and small-town paternalism.[93]

The festive moment of class consciousness and united struggle of 1919 – these dramatic events, which at once preserved, extended, and undermined the tamer progressivism of the middle class – receded as the recession advanced in the spring of 1920. Hope gave way to caution, impassioned radical solidarity to a looming sense of fragmentation and

Labour Council float, Victory Bond parade, Saint John, 1919. Expectations of remodelling post-war society contributed to intense labour activity in 1919.

helplessness. Workers who a year before had struck defiantly for wage increases and shorter hours now confronted wage reductions and lay-offs. In Amherst, a minor disagreement over a foreman gave the management of the woollen mill an opportunity to close the factory 'for repairs' for several weeks; the town's moulders were also humbled under the threat of plant closure. The most grievous collapse, perhaps, came in Halifax in 1920, where radical politics and labour activism had meshed so effectively a year before. Shipyard workers mounted the city's biggest-ever strike – indeed, one of urban Canada's largest single-industry strikes on record. These workers were full of the radicalism and confidence of 1919. Then came the chill realization that their bargaining power was fast eroding, as it became evident that capital might simply pull out. They then faced questions that all the region's organized workers have faced ever since: What becomes of labour if capital simply moves away? How should organized labour respond to lay-offs and plant closures? Against the emergent reality of de-industrialization, labour relied on its traditional weapons with diminishing effect.[94]

Against this emergent reality, many of the laws, programs, institutions, and ideals of the progressives would prove no more durable. Prohibitionists would be undermined not only by their own failure to fulfil the Utopian expectations aroused by their campaign, but also by the fiscal weakness of dependent provincial states expected to provide citizens with social services. Advocates of technical education, who had once dreamt of responding to the needs of a rapidly changing society through sophisticated schools equal in quality to the Massachusetts Institute of Technology, started to think of ways they could subsist on the margins of a de-industrializing economy by offering courses in homemaking, automobile operation, and clerical work. Landmark attempts (through the Massachusetts-Halifax Health Commission) to make comprehensive public health (including 'mental hygiene,' social psychology, and fully professionalized nursing) routine elements of a new post-war civil society proved no more durable in a climate of retrenchment and underfunding. Progressive advocates of women's rights, many of them exhausted by the demands of war, would discover that the expanded state and the new professionalism for which they had fought so hard ironically empowered male bureaucrats and professionals, while undermining the authority and public presence of women.[95] For middle-class progressive reformers no less than workers, what could be preserved from the débâcle were a few shards and stones as souvenirs from a once-almost-real 'city on the hill.'

In an editorial, the left-wing Halifax *Citizen* confidently predicted early in 1920 that the 'hour of Midnight' was striking for the 'old order' and that the working class was no longer willing to have politicians think and act on its behalf: 'The new day will be ushering in a new era, in which the working class must be prepared with leaders and policies that will direct and build a new nation conceived in brotherhood and devoted to the cause of humanity.'[96] The hour of midnight was indeed tolling, but it was not tolling for the 'old order.' It was tolling for everyone in the region – especially the middle-class progressives and the working-class radicals – who, since 1910, had constructed public lives around the problems and challenges of capitalist modernity. In the 1910s, Maritimers had seen their region as one of advanced and advancing capitalism; its central problems were those of industrial societies the world over. But in the 1920s, the region would be seen anew, as industries collapsed, as workers and their radical leaders were obliged to emigrate in large numbers, and as a conservative regionalism came to replace what had been a progressive 'common sense.' Many legacies have endured from the 1910s: town planning, steel shipbuilding, workers' compensation – above all, the real if incomplete empowerment of women as potential equals of men in public life. What could not survive was the decade's reforming certainty, that marvellous and contradictory sense Maritimers then had of being in step with the progress of a wider modern world. The 1910s were the region's last years of abundant hope. Anyone who writes of them writes an elegy for a vanished continent of aspiration, long lost beneath a sea of misfortunes, but still, for all that, not quite forgotten.

PART THREE
LIVING WITH DISPARITY, 1920–1950

# CHAPTER SEVEN

# The 1920s
## Class and Region, Resistance and Accommodation

I

The decade began with a sad, lonely voice of protest. In the summer of 1920 a young Welshman left his wife and child in Swansea and sailed across the Atlantic to the New World. A miner by trade, William Ambrose John had answered advertisements placed by the Dominion Coal Company and borrowed money for the passage. On 27 July, Will John and his friend Robert Johnston landed in Sydney. They went to work at No. 16 colliery, New Waterford, on 2 August. 'Then came the awakening,' John later wrote. 'We found the promises of the company were like all promises – made to be broken.' The two men soon discovered they were earning much less than the company's agent in Liverpool had promised. When Will John went to collect his first pay on 6 August, the pay slip showed $18.16 for five days' work. The entire amount was taken up in deductions and there was no cash coming to him. The following week he earned $12.61 for three days' work and received $3.02 in cash. There was little hope of sending money home or bringing his family to join him as planned. The discouraged immigrants left the coal mines and headed for New Brunswick. In Saint John they found work washing bags at the Atlantic Sugar Refinery. It was hot, gruelling, soaking-wet work, eight hours a day, six days a week. Johnston went up to the coal mines at Newcastle Bridge to look for employment, while John continued to work overtime at the refinery. He was now hoping to get a job on one of the New England boats or to work his way back to Wales. He also continued to write letters home to his wife. On 1 September: 'If I had wings I would fly over the Atlantic in order to take you in my arms and comfort you.' On 3 September: 'From now on it is going to be a battle ...' On 5 September: 'Your Ambrose has been through hell this last six weeks ...' Then, at about 7:00 p.m. on the evening of 8 September, lying on his bed at the People's Palace, the Salvation Army hostel in Saint John, with one foot on the floor, William Ambrose John picked up a revolver and shot himself through the heart. It was a personal act of despair, but, as Walter Benjamin has said, suicide is also the ultimate individual act of protest. On a chair beside the bed Will John left a letter addressed to the chief constable of Saint John, giving a detailed account of his experiences and concluding: 'will you please try to stop the Dominion Coal Company from luring any more men from the Old Country under false promises ...'[1]

For the Maritime provinces the death of William John marked the beginning of a bleak decade. During the summer of 1920 the short boom associated with the end of the First World War came to an abrupt end, and as the world economy returned to normal, the Maritimes lost the temporary advantages created by wartime conditions. Exports now faced increased competition in world markets, and there were lower prices for fish and lumber. In the coal and steel industries Maritime producers were restored to their peripheral place in the national market. Local manufacturers, facing up to the logic of national integration, continued to sell out to the competition or to go under. Efforts to establish steel shipbuilding in Halifax, encouraged by the government during wartime, were suspended. Wages fell and unemployment increased.[2]

The great historic response to underdevelopment was 'the exodus.' For generations Maritimers had registered dissatisfaction with local conditions by boarding the Boston boats and the westbound trains. Out-migration continued to be a workable survival strategy during the 1920s, and Maritimers continued to contribute their labour power to the larger labour markets outside the region. Women went to the big cities to work as domestic servants, nurses, and office workers. In the summers, men joined the great harvest excursions that ran packed trainloads of Maritimers into the prairie West to help bring in the grain crops that were the country's leading staple export. Similarly, massive construction projects, such as the pulp-and-paper mill at Corner Brook, drew under-employed workers from the Maritime provinces. During the decade of the 1920s the population of the region grew less than 1 per cent. While the population of New Brunswick increased slightly, both Prince Edward Island and Nova Scotia registered losses. Demographers estimate that about 122,000 people left the Maritime provinces during the 1920s. It was the largest exodus experienced by the region in a single decade.[3]

Little of this was new to the Maritimes, however. The conditions of crisis in the 1920s marked the culmination of developments that had been in the making for at least a generation. As the spatial consequences of capitalist development became apparent during the first half-century of Confederation, both political and economic power had become concentrated in fewer hands and more distant places. The rise of national

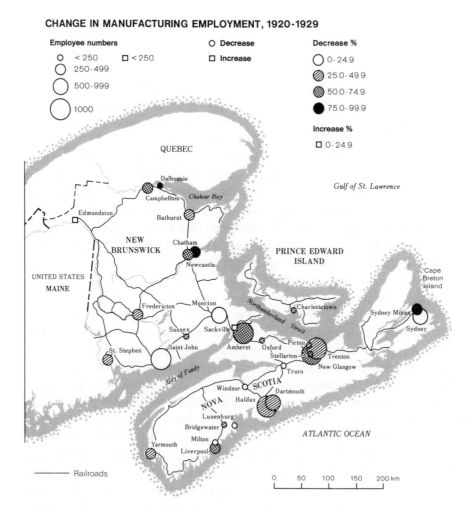

CHANGE IN MANUFACTURING EMPLOYMENT, 1920-1929

Figure 9  The collapse of manufacturing in Maritime towns and cities, 1920–9

markets in goods, labour, and capital all seemed to reduce the Maritimes to one of the hinterlands of the new Dominion. For many Maritimers it seemed as if the fate of the region was tied to powerful forces that were hard to identify and even more difficult to control.

A recognition of the imbalances in Confederation has always been implicit in the historiography of nation building, but more recent approaches grounded in social history and political economy have been more concerned to underline the consequences of uneven development for the country's subordinate classes and regions.[4] 'As for the Maritime Provinces, nothing, of course, ever happens down there': Frank Underhill's comment was an unfortunate one, for it was in fact made as part of a lament for the lack of a vigorous national protest tradition in Canada in the 1920s and 1930s, one that Underhill hoped might have provided 'a popular balance against too much authority in the hands of an oligarchy at the centre.'[5] Recent work on the history of the 1920s in the Maritimes contradicts the stereotype of conservatism that earlier writers have been too ready to accept. In its place we can see that some important groups of Maritimers failed to accept the decline of the region with equanimity and mounted a struggle against the legacy of under-development. This was a time of difficult adjustments for the people of the region. Maritimers in the 1920s still shared the limited optimism of the first half-century of Confederation, and they had not yet accepted the recognized dependency of the future. In part the history of this decade was a story of local protest and resistance; at the same time this was also a history of containment and accommodation.

II

In the summer and autumn of 1920 the apparent conservatism of the political system in Nova Scotia and New Brunswick was shaken by the emergence of large numbers of independent candidates in the provincial elections that year. In Nova Scotia the United Farmers nominated sixteen candidates. Together with eleven labour candidates, they received more than 30 per cent of the vote in the July election. Seven farmer and four labour members were returned to the Legislative Assembly. In the October 1920 provincial election in New Brunswick, the United Farmers of New Brunswick ran twenty-six candidates for the House of Assembly. They received 21 per cent of the vote and elected eleven members, two of them on a joint Farmer-Labour ticket in Northumberland County. More than a year later, when Islanders went to the polls in the Dominion election of 1921, the United Farmers of Prince Edward Island ran three candidates, advancing the cause of 'the common people' against 'the special privileged interests.' Their leader, Horace Wright, won 20 per cent of the vote in Prince County, and overall the three progressives and one labour candidate received 17.1 per cent of the vote. Meanwhile, in the constituency of Victoria-Carleton in New Brunswick the president of the United Farmers, Thomas W. Caldwell, was returned to the House of Commons, the only progressive candidate to be elected east of Ontario in the 1921 election.[6]

The farmers were perhaps the largest and the most threatened social class in the Maritimes in the early twentieth century, and it was hardly surprising that farmers in the Maritimes, as elsewhere in Canada at this time, should voice their protests against the contemporary preoccupation

Digging potatoes, c. 1920. Farm life involved men and women, young and old, working together; it may not have produced much in the way of surplus earnings, but most farm families could at least feed themselves; some urban workers sought refuge on farms when town jobs failed during the industrial downturn.

with urban and industrial development. Urbanization and emigration both seemed to undermine the vitality of rural society, and the attractions of the North American labour market acted powerfully on the rural parts of the region. The number of farms was beginning to enter its steady decline, even as the average size of the surviving farms was beginning to grow. In New Brunswick, for instance, the number of farms declined by 6 per cent during the 1920s, and the total acreage declined by 3 per cent, while the average farm size increased by 5 per cent. This was the beginning of a long-term trend that would widen the gap between a diminishing number of progressive, industrializing farmers and a growing body of rural residents for whom agriculture no longer offered the principal means of making a living. If the balance of the population was not shifting from rural to urban as quickly as in central Canada, there was a pronounced increase in the number of households that could be described as rural non-farm. Those who continued to live on the land hoped to make a living by going fishing and cutting wood, and there might even be seasonal or temporary work for wages in construction, in industry, on the docks, and on the roads.[7]

The most articulate farmers' voices of the 1920s, however, did not come from the rural dispossessed but from the advocates of a more progressive agriculture. Their protest was not so much a gasp of protest against rural decline as a call for the extension of progressive development into the countryside. The farmers worried that the provincial governments in New Brunswick and Nova Scotia were too sympathetic to the interests of the pulp-and-paper, coal, and steel companies and consequently neglectful of agricultural concerns. The farmers' political platforms avoided broad statements of principle and called instead for practical measures such as the building of more country roads to improve access to markets, the elimination of tariffs on imported farm machinery and fertilizers, the increased reporting of crop statistics and market conditions, more abattoirs to promote the livestock trade, greater use of trained specialists in the departments of agriculture, and further extension of electricity and postal services into the countryside.[8]

The farmers' movement demonstrated its greatest strength in New Brunswick, where the United Farmers reported 141 locals with 10,000 members and considered itself the voice of progressive agriculture in the province. Supporters tended to be located in the more successful farming areas, such as the Upper Saint John River Valley, where there was rapid expansion in the production of such commercial export crops as potatoes. The movement here was not only a political protest but an economic-reform movement as well. The United Farmers established a network of co-operative stores for buying seed and equipment, and by 1920 the United Farmers Co-operative Company of New Brunswick had twenty-three local stores, mainly in the Upper Saint John River Valley. The Farmers' MP, Caldwell, was himself a successful East Florenceville farmer who was reluctant to have the organization enter politics and did so himself only when he became convinced that the farmers must go into politics in order to advance the larger agricultural cause. In 1921 William Irvine, who worked as an organizer for the United Farmers, continued to believe that the economic potential of the movement was more significant than its political objectives: 'People are beginning to see that it is even more important that they take a hand in the management of their business affairs than it is to elect a representative to Parliament. It is just as foolish to leave the manufacturing and distributing of the necessities of life to the caprice of a profit hunting individual as it would be to leave our government in the hands of a kaiser. It seems as if a real democracy in industry and commerce might be reached through the cooperative ideal.'[9]

The experience of the United Farmers in the Maritimes underlined the extent to which the agricultural interest was far from homogeneous. There were problems in combining the interests of the small subsistence farmers struggling for survival with the ambitions of the export-oriented agriculturalists. On the tariff issue there were divisions between the export-oriented potato farmers, who favoured tariff reductions, and the mixed-farming areas, where farmers relied on the demand of local urban markets and the tariff was expected to protect local industry. There were also difficulties in making alliances with labour groups in the region and extending the movement into the Acadian districts. As well, the co-operative stores established by the farmers lacked financial strength and faced organized competition from their rivals.

Yet the farmers' turn to politics in the 1920s was not entirely a failure. The farmers succeeded in reminding provincial governments that they remained the largest single occupational group in the Maritimes and that it would be difficult to govern without their support. In both New Brunswick and Nova Scotia the traditional parties were not slow to adjust their sights and re-establish their hegemony over the political process. A number of farmer candidates from the 1920 elections subsequently appeared as Liberal and Conservative nominees in the 1925 provincial elections. The Conservatives in particular were able to capture much of the movement's support with their own brand of regional protest. In Prince Edward Island some Progressives eventually found their way into the Co-operative Commonwealth Federation in the 1930s, while others, such as Walter Jones and Horace Wright, later came to power as Liberal politicians during the 1940s. In response to the farmers, governments soon demonstrated that they were prepared to take greater action to promote farm interests. Agricultural representatives employed by the Dominion and provincial governments promoted co-operative marketing and, through agencies such as co-operative shipping clubs and marketing boards, helped drive up prices paid to Maritime farmers.[10] The farmers' case was vindicated by the findings of the federally appointed Royal Commission on Maritime Claims in 1926, which reserved some of its strongest words to condemn provincial governments for the failure of agriculture in the region.[11]

The farmers were only one of the groups of small commodity producers who struggled with the challenges of the 1920s. Like farmers, the fishermen of the Maritimes often enjoyed a position of economic independence that was more formal than real. As owners of boats and gear, the inshore fishermen appeared to stand on an equal footing with the merchants and fish companies. In practice they had little choice but to accept the fish prices determined by local merchants and distant markets. During the 1920s the rise of new firms employing offshore trawlers and freezer plants represented a significant industrializing movement in the region's ancient staple trade. Companies such as Lunenburg Sea Products demonstrated that Maritime business was successfully adapting

Silver-fox farming, c. 1910. Fox farming was one of the success stories of progressive agriculture during the inter-war years, especially around Summerside, P.E.I. Unfortunately, the boom collapsed in the 1930s, highlighting the dangers of depending on a single specialized commodity.

to the changes in markets and technology involved in the transition from the salted fish trade to the fresh- and frozen-fish trade. Progressive developments such as these required large amounts of capital investment and brought the industry increasingly under the sway of New England companies such as Atlantic Coast Fisheries, which by 1929 controlled much of the fresh-fish trade through its wholly owned subsidiary, Maritime-National Fish. These changes threatened the livelihood of the inshore fishermen in several ways. As in farming, a gulf was growing in the 1920s between the industrializing, capital-intensive parts of the fisheries and the majority of the inshore fishermen, who worked in the context of a seasonal, household economy, subsidized by less-than-subsistence prices and relying heavily on the unpaid domestic labour of women and children.[12]

To counteract their declining influence as producers, the fishermen also attempted to mobilize their economic power. There was nothing in the Maritimes to compare to the great crusade led by the Fishermen's Protective Union in Newfoundland, but there were continual efforts to establish associations and co-peratives among the fishermen. Fishermen's organizations were formed on Prince Edward Island at Tignish in 1924 and Alberton in 1930. The first of these was led by Chester McCarthy, a young lawyer who in 1930 became the first president of the United Maritime Fishermen. Similarly, in the Caraquet and Shippegan area a co-operative formed by Acadian fishermen considered one of its goals to be 'to cause the fishing industry to be liked, to make it attractive for the young people and to prevent them from emigrating to the cities and to the United States.' The members aimed to secure better prices by improving local methods of curing and packing fish. They also worked to strengthen the position of the fishermen by establishing insurance programs and pressing governments to provide loans for boat building.[13]

The loudest voices of protest during the 1920s focused on the threat represented by the introduction of trawler fleets to serve the new fresh-fish plants. Centralization of the industry around a smaller number of centres reduced the average fisherman's access to markets. The fresh-fish trade required year-round supplies, which the companies sought to meet in part with their own boats. By 1927 there were ten trawlers operating out of Halifax, Port Hawkesbury, Saint John, North Sydney, Canso, and Digby. These efficient offshore vessels were landing large quantities of fish and helping to drive down prices for the inshore fishermen. On the sixtieth anniversary of Confederation in July 1927, the fishermen of Canso were holding what they called 'indignation meetings' to protest the presence of steam trawlers in the fisheries. The result was the appointment of a royal commission, under Justice A.K. Maclean, which recommended that the use of steam trawlers be limited by legislation. It appeared to be a victory, but one that was qualified by the fact that subsequent legislation did no more than impose a tax of one cent per pound on fish caught on foreign trawlers and slightly less for domestic trawlers. Moreover, the fishermen's resistance was closely bound up with a defence of the schooner captains and the fish merchants, who had not been the most generous of partners in the past. Ironically, the inshore fishermen were also helping to perpetuate a system under which the fishing companies would continue to regard them as equal partners in distributing the investment risks and low prices of the industry.

The royal commissioners did not fail to observe that co-operation among producers could be one way to increase returns to the fishermen. In the final report the existing co-operatives of fishermen thus received official encouragement. Specifically, the report proposed that the Dominion government appoint an organizer to promote the growth of co-operative organizations among the fishermen, to enable them to adapt better to the changes taking place in the industry. In September 1929

Father Moses M. Coady of St Francis Xavier University, an advocate of adult education and self-help among small producers in the region, was hired by the Department of Marine and Fisheries to promote the cause. It is clear that many fishermen did not wait for Coady's arrival to take the initiative, and by the end of the decade, a vigorous local co-operative movement was running through the fishing communities. Under the guidance of Coady, many of these co-operatives would join together in 1930 to create the United Maritime Fishermen's Co-operative.[14]

The one sector of the regional economy that seemed to benefit from the larger prosperity of the North American continent during the 1920s was the forest industry. While the lumber trade, the traditional mainstay of the forest industry, was in difficulty, considerable expansion took place in pulp and paper, particularly during the later part of the decade. In 1911 New Brunswick had followed the lead of Ontario in limiting pulpwood exports; as a result, pulp mills were soon established at Bathurst and Edmundston in northern New Brunswick. In the late 1920s the decline of the lumber trade was offset by considerable expansion in the pulp-and-paper industry in both Nova Scotia and New Brunswick. In 1928 the New Brunswick government signed a fifty-year lease of Crown lands with the International Paper Company, and the result was the opening of a $15-million newsprint mill at Dalhousie in 1929. Expansion of this kind attracted capital to the province and created more work not only in constructing and operating the mills but also in cutting wood for this expanding industry. Pulpwood production more than doubled between 1920 and 1930. While lumber towns such as Chatham and Newcastle lost population during the decade, pulp-and-paper towns such as Dalhousie and Edmundston were among the few Maritime communities to report significant increases in population. By the end of the decade it was likely that as many as one out of every four farmers and fishermen in New Brunswick and one in every five or six in Nova Scotia was working in the woods for some part of the year.[15]

Although the most enthusiastic promotional prophecies of New Brunswick premier J.B.M. Baxter were not realized, few New Brunswickers were prepared to question the attractions of the industry. Yet there were parallels with the changes that were taking place in the farming and fishing parts of the region. While pulp and paper represented a progressive application of new capital and technology to regional resources, the traditional forest industry was simultaneously suffering from neglect. As in farming and fishing, the forest industry was also dividing into developing and underdeveloping sectors. In many parts of the region the decline of the small local sawmill, producing lumber for local use as well as for export, could not be compensated for by the rise of distant mills in the northern parts of the province. The small mills, often

In the woods. Farmers and fishermen often earned extra cash working in the woods during the winter. Even though lumber markets were in trouble, pulp-wood output doubled in the 1920s.

operated by local owners who practised a well-developed paternalism within their territory, did not have access to the capital resources, Crown lands, and government favours available to the large new companies. Moreover, because the pulp-and-paper mills depended especially on smaller trees and softwoods, the strategy may also have helped to discourage the development of hardwood stands that could be used to develop a more diversified forest industry.[16] Ultimately, the arrival of the pulp-and-paper industry represented a development strategy that depended on outside investment and outside markets. It was Canada's traditional strategy for the exploitation of natural resources, yet it was also fraught with dangers. The potential for disastrous results had already been demonstrated in the case of the nineteenth-century timber trade, and more recently in the case of the Nova Scotia coal industry.

III

The wage earners belonged to the most vulnerable social class in the Maritimes. Compared to the rural small producers, they were even less able to respond to economic difficulties by falling back on the hidden productivity of the household economy and the resources of land, sea, and woods. Any change in the economic condition of the region was at once registered in the weekly wages of the dependent workers who made up the region's working class. The rise of the labour movement in the Maritimes represented an effort to exert greater control over the economic status of workers within the local labour market. As in other parts of Canada, labour organizations in the Maritimes emerged from the First World War with an enhanced sense of purpose and solidarity. For labour leaders across the Maritimes this was to be the beginning of an age of social reconstruction in which the needs of the people would be placed ahead of the interests of profit. After 1920 these radical ambitions were forced to recognize the ongoing crisis of the regional economy. Workers who had fought for wage increases during the inflationary years of the later 1910s found themselves on the defensive after 1920, battling against efforts to drive down wages.

The most remarkable of the union leaders was James Bryson McLachlan, a Scottish-born coal miner whose fiery rhetoric and resourceful tactics impressed friends and enemies alike. A coal miner himself from the age of eleven, McLachlan articulated the ambitions of the coal miners more effectively than any other leader. By the 1920s he was a veteran of the local class struggle in Cape Breton and enjoyed the enthusiastic support of the coal miners, who elected him to union office and supported him in elections. His own inspiration came from what he described as a tradition of preachers running from Moses and Jesus through Carlyle and Marx. He had long since abandoned organized religion for the cause of socialism, and to the coal miners McLachlan preached an economic gospel that promised to 'redeem the world from the chaos of capitalism.' As a socialist, and by 1922 a Communist, McLachlan fully expected the capitalist system to collapse of its own contradictions; in the meantime, however, he knew that collective bargaining could be used effectively to improve wages and conditions. By 1920 the coal miners had won recognition of their union, the United Mine Workers of America (UMW), for which McLachlan had battled for more than a dozen years, and union contracts were securing important improvements in wages and conditions. At a time when organized labour across Canada was often in retreat following the defeat of the Winnipeg General Strike of 1919, the Nova Scotia coal miners found themselves in the vanguard of the class struggle in Canada.[17]

The labour leaders faced a formidable adversary in the person of Roy Mitchell Wolvin. Wolvin was a Montreal financier who took control of Dominion Steel in 1920 and completed a huge merger in 1921. The British Empire Steel Corporation (BESCO) was a holding company that included virtually the entire coal and steel industry of Nova Scotia, as well as the Halifax shipyards. The new corporation's highly optimistic financial structure inflated the value of the merging properties by some $19 million and promised shareholders an enhanced return on these assets. All this was controversial, and eyebrows were raised in more cautious financial circles; but there was nothing illegal about BESCO's financial arrangements. The corporation's ability to float its stock and bond issues testified to the credibility of its promotional efforts. This corporate strategy, however, depended on levels of stability in markets for coal and steel and in relations between labour and capital that, in the context of the 1920s, proved unrealistic.[18]

The troubles of the coal industry in part reflected the weak position of the industry within the national economy, particularly at a time when over-production of coal in the United States and the development of hydroelectric power were both driving down energy prices in central Canada. Even as the price of coal increased, the coal tariff remained pegged at fifty-three cents per ton, which itself was a reduced level of the protection established in 1897; furthermore, slack coal was admitted at fourteen cents per ton, and after 1907 iron and steel producers in central Canada were entitled to a 99 per cent rebate on the coal tariff. Although Nova Scotia had been highly important in building up the industrial capacity of central Canada, the country lacked a national fuel policy that would reserve the domestic market for Canadian suppliers. When BESCO ran into financial difficulties and was compelled to reduce its costs, the reduction of workers' wages seemed to be the obvious strategy for corporate survival.

The coal miners' resistance drew much of its energy from traditions of solidarity within the industrial community and of workers' control within the coal industry. The industrial communities were made up largely of men and women who shared common roots within the Maritimes. The coal towns themselves had ceased to be company towns at the end of the First World War, and by electing labour candidates as mayors and councillors, the residents had turned their communities into labour towns. Distinctions between corporate and community interests were sharply drawn over issues such as taxes and assessments, support of strikers, and the use of armed force during strikes. Similarly, the ability of the coal companies to exert control over the workplace was limited by the miners' traditions of workplace control. Between 1920 and 1925 there were at least fifty-eight individual strikes in the Sydney coalfield, most of them over not wage issues but such matters as work assignments, fines and suspensions, and the role of the pit committees and the union within the workplace. In the major wage struggles of the 1920s the miners relied on this latent ability to control production by restricting output or holding the mines hostage to the forces of nature. The coal miners also endorsed the more ideological socialist critique advanced by their leaders, who advocated policies of public ownership and democratic control in the coal industry. President Wolvin often complained that the coal mines were not being run by the company but by the workers, and he made no secret of his desire to drive the union out of the coalfields.[19]

The first great battle took place in 1922 when the corporation implemented a one-third reduction in wages. The miners were not anxious to go on strike during the harsh winter months, especially without guarantees of support from union headquarters in Indianapolis. Instead they met the wage cut with a one-third reduction in output, loading six boxes of coal in a shift instead of the usual ten. Restriction of output, McLachlan pointed out, was a traditional tactic of the Scottish coal miners and a highly appropriate response to reduced wages: 'War is on, and it is up to the workers in the mines of the British Empire Steel Corporation to carry that war into the "country" of the enemy.' In taking on BESCO, McLachlan proclaimed that the coal miners were fighting a loyal and patriotic battle for 'a living wage, home and children against stocks, bonds and dividends.' The situation attracted national attention and precipitated a long debate in the House of Commons in which the minister of labour was taken to task for denouncing the coal miners as 'un-British, un-Canadian and cowardly.' In the summer of 1922 the coal miners adopted a series of resolutions calling for the abolition of the capitalist system – 'peaceably if we may, forcibly if we must.' Toronto Communist Tim Buck, who was present at the meetings, was surprised by the forcefulness of the declarations, which owed as much to the language of Chartism as to Bolshevism. By the end of the summer the dispute was settled through the intervention of the provincial government, but it was clear that the war was far from over.

The following summer the demands of class solidarity brought the coal miners out again. The steelworkers of Sydney, also employed by BESCO, had been battling for union recognition for almost twenty years and in 1923 seemed close to success. A strike erupted at the steel plant, and when provincial police charged through the streets in a bloody riot on 1 July, McLachlan called the coal miners out in support: 'No miner or mine worker can remain at work while this Government turns Sydney into a jungle; to do so is to sink your manhood and allow Armstrong and his miserable bunch of grafting politicians to trample your last shred of freedom on the sand.' This was a fateful decision, one that brought down the wrath first of the provincial government and then of the international union. For his call to arms McLachlan was charged with seditious libel and subsequently sentenced to two years in jail. For his

Bootleg pits, 1925. During coal strikes or shut-downs idle miners dug coal in abandoned pits, violating the exclusive leases of coal companies in order to meet local needs for fuel.

violation of international union policy in calling the sympathetic strike he was removed from office by John L. Lewis of the United Mine Workers. McLachlan's conviction gave the labour cause a popular hero, but his removal from office deprived him of his position of greatest public influence. After his release from the penitentiary, McLachlan was installed as editor of the *Maritime Labor Herald*.

In the final confrontation with BESCO, McLachlan was effectively on the sidelines, his print shop mysteriously burning down just as the long strike began in March 1925. The company, again seeking wage reductions, closed the company stores on which so many families depended in the winter months and refused to meet the union leaders. There was no doubt that the company saw this as a final effort to bring the coal miners into line, and vice-president J.E. McLurg declared: 'We hold the cards ... Things are getting better every day they stay out ... Let them stay out two months or six months, it matters not; eventually they will have to come to us ... They can't stand the gaff.' The crisis came on 11 June 1925, in a violent confrontation at the power plant near New Waterford, where company police did battle with unarmed miners. One coal miner, William Davis, was shot and killed and a half-dozen more were wounded. In the following nights fires swept through the company stores.

The Canadian army was brought in to restore order, and the provincial government went down to defeat for the first time since the 1880s. A hurried truce was arranged, and a royal commission was appointed to look into the troubles.[20]

The explosive confrontations in the coal and steel towns attracted national attention. Social workers and clergymen documented the deplorable conditions of industrial life. There were long debates in the House of Commons and national speaking tours by local union leaders. In the times of greatest hardship there were shipments of food and clothing and donations of money from sympathetic churches, industrial workers, and ex-Maritimers across the country. Under the provisions of the Militia Act, BESCO did not hesitate to call on the armed force of the state to help impose its will. Much to the dismay of the prime minister, hundreds of Canadian soldiers became accustomed to spending their summers on strike duty in Cape Breton. Under pressure to demonstrate its concern, the Dominion government amended the Militia Act in 1924 to restrict the ease with which local magistrates could call out the armed forces.[21]

Since collective bargaining enjoyed no protection under the law, the industrial struggle often took the form of direct action. Still, the voice of labour was also heard in the political field. Independent labour candidates appeared in the provincial elections of 1920 in Nova Scotia and New Brunswick, often collaborating with the farmer candidates. The coal miners of Cumberland and Cape Breton were responsible for the election of the four labour MLAs in Nova Scotia in 1920, and they had high hopes that McLachlan would be sent to Ottawa as the MP for Cape Breton South–Richmond in 1921. In that election McLachlan easily captured the mining polls with absolute majorities and emerged from the industrial area as the leading candidate, only to be defeated by Liberal and Tory votes in the rural parts of the far-flung riding. McLachlan was obviously the miners' choice; his poll of more than 8,914 votes in 1921 was greater than the number of votes that elected J.S. Woodsworth in Winnipeg that same year, and Woodsworth himself keenly regretted McLachlan's absence from the House. For the coal miners, McLachlan's defeat underlined the limitations of parliamentary democracy as an instrument of working-class action. On several occasions the coal miners later advanced proposals for the reform of the parliamentary system to provide representation for occupational groups and social classes.[22]

In 1925 the new Conservative government in Nova Scotia appointed a royal commission, headed by a British coal-mining authority, Sir Andrew Rae Duncan. Not so well noted was the fact that Duncan was the vice-president of an employers' federation whose members included several BESCO directors and was also a former Liberal candidate who had been twice defeated by Labour candidates in the British elections. Although the Duncan Report scolded the company for its bad faith and intransigence towards unions, the royal commission accepted the logic of wage reductions as inevitable and predictably failed to endorse the union's call for public ownership of the industry. One of the commissioners, Ontario businessman Hume Cronyn, appealed to the people of central Canada to support this important Maritime industry in the interests of national unity, even at the expense of higher energy prices. Duncan himself did not endorse this appeal, and Cronyn included it as a personal addendum to the report. Privately, Cronyn was prepared to go even further and point out that there could be no solution to the industry's difficulties as long as Roy Wolvin remained at the helm.[23] But the provincial government had little taste for drastic measures. When the corporation failed to meet its required royalty payments in 1926, as required under the original leases granted to Dominion Coal in 1893, this presented the province with an opportunity to repossess the coal leases and reorganize the coal industry on a new basis. The province's deputy attorney general pointed out that this was a once-in-119-years' opportunity to correct the short-sighted terms of the coal leases. Hector McInnes, an influential Conservative and a member of the BESCO board, advised the premier to avoid rash action that might threaten the confidence of investors. As a result the business-minded Rhodes government shrank from taking action and instead allowed BESCO to slide gradually into bankruptcy.[24] By the end of the decade the industry had been reorganized on a more modest basis by Sir Herbert Holt and the Royal Bank of Canada.

The coal miners also hoped to offer leadership to a regional labour movement that transcended the coal industry itself. They were instrumental in promoting the growth of a provincial federation of labour and a labour party, and they underwrote the publication of the *Maritime Labor Herald*. The coal miners' rebellion was re-enacted, in more modest ways, by other groups of workers. The labour vote was apparent in the provincial elections and also in municipal politics in centres such as Saint John, Moncton, Amherst, New Glasgow, and Halifax. Already in the summer of 1920 there were strikes in the coal mines and shipyards and on the railways and street railways. Again, the issue of wage reductions was paramount as employers whittled away the gains achieved at the end of the war. In 1919 the Halifax carpenters had won a wage of sixty-six cents an hour, but by 1922 some carpenters were said to be earning only twenty-five cents an hour. Expressions of protest were found in the pages of the local labour newspaper, the *Citizen*, and at the meetings of the Halifax Trades and Labour Council, but the traditions of industrial militancy and political action that had marked the Halifax

The people's champion. J.B. McLachlan, a committed socialist, led the Nova Scotia coal miners' crusade for economic democracy.

labour movement in the previous decade were quickly disintegrating. The skills of urban craftsmen were more portable than those of the coal miners, and skilled workers joined the exodus to the more prosperous urban centres of North America. Those who remained devoted themselves to a narrower conception of trade unionism.[25]

Most workers, however, had not yet benefited from the appeals of union organization, and the working-class experience remained a fragmented one across the region. Unlike the Nova Scotia coal miners, the miners of the Minto coalfield in New Brunswick repeatedly failed to win recognition of the United Mine Workers, in part because the operators in this smaller coalfield continued to practise an effective politics of paternalism. Another unorganized group, the offshore fishermen employed in the schooner fishery, were especially vulnerable. When disastrous gales struck the Lunenburg fleet in August 1926 and again in August 1927, six vessels went down and 138 men were lost. Instead of taking steps to improve safety and require radios on the boats, the Nova Scotia government was concerned about the high cost of compensation claims. As a result fishermen were written out of the existing Workmen's Compensation Act and turned over to private insurance companies.[26]

In the 1920s most workers remained primarily concerned with the daily needs of their work and household. This was particularly true in the case of women workers. With a few exceptions, women's work in the household was rarely acknowledged as productive labour. The exceptions were those who were in a position to hire domestic servants. Women's work in the household also received recognition from the women's institutes that celebrated the skills of rural women in province-wide 'Thrift Exhibits,' and from the miners' wives who joined branches of the Women's Labour League and made their case in the labour press: 'A house is a woman's work-shop and she is there night and day the whole year through.' When women entered the paid labour market they inevitably found employment in what were considered to be women's jobs in stores, offices, factories, homes, and hospitals. Black women had even fewer options, recalled Carrie Best, a New Glasgow woman who went to Chicago to train as a nurse: 'Stenographers, clerks, waitresses, nurses or in fact any position other than a domestic or teacher in a black community was unheard of in those days in Nova Scotia.' Occasionally women workers confronted their employers, as in the case of a wage dispute between women operators and the Maritime Telephone Company in 1925. But there were no important changes in the condition of women employees during the 1920s. In Halifax women's annual wages in 1921 amounted to 50 per cent of male earnings, 52 per cent in Saint John, and little had changed ten years later.[27]

All was not defeat. The highly politicized class consciousness of the early 1920s, with its emphasis on the broad interests of the working class as a whole, was replaced by a more modest form of class consciousness that aimed to protect the interests of the smaller occupational group. Thus the coal miners continued to negotiate and sign contracts with their employers, a necessity that BESCO had been anxious to repudiate entirely. Under amendments to the Coal Mines Regulation Act in 1927 the check-off of union dues in the coal industry was protected by law. Similarly, the Halifax carpenters proved steady defenders of their members' interests. The building-trades council established a rigorous system of job protection through a card system and insisted on fair wages and conditions on public contracts. The carpenters themselves enforced a closed shop and by the end of the decade won back the acceptance of employers and the wage levels of 1919. In New Brunswick the provisions of workers' compensation were broadened to include loggers; when the employers protested the costs of such an insurance program, organized labour rallied successfully to defend this modest extension of government protection to workers. Even in the case of women workers there were some small symbolic signs of advance. In Nova Scotia a minimum wage for women workers was recommended in 1920, although there was no action until 1930; in New Brunswick a commission reported in favour of minimum wages in 1925, though action again was slow. These were ambivalent achievements in some respects, for the price of these limited forms of industrial legality and workers' rights appeared to be the sacrifice of more visionary hopes for economic democracy and social reconstruction. Yet these developments were not unique to the Maritimes and anticipated the historic accommodation between labour and capital that was to take place across North America in the 1930s and 1940s.[28]

IV

While labour radicals were battling to advance the cause of class struggle and economic democracy in the region, some of the most vocal protests of the 1920s spoke the language of regional protest and political reform. The coalition of interests and opinions that became known as the 'Maritime Rights' movement hoped to encourage solutions to the region's difficulties by mobilizing a sense of regional patriotism. Defenders of Maritime Rights acknowledged that the region had fared poorly in the years since Confederation, and they believed that solutions could be found by correcting the political imbalances. Accordingly they sought changes in those Dominion fiscal and transportation policies that they considered responsible for many of the region's difficulties. Accommodating themselves to the realities of the capitalist economy and the Canadian state, they simply sought to increase the political power of the region within Confederation.[29]

It was a challenging task, since representation in Parliament depended on the region's population. The number of Maritime seats in the House of Commons had declined from 43 seats in the 1870s to 31 in 1921. New Brunswick's representation had been reduced from 16 to 11, Prince Edward Island's from 6 to 4, and Nova Scotia's from 21 to 16. The size of the House of Commons meanwhile increased from 206 seats in 1874 to 235 in 1921. Nova Scotia would lose another 2 seats before the 1925 election, while the commons was increased by 10 seats. It also seemed that Maritime MPs often failed to exploit what influence they did have on the national scene. Powerful cabinet ministers such as W.S. Fielding, the former Nova Scotia premier and secessionist of the 1880s, had long since left the Maritimes and no longer identified themselves with the causes of the region. When the Liberals chose Sir Wilfrid Laurier's successor in 1919, however, the new party leader, William Lyon Mackenzie King, entered the House of Commons as the member for Prince County, Prince Edward Island. As leader of the opposition prior to the 1921 election, King did not hesitate to advance regional causes. The veteran MP from Cumberland, Hance J. Logan, who was also president of the Maritime Board of Trade in 1920, considered standing as an independent Maritime Rights candidate in 1921 until King convinced him that the

The people's railway  In the 1920s the Intercolonial Railway was swallowed up by the new Canadian National. The loss of regional control soon brought huge rate increases.

region's interests would be better served by the Liberal Party.

In the 1921 election Maritimers gave the Liberals twenty-five of their thirty-one MPs. Nevertheless, within the 1921 Parliament this contingent failed to mobilize its influence successfully in defence of regional interests. Had the Maritime Liberals been able to forge an alliance with the Labour and Progressive MPs, their numbers would have equalled those of Mackenzie King's Liberals in the minority 1921 Parliament. Instead King (now sitting for an Ontario seat) pursued a strategy of enforcing strict party discipline among the Maritimers and courting the Progressives with selective concessions. The most telling instance of such regional favouritism was the renewal of the Crowsnest Pass freight rates for western farmers in 1922; meanwhile, the Maritimers' objections to a 40 per cent increase in freight rates on the Intercolonial Railway remained unsatisfied.

Frustration in Parliament led Maritimers to pursue Maritime Rights through a public campaign to educate regional and national opinion on the subject of Maritime grievances. The agitation was most apparent in local boards of trade around the region. The boards arranged public meetings on regional issues and organized trainloads of delegates to carry their cause to Ottawa. The campaign was also prominent in the Conservative newspapers of the region, where publishers such as W.H. Dennis of the Halifax *Herald* and J.D. MacKenna of the Saint John *Telegraph-Journal* ably promoted the regional cause. A lively pamphlet literature fanned the flames, including F.B. McCurdy's strident tract *Nova Scotia's Right to Live* (1924). A wealthy financier and disillusioned former Conservative cabinet minister, F.B. McCurdy came to believe in a kind of sovereignty-association for the Maritimes in relation to continental Canada, an arrangement that would allow the region independence in commercial policy. Although he was regarded as a potential leader of the Nova Scotia Conservatives, by 1926 McCurdy had moved out of party politics and was promoting the League for the Economic Independence of Nova Scotia. Meanwhile, in April 1923 H.W. Corning, MLA for Yarmouth and leader of the Conservative Party in the Nova Scotia House of Assembly, presented a resolution proposing a referendum on 'the restoration of Nova Scotia to the status of an independent self-governing dominion.' This separatist resolution was voted down fourteen to four in the assembly but served to identify the Conservative Party with the issue of Maritime Rights.

Only a minority of Maritimers was prepared to follow the logic of regionalism far enough to contemplate some form of autonomy or independence under the British Crown. The radical regionalists such as McCurdy and Corning were soon superseded. Dennis and other back-room leaders of the Conservative Party secretly disowned Corning's separatist policy, but moved quickly to mobilize regional opinion behind the Conservative Party as the expression of regional sentiment. Corning died of typhoid in 1924, and party leader W.L. Hall was deposed amid reports of scandal, thus clearing the way for Dennis and his associates to recruit a distinguished expatriate Maritimer to serve as party leader and future premier. E.N. Rhodes was not only an Ontario businessman and former speaker of the House of Commons but also the son of the Amherst manufacturer Nelson Rhodes, founder of Rhodes, Curry and Company.

The movement proved its appeal at election time, when Maritime Rights was a common cry in provincial and Dominion elections. In December 1923, running the aged W.A. Black of the ancient shipping firm Pickford and Black, the revitalized Conservatives won a federal by-election in Halifax. Then in Kent County, New Brunswick, the Conservatives surprised themselves by winning a second by-election in a largely Acadian district, traditional Liberal territory. In this case Alexandre Dou-

# Where's My Boy?

THIS is the cry that is going forth from every home, from every hamlet in Nova Scotia. For, after 43 years of Provincial misrule, and in spite of the bountiful gifts of Providence, close to two hundred thousand Nova Scotians have been driven into exile, forced across the border to earn the living denied them at home.

**We have shrunk from third to seventh place in the list of Canadian Provinces**

**We have lost one third of our representation at Ottawa.**

We have seen sections of our country side die, our villages decay, our towns and cities lose pride of place to cities that weren't founded when partisan politics laid its blighting hand on our prosperity.

Sadder than this, more serious than this, is the shadow of this misrule as it falls across the thresholds of Nova Scotia. Sons, daughters, husbands, fathers—a hundred thousand homes have experienced the pang of parting from the loved ones

All that is yesterday. TODAY THE TIDE IS TURNED. The people of Nova Scotia are through forever with partisan politicians, promises, personalities. There is only one issue in this election. Only one object before every elector—to throw the burden of a discredited Government off our backs and put in power a party of earnest men, who, taking charge of affairs of the Province, will make it the land Nature intended it to be.

For the sake of our families, for the sake of our future, for the sake of our country, we are going to think of the loved exile on election day and

IN the year 1923 one single steamship line took out 15,273 Nova Scotians MORE than it returned. The leak is going on by all steamers, schooners and trains. The Machine Politicians are responsible. SCRAP THE LOT AND STOP THE LEAK.

# Vote Him Back Home

### Vote Against The Government That Drove Him Into Exile
### Vote For a change that will give A Good Living For All Nova Scotians

On Thursday, June 25th, Place the Interests of Your Province ABOVE Party
--DO IT FOR NOVA SCOTIA.

'Where's My Boy?' In the provincial election of 1925 Nova Scotia's Conservatives encouraged women voters to support Maritime Rights as a way of restoring jobs that would, they suggested, allow thousands of migrant workers to return home.

cet, an independent farmer candidate in 1921 and a leader of the local branch of the Société l'Assomption, had emphasized local grievances rather than his loyalty to the party of Arthur Meighen. Provincially, the Liberals lost power in Prince Edward Island in 1923, and then in Nova Scotia and New Brunswick in 1925. In the Dominion elections of 1925

Maritimers also abandoned the Liberals and voted heavily for the Conservative Party. In 1921 the Liberals had won twenty-five of the region's thirty-one seats, but in 1925 the Conservatives won twenty-three of twenty-nine seats, enough to place King's Liberals second to Meighen's Conservatives in the new House of Commons and help precipitate a period of political and constitutional confusion in Ottawa. Despite King's appointment of the Royal Commission on Maritime Claims, in the 1926 election twenty of the twenty-nine seats remained Conservative. In 1927 the Conservatives named an ex-Maritimer as the party's national leader, and in the 1930 election R.B. Bennett's party won twenty-three of the region's twenty-nine seats.

The broad rhetoric of regionalism tended to obscure the narrow social base of the movement. Maritime Rights was dominated by the professionals and businessmen of the region, especially those in the port cities and railway towns, which stood to benefit the most from improvements in federal policies. The rank and file of this social movement were found in the local boards of trade, and Maritime Rights can be credited with briefly restoring the hopes and expectations of the region's business community. When the 'Great Delegation' travelled to Ottawa in February 1925 to present the region's grievances at a Maritime Day in Ottawa, the composition of the delegation was heavily dominated by the region's boards of trade and members of Parliament. The majority of the 300 delegates came from the single city of Saint John, and representatives of such groups as farmers, fishermen, and industrial workers were conspicuously few in number. The Maritime case, as presented in the railway committee room of the House of Commons, was unsystematic and largely devoted to the pleas of Saint John for a greater share of the Dominion's export trade.

More than any other social class, the region's business community succeeded in identifying its interests with the larger cause of regional patriotism. Nevertheless, the business community in the Maritimes occupied an ambivalent position, and the region could not rely fully on the patriotism of its capitalists. Many successful local entrepreneurs had found that their best interests lay in making an accommodation with the banks and corporations of central Canada. While industrial employment in towns such as Amherst was virtually wiped out by shutdowns in the 1920s, the responsibility could not be placed entirely with malevolent outside interests. When Canadian Car and Foundry closed its doors in Amherst in the 1920s, it was only following a strategy of centralizing the production of rolling stock in its Montreal and Fort William shops; this strategy had been under way ever since the company was created in 1909 and was supervised by Nathaniel Curry, the former president of Rhodes, Curry. As a result, he was now in a position to pursue a successful industrial and financial career from a new base in Montreal. Similarly, the collapse of another old family firm, Robb Engineering, was arranged by the Dominion Bridge Company of Montreal, which had gradually acquired control of the local firm. While tariff and freight rates exacerbated the difficulties of local industry, it was also true that the day of the community-minded entrepreneur had given way to an age of industrial consolidation and financial centralization. At best, adjustments in federal policy promised only to prolong the decline.[30]

Maritime businessmen also perceived that alliances with metropolitan business were capable of producing increased economic activity within the region. If industrial employment was collapsing in factory towns such as Amherst, increased activity in the distribution of goods on behalf of the metropolis was bringing some limited expansion to centres such as Moncton. While some 1,500 people lost their factory jobs in Amherst in the 1920s, in Moncton the establishment in 1920 of a mail-order centre by the T. Eaton Company of Toronto created more than 750 new jobs.[31] Similarly, if few Maritime Rights spokesmen were prepared to defend the British Empire Steel Corporation, they could be grateful that they were not called upon to evaluate the regional loyalties of other major regional businesses, such as the Bank of Nova Scotia, which for at least a generation had been responsible for the transfer of spectacular quantities of investment capital out of the region.[32]

On the whole, Maritime Rights had a favourable view of Canada as a progressive, modernizing nation. The main body of opinion within the movement favoured policies of economic nationalism and increased integration of the Maritimes into the Canadian economy. Nowhere was this better reflected than in the assiduous campaign for improvements in Maritime transportation. The integration of the region into the national transportation network was far from complete. The troubles of the Intercolonial Railway in maintaining a semblance of regional autonomy and protecting its status as a public enterprise became one of the *causes célèbres* of the 1920s. Similarly, the claims of Saint John and Halifax to be regarded as the winter ports of the Dominion, in preference to Portland, Maine, and other American outlets, represented a long-held ambition to be recognized as the wharf of the Dominion, particularly for the purposes of the nation's leading export, the grain trade. In the case of Prince Edward Island, the fulfilment of the Confederation agreement to provide 'continuous communication' between the province and the mainland had been perfunctory at best.

It was predictable that the appeal of Maritime Rights would often ring false in labour circles, where it was recognized that employers were always keen to appeal to workers to make sacrifices for the benefit of their employer. Although longshoremen's leader James Tighe in Saint

John participated in the Great Delegation of 1925 and defended the interests of the port city, other labour leaders were less enthusiastic about Maritime Rights. Opposition to a regional rate of exploitation represented by longer hours and lower wages had become one of the staple themes of labour protest in the Maritimes in the first decades of the twentieth century. In the case of the coal industry, labour spokesmen recognized that their industry faced a crisis of markets and were inclined to favour the protection of a national market for coal. Their concern over tariff policy, however, was eclipsed by the battle against their principal enemy, popularly referred to as the British *Vampire* Steel Corporation. When the Associated Boards of Trade of Cape Breton Island organized a delegation to Ottawa in the fall of 1924, the miners and steelworkers rejected invitations to participate. The lone representative from Glace Bay proved to be a colourful local Liberal magistrate, A.B. MacGillivray. Later the *Maritime Labor Herald* would describe the Cape Breton Maritime Rights delegation to Ottawa as the 'direct and open result of the underground manipulation of Besco.' In the atmosphere created by BESCO an appeal for protection of the coal and steel industries was doomed to receive little support in the local community.[33]

The principal achievement of the Maritime Rights movement was Mackenzie King's decision to appoint a royal commission to investigate 'Maritime Claims.' The investigation was chaired by Sir Andrew Rae Duncan, whose pacification of the coal miners after the 1925 strike was regarded as a notable success. The other two appointees were distinguished Maritimers, a Halifax judge and a McGill professor, who both enjoyed good credentials as Liberals. The Duncan Commission hearings provided an opportunity for Maritimers to air their grievances, and they did not fail to do so. When Duncan and his commissioners submitted their report to the Dominion government in September 1926, the Nova Scotia government was still continuing to distribute copies of the province's submission from July. Judged by the expectations of that extensive catalogue of grievances, the final report failed to vindicate the Maritime Rights claim that Dominion policies had forced the region into a condition of 'dilapidation and decay.'[34]

The distinction between 'Maritime Rights' and 'Maritime Claims' was not lost on the commissioners. The Duncan Report was a highly political document. It repudiated the Maritime Rights version of regional history while admitting the necessity of a sympathetic hearing for the region's pleas of incapacity. The attempt to blame Confederation for the decline of the region stood condemned as a historical fallacy. It was true 'that the Maritime Provinces have not prospered and developed, either in population, or in commercial, industrial and rural enterprise, as fully as other portions of Canada.' But, the report continued, 'We are unable to take the view that Confederation, is, of itself, responsible for this fact ...' The region's troubles were said to be 'unrelated to Confederation' and 'would have taken place whether or not the Maritime Provinces had been independent units outside of Confederation.' Nevertheless, 'a better balance of territorial prosperity' was considered a desirable national objective, and Maritime claims deserved 'sympathetic consideration and understanding.'[35]

Pleas of poverty received the most sympathy, and the Duncan Commission recommended a complete revision of the financial arrangements between the Dominion and the Maritime provinces. The commissioners refrained from making specific suggestions, however, and pending further action by the Dominion, the commission simply advocated that the annual Dominion subsidy be increased by $875,000 to Nova Scotia, $600,000 to New Brunswick, and $125,000 to Prince Edward Island. In the realm of transportation, it was agreed that some unfairness might have entered into the fixing of freight rates in recent years. There were recommendations to assist Maritime exports by reducing railway freight rates by 20 per cent both within the Maritimes and on traffic to central Canada, with a view to restoring these rates to what was considered to be the national average. The railway itself was gently treated: Canadian National Railways could expect to be compensated for any resulting loss of revenue. In his automobile tours around the region Duncan had personally witnessed the extraordinary complications involved in travel to Prince Edward Island, and improvements in rail and ferry service for this province were also included among the recommendations.

The report also recommended the establishment of port commissions for Halifax and Saint John harbours. The commission endorsed the view that harbour development could be as important to Canadian development as the earlier development of railways and canals. It is interesting that the report's only direct critique of private entrepreneurship was directed at the ports, where it was said that 'under existing conditions of proprietorship at these ports, there will neither be inducement enough, nor impetus enough, to create really great ports.' These remarks also included an implicit critique of Canada's lack of an adequate 'ocean policy,' though it was pointed out that the use of public authority for the development of railways and canals ahead of ports 'has naturally come first.'[36]

On a number of other issues, the report offered little. The problem of the region's declining representation in Parliament was conveniently considered to be outside the commission's terms of reference. In respect to commercial policies, the report pointed out only that trade treaties with the United States for fresh fish and forest products might be considered. At the same time, increased tariff protection for coal and steel was deferred to a tariff advisory board for consideration. There was strong criticism of the condition of agriculture, where it was judged that 'the responsibility for its backward condition rests primarily upon the industry itself and upon the provinces.' No specific recommendations were made, except that the provinces should introduce more vigorous agricultural-development policies and recognize the significance of improved distribution and co-operative marketing methods. The provinces were also advised to do more to encourage the tourist trade.[37]

Regional politicians made the best of the disappointing report, but they may have made a tactical error in describing it as the Maritimes 'Magna Carta.' Following the report of the Duncan Commission, Premier Baxter of New Brunswick said, the Maritimes stood before Canada in the position of a plaintiff whose cause has been endorsed by the courts. The Maritime Freight Rates Act (1927) implemented some of the railway recommendations, and the Dominion Fuel Act (1927) allowed subsidies to coking plants using Canadian coal. Similarly there was harbour-board legislation for Halifax and Saint John and funding for a new Prince Edward Island ferry. Indeed by 1928 P.J. Veniot, the former New Brunswick Liberal premier and now a member of King's cabinet, claimed that the government had already implemented eight of the ten main recommendations.[38] Regional solidarity was breaking down, and by 1929 the new Liberal premier of Prince Edward Island, A.C. Saunders, hoping for more prompt action to adjust the Island's provincial subsidy, was failing to co-operate with his fellow Maritime premiers, both Tories.[39]

Of all the issues raised by Maritime Rights, that of discriminatory freight rates and underdeveloped transportation ties to the rest of the country probably received the most national attention. The Maritime Freight Rates Act was acclaimed as the Maritimes version of the Crow's Nest Pass Agreement. The establishment of harbour boards in Halifax and Saint John represented a rare resort to the strategy of nationalization and public enterprise by the Canadian state in the 1920s, and considerable investment and expertise would be poured into the improvement of these ports. In 1928, Parliament approved an expenditure of $1 million for the construction of a second ferry to link Prince Edward Island to the mainland; the ss *Charlottetown* was finally launched in 1931, in time to replace the weatherbeaten *Prince Edward Island* as the province's only link with the mainland. Flawed as they were in implementation, these measures represented tangible concessions to regional interests. In retrospect, however, they seem to have had little force in affecting the shape of regional development in the Maritimes. Soon afterwards Harold Innis would feel obliged to remind Maritimers that adjustments in transportation policy could not solve the region's problems; indeed, the economic conquest of the region had been steadily advancing along the railway lines for more than fifty years, bringing western goods in and taking eastern people out.[40] The tragedy of the Maritime Rights movement was that some of the causes it championed tended to increase the dependency of the region. Yet the increased integration of the region into Confederation would not necessarily increase the stability or independence of the regional economy. Much of what Maritime Rights had wanted and the Duncan Report had provided was designed to increase the integration of the region into Confederation. In this sense the Maritime Rights movement was not regionalist but nationalist in its ambitions.

The Duncan Report markedly failed to revive enthusiasm for the Liberal government among Maritimers. The best that can be said is that, in the 1920s, the Dominion was still groping towards a recognition of its responsibilities for the uneven development of the Canadian economy. In the short run, the cause of Maritime Rights reinvigorated regional politics and provided Maritimers with a powerful myth of regional grievances against Confederation. This would remain a lasting staple of regional politics and culture. Nevertheless, the failure of the report and the weakness of subsequent action may simply have increased Maritime cynicism about the prospects of achieving significant changes through the political process. For some it may have increased the appeal of nonpolitical solutions to regional problems. But for many Maritimers it simply confirmed their sceptical appreciation of the weakness of the hinterland within the Canadian state.

V

From a late-twentieth-century perspective, it is easy to exaggerate the significance of the state in shaping the region's experience in earlier times. Just as many Maritimers failed to recognize the significance of Confederation until long after the event, so too did many Maritimers seek less formal solutions to the challenges of regional underdevelopment and regional identity. As Antonine Maillet has written, in the case of the Acadians in the 1920s, the laws made in places such as Ottawa and Fredericton often took some time to filter down to the local communities and to be deciphered and interpreted in appropriate ways.[41]

One of the region's few boom industries in the 1920s was certainly the unintended result of state intervention by Dominion, provincial, and American governments. While moral reformers had expected prohibition to bring about a brave new world, many Maritimers regarded it in a more matter-of-fact fashion. The context of prohibition offered economic opportunity for the region, and it was soon apparent that the entrepreneurial spirit was alive and well along the coastlines of the Maritime provinces, where unemployed fishing vessels found new scope in carrying cargoes of rum into isolated coves and inlets. For their fish, schooners could expect a price of around two cents per pound from local merchants, about two-thirds of which would be consumed by the cost of bait, provisions, gear, gas, and owners' shares. It was not surprising that fishing schooners were soon converting to the more lucrative liquor trade. The carrying trade brought rum, whisky, and wines from the Caribbean through warehouses at St Pierre and then on through the Maritimes into New England. The end of prohibition in Nova Scotia and New Brunswick did not bring the trade to a close, for as long as prohibition remained in effect in the United States local schooners would continue to make regular deliveries to 'Rum Row' in offshore New England, and the newly constructed highways of New Brunswick would carry carloads of Canadian booze to the American border. The more times a cargo changed hands, the more widely the risk was distributed and the more widely the income shared as well. Yet Maritimers were rarely more than middlemen in the traffic, the small fry in an increasingly monopolized and internationally controlled commerce. The end of prohibition in New Brunswick in 1927 and in Nova Scotia in 1929 in favour of state control of liquor sales represented not only the abandonment of an experiment in social engineering but also the expropriation by the government of a successful, cash-producing economic sector.[42]

Another ambitious social reform of the decade was the attempt to bring the region's six most important universities together in some form of union. A small region within the North Atlantic community, the Maritimes could nevertheless strive to excel in the educational field. Progressive reformers understood that a good education was like a passport to the opportunities of the outside world. Indeed, no single institution was more responsible for promoting the exodus of educated Maritimers than the well-established educational establishments of the region. Local school boards constantly lamented the departure of young, able teachers, while reports of alumni activities disclosed disturbing evidence of the continuing exodus. More than one-third of the graduates of Acadia University in the 1920s moved to the United States. From his position as vice-president of St Francis Xavier University at Antigonish, Father Jimmy Tompkins perceived the ambivalent promise of education more clearly than most of his contemporaries. Experienced in attracting alumni support, he aroused the interest of the Carnegie Corporation of New York in the region's educational problems. Following a study that documented the weaknesses and fragmentation of higher education in the Maritimes, the foundation announced that it was willing to provide $3 million for the establishment of a federated university of the Maritime provinces. Tompkins' own hopes for federation were linked to a belief that the educational facilities could be adapted to the larger needs of the region, yet the individual universities, including his own, failed to see how this could be achieved by centralization in Halifax. The whole enterprise foundered on the failure of the individual universities to subordinate local interests to a larger regional cause. The only development was the removal of King's College from Windsor to Halifax. Tompkins himself almost disappeared into obscurity, exiled to the outports by the church hierarchy, but the aging priest found a new cause in his contact with the fishermen of Canso. He became an enthusiastic defender of adult education and co-operative solutions to their problems, and ultimately the Antigonish Movement of the 1930s succeeded in accommodating much of the rural discontent of the 1920s. Meanwhile, the philanthropy of the Carnegie Corporation and other agencies was funnelled into individual projects for the improvement of public-health and educational facilities in the region, anticipating the future role of the welfare state in compensating Maritimers for the effects of regional underdevelopment.[43]

Meanwhile, a more successful unity movement was taking place within the Methodist and Presbyterian churches. Catholics and Anglicans watched in curiosity as the new United Church of Canada officially came into being on 10 June 1925. The new church had been in the process of formation for more than twenty years, and the major architects included Maritime progressives such as Clarence MacKinnon, moderator of the Presbyterian Church in 1924 and principal of the church's Pine Hill divinity college in Halifax since 1909. Many of the strongest proponents of church union on the national scene were former Maritimers, such as Robert Falconer of the University of Toronto and Walter Murray of the University of Saskatchewan. Indeed, in many respects, the call for church union was a response to national challenges. The rapid growth of a foreign immigrant population in the big cities and in western Canada presented the Protestant churches with an immense missionary challenge, and it was not hard for many supporters to see the United Church as a national church dedicated to the Christianization and Canadianization of the population. Even at the most practical level of supplying ministers, whether it was to the burgeoning western frontier or to the depleted districts of the Maritimes, the merger promised a better allocation of resources and greater efficiency in church work. The impact of the Social Gospel, with its emphasis on pragmatic moral and social reforms such as prohibition and public health, had helped to undermine theological obstacles to church union; for many supporters of church union the prospect of establishing God's kingdom on earth was more important than the perpetuation of separate establishments or doctrinal differences. Before the union there was co-operation in settlement houses and missionary work, and indeed by 1924 in the Maritimes more than 30 congregations of Presbyterians and Methodists were already meeting to worship jointly. Those who opposed the union tended to be associated with more conservative views of the role of the church. Many also had reservations about the power of the state to legislate church members into a new church from which they would then be required to withdraw. As a result there were some heated moments in the provincial legislatures in 1924, and in Prince Edward Island the lieutenant-governor initially refused to sign the union legislation into law. But there was nothing to distinguish the region as a stronghold of conservatism or parochialism. The call to build a new national church received a favourable response in the Maritimes, and in the end all the Methodist congregations and 498 of the 634 Presbyterian congregations joined the union.[44]

Meanwhile Maritimers also did their best to join the automobile revolution, which was well under way across North America during the 1920s. Like the building of the railways, the construction of highways helped to integrate the region into the continental transportation network and allowed some Maritimers to benefit from new opportunities. New Brunswick premier P.J. 'Good Roads' Veniot took quick advantage of Dominion legislation to secure subsidies of more than $1.2 million for the building of highways, until the program was discontinued in 1924. New Brunswick was successful in laying down an extensive network of gravel roads during the decade, and in 1929 it was noted that as many as twenty thousand people received some employment in road construction during that year. In Buctouche a young Kenny Irving became fascinated by the attractions of the Model-T, turned his back on his father's lumber business, and began selling cars and building service stations; eventually K.C. Irving would control the largest personal business empire in the Maritimes. Meanwhile, Maritimers also did their best to attract motor-driving tourists, especially from the New England states, and the gasoline taxes paid by these travellers were especially useful in helping to pay the costs of the roads. To conform with American practice, the rule of the road was shifted from left to right in Nova Scotia and New Brunswick in 1922.[45]

Almost as compensation for the difficulties of the decade, the 1920s also witnessed the upsurge of a romantic regional culture. In historical literature it was typified by evocations of the golden age, such as F.W. Wallace's *Wooden Ships and Iron Men* (1924). A film version of Wallace's novel *Blue Water* was filmed near Saint John in 1922, though it was found that 'New Brunswick sea water was too chilly for many of the situations required,' and the film was completed in Florida. In poetry an eclectic group of Song Fishermen, including Robert Norwood and Andrew Merkel, celebrated a romantic vision of the Maritimes, conjuring

Right turn. With the coming of the automobile, the rule of the road was shifted from left to right, largely to accommodate the droves of motor-tourists from the United States who were expected to fill the roads and help pay for them with their gasoline taxes.

with the imagery of ships and shorelines. Meanwhile Michael Whelan's *Canada, Queen of the North* (1927) underlined the extent to which the regional culture had associated itself with the promotion of a pan-Canadian national identity. Some of the characteristic dilemmas of the region were explored by young Acadian writer James Branch; his play *L'émigrant acadien* (1929) offered the official view that a return to the soil offered the best promise of survival in the modern world. Realistic novels such as Louis Arthur Cunningham's *This Thing Called Love* (1929) and Frank Parker Day's *Rockbound* (1928) found little favour upon publication. A voice of social protest such as that of the worker-poet Dawn

Fraser in Cape Breton achieved considerable local popularity in the industrial community with his *Echoes from Labor's War* (1924), but received no recognition at all in literary circles.[46]

While the fisheries charted a troubled course in the 1920s, the industry was entering the realm of legend. The sailing skills of the fishing crews were being celebrated in an international racing competition organized by W.H. Dennis of the Halifax *Herald*. The North Atlantic Fishermen's International Trophy was open only to bona-fide fishing schooners and immediately became a contest between New England and Nova Scotia vessels. In 1920 the trophy and prize money of $4,000 were carried off by a Gloucester schooner. The following year a sleek new fishing vessel was built and launched by Smith and Rhuland at Lunenburg in time for the fishing season. Captained by Angus Walters, the *Bluenose* captured the prize that fall and triumphed again in 1922. In 1923 the races ended in controversy when the judges decided that the *Bluenose* had committed a minor infraction of the rules. The races were suspended until 1931, when the *Bluenose* finally entered regional mythology as the ultimate of the fishing schooners.[47]

The Acadians were also in danger of being relegated to the realm of the picturesque. This was partly the doing of the tourist promotions and literary representations of the region, which underlined the romantic image of the vanished land of Evangeline; contemporary Acadians were seen as little more than residual figures in the landscape, occasionally dressing up in peasant costumes for the benefit of the passers-by. The traditional leadership of Acadian society was also complicit in encouraging Acadians to regard themselves as a people who did not belong in the modern world; conservative clerical teachings prescribed loyalty to the church and to the land as the best guarantees of Acadian survival in a threatening world. Under the influence of priests such as the Quebec-born Louis-Joseph-Arthur Melanson, who later became bishop of Moncton, Acadians in New Brunswick were encouraged to settle new lands under difficult frontier conditions. In practice the Acadians on the land often turned to the woods, working in local sawmills or cutting pulpwood for contractors. Like other rural Maritimers they also left their homes to settle in urban centres such as Moncton or to migrate long distances to work on construction sites and in milltowns in New England and northern Ontario. In doing so, individuals and families were pursuing their own makeshift survival strategies in Acadia as in the rest of the region.

Still the Acadians were an especially vulnerable group within the region's population, accounting in 1921 for 31.2 per cent of the population in New Brunswick but only 13.5 per cent in Prince Edward Island and 10.8 per cent in Nova Scotia. The crisis of leadership in Acadian

The *Bluenose*. Built at Lunenburg in 1921, this sleek fishing schooner captured the imagination of Canadians. But, while the *Bluenose* was winning trophies, most fishermen were struggling for survival and some were rum-running.

society was manifested in 1926, with the shutdown of *Le moniteur acadien*, the traditional voice of the Acadian leadership. Moreover it was all too obvious that Acadians were underrepresented in the broader regional causes of the decade and that the provincial legislatures contained disproportionately low numbers of Acadian representatives. It was true that P.J. Veniot became premier of New Brunswick in 1923, but he was not able to win the 1925 election. In that election the province divided sharply along ethnic lines, with the Liberals electing members only in the Acadian districts. The Liberals charged that Ku Klux Klan organizers had infiltrated the province to help bring down the government with racist propaganda. The other key election issue was the government's decision to promote publicly owned hydroelectric power, a decision that brought down the wrath of the large lumber operators, who preferred to reserve the project for private enterprise; they were also unhappy with high stumpage rates for wood cut on Crown lands and with the Liberals' administration of the Workmen's Compensation Act. Veniot himself represented a new kind of Acadian politician, a successful businessman and a member of the secular élite who was not closely associated with traditional causes. In this respect he was a forerunner of the new Acadian bourgeoisie, which would begin to come into its own in the 1960s. Following his defeat in 1925, Veniot entered federal politics and served as a cabinet minister in the Liberal government of the late 1920s.[48]

Regional consciousness was especially strong in some of the larger cities of North America that had become home to the emigrant Maritimers. In Winnipeg and Boston, for instance, there were clubs and publications that maintained a sense of regional identity in faraway places. They commented on news from home and, in moments of crisis such as the great strikes of the coal miners in the 1920s, organized support in the form of fund raising and bundles of food and clothing. Yet the rise of sentiment and nostalgia in regional culture was also a sign that the region's culture was becoming a home for the residual traditions and folkways of North America. Throughout North America local cultures were waning before the advance of the mass popular culture transmitted by radio and movies. The cultivation of nostalgia was a particularly appropriate function for a region that had suffered such a large loss of population. The New Brunswick Tourist and Resource Association sponsored a steamship pilgrimage to Boston, and Nova Scotia sponsored an Old Home Week, all designed to attract former Maritimers with the lure of nostalgia. Such episodes as the designation of Louisbourg as a national historic site in 1928 marked the beginning of concerted efforts to commemorate and exploit the region's historical heritage. For those with an anti-modernist urge to locate primitive frontiers and simple folk, there had always been the Acadians, but in the 1920s Nova Scotians also began to promote picturesque locations such as Peggy's Cove – which was not only rough and exotic but also conveniently close to Halifax.[49]

Regional identity also found expression in the realm of sports. International victories such as that of Sydney Mines native Johnny Miles, who won the Boston Marathon in record time in 1926, were seen as vindications of the rugged regional spirit. The Maritime Championship in rugby football, symbolized by the McCurdy Cup, donated by the promoter of Maritime Rights, was the subject of intense rivalries. In the wake of the bitter coal strikes of the first half of the decade, much of the community spirit of Glace Bay focused on the achievements of the Caledonia Amateur Athletic Club. Under coach John McCarthy, the club's rugby team perfected a style that relied on precision in passing and the sturdy physical skills and team spirit of the coal miners. In competing for the McCurdy Cup against Halifax college students, it was clear that the coal miners were defending both local and class loyalties. In 1929 they became regional heroes when they brought home the McTier Cup from the Eastern Canadian Championship in Montreal.[50]

But the sporting world remained an essentially male preserve. There were perceptible class differences in female sports: the ladylike sports were confined largely to golf, tennis, badminton, curling, and skating; working-class women were more likely to participate in softball, volleyball, hockey, track and field, and speed skating. A Maritime Ladies' Track and Field Championship was organized for the first time in 1927, providing opportunities for talented athletes such as Gertrude Phinney to demonstrate their abilities. Phinney subsequently set several Canadian records and won the Canadian championship in the 220-yard dash. She qualified for the 1928 Olympic team, but yielded to her father's advice, based on the medical orthodoxy of the times, that strenuous exercise could be dangerous to the feminine physique.[51]

Nor did the arrival of the franchise do much to undermine the conventional wisdom regarding the role of women. In 1922 Prince Edward Island was the last of the three Maritime provinces to extend the franchise to women (Newfoundland would do so in 1925). Liberal premier John Bell had included the pledge in his 1919 election campaign and considered that, particularly with the arrival of the Dominion franchise in 1918, the province 'must recognize and keep pace with the march of public sentiment.' As had happened in Nova Scotia in 1918, women were at the same time also permitted to hold office. This was not the case in New Brunswick, where the franchise was extended in 1919 but the right to hold office was withheld until 1934. There were no victories by woman candidates in provincial or federal elections in the 1920s, and it appears that woman voters were prepared to join the men in voting along lines of class and regional interest. One of the few woman candidates in the 1925 Dominion election, music teacher Minnie Bell Adney, received only eighty-four votes running as an independent candidate in Victoria-Carleton. For married women domesticity remained the rule. Muriel McQueen, the daughter of a prominent Liberal and a lawyer in her own right, campaigned in support of the New Brunswick Liberals in 1925, but following her marriage in 1926 she retired in support of her husband's law practice. Her public activity was limited to the Imperial Order of the Daughters of the Empire and the Grand Falls Literary Society; later she opened a tea-room and a bed-and-breakfast establishment. It was only her husband's lengthy illness and early death that brought her back into legal practice and eventually in the 1950s into politics.[52]

VI

On a Saturday night in the winter of 1923 in the crowded ballroom of Montreal's Windsor Hotel, Winnifred Blair of Saint John, New Brunswick, was crowned as the first Miss Canada. Miss Blair returned home from the Montreal Winter Carnival in triumph. At railway stations Miss Canada was greeted by cheering crowds, and a short tour of the region followed. In Fredericton she was honoured at the opening of the provincial legislature, and in Glace Bay she descended No. 2 colliery and tried her hand at mining coal. Although the city of Halifax was also represented in the Montreal contest, the Halifax *Herald* commented with satisfaction that 'the contest which had resolved itself into one of East versus West has been decided in favour of the Maritime Provinces. The decision of the five judges ... was considered satisfactory, excepting perhaps to a section of the western party.' In Cape Breton, Dawn Fraser, best known for his verses of social protest on behalf of labour radicalism, attributed Miss Blair's victory directly to the existing sense of regional grievance:

These Maritimes, the papers say,
Are falling backward every day.
'Cause all the cream and all that's best
Is grabbed up by the Middle West.
Miss Canada, we wonder how
You keep the laurels on your brow;
Brave little champion of the East,
We got our rights for once at least.

Yet the excitement surrounding Miss Blair's victory was short-lived. Although she did travel briefly to the United States during her reign, she had little desire to exploit her position or to seek fame and fortune. There would be no movie career, no national tour, and no audience with Queen Mary. Like most residents of the region, she was preoccupied with the problems of making a living. As a stenographer she was earning ten dollars a week. Her father, a former telegraph operator, had died of wounds received in the First World War. At nineteen years of age, Miss Blair was helping to support her widowed mother and a younger brother and sister. In the Maritimes, regional and class loyalties have always been closely entangled, and Miss Blair's short reign as a regional hero was followed by a return to the office. Like most Maritimers she was only recognizing that the demands of class could not be extinguished by the appeals of region.[53]

Like the residents of other peripheral regions within the industrial states of the early twentieth century, the people of the Maritimes adjusted uneasily to their condition of dependency in the modern world. There was no uniform response shared equally, for the region was unevenly touched by the forces of industry and capital. Identities based on class and region contended for hegemony, but neither fully succeeded in harnessing the dissatisfaction of Maritimers, and the radical moments of resistance in the early 1920s gave way to a more conservative regionalism after 1925. The Canadian state intervened in modest ways to maintain the legitimacy of Confederation, but none of these efforts resolved the historical and structural inequalities confronting the region. In retrospect, we may conclude that the 1920s helped place issues of regional disparity and economic democracy on the Canadian political agenda. But it was an agenda that Canada would be slow to recognize. When the Great Depression of the 1930s arrived, other Canadians would also know what it meant to be the victims of forces they could not control.

CHAPTER EIGHT

# The 1930s
## Depression and Retrenchment

The decade of the 1930s was coloured throughout by the Great Depression. Dependent upon primary production and international trade, the Maritime economy was hit harder than that of any region east of the Prairies. No stranger to economic recession, the Maritimes found this one particularly severe because their primary source of relief in the past – emigration – was closed to them. The Americans sealed their borders, and other provinces hedged their social programs with long-residency requirements. With the Depression's threat to personal economic security so widespread, people and governments often appeared at their worst. Anomalies in Canada's constitution made it convenient for different levels of government to disclaim responsibility for the needy. Moreover, Canada's initial ventures in social welfare discriminated against poorer provinces by making their participation conditional upon their ability to match federal contributions. In those provinces unable to do so, the system often translated into harsher treatment for those requiring aid.

Though threatened with destitution, many Maritimers fought back through organization. The unemployed formed unions to protect their interests, traditional labour organizations fought to defend previous advances, and farmers, fishermen, and woods workers experimented with new structures featuring study groups, co-operatives, and credit unions. Cultural institutions expanded, and although women's institutions made little progress, there were individual gains. The most successful politicians were those skilful in giving the illusion that more was being done with less. The sense of regional grievance, which had peaked during the 1920s, persisted in discussions of constitutional reform. Although Maritime provincial governments were reluctant to admit the disparity between their social programs and those of other provinces, they ultimately focused their demands for reform on the principle of fiscal need as the basis for federal subsidies.

Pulp mill under construction, Dalhousie, N.B., 1929. The transition from saw logs to pulp and paper was accelerated during the 1930s. Such mills were the only factories built in the Maritimes for some time.

THE WELFARE CRISIS

As the decade opened, the region was enjoying a rare construction boom, as projects arising from regional agitation and the Duncan Commission came to fruition. Investments in pulp and paper saw the completion in 1929 and 1930 of new plants at Liverpool and Dalhousie and the expansion of existing facilities at Grand Falls and Bathurst. Government and private funds were channelled into the development of tourism, as provincial governments used a portion of their increased subsidies to finance borrowing for road-building schemes of which the federal government paid a share of the cost. Meanwhile, private capital was attracted to major hotels in Halifax, Saint John, Charlottetown, Digby, and Pictou. In 1929 the National Harbours Board borrowed several millions of dollars to begin the renovation of port facilities at Halifax and Saint John. With business good at the beginning of the decade, the region's promoters and press continued to boast of better conditions as part of a campaign to attract investment.[1] Their efforts backfired, however, as there was little investment to attract, and the resulting myth of Maritime prosperity gave federal politicians an excuse for limiting relief funds to the region and for resisting its demands for constitutional reform.

The reality was very different. Closed out of traditional markets by the American Smoot-Hawley tariff of 1930 and Canada's later failure to follow Great Britain in devaluing its currency, primary producers in the Maritimes saw their products decline in value even more sharply than those of their counterparts in the central provinces. From 1929 to 1933 the value of timber production dropped 75 per cent, fish production 47 per cent, agriculture 39 per cent, and coal 45 per cent. The numbers employed in manufacturing declined by 38 per cent, and steel production fell 62 per cent.[2] By 1933 per-capita income for the region dropped to $185, a figure marginally above the Prairies' $181 but far below the Canadian average of $262.[3]

Declines in production meant lost jobs. The percentage of unemployed wage-earners by June 1931 rose to 19 for the Maritimes compared to 18.4 for the country as a whole. The problem surfaced soon after the stock-market crash of October 1929 as winter traffic through Halifax and Saint John declined sharply, leaving about half the longshoremen out of work.[4] Unemployment, also high among woods and mill workers went from bad to worse; for example, all the major lumber mills in Northumberland County, its economic mainstay, closed before the end of 1931. In Nova Scotia, the Dominion Steel Company, or DOSCO, as the former British Empire Steel and Coal Corporation was called after the reorganization of 1928, limited production in both steel works and mines and in that year announced a plan to close permanently collieries employing 2,750 men.[5] Fishermen were hit hard by slumping prices, although their numbers increased as the unemployed in other sectors turned to the fisheries as what Parzival Copes called the 'employer of last resort.'[6] Farmers sold their crops at strong prices in the fall of 1929, but the inevitable and sustained collapse of their markets eventually drove many out of a market economy to swell the ranks of the unemployed.

Responsibility for relief officially belonged to the municipalities, which varied in size from two thousand to sixty thousand. These bodies were poorly equipped to handle an industrial crisis of such magnitude. Theoretically, the level of government closest to those needing help should know best the nature of the aid required.[7] In practice, many Maritime municipalities, their revenues from property taxes in sharp decline, were unable to borrow the cost of the relief needed by their people. Appeals to the federal government for aid to the provinces to help their municipalities brought the infamous statement by Mackenzie King in the winter of 1930 that he might help provinces with Liberal or Progressive governments, but as for Tory-led provinces, he 'would not give them a five-cent piece.'[8] After the federal election in the spring of 1930, R.B. Bennett kept his promise of aid with a relief grant of $20 million. Those municipalities and provinces providing relief work received a rebate of one-quarter the cost. For those providing direct relief, the cost was shared on a one-third, one-third, one-third basis, but the municipality had to come up with the first third and administer the program. As the Depression continued this became the basic formula for the distribution of relief funds.[9]

Granted in this form, federal assistance did little to alleviate the plight of the poorest municipalities. After decades of rural depopulation, Guysborough County, for example, had no reserves with which to cushion the disruption of its lumbering and fishing industries. Unable to collect more than a third of its taxes and denied bank credit, it was virtually bankrupt by June of 1931. New Brunswick's northern counties, including Northumberland, Restigouche, and Gloucester, were in similar condition by mid-1934.[10] Direct appeals for help were referred to the provinces. When Northumberland's county council telegraphed 'large numbers destitute to danger of starvation' to former local resident R.B. Bennett, it received the reply that there could be 'no contact between the Dominion and municipalities.'[11] Because of their own financial plights, however, Maritime provincial governments were most reluctant to accept the responsibility.

Indeed, the Depression highlighted existing disparities in welfare services between the Maritimes and the rest of English Canada. Maritime governments had followed the national trend to provincial public-health programs and workers' compensation, but they claimed to be financially unable to imitate Ontario and the western provinces in the introduction of mothers' allowances and old-age pensions. Although they initially talked of the need for standardized and centrally administered welfare services to assist the municipalities – Nova Scotia's mothers' allowances program of 1930 was explained as a step in that direction – with the sudden growth of unemployment they forced the responsibility for relief back upon the municipalities.[12]

The financial problems of the three provinces were real enough. The Duncan Commission had found their taxes in relation to their resources to be the highest in the country. By 1929 New Brunswick and Nova Scotia were devoting respectively 28 and 26 per cent of their revenues to the servicing of the public debt, compared to about 15 per cent for all provinces. Only by devoting to them a disproportionate share of their revenues could they have participated in national matching-grants programs in road building, technical education, and old-age pensions. By 1933, with debt charges consuming respectively 55 and 35 per cent of their revenues, their claims to be unable to finance greater relief expenditures appeared to have substance.[13] Their failure to do so, and the poverty of many of their municipalities, meant that the region as a whole was given only a fraction of the federal funds it would have received had the money simply been distributed on a per-capita basis. In 1933 the federal contribution to direct relief in the Maritimes, with almost 10 per cent of Canada's population, was just 3.5 per cent of the total, and by 1938–9 this had declined to 2 per cent.[14] The inability to match federal funding meant that the poorest areas of the country tended to receive the least assistance.

The amount of relief paid by the municipalities varied dramatically. The town of Amherst, with a reputation for wealth and labour militancy, supported almost two thousand people on relief through 1933 at an average cost of $5.70 per month – a figure close to the national average.[15] At a relief conference of Nova Scotia municipalities in 1934, Mayor Read defended his town's greater largesse by noting that its grant for food worked out to four and a half cents per person per meal for a family of four and invited the other mayors to explain 'how anyone can live on less.'[16]

This was a question that the unemployed had to answer for themselves; in every other municipality, less was what they received. In the industrial communities of Sydney, Glace Bay, New Waterford, and Springhill, relief payments averaged close to four dollars per month. Sydney steelworker George MacEachern attributed the survival of his own family on relief totalling a dollar a week per person to assistance from his brother-in-law in the form of weekly donations of milk for his children. As he recalled, there was no money for rent or clothing, and fuel was regularly stolen from DOSCO's coal banks.[17] In other towns, such as Inverness, Pictou, and Stellarton, relief payments averaged little more than half as much. Of the rural municipalities only the two largest, Pictou and Cape Breton counties, paid relief on a twelve-month basis. Others tended to cut off funds during the summer months, and the poorest, such as Guysborough County, might make available a dollar per person to several hundred unemployed one month and give them nothing the next. The stronger municipalities in New Brunswick, such as Moncton and Saint John, paid comparable amounts through the winter, but reduced payments when the province cut off funding during the summer months. In the poorer municipalities, payments were much lower. In Gloucester, for example, in the winter of 1936, the twelve thousand people on relief received little more than a dollar a month. In Prince Edward Island, residents of Charlottetown averaged almost four dollars while the others secured less than two. That province, too, cut off most relief payments through the summer months. In the peak month,

March of 1933, 123,733 Maritimers, or more than 12 per cent of the population, received direct relief.[18]

With the relief from governments so limited in the Maritimes, people were more dependent on support from relatives and volunteer agencies. Aid for clothing and sometimes milk for children were distributed through the Red Cross. Meals, clothing, and other assistance were provided through church organizations, such as Charlottetown's Zion Presbyterian Church Benevolent Society or its Catholic Social Service.[19] But the help thus provided was neither comprehensive nor permanent. People died from malnutrition and related diseases. George MacEachern recalled the reaction of a friend to the report of the death of a Sydney resident, a frequenter of the Sydney Mission, from malnutrition: 'Malnutrition be damned, he died of starvation and Christian sympathy.'[20] Maritimers seemed more perceptive of relief needs at a distance than they were of those in their own region. Throughout the 1930s they collected hundreds of railway carloads of clothing and foodstuffs for the drought-stricken Prairies where governmental assistance was usually more generous than in the Maritimes.[21]

The concern was great lest some receive relief unnecessarily. Traditionally, the stigma attached to the municipal 'homes' or poorhouses was assumed to be protection enough for the public purse. With the granting of relief outside these institutions, such concerns were met by professional social workers. In Saint John the Social Service Exchange, staffed by women professionals, maintained card files on all families needing assistance either from governments or volunteer agencies.[22] Federal and provincial regulations required that, before relief was given, each family or individual should be investigated to ensure that their need was genuine. Since the social workers were usually concerned to justify their positions in terms of the money they could save municipalities, their rigid application of means tests, ferreting out of bank savings, and interviewing of neighbours gave them an unattractive image.[23] Relief monies were paid in the form of vouchers, which allowed the individual to purchase groceries from a specified list of the cheapest staples available.

As public-relief costs mounted, fear that these might become endemic led to demands that the indigent perform some kind of service for the assistance received. In rural areas this might mean the cutting of fuel for other unemployed. In cities it might involve work in public street-building projects. To defend themselves, the unemployed, often encouraged by radical labour leaders, developed their own organizations. These were known as the Workers' League (later the Workmen's Protective Association) in Saint John, the Unemployed Union in Sydney,

# "Premier Tilley Had a Province, I. O., I. O. U."

'Free Spender,' 1935. Though modern scholars might criticize Maritime governments for failing to spend more on relief, to contemporaries their borrowings already held frightening implications for local taxpayers.

Urban gardens, Fredericton, 1932. Governments cut relief payments during summer months. Unemployed workers were expected to plant garden plots, the seed and fertilizer for which were supplied by local service clubs.

and the Unemployed Workmen's Association in Charlottetown. Through organization the unemployed agitated for municipal participation in federal relief programs, protested cutbacks, opposed work projects paid for in relief vouchers alone, and, in general, served as a competing pressure against those whose primary concern was to lower the burden upon local taxpayers. They also worked to reduce the sense of guilt and failure for individuals by blaming the Depression on the society in which they lived.[24]

In rural communities, relief was handled by volunteer committees or parish officers, sometimes called overseers of the poor. It was their responsibility to stretch as far as possible the limited funds accorded them. In northern New Brunswick, where people were starving, they sometimes arranged loans on their own credit. They also prosecuted for the crime of bastardy those who illegally created new mouths to feed.[25] Theirs too was the responsibility for deciding whether or not the families of the unemployed would be allowed the services of a doctor. The admission of indigents to hospitals was a matter of decision by the finance committees of the municipalities. As tuberculosis ravaged the northern counties in New Brunswick during the second half of the decade, the municipalities, a witness told the Rowell-Sirois Commission, often failed 'to allow treatment in the early stages when it is the most effective.'[26] On Prince Edward Island, where upwards of 1 per cent of the population

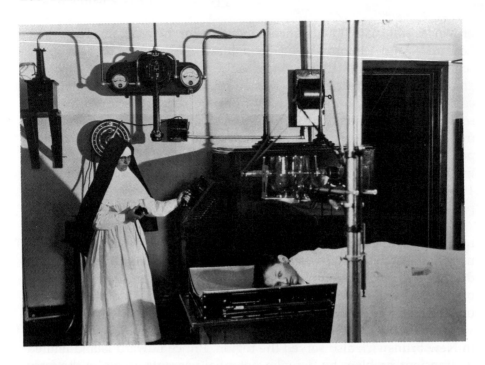

X-ray machine, St Joseph's Hospital, Campbellton, N.B. Tuberculosis was a major cause of death. X-rays allowed early diagnosis, but many victims of the disease could not afford the treatment, which usually meant a lengthy convalescence in a sanatorium.

had tuberculosis in some form, the waiting list for the tiny sanatorium had a similar effect.[27] In Nova Scotia regulations requiring medical services for the indigent were resented by municipalities. Efforts by New Brunswick's health minister, W.F. Roberts, to allow hospital admissions upon the recommendation of public-health officers failed to gain the support of his colleagues.[28]

One apparent break in the restraint imposed by the Depression was the introduction of old-age pensions in all three provinces. Here extension of the provinces' commitment to social welfare was more illusion than substance. Pensions were a hot political issue in the region. Unable to afford the 50 per cent initially required for participation in the federal program, Maritime governments were encouraged by R.B. Bennett's pre-election promise 'to see to it that old age pensions are paid to every province' and his suggestion that the federal government might pay up to 99 per cent.[29] But the revised scheme introduced in the summer of 1931 set the federal contribution at only 75 per cent. Amid the Depression, and faced with a disproportionate number of elderly, the three provinces still lacked the finances to implement the program. The Prince Edward Island cabinet solved its political dilemma by developing a scheme that even their province could afford. By scaling down the amounts paid and drastically tightening the rules for eligibility, they could transfer the indigent elderly from the relief rolls to the pension rolls at little additional cost to the province. Under their program, introduced in 1933, only one in five of those over seventy qualified for a pension, and the pensions averaged less than 60 per cent of those paid in Ontario and western Canada. Nova Scotia adopted a similar plan in 1934, and New Brunswick followed in 1936. The disparity in the federal pension structure continued to the 1950s.[30]

Assistance by the state was not confined to pensions or relief. Direct relief was available only to those who met stringent residency requirements. Those who had left their communities to look for work, often described as single unemployed transients, were given shelter in camps organized by the Canadian army. In 1931 they were admitted to work on the Halifax Citadel, where approximately 900 resided when they were turned out in 1937 at the termination of the program. Several camps in New Brunswick also served the region. Prince Edward Island limited its transient problem by denying potential vagrants access to the ferry and expelling those who did appear. For camp residents the standard of living could be higher than for other unemployed in the region. They received food, shelter, medical care, and twenty cents per day. But camp life in exclusively male company under military discipline for an indefinite period was unattractive for the young men who composed a major portion of this group.

The back-to-the-land movement served a similar constituency. In 1931 the federal cabinet proposed a scheme by which relief monies from all three levels of government would be used to establish people upon farms where they could become self-supporting. The proposal dovetailed with Nova Scotia's and New Brunswick's aspirations to rehabilitate depopulated rural areas and, in the case of New Brunswick, to open new lands for settlement. In 1932 Nova Scotia expropriated approximately 600 vacant farms, which were made available to unemployed families – chiefly miners. The scheme was a mixed success, as more than one-third drifted away by 1938 and another third were behind in their repayments. Only twenty-four fulfilled the conditions giving them title to their farms.[31]

In New Brunswick the enthusiasm was greater as the government proposed to open new lands to 'pioneer' settlement. Acadians, whose clergy had traditionally endorsed colonization as an antidote to emigration, were particularly responsive. But when the municipalities learned that their share of the capital required to outfit the farmers was much

'Back to the land.' With photos like this one, New Brunswick attempted to lure welfare recipients out of its towns. Since little in the way of public support was provided, success was limited.

more than they were paying for relief in other forms, they refused to participate. The unemployed took out land but did so under nineteenth-century settlement legislation, with only a fraction of the support provided by the national program. The provincial government built roads, gave the settlers a few implements, supplied $4.07 worth of groceries four times a year, paid bonuses for land cleared and planted, and periodically allowed settlers to cut and sell timber from Crown lands. By 1936 new families were taking out land at a rate of about 600 per year. Concentrated in the northern counties, they created a few dozen new communities, including Allardville in Gloucester County, Trout Brook in Madawaska, St Arthur in Restigouche, Alnwick in Northumberland, and Bronson in Queens. By 1939 the new settlers remaining on their grants totalled 11,165.[32]

The pioneer settlements had an attraction other than the lack of alternatives. In a decade when national marriage rates declined by 12 per cent in the first five years, pioneer settlement offered young people an opportunity to escape the parental roof, marry, and raise families of their own.[33] In employing the pioneer analogy, clerics and politicians pointed out that the modern settlers would have equipment and resources equivalent to those of their forefathers in previous centuries. Probably they did. The original settlers too had gone without schools, medical services, and modern machinery. But the standards for judging success or failure had altered. A federal study of some of the settlements at the end of the decade suggested that, because of the lack of machinery, much of the enormous effort of the settlers had been wasted.[34] A confidential provincial study implied that the expenditure in public land, timber, and roads for such communities was unjustified.[35] Both studies give an impression of rural slums in which illiteracy was high and few of the people were genuinely self-supporting.

ETHNIC TENSIONS

Non-white minorities were particularly hard hit by the Depression. At the margins of the Maritime economy, Blacks and Native people were traditionally the last hired and the first fired. Although both had evolved a partially subsistence economy, the elimination of their modest income from wages and handicrafts caused severe hardship. The Native people's peculiar relationship with the federal government provided a rationale for overt discrimination. They did not need their jobs, the reasoning went, because the federal government would look after them.[36] The prejudice against Blacks surfaced in the protests of municipal officials against provincial legislation that required local taxpayers to pay for medical services for 'the descendants of those who were brought here as slaves.'[37] Native people, too, were discouraged from the use of federally funded medical services by reference to doctors distant from their reserves.[38]

The economic insecurity of whites during the Depression was not conducive to any relaxation in the subordination of the non-white groups. In 1937 in Trenton a mob of 400 whites destroyed the home of a Black family that had crossed the de facto segregation lines by buying a house in a 'white' neighbourhood. The only arrest was that of a Black man accused of assaulting a white woman during the riot.[39]

The Depression also exacerbated tensions between Acadians and English-speaking Maritimers, tensions that leaders on both sides worked to defuse. As usual, education provided a flashpoint. Illiteracy was a particularly acute problem for Acadians. Forced to cope with two languages in their first year of school, as well as residing in some of the poorest school districts, Acadian children tended to fail and drop out. Surveys would later show that, in the three French counties of Madawaska, Gloucester, and Kent, only 40 per cent of students beginning grade one in 1931 entered grade five in 1935. The comparable survival rate in three English counties was 75 per cent.[40] Acadian leaders had earlier won the

Buctouche Convent School, 1931. Private convent schools continued to help Acadian girls to acquire both literacy and household skills as well as to learn the tenets of their faith.

support of Conservative premier J.B.M. Baxter for their campaign for educational reform, and in 1928 Regulation 32 had provided the option of French as a language of instruction for grades one and two and for particular courses in subsequent years. But in the face of a flurry of petitions from the Orange Lodge and other anglophone groups, the regulation was rescinded.[41]

The dilemma for Baxter seemed insoluble. By responding to Acadians' problems he could hope to make long-term electoral gains among a people whose majority support for more than a decade had gone to the Liberals. But with anglophone New Brunswick worried about the relative growth of French population in the north and east, the Orange claim of the 'Frenchifying' impact of the new policies evoked a response that threatened the Conservatives' traditional electoral power bases. Baxter held open the possibility of reform with the promise of a commission of inquiry. Having won the election, he implemented his promise in the spring of 1931 just before retiring to the bench.

The commission, an unwieldy body representing universities, business, labour, farmers, women's institutes, and the Acadian national societies, focused primarily on the inequity in financial resources among the 1,341 school districts. School taxes on one dollar of assessed property, the commissioners reported, varied from a county average high of 45.5 mills, or tenths of a cent, in poverty-stricken Gloucester to a low of 9.5 in the city of Saint John. The commission proposed to establish the county as the basic unit for financing and managing schools and to create a 'Provincial Equalization Fund' to allow minimal services to be maintained in all counties at similar rates of taxation. At the insistence of the Acadian representatives, it also considered the language problems of the Acadian children and endorsed a program of first-language instruction similar to that provided by Regulation 32.[42] The government then gave the economic crisis as the reason for not implementing the financial recommendations and stalled the Acadians on the language question with the claim that more time was needed to prepare the legislation.

When no legislation materialized in the session of 1934, a bitter Calixte Savoie, who had spearheaded the Acadians' campaign on education, interfered in the sensitive matter of store lay-offs, which Acadians believed tended to discriminate against them. In a circular letter to Acadians in the Moncton area, he urged them to demand service from English businesses in their own language as a means of preserving jobs for bilingual francophones. Tensions mounted as anglophone clerks reacted angrily to this perceived threat to their livelihood. Acadian leaders divided upon the wisdom of this strategy. Soon a letter from four prominent Acadians, including provincial cabinet minister A.J. Léger, claimed that the circulars did not represent the sentiments of the 'vast majority' of Acadians.[43]

The Acadian nationalists continued their campaign in less confrontational terms. In 1936 they realized a long-standing dream when Moncton became a separate archdiocese under an Acadian bishop.[44] In the same year prominent Acadians established an educational association. Summer school programs for teacher training were later launched at Sacré-Coeur and Saint-Joseph colleges, although these were not recognized or funded by the province.[45] The Acadians' educational campaign bore fruit in Prince Edward Island, as inspectors in primarily Acadian communities in 1935 reported the use of French texts and advertisements for teachers who had French and were willing to use it. Unable to obtain adequate language instruction in the local Normal School, Island Acadians secured the support of the language committee of the Saint-Jean-Baptiste Society of Montreal and other nationalist groups to fund summer courses in French at Miscouche beginning in 1940.[46] In Nova Scotia low-key negotiations between the Acadian Société l'Assomption and education officials resulted in 1939 in a program to provide, in certain designated schools, close to 90 per cent of instruction in French during the first six grades.[47]

ORGANIZATIONAL RESPONSES

The large-scale unemployment left labour unions on the defensive throughout the 1930s. With labour surpluses so apparent, the strike became a weapon of dubious value. In the coal areas of Cape Breton, patterns of past militancy ensured that DOSCO would move carefully in its plans to reduce wages and close four major collieries. In 1932 the provincial government invited Sir Andrew Rae Duncan, whose previous investigations had appeared to win the respect of the miners, to pronounce judgment on the corporation's proposal. This time Duncan supported DOSCO, claiming that the changes were in fact necessary to preserve the solvency of the corporation. The permanent reduction in jobs was difficult for union members to accept. The United Mine Workers of America (UMW), District 26, voted against their leaders' recommendations to endorse the proposed contract, and in the summer of 1932, dissidents within the district organized the rival Amalgamated Mine Workers.

Although not directly an instrument of the Communist Party, the new union was compatible with CP policies of labour militancy and of bypassing the internationals in organizing both employed and unemployed workers in broad industrial unions. The new organization included a substantial group of radicals and had the enthusiastic support of J.B. McLachlan, whose radical *Nova Scotia Miner* repeatedly denounced the UMW and his personal nemesis, international president John L. Lewis. Indeed the radicals appeared to dominate the AMW, which enjoyed the support of an estimated 60 per cent of the miners.[48]

Despite its numbers, the new union faced an immediate dilemma in seeking recognition. DOSCO and the provincial government, who tacitly favoured the UMW, refused a referendum and the AMW request to participate in contract negotiations. The new union could force recognition only through a strike, but in 1933, at the nadir of the Depression, such action seemed impractical even to a radical leadership. The UMW simply held its ground and, as frustration mounted among the AMW rank and file, increased the pressure on its rival with brief strikes for a closed shop in areas of its own strength, such as Springhill.[49] In 1935 the Communist Party, in an abrupt change of tactics, disbanded its Workers' Unity League and sought again to rally labour in established union structures. In 1936 the AMW, in financial difficulties and stressing the need for unity, accepted the terms of surrender arranged by a miners' committee.

With confrontation usually inadvisable, trade unionists sometimes employed to advantage the plant councils organized by the corporations as alternatives to the international unions. In the new International Pulp and Paper mill at Dalhousie, veteran unionists, with active support from a mixed-language work-force, dominated the plant councils and, by 1936, with a judicious mixture of co-operation and pressure, persuaded the corporation to tolerate the same people in charge of a local of the International Pulp and Paper Workers.[50] In Sydney, radical unionist George MacEachern recalled how steelworkers' membership in the DOSCO plant council had been useful in the organization of an independent union.[51] In the coalfields of Minto, however, local and plant unions yielded no such accommodation. Here the number and insecurity of the owners led to labour policies as varied and unyielding as those in the timber woods. As wages fell and hours lengthened, the provincial government of L.P.D. Tilley amended the province's mining act to include belated provisions on child labour and safety inspection, and limited underground work to eight hours a day – a restriction bitterly resisted by some employers.[52]

Most vulnerable were the unorganized workers, whipsawed between invitations to work for unreasonably low wages and threats that those who refused would be denied relief. In 1936 the Dysart government appointed a fair-wage officer to investigate complaints of unfair labour practices. The following year the Fair Wage Act was amended to create a Fair Wage Board, representing both business and labour, with authority to adjust wages, hours, and other conditions of work.[53] Labour made a more significant breakthrough in Nova Scotia through its Trade Union Act of 1937, Canada's first legislation requiring union recognition and compulsory bargaining. The Committee for Industrial Organization (CIO), supported by the international unions, and a new Steelworkers' Organizing Committee, led by Silby Barrett, formerly of the UMW, had signed up about 3,000 workers or about 90 per cent of the employees at the Sydney steel plant near the end of 1936. When DOSCO refused to bargain with the new union, its leaders met privately with Premier Angus L. Macdonald and then mounted a campaign to win over the rest of the cabinet.[54] With an election approaching, they were successful, and the legislation introduced early in 1937 permitted a burst of activity among previously unorganized workers.[55] In New Brunswick, efforts by Minto coal miners to secure recognition for a UMW local met solid opposition from employers. A bitter three-month strike involving almost 1,000 workers ended without recognition for the miners' local. In 1938, acting minister of labour J.B. McNair introduced the New Brunswick Labour Bill. Though failing to go as far as the Nova Scotia legislation in requiring union recognition, it did assert the right of workers to form and join unions without being penalized by their employers.

The Protestant churches responded to the Depression through social-reform agencies created during the flowering of the Social Gospel. The

Anglican dioceses of Nova Scotia and New Brunswick, the Maritime United Baptist Convention, and the Maritime Conference of the United Church all maintained boards or committees devoted to local reform and affiliated with other reform organizations at the national level. They applauded welfare innovations by any of the three provinces and urged the other two to keep pace. Their leaders continued the rhetoric of realizing God's kingdom on earth. Their boards reiterated proposals of support for the League of Nations, co-operatives, aid to the unemployed, and other measures to advance the welfare state.[56] Yet the belief in rapid or even steady progress was difficult to maintain amid a growing climate of pessimism.

Religious conservatives, emphasizing fundamentalism, literalism, and evangelism, assumed a greater prominence within the larger denominations, and the appeal of their message was reflected in the rapid growth of fundamentalist sects. The Maritime United Baptist Convention came under attack from a seceding fundamentalist group led by the Rev. J.J. Sidey, who claimed in a dramatic trial over the ownership of a parsonage that the convention had forfeited its claim to be Baptist through its excessive liberalism. While retaining the property in question and heading off a major schism, the convention mounted its own evangelical response.[57] Popular among the Anglicans, but also winning approval from the Baptists, was a crusade led by the British 'Oxford Group.' Conducted in Canada and the United States by visiting 'teams' from Britain, the Oxford Group's campaign for 'moral rearmament' emphasized individual virtues that appealed to businessmen; in 1939 it was formally endorsed by the Canadian Federation of Mayors and Municipalities.[58] Meanwhile, fundamentalist sects proliferated outside the traditional denominations, with membership in the Disciples of the Church of Christ growing from three to five thousand in the region during the decade, and the Pentacostals, concentrated in western New Brunswick, almost tripling their membership from 2,592 to 7,168.

Social theology had its most striking impact in the 'Antigonish Movement,' led from St Francis Xavier University, where Catholic social activists campaigned for rural reform through co-operatives and adult education. They evolved a critique of the exploitive nature of capitalist society and the élitist educational system it perpetuated.[59] Although their rhetoric embarrassed conservative Catholics, they invoked in their support the papal encyclicals *Rerum Novarum* (1891) and *Quadragesimo Anno* (1931), which, though condemning Marxist socialism, clearly asserted the church's social responsibility. With the support of two local lay organizations, the Scottish Catholic Society and the University Alumni, they launched a Department of Extension with the charismatic Rev. Dr Moses Coady as director, the efficient A.B. MacDonald as sec-

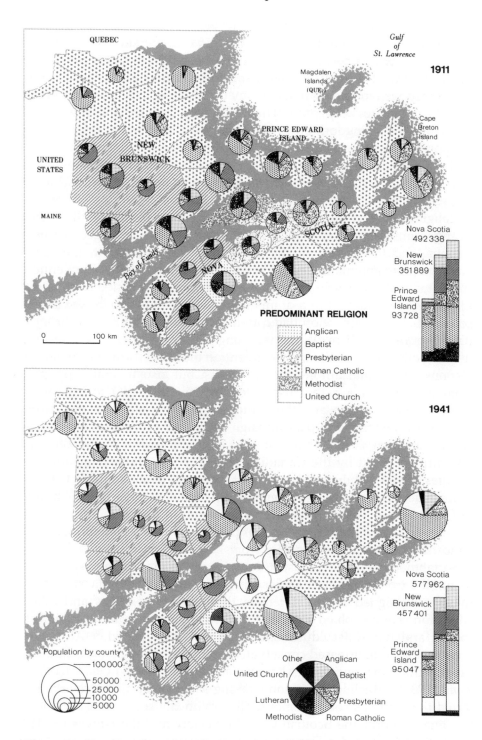

Figure 10 The changing geographical distribution of religious denominations in the Maritimes, 1911–41

retary, and the Rev. Dr J. Tompkins as resident guru and critic.[60]

The Antigonish method of organization, which began with the study group, was eminently suited to people thrown back upon their own resources. Farmers and fishermen were invited to identify their problems and to propose concrete solutions. Their proposals, with some prompting, often called for co-operation in production, through local creameries, canneries, or fish plants, in transportation, and in marketing, as well as in the bulk purchase of supplies.

Co-operatives were a familiar theme to farmers. The United Fruit Companies of Nova Scotia, based in the Annapolis Valley, the Moncton-centred Canadian Livestock Co-operative (Maritimes), and the Maritime Co-operative Egg and Poultry Exchange still survived, as did some twenty-eight retail co-operative stores. Most of the stores had originated with the United Farmers' movement after the First World War. The field workers of the provincial Department of Agriculture, who had promoted co-operatives to strengthen rural communities, embraced the Antigonish techniques and became virtual agents of the movement.[61] So did many priests. It was further consolidated as 'grass-roots' leaders received 'short-course' training at the university.

The spread of the movement was hampered by the social gulf between Catholic and Protestant communities. Coady's statement that its goal was 'the realization of the Sermon on the Mount' struck a responsive chord among proponents of the Social Gospel.[62] The Maritime Conference of the United Church endorsed co-operatives, and a few of its clerics, such as J.D.N. Macdonald, became leaders.[63] But for many it was difficult to accept the Catholic leadership. Among those taking the 'short course,' Catholics outnumbered Protestants by about four to one.[64]

Most conspicuous was the movement's impact on the fisheries. In the hearings before the MacLean Commission of 1927–8 the inshore fishermen had expressed interest in co-operative organization and entered a tacit alliance with the Catholic clergy. The federal department of fisheries approached Moses Coady to organize the fishermen. In a whirlwind tour of the province, Coady laid the groundwork for the 1930 convention that established the United Maritime Fishermen (UMF). The central council was to be principally concerned with lobbying and education. Individual locals would build canneries, organize marketing agencies, and generally conduct the economic business of the organization.[65] Chester McCarthy, a former fisherman and lawyer, who had helped organize, at Tignish, Prince Edward Island, the oldest surviving co-operative lobster cannery in the region, emerged as president. As the UMF activities highlighted the shortage of credit in rural communities, Coady, in 1932, began organizing credit unions through which people could pool their savings for individual or community use. For the fishermen this had the

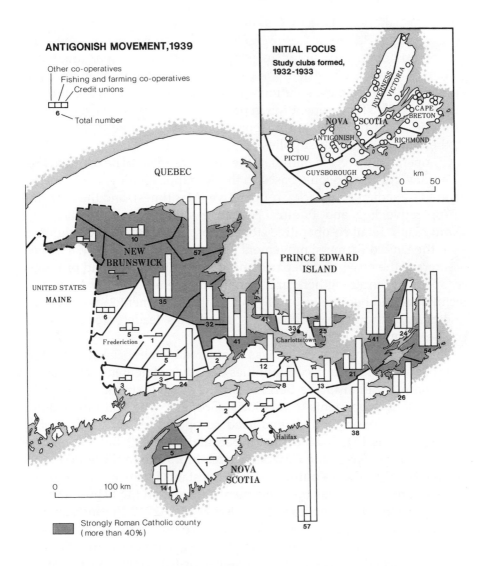

Figure 11 The Antigonish Movement in the Maritimes in the 1930s

benefit of lessening their dependence upon the merchants, whose provision of credit was often conditional upon exclusive patronage regardless of price.

Organization did not advance smoothly. The secretary misappropriated funds and, with Chester McCarthy forced out of the executive by a rule restricting membership to fishermen, the Prince Edward Island delegation withdrew to form a separate association. As the Depression reached its nadir, paid memberships among the inshore fishermen, whose income averaged just $75 a year in some communities, declined to about

The Rev. Dr Moses Coady

800. Yet the benefits from organizing extended well beyond the formal membership; fish companies were forced to offer higher prices to limit the spread of the movement.[66]

Important too was the UMF's role in lobbying the federal government. The alliance of fishermen and clerics secured the 1929 legislation taxing trawler-caught fish, and when that was thrown out by the courts, its replacement by the 1931 legislation limiting trawlers in the Atlantic fisheries to the six then operating. The fishermen needed their allies, as the fish companies, bitter about losing the trawler dispute, closed fish plants in communities such as Canso that had been most vocal in the anti-trawler campaign. The companies also lobbied against federal financial support for co-operatives[67] In 1934 Ralph P. Bell, president of the Lockeport Cold Storage Company, advised J.L. Ralston that the United Maritime Fishermen was 'a cloak for the activities of a socialistic and radical band of Roman Catholics.' He threatened to withdraw his support from the Liberals unless they cut off financial support for the UMF.[68] Other fish merchants complained of what they called plans to 'Sovietize the fishery,' and argued that the federal grant to the UMF was using their tax money to subsidize a competitor. On taking office in 1935 the Liberals

The sardine industry, Bay of Fundy, c. 1940. The sardine fishery expanded during the 1930s. At Blacks Harbour, the small herring taken in weirs along the New Brunswick shore of the Bay of Fundy were packed in flat rectangular cans and shipped throughout the world.

reduced the federal subsidy to the UMF and designated it for educational purposes. They then gave much larger grants to the extension department at St Francis Xavier University and returned Coady to the government payroll as a co-operative organizer.[69]

Aided by these grants and others from the American Carnegie Foundation, the Antigonish Movement spread to Prince Edward Island and New Brunswick. In the former province, J.T. Croteau, a young social scientist imported from the United States to a Carnegie-financed chair that served both St Dunstan's University and Prince of Wales College, became an enthusiastic proponent. In 1936 he helped organize the Adult Education League of Prince Edward Island, which promoted study groups, brought in speakers, and secured provincial support for the training of leaders at Antigonish.[70] In New Brunswick, St Thomas University at Chatham created an extension department to serve anglophones in the province, while Father Livain Chiasson of Shippegan, who had earlier acted as Coady's interpreter and guide while organizing Acadian fishermen, was employed by the St Francis Xavier extension department as a director of adult education among the Acadians.[71] By late 1938, spokesmen for the Antigonish Movement claimed direct involvement by approximately 50,000 in activities including 42 co-operative stores, 17 co-operative lobster canneries, 10 fish-processing plants, 140 credit unions, and 2,390 study clubs – 1,500 in Nova Scotia, 500 in New Brunswick, and 390 in Prince Edward Island.[72]

In 1933 the movement penetrated the Nova Scotia mining communities, where it was promoted as an alternative to Communism. An experiment in running a bankrupt coal-mining operation in Inverness as a co-operative failed when miners objected to the deterioration in their working conditions.[73] In most coal-mining communities the movement was limited to stores, credit unions, and a few libraries. In 1938 a co-operative housing scheme at Reserve Mines offered miners a chance to secure their own homes as an alternative to company housing. It spread the following year to Glace Bay and Dominion.

The Farmer-Labour Union, which developed in the sawmilling and port towns and villages on the Miramichi in northern New Brunswick, was, in part, a by-product of the Antigonish Movement. Formed in a convention of farmers, woods workers, and longshoremen at Nelson on the Miramichi in 1936, the new organization focused on the economic needs of the people of that locality. It encouraged study clubs, co-operatives, and credit unions. Its goals included increasing the processing of resources within the region, forcing timber companies either to exploit their leases or to give them up, and securing a greater share for labour from any improvements in market conditions.

Initially, the union's leaders, an unorthodox group that included a farmer and a priest and was headed by Gregory McEacheron, a professional boxer-turned-merchant, put pressure on the provincial government to achieve their goals. Premier Allison Dysart was moving in that direction with legislation to withdraw timber leases from firms that did not use them and the appointment of a fair-wage officer and board. But the board was slow and the situations calling for investigation many. In August of 1937 the Farmer-Labour Union called a general strike to demand better wages and hours of work. At the time, wages and hours varied dramatically among employers. To lumbermen such as G.P. Burchill and W.H. Miller, their efforts in keeping their operations open during the Depression entitled them to require sacrifices from their employees. To the woods workers, allowing lower wages and longer hours for some undercut the bargaining position for others. The strike lasted ten days and involved about 1,500 workers. A citizens' committee intervened to help negotiate a settlement that gave both woods workers and longshoremen standardized wages and a nine-hour working day.

Although the general strike offended some supporters, and the New Brunswick Council of Labour looked askance at an organization that poached on the turf of international unions, the Farmer-Labour Union continued to grow until, by 1939, it included twenty locals in five counties. Relations with the Dysart government remained strained as the union demanded work for the unemployed and considered the alternatives of direct political action or support for the Co-operative Commonwealth Federation (CCF), William Herridge's New Democracy movement, or the suddenly labour-conscious Conservatives. Ultimately, though seeking pro-labour candidates from the Conservatives, the union remained officially unaligned in the provincial election of 1939.[74]

With the United Maritime Fishermen serving mainly inshore fisheries in eastern Nova Scotia and New Brunswick, schooner fishermen, fish-handlers, and trawlermen on the 'South Shore' sought other forms of organization. Stimulated by the upsurge in union activity encouraged by the CIO campaign and the province's 1937 Trade Union Act, they revived the Fishermen's Federation of Nova Scotia. Emerging first as an alliance between schooner fishermen and their captains, it was joined by fish-handlers, whose union was also affiliated in the American Federation of Labour. When the fish companies refused to negotiate with either – the Trade Union Act had left companies to decide what constituted a majority of their employees – the schooner fishermen of Lunenburg tied up their boats in January of 1938. They were joined by other schooner fishermen and some shore fishermen in Lockeport and Halifax. In all three communities fish-handlers refused to accept 'scab' fish. The National Fish Company struck back by firing union militants and replacing them from the unemployed. With support from organized labour, the fish workers secured the intervention of Angus L. Macdonald and a settlement that provided for a certification vote for the employees of the National Fish Company. Even so, the company won a majority vote against union organization, aided by new fish workers hired for the occasion.

The fishermen and fish-handlers of Lockeport then turned to the Communist-led Canadian Seaman's Union. Efforts to gain recognition in the fall of 1939 again met staunch refusal and a lockout for the fish-handlers. Although supported by new locals that sprang up in Shelburne, Liverpool, Yarmouth, and five other communities, the fish workers discovered the limitations of a trade-union act that failed to recognize fishermen as employees and excluded fish-handlers because they had incorrectly applied for certification before being locked out. Supported by labour organizations throughout the province and vigorously picketing, the fishermen found themselves in confrontation with 160 RCMP officers, who had been rushed in to maintain order. Violence loomed, and the premier again undertook mediation. This resulted in the recognition of the fish-handlers, but left the fishermen still formally excluded from the union process on the grounds that they were not employees.[75]

Another group that developed effective organizational techniques in the face of the Depression was the region's visual artists. In the mid-1920s a former medical scholar at the University of Chicago, writing from his native Shediac, had castigated the region for its 'stagnation and decadence in cultural and educational standards and in the higher thought of the country.'[76] J.C. Webster backed his social criticism with skilful leadership in a drive for reform. He used his position on the National Historic Sites and Monuments Board of Canada to press for the preservation of Louisbourg as a national park and the development of museums devoted to the cultural education of the public. He personally led the drive for private subscriptions to create a museum in Saint John, to which he donated his private collection of books and memorabilia. Begun in 1931 and completed in 1935 the New Brunswick Museum was intended to educate the people in their history, natural history, and fine arts. Webster had also pressed the federal government for a museum at Beauséjour. This opened the same year, and he canvassed his friends to contribute manuscripts and other antiquities.[77] Thus, when Walter Abell, a young fine-arts professor at Acadia University, suggested a regional association to publicize the work of local artists and expose Maritime audiences to travelling exhibitions of works by regional, national, and international artists, he won Webster's enthusiastic support.[78]

The timing of their efforts also coincided with the American-based Carnegie Foundation's interest in assisting museums throughout North America. Founded in 1935, the Maritime Art Association included thirteen local art groups and launched a vigorous program of exhibits. By 1940 its 'Bulletin' had evolved into *Maritime Art*, Canada's first full-fledged art magazine. Aided in part by these developments, several of the region's artists, including Jack Humphrey and Miller Brittain, attained formidable international reputations.

More than the region's literature, in which, with a few notable exceptions, romanticism and escapism tended to dominate, Maritime artists led in trying to capture the Depression images of the decade. Their realism was sometimes not appreciated locally. A mural by Miller Brittain, commissioned by the Saint John hospital and depicting the hunger and determination of the workers of the period, was later rejected by the administrators who had commissioned it.[79]

The Depression did not encourage organization or gains in status by women. Although women were often forced to assume a more prominent economic role in households where the traditional breadwinner was unemployed, such changes were considered temporary.[80] Individual women did set precedents in entering 'male' occupations, but these usually remained isolated incidents. The cult of domesticity was still the dominant ideology, though women held a fairly constant percentage of paid employment throughout the decade.[81] The unwritten rule of the period was that priority in employment should go to males with families to support.

In Nova Scotia early in the decade a combined lobby by the Trades and Labour Council and the YWCA during a critical Halifax by-election secured mothers' allowances and minimum-wage legislation. The Minimum Wage Board of 1930, composed of a former retail merchant, the president of the Halifax Trades and Labour Council, and an ex-newspaperwoman, tried to find a reasonable compromise between women's needs and the concern of Nova Scotia's manufacturers to remain competitive. The rulings of the board, enforced by the courts but restricted to the towns and cities, raised wages for experienced women workers from about six dollars to eleven dollars per week. Although the board reduced women's wages as the Depression worsened, such reductions were probably less and came more slowly than if the board not been in place.[82]

Women made sporadic inroads in business, the professions, and politics. Muriel Fergusson of Woodstock, who had consciously chosen marriage instead of the legal profession for which she had trained, took over her husband's practice during the mid-thirties when the latter was incapacitated.[83] Frances Fish, PhD, and, in 1918, the first female graduate of the Dalhousie Law School, returned from employment with C.H. Cahan's law firm in Montreal to her home community of Chatham where she sought to succeed her late father as the local magistrate. Despite her strong political credentials, the appointment went to a man with a family to support.[84] The provincial Conservatives did oblige her to the extent of new legislation allowing women to run for election to the legislature. With the political outlook for Conservatives especially dismal in destitute Northumberland in 1934, competition for the nomination was limited. Fish ran, but, like most Conservatives, was overwhelmingly defeated. Women gained the right to run, but were immediately saddled with the myth that they could not win in New Brunswick.

In the mining areas of Nova Scotia, women pushed for formal recognition of their role in the labour movement. The organization of the AMW was followed by the creation of a Women's Auxiliary, which took a particular interest in investigating and exposing the insufficiencies of workers' wages and of relief structures. The women failed to secure a vote for miners' wives in the approval or rejection of contracts, however, and the auxiliary disappeared with the defeat of the AMW.[85] Women also played a significant role in the Antigonish Movement, supplying about one-third of the study clubs organized.[86] Lottie Austin of Mabou, Cape Breton, even won appointment as the provincial agricultural representative for Inverness – reputedly the first woman to hold such a position in Canada.[87] Another 'first' was recorded by 'Molly' Kool of

Alma, New Brunswick. Having served three years on her father's scow as cook and able seaman she studied for her mate's papers in 1937 and two years later qualified for her master's ticket in steam.

## POLITICAL RESPONSES

The shortage in public revenues left by the Depression encouraged cynicism as political parties tried to persuade the public that they could do more with less. The Conservatives were unfortunate in their timing. In office provincially at the lowest point of the Depression, they were also associated with a federal party that had failed either to solve the problems of unemployment or to reform the welfare programs that discriminated against the poorest provinces. Their obvious failures allowed the Liberals to develop policies that appeared positive by comparison and to consolidate their hegemony over the region.

When the Conservatives won the federal election of 1930, Premier E.N. Rhodes of Nova Scotia resigned to enter R.B. Bennett's cabinet as minister of fisheries. His successor as premier, Gordon Harrington, required all his reputed skill as a labour conciliator to avoid a major confrontation in the mining districts. His strategies included another Duncan Commission to investigate the coal industry and lobbying the federal government for increased coal and steel tariffs and larger transportation subsidies. But he could not keep his party's promise on old-age pensions or solve other economic problems of the Depression. His tactics of cultivating the industrial communities gave some electoral success in these areas, but efforts by party organizers to manipulate voters' lists backfired in the election of 1933, adding a legend of Tory election-rigging to the myth of the Tory responsibility for the Depression.[88]

The Liberals rebuilt their fortunes under the leadership of Angus L. Macdonald, one of a group of 'young Liberals,' including J.L. Ralston, J.L. Ilsley, and Norman Macleod Rogers, who had worked to rehabilitate the Nova Scotia party after the débâcle of the previous decade. Defeated in the constituency of Inverness in the 1930 federal election, Macdonald won a last-minute bid for the provincial leadership at the convention a few months later. A Dalhousie law professor and the first Roman Catholic leader to win election as premier, Macdonald preached a brand of provincial nativism that sought to bridge religious divisions through pride in Scottish ancestry.[89] Following a strategy that had previously worked for his opponents, he also developed the theme of regional protest in a demand for a royal commission investigation of Maritime problems. He parlayed a remark by Rhodes to the effect that, back in 1926, Prime Minister Arthur Meighen had told Duncan that little could be done with the tariff into a charge that the Conservatives had prevented the federal Duncan Commission from considering reforms involving the tariff.[90] Thus Macdonald could promise a more far-reaching investigation as his solution to the province's economic and constitutional woes.

In power Macdonald implemented the more prominent of his pledges. Following Prince Edward Island's lead, he introduced a scaled-down version of old-age pensions and appointed the promised royal commission on the province's disabilities in Confederation. Despite federal opposition, he secured the services of John Harry Jones, a British economist from Leeds University as chairman, and as members, University of Toronto economist Harold Innis, and Alexander Johnston, a former journalist, politician, and deputy minister of marine and fisheries.[91]

Norman Macleod Rogers, a reform-oriented Liberal from Nova Scotia then teaching political science at Queen's University, was drafted to prepare the province's case, which centred on the tariff. By calculating the amount by which the tariff raised prices in each province and by subtracting any increases deemed beneficial, Rogers arrived at a rough estimate of the tariff's net cost or benefit for each province. The Maritimes came out as heavy losers. Neither Rogers' submission nor the two commission reports (Innis prepared his own) sought to abolish the tariff or endorsed demands for regional control. Instead they used the issue of the tariff to justify a demand for compensation to the poorer provinces. Nova Scotia's financial difficulties were to be alleviated through the central government as the commissioners reiterated the necessity of determining federal subsidies on the basis of actual need. Essentially the commissioners were trying to get at the problem of a Canada that was national in encouraging the development and centralization of industry but provincial when it came to paying for social services. Less radical and less directly partisan than expected, the commission's report enjoyed a largely favourable press across the country.

Placed on the defensive by the Nova Scotia investigation, the federal Conservatives decided to complete the long-promised review of federal-provincial subsidies that Duncan had earlier recommended. Bennett appointed a royal commission headed by Sir Thomas White, former minister of finance and vice-president of the Canadian Bank of Commerce. With two of the three commissioners from Ontario and represented by lawyers to fight the Maritime case, the government's intent was to close off the subsidy issue as cheaply as possible. Duncan had suggested a broad rationalization of subsidies that would consider the needs of all provinces. The Mackenzie King government, however, had followed the Duncan inquiry with a series of limited investigations that had recommended multimillion-dollar settlements for each of the prairie provinces. The White Commission represented a continuation of the practice of dealing with each region separately. Ultimately, the commissioners rejected the argument of fiscal need as the basis for determining subsidies, but recommended a modest increase for the Maritimes of $425,000 annually for Nova Scotia, $300,000 for New Brunswick, and $150,000 for Prince Edward Island.

The White recommendations, implemented in time for the federal election of 1935, did not restore the fortunes of the Conservatives in the region. Dissatisfied with the government, Maritimers were split over the alternative. In Nova Scotia and New Brunswick, some erstwhile Conservatives turned to Harry Stevens, a British Columbian whose price-spreads investigation had exposed the exploitation of primary producers and who had broken from the government to mount his own reform platform. At 14 and 10.5 per cent of the popular vote, respectively, the two provinces gave Stevens' Reconstruction Party some of its strongest support.[92] In industrial Cape Breton, the 'left' divided; UMW leaders and CCF supporters threw their weight behind a labour candidate running under a Reconstruction banner. This was part of an unsuccessful attempt to upstage the Communists who were running J.B. McLachlan. Despite the split in the labour vote, McLachlan came third, several hundred votes ahead of his Reconstruction opponents.[93] But here, as in the region overall, most of the disaffected went to the Liberals, who won a clear majority in both seats and share of the popular vote.

The Liberal victory enhanced the position of the party in Nova Scotia. With J.L. Ilsley, a Kentville lawyer, replacing J.L. Ralston in the cabinet (Ralston left the federal political scene temporarily, rumour had it, to help a financially troubled law partner) and Norman Rogers representing Kingston, Ontario, as minister of health, Premier Macdonald could claim friends in high places. Although economic recovery was slight by the provincial election of 1937, Macdonald boasted of a series of successes that included the introduction of old-age pensions and the work of the Jones Commission. He claimed credit for instigating the federal White Commission, while blaming his opponents for its deficiencies. He escaped embarrassment for the federal reductions in relief grants to the Maritimes, since these had been slipped through in supplementary estimates and effectively concealed from the press.[94] Other federal sins could be excused while Canadians awaited the work of a newly announced Royal Commission on Dominion-Provincial Relations (The Rowell-Sirois Commission). The compulsory bargaining legislation for trade unions helped Macdonald's party shed its anti-labour image and allowed it to challenge the Conservatives more effectively in the industrial areas. Winning twenty-five of the thirty seats in the election of 1937 – up three from 1933, the Liberals would develop the legend of

'Angus L.' as a factor in their domination of the province over the next two decades.

In Glace Bay the 'left' united, as Communists, UMW leaders, CCF supporters, and Antigonish Movement organizers joined forces in an attempt to elect W.T. Mercer, a United Church clergyman and Social Gospel enthusiast, as an Independent Labour candidate. Though running well ahead of the Conservatives, Mercer failed to beat the Liberal candidate. The following year the UMW, after surveying alternatives, affiliated with the CCF. The union's unexpected overtures were received cautiously by a national party fearful of Communist infiltration. The new electoral strategy finally yielded some victories for the 'left' as Douglas Macdonald, a UMW board member, won a provincial by-election in Cape Breton Centre in December 1939 and Clarie Gillis, an anti-Communist labour leader and former vice-president of the AMW, took Cape Breton South in the federal election of 1940.[95]

In New Brunswick the Conservatives won a second term early in the Depression. Their victory was a matter of timing and tactics. The tactics included legislation on mothers' allowances and old-age pensions, which they subsequently failed to proclaim into law. The timing involved calling the election before the federal Conservatives announced their decision on old-age pensions and before they had begun their own promised study of educational reform. J.B.M. Baxter's subsequent resignation as premier suggested the difficulty of governing amid a climate of shrinking revenues, rising taxes, and mushrooming public debt. Baxter's successor, C.D. Richards, lasted two years before giving way to L.P.D. Tilley, a grandson of the illustrious Sir Leonard.

As the government's problems multiplied, the Liberals rebuilt their forces under the leadership of Allison Dysart, who, like his Nova Scotia counterpart, was personable, a lawyer, and the first Roman Catholic to be elected premier in his province. Key players on the Liberal team included A.P. Paterson and J.B. McNair, men who shared a common interest in Canada's constitution and the Maritimes' place in it, but who came to the subject from very different backgrounds. Though one of the original propagandists of the Maritime Rights movement, Paterson had remained aloof from the regional celebration accompanying the supposed implementation of the Duncan Commission. In the late 1920s and early 1930s Paterson continued to propose an agitation demanding the region's rights under the original Confederation compact. As New Brunswick's financial position deteriorated during the Depression and the inequities in old-age pensions and other social programs became apparent, Paterson's arguments became increasingly popular. They also received an element of academic credibility when endorsed by McNair, a Rhodes scholar and specialist in constitutional law. Paterson's speeches and the interest aroused by the Jones and White commissions, enabled the Liberals to build their demand for constitutional reform into a substantial issue. In vain Tilley tried to defuse the question with his own commission, which reported that there was no legal basis for Paterson's claims.[96]

With the Liberal victory in the fall of 1935, McNair became attorney general and Paterson minister of education, a portfolio shortly to be combined with a new ministry of federal and municipal relations. The heaping of responsibility upon Paterson may have reassured the Saint John business community of which Paterson, a wholesale grocer, was a senior member, but it left to a legislative novice of unorthodox views the responsibilities of constitutional negotiation with the federal government and relief assistance to the municipalities.

The provincial government had barely settled into office when it faced a critical constitutional decision. The new federal Liberal administration was reconsidering basic relief policy in the light of demands from the Canadian Union of Municipalities that the federal government, as the only level of government with adequate financial resources, take full responsibility for the relief of the unemployed. Prime Minister King, who liked to hide behind the constitution on such issues, found himself unexpectedly exposed at the Dominion-Provincial Conference of 1935 when Premier Alexandre Taschereau of Quebec proposed the patriation of the Canadian constitution to facilitate whatever amendments were necessary. The other eight provinces fell into line, leaving the New Brunswick delegation to raise the only objection. This took the form of an amendment to Taschereau's resolution calling for a conference to negotiate specific constitutional revisions. New Brunswick was not prepared to sign a blank cheque. At a subsequent conference, New Brunswick vetoed a proposal for an amending formula that would have allowed changes providing that six of the nine provinces, including both Ontario and Quebec, agreed.[97]

For a generation familiar with the financial transfers to the poorer provinces implicit in modern welfare programs, New Brunswick's position is hard to appreciate. Having campaigned on a plank of constitutional revision, the Liberals would be guilty of a sharp reversal if they then surrendered both the province's and the region's veto over constitutional change without any concessions in return. Moreover, there was nothing in the Maritimers' experience to suggest that they would be better served in a national program than in a provincial one. They had not received equity in past programs, Paterson argued, citing specifically the case of the Intercolonial Railway. How could they expect to fare better by increasing the responsibilities of the federal government? Above all, New Brunswick leaders were sceptical (and modern historians share their scepticism) that the constitution, rather than lack of political will, was the real barrier to federal aid to the unemployed.[98] If federal politicians genuinely wished to help the unemployed, why did they not make specific proposals? Nevertheless, New Brunswick's sudden emergence as a defender of provincial rights allowed King to sustain the myth that the constitution, and specifically New Brunswick's opposition to reform, had blocked federal efforts to aid the unemployed. New Brunswick's further rationalization of a provincial-rights stance before the Rowell-Sirois Commission – although it also endorsed the Jones Commission's principle of subsidies based on fiscal need – made New Brunswick appear as an awkward anomaly amid the centralizing reform currents of the period.

Helped by a slight economic recovery during its term in office, the Dysart government cultivated a positive image in combatting the Depression. Following the lead of Nova Scotia and Prince Edward Island, it introduced scaled-down old-age pensions and was the first to participate in a federal program that lowered the age of eligibility for pensions to the blind. It initiated public works to create jobs, appointed a fair-wage officer and board, and required timber companies to exploit their leases in order to hold them. Although the province was virtually bankrupt, the Liberals were successful in concealing this fact from the public. Robert Tweedie, Dysart's personal secretary, later suggested that part of their problem in the election of 1939, which the Liberals came close to losing, was 'over-confidence.'[99]

Such confidence, if it did exist, was certainly not justified. Many were discontented with the Liberals' labour, employment, and relief policies. Moreover, the opposition had acquired an effective leader in Frank Squires, whose image helped to nullify the Liberals' constant reiteration of past Tory sins. Though the provincial Liberals had been able to conceal some of their internal quarrels, others had spilled over into the legislature. The session of 1939 opened with Liberal members criticizing government policy. Frank Bridges, a native of Fredericton then practising law in Bathurst, devoted most of a speech explaining his break with the government to an attack on A.P. Paterson. While Bridges focused on the threat to national unity and the Liberal Party implicit in Paterson's doctrine of provincial rights, his speech also suggested intense dissatisfaction among northern municipalities in the matter of relief. Paterson's ineffective rejoinder served to highlight the eloquence of J.B. McNair's defence of the government's constitutional position, which ran to thirty pages in the *Synoptic Report*.[100]

The election itself brought a reshaping of the administration, as Paterson was defeated after receiving substantially fewer votes than the other Liberal candidates in Saint John. Bridges did not stand, but would later enter the federal cabinet. Dysart, ill and perhaps discouraged by the narrowness of his victory and the province's continued economic plight, resigned in favour of McNair. With the outbreak of war McNair emphasized his own abandonment of a defensive stance on the constitution by publicly urging Quebec premier Maurice Duplessis to drop the issue of provincial rights in support of the war effort.

On Prince Edward Island, Albert Saunders in May 1930 resigned as premier to accept appointment to the province's Supreme Court. With unusual candour, he later told a journalist that this was his ultimate goal in entering politics. Saunders left to his successor a troublesome legacy of promises, including higher salaries for teachers, greater support for the treatment of tuberculosis, and old-age pensions – all contingent upon subsidy increases from the federal government.[101] Despite Saunders' earlier efforts to be ingratiating, including dropping out of the regional protest, the expected help from the King government did not materialize. Past promises to make prohibition effective also came home to roost. The abandonment of prohibition in New Brunswick and Nova Scotia meant a greater concentration by rum runners on trade with the Island and resulted in a series of liquor-related scandals. In the election of 1931 the Dominion Alliance, which had previously supported the Liberals, remained officially neutral.

The election saw the Conservatives under J.D. Stewart defeat Walter Lea, the first farmer premier of the province, by a majority of six seats.[102] Stewart's victory ensured that, in yet another province, the Tories would be associated with the Depression. Having made much of the pension issue in his campaign, and with his own party in power federally, Stewart, in consultation with federal officials, worked out a plan to squeeze pensions to fit the province's limited revenues. Most active in the health field was W.J.P. Kennedy, physician, surgeon, and leader in Red Cross and anti-tuberculosis campaigns. In 1939, as the head of a new Department of Health, Kennedy had the government take over from the Red Cross responsibility for nurses' inspection of the schools and transferred the nurses to the public payroll. In the same year the new sanatorium opened under his department's auspices.[103]

The persistence of the Depression contributed to the Island's disillusionment with the Conservatives in the provincial election of 1935. With opposition leader Walter Lea seriously ill, the Liberals turned to Thane Campbell, a forty-two-year-old Rhodes scholar who had practised law with Albert Saunders. The youthful Campbell waged an energetic campaign that ended with the Liberals' winning every seat in the assembly. When in power, Campbell established a permanent civil service and encouraged co-operative organization and marketing boards. He also transferred prohibition enforcement back to the government from an independent commission and lightened some of its penalties. Perhaps learning from Saunders' experience, Campbell became a defender of regional solidarity, supporting the Maritimes Transportation Commission in its protest against the dissolution of the National Harbours Board and its attempts to equalize rates for port services. In the matter of constitutional reform Campbell carefully dissociated his province from New Brunswick's provincial-rights stance and reiterated to the Rowell-Sirois Commission Nova Scotia's call for a redistribution of subsidies based on fiscal need.

The outbreak of war in September of 1939 allowed the Maritimes to leave the decade with some of the optimism with which they had entered it. Since war had meant prosperity for the region in the past, producers waited impatiently for the expected contracts to come their way. But the anticipation of boom could not conceal the relative decline of the region. Trends of economic consolidation in central Canada continued, as the Maritimes' share of the nation's manufacturing declined by about 16 per cent. The mail-order houses continued their inroads into the retail trade, and Toronto and Montreal firms maintained and extended their hegemony over the wholesale. A more insidious factor was reflected in the three provinces' chronic financial difficulties, as the federal government continued to promulgate the welfare state in a form that limited the Maritimes' participation. Unemployment relief played a more restricted role in the Maritimes, old-age pensions were qualitatively different there, and per-capita expenditures on health and education fell far below those in the rest of the country and resulted in higher rates of illiteracy and infant mortality.[104] Through the various royal commissions, Canadians had begun to identify the constitutional basis of the problem, but stronger provinces were not disposed to forego any advantages. Despite disproportionately high expenditures on roads and other public works, the Maritimes lagged behind the rest of the country in infrastructure and were unable to afford the assistance to industry provided by other provinces. Maritimers confidently expected to participate in the industrial expansion of a wartime boom, but never before had they been in such a weak position to do so.

# CHAPTER NINE

# The 1940s
## War and Rehabilitation

'You never meet a man who thinks of himself as a Maritimer,' a contemporary central-Canadian commentator complained after a tour of the region in 1948.[1] This absence of a strong sense of regional identity proved a serious liability during the 1940s when war and insecurity bred a highly directive federalism that banished the Depression, contributed to the military victory in Europe, recast Canada's social-security system, and reshaped the political economy of Atlantic Canada. Although Canadian business mounted the most concerted opposition to the growth of federal powers, their own industrial strategy was no less centralist. Most Maritimers, caught between their commitment to the war and their need of employment and social security, and divided and distracted by post-war adjustment and cold-war rhetoric, seemed content to leave the solutions to their problems to the interventions of the federal government and the operation of the 'free' market.

Although Canada had declared war on Germany on 10 September 1939, the nature and magnitude of the European conflict became clear only in the spring of 1940. The limited extent of the initial conflict, the peace proposals, and the confusion that marked the first seven months of the war created a deceptive air of unreality. Hitler's sudden invasion of Denmark and Norway in April 1940 and his 'sickle cut' through Luxembourg, Belgium, the Netherlands, and France ended the 'phoney war.' The flight of the 337,331 British and Allied servicemen from Dunkirk from 28 May until 3 June, the entry of Mussolini's Italy into the war on 10 June, and the fall of France on 22 June dramatically demonstrated Hitler's intentions and transformed the war into a global confrontation.

By July only Britain had escaped Hitler's European grasp. How long Britain would remain so was unclear, as the German Luftwaffe rained bombs upon British airfields, defence industries, and the civilian population, to prepare Britain itself for invasion. What followed was the Battle of Britain, a tense, year-long air battle, in which Canadian men and *matériel* helped keep Britain in the war.

A few days before France negotiated its peace with Germany, a shaken Canadian War Cabinet held a sombre but crucial meeting. After consulting the opposition leaders, the government vowed that Canada would fight so long as Britain and France, or Britain alone, remained a belligerent.[2] Before either the Soviet Union or the United States entered the war, this onerous commitment meant that for a decisive period Canada would be Britain's largest, most powerful ally.

In contrast to the government's timorous, vacillating, and contradictory response to the Great Depression, Canada's war effort was a monument to public planning, co-ordination, and initiative. Immediately upon the outbreak of war the federal government assumed the emergency powers specified in the British North America Act, the chief legislative instrument of which was the War Measures Act, which 'for practical purposes ... became the constitution of Canada.'[3] The War Measures Act gave the federal government power to promulgate, without parliamentary debate, regulations and orders that had the force of law on any matter affecting Canada's 'security, defence, peace, order and welfare.' Little remained outside its purview. Under the act's provisions, the federal government promulgated 6,414 orders, affecting all aspects of Canadian life.

The spirit of total war pervaded all levels of society. Scarcity of supplies, government regulations, and popular taste altered the colours and styles of civilian clothes.[4] Children played with wooden soldiers, gas masks, and cigarette cards; collected bones, cooking fats, and scrap metal to recycle for war production; planted victory gardens, purchased war savings stamps and certificates, or were awarded them as school prizes. They read Canadian rather than American comics, American comics having been banned as a 'non-essential' import. Among the most popular of Canadian war comics was the Johnny Canuck series, 'Canada's answer to Nazi oppression.'[5] Perhaps nothing caught the imagination of Maritime war workers more than the work of Nova Scotian Walter Callow, the blind, paralysed First World War veteran who turned a Cigarette Fund for soldiers into a wheelchair coach service for disabled veterans, with the enthusiastic support of annual, school fund-raising drives.[6] To build and maintain civilian support for the war, a Wartime Information Board surveyed public opinion and made and distributed films, posters, radio broadcasts, and pamphlets. It curtailed, edited, and provided news to local papers.[7] Radio was one of the board's most effective mediums, and listeners were treated to a variety of programs,

'Pinch Till It Hurts,' 1944. Coupons and food stamps became a way of life for Canadians under rationing, but belt-tightening was getting a bit excessive for some.

from dramatic, uplifting newscasts to the 'Arsenal of Democracy' and the 'Theatre of Freedom' theatre series and the popular soap opera 'Soldier's Wife.'

No Canadian region appreciated the imperatives of national defence more than the Maritime provinces; and no one could fault the region's generous response to the war's demands. During the war Maritime men and women between the ages of eighteen and thirty-five, moved by

'Doesn't He Look Natural!' 1941. Cartoonist Chambers's assessment of the fate of the Rowell-Sirois Commission recommendations was accurate, at least for the next sixteen years.

their traditional loyalties, proximity to the war front, and economic necessities, joined Canada's armed forces in record numbers. For example, 48.1 per cent of Prince Edward Island's eligible male population joined one of the armed forces, the highest percentage of volunteers from any province except British Columbia. Nova Scotia followed Prince Edward Island with 47.6 per cent participation; and New Brunswick, with 46.8 per cent, was surpassed only marginally by Ontario and Manitoba.[8] Civilians authorized salary deductions to purchase war certificates, undertook voluntary war work, and contributed to a variety of relief funds. In the same co-operative spirit, Maritime provincial governments readily surrendered their taxing powers (Nova Scotia was the only Canadian province with an income tax) to the federal government and delegated the powers of their Labour Relations Act to the Canada Labour Board.

Maritimers had good reasons to support the war, quite apart from their strong traditional loyalties. Since the Maritimes were geographically closer to the European war zone than any other region, the Canadian military authorities realized that, should Britain fall and the war continue, Canada's east coast would become a primary target, and made every provision to cope with east-coast air and naval raids.[9] Already off the Maritime coast German submarines (or 'U-boats') hunted in wolf packs, seeking and often finding opportunities to disrupt the Canadian convoy service or cripple its military strength.[10] To protect Atlantic ports from German submarines, the Royal Canadian Navy installed underwater defences at Halifax, Saint John, Sydney, and Shelburne. The Royal Canadian Air Force established operational bases at Chatham, Moncton, Saint John, Yarmouth, Shelburne, Eastern Passage, Debert, Sydney, and Summerside. British Commonwealth Air Training bases were opened at Stanley and Greenwood. Large army training bases were built or expanded at Edmunston, Sussex, Little River, Debert, and Aldershot; and a prisoner-of-war camp at Ripples, New Brunswick, was staffed by the Home Guard. The navy operated training bases at Deep Brook and Cornwallis. Additional defences were built at Louisbourg, Yarmouth, and Moncton. Anti-aircraft guns and searchlights guarded these larger installations, and radar stations and militia units monitored the coast. At Sydney, the Cape Breton Highlanders, six RCAF seaplanes, and anti-submarine and torpedo nets guarded this important but vulnerable strategic industrial centre. There and elsewhere civilian groups, Boy Scouts, the Red Cross, the St John Ambulance Corps, and various women's organizations set up guards around power stations, dams, and transmission lines. In large urban areas and populous danger points designated by provincial or federal authorities, civil defences (including an air-raid precaution operation) were organized: volunteer doctors, nurses, stretcher-bearers, fire-fighters, drivers, police, and telegraphers were drilled in emergency procedures; electric sirens were posted, and proprietors were advised to keep on hand a bucket of sand for extinguishing incendiary bombs and a gas mask (which could be purchased from the T. Eaton or Robert Simpson stores) for each resident.[11] To co-ordinate regional defences, in June 1940 the government created Maritime Command. Confronted by newspaper headlines such as 'WAR MOVES NEARER NOVA SCOTIA,' residents worried lest one electric light serve as a target of enemy aircraft. Increasingly the region took on the appearance and feeling of an armed camp; rumours of spies and saboteurs, black-outs, and air-raid drills fed the region's sense of fear and apprehension.

Portable sawmill, Shepody, N.B., c. 1940. Wartime demand doubled the number of sawmills during the 1940s. Portables such as the one depicted here allowed substantial production with limited investment.

Above all the war brought an end to the grinding poverty of the Great Depression. Employment opportunities were unevenly distributed in time and space, and pockets of unemployment persisted in some areas, especially during the early years of the war.[12] Generally, however, work was not only plentiful, but workers were in short supply, especially in Halifax and Saint John. The absorption of large numbers of men and women into the armed forces and the departure of others for work in central-Canadian war industries decimated the ranks of the unemployed. The influx of servicemen (and their dependants) with regular paycheques proved a boon to merchants, created new jobs in the service and civilian support industries, and placed a severe strain on public services. Labourers, plumbers, welders, and carpenters were in especially great demand in the shipyards and the construction industry. Building permits in cities like Halifax and Moncton doubled between the years 1939 and 1941. Military bases at Debert, Stanley, and Cornwallis transformed these small communities into towns almost overnight.

Stevedores worked day and night in Saint John and Halifax, since the bulk of 'Canada's wartime, waterborne traffic'[13] flowed through these

Pouring brass, Lunenburg Foundry, 1942. War revitalized some declining industries, though the naval castings being poured in this foundry would have
no market after the war.

two ice-free winter ports. The shortage of vessels and the dangers from
German submarines in the St Lawrence forced much of the summer
traffic through Canada's Atlantic ports. Moreover, the federal government's ambitious program of naval and merchant marine construction
revived and expanded the region's dormant shipbuilding industry.[14]
More urgent still were facilities for the repair of worn and damaged
vessels, veterans of the Battle of the Atlantic, Germany's attempt to cut
Britain's lifeline to North America. To meet these demands, the federal
government constructed, or subsidized the construction of, graving docks,
piers, floating dry docks, and marine railways. By 1943 'more than 75,000
men and women, exclusive of those employed by various contractors
supplying components, were at work in regional' shipyards, building or
repairing damaged vessels in Maritime Canada.[15] According to a 1943
survey of shipyards, the region was still short an estimated 4,872 qualified shipyard workers.[16]

Much ship construction was done in British Columbia or at Great
Lakes and St Lawrence ports, while Maritime ship workers specialized
in the more pressing task of ship repairs. Nevertheless, there was usually

Convoy preparing for departure. Large convoys of supply and troop ships assembled in Bedford Basin for the dangerous Atlantic crossing.

more than enough work for all. The Dominion Steel and Coal Company (DOSCO), which owned Halifax Shipyard Limited, boasting a work-force of 'more than 3,000 civilian employees,' soon outgrew its Halifax facilities and expanded across the harbour to Dartmouth, but still there was insufficient space. Other Halifax shipyards, Purdy Brothers, Webb and Sparks, T.E. Hogan, and Dartmouth Repair also lacked space. On all these sites men and women worked around the clock, at night 'under the cluster of flood-lights ... and the intense violet flare of arc-welders.'[17] Despite their efforts, work-loads backed up so badly at Halifax and Saint John that 'the navy opened new repair facilities at Shelburne and Point Edward.' Small vessels were also built or repaired at Meteghan, Parrsboro, Buctouche, Gagetown, Weymouth, Bridgewater, Hebbville, Lunenburg, Liverpool, Charlottetown, and Sydney. At Pictou, a Crown-company-built shipyard operated by Foundation Company of Canada constructed twenty-four, small 4,700-ton freighters;[18] while ship repairs were done by Pictou Foundry. At these plants women and teenage boys too young for military service worked as riveters, welders, and labourers.[19] At the peak of its production the Pictou shipyard employed some 3,800 persons, close to half of them women. The Trenton Steel

Works, whose capacity was well above its normal production, and the Eastern Car Company were also pressed into service.

Elsewhere, dormant industries, or those operating below capacity, such as Canadian Cottons at Marysville and Milltown or Enterprise Stoves at Sackville, took on new life. The DOSCO steel plant at Sydney, whose vulnerable location had been the concern of pre-war military planners,[20] increased its run of primary steel, produced wire fencing for the battlefields, and, thanks to a $1.75 million federal grant, reopened its ships' plate mill, which shortly produced 'more than one-third of Canada's output of regular ships' plate,'[21] used to build or repair war vessels. At DOSCO's Trenton Steel Works, shells and gun mountings were manufactured as well as bolts and nuts.

Employment opportunities drew rural and village workers away from traditional occupations to the region's towns and cities. An increase in population from 98,636 persons in 1941 to 133,931 in 1951 allowed metropolitan Halifax to retain its position as Canada's twelfth-largest city. Most of this growth took place in the city's suburbs of Armdale, Fairview, Dutch Village, Spryfield, Herring Cove, Rockingham, and Bedford. Across the harbour Dartmouth's population rose from 10,847 to 15,037, with the population of the Dartmouth lakes area growing from 3,497 to 8,231.[22] A large air base at Eastern Passage with a consignment of some 3,500 airmen, many with wives and children, turned Cole Harbour–Eastern Passage into a sizeable suburb. The growth of war industries on the eastern side of Halifax Harbour led to a similar transformation at Woodside and Imperoyal.

In Saint John the construction of a government-owned dry dock, the arrival of transient and fixed military personnel, the increased orders for the DOSCO nail mill, and the transfer to the area of Woodside's Acadia Sugar Refinery, revived the city's depression-ravaged economy. The city's metropolitan population grew from 70,927 in 1941 to 78,337 in 1951. Here, all the increase and more took place in the suburbs of Lancaster, Rothesay, Simonds, and Westfield. In fact the population of the inner city fell by almost 1,000 as a program of urban renewal reduced the amount of high-density, low-cost accommodation available within the city's borders.

The war also stimulated population growth in towns such as Chatham, Amherst, Pictou, New Glasgow, and Trenton, towns that had stagnated since the First World War. Summerside, Sydney, Fredericton, and Moncton, whose populations had grown steadily since the Armistice, continued to expand. During the 1940s the population of Fredericton increased from 10,062 to 16,018, and that of Moncton from 22,763 to 27,334. Consequently, at the end of the decade 54 per cent of Nova Scotia's population lived in urban centres, as opposed to 44 per cent at the beginning; in New Brunswick 32.4 per cent of the province's population were urban dwellers in 1951, 6 per cent more than in 1941; in Prince Edward Island only 25 per cent of its population lived in urban centres in 1951. Increasingly the region's towns and cities offered rural dwellers, too, both permanent and occasional employment.

Employment opportunities, price controls, and national wage and work standards narrowed 'slightly' the gap between social groups;[23] in particular, wage earners and women improved their positions. Estimated general wage rates increased as much as 21 per cent, while the cost of living during the war rose no more than 18 per cent above pre-war levels.[24] Some occupations fared much better than others. In Halifax the average hourly wage of a labourer rose 48 per cent, and the wage of a carpenter rose 35 per cent above pre-war rates. Steady employment, long hours, and overtime swelled family incomes. Patriotism, money, and the pursuit of adventure, freedom and self-respect drew women into the armed forces and war-related industries. While many of the new jobs, including those in the military, were in the nurturing, sales, and service sectors, some women found work in shipyards and industrial plants as welders, fitters, and instrument makers. Domestic servants, who composed 37 per cent of the female work-force in Nova Scotia in 1941, could make three times their wages in the aircraft, transport, and shipping industries. Other women staffed the multitude of voluntary organizations that contributed to the material and emotional welfare of their communities.[25]

War employment offices helped workers, male or female, find jobs; the War Emergency Training Act enabled workers to retrain or upgrade their skills; cost-of-living allowances (restricted to wage earners) insulated workers from inflation; government-sponsored labour-supply pools guaranteed vital war workers, such as stevedores, year-round board, lodging, and wages; and a compulsory unemployment-insurance scheme cushioned workers from periods of temporary unemployment. The scarcity of labour and the 1943 Privy Council Order 1003, which made collective bargaining compulsory in all industries across the country, strengthened the power of organized labour. Labour's enhanced importance led the New Brunswick government in 1944 to create a separate Department of Labour, increase workers' compensation, and improve technical education. The following year a minimum wage was established. Although war work often entailed authoritarian managerial structures and hazardous working conditions,[26] on balance, at the end of the war the region's working class had more money, better skills, and increased knowledge, and was better organized and conscious of its 'social significance';[27] and women had broadened their range of occupational opportunities.

The strains and demands of wartime employment also altered social patterns and fed conflicts. Prolonged separation of wives and husbands, particularly among service personnel, brought marital tensions and family breakdowns. In recognition of this war problem, the Canadian Legion campaigned for easier and cheaper divorce procedures; more particularly, the Island chapter called for a provincial divorce court,[28] and the Canadian Bar Association offered veterans free legal service for divorce. Parents' absence from home and the refusal of men to accept their wives' economic independence and make the necessary domestic accommodation led to what one observer colourfully described as 'a sort of domestic rebellion.'[29] Wartime social problems changed. In contrast to the pre-war period, when children died in Saint John 'for no other reason than that they were undernourished,'[30] social workers in Saint John and Halifax reported more cases of 'drunkenness, more drifting apart of families, more licence, more problems of sexual behaviour, but less malnutrition and the wretched domestic concomitants of poverty.'[31]

None the less, living conditions in Halifax, Saint John, Sydney, and elsewhere were often deplorable. Crowding in Halifax was perhaps the most obvious and stubborn problem. Even before the war Halifax had a shortage of an estimated 4,000 dwellings.[32] The influx of large numbers of military and civilian war workers and transients strained housing facilities to the limit. The naval establishment alone grew from a few hundred to almost 20,000 within a very short period; before the war ended there were almost 100,000 military personnel in the city. With them came dependants, supply staff, and a host of unsolicited camp followers – prostitutes, bootleggers, and drug dealers anxious to profit from the situation. (Bootleggers benefited immensely from the provincial government's stringent liquor ration of two quarts of gin or one quart of rum or whisky or two dozen quarts of beer a month to ration-card holders.)[33] The dated 1941 census reported that Halifax had an average of 4.9 persons per room; in some cases 10 persons shared one room. About 62.5 per cent of the city's residents were tenants, housed in flats, apartments, row houses, or semi-detached buildings, at least 29.3 per cent of which were in need of repair (as opposed to a national average of 20 per cent). Those in a bad state of repair possessed leaking roofs, defective doors and windows, sagging floors, and rotting woodwork.

A pre-war sanitary survey conducted by the Halifax Board of Health for the Citizen's Housing Committee condemned 192 buildings containing 370 families as beyond repair and unfit for habitation, while another 1,273 dwellings would pass inspection only if extensively repaired. According to a 1943 Halifax Board of Trade study on housing, things had deteriorated considerably since then. Although only 2.7 per cent of Halifax residents were without flush toilets, 18.7 per cent of the city's dwellings possessed neither bath nor shower. Many were poorly heated, and others were a fire hazard.[34] To meet the chronic housing shortage the federal Wartime Housing Corporation built more than a thousand small houses, and the naval authorities erected 'masses' of cheap 'pre-fabricated cottages.'[35] Although voluntary organizations such as the Salvation Army, the Knights of Columbus, the YMCA, and the Canadian Legion expanded their hostel accommodation (the YMCA converted the Halifax Ladies' College at Barrington and Harvey streets into a 750-bed hostel), it took only an additional consignment of troops or refugees, like that in December 1940, to leave an estimated 400 to 500 men without accommodation.[36]

Problems of provisioning, transporting, caring for and entertaining Halifax's expanded and fluctuating population stubbornly resisted solution. The shortage of food and fuel in the city obliged public authorities to ration meat, vegetables, and gasoline more stringently than in the rest of the country, and sometimes for long periods of time. For example, Maritimers were permitted only two gallons of gasoline per week, while the rest of the country enjoyed five. While the local authorities struggled to overcome the provisioning difficulties created by the city's limited, overburdened transportation system, many Haligonians were convinced that their severe shortages were caused more by the fact that the federal war planners insisted upon using the dated 1941 population figures in calculating the city's requirements. Nor did the federal government seem ready to recognize the extra strain on the city's financial resources caused by the need to maintain and expand its overburdened roads, public transit system, schools, and hospitals. At the Grace Maternity Hospital, beds were set up in the waiting-room; and a diphtheria epidemic (related to crowded housing) in the early part of the war pushed the city's hospitals to the breaking point.

Recreational facilities, too, were in very short supply, despite the generous efforts of the churches and various voluntary organizations such as the YMCA, the Canadian Legion, the Salvation Army, the Red Cross (a third of Nova Scotia's population belonged to a Red Cross organization by 1945), the Navy League, the Victorian Order of Nurses, the Knights of Columbus, and the Imperial Order of the Daughters of the Empire. Between their more limited, sedate entertainment of concerts, dances, socials, and milkshake canteens and the brothels, drug dealers, and bootleggers, however, there was relatively little middle ground. The city possessed only nine cinemas, with a total capacity of 7,500 seats.[37] And apart from the Allied Merchant Seaman's Club on Hollis Street (which the American authorities objected to because it possessed 'no segregation as to race or colour')[38] and a few wet canteens, the only other licensed service club, the Ajax Club, run by Mrs Janet McNan,

Waiting in line, the Orpheus Theatre, Halifax, 1941. Over-crowding and shortages caused frustration to both civilians and military personnel in Halifax. Sailors wait their turn to see a movie under the vigilant eyes of the military police.

had its liquor licence revoked, through the pressures of the revitalized prohibition movement, led by men such as the Rev. Gerald Rogers, the minister at Fort Massey United Church.

Throughout the war the combination of scarce, poor, expensive housing, food and fuel shortages, and overcrowding, and the addition of a multinational population of military and civilian personnel, gave Halifax the air 'of a beleaguered and refugee-crowded city in Europe.'[39] So acute had these problems become that the civilian and military authorities drew up – though they did not implement – a plan to expel from the city all but essential war workers.[40] Consequently, by the war's end the social tensions in Halifax made it almost as volatile as the navy's magazine on the shores of the Bedford Basin, and when released, those tensions were almost as destructive.

Halifax exploded on Monday, 7 May 1945, when sirens, ships' whistles, and church bells announced Germany's surrender. Thousands of celebrating sailors, soldiers, and civilians poured onto the streets. That night fireworks on Citadel Hill drew up to 15,000 people, including 7,964 sailors – from the shore establishment and the troop ships *Scotian*, *Stadacona*, and *Peregrine* – with no orders to return to their barracks until 7:00 a.m. the next morning. (Army and air-force personnel had curfews of 10:15 and 11:45 p.m.) With only two clubs and a few wet canteens in the city, and the restaurants and cinemas closed or closing – their staff having joined the celebrants – there was little for the men to do.

Trouble began about 10:30 p.m., soon after the Citadel's fireworks ended, when some navy ratings stopped tramcar 126 not far from the dockyard, chased its driver and passengers from the car, smashed its windows, and set it afire. A police car and a fire truck whose drivers tried to intervene were similarly roughed-up. From there, things deteriorated rapidly.

Liquor stores and breweries were the mob's first objective. Once a civilian mob overcame the lone watchman at the Sackville Street liquor store and smashed its windows, a horde of thirsty blue-jacketed servicemen helped them confiscate its contents. The Liquor Commission's stores on Hollis and Buckingham streets were next. Soon the city's streets, parks, and cemeteries became beer gardens full of drunken sailors and civilians. Others turned on shops and restaurants, smashing windows and looting their contents. Although drunkenness immobilized a number of active rioters, the disturbance had not run its course.

Reinforced by ten thousand rested, happy warriors who had been retained in barracks and others who simply deserted their posts, the rioters and looters resumed their activities the next day shortly after noon, when the victory ceremonies and thanksgiving service at St Paul's Anglican Church ended. The subsequent riot followed a familiar pattern: an attack on another tramcar (151) followed by an assault on Oland's and Keith's breweries. The owner of Keith's Brewery, realizing the futility of resistance, opened the doors and appealed to the crowd to leave the building intact. From there an increasingly drunken crowd fought, vandalized, looted, and consumed its ill-gotten gains, undeterred by the ineffectual naval shore patrol and the city's feeble eighty-three-man police force, assisted by a small detachment of RCMP officers. Many of the two hundred-man Navy Shore Patrol, detailed by the civilian and military authorities to help contain victory rioters, had inexplicably been reassigned to other duties; and those on duty had been instructed simply to do what they could to contain but not provoke the rioters.

At the end of the second day two navy men were dead, one from a skull fracture the other from alcohol poisoning. Seventeen persons had been injured, 251 persons had been charged, largely with looting, robbery, drunkeness, disorderly behaviour, and rape. About 564 businesses were damaged, and an estimated $5 million worth of property damage

V.E. Day, Halifax, 7 May 1945

closed some shops for weeks. With insufficient force to quell the riot and balked by naval authorities in his efforts to impose martial law, the newly elected mayor of Halifax, Alan M. Butler, backed by outraged merchants and townspeople, sought 1,000 paratroopers from the Debert Army Camp and 60 provosts from Camp Borden to stand by in case of an anticipated third attack the next day. Fortunately, Butler's precautions were unnecessary. The conflict was over, except for an acrimonious but revealing verbal battle over the responsibility for this costly victory riot.[41]

Canadians' deep sense of insecurity and fear of post-war recession had been detected by an early public-opinion survey by the Wartime Information Board, and Canada's first Gallup Poll in 1943 had placed support for the Co-operative Commonwealth Federation (CCF), with its promise of social security, one percentage point ahead of both the Conservative and Liberal parties. In Cape Breton, where the CCF enjoyed the backing of the United Mine Workers union, three CCF members had been elected to the Nova Scotia legislature in 1941, only one less than the Conservatives, whom they replaced in 1945 as the official opposition. Moreover, the party's capture of 11 per cent of the popular vote in the New Brunswick provincial election of 1944 demonstrated that the CCF's appeal was not confined to central and western Canada. Spurred on by partisan political considerations, W.L.M. King's Liberal government created a new Department of Reconstruction under the dynamic direction of C.D. Howe and invited provincial governments to appoint their own reconstruction committees and co-operate with the federal planners.

All Maritime provinces, drawing upon the abilities of several of their well-placed native sons, complied with the federal request, though in varying degrees. Nova Scotia ordered a full-blown Royal Commission on Provincial Development, chaired by Canada's foremost political scientist, Robert McGregor Dawson of the University of Toronto, ably assisted by Henry Marshall Tory, the former president of the University of Alberta and the National Research Council. New Brunswick commissioned a thorough report, its investigation chaired by the Nova Scotia-born president of the University of New Brunswick, Norman A.M. MacKenzie.[42] Prince Edward Island contented itself with a more modest *Interim Report*, with its inquiry headed by Dr J.E. Lattimer, the chairman of the Department of Agricultural Economics at Macdonald College, McGill University.

All three recognized the temporary and superficial character of the region's war-induced prosperity, as did other informed regional observers. They realized that much of the region's well-being was the result of federal war expenditures on payrolls and short-term construction projects, such as airports, military bases, housing, shipping facilities, and the production of raw materials, principally coal, wood, wood products, and newsprint. Few of these projects promised lucrative long-term employment. Meanwhile, the concentration in central Canada of wartime industrial production readily adaptable to labour-intensive peacetime production accentuated the growing industrial disparity between the centre and the periphery and left the Maritimes more exposed, defenceless, and dependent than before the war. In the words of the *Report of the New Brunswick Committee on Reconstruction*, the underlying causes of regional maladjustment not only remained unchanged but were aggravated by the war.[43]

The exigencies of war disrupted many traditional regional industries, some temporarily, some permanently. For example, owing to the scarcity of oil and shipping and the fear of German submarines, the Acadia Sugar Refinery at Woodside, which employed about 800 men, was closed in 1942 and relocated in Saint John. Similarly, public works such as the construction of water terminals at Charlottetown were discontinued upon the outbreak of war. Industries not favoured by guaranteed supplies, markets, and production incentives faced a competitive disadvantage in securing labour and capital. To add insult to injury, the migration or assignment of skilled labour to war industries in central Canada gave federal war planners additional reasons to establish war production outside the region.

Recruitment, better employment, unemployment insurance (small commodity producers such as farmers and fishermen were excluded from the scheme), and higher wages in urban centres made rural labour scarce and expensive. Labour scarcity, together with the Wartime Prices and Trade Board's refusal to authorize (or its delay in authorizing) new farm machinery to replace the old and/or compensate for the loss of labour, caused periodic problems for farmers, especially on Prince Edward Island.[44] There, farmers encountered additional marketing problems owing to the loss in 1941 of the *Charlottetown*, one of the Island's two Borden ferries. Initially because of war scarcity, and later simply due to technical and political bungling, the *Charlottetown* was not replaced by the *Abegweit* until 1947.[45]

Many persons left farms for good during the war. At the end of the decade Nova Scotia had 17 per cent and New Brunswick 11 per cent less acreage in cultivation than in 1941. Similarly, fewer persons over fourteen years of age found employment in agriculture (19 per cent in Prince Edward Island, 13.9 per cent in Nova Scotia, and 16.1 per cent in New Brunswick). Despite labour and machinery shortages, Maritime farm productivity increased significantly. Average farm sizes in all three provinces expanded; moreover, owing to the growth of internal markets and aided by price supports, Maritime farm incomes increased temporarily more rapidly than national averages.[46] In the case of fishing, the

Another 'Displaced Persons' Problem. The government offered generous help in resettling war refugees in Canada, while farmers were compelled to destroy their orchards because of loss of markets overseas. The irony was not lost on Maritimers.

presence of German U-boats prevented primary producers from exploiting their temporary advantage; nor did the war bring any permanent improvement in technique or equipment that might have given the region's fishermen a competitive edge in the post-war era.[47]

No sector suffered more from the disruption of traditional markets than the apple industry, located primarily in the Annapolis Valley but also in the Saint John River Valley and on Prince Edward Island. Closure of the British market, which had absorbed up to 80 per cent of the

Annapolis Valley's pre-war crop, was cushioned temporarily by the federal government's creation of the Nova Scotia Apple Marketing Board, to dispose of the Nova Scotia crop on the domestic market by encouraging the creation of food-processing plants to turn the apple surplus into juice, sauce, and pie fillings, while awaiting the reopening of the British market. The post-war sterling crisis, however, coupled with Britain's increasing ability to supply its own needs, meant that the British market never reopened, and Maritime apple growers, unable to break into the saturated Canadian and American markets, were obliged to uproot their orchards, close their warehouses, and nail 'For Sale' signs on their property. The federal government compensated them to some extent for their considerable loss,[48] but by the end of the decade all three provinces counted half the apple trees they had possessed at its beginning.[49] So dire was the Annapolis Valley's perceived plight that the Nova Scotia minister of agriculture, A.W. MacKenzie, speculated publicly that 2,000 families might be obliged to leave the area (speculation that George Nowlan used to help him capture the Digby-Annapolis-Kings federal constituency for the Conservative Party in the by-election of 1948); fortunately, it was a false prophecy.[50]

With the end of the war, the Canadian military establishment shrank from 478,000 in May 1945 to 31,000 in September 1946. Employment in Maritime shipyards, which had reached a peak of 75,000 persons in 1943, shrank to a mere 12,000 by 1950. Heavily dependent as it was upon defence expenditures, the Maritime economy was in general poorly placed to face the post-war world, perhaps more poorly placed than at the war's beginning.

Many contemporary federal war planners and politicians thought they knew what had gone wrong. According to them, the failure of Maritime industry to benefit from the war was due to the region's lack of hydro-electricity, the pre-war decay of its industrial base, the scarcity of skilled labour, its distance from markets, its lack of entrepreneurial initiative, and its vulnerability to attack. All three provincial reconstruction committees, however, disagreed with the wartime planners. They concluded that the war planners and politicians themselves were responsible for much of the region's plight, an argument reinforced by the research of Professor E.R. Forbes. According to Forbes, federal planners and politicians not only failed to redress regional disparity during the war, but often made decisions detrimental to the Maritimes' long-term economic development, thereby consolidating rather than alleviating regional disparity. As he explains, none of the new 'crown corporations was located in the region' and, of the Department of Munitions and Supply's extensive investment in the creation and the equipment of Canadian industry by 1944, only about 3.7 per cent had been placed in the Maritimes, chiefly in Nova Scotia, and mostly for aircraft and naval repair. Much of the shipbuilding had been done outside the region, particularly in British Columbia, with the Maritime share accounting for only 6.2 per cent of the value of total contracts. In their placement of orders and the distribution of capital-equipment grants and depreciation allowances, as well as their deafness to pleas from Maritime industrial and political leaders, federal politicians such as C.D. Howe and his bureaucrats favoured the concentration of manufacturing in central Canada.[51] Howe's personal dislike for DOSCO, which controlled much of the region's war industry, made efforts to loosen federal purse strings more difficult still.

But why did Maritime leaders permit this to occur? The region did not lack influence in the wartime federal cabinet. With four key cabinet ministers, James Layton Ralston, senior minister of national defence, Angus L. Macdonald, minister of national defence for naval services, James L. Ilsley, minister of finance, and Joseph E. Michaud, minister of transport, the Maritimes had rarely been better represented in Ottawa. (Some might even have counted Howe, the powerful, American-born minister of munitions, who had come to Canada in 1908 to become a professor of civil engineering at Dalhousie University and later became its first chancellor.) Moreover, all four Maritime ministers sat on the ten-man War Committee of the Canadian cabinet. In the Commons, too, sat Cyrus MacMillan, a member of the 1920s Duncan Commission and other regional commissions, who had briefly occupied the ministry of fisheries and now represented the P.E.I. constituency of Prince.

Of the four cabinet ministers, the forty-nine-year-old, once-and-future premier of Nova Scotia, Angus L. Macdonald, thought by some to be W.L.M. King's logical successor, was probably the person most committed to the region; certainly he was best placed to co-ordinate a regional offensive. But Macdonald, equally committed to the war, was fearfully overworked and anxious during these years, building the Canadian Navy from a 13- to a 560-ship force and overseeing the perilous convoy service. In poor health, uncomfortable in Parliament, at odds with the press, and increasingly out of sympathy with the prime minister, Macdonald had neither the time, the energy, nor the political clout to assume this onerous task.[52] And none of the other Maritime ministers, whether through overwork or partisan loyalty, proved a more effective regional advocate.

The role of regional watch-dog, therefore, fell by default to the provincial premiers, all able enough men, but captives of their political loyalties and their commitment to the war, and unwilling to venture much beyond their provincial borders. The least able of the three was A.S. MacMillan, Macdonald's stand-in as premier of Nova Scotia. A seventy-year-old contractor and lumberman from Upper South River,

Antigonish County, MacMillan was not always in good health, though he held concurrently the offices of premier, provincial secretary, minister of public works, and minister of highways (until 1942). MacMillan also led a divided cabinet, as many of his colleagues saw him for what he was: a caretaker, marking time until Macdonald, their man in Ottawa, returned – which he did less than a week after the capitulation of Japan in September 1945.[53]

In contrast to MacMillan, fifty-three-year old John Walter Jones, who succeeded Thane A. Campbell in 1943 as the Liberal premier of Prince Edward Island, had qualities that might have made him a forceful regional leader. Behind his carefully cultivated rustic image of 'Farmer Jones' was a well-educated, widely travelled, articulate author-and-teacher-turned-farmer. Born in Pownall, this peppery, popular politician and former member of the Farmers' Progressive Party was not afraid to challenge the great and powerful or question the virtues of Confederation, or, if need be, of the free market.[54] His fief was small, however, and increasingly dependent upon federal largesse, and his province's needs were often different and sometimes in competition with those of Nova Scotia and New Brunswick.

When John Babbitt McNair, the stately, fifty-year-old, Andover-born Rhodes scholar and Fredericton lawyer, replaced A.A. Dysart as premier of New Brunswick in 1940, his province's finances were in a precarious condition. The province's Montreal bankers were threatening to foreclose; ironically, when McNair left politics in 1952 his province faced a similar threat. Throughout McNair's term of office he wrestled with the seemingly impossible task of managing the province's strained financial resources, aware that his most immediate source of salvation was Ottawa. An able advocate, in September 1940 McNair asked the federal government for $4.5 million to construct hydroelectric plants and roads, in order to counteract the wartime planners' refusal to decentralize war industry owing to the Maritimes' lack of infrastructure. When he was offered a mere $100,000, the desperate state of the province's finances gave McNair, a devoted Liberal and committed war supporter, little option but to accept what he had been offered and wait for a more opportune moment.[55]

Given the critical character of the war and the promise of regional equity contained in the recently published report of the Rowell-Sirois Royal Commission on Dominion-Provincial Relations, this was not an unreasonable position. The commission had been appointed in 1937, at the insistence of a broad network of English-Canadian nationalists, intellectuals, and social democrats distressed by the retreat of government, the resurgence of provincial rights, and the failure of the British North America Act to provide the central government with the power to cope with the Great Depression.[56] The commissioners had examined a wide range of subjects, including the country's social-security system, municipal institutions, and educational institutions. Their report called for a drastic overhaul of public services, a modest redistribution of federal-provincial powers, and a redress of regional inequalities.

The royal commission's recognition of regional disparity was applauded by even such traditional opponents of the extension of federal powers as the Saint John Board of Trade, though that body remained reluctant to relinquish its moral claim for better terms.[57] The commission's insistence upon basic national standards for social and public services promised relief to hard-pressed provincial and municipal governments. A preliminary provincial assessment of the benefits of a proposed 'equalization' or National Adjustment Grant suggested that New Brunswick, with a $5.51 per-capita federal grant, would fare better than any other province, including Prince Edward Island with $2.95 and Nova Scotia with only $1.56 per capita.[58] McNair, therefore, had every reason to be patient and hopeful in September 1940.

As King's Reconstruction Committee elaborated its plans, Maritimers had even more cause to be optimistic. Inspired by the British government's Beveridge Report of December 1942, and driven by a Depression-bred confidence in planning, counter-cyclical financing, and social security, by April 1943 Canadian social planners recommended a 'Charter of Social Services,' including measures to provide full employment, cradle-to-grave social security, health insurance,[59] better schools and transportation facilities, and the more efficient exploitation of natural resources. These suggestions were particularly attractive to a region with a disproportionately large number of the country's unemployed, elderly, young, ill, and illiterate, and with an economy that was increasingly dependent upon natural resources and sensitive to transportation costs.

All Maritime reconstruction committees, for example, had deplored the region's relatively poor health services. A national health survey in 1943 had found that Prince Edward Island had only half the number of doctors needed to meet the national standard of one doctor per thousand people.[60] The Nova Scotia reconstruction committee argued that Nova Scotia's lower per-capita income and living standard created higher rates of infant mortality, dietary deficiencies, and, according to military service records, 'a lower average height.'[61] Similarly, the New Brunswick committee had tied that province's high infant and maternal death rate – the highest in Canada – to the province's woefully inadequate health services.[62] In anticipation of further post-war federal largesse, optimistic provincial and municipal officials drew up long shopping lists of public works: roads, power facilities, land reclamation, national parks and sewers.

The federal government itself seemed ready to proceed with these plans, or so it appeared during the Dominion-Provincial Reconstruction Conference that opened in Ottawa on 6 August 1945, the day the Americans dropped their atomic bomb on Hiroshima. At that conference King, perhaps hoping to achieve at the end of his long career what he had promised at the beginning, outlined to Canada's nine premiers and their 150 advisers plans for a comprehensive program of social security as well as grants-in-aid to assist provinces to undertake important public works and maintain a wide range of social services. In return, the provinces would be asked to continue the wartime arrangement to centralize tax revenue in Ottawa[63] and extend federal legislative powers.

King had scarcely completed his speech before the premiers of Ontario and Quebec denounced the reform package, which Ontario premier George Drew, hysterically characterized as 'Hitlerism.'[64] The central-Canadian premiers' opposition confirmed the Maritime premiers' good opinion of King's plans. To MacMillan, McNair, and Jones, a program of public works and social security that promised to inject revenue into the region's economy was an offer they could not refuse, despite their rhetorical attachment to the virtues of local autonomy.

The Drew-Duplessis refusal to accept King's social vision – or, more importantly, to permit the federal government to control their provincial tax revenue – at this and subsequent conferences in November 1945 and April 1946 severely crippled King's plans and obliged the federal government to proceed with caution. Although the Unemployment Insurance Act (1940) and the Family Allowance Act (1944) had been enacted with relatively little difficulty during the war, the government's plans for a non-contributory Old Age Security Act was held up until 1951, and a national health insurance plan for two decades. In 1948, however, the federal government established a program of general health grants designed to encourage provinces to survey their health needs, create and enlarge their health facilities, and establish special programs to deal with mental health, cancer, tuberculosis, and venereal disease. Under the provisions of this program hospitals were built, renovated, or enlarged: for example, extensions were added to Prince Edward Island's crowded Falconwood Infirmary and to Halifax's Victoria General Hospital.

Roads, resource development, and housing received a high priority in the federal government's public-works program. Its Wartime Housing Corporation, which had built some 45,930 housing units during and immediately after the war, in 1947 was placed under the Central Mortgage and Housing Corporation, created a year earlier to administer the Canada Housing Act and designed initially to help returned veterans to construct homes. Through grants, loans, and the insurance of mortgages it assisted the construction of some 367,900 new living units between the years 1945 and 1949. A full range of demobilization assistance, outlined in the Veterans Charter of 1944, eased the veterans' transition to civilian life. Grants were available to facilitate land purchases and assist small businesses. Similarly, medicare and disability allowances and unemployment and retraining assistance infused funds into provincial services and helped sustain provincial economies.

No provision of the Veterans Charter seemed more portentous than the generous program to underwrite the veterans' university education, a plan pioneered during the First World War by Nova Scotia's Henry Marshall Tory. The post-Second World War Khaki College program doubled staff and student numbers at the Maritimes' numerous universities and colleges and challenged and transformed the character of these staid institutions. It also underlined these institutions' dire need for funds beyond the capacity of private and provincial bodies to provide. Consequently, in their presentations to the federal government's Massey-Lévesque Royal Commission, established in 1949 to examine the status of Canadian arts and letters, spokesmen for Maritime universities pleaded eloquently for federal funding.

That same year, federal-provincial negotiations produced a shared-cost agreement to subsidize construction of the Trans-Canada Highway. This agreement enabled the provinces to build and renovate some of the region's main highway arteries, a service demanded by an increasing number of car owners, though well beyond the public resources of most provincial governments. Moreover, motor vehicle licensing and the gasoline tax provided a lucrative source of provincial revenue. Similarly the Maritime Rehabilitation Act (1948), a federal program designed to meet the region's particular needs, enabled Nova Scotia, New Brunswick, and Prince Edward Island to reclaim hundreds of thousands of acres of wasting agricultural lands, especially along the Fundy Shore, and to aid the development of a Maritime beef cattle industry on these lush grasslands.[65]

Welcome though they were, the infusions of federal funds into the region were a palliative not a cure for the region's ills. For one thing, King's new federalism fell far short of the reform package suggested by the Rowell-Sirois Commission or the Reconstruction Committee, though both were endorsed by an articulate body of opinion, aided and abetted by the Canadian Broadcasting Corporation, which saw the war as a 'vehicle for social change.' Unfortunately, too, the reform recommendations had aroused public expectations beyond the means of hard-pressed provincial treasuries.

Nowhere was public pressure for funds stronger than in education, which the educated federal and provincial planners saw as the region's 'most promising weapon' for social change.[66] The rate of illiteracy in

New Brunswick, where 6.9 per cent of the population over ten years of age could neither read nor write, was the highest in Canada.[67] In Prince Edward Island things were only marginally better. In 1944, of the Island's 473 schools, 405 had only one room (and of these 184 were in need of repair and 69 were beyond repair); 42 two rooms; 9 three rooms; 7 four rooms, and only 10 five or more rooms.[68] Nor did the Island yet possess a vocational, or technical school. The qualifications of many of the teachers were commensurate with their low salaries. Although the June 1942 federal regulation froze teachers to their positions during the war, the rescinding of this regulation in September 1945 created an exodus, as the better-qualified, more-mobile teachers sought more lucrative employment elsewhere.

The plight of the region's colleges and universities was little better. A few, notably the University of New Brunswick, might count upon the private benevolence of wealthy benefactors (such as UNB's chancellor, Lord Beaverbrook, installed in 1947) to establish scholarships or improve university facilities such as the Lady Beaverbrook Residence.[69] Most, however, lived simply upon student fees, alumni contributions, denominational support, the generosity of foreign funding agencies such as the Rockefeller or Carnegie foundations,[70] the goodwill of their over-worked, underpaid staff, and inadequate grants from hard-pressed provincial governments.

All provinces made efforts to improve education, perhaps none more than Prince Edward Island, whose premier, a former school teacher, believed that 'education should form the basis of post-war reconstruction.'[71] Correspondence courses were created and extended, using radio wherever possible; teacher training was upgraded and teachers' salaries were improved; basic provincial minima for curriculum and school maintenance were established; vocational and technical training were improved, using the facilities and experience of the federal government's War Emergency Training Act and its post-war, peacetime successor, and tentative steps were taken towards school consolidation, especially of rural schools. Even so, especially after 1948, increased school attendance owing to the baby boom and the Family Allowance Act, which tied payment of allowances to school attendance, made it difficult for local governments to maintain existing services. The problem was money. Both New Brunswick (at $8.33) and Prince Edward Island (at $6.90) spent less per capita on education than any other province, not because they valued education less but because they had less to spend; indeed, as a percentage of the provincial budget only Alberta spent more on education than Prince Edward Island, followed by Nova Scotia.[72] The Rowell-Sirois Report, the reconstruction committees, and the staunchly provincialist Saint John Board of Trade all recognized that Maritime

Federal offices, Charlottetown, 1945. The new family-allowance offices that opened in Charlottetown – evidence of a growing federal bureaucracy – served as a pilot project for implementing the new social services.

education would reach national standards only through the infusion of federal funds. Unfortunately, that possibility became a casualty of federal-provincial bickering.

Whatever its setbacks, the 'new' federalism swelled the ranks of professionals, such as doctors, nurses, social workers, and professors, who were organized nationally and became increasingly dependent upon federal funds and policy. The tendency to look more and more to Ottawa may also have undermined regional self-help efforts such as the Antigonish Movement.[73] It certainly raised expectations, imposed national priorities, drained scarce provincial revenue into matching-grant programs, and left provincial governments with a growing burden of operating costs that severely reduced their financial ability to initiate projects more appropriate to the region's needs. All were obliged to expand their civil service and spend time and resources on an army of public servants. In recognition of the growing importance of the public sector, in 1943 New Brunswick passed a Civil Service Act providing tenure for government employees. By 1946 all three Maritime provinces had established departments of health and welfare to administer their new and improved social services. Similarly, the growth of highways and licensed vehicles and the need to test, licence, and regulate traffic swelled the payroll of provincial departments of highways.

As the Rowell-Sirois Report had warned, much of the administrative and financial burden for expanded social and educational services and public works fell upon impoverished municipal institutions, to which the provinces had delegated their powers under Section 92 of the British North America Act. The income of municipalities was restricted, however, and their powers to levy personal income tax and 'personal' property taxes on banks and other businesses had been assumed by the federal government in 1942. Although the provinces compensated municipalities for the loss of revenue and provided funds for the establishment and maintenance of new programs, finding an equitable funding formula took time, and the monies distributed never seemed sufficient. The implementation of these programs eventually precipitated a 'post-war revolution'[74] in provincial-municipal relations, in which the provinces established basic standards for public services and assumed a greater responsibility for funding and maintaining schools, roads, and health services. During the 1940s, however, the demands upon municipal institutions proved so onerous that three Nova Scotia towns, Port Hood (1946), Wedgeport (1947), and Joggins (1949), surrendered their incorporated status.[75] To alleviate some of the burden, in 1945 the New Brunswick government took over responsibility for secondary and rural roads from the municipal authorities. Religious groups, principally the Catholic Church and the Salvation Army, and volunteer organizations such as the Red Cross were placed under similar financial constraints in maintaining their traditional commitment to medical and, in the case of the Catholic Church, educational services.

More important than the character and insufficiency of federal assistance was the region's inability to generate sufficient personal or public revenue to support policies tailored more closely to the region's needs. Though it is fashionable to blame the public sector, that failure was as much the responsibility of private as of public policy. The stagnation of Maritime industrial development, especially the decline of industrial Cape Breton and the failure of the government to arrest that decline during the war, left the post-war Maritime economy increasingly dependent upon the relatively low income generated from seasonal primary production, construction, and the growing sales sector of the economy. To augment their revenue, provincial governments raised taxes on gasoline, alcohol, cigarettes, entertainment, and other consumer goods. Prince Edward Island's premier even precipitated a constitutional crisis with his lieutenant-governor in order to abolish prohibition and tap the lucrative source of revenue that liquor sales would provide. The dispute was resolved by a 1948 plebiscite, which Jones won by a three-to-one margin.[76]

Apart from providing additional provincial revenue, the post-war spending spree triggered by the end of rationing and the conversion to peacetime production benefited the Maritimes relatively little, since few of the prized post-war consumer goods, such as cars and electrical equipment, were manufactured in the region. Meanwhile, money was drained from the region to procure these goods, as was labour, especially skilled labour, in search of better opportunities in central Canada and the West. Left behind was a population disproportionately composed of the young, the old, and the unskilled – those least able to contribute to provincial income and most likely to need government assistance. Maritimers enjoyed some of the benefits of post-war prosperity, and their enjoyment dulled the edge of regional dissatisfaction. Nevertheless, though their earned income as a percentage of national income had risen during the war years, it now fell an average of 8 per cent between the years 1946 and 1951, as the country converted its economy from war production to peacetime consumption.

Unfortunately, the conversion only accelerated a trend that the Rowell-Sirois Report had described as a 'natural shift of industry and finance and the consolidation of wealth and income in Central Canada.'[77] Some, including New Brunswick's obsessive Maritime Rights crusader A.P. Paterson, saw this trend as an almost conspiratorial continentalization of the Canadian economy, with the continent's industrial core concentrated along the shores of the Great Lakes, and the Maritimes reduced to providing cheap labour and primary products.[78] Whether the result of conspiracy or not, the pattern was unmistakably accelerated by war and post-war public and private policy. For example, the rationalization of Canadian-American war production under the Hyde Park Agreement of April 1941 led to the concentration of war industries in central Canada and the subsequent shipment of their production through American ports, a development that the Saint John Board of Trade had vigorously denounced.

Although business leaders, whose industries had often been resuscitated by the government's wartime initiatives, viewed the King government's 'socialistic' control of the economy as a 'national calamity' and threat to the free market,[79] these federal policies and politicians frequently proved indispensable to the free market's own centralist economic strategies. The 'free' marketers did not lack friends in the cabinet and the civil service who all-too-obligingly emasculated the more advanced plans for regional equity and the restriction of monopolies suggested by the post-war planners. Moreover in the post-war privatization

'Cure by Bleeding.' Policies that economists would later rationalize as 'equilibrium theory' were viewed with scepticism by many.

of public war industries, C.D. Howe's preference for large multinational corporations as buyers, on the pretext that they were more capable of sustaining the industries' development and management, accelerated the concentration of Canadian industry and of American control over it. Few Maritimers believed that the sale of the 200 or more government-owned ships of the Park Steamship line to foreign interests did anything to aid Canada's ailing merchant marine!

Nothing symbolized the continentalization of the Canadian economy more than the proposed St Lawrence Seaway project. Much to the dismay of Maritime politicians and businessmen, in March 1941, nine

Red Cross mobile clinic, Charlottetown, 1948. Some wartime voluntary services, such as the Red Cross supply of blood through donor clinics, were converted to peacetime ends.

months before the United States was forced into the war, Canada and the United States signed the Great Lakes–St Lawrence Basin Agreement, a package plan to dredge a twenty-seven-foot channel from Montreal to the eastern end of Lake Erie and construct hydroelectric dams to overcome central Canada's energy shortages. The federal project was designed to decrease central Canada's dependence upon coal and oil, increase its industrial competitiveness, and give ocean-going vessels direct access to the head of the Great Lakes, bypassing Atlantic ports.[80] The federal government failed to proceed with the project at that time not because of the Atlantic region's concerted opposition, but because of the U.S. Congress's refusal to ratify the agreement and the scarcity of wartime resources. In fact, Maritime opposition to an initiative had rarely been so unequivocal – or as revealingly impotent in the face of the solid phalanx of central-Canadian political and business interests.

Failure to find a solution to the Maritimes' economic plight cannot be explained solely in terms of the conspiratorial continentalist machinations of central-Canadian businessmen and politicians. The inchoate character of the 'new' federalism, the ideological appeal of the 'free' market, strong partisan loyalties, competing post-war preoccupations, and intraregional social conflicts made concerted regional opposition to central-Canadian private and public policy difficult to mobilize. In welcoming the 'new' federalism, Maritimers had been reassured by the Rowell-Sirois Report's talk of the delegation of powers, the co-operative approach of the federal Reconstruction Committee, and the support of the British Beveridge Report (the Ottawa social-planners' Bible) for the devolution of central powers to regional agencies.[81] Few seemed to have anticipated the Ontario and Quebec premiers' emasculation of social programs and plans for full regional equity, the depth of the commitment of the Ottawa bureaucracy and the 'free' marketers to centralization, and the courts' refusal to countenance the delegation of powers. Anxious to benefit from the federal largesse and eliminate the cost of duplication, Maritimers were all too willing to co-operate, and give the 'new' federalism a chance.

The most conspicuous exception was Angus L. Macdonald, who resumed the premiership of Nova Scotia on 31 August 1945. Macdonald had lost his appetite for 'assailing the citadel in which central Canada's millionaires have fattened at the expense of the people of the Maritimes.' After five years in Ottawa he had become conservative and fearful of 'state socialism'; his only answer to unemployment in Cape Breton coal towns seemed to be to dress men in Highland costume 'to entertain the tourists.'[82] Fiercely jealous of provincial autonomy, and convinced of the traditional virtues of independence, self-sufficiency, and individualism, at the federal-provincial conferences of November 1945 and April 1946 Macdonald joined the Ontario and Quebec premiers' attempts to block or retard the federal government's initiatives. Whether because of ideology or provincial penury, Nova Scotia and P.E.I. were the only provinces to refuse federal aid to housing. Although Macdonald's opposition to the federal government's proposed tax-sharing agreement, which he took to the courts, led eventually to a larger financial settlement for his province, his failure to undertake comparable initiatives, together with his homilies on the importance of traditional values and a romanticized provincial identity, proved a poor substitute for – and a weak defence against – the political dynamics of the 'new' federalism and the 'free' market.

Whether because the Maritime premiers lacked resources, imagination, and political will, or simply because they had a shrewd appreciation of immediate economic and political realities, none chose to formulate a regional alternative to federal policy, or to challenge the logic of the 'free' market. In keeping with traditional political habits and the recommendations of their provincial reconstruction committees, they concentrated upon providing public services and facilities designed to stimulate income and employment in the primary sector of the economy.[83] This was not an unreasonable short-term policy, given the post-war market for the region's fish, wood, mineral, and farm products during the period of relief and reconstruction in Europe.[84] All three premiers made a major commitment to rural electrification, the building and paving of roads, tourism, research, technical education, farm and forest surveys, reforestation, marshland reclamation, fire protection, and refrigeration services: more modest were their conservationist efforts. The post-war return of labour and the reorganization of provincial fishermen's loan plans, together with the activity of the federal government's Fisheries Price Support Board (1947), stimulated a marked growth in the Maritimes' fishing fleet, especially in capital equipment and the deep-sea fleet. Federal war assets, military buildings and runways, and technical equipment were also used to extend health, educational, transportation, and communications facilities. All three provinces invested in the development of power. In New Brunswick the promotion of many of these initiatives was entrusted to the province's Resource Development Board, created in 1944 to stimulate the growth of primary and secondary industry. A more academic body, the Nova Scotia Research Foundation, was established in Nova Scotia in 1946 to find solutions 'to the problems of economic development and rehabilitation' by working through the province's universities and the National Research Council.

Less energetic and successful were the provinces' attempts to encourage the growth of secondary industry. In contrast to their efforts on behalf of primary producers, the provincial premiers failed to follow their reconstruction committees' call to curb monopolies and combines, create effective marketing boards, develop attractive capital-assistance programs, or challenge the 'market prerogatives and traditional position of established elites.'[85] Jones expanded the Island's facilities for packing meat, vegetables, and fruit, built government-owned cold storage, and provided government support to improve the Island's air, rail, and water facilities; and McNair induced Fraser Companies to establish a small paper mill on the Miramichi and K.C. Irving to acquire and modernize another mill in Saint John. Nevertheless, relatively little secondary industry was established in the region during the decade. In this respect the provincial premiers were content to complement rather than challenge the economies of the market-place.

Partisan loyalty also constrained their criticism of federal policy. Despite the region's anger with the steep 1948 freight increases, Macdonald refused to embarrass his party during the Liberal leadership convention of August 1948, in deference to the objections of Robert Winters, the thirty-eight-year-old Liberal MP for Lunenburg-Queens, who feared that a spirited protest might spoil his chance for a cabinet post. McNair and the New Brunswick Liberal delegates had wanted to nominate Macdonald for the leadership of the federal party and withdraw only after putting a case for a better deal.[86] Macdonald's submission to the claims of partisan interests was not unique; Maritime Liberal MPs also bowed to the pressure of party discipline and voted for the 'rationalization of freight rates.' Similarly, though the Liberal editor of the *Maritime Advocate and Busy East*, C.C. Avard, called upon his fellow Maritimers during the 1949 federal election to 'vote for the men who will stand valiantly and persistently for the Atlantic provinces, rather than for those who are mere voting machines,'[87] the Liberals increased substantially their popular vote and took twenty-six of the thirty-four federal seats allotted to the region (now including Newfoundland). Premiers rushed to the defence of their federal colleagues during elections, and even such an implacable Maritime Rights advocate as A.P. Paterson rallied loyally to his party's cause, ready to forget its repeated failure to redress regional grievances.

Perhaps they realized that there was little public support for an anti-federalist offensive in the post-war Maritimes. After fifteen years of economic depression and war, with their attendant privations and restraints, people seemed tired of fighting. They sought escape, diversion, and personal security and welcomed the opportunity to rebuild their lives, continue their education, resume their civilian occupations, rejoin or establish families, and enjoy the flood of consumer goods and services made available through the conversion to peacetime production and large-scale public and private spending. For veterans, many with war brides, and for displaced persons with different cultures, values, habits, and manners, it was a period of readjustment. A buoyant central- or western-Canadian economy provided a safety valve for those dissatisfied with opportunities in the region.

Chief among the sources of public entertainment was the radio, which a growing number of radio sets and stations made increasingly accessible to Maritime listeners. In radio, as elsewhere, service, social concern, and criticism gave place to reassurance, consumerism, and escapism. Among the most popular radio programs were 'Mrs. Housewife, You're on the Air,' the 'Danny Galavan Show,' the 'Eddie Arnold Show,' 'The Lone Ranger,' 'Tops in Pops,' 'Moonlight Serenade,' and 'Hockey Night in Canada.'[88] At movie theatres in the region's towns and cities, American, and only American, films were shown: 1948 featured such offerings as *Rage in Heaven* with Ingrid Bergman, *Unconquered* with Gary Cooper, *Dark Passage* with Humphrey Bogart, *The Lady from Shanghai* with Rita Hayworth and Orson Welles, and *Tycoon* with John Wayne and Laraine Day.[89] Preoccupation with war service died slowly in the Maritimes: as late as 1948 Maritime Red Cross members were still packing parcels for 'the needy of Britain.' Churches recorded increased attendance, and a renewed interest in religion. The union of the Full Gospel and United Pentecostal churches in 1946, and the revived activities of the Watch Tower Bible and Tract Society, which had been banned under the War Measures Act, made these groups more visible among the region's traditional religious denominations, such as the Baptists and Presbyterians, both of which declined in numbers during the decade. Their decline, and the marked growth of the Anglican, United, and Catholic churches brought Maritime religion closer to the national character.

In other ways too the Maritimes became more integrated into national patterns. They shared the country's fascination with the spectacular career of Ottawa's famous figure skater, Barbara Ann Scott, as she moved from Canadian (1944) to North American (1945) to World (1947–8) championships, and then to an Olympic gold medal (1948) at the age of twenty. Children played with 'Barbara Ann' dolls, people showered her with gifts, and receptions were held in her honour.[90] Among sports fans only the Toronto Maple Leafs' record of six Stanley Cup championships during the decade rivalled the achievement of Barbara Ann Scott in attracting popular interest. Closer to home, the return of veterans revived the quality of amateur sports and interest in them. Perhaps none was more popular in the region than baseball, played informally or by various intra-urban, regional, or provincial leagues, as well as school, club, and community organizations.[91]

Some Maritimers exploited wartime and post-war economic opportunities to accumulate and consolidate their wealth. Chief among these was Kenneth Colin Irving, 'New Brunswick's first modern entrepreneurial industrialist.' Irving not only expanded his father's lumber company into pulp-and-paper production and newspaper ownership, but also organized his oil-and-gas company to take maximum advantage of increased post-war highway construction and car-ownership. During the war he turned Canada Veneers into the world's largest supplier of aircraft veneers and bought bus lines, railways, and shipyards. Frank H. Sobey also spent the decade expanding his cash-only, self-service grocery chain, in 1946 buying out his largest competitor, Barker's of New Glasgow, with its eight stores, bakery, and warehouse.[92] The wartime and post-war building boom proved equally profitable to the L.E. Shaw Limited brick factories in Chipman, New Brunswick, and Elmsdale, Nova Scotia. Building-materials supplier and general contractor M.F. Shurman Company Limited of Summerside expanded its business beyond the Island, specializing in airport construction.[93] Similarly a St François furniture factory specializing in school desks, New Brunswick's Nadeau and Nadeau Company, incorporated in 1946 by Docithe Nadeau, an Acadian farmer, MLA, and woodworker, profited from the post-war boom in school construction.[94] The decade's most striking entrepreneurial success was Carl Burke's creation of Maritime Central Airways. When Canadian Airways closed its Maritime routes in 1941, leaving Charlottetown without a regular commercial air link to the mainland (except for Trans-Canada Airlines' stop-gap service), Carl Burke, an ex-Canadian Airways pilot, purchased three aircraft and, with much help from the provincial government,[95] began regular flights to various Maritime towns, and eventually to Quebec. By 1945 he had ten planes in service, and by 1948 he was able to offer regular air service to Saint John, Fredericton, Summerside, Halifax, New Glasgow, Moncton, Sydney, Charlottetown, and the Magdalen Islands. Unfortunately, regional ventures of this nature were far too infrequent.

Too often intraregional rivalry and social and ethnic tensions compromised regional co-operation and co-ordination. While the Maritime Board of Trade had no difficulty in agreeing upon the importance of a Maritime electrical grid, a Canso causeway, the promotion of tourism, and the creation of a Green Gables or Blomidon–Cape Split National Park, conflicting intraregional interests continued to impede concerted initiatives.[96] The Saint John Board of Trade, a bastion of Maritime Rights advocacy, jealously promoted its city's interests over the rival claims of Halifax, Moncton, and Fredericton and fussed constantly lest more public monies be spent in the north of the province than in the south.[97] In attempting to persuade the Wartime Hospitals Committee to establish a 120-bed veterans' hospital in Charlottetown rather than enlarge Camp Hill Hospital in Halifax, Premier Jones reminded the federal authorities that Halifax was as distant from the Island as Montreal and regretted that there appeared to be no one in the federal cabinet to defend Island interests.[98] Herbert Jones, the president of the Island local of the United Steel Workers of America, agreed with the premier. Alarmed by the Charlottetown shipyard's failure to secure contracts for naval repairs, in contrast to the Halifax shipyard's success in gaining contracts to build the tribal class of warships for the navy, Herbert Jones accused the naval authorities and Angus L. Macdonald, 'the Minister himself,' of 'grossly discriminating against both Prince Edward Island and New Brunswick in favour of Nova Scotia.'[99] Nor were private interests always compatible with public interests, as Premier Jones discovered when he attempted to improve the rail service between the Borden Ferry and Charlottetown, an improvement that K.C. Irving feared would divert business from his Island Motor Transport, a subsidiary of his Saint John-Moncton Transport (SMT) Limited.[100] Local reconstruction planners had good reason to warn that petty intraregional and personal jealousies posed a major impediment to political action.[101]

Social conflict had a comparable effect; the most pervasive example

Clarie Gillis. First elected to Ottawa in 1940 to represent the coal-mining towns, Gillis remained a stout defender of Cape Breton's working men and women for the next seventeen years as the lone CCF MP east of Ontario.

was the concerted campaign by Maritime boards of trade and politicians to combat socialism and reduce the power of trade unions. The growth of the CCF, measured by its wartime electoral success in Nova Scotia and New Brunswick, its access to press coverage and radio time, and its respectability among the region's intelligentsia, combined with the increased power of organized labour to alarm many business and political leaders. As early as 1944 Maritime boards of trade agreed, during a boards of trade secretaries' meeting in Montreal in October 1944, to co-ordinate their 'fight against socialism.'[102] Subsequently, employees were warned against the evils of socialism and of the dangers to their jobs should a CCF government take power. In Liverpool, Hartland, Bridgewater, and Edmunston, recalcitrant 'CCFers were fired.' The Cold War warriors, however, had little to fear, since after 1945 the CCF experienced a 'serious and steady decline.'[103] Its paper, the Glace Bay *Gazette*, ceased publication and membership shrank. Moreover the CCF and the 'Catholic graduates of St. Francis Xavier' had emasculated the Communists in the United Mine Workers union.[104] The paper chase, nevertheless, continued unabated. National magazines such as *Saturday Night* and *Maclean's* crusaded relentlessly in defence of private ownership, as though it were in imminent danger, despite the findings of a 1945 Gallup Poll that only 18 per cent of Canadians favoured government ownership. Fortunately, few went to the hysterical lengths of *Social Suicide*, a booklet written by B.A. Trestrail, in which he compared the CCF to the Nazi party 'and somewhat inconsistently stressed the Jewish background of David Lewis.'[105] In some areas the CCF was seen as too close to the Catholic Church; in others it was depicted as a party dominated by Protestant parsons. Maritime business and political leaders endorsed the Cold War and the subsequent hunt for Communist conspirators, especially among workers. At the 1948 Maritime Board of Trade meeting the Halifax Board called upon governments to revoke certification of unions having officers who were Communists or members of other subversive organizations.[106] A highly effective weapon, red baiting united its proponents, divided labour unions, and attracted the support of politicians.

During the post-war years, this concerted antisocialist campaign and the declining demand for industrial employment made organized labour particularly vulnerable; and its opponents were quick to press their advantage, as Maritime coal miners learned in 1947. During the war the coal industry had suffered from poor labour relations, characterized by chronic absenteeism and unauthorized strikes, including a ninety-day strike in 1941 that the *Globe and Mail* called 'a crystal clear case of deliberate sabotage of the national war effort.'[107] Labour discontent continued after the war and led to a series of three strikes, between 31 January and 30 May 1947, to secure wage increases and other benefits.[108] When Macdonald's lecturing and moralizing failed to bring the more than 14,000 Nova Scotia and New Brunswick miners back to work, the Nova Scotia legislature passed a Trade Union Act that made certification of unions and strike votes dependent upon the support of 60 per cent of the workers and limited check-off privileges.[109] The same year the Prince Edward Island government, whose 1946 Speech from the Throne 'rejoiced' that no effective labour organization existed on the Island, proved even more high-handed during a nation-wide Canada Packers strike that defied the mediation efforts of provincial governments. Convinced that labour organizations were as dangerous as monopolistic capitalism, Jones seized the factory, placed it under a controller, hired scab labour, outlawed labour affiliation with any extraprovincial organization, and ordered the resumption of production.[110] Subsequent trade-union legislation in 1948 extended these restrictions to all organized workers and prohibited the closed shop or affiliation with any national or international union. These restrictions were moderated only under threat of federal disallowance.[111] Attempts to emasculate labour organizations did nothing to help the region's workers retain a larger share of the value of their labour.

In contrast to their willingness to act to curtail the demands of labour, in 1949 no government, federal or provincial, made an effort to intervene when conservative labour representatives and shipping company executives, with the support of the federal government, invited Harold ('Hal') C. Banks, an American gangster, into Canada. Bank's mandate was to break up the Communist-controlled Canadian Seamen's Union and replace it by the Seafarers' International Union, and his goon squads terrorized the Halifax waterfront during that city's bicentenary. Perhaps nothing demonstrates the contempt for organized labour among some of the region's employers more than K.C. Irving's treatment of striking workers at his east Saint John oil refinery in 1948. The strike had been called after Irving rejected a New Brunswick conciliation board's unanimous recommendation for a settlement. 'When a trucker refused to drive his rig through an angry mob of strikers, Irving angrily pushed him aside, took the wheel and crashed ahead'; Irving was charged with reckless driving but was never prosecuted.[112] Class interests often made a mockery of regional solidarity.

Women fared little better in the post-war era. Discouraged by the lack of opportunity, many women returned to traditional roles. Although domestic technology mitigated the drudgery of female domestic life, the post-war baby boom and the emphasis on traditional family values, reinforced by government social policy, eroded wartime gains towards gender equality.

Intraregional ethnic tensions also divided and distracted Maritimers. Although each of the Maritime provinces had its own Acadian pressure group, New Brunswick Acadians, the most numerous and best organized, led the struggle for a better deal within the region. Conscious of the Acadians' high rates of illiteracy and the relatively inferior qualifications of their teachers and physical facilities, they focused much of their effort on education. In the past, Acadians had depended on the slender resources of the church, and the generosity of the Société l'Assomption. In 1940 New Brunswick Acadians wrung authorization from their government to use French texts in public schools. More important, for some, was the public recognition by New Brunswick's minister of education, C.H. Blakeney, in August 1943, during a meeting of the Association Acadienne d'Education, of the importance of making French the language of instruction in Acadian schools. In 1944, New Brunswick's first francophone radio station, CJEM, went on the air, and in 1945 a third francophone classical college, the Eduiste-run Saint-Louis, was established at Edmunston. These gains, coupled with the development of a bilingual Canadian military base, also at Edmundston, helped make this dynamic industrial and administrative centre, close to the Quebec border, an important pole of francophone development. Determined to play a role in their province commensurate with their numerical importance, New Brunswick's francophones rejected their political élites' support of W.L.M. King's conscription plebiscite, and decided in 1949 to make *L'Evangéline* a secular daily journal. Clearly, Acadians were more than the reflection of their religious and political élites, despite the important leadership role of a second generation of Acadian bishops such as Mgr Norbert Robichaud. The creation of a commercial course at Collège Saint-Joseph in 1942, the establishment of the federation of caisses populaires in 1946, and the formation of a caisse populaire insurance company in 1948 underscored the pre-eminently pragmatic character of the Acadian survival strategy during the decade.[113]

The Maritime Black community, centred principally but not exclusively in Nova Scotia, spent much of the decade establishing and extending its civil liberties. In some respects the integration of Blacks into the armed forces had forced the issue. Although some Black Maritimers looked to the CCF[114] for assistance, most followed the more conservative path of the Nova Scotia Association for the Advancement of Coloured People (NSAACP). Founded in 1945, the NSAACP, together with the *Clarion*, a monthly newspaper published in New Glasgow from June 1946 to 1956, and edited by Carrie W. Best, 'in the interests of Canada's negroes,'[115] pursued the cause of Black rights with firmness. Under the dedicated leadership of the Rev. W.P. Oliver, the minister at Halifax's Cornwallis Street Baptist Church and a chaplain in the armed forces from 1942 to 1945, education was regarded as the surest road to respect and justice.[116] But neither Oliver, the NSAACP, nor the *Clarion* hesitated to use the courts to force the issue in the celebrated Viola Desmond case. Unable to find a seat in the balcony of New Glasgow's Roseland Theatre, the area known as 'nigger Heaven,' Viola Desmond insisted upon sitting in the whites-only 'parterres.' When the theatre management accused Desmond of trying to evade a government tax (the price of the balcony seats being thirty cents plus two cents tax as opposed to forty cents plus three cents tax in the parterre) the case, which was really about segregation, went to the Supreme Court before it was settled in Desmond's favour. A legal, political, and moral victory for the region's Black community, this judgment was a significant landmark in a long, difficult struggle for respect and equality.

Meanwhile the region's 4,677 Native people, half of that number located in Nova Scotia, spent the decade fighting to retain their right to live in scattered communities, undisturbed by federal bureaucrats' attempts to reduce social-service costs by confining them to six service points: Richibucto, Perth, Fredericton, Shubenacadie, Eskasoni, and Summerside. This policy, established in 1941, was in ruins by the decade's end. The bureaucrats had failed to provide sufficient resources to persuade many people to move. Those who did move were reluctant to stay in an artificial social environment divorced from their traditional employment, family, and friends. The Newfoundland and Quebec governments would attempt a similar social experiment in later decades, with little more success. In waging their lonely battle against this insensitive, bungling centralization policy, the Micmac people found that passive resistance and resilience were their most effective weapons.[117] In this respect they were typical of their fellow Maritimers during the 1940s.

While the war had brought the Maritimes temporary material prosperity and the post-war period a degree of social security, both had accelerated the region's growing vulnerability to and dependence upon central-Canadian public and private policy. During the decade the federal government, in the name of national and social security, had seized the agenda and defined national interest; and it was difficult to argue with its wartime success or to question its post-war direction. Caught between their penury, the 'new' federalism's promise of employment and social security, and their loyalties and apparent commitment to the rhetoric of the 'free' market, Maritimers ended the decade divided, preoccupied, and without an alternative regional strategy. Consequently, at the decade's end the Maritimes were more poorly placed than before the war to resist the centralist claims of either the 'new' federalism or the 'free' market.

PART FOUR
THE ATLANTIC PROVINCES, 1950–1980

# CHAPTER TEN

# Newfoundland Confronts Canada, 1867–1949

April can be a cruel month in eastern Newfoundland, characterized by heavy, dense fogs, the ice pack pressing against the coast, bitter winds, and damp snow. The first of April 1949, the day on which Newfoundland passed from rule by a British-appointed Commission of Government to the status of a Canadian province, was typically cold and gloomy. It fitted the mood of the predominantly anti-Confederate town of St John's. Some houses flew black flags,others the Union Jack at half mast, yet others the old, unofficial flag, the pink, white, and green. There were drawn blinds and black ties. In Government House, though, fires had been lit; and in that cheerful enclave Sir Albert Walsh was sworn in as the first lieutenant-governor, and Joseph Smallwood as the first premier, together with his cabinet.[1] In the Ottawa sunshine, brief, parallel ceremonies took place on Parliament Hill. Gordon Bradley, Smallwood's partner in the Confederation campaign that had started in 1946, was sworn in as secretary of state. 'This is a day which will live long in North American history,' he said.[2]

> It is a day of fulfillment – fulfillment of a vision of great men who planned the nation of Canada more than 80 years ago; and as we stand here on this day of destiny, our thoughts fly back through the years to those far-seeing men of the past – Macdonald, Brown and Cartier in Canada and Carter and Shea in Newfoundland ... In fancy we see them now, bending over this scene in silent and profound approval ... Thus we begin life as one people in an atmosphere of unity. We are all Canadians now ...

In stark contrast to Bradley's optimistic portrayal of Confederation as the positive conclusion of a long historical process, Albert Perlin, Newfoundland's most intelligent political commentator, published a lament in verse in the St John's *Daily News*:[3]

On this day of final parting sad nostalgic
  thoughts arise,
Thoughts to bring hot tears surging to the
  Newfoundlander's eyes.

Thoughts that bring to mind the story of the
  struggles of the past,
Of the men who built our island, nailed its colours to
  the mast.

He reviewed the country's history in couplets, and finished with an expression of the bitterness with which the anti-Confederates viewed their failure:

Let us climb the steep road winding to the top
  of Signal Hill,
There to seek in last reflection surcease from
  our present ill.

See the old familiar places where our history
  was made,
See the men who helped to make it passing in a last
  parade.

Cabot, Gilbert, Guy and Whitbourne, Carson, Morris,
  Hoyles and Kent,
And the men who followed after with their
  hearts on progress bent.

Praise their sturdy independence, tell them if
  they were betrayed,
It was by but half the voters that the fatal
  choice was made.

...
Sold by only half the people, all too willing
  to deny
For illusionary profits what the future might
  imply.

They have bought confederation paying in the
  country's pride.
Let us hope their expectations will be amply
  satisfied.

Those who lost the fight for freedom have the
  greater pride this day,
Though their country's independence lies the victim
  of the fray.

For Perlin, Confederation was a betrayal, an indignity, an insult to a country that had struggled with some success, he would have argued, to maintain and strengthen its independence. Newfoundland had been bullied into Commission of Government in 1934, and into Confederation in 1949. His was a romantic view of the country's history, which, as was always the case in such accounts, placed great emphasis on external scapegoats for its ultimate failure: English west-country merchants, fishing admirals, naval governors, French treaty rights, Canadian malevolence, and a British government that, over the years, had displayed both indifference and manipulative skills of a high order. Against these hostile factors Newfoundlanders had struggled; they had achieved independence in 1855, only to have it snatched away by no more than a mere majority of voters who had been bribed into voting for Confederation in July 1948.

This view of Newfoundland's past still has currency, and some of the more egregious embellishments of the myth continue to circulate. The romantic interpretation has a pedigree stretching back to the early nineteenth century, when a reform movement emerged in St John's seeking the grant of a local legislature and the repeal of the old fishery laws. Its principal spokesmen, William Carson and Patrick Morris, added to the mix a belief that the island possessed rich natural resources apart from the fisheries, resources that, once developed, would make the country 'rich and great.'[4] Newfoundlanders, then, tended to see themselves as settlers in a land that had great economic potential but was held back by the hostile action – or the failure to act – of an array of bogeymen. Add to this a strong dose of local patriotism, and one has the mentality that lay behind the rejection of Confederation in 1869: the crucial decision that Newfoundland would try the experiment of independence. The road was to lead to 1 April 1949, and for reasons that Perlin never fully appreciated.

The defeat of Confederation in the 1869 election was so overwhelming that serious discussion of the issue was effectively ended, not to be revived until the 1940s. The colony's leaders had to base their policies on the assumption that Newfoundland would remain independent; their task, therefore, was to attempt to make that independence viable and permanent. It was a daunting prospect. A population of approximately 162,000,[5] less than half that of Nova Scotia, lived for the most part in small settlements and towns perched along the coast. Eighty-nine per

Weighing salt cod. Before being shipped, fish had to be graded and weighed. Credit was given for the catch based on the merchant's judgment regarding its grade and weight.

cent of the work-force was engaged in the fishery,[6] and fish and seal products represented 95 per cent of exports.[7] There was little market agriculture, though subsistence farming was widespread. There was a tiny secondary sector. Sawmilling and lumbering were in their infancy, and the interior was only slowly becoming known, as the colony's Geological Survey, started in 1864, produced its annual reports. J.D. Rogers' description of Newfoundland as 'a husk without a kernel' has truth for this period, and for long after: 'The sea clothes the island as with a garment, and that garment contains the vital principle and soul of the national life ... To the Newfoundlander the land is a forest or a "barren"; the sea a mine or harvest field, and on the foreshore the yield of the sea is prepared for market.'[8] Virtually all the country produced was exported to Europe, the West Indies, and Brazil; almost all it consumed was imported, about 65 per cent from Britain and the United States, 25 per cent from the mainland colonies, and the balance from elsewhere.[9]

The economy was presided over by a small group of merchants based for the most part in St John's and Conception Bay. They were both importers and exporters, and they ran the fisheries on a credit system: that is, fishermen were advanced supplies on credit in the spring, and they sold their catch to their supplier in the fall, receiving payment – assuming they had a credit balance – in goods rather than cash. Cash was a scarce commodity in outport Newfoundland. Merchants tended to charge as much as they could for supplies advanced on credit, and to pay as little as possible for the fish.[10] This practice, together with the natural uncertainties of both the seal and cod fisheries, and the vagaries of the markets, kept most fishermen either in poverty or on the brink of it. By the mid-nineteenth century the seal fishery, which in the 1840s had represented about a quarter of the colony's exports by value, and which employed as many as 14,000 men in the late 1850s, was starting to decline. In the 1860s merchants turned to steamers to increase both yield and profitability, a process that centralized the sealing industry in St John's and Conception Bay and severely reduced the number of men involved: by 1870–4, the number had declined to an annual average of 9,600, falling to 3,600 by 1900.[11] This helped to intensify the degree and extent of poverty in the colony, and relief bills were starting a dramatic climb. Given the absence of opportunities outside the fisheries, the problem arose of how to provide for an expanding population (it increased by 35 per cent between 1869 and 1884) that a single-staple economy could no longer support.

If poverty and underemployment were two characteristics of the population, another was widespread illiteracy. In spite of a gradually expanding school system, it has been calculated that in 1900 about a third of Newfoundlanders were totally illiterate, compared to 13 per cent in the Maritimes; and this was an improvement over the situation in the 1870s.[12] This appalling fact obviously affected Newfoundland's ability to meet the challenges it faced as an independent country. It also helped to perpetuate the wide gap between the élite and the mass of the population, breeding deference among the latter, and among the former, 'a sluggish intellectual life and an unimaginative and inefficient debate about the goals of society ....'[13] Certainly illiteracy, poverty, and the chronic drain of many of the best and brightest to mainland centres placed the colony at a distinct disadvantage when compared to other parts of the North Atlantic world.

As well, though a strident local patriotism was emerging, the population was marked by sectarian and racial divisions that persisted well into the twentieth century. Newfoundlanders were descendants of migrants from the west of England and the southeast of Ireland, most of whom had arrived in the period 1760–1830. The Irish settled mainly on the Avalon Peninsula, and the English to the north and west, though there were areas of significant overlap in St John's, the north shore of

Conception Bay, and the Burin Peninsula. Each group arrived imbued with the prejudices and animosities of its homeland, and these received a formal platform with the advent of political activity in the 1830s.[14] The mutual hostility of Catholics and Protestants, Irish and English, played a significant part in the island's political and social life. The situation was further exacerbated in the mid-nineteenth century by the overt animosity that existed between Anglicans and Methodists. These entrenched divisions were formally recognized and expressed by the creation of a denominational school system by the education acts of 1843 and 1874, in which each church was provided with government funds to manage its own schools – a step that did little to improve educational standards. Further, after thirty years of politics in which sectarian division and denominational rivalry had played a significant part, an unwritten agreement was reached in the 1860s whereby each of the three major denominations – Roman Catholic, Anglican, and Methodist – would be proportionately represented in the two houses of the legislature, the executive council, and the civil service. By embedding sectarian division in the system, it was hoped and expected that non-denominational political parties would emerge – which in time they did – and that the country's problems could be faced free from constant bickering over place and patronage. This agreement, and the confessional school system, incorporated the churches into the state, and politicians had to be careful to respect this influential and conservative interest.

Similarly, the colony's leaders had to be wary of another important interest known in shorthand as 'Water Street,' the larger merchants of St John's. Its members controlled the economy, the two local banks, and the few manufacturing concerns that emerged in the later nineteenth century. They rarely sat in the Assembly, but dominated the Legislative Council. The Chamber of Commerce, replaced in 1909 with a Board of Trade, acted as their lobby. Imbued with a competitive *laissez-faire* philosophy, the merchants saw the fisheries as their preserve and opposed any outside interference. There was as a result no Department of Marine and Fisheries until the late nineteenth century; no systematic collection of fisheries statistics; no effective state intervention in the industry until the 1930s; and no financial assistance to compare with that provided by the French government to its fishery, and later by the Icelandic and Norwegian governments. The attitude of the merchants explains, at least in part, the stagnation and backwardness of the Newfoundland fishery when compared to those of its major competitors.

As if these problems were not enough, Newfoundland under responsible government had also inherited treaties regarding fishing rights signed with the United States and France in the period when the country was regarded as no more than a fishing base. The French rights derived from the Treaty of Utrecht (1713), and were complicated by an ambiguously worded declaration purporting to define them appended to the Treaty of Versailles (1783). French fishermen had the right to fish in season on the coast between Cape St John and Cape Ray – the 'French Shore' – but disputes arose from French claims that they had an exclusive fishery, that they were not amenable to local law, and that the settlement and industrial development of the French Shore was, strictly speaking, illegal.[15] Moreover, the French presence on the islands of St Pierre and Miquelon and on the Grand Banks was a constant irritation. American rights derived from the 1818 fisheries convention, which awarded the right to fish on the Labrador and west coasts and part of the south coast. These did not become the cause of serious dispute until the early twentieth century, and then only briefly. The major problem for nineteenth-century governments was the French Shore, where colonial sovereignty was clearly limited, where the imperial government claimed a right of supervision, and where settlement and the desire to develop resources was steadily growing. So far as the Colonial Office was concerned, Newfoundland meant French fishing rights and constant friction with the local government: 'The affairs of Newfoundland,' minuted the permanent undersecretary, Sir Robert Herbert, 'except where they are insignificant, are Imperial.'[16]

In the 1870s the French Shore was only geographically part of Newfoundland. The settlers there – about 8,600 in 1874 – had no political representation, paid no taxes, and managed their affairs under the guidance of a few clergymen and merchants, their disputes being adjudicated by the officers of the naval squadron that patrolled the shore each summer. Their trade links were with Nova Scotia rather than with the rest of the island. In the late 1870s and 1880s the French Shore was brought firmly within the colony's administrative structure, but the legality of land, mineral, and forest grants remained in dispute until the French Shore question was settled in 1904. Labrador, its interior boundary undefined until 1927, was another distinct region. It was regarded on the island as a summer fishery – as Newfoundland itself had been regarded in England until the early nineteenth century – which needed a minimum of administrative machinery. Elsewhere the pattern of local government was distinctive. There were no incorporated towns; St John's did not receive a 'municipal board' until 1888, and most town councils were formed after 1949. The basic administrative unit was the electoral district, whose member or members of the Assembly acted as the link between the central government and the locality, the fount of patronage and the conduit of public money. Most settlements or groups of settlements had government-appointed road and school boards, which administered funds transferred from St John's. The larger places had a magistrate, and perhaps a customs officer, who, together with the doctor (if any), the clergyman, and the merchant, formed influential local oligarchies.

Surveying the state of Newfoundland in the 1870s, almost all politicians agreed that their first priority had to be an attempt to diversify and strengthen the economy. This alone would improve the standard of living and the quality of life, stem out-migration, and bring Newfoundland to a position of equality with its mainland neighbours. They did not look to the sea for salvation, however, but to the land. The seal fishery was past its peak, and it was generally assumed that the cod fishery had reached the limit of its productive capacity and would not be able to generate an income sufficient to support the population at an adequate standard. As a joint committee of the legislature reported in 1880,[17]

> The question of the future of our growing population has, for some time, engaged the earnest attention of all thoughtful men in this country ... The fisheries being our main resource, and to a large extent the only dependence of the people, those periodic partial failures which are incident to such pursuits continue to be attended with recurring visitations of pauperism, and there seems no remedy to be found for this condition of things but that which may lie in varied and extensive pursuits.
>
> Our fisheries have no doubt increased, but not in a measure corresponding to our increase in population. And even though they were capable of being further expanded, that object would be largely neutralized by the decline in price that follows a large catch, as no increase of markets can be found to give remunerative returns for an augmented supply.
>
> It is evident, therefore, that no material increase is to be looked for from our fisheries, and that we must direct our attention to other sources to meet the growing requirements of the country.

The Conservative governments of the 1860s had taken the same point of view, and had started a geological survey – the main purpose of which was to identify opportunities for land-based development – and passed legislation to encourage agriculture. The 1870s saw the implementation of a more dramatic solution, which might be termed a Newfoundland national policy.[18]

The basic element of the plan was the construction of a railway across the island, from St John's to a point on the French Shore, to provide access to the undeveloped resources so enthusiastically touted by the geological surveyors. Steam, that symbol of modernity and progress, would usher in a new, diversified economy in which lumbering, farming, and mining would supplement the fisheries. The 'promised land' of the west coast, freed in time from French control, would at last be fully developed. It was an exciting vision. This meant, wrote the Rev. Moses Harvey, who provided a Niagara of propaganda,[19] 'the opening up of this great island – the union of its eastern and western shores – the working of its lands, forests and minerals; its connection with the neighbouring continent. It means the increase of population; the conversion of the country into a hive of industry; the commencement of a material and social advance to which no limits can be set ...' It was a policy that owed much to mainland examples, and to the Canadian experience. What others had done, Newfoundland could do also; and who was to say that the island's natural resources were in any way inferior to those possessed by the sister provinces?

The most prominent political backer of the railway scheme was William Whiteway, a St John's lawyer who became premier in 1878. Once his determination to build the line became evident, the guardians of the traditional economy revolted, and a debate began on the country's future direction. It was a debate that Whiteway won, principally because he could present a coherent and attractive policy, unrealistic as it may have been. His opponents, mainly merchants and their allies, fell into the trap of allowing themselves to be presented as backward-looking conservatives, fish-bound exploiters, and monopolists. Nevertheless, they did express, albeit ineffectively, an alternative model. In their view the railway policy was inappropriate, given that the fisheries were the foundation of the local economy and likely to remain so. The policy was built on Utopian assumptions and would be extremely expensive. Far wiser, they argued, to concentrate on agricultural and rural development in general in connection with the fisheries, and to build roads rather than railways. Development should be linked to the existing resource base and to the country's capacity to pay.

The early 1880s saw the most serious polarization of opinion since the Confederation debates. It was appreciated that the railway issue and all it represented was of crucial importance – 'an experience so new, so expensive, so divergent from our ordinary habits and wants, and at the same time so irretrievable in its results for good and evil.'[20] The debate took place during a period of considerable economic difficulty, a fact that added to its urgency and sharpened the rhetoric. The last twenty years of the nineteenth century was a period characterized by growing competition in foreign markets from French and Norwegian producers. Between 1870 and 1899, the average price for cod fell by some 25 per cent and for seals by 35 per cent. Over roughly the same period, not surprisingly, the proportion of the labour force employed in the fishery declined by 25 per cent. Indeed, for the first time the island experienced a net population loss in migration terms.[21] Merchants found it increasingly difficult to realize a steady profit, credit was tightened, and poverty and unemployment were endemic. Each side had its panacea. Whiteway promoted railway building, land-based development, and a compromise settlement with the French that would allow the exploitation of the resources of the west coast. His opponents argued that the first priority should be the passage of legislation to prevent the sale of bait fish to French Bank schooners, no matter what the repercussions might be for a French Shore settlement or the railway. They hoped that such a bill would ruin the French Bank fishery, reduce French fish exports, and so relieve glutted markets and drive up prices. The fishery had to come before the speculative advantages of interior development. It is significant that they had few concrete proposals for the solution of the fishery's internal problems, which centred on quality control and marketing. Effective action here could have gone far to improve the competitive position of Newfoundland fish.

The construction of the narrow-gauge railway began in 1881, and Whiteway was confirmed in office in the 1882 election. His opponents then regrouped and, by means of a series of complicated, desperate, and unsavoury manoeuvres, managed to gain control of the government three years later.[22] This was their chance to set Newfoundland on another course. But Robert Thorburn and the Reform Party failed to rise to the occasion. The Bait Act had little positive impact on the health of the fishery, whose domestic problems were examined, but not addressed in any determined manner. Rural development schemes faltered and failed. By the end of its term in 1889, the government was building railways and had floated the colony's first loan on the London market. Whiteway's Liberal Party swept back into power, its policies unchanged.

This passage of events is crucial in Newfoundland history. 'The model,' R.E. Ommer has written, 'did not fit the economic facts ... Its strategy built on Newfoundland's weaknesses, not her strengths, and was doomed to failure. Attempts to generate future development should have been grounded in Newfoundland's one great renewable resource. The path should have led through linkage development to a regional multiplier effect stemming from the existing export sector.'[23] Given the country's isolation, the lack of a hinterland, its small domestic market, and a pervasive conservatism, this might well have been difficult to achieve.[24] Perhaps this was one reason, and a sensible one, why the country chose a continental development strategy; but a serious implication of that choice was a comparative neglect of fisheries reform and development and of the potential of the marine sector in general. Merchants adjusted to the situation. As profits in the fisheries declined, some began to speculate in timber lands and mining leases, others to invest in heavily

Laying track on the Newfoundland Railway. A costly railway-building program in the 1880s and 1890s contributed to the debt problem that would lead
to loss of responsible government in the 1930s.

protected local manufacturing industries. There was a trend, accelerated
after the crash of the local banks in 1894, to abandon the direct outport
trade to smaller traders and to concentrate on the wholesale and import-
export business. Such attempts as were made to diversify within the
marine sector were largely unsuccessful, and the fishery's much-dis-
cussed and well-understood problems – an apparent inability to produce
saltfish of a consistently high quality, and to sell it effectively – remained
unresolved. As Eric Sager put it, the merchants were, on the whole,
'conservative and mercantilist ...':[25]

> the fishery was not a processed food industry requiring skilled production
> and organised marketing. The fishery was a rich vein of the New World
> which produced a commodity for exchange in domestic and international
> markets. Fish was a form of bullion from the sea ... When the fishery failed
> to respond to the men and ships who worked it, it seemed that the vein
> must be exhausted and the merchants turned their attention to other items
> of commercial exchange.

Whether the effective adoption of what in retrospect seem more appropriate policies could have saved the colony from the crisis through which it passed in the 1890s is improbable, though the crisis might have proved less severe. As it was, continuing French and Norwegian competition in European fish markets, coupled with an overall decline in primary-product prices, placed Newfoundland fish exporters – and the local banks that financed them – under severe pressure. At the same time the public debt began a steady increase as the railway line pushed into the island's interior. Hopes that an independent reciprocity treaty with the United States might alleviate the situation were dashed when a draft convention, agreed on in 1890, ran into implacable Canadian opposition and, as a result, a British veto. In December 1894, after a year of political upheaval that destroyed confidence in the country's stability, the two local banks suspended business. Most of Water Street followed; and the government, unable to float a loan, hung on the edge of bankruptcy.[26]

Canadian banks soon arrived in St John's – the Bank of Montreal taking over the government's accounts – an event that certainly helped to stabilize the situation, but that, in the longer term, marked a significant loss of local autonomy. Newfoundland's political autonomy hung in the balance as well, since the crisis drove the government to investigate the possibility of Confederation. Since the mid-1880s, amid the uncertainties created by the expiry of the fishery clauses of the Treaty of Washington, the Canadians had been quick to express enthusiasm for Confederation whenever Newfoundland had showed signs of looking for an independent reciprocity treaty. But once it became clear that Britain was unlikely to allow such a treaty over Canadian objections, Canada lost interest. Indeed, there were many Canadian politicians who feared both the expense of Confederation and the additional internal problems that might be generated by the French Shore question. Nevertheless, the April 1895 negotiations came close to success. They failed in the end because the Canadian government proved overly cautious on the financial terms and the British government unwilling to provide the substantial dowry that might have overcome the difficulty.[27] Newfoundland managed to borrow sufficient funds to avoid disaster and resumed its independent course. There were to be no further serious negotiations until 1947.

By the end of the nineteenth century, Newfoundland had gained relatively little from its national policy. While there had been some economic diversification – in mining, forest industries, local manufactures, and transportation – the economy still remained dependent on the stagnating, archaic fishery. Products of the cod and seal fisheries together made up, on average, 85 per cent of exports between 1895 and 1904. The railway, that herald of progress, ran through a largely empty interior.

It was at this point that Newfoundland began its stormy relationship with finance capital and the international corporation, and became subject to pressures that gradually drew it away from the old North Atlantic merchant economy. Political and diplomatic pressure from London now became supplemented by the pressures of the Canadian banks and of business interests based on the mainland and in England. The first manifestation of this shift was the arrival of Robert G. Reid and his sons, who came to Newfoundland in 1890 from Montreal to complete the construction of the railway. Reid rapidly became a powerful force in the colony, admired by many, but regarded with suspicion by others because of his close links with the CPR, the Bank of Montreal, and the Royal Trust.

In 1898 Reid signed a contract with the Tory administration of Sir James Winter that, in summary, sold him the railway and the St John's dry dock, awarded him the contracts for much of the coastal steamer service and the Gulf ferry, transferred to him the telegraph system, and gave him a total fee-simple land entitlement of 6,400 square miles.[28] The ensuing impassioned debate clearly delineated the options that now faced Newfoundland. If it wanted significant new industries to develop out of its investment in infrastructure, it would have to attract entrepreneurs from elsewhere, since local businessmen lacked either the capital, or the enterprise, or both. Edward Morris, a future premier, was among the enthusiasts:[29]

> the development of the country is better in the hands of a reliable Contractor than in the hands of the Government. All his interest henceforth lies in opening up and developing the country ... If he becomes rich so do we ... No man had more faith in this country and its resources than I have, but it won't do to spend our lives boasting about the capabilities of the country and permit the people of the country to be starving and perishing all around us. We have been hugging these phantoms to our bosom too long ...

To Robert Bond, the Liberal leader, the 1898 deal represented a sell-out that would allow Reid to 'bid defiance to the Legislature':[30] 'I am not prepared to thus barter away the property of the people of this country and of those who shall come after us ... We hold this country in trust for future generations ... The whole complexion of the destinies of the country depends on the action of the Government. By whom, by what influence, from what quarter, are its rich resources, its hopes, its fortunes to be controlled? That is the question we have now to decide.'

When Bond himself became premier in 1900, he found that he too faced the same problem as his predecessors. He managed to revise the 1898 Reid contract in the colony's favour, but it still recognized the perceived need to make large concessions to stimulate development and in no way represented a rejection of large-scale outside investment.[31] In 1905 his government signed an extraordinarily generous agreement with the Anglo-Newfoundland Development Corporation, a subsidiary of the English Harmsworth newspaper empire, in order to obtain a pulp-and-paper mill at Grand Falls.[32] Bond introduced the relevant legislation in words similar to those used by Morris in 1898, arguing that interior development demanded and justified special concessions.

In general, Newfoundlanders were satisfied with Bond's handling of the Reid and Harmsworth deals, which seemed to promise solid economic development at long last. Indeed, the early twentieth century was perhaps the most optimistic period in the country's history. Fish prices revived. Employment was created by the Reids, the Harmsworths, and by the Cape Breton steel companies in their mining operations on Bell Island in Conception Bay. Sawmilling expanded. In 1904 the French Shore question was settled as part of the *entente cordiale* – thanks more to Lansdowne and Delcassé than to Bond – and it was hoped that the much-touted riches of the west coast would come into production. Further, it seemed as though Newfoundland might finally be able to complete an independent reciprocity treaty with the United States, trading access to bait for free entry for fish into the American market.[33] For a brief moment it looked as if the national policy had paid off after all, and that a firm independence had been achieved. The country needed an anthem, which Governor Sir Cavendish Boyle provided in the 'Ode to Newfoundland' (1904), set to music by his old school friend Sir Hubert Parry.

The euphoria did not last. Bond became embroiled in a complicated and obsessive dispute with both Britain and the United States after his reciprocity treaty was rejected by the U.S. Senate in 1905. Sanctions against American fishermen in Newfoundland waters hurt local fishermen more than the visitors, and, coupled with a tendentious interpretation of the 1818 convention, roused widespread hostility. Bond also precipitated an expensive, long-lasting dogfight with the Reids, a conflict that turned the latter into an actively hostile force and helped create a bitter political atmosphere. In 1909 Bond lost the government to the Reid-backed Sir Edward Morris and his People's Party. An amalgamation of old Tories, dissident Liberals, and ambitious new politicians, it was, on the whole, far less principled than its predecessor.[34]

The new government had to contend with more than the demoralized Liberals. Coincidentally with its election, the Fishermen's Protective Union (FPU) was founded by William Coaker at Herring Neck, in Notre Dame Bay. The FPU grew swiftly under Coaker's dynamic leadership, earning the hostility of Water Street and of the Roman Catholic Church,

William Coaker

which prevented its adherents from becoming members. The union was the voice of rural workers, fishermen, lumbermen, and sealers and demanded that both they and the fishery receive the attention that had been so long denied. The FPU motto was 'To Each His Own.' Did the fisherman receive 'his own,' Coaker asked,[35] when

> he boards a coastal or bay steamer ... and has to sleep like a dog, eat like a pig, and be treated like a serf? ... at the seal fishery where he has to live like a brute, work like a dog and be paid like a nigger? Do they receive their own when they pay taxes to keep up five splendid colleges at St. John's ... while thousands of fishermens' children are growing up illiterate? Do they receive their own when forced to supply funds to maintain a hospital at St. John's while fishermen, their wives and daughters, are dying daily in the outports for want of hospitals?

The union demanded state intervention in the fishery to control both processing and marketing, and reforms that would ensure that fair prices were charged and paid to fishermen. It demanded a better and expanded education system, rural health services, and old-age pensions. And it demanded political reforms at the centre and at the local level that would enable fishermen to gain political experience and so challenge the stranglehold of the élite, the 'long-coated chaps' of St John's. The union challenged the basis of the Newfoundland state. It attacked the mer-

Fishermen's Protective Union MLAs, 1919

chants, the churches, St John's, and the politicians, voicing its concerns in firm, class-based rhetoric.

Coaker rapidly concluded that to achieve its goals the union would have to enter politics. The FPU therefore made an electoral alliance with Bond's Liberals and won eight seats in the 1913 election. Morris was astute enough to realize that the Liberal party was moribund, and that the FPU represented a real threat to his dominance. He was prepared as a result to make such concessions as would be tolerated by his Water Street and Roman Catholic backers. It is difficult to predict what might have happened if the First World War had not transformed the situation. It is possible that, if the FPU had maintained its momentum, and Coaker had overcome his reluctance even to consider becoming prime minister, the union might in time have formed a majority government. But the outbreak of war intervened and proved to be a watershed in the country's history.

As an independent member of the Empire, Newfoundland responded with enthusiasm to the call to arms. With all-party support, a Newfoundland regiment was formed, a venture that was to prove enormously expensive in terms of both lives and money.[36] An imperial loyalist, Coaker fully supported the war effort and urged his followers to volunteer for service overseas. Though he maintained his hostility to Morris, he was eventually persuaded to join him in a National Government formed in 1917. Once this had been done, Morris departed for London and a peerage, leaving the new government, now led by William Lloyd (a Liberal), to face the appalling problem of conscription. The regiment had suffered heavy losses – of the 6,000 Newfoundlanders who enlisted between 1914 and 1918, 20 per cent were killed and 37 per cent wounded[37] – and its existence as an independent unit was in question. Liberal and People's Party members of the National Government supported conscription, since voluntary enlistment was failing to produce a sufficient number of recruits. But in outport Newfoundland the fishery was booming. The average price for fish between 1915 and 1919 was 65 per cent above the 1910–14 average, and volumes increased by about 13 per cent. Fishermen were temporarily relatively prosperous and understandably reluctant to join the regiment. Conscription threatened the viability of family-based crews by taking away the younger men, and opposition was widespread – particularly since both the regiment and the war effort were seen as very much a St John's affair. FPU members let Coaker know what their views were. After a period of indecision, Coaker decided that in spite of this pressure he would have to support conscription. He recoiled from precipitating a political crisis in wartime, and from totally alienating the St John's merchants with whom he would have to work if the fishery was to be reformed. To his followers, however, he had sold out. Though conscription was accompanied by income and profits taxes, and by controls on food prices and profiteering, Coaker was widely thought to have himself become one of the 'long-coated chaps.' The crusader had become the politician. The irony was that no conscript went into action.

At the end of the war the fishing industry was over-extended and vulnerable. Fishermen and merchants alike had borrowed in order to expand operations and profit from the boom, and a number of the newer firms were undercapitalized. Fish prices began to drop, yet the price of imports remained high. Market conditions became difficult as competitors' fish began to arrive once again. Both the mining and newsprint industries were also facing difficulties, though in the case of the latter, these proved to be of short duration. The railway, which had handled an unprecedented volume of traffic during the war, was in poor condition, and the Reid Newfoundland Company was in financial difficulties. The government itself was now hamstrung by debt. The war effort had been funded by loans, and the public debt stood at $42 million, an increase of 38 per cent over the 1913–14 financial year. The political scene was likewise uncertain. The National Government collapsed in 1919, principally because the Roman Catholic archbishop put heavy pressure on the Catholic politicians of the People's Party to sever their links with the FPU. Thus there were three parties competing for power, none of them in a position to gain an overall majority, and a group of unaffiliated malcontents who swarmed around Richard Squires, a former People's Party member who had been left out of the National Government. It was Squires rather than Coaker who took advantage of the situation. He formed a Liberal Reform Party, claiming that it was the direct descendant of the old Liberal Party of Whiteway and Bond, from whom he obtained a guarded laying on of hands. He then negotiated an alliance with Coaker and the FPU, and together they won the 1919 election. Squires became prime minister[38] and Coaker minister of fisheries: he now had the opportunity to implement the FPU program, but in the midst of crisis conditions.[39]

It is indicative of the attitude of the mercantile community that the only far-reaching proposals for reform of the fishing industry while Newfoundland was under responsible government should have come from a relatively conservative fishermen's union. Coaker prescribed a dose of state intervention: the quality of fish and of cargoes would be controlled by government cullers and inspectors, and marketing would be managed by a government board working in collaboration with the exporters. Enacted in 1920, the new regulations had a short life. Squires did not provide the necessary political and financial support, and the legislation was flawed in that penalties were weak and the consent of a majority of exporters was needed to impose export licensing for a given market. Faced with a credit squeeze imposed by the banks, tight markets, and heavy competition, the exporters soon became panicky, divided, and prone to listen to irresponsible attacks on Coaker and the regulations from his political opponents. As a result the experiment collapsed in 1921.[40]

There is no question that the adoption of the Coaker regulations would have helped Newfoundland to maintain its position in the markets. Norway and Iceland were better organized to begin with, and were moving towards an acceptance of direct state intervention. The former adopted export controls in the late twenties and the latter in 1932. Moreover, importing countries were starting to introduce centralized purchasing: Italy did so in 1918, followed in the 1930s by Spain, Portugal, and Greece. It would be an exaggeration to say that the marketing of Newfoundland fish was totally disorganized, since merchant combines did exist for certain markets. But the quality of exports remained a serious problem, and the state did not effectively intervene either in that area or in marketing until the mid-thirties, when the Commission of Government created the Newfoundland Fisheries Board.[41] By then Newfoundland's share of European markets had declined significantly.

The defeat of the fishery regulations at the hands of Water Street was

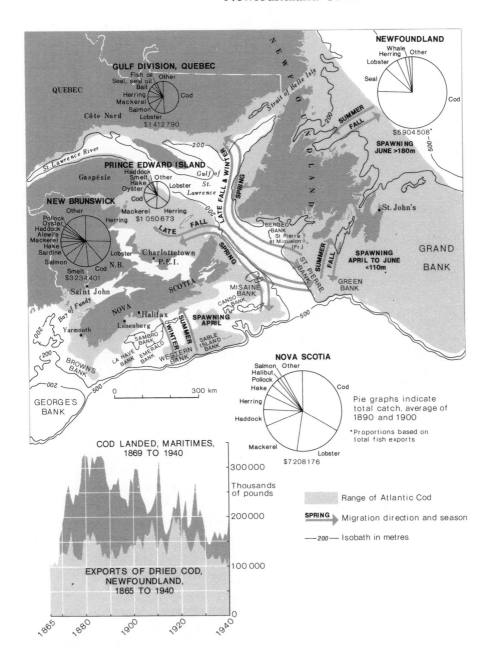

Figure 12 The fishing industry of the Maritime provinces and Newfoundland in the late nineteenth and early twentieth centuries

probably a more severe blow to Coaker and the FPU than the conscription crisis. Fishery reform had always been at the heart of the union move-ment, and its failure was crushing. It meant the effective end of the FPU,

On the ice. Sealers harvested seals from the drift ice in the early spring. Several disasters saw ships and men lost in severe storms; here sealers manhandle their ship through the ice towards open water.

weakened as it was from the start by the success of the Roman Catholic Church in frustrating its goal to organize all fishermen, regardless of creed. The FPU had defied the twin pillars of the Newfoundland state, and had lost. Coaker and the union rapidly lost momentum and influence and ceased to be a power in the land. The FPU had been the only political grouping with a coherent view of the country's future, with concrete and practical proposals for refurbishing its economy and society. As it faded, Newfoundland found itself in the hands of a succession of political chieftains and a highly conservative commercial and social élite.

When considering Newfoundland's experience in the 1920s, however, and the performance of its leaders, it is essential to remember the economic difficulties of the period. The inevitable dislocations caused by the return to a peacetime economy were followed by a period of weak and uncertain primary-product prices. The fishery, which still employed about half of the work-force, experienced a serious contraction in real-output growth; David Alexander calculated a decline of 27.8 per cent over the period 1916–39, or about 2.3 per cent per year.[42] Fish prices fell by about 15 per cent during the twenties, before the Depression reduced them even further. Moreover, the decade saw a decline in the value of fishery products as a percentage of total exports from 64.3 per cent in 1921–5 to 46.3 per cent in 1926–30.[43] Given the importance of the fishery to labour, this situation severely compromised gains made in the pulp-and-paper industry, which, by the late twenties, as volumes dramatically increased, was providing in excess of 40 per cent of the value of total exports. Though this industry provided a large number of seasonal jobs for fishermen-loggers, it directly employed only a small fraction of the work-force – no more than 10 per cent – and as an enclave industry was far less valuable to the economy than the fishery might have been. It was not without its problems either, as paper prices began a significant and persistent decline after 1925. The mining industry likewise experienced a growth in its share of export values over the decade, but it was an even smaller employer, and at the largest centre, Bell Island, production fell below pre-war levels – no doubt a reflection, in part, of poor management by the British Empire Steel Corporation (BESCO). Since both the work-force and the population were increasing, the perennial problems of poverty and unemployment were exacerbated. There were few other employment opportunities, unless a man wished to join the stream of migrants travelling, on a seasonal or permanent basis, to Sydney and other mainland centres – a safety valve that was closed off in the Depression. The government's ability to respond constructively to this dismal situation was limited. In 1920 the debt service absorbed 20 per cent of revenue. This charge largely accounted for the deficit, which in turn caused further borrowing until, in 1930–1, the debt stood at $92.6 million, and the cost of its service at 65 per cent of revenue. Given the state of the public finances and the problems besetting the economy, Newfoundland would have experienced serious difficulty in the Depression even if it had elected governments composed of saints and scholars.

Following the failure of Coaker's fishery regulations, the Squires government turned for salvation to a second newsprint mill to be built at Corner Brook. This originated as a joint venture between the Reid Newfoundland Company and the British engineering firm of Armstrong, Whitworth and Company. Funding was guaranteed by the British and Newfoundland governments, and the latter provided in addition a range of financial concessions that in time exceeded those granted to the Harmsworths at Grand Falls.[44] Construction started in 1923, and Squires, playing the role of industrial developer, was able to win a second election. At the same time he managed to solve a crisis that was developing over the railway. In 1920 the Reids had informed the government that they were no longer prepared to operate the line without assistance. The government in turn proved accommodating, to the extent that it provided $4.2 million in stop-gap financing between 1920 and 1922 while searching for a permanent solution. By the latter year each side was about to sue the other. The impending litigation threatened the Corner Brook development, since the Reids held most of the forest lands involved. Belatedly, Squires stepped in, dropped the lawsuit, and arranged for the government to buy out all the Reid interests, except their lands, for $2 million. It was a sensible move. Though the government had now to shoulder the financial burden of the railway, the Reid company was no longer a powerful force, able to manipulate and intimidate politicians and employees.

Soon after the Corner Brook legislation was passed, the second Squires government collapsed amid accusations – later substantiated – of graft and corruption.[45] Three weak governments came and went in rapid succession over the next year, to be followed by a conservative, mercantile administration led by Walter Monroe in June 1924. Presenting himself as 'a plain man of business,' Monroe promised clean government, retrenchment, and reform. Reform, however, consisted of abolishing direct and raising indirect taxes, increasing ministerial salaries, and providing comfortable tariff protection for manufacturing concerns owned by members of the cabinet. The plain man of business also managed to increase the public debt by $19 million in four years. Weakened by defections and growing unpopularity, he barely managed to hang on for his full term.[46] In 1928 Squires returned to power, this time without any formal alliance with the FPU. It was he who had to face the onset of the Depression.

Its impact was devastating. Between 1928–9 and 1933–4 fish prices fell by 48 per cent and newsprint prices by 35 per cent. The value of total exports fell by 27 per cent over the same period, imports by 44 per cent. Government revenues, still largely derived from customs duties, declined by 11 per cent, though there were increasing demands for relief payments, occasioned in part by fisheries failures in 1930, 1931, and 1932. The cost of debt servicing was becoming unbearable. Squires reduced expenditures as far as he could and continued to borrow until 1931. In that year the country failed to float an $8 million loan and found itself on the verge of bankruptcy. The government-supported Savings Bank was also in serious difficulties. Newfoundland survived the year only because the Canadian banks operating in the Dominion reluctantly agreed, under pressure from R.B. Bennett, to provide funds. They imposed stringent conditions, including the appointment of a British Treasury official to investigate and supervise the public finances, the payment of customs revenue into a special account to be used principally to service the debt, and a guarantee that Labrador would not be sold or leased until they were reimbursed. The government also undertook further to reduce expenditures. There were immediate cuts in salaries

The 'Great Riot' of 1932. A demonstration by unemployed workers deteriorated into a riot outside the legislature in St John's.

of from 20 per cent to 33 per cent, as well as in pensions and the
education and road grants. Such action only added to the social unrest
and misery already caused by the economic climate.[47]

In St John's, where there was a large concentration of unemployed,
the situation was particularly tense. It became explosive when Peter
Cashin, the minister of finance, resigned from the government in February 1932 and accused Squires of diverting public funds to his personal
use. Opposition politicians used the opportunity to organize a parade
of the unemployed to the legislature, an event that degenerated into a
serious riot. Squires obtained a dissolution. In the election that followed
the demoralized Liberals were defeated by the United Newfoundland
Party, led by Monroe's nephew, Frederick Alderdice. This conservative,
mercantile grouping won all seats but two.[48]

The new government, supported by the British Treasury representative, rapidly concluded that additional revenue was unavailable and
further retrenchment impossible. It therefore proposed, in the fall of
1932, a partial default on debt payments. There was immediate con-
sternation in London and Ottawa. Fearing the impact of default on Canadian credit, on colonial securities traded in the London market, on
the Canadian banks, and – more vaguely, but none the less sincerely –
on the reputation of the Empire, the two governments agreed to help

Newfoundland meet debt payments on condition that it agreed to a royal commission of inquiry. Alderdice had no choice but to agree. Chaired by Lord Amulree, and with two elderly Canadians as its other members, the commission began its work in the spring of 1933.

By the time Amulree returned to London in the late summer, his central recommendations had been worked out for him by the Dominions Office, the Treasury, and the Bank of England. They had decided that since an obvious unilateral default could not be allowed, the Newfoundland debt would be rescheduled and guaranteed by the British government. For its part, Newfoundland would have to accept the suspension of responsible government and rule by an appointed commission until such time as it was once again self-supporting.[49] The Amulree Commission made precisely these recommendations. English bureaucrats wanted a quick solution to an urgent financial crisis that was expected to be of short duration. The report had to provide a more elevated rationale for the suspension of democratic institutions, however. It did so by blaming Newfoundland's plight less on the impact of the Depression than on years of maladministration, corruption, and an array of other sins of commission and omission. Newfoundland, the report stated, needed more than financial aid: it needed thorough reconstruction and reform.[50] It was a political rather than an economic interpretation of Newfoundland's experience as an independent country, one that proved acceptable both to the British Parliament and to Newfoundlanders themselves, wearied as they were by economic depression and uncertainty, disillusioned with their politicians, low in morale, and anxious to find a way out of the impasse. 'The Report,' said Alderdice in the House of Assembly,[51]

> itself gives the Commission's idea of the low state of political morality in this country during the last quarter of a century. The picture they paint is a dark one but we must ... admit its truthfulness ... Every passage of the Report holds the mirror up to our faults ... in order to enable us to realise the true state of affairs and govern ourselves accordingly ... So I feel that Responsible Government is only a theoretical boon, and in our case it has proved a curse instead of a blessing. If we accept the proposals of the Home Government, not one man in five hundred will know the difference except that he will see prosperity restored to the country ...

Once the panic of 1933–4 had subsided, many Newfoundlanders came to the conclusion that the Amulree Report was in many ways inaccurate and unfair. Newfoundland did not collapse because Sir Richard Squires had twice been caught with his hand in the till, nor because the civil service was riddled with jobbery. It collapsed because the public debt had become too heavy a burden; and the debt was largely a monument to the implications of Newfoundland's decision in 1869 to remain independent:[52] 'Analysis of the Newfoundland public debt in 1933 shows that 35 per cent was attributable to the development of the railway; 60 per cent was accounted for by the railway and other development expenditures ...; that over 70 per cent was chargeable to these and the war debt; and finally that the lion's share of borrowings made to cover budget deficits was in order to keep the railway operating.' The two largest single items in the debt statement were the railway and the cost of the First World War, both the result of political independence. Such expenditures might be criticized in hindsight as being perhaps unwise or unfruitful; but it is hard to find them irresponsible. The debt could not be afforded because, for all the hopes and dreams of the late nineteenth century, the economy had not developed any degree of insulation from international price movements. Though there had been a significant amount of diversification, it remained dependent on export markets, and the inefficient fishery was still the largest employer. Newfoundland had chosen independence and, subsequently, a development model that concentrated on expensive infrastructure and the resources of the land rather than on the potential of the marine sector. The crisis of the early thirties had its roots in the nineteenth century.

The Commission of Government, composed of the governor and six commissioners – three British civil servants and three Newfoundlanders – was sworn in, ironically enough, in the ballroom of the Newfoundland Hotel on 16 February 1934. The Amulree Report had made numerous suggestions for reconstructing the economy, and the Dominions Secretary had spoken grandly of the great task ahead.[53] As a result the commission was expected to usher in a new era. This was not to be, however, for the commission had to fulfil irreconcilable purposes. It was supposed to be the harbinger of rehabilitation and prosperity; but at the same time it had to act as receiver. The former role demanded expenditure, the latter parsimony and close supervision by the Treasury. Caught between these rival demands, the commission could not live up to expectations: it simply had neither the funds nor the financial independence to do all that it would have liked. The situation was further complicated by the commission's concern over its legitimacy. Of its legality there was no doubt; but its members and the Dominions Office became acutely conscious of the fact that it was a self-perpetuating bureaucratic dictatorship imposed on a people with long democratic traditions. There was no consultative forum, no representative body through which to legitimate its actions or to gauge public opinion. The commission became highly sensitive to criticism and fearful that some former politician such as Squires might lead a revolt. As a result it tended not to invite consultation but to avoid it, retreating all too often into secrecy and carefully drafted public statements.[54]

In these circumstances disillusionment soon set in, though during the thirties the commission implemented far-reaching and long-overdue bureaucratic reforms, attempted to tighten up local administration, made a start in improving the inadequate and ramshackle provision of social services, and tackled the problems of the fishery by instituting regulated marketing and government inspection. It also began to develop imaginative, long-term, rural-development schemes. What preoccupied contemporaries, however, was the persistence of poverty and unemployment. By 1939 a monthly average of 58,187 persons were receiving able-bodied relief, an increase of 82 per cent over 1934. There were marches on the old legislature, public meetings, and growing resentment among the articulate and politically frustrated of St John's. Structural changes to allow for a representative element in the new constitution might well have been made in order to soften some of the discontent, had it not been for the outbreak of war in 1939. It was accepted on all sides that change would have to await the war's end.

War brought with it a sudden and jolting prosperity. In 1940 Canada, which had overall responsibility for the defence of Newfoundland, moved swiftly to safeguard the airport at Gander and the seaplane base at Botwood, and sent infantry, aircraft, and naval personnel. Canadian armed forces later moved into St John's and constructed a large air base at Goose Bay in Labrador. Under the destroyers-for-bases deal (1940), the United States built important installations at St John's, Argentia, and Stephenville, as well as stationing detachments at Gander and Goose Bay. At the height of the military occupation in 1943, there were approximately 10,000 American and 6,000 Canadian personnel in Newfoundland. The construction of the new bases provided, at the peak in 1943, some 20,000 jobs. Though paid less than an American worker, a Newfoundlander employed as a labourer on the bases could expect to earn $1,500 annually in 1941, as opposed to $333 had he remained in the fishing boat. The number on able-bodied relief plummeted. The war, in fact, created virtually full employment. Besides the work created by the bases, about 11,000 Newfoundlanders enlisted, and hundreds of others found work on the mainland. With the revival of the fishery, and strong prices, those laid off from the bases had a viable alternative. The financial situation of the government was likewise transformed. The revenue began a dramatic climb in 1941, until in 1944–5 it stood at 197 per cent of the 1938–9 figure. Expenditures increased by 53 per cent over the same period, and the commission enjoyed a comfortable surplus, part of which was loaned, interest-free, to Britain.[55] It was clear that Newfoundland was once again self-supporting, and that the prin-

Gun emplacement, St John's. The presence of German U-boats, the threat of raids on convoys, and the sinking of the Newfoundland ferry to Cape Breton in 1943 brought the war very close to home.

cipal justification for the suspension of responsible government had disappeared.

Neither the Canadian nor the British government, however, was persuaded that the return of responsible government after the war would be desirable. Officials in the Department of External Affairs had concluded by 1945 that it would be in Canada's best interests if Newfoundland joined Confederation. The war had clearly demonstrated the country's strategic importance, and there existed lively, if exaggerated, fears of the expansion of American influence there.[56] The British were concerned that the economy was still inherently unstable and that, once the wartime boom ended, an independent Newfoundland would soon find itself in difficulties and reappear with a begging bowl at the doors of the Treasury. Assuming at first that Confederation would be politically impossible, the Dominions Office and the commission had developed an elaborate and expensive reconstruction scheme designed to stabilize the economy before the return of full independence. This had collapsed once the Treasury had indicated that it was not prepared to borrow the necessary dollars, and Canada that it was not willing to lend them. As a result, the Dominions Office also began to examine the practicability of Confederation.[57]

By 1946 both governments had agreed that Confederation would be the best solution to the 'Newfoundland problem,' but that it would have to be approved by a vote. The British government decided that the best way to set the stage would be with a 'National Convention.' After thirteen years of commission rule, it was thought necessary to provide a forum that would reawaken political debate, provide political education, and air the issues. Thus the convention, which was elected in June 1946, was provided with terms of reference that instructed it to examine Newfoundland's financial and economic condition and, on the basis of that examination, to recommend which forms of future government should be placed on the ballot in a referendum.

The convention did not proceed precisely as planned, mainly because there existed from the outset the nuclei of anti-Confederate and Confederate parties. The former, whose main spokesman was Peter Cashin, held that the convention represented a breach of faith by the British government, which, once the war was over, should have restored responsible government. They sought to use the convention, therefore, to ensure that this indeed happened, confident that they would receive widespread support in the referendum. They also made no secret of their contempt for the commission government. The leading Confederates, Gordon Bradley and Joseph Smallwood, realized that the convention presented a golden opportunity to bring about a constitutional change that they were convinced would transform the lot of the ordinary Newfoundlander.[58] They appreciated, however, the extent of popular support for both responsible and commission government and the need to do all they could to turn public opinion towards Confederation. It was Smallwood, against the cautious Bradley's better judgment, who brought the division into the open. In October 1946, as the convention was starting its committee work, he formally proposed that a delegation be sent to Ottawa to ascertain possible terms of union. From that point on the convention's proceedings were dominated by debate over future forms of government. Its members split into groups favouring responsible government or Confederation, with a subgroup of the former arguing for closer economic ties with the United States. Nevertheless, the convention considered and debated at length reports on the economy. It sent a delegation to Ottawa that obtained draft terms of Confederation, and to London, where officials coldly indicated that there could be no guarantee of financial assistance for an independent Newfoundland. The convention's debates were broadcast in edited form each evening, and as the political temperature rose within the chamber, so did public interest in the issues under consideration. In 1946 there had been a very low turnout for the convention elections, an indication of the general apathy. By January 1948, when the convention closed, the country was obsessed by the constitutional question and as deeply divided as the convention itself.[59]

In its final vote, the convention recommended that only two options be placed on the referendum ballot: continuation of commission government, and responsible government. Smallwood and Bradley thereupon gathered thousands of signatures and petitioned the Commonwealth Relations Office to add Confederation. This would in all probability have been done anyway, given the British desire to conclude Confederation if at all possible and the plausible argument that the voters should not be denied an opportunity to consider any option for which significant support existed. But the petitions added political justification, and Confederation was added to the ballot to the fury of the anti-Confederates, who by now were confirmed in their conviction that there existed a dark Anglo-Canadian plot.

Smallwood became the key figure in the Confederate Association, which began a well-organized and highly professional campaign in preparation for the referendum. He stressed tirelessly the economic advantages of union: the family allowance, unemployment insurance, better pensions, and a higher standard of living. He set up Water Street as the whipping boy, claiming that it wanted to prevent the 'toiling masses' from taking 'the best chance they EVER HAD to make Newfoundland a better place for themselves and their families.'[60] In contrast, the anti-Confederates were divided, badly organized and poorly led. The mainstream antis backed the Responsible Government League, which had been formed in 1947. Though it had widespread support in St John's and the southeast of the island, no leader to rival Smallwood emerged other than Peter Cashin. Cashin was unreliable, volatile, commanded only a small personal following, and was too closely identified with the old days of Squires and the six-cent dole. The younger antis, impatient with the old guard, formed another party to advocate economic union with the United States (dubbed 'Comic Union' by the Confederates), and persuaded a St John's businessman, Chesley Crosbie, to lead it.[61]

In spite of their divisions, the responsible-government forces could

count on the support of the Roman Catholic Church and the majority of merchants. The former argued that the material attractions of Confederation should be subordinated to other values. What was best for the country, stated the *Monitor*, the newspaper of the St John's archdiocese, was that option which would allow Newfoundlanders to continue 'to live decently, soberly and honestly, continuing to recognize that there has grown up with us during the past four and a half centuries a simple, God-fearing way of life which our forebears handed down to us, and which we must pass on untarnished to posterity.'[62] Water Street feared for the future of its local industries under Confederation, it also feared a loss of economic dominance and the prospect of increased taxation. The antis could also play on the traditional, ingrained antipathy to Canada, and they made appeals to local patriotism, presenting themselves as the true Newfoundlanders.

Yet to many voters, Canada was no longer a foreign and hostile coun-

try. Over the eighty years since 1869, Newfoundland had moved slowly but steadily from a North Atlantic to a North American orientation, and its links with Canada had grown and proliferated. In the period 1900–14, Canada had provided about a third of Newfoundland's imports and bought about 9 per cent of its exports; by 1945–9, these figures had increased to 57 per cent and 14 per cent respectively. In terms of gross value, imports had increased by 1,500 per cent, exports by 972 per cent. Improved rail and steamship connections had helped stimulate this trade and had also encouraged the emigration of Newfoundlanders to Canada where, by the early 1940s, about 26,000 were living, the largest concentration being in Nova Scotia. Newfoundland currency was tied to the Canadian dollar, and Canadian banks had been a familiar presence since 1894. Newfoundland Methodists had joined the United Church of Canada, and increasingly Newfoundlanders were going to Canada for higher education – principally to the Maritimes – rather than to

Britain.[63] The war had further strengthened the relationship between the island and the mainland, and in general had created a climate in which Confederation could be seen as an attractive option.

Newfoundlanders had become accustomed to a significantly higher standard of living than they had enjoyed before the war, and the American and Canadian bases had served as local showcases for the North American way of life. Those who had worked or served abroad had lost much of their parochialism. Such people remembered the political scandals of the inter-war period, the Amulree Report, and the misery of the Depression; and they hesitated to take the risk of independence again and to hand the country back to those who had bankrupted it. Smallwood and his Confederates not only offered the chance of a better material life, but were perceived as being removed from the old élite; they were identified with neither St John's, Water Street, nor the old politics. They represented a new departure and the promise of economic and financial security.

The results of the first referendum (3 June 1948) showed that a majority of voters opposed responsible government. It received 44.6 per cent of the votes, but Confederation received 41.1 per cent and commission government 14.3 per cent. Given the strident hostility to Confederation that had existed prior to 1934, this was a remarkable result, which reflected both Smallwood's skill as a propagandist and the fundamental changes that had occurred during the war. In the second referendum (22 July 1948), commission government was dropped from the ballot. The referendum was preceded by a sharp campaign in which Smallwood played the anti-Catholic card and managed – significantly – to gain the open support of some members of the St John's élite. He increased his vote by 11 per cent, sufficient for a 5 per cent majority. It was enough for the Commonwealth Relations Office, and enough for Mackenzie King, once J.W. Pickersgill had talked him out of an attack of hesitancy. A delegation appointed by the commission negotiated the final terms of union,[64] and on 31 March 1949, Newfoundland became a Canadian province. There was satisfaction in Ottawa and London; and in St John's a mixture of jubilation and sad resentment.[65]

There can be little doubt in retrospect that, whatever their individual reasons may have been, the majority of Newfoundland voters made a wise decision in 1948. They had learned from their history that independence as a small country with an economy built on fish, newsprint, and iron ore was a precarious business. Periods of prosperity had been few and far between, and already the wartime boom was fading. The public accounts showed a deficit again from the 1947–8 financial year, and the fishing industry was facing severe market and currency problems in Europe and the Caribbean. Ninety-four years of responsible government had demonstrated, it seemed, that Newfoundland did not after all have the resources with which to build a viable independence. Had the country been able effectively to build on its potential strengths in the marine sector, and had it resisted the mirage of development presented by railways and the interior, it is possible that the result might have been different. But by the 1940s that was past history, and the legacy could not be undone.

As interim premier, Smallwood was clearly identified with the Liberals, and he moved to transform the Confederate Association into the Newfoundland wing of the party. This was done formally at a large and enthusiastic convention in late April 1949, where Smallwood announced a provincial election for 27 May. The antis had already formed the provincial Progressive Conservative Party on 8 April, but they were a demoralized, divided, and poorly organized group, which was no match for its opponents. As for the Co-operative Commonwealth Federation (CCF), it found it virtually impossible to establish itself in the new province, where the union movement remained divided in the wake of the referenda campaigns. As well, Smallwood, given his union background and populist rhetoric, attracted many potential CCF supporters. The provincial campaign overlapped with the federal, a circumstance that gave the Liberals a considerable advantage, as did the fact that Smallwood was able to take the credit for the immediately tangible benefits of Confederation, such as the arrival of family-allowance payments. In the provincial election, the Liberals won a landslide victory with a majority of sixteen and 65.5 per cent of the vote. Federally, they carried five out of seven seats.[66] Smallwood was now the uncrowned king of Newfoundland and was to remain so for twenty-two years, establishing what he himself called a 'democratic dictatorship.'[67]

While this development had much to do with Smallwood's skills as a politician and propagandist, it was also a legacy, as an increasingly bitter Gordon Bradley pointed out, of the suspension of responsible government and the years of commission government. The political hiatus of 1934–49, he argued, by denying a generation any experience of democratic government, had left Newfoundland 'with very little above the grade of kindergarten politicians,' thus leaving the way open for Smallwood.[68] In this sense, then, the dominance of Smallwood after 1949 is closely linked to Newfoundland's previous history. And Smallwood himself, though proudly calling himself a Canadian, always emphasized his own political lineage in local terms, seeing himself as the successor to Whiteway, Bond, and Squires, from the last of whom he had received his early political instruction. The new Newfoundland of the 1950s had its roots in a long and complex history, and its leader faced many of the same problems that had perplexed his predecessors in the 1870s.

# CHAPTER ELEVEN

# The 1950s
## The Decade of Development

THE CONTEXT OF DEVELOPMENT

It was a week before election day. A gentleman called on an elderly couple to make sure they were voting – right. The couple were sitting on their little front porch pouring over some tourist literature which they had somehow acquired. After the election talk was over, the old man pointed to some of the pictures in the tourist literature – important scenic points in the Maritimes – and asked the vote-getter, with a note of actual wonderment in his voice, 'You don't mean to tell me that all the beautiful places in these pictures are right here in the Maritimes! Well, if they are, I ain't seen none of 'em!'

'Of course they're here, Henry!' reproved his wife. 'But they're just for them there tourists – Americans most!' Having settled this point for her husband she turned to their caller and remarked eagerly, 'Well, you won't forget to send your car for us on election day – to take us to vote?' and, a bit pathetically, 'I don't believe I've had a car ride since last election day.'[1]

In 1950 there were two Atlantic Canadas, one largely rural and isolated, like Henry and his wife, the other essentially urban and fully integrated into mainstream North American culture, like the politician who sought their votes. Within ten years, the forces of change would sweep away most of the remnants of the traditional way of life and replace it with highly bureaucratized and centralized structures from which few could escape.[2]

This transformation had been working its wonders in Atlantic Canada since Confederation. Only the pace of change in the 1950s, like the 'muscle' cars that sped down the beckoning highways, seemed to have accelerated.[3] For many Atlantic Canadians the change was symbolized by material acquisitions such as electric lights, indoor plumbing, a refrigerator, or that much-prized family car. Others would remember the

1950s as the time when they saw their first television program, received an old-age pension cheque, or took a trip on a school bus. Monuments to the development ethic of the dynamic decade still grace the landscape in the form of the Angus L. Macdonald Bridge, the Canso Causeway, Beechwood Power, and Labrador City, as well as a host of consolidated complexes that were rapidly replacing the one-room schoolhouses in the region. In every corner of Atlantic Canadian society, mass consumer culture, with its cheap manufactured products and hard sell, replaced the old order based on scarcity and hard work. For some people, the appearance of tranquillizer drugs in 1956 perhaps helped to relieve tensions in the fast-paced age, just as the birth-control pill served as an antidote to the emerging sexual revolution symbolized by the publication of *Playboy* Magazine in 1954.[4]

Technology was the mainspring of the decade, and every day seemed to bring exciting new products and ways of doing things. In 1955 the first transatlantic telephone cable was completed from Clarenville, Newfoundland, to Oban, Scotland. Like television and computers, which were on the cutting edge of technology in the 1950s, it was a significant step in the communications revolution that was rapidly turning the world into a 'global village.' Other technological developments were more sinister. As the Cold War intensified and its warriors exploded ever-more-powerful nuclear bombs into the earth's atmosphere, people began to wonder whether there would be any world left to develop. To the surprise of many Atlantic Canadians, Pugwash became the site of one of the most ambitious efforts to influence the course of human events. In July 1957, twenty-two scientists from ten countries, including the United States and the Soviet Union, converged on Pugwash to discuss nuclear disarmament. They were there at the invitation of Nova Scotia-born industrialist Cyrus Eaton, who offered his summer residence as the site for the conference, proposed by such eminent scholars and scientists as Bertrand Russell and Albert Einstein.[5]

Atlantic Canadians responded in a variety of ways to the events overtaking them. Women and men in the labour force organized to gain some control over their working conditions. Even teachers and civil servants – white-collar employees not noted for their militancy – considered strike action as a way to make their voices heard. Entrepreneurs such as Chesley Crosbie, K.C. Irving, the McCain brothers, and Frank Sobey found the 1950s a decade of opportunity, riding the crest of the wave in the expanding service sector with airlines, gas stations, processed foods, and supermarkets. Others cursed the new-fangled notions invading Atlantic-Canadian society, undermining a way of life that somehow seemed less grasping and impersonal than the new trends.

Harvesting grain, Annapolis Valley, N.S. Unless they were prepared to organize into co-operatives for marketing their products, farmers found even their own markets increasingly difficult to penetrate.

Although there were many perspectives on the development ethos of the decade, on one point all could agree: the whole fabric of Atlantic Canadian society was being rapidly altered.

The social impact of a decade of change can be deduced from the statistical evidence. Between 1951 and 1961 the number of men engaged in primary industry in the four Atlantic provinces dropped by more than 50,000. In percentage terms those working in agriculture declined by 49 per cent, in fishing and trapping by 37 per cent, in forestry by 24.5 per cent, and in mining by 22.2 per cent. The manufacturing sector also showed a slight decline, with 4,000 fewer people engaged in secondary industries in 1961 than ten years earlier. Unable to find employment, 82,000 people left the region in the 1950s. Those who stayed worked in the expanding trade and service sectors where in excess of 75,000 jobs were created. By 1961 direct government employment accounted for more than 100,000 jobs in the region. Many of the new jobs were in areas traditionally dominated by women. While the number of jobs held by men actually decreased by 5,000 during the decade, the number of women in the labour force grew by 35.9 per cent to 135,000.[6]

Stanfield's textile mill, Truro. Stanfield's, first famous for its 'long-john' winter underwear, is one of the few regional textile mills to survive into the modern era. Working on a production line for shirt tops in one of the many non-unionized work sites in the region, the women pictured here put in long hours for little more than the minimum wage.

Military spending associated with the Korean War and the Cold War accounted for many of the new jobs in Atlantic Canada during the 1950s. By 1961 the number of people working in defence in the region – more than 41,000 – was more than in agriculture or construction, and almost as many as in fisheries and forestry combined. While the value of defence contracts for construction, supplies, and research awarded in Atlantic Canada was typically negligible, nearly one-quarter of all those employed by the Canadian armed forces were based in the region, and military spending was approaching $200 million annually by the end of the decade. One-quarter of the Halifax labour force was dependent on employment associated with the Atlantic Command headquarters,

HMCS *Stadacona*, HMCS *Shearwater*, and the Navy Dockyard. The establishment of Camp Gagetown brought investment to the Fredericton-Oromocto area, where by 1961 more than one-third of the labour force depended on defence spending. Similarly, the air-force bases at Summerside and Greenwood had a stimulating impact on the areas surrounding them. In Newfoundland, the American presence at Argentia, Harmon Field, and Goose Bay contributed substantially to the economy, the combined employment on Canadian and American bases accounting for nearly 8 per cent of the provincial labour force. Defence employment was higher than the national average of 2.7 per cent in all four Atlantic provinces, but Nova Scotia, with 11.4 per cent of its labour force in defence, was particularly vulnerable to military spending cuts that were being mooted by the end of the decade.[7]

As dramatic changes worked their way through the Atlantic Canadian economy, few escaped their impact. Centralizing pressures tolled the death knell for many of the region's rural areas, sapped the initiative from Native and Black communities, and concentrated power in provincial capitals. Towns dependent on the fishing industry were perhaps the hardest hit. Squeezed by the efficiency of offshore fleets, the centralization of port and processing facilities, and stiff foreign competition, the inshore fishermen faced a bleak prospect. 'Outport people' in Newfoundland were offered government grants to help them locate in more accessible communities, but would not face wholesale relocation until the 1960s.[8] Farmers also faced enormous pressures. In the Annapolis Valley, apple growers were paid to uproot their orchards because there was no longer a British market for their apples. Quotas, marketing boards, and nationally defined standards signalled the end of part-time production for many in the region. While the exploitation of industrial minerals brought growth to communities in northern New Brunswick and Labrador, the decline of the coal industry was a singular feature of the decade. In Springhill in 1956 and 1958 two major mine disasters, which together took the lives of more than 100 men, tragically documented the inadequacy of safety measures in the increasingly obsolete mines.[9] Indeed, occupational and environmental safety emerged as a major concern of the decade. On the Burin Peninsula, for instance, workers in the fluorspar industry began to experience the disastrous consequences of exposure to carcinogenic substances in the mines.[10] Other environmental problems took longer to surface. Spraying for the spruce budworm in New Brunswick's forests got under way in the 1950s, as did general herbicide and insecticide programs. Few considered the health risks of such activities, not even the housewives who freely sprayed DDT in their homes.[11]

Women in Atlantic Canada in the 1950s, as elsewhere in North Amer-

Trawler off the Grand Banks, 1949. The offshore fishery became more mechanized and efficient through the use of large trawlers. Since they were often owned and operated by fish-plant owners, the trawlers were given priority as suppliers to plants. Inshore fishermen, using smaller boats and operating more seasonally, found it increasingly difficult to make a living.

ica, were largely defined by their unpaid reproductive and service roles. Most of the women who comprised over 20 per cent of the paid labour force were single, divorced, or widowed. A federal law barring the employment of married women in the civil service was repealed only in 1955, and provincial jurisdictions were slow to follow the federal lead.[12] In 1956 Nova Scotia passed legislation requiring equal pay for equal work, but no attempt seems to have been made to enforce the law; and, in any event, because men and women were segregated in the workplace, comparisons were difficult. Nor were women encouraged to raise their employment aspirations. Strict quotas were placed on the number of women accepted into many of the professional programs in the region's universities, and women were barred by law and custom from the boardrooms, clubs, and taverns where power was often mediated. While women could legally vote and hold public office, they were marginalized in auxiliaries to major political parties and restricted in such civic duties as jury service. Young women coming of age in the 1950s

Waiting for the survivors. The Springhill disaster of 1958 riveted the nation's attention over several days during the rescue attempts. Seventy-four men were killed; the mine, one of Nova Scotia's biggest, never reopened.

were encouraged to take up one of the traditional female professions of teaching, social work, nursing, and clerical work, or train on the job to be a stewardess or bank teller. Their primary objective, reiterated by books, movies, television, and time-honoured social conventions, was to find a husband. For women seeking higher professional and administrative positions, the chief requirement was an uncommon determination to achieve their ambitions.

Married women in the 1950s were experiencing a particularly difficult transition. In farming and fishing families, wives found themselves excluded from their traditional productive roles by male-dominated corporate structures that increasingly managed primary industries.[13] At the same time, wives were often the ones made responsible for the mounting paperwork associated with such enterprises. Increasingly, too, woman's role was becoming that of consumer to meet her family's needs, rather than producer. This transition was underlined during the decade by the creation of provincial branches of the Canadian Association of Consumers (renamed the Consumers' Association of Canada in 1962), the goal of which was to produce a better-educated consumer.[14] In the 1950s

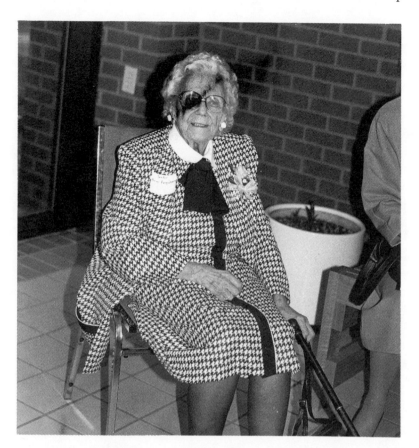

Muriel McQueen Fergusson, c. 1990. New Brunswick's Muriel Fergusson broke down barriers to women's participation in regional politics. She served as the region's first female regional director of family allowances, Fredericton's first female alderman, and, in 1953, the region's first female senator.

wives were still expected to care for the young and very old as well as their wage-earning husbands and to serve as crisis-managers for the increasingly beleaguered family. Social-welfare legislation passed in the late 1950s finally put to rest the haunting spectre of being sent to the poorhouse if sick, insane, or infirm, but most care-giving activity was still performed by women in the home. Ironically, the well-being of the care-giver was particularly tenuous. A woman who left her husband because of cruelty or uncondoned adultery was ineligible for social assistance in most jurisdictions. Even with such help, a woman raising her children by herself was often considered a pariah and lived a life of poverty and isolation.

Despite these legal and attitudinal barriers, women were beginning to carve out new roles in the public world and press for changes in the laws that governed their private lives. Following an amendment to the Indian Act in 1951, Irene Bernard of Tobique became the first woman in Canada to be elected to a band council. Muriel Fergusson, New Brunswick's first female regional director of family allowances and Fredericton's first female alderman and deputy mayor, followed these triumphs in 1953 by becoming the first woman from Atlantic Canada to be appointed to the Senate.[15] Former Kentville mayor Gladys Porter became the region's first woman to be elected to a provincial legislature in 1960. In the same year a few brave souls in Halifax were inspired to form a branch of the Voice of Women to work for disarmament and peace.[16] Other women unintentionally found themselves involved in new political situations. Organizers of the International Woodworkers of America, who were attempting to negotiate their first contract for Newfoundland loggers in the 1950s, understood that 'more strikes have been lost in the kitchen than have ever been lost on the picket line.' When the strikers were threatened with fines or jail sentences, H. Landon Ladd called the women of Grand Falls to a meeting. According to his account:

> they came, every one of them. Christian, decent women, mothers, law-abiding people who had all their lives gone to their churches and abided by the law in every respect ... I got up there and said, 'Sisters of the IWA, I have a message for you, I have the list of every man who has been fined ... and I want you to meet with your husbands in just a few minutes and I'm asking each of you women to tell your husbands to go to jail.' The place was stunned silent, tears were rolling down the faces of these wonderful women. I said, 'I'm asking you to do it,' and I said, 'I'm going to leave you and take a vote' ... we went back into the room a short while later, and the women had voted unanimously (to send their husbands to jail).[17]

The 1950s was a tough period for the region's organized labour. From a high of 32 per cent in 1953, trade-union membership in Atlantic Canada declined to a low of 21 per cent a decade later.[18] The merger of the Trades and Labour Congress and the Canadian Congress of Labour to create the Canadian Labour Congress in 1956 forced difficult organizational adjustments on regional locals, while structural changes in the economy put labour on the defensive. Coal miners and steelworkers, once the élite of organized labour, were faced with a dramatic decrease in demand for their products, a result of competition from new sources of energy, the increasing obsolescence of mining and milling operations and bad management by distant directors. Dominion Steel and Coal Corporation (DOSCO), the holding company for most of the region's coal and steel industry, was taken over by A.V. Roe in 1957. A Montreal-based conglomerate, A.V. Roe was more adept at seeking government

Supplies for strikers. The International Woodworkers strike in 1959 ended with the arrest of the strikers and their imprisonment in the Grand Falls Armoury. Their harassment by government and squads of RCMP won national attention. Their families, who rallied to supply food and other necessities, are shown waiting to deliver parcels to those in jail.

grants than investing in the region's future, with the result that labour and management were forced into collaboration simply to keep the Atlantic operations going.[19] At the same time, the Cold War battle against Communism in the United States continued to wreak havoc in the Canadian labour scene. Unions were purged of alleged Communist sympathizers, and any suggestion of dramatically altering the structure of the workplace was quickly buried. Labour discipline was also imposed by the elaborate bureaucratic apparatus accompanying government legislation relating to unions. By the 1950s, the rank and file of union members had relinquished their control over collective bargaining to full-time union agents who sought better wages and working conditions in negotiation with management along lines laid down by the state. With hierarchical structures, bureaucratic processes, and limited goals, unions came to resemble the very businesses and governments they struggled against and no longer offered a radical critique of a system that sustained such inequities in wealth and power.[20]

The development ethic was also turned against the region's workers, who were often accused of scaring away elusive capital investment by their attempts to resist exploitation. In 1957–8 400 quarry workers in Windsor, Nova Scotia, remained off the job for more than a year in their efforts to achieve union security and better working conditions from the American-owned Canadian Gypsum Company.[21] As a member of the

Canadian Labour Congress, the Nova Scotia Quarry Workers Union was entitled to financial aid from the parent body, but most of the support came from various provincial locals whose members recognized the significance of the strike for all workers in the region. In 1959, the International Woodworkers of America's aggressive organizing drive in Newfoundland ended in a disastrous confrontation with the provincial government. Opponents of unions used nativist arguments to discredit such 'foreign' organizations, conveniently ignoring the fact that the advent of multinational corporations made it necessary for labour, too, to organize on an international scale.

As the fisheries became increasingly controlled by large corporate structures, the workers in the industry, especially those defined as part-time or occasional, were required to make major adjustments. Many fishing families decided to abandon a way of life that seemed to offer only soul-destroying working conditions and unrelenting poverty. Others urged reorganizing the fisheries along industrial lines. In 1956 fishermen became eligible for unemployment insurance, a sign that they were now considered wage earners rather than self-employed entrepreneurs. When the members of various fish-handlers' unions in the Maritimes formed the Canadian Seafood Workers' Union in 1957, the resolutions passed at their founding convention testified to the new goals sought by men and women in the industry. In addition to demanding that the government establish a coast guard, place a twelve-mile limit on foreign fishing vessels, and reduce the premium on the Canadian dollar, they also called for workers in the fishing industry to be brought under the Workmen's Compensation Act and to be given paid vacations and pension plans.[22]

While workers in the primary and secondary sectors faced major obstacles in their efforts to improve their bargaining position, white-collar workers were beginning to flex their muscles. The right of employees to organize in New Brunswick's rapidly expanding power industry was an issue in the 1952 election in that province, and in the same year teachers in Nova Scotia voted to go on strike for better wages and working conditions. In 1958 the Nova Scotia Civil Service Association was organized to give government employees a collective voice, a major milestone on the road to union status.[23] The employment trends of the decade made it virtually inevitable that service-sector unionism would represent the wave of the future, offering a new look to the 'big labour' that would stand up to the power of 'big business' and 'big government.'

During the 1950s, even those who had never participated in the wage economy felt the impact of the state. The universality of mothers' allowances and old-age pensions helped to take some of the stigma away from the word 'welfare' and enabled more people to plan around a monthly income, however small. Though still suspect in some circles, unemployment insurance brought important benefits to a region where seasonal and structural unemployment was consistently higher than in other areas of the country. Federal cost-sharing programs also made it possible for the poorer provinces to improve their treatment of dependent citizens. Such improvements were long overdue. By the 1950s the Atlantic provinces were being singled out as a social-service backwater. A Canadian Welfare Council report published in 1949 documented appalling conditions in New Brunswick, where the mentally ill, alcoholic, bed-ridden, blind, aged, and paraplegic, as well as unwed mothers and their children were herded together into municipal poorhouses. The track record of other provinces in the region was scarcely better.[24] In 1956 Nova Scotia passed a social-assistance act that ushered in a new era of public welfare.[25] The mentally ill were thereafter treated separately from the poor and dependent, who were now more likely to maintain themselves on their meagre social-assistance income rather than being committed to custodial care. For the sick and elderly, nursing homes, though still offering less than ideal conditions, began to serve as alternatives to municipal poorhouses. Nevertheless, these embarrassing monuments to a more brutal age continued to survive on the landscape of Atlantic Canada until well into the 1960s.

Improvement in general standards of health and hygiene was a welcome trend of the 1950s. A national hospital-insurance plan came into effect in 1958, making institutional care accessible to more people. Dr Salk's vaccine discovered in the early 1950s conquered the crippling childhood disease of poliomyelitis, but not before a major outbreak in 1953 had reaped another harvest of victims. Although all provinces benefited from the strides made in medical care during the decade, none moved forward faster than Newfoundland, where health services outside the major centres had been pitifully inadequate. Such diseases as tuberculosis and gastro-enteritis took an alarming toll, especially in the Native communities of Labrador. Though not fully eradicated during the 1950s, these scourges were gradually being brought to submission. In outport communities diagnosis was significantly improved by the *Christmas Seal*, a vessel carrying X-ray equipment.[26]

THE CULTURE OF DEVELOPMENT

The 'quaint' mixture of 'traditional' and 'modern' elements in Atlantic Canada in the 1950s elicited a variety of responses.[27] Those promoting tourism in the era of the motor car underlined the slower pace, older ways, and friendly people that awaited the visitor to the region. 'In the scenic land of Longfellow's Evangeline, the haven of Grand Banks fishermen, the home of heroes, you'll find a friendly remoteness from the confusions of the world,' readers of *Holiday* were told in 1953.[28] Award-winning film maker Margaret Perry produced films for the Nova Scotia Tourist Bureau that echoed this romantic notion of the region's culture and society. Since the 1940s the Nova Scotia government, through its Handcrafts Division of the Department of Trade and Commerce, encouraged those who still engaged in traditional crafts to produce for a commercial market. Among the many products of this initiative was Bessie Murray's design for a Nova Scotia tartan, developed for the province's Sheep Breeders' Association in 1953. Most people in the region, however, considered their 'homemade' products an embarrassment and were eager to join the ranks of the consumer society. In the late 1950s a vacationing dealer bought 1,200 spinning wheels in Cape Breton, a testimony to the changing values of both modern and traditional cultures.[29]

It is not difficult to understand why Atlantic Canadians wanted to abandon their traditional ways as quickly as possible. Antique dealers and craft promoters might well wish to exploit the post-war nostalgia for the past; they certainly did not want to live in the past themselves. By the 1950s social scientists had begun to emphasize the human problems fostered by isolation and underdevelopment. The most ambitious of the academic analyses of the region was the 'Sterling County' study conducted by scholars from Cornell University.[30] Drawing a distinction between 'disintegrating' and 'integrating' areas in Digby County, Nova Scotia, Alexander Leighton and his team found exactly what they had expected: a higher incidence of psychiatric disorder in 'Depressed Areas.' Those 'people of cove and woodlot' who had unwittingly collaborated in the investigation heaped ridicule on the findings, which were unnecessarily alarmist and couched in condescending terms. But the study was widely acclaimed in academic circles, where 'Sterling County' became a euphemism for the unfortunate consequences of underdevelopment.

Atlantic Canadians, of course, had their own academic approaches to the problem of poverty in the midst of plenty. By the 1950s, the program of adult education and co-operation developed by Moses Coady and his colleagues at the Extension Department of St Francis Xavier University was gaining world-wide recognition. Upon Coady's death in 1959, the Coady International Institute was established to export the Coady system to developing nations.

Given the tensions under the surface during the decade, it is perhaps not surprising that many people took refuge in the region's long history. There was much to commemorate in the 1950s. While Acadians remembered the *grand dérangement*, descendants of the Lunenburg County

Germans and New England Planters reflected upon the arrival of their ancestors two hundred years earlier. Annapolis Royal celebrated the founding of Port Royal by Champlain in 1605; Charlottetown, its centenary as a city. New Brunswick, Prince Edward Island, and Newfoundland boasted a century of responsible government; Nova Scotia trumpeted two hundred years of representative government. In the summer of 1955 Portuguese fishermen from the *Gil Eannes* bested them all when they staged a spectacular pageant in St John's marking the five hundredth anniversary of the Grand Banks fishery.[31]

Writers from the region seemed to catch the spirit of nostalgia that gripped Atlantic Canadians as they sped forward to a future that promised to be vastly different from the past. Will R. Bird, George Clarke, Emery LeBlanc, Hugh MacLennan, Marguerite Michaud, Ron Pollett, Thomas Raddall, Evelyn Richardson, Ted Russell, and Esther Clark Wright all found inspiration in the region's history or rural distinctiveness.[32] Ernest Buckler perhaps best captured the transitional nature of the decade in his widely acclaimed novel *The Mountain and the Valley*, published in 1952. Other talented writers were just launching their careers, most notably Harold Horwood, who spent much of the 1950s as a columnist for the St John's *Evening Telegram*, and Antonine Maillet, whose first novel, *Pointe-aux-Coques*, appeared in 1958. Prince Edward Islanders remained the region's most avid readers. A Carnegie-endowed library system with twenty branches made books easily available to everyone on the Island, with the result that book circulation there was greater than that of New Brunswick with five times the population.[33] A rich oral culture in the region continued to attract attention. Helen Creighton, no longer encumbered by the old-fashioned Presto machine with its accompanying converter, batteries, and blank disks, was more efficient than ever with her new reel-to-reel tape-recorder in capturing for posterity traditional songs and folklore. She, together with Sandy Ives and Louise Manny, figured prominently in the first Miramichi Folk Song Festival that brought singers and collectors together in 1958.[34] In the Acadian community, Father Anselme Chiasson continued his monumental task of documenting the folk-songs and folklore of his people.

Most Atlantic Canadians were not, however, inspired by their writers and folklorists. Instead they sat spellbound in front of television sets watching such delights as 'The Honeymooners,' 'I Love Lucy,' and 'Our Miss Brooks.' English-language private and public stations broadcasted in all provinces by mid-decade.[35] By the end of the decade the Canadian Broadcasting Corporation (CBC) network beamed its own French and English programs as well as popular American shows simultaneously from Victoria to Sydney. A few productions, including the highly popular 'Don Messer's Jubilee' and various news and talk shows, originated in the region. Enterprising individuals like Don Jamieson in St John's actually experimented with locally produced drama.[36] The vast majority of programming, however, came 'from away,' and Elvis Presley's performance on 'The Ed Sullivan Show' provoked as much interest as any local event. Television, even more than the ubiquitous radio, which had dominated communications for more than a generation, brought mainstream North American culture to everybody's living-room, defining values, goals, and even speech patterns.

Ironically, a decade of centralization seemed to strengthen local initiatives and inspire regional cultural expression. In sports, improved transportation made minor- and little-league baseball teams more vital than ever.[37] Hockey and harness-racing flourished. Individual achievement and endurance in sports were particularly emphasized during a decade that prized such virtues. In 1951 Evelyn Henry, a nineteen-year-old nurse from Keppoch, became the first person to swim the Northumberland Strait. Yvon Durelle slugged his way to fame in the boxing ring in the 1950s, but two defeats at the hands of world light-heavyweight champion Archie Moore in 1958 and 1959 signalled the end of world-championship prospects for the 'fighting fisherman' from Baie Ste Anne.[38] In the Acadian community, choral festivals reached new levels of achievement, and throughout the region drama festivals drew large audiences. Truro-born contralto Portia White was at the height of her international singing career in the 1950s, her name mentioned in the same breath as that of Marian Anderson and Mahalia Jackson. At Mount Allison University, Alex Colville, Lawren Phillips Harris, and Ted Pulford were training a generation of artists, including Tom Forrestall, Mary Pratt, and Christopher Pratt, who, together with their mentors, drew inspiration from regional settings. By the end of the decade, Frederictonians boasted a world-class art gallery, sponsored by the bombastic and irresistible Lord Beaverbrook, after whom the gallery was named.

Ethnic identities also thrived in the 1950s. In the wake of events commemorating 1755, Acadians in the three Maritime provinces developed a new sense of solidarity and purpose. The Société Nationale l'Assomption, reorganized as the Société Nationale des Acadiens in 1957,[39] reflected the spirit of the times. Although Acadians would not give up their strong sense of history and culture, which had sustained their identity for more than two centuries, secular goals relating to language, education, and economic opportunity demanded new strategies. Jean Hubert, editor of the Moncton-based French-language daily newspaper L'Evangéline during the 1950s, was a spirited advocate of change. Urging his fellow Acadians to abandon their parochialism, he condemned the Acadian élite for failing to provide the the necessary leadership. 'Nos organismes, nos associations, nos institutions font preuve du plus grands mutism, comme si toutes leurs activités devaient se passer

The 'Fighting Fisherman.' Yvon Durelle from Baie Ste Anne, New Brunswick, challenged the world light-heavyweight champion, Archie Moore, in 1958 and 1959. Though Durelle lost both bouts, his heroic performance captured the imagination of Canadians.

dans le secret absolu,' he proclaimed in an editorial in April 1959. 'Nos sociétés pourraient avoir une influence beaucoup plus grande si elles commençaient par avoir une présence ...'[40]

The new sense of purpose emanating from the Acadian community in Atlantic Canada was fuelled by alarming demographic trends. In absolute numbers the Acadian population was growing rapidly, but, even in New Brunswick where they represented more than one-third of the provincial population, emigration and assimilation were threatening the survival of Acadian culture. Those claiming French as their mother tongue actually declined in Prince Edward Island in the 1950s and increased only marginally in Nova Scotia.[41] The irresistible lure of urban centres, the anglophone dominance of the media, and the poverty of the rural areas in which many Acadians lived made it difficult to organize for political action. At the same time, improved communication and rapid change helped to stimulate a collective response to the homogenizing trends of the decade.

Unlike the Acadians, the Scots in the Atlantic region were well represented in the leading ranks of society. Scots reaffirmed their language and culture at St Anns Gaelic College, founded in 1939. In 1950 the Adult Education Division of the Nova Scotia Department of Education hired a Gaelic adviser. As long as Angus L. was at the helm in Nova Scotia, Scots wishing to preserve their heritage had a ready ally. Bagpipes and tartan kilts often graced public occasions in Nova Scotia, creating an impression outside the province that it was in fact as well as name a 'New Scotland.'

The Black community in Atlantic Canada had fewer institutional resources. While Nova Scotia's Black population had been organized since 1945, the New Brunswick Association for the Advancement of Coloured People was not formed until in 1959.[42] Minorities of colour still faced crippling discrimination in Atlantic Canada, but there were signs of change, spurred by the powerful civil-rights movement in the United States. In 1954 the Nova Scotia government quietly dropped a clause in the province's education act that sanctioned separate schools for its Black population, and in 1955 it passed legislation making discrimination on the basis of race, national origin, colour, and religion illegal in employment and union membership.

If development was the dominant ethic of the 1950s, education was seen as the key to its success. Indeed, education, revolutionized by dynamic growth, centralization, and bureaucratic organization, represented in microcosm the larger trends of the decade. All four provincial governments were pressed to accommodate the region's expanding elementary-school population and anticipate the demand for higher education. Consolidation seemed to be the answer, both for the schools

Piping in the tourists, 1957. A focus on Nova Scotia's romantic Scottish heritage attracted tourists looking for the quaint or exotic and also served to divert attention from the problems of the industrial economy.

and the structures that administered them. With their gymnasiums, science laboratories, and home-economics and industrial-arts facilities, the new education factories were a sharp contrast to the one-room schoolhouses that they replaced. The teaching profession, too, was changing, becoming more highly trained and specialized. Despite the growing prestige of the profession, it was not always easy to find teachers to fill the new classrooms, in part because the region's salaries lagged behind those of the rest of the country. In an effort to find a solution to the problem of supply and demand, in 1957 Newfoundland hosted a conference to address the issue of teacher shortages, and departments of education in all provinces offered teacher-training courses in summer schools.

The most obvious feature of the revolution in education was the increasing costs. While the school population in the four Atlantic provinces grew by more than one-third during the decade – from 338,364 to 485,051 – costs of education more than doubled.[43] In Nova Scotia expenses of the Department of Education shot up from $13.6 million to $35.6 million between 1950 and 1960. Prince Edward Island's education bill was much smaller but subject to the same expansion, rising in the same period from $1.4 million to $3.8 million. As alarming as the escalating costs was the growing disparity in educational opportunities offered in rich and poor school districts. Provincial governments had little alternative but to centralize funding mechanisms so that poorer areas would not fall behind in the educational services offered to their young people.

Expansion in enrolment, programs, and budgets also characterized the region's universities in the 1950s. When the veterans graduated and joined the work-force, their grants from the Department of Veterans Affairs also disappeared, leaving university administrators with dwindling coffers. In 1952, federal grants-in-aid to universities were forthcoming as a result of a recommendation of the federal Royal Commission on National Development in the Arts, Letters and Sciences, but they fell far behind the sky-rocketing costs of higher education. By the mid-1950s enrolments were higher than ever and the demand for expensive new programs such as Education or Commerce was difficult to ignore in a region endeavouring to improve the quality of its work-force.[44] In Newfoundland, Memorial College, raised to university status in 1949, was forced to restrict enrolment in 1957, a measure that remained in effect for three years while a new campus was being built.[45] In the three Maritime provinces the existence of a number of small denominational colleges made higher education accessible to a larger proportion of the population but also threatened a costly duplication of services. Moreover, regional underdevelopment was reflected in faculty salaries, which were the lowest in Canada, a fact that made it difficult to hire and hold the best-qualified professors. Pressure to resolve these and other problems facing the region's universities would be even greater in the 1960s, when the post-war generation reached adolescence. In the meantime, university administrators did their best to cope with an increasingly untenable situation.

Vocational education in the region was spurred by federal cost-sharing programs introduced during the decade. Adult education, widely proclaimed as a solution to the region's unemployment problems, also became the focus of much attention. The first Atlantic Conference on Adult Education held in Amherst in June 1951 was devoted to 'an extensive study of community problems through group discussion.'[46] Guy Henson, director of the Adult Education Division of the Nova Scotia Department of Education, argued in an address delivered to the Atlantic Regional Conference on Adult Education in Charlottetown in 1955 that education was a crucial factor in regional development.[47] He subsequently took a position as director of the reorganized Institute of Public

Affairs associated with Dalhousie University where he created a receptive environment for discussions about new strategies for labour-management co-operation.

It is this transformation – in family life, education, work, arts, and leisure – that provides the context for political developments in Atlantic Canada in the 1950s. Although subsistence production continued to sustain a relatively high proportion of the region's population, the commercialization of primary pursuits and the welfare state drew farmers, fishermen, forestry workers, and housewives into the political-bureaucratic maze that dominated the processes of making a living. Most people, if they were not totally dependent on wage labour for survival, now worked for a wage at least part of the year or part of their life cycle. Young people who stayed in the region moved to urban centres to work on the construction sites and in the banks, hospitals, and government offices that housed the new economic order. By 1960 more than half the region's population lived in towns and cities. New suburbs near Halifax, Fredericton, Charlottetown, and St John's – stimulated by financing made available by the Canada Mortgage and Housing Corporation and, after 1954, federally insured mortgages – may have lacked individuality, but many Atlantic Canadians longed for the conveniences that suburban homes contained and the status they symbolized.

THE POLITICS OF DEVELOPMENT

The economic and social transformation experienced in Atlantic Canada during the 1950s was largely orchestrated by the state. It is therefore not surprising that provincial capitals became the locus of most of the organizational activity surrounding efforts to bring prosperity, now seemingly within reach, to a long-suffering Atlantic Canada. As in earlier periods of post-Confederation Canadian history, efforts to improve the region's economic climate depended upon co-operation from Ottawa. So significant were the political activities of the 1950s in the ongoing federal-provincial struggle that historian W.S. MacNutt has described them as constituting an 'Atlantic Revolution.'[48] This is a useful term to apply to political events of the 1950s not only because it helps to differentiate these activities from those movements for 'better terms,' 'repeal,' and 'Maritime Rights' that went on before, but also because it captures the dramatic nature of the economic and social changes occurring during the decade.

In many ways the economic conditions that gave rise to political action in the 1950s were similar to those that sparked the Maritime Rights movement of the 1920s. Emerging from the Second World War with a per-capita income 24 per cent below the Canadian average, the region sank to 33 per cent in 1955 (and 37 per cent when Newfoundland is included in the tabulation).[49] Newfoundland had the dubious distinction of being the poorest province in the nation, its personal income only 51 per cent of the Canadian average in 1950, rising slowly to 54 per cent by 1955. Secondary industry in the Maritimes summoned up a miserable 2.2 per cent of the national increase between 1946 and 1953, while Ontario's share in the corresponding period was 56.6 per cent. In 1953 the net value of secondary industry in the Atlantic provinces was $94 per capita, while the national average was $405 and Ontario's average $696.[50] At the same time, the expansion of state services in the post-war period put a severe strain on provincial treasuries. In 1951 the New Brunswick government was forced to accept an 'adviser' by its creditors; Prince Edward Island annually gave evidence of its inadequate financial resources; and even the Newfoundland government, which had entered Confederation with a surplus of more than $40 million, found its treasury rapidly dwindling under the twin demands of social services and economic development. Nova Scotia, often in a better financial position than other provinces in the region, was faced with a crisis in the coal and steel industry that threatened to dwarf all other demands on the provincial government.

The double-barrelled challenge of decline relative to the rest of Canada and rapid transformation within their own boundaries moved regional leaders to action. People in Atlantic Canada had been keen observers of Roosevelt's New Deal policies, had witnessed the apparent success of the Commission of Government in Newfoundland, and had seen the results of government planning for wartime production and peacetime reconstruction. While a few cynics still felt that governments could do little to shape economic forces, many Atlantic Canadians now expected the interventionist state to rectify what was ailing the region. Working through such organizations as the Maritime Provinces Board of Trade, the Maritimes Transportation Commission, co-operative organizations, provincial federations of labour, the region's universities, and various quasi-governmental agencies, they turned to their provincial governments for action and counselled self-help and co-operation to overcome their common problems. Pressed by departmental experts and by public opinion that had moved well in advance of government policy, Atlantic premiers gradually accepted what was becoming the conventional wisdom of the age: that state planning was the only alternative to economic backwardness, and that federal aid was the necessary condition for the success of such planning.

Federal MPs were also spurred to action. Longtime Maritime 'booster' C.C. Avard, editor of the *Maritime Advocate and Busy East*, argued on the eve of the 1949 election that 'we should vote for the men who will stand valiantly and persistently for the Atlantic provinces, rather than for those who are mere voting machines for their particular party.' He suggested that the Maritimes join with Newfoundland to create a 'united Atlantic front' that would 'demand Maritime rights from Ottawa.'[51] Although the region's politicians shrank from block voting, and, indeed, had disgraced themselves by bowing to the party whip on the freight-rates hikes of 1948, few could escape the growing body of public opinion that 'something must be done' for the Atlantic region. Members of the opposition needed little encouragement to criticize the federal Liberals. Cape Breton's Clarie Gillis of the Co-operative Commonwealth Federation (CCF) was a strong voice for regional interests until his defeat in 1957. So, too, was Conservative Alfred J. Brooks from New Brunswick. In 1948 George Nowlan won the Digby-Annapolis-Kings riding on a Maritime Rights campaign that he carried into the House of Commons and eventually into the national presidency of the Progressive Conservative Party. So widespread was the discontent that even Liberals began to point out the error of their party's ways. Gordon B. Isnor, speaking from the safety of his Senate seat in February 1951, cited figures showing that nearly 90 per cent of government contracts in 1950 had been placed in Ontario and Quebec. Isnor called for decentralization not only of government purchasing but of the country's industry as well.[52]

Provincial administrations in the three Maritime provinces, suffering from poverty, longevity, and the accumulated weight of past defeats in federal-provincial battles, were slow to respond to the groundswell of regional discontent and demands for dramatic action. The same cannot be said for Joey Smallwood's Liberal government in Newfoundland. Fresh from a successful campaign to bring his country into Confederation, Smallwood promised that 'every bit of our strength and energy as a government will be used in this great work of development.'[53] He was true to his word, taking the Economic Development portfolio himself and badgering any capitalist who would listen to invest in Newfoundland. Nor did he leave Ottawa off the hook. By Term 29 of Newfoundland's Confederation agreement, a royal commission was promised within eight years of Confederation to review the province's financial position. In December 1953, more than three years before the royal commission was to become operative, Smallwood began building up his case for a generous federal grant under Term 29. He was also instrumental in luring J.W. Pickersgill to the riding of Bonavista Twillingate. As former assistant to prime ministers King and St Laurent, and briefly clerk of the privy council, Pickersgill had uncommon access to the levers of federal power. In 1953 Pickersgill replaced Gordon Bradley as the cabinet minister from Newfoundland, a move that underscored the weakness of the province's Liberal members but gave Smallwood a powerful voice in the St Laurent administration. Meanwhile, the outspoken Newfoundland premier kept the pressure on Ottawa by criticizing national policies that made Quebec and Ontario economic giants and left the Atlantic provinces to their own resources. 'Before we become second-class citizens of Canada,' he announced to an Atlantic Association of Broadcasters meeting in June 1955, 'we will show the other Maritime Provinces how to get out of Confederation.'[54]

Smallwood's feisty example was an inspiration to Maritime premiers, especially to Hugh John Flemming, who led the New Brunswick Progressive Conservative Party to victory in September 1952. A successful lumberman and the son of an earlier New Brunswick premier, Flemming had a deeply felt patriotism for his province and a strong drive to reduce the poverty of New Brunswickers. Once in office Flemming found that he had important allies in his war on poverty in the rapidly expanding faculty of the University of New Brunswick, in his own public service, and in the expanding bureaucracy of the New Brunswick Electric Power Commission.[55] Faced with a bankrupt treasury, Flemming pressed Ottawa to contribute to the costs of power development at Beechwood on the Saint John River. When the St Laurent government, already committed to the St Lawrence Seaway, refused to see Beechwood as deserving of federal assistance, Flemming made it his mission to get his province's share of development money out of a tight-fisted federal government.

People in the other Maritime provinces also experienced, to their regret, the rigidly bureaucratic notion of equity that seemed to inform the national policies of the period. Prince Edward Island premier Alexander Matheson, a man of enormous stature and with a temper to match, was apoplectic with rage when in 1956 the federal minister of finance, Walter Harris, demanded that Prince Edward Island return $1.4 million that had been mistakenly paid out in per-capita grants.[56] In the same year, the federal government resisted helping the victims of the mining disaster in Springhill until embarrassed into doing so by references to the sums of money offered to fleeing Hungarian refugees.[57] J. Angus MacLean, an Island Progressive Conservative who had been elected to the House of Commons in 1950, echoed the feelings of many Atlantic Canadians when he reflected that Maritimers felt that they would have received more sympathetic treatment from the Canadian government if they had lived in developing countries somewhere else.[58]

Fuelled by their renewed sense of collective grievance, Atlantic Canadians set out to challenge Ottawa's crude definition of national policy. In 1951 the Maritime Provinces Board of Trade (MPBT), an organization with more than 100 affiliated boards representing nearly eight thousand members, established a regional office in Moncton and hired a full-time manager. At their annual meeting held in Sydney in October 1951, MPBT members heard L.W. Simms of the Maritimes Transportation Commission describe the pernicious effects of horizontal freight-rate increases on Maritime trade and the failure of the Turgeon Royal Commission on Transportation to offer satisfactory redress.[59] They also received a report from former New Brunswick minister of education Dr C.H. Blakeny entitled 'The Industrial Development of the Atlantic Provinces.' Blakeny recommended an aggressive 'Buy Maritime' campaign, increased immigration, interprovincial co-operation to develop power resources, and the creation of an industrial development committee to promote economic growth.[60] In the following year, at Charlottetown, the MPBT membership endorsed Blakeny's report and his subsequent suggestion that the Atlantic provinces appoint a royal commission to investigate all matters concerning the economic well-being of the region.[61]

The MPBT executive sponsored a joint meeting with the Atlantic premiers in Moncton on 14 September 1953.[62] Topics discussed included a uniform highway code for the Atlantic provinces, improved regional standards of education, creation of a joint tourism-promotion program, co-operation for development of industry and natural resources, and a royal commission to survey the economic conditions of the Atlantic provinces. Nova Scotia premier Angus L. Macdonald was lukewarm on Blakeny's idea of a royal commission. Arguing that 'We must stop looking to governments for money,' Macdonald suggested that the MPBT follow the New England precedent by establishing an Atlantic provinces council funded by the businessmen themselves to conduct their proposed survey. At the MPBT annual meeting held in Saint John the following month, delegates agreed to co-operate with governments in establishing a twelve-man plenary committee to consider how to set up an Atlantic council. It was left to the pleasure of Premier Macdonald to call the committee, but his death in April 1954 left the job to his successor, Henry Hicks.

Hicks was a stark contrast to Angus L. Renowned for his efficient energy as minister of education, Hicks had announced at the leadership convention that his party was living too much upon its past and should now devote itself to creating new records of public service against future appeals to the people.[63] Within two weeks of being chosen premier on 15 September, Hicks presided over a meeting of the twelve-man plenary committee, representatives from the MPBT , and the premiers in Halifax. They decided to create the Atlantic Provinces Economic Council (APEC), whose task was to survey, study, stimulate, and co-ordinate activities relating to the economic well-being of the Atlantic provinces.[64] At meetings early in 1955, a budget of $26,000 was approved for the first year of operation, and Nelson Mann, a Cape Bretoner with experience in

The road to the isles, 1955. At a ceremony attended by thousands of grateful mainlanders, the Canso Causeway was opened, connecting the rest of Canada to Cape Breton.

both industry and public service, was appointed as first executive manager. R. Whidden Ganong of the well-known candy-manufacturing company in St Stephen was chosen president of the organization. Vice-presidents represented each province. Twenty-five directors, seven from each of the Maritime provinces and four from Newfoundland, were elected to the first APEC board. Newfoundland initially played a smaller role because its officials were so busy with their own development strategies, particularly those relating to the upcoming royal commission on Term 29. Nevertheless, Smallwood agreed to help finance APEC, making

Newfoundland the only province to provide direct assistance to the 'independent' body.[65]

The creation of APEC coincided with the announcement of the Royal Commission on Canada's Economic Prospects chaired by Walter Gordon. The thrust of the commission suited the needs of APEC, the premiers, and organized groups in the region. Twenty-three briefs were submitted from the Atlantic provinces, virtually all of which were couched in the now-familiar language of regional grievance.[66] The flurry of research surrounding the royal commission hearings focused thinking on the region's economic problems and inspired enthusiasm for remedial action that carried over into the federal-provincial conference in the fall of 1955. Flemming was insistent that national adjustment grants over and above a more generous equalization formula be approved.[67] Even in the empire province of Ontario there was some sympathy for the Atlantic position, especially if grants to the region were coupled with an across-the-board increase in the federal formula for all the provinces.

With an election looming on the distant horizon, the St Laurent government was on the defensive. The 1956 budget, which included plans for an equalization formula based on the income of the two wealthiest provinces, was a sign that Ottawa was beginning to bow to pressure from the poorer provinces. And more was to come. Speaking to the Canadian Congress of Labour in Toronto on 24 April 1956, St Laurent challenged the Atlantic provinces to produce 'the initiative and ideas' to accomplish the redevelopment they were demanding.[68] St Laurent might have chosen a more appropriate location than Toronto to make such an announcement, but his timing could not have been better. Hugh John Flemming was facing an election as well as huge debts on behalf of Beechwood. He could not let such an opportunity pass. Encouraged by Michael Wardell, the British-born publisher who had recently purchased the Fredericton *Daily Gleaner* and the *Atlantic Advocate*, Flemming fired off a telegram to each of his Atlantic colleagues (with a copy to St Laurent) inviting them to a meeting in Fredericton to make plans for co-operative action.[69] Flemming gave his telegram to the press, an action that not only put the other premiers on the spot but also brought an offer from the president of APEC to help in co-ordinating the regional response to St Laurent.[70] Of course, it was an easy invitation for Flemming to make. If he failed to win the New Brunswick election announced for 18 June, his successor would have to entertain the invited guests.

The Atlantic premiers, their advisers, and representatives from the Maritimes Transportation Commission and APEC met in Fredericton on 9 July. Flemming had won his election handily, and the Liberal premiers appeared apprehensive about the motives behind what became the first Conference of Atlantic Premiers. Hicks announced that there was noth-

Atlantic premiers' meeting, Fredericton, 9 July 1956. This meeting of the Atlantic provinces' first ministers foreshadowed the conferences that would become commonplace in the following decade. Front row, centre: premiers
Hugh John Flemming (N.B.), Henry Hicks (N.S.), Joey Smallwood (Nfld), and
Alexander Matheson (P.E.I.). Others in attendance include cabinet ministers
and members of the Atlantic Provinces Economic Council and the Maritimes
Transportation Commission.

ing new in St Laurent's challenge, Matheson served notice that Prince
Edward Island would not countenance any discussion of Maritime union,
and Smallwood pinned his hopes on the Royal Commission on Canada's
Economic Prospects and Term 29.[71] Flemming, however, following the
counsel of his economic adviser William Y. Smith,[72] came to the conference with concrete proposals that were impossible for the other premiers to trivialize. Flemming argued that the Atlantic provinces should
demand from Ottawa 'fiscal need' subsidies, assistance for resource development, a regional transportation policy, monetary and fiscal policies
to stimulate regional growth, and a tariff policy designed to help the
region sell its primary products in foreign markets. His colleagues balked
at tinkering with monetary and fiscal policy, but they added their own
items to the shopping list, including improved trade relations with the
Caribbean area. At Hicks's suggestion, it was decided to ask the federal
government to place defence industries and contracts in the Atlantic
region. A 'continuing committee' composed of three representatives from
each of the four governments, with the ubiquitous Nelson Mann as
secretary, was charged with producing a report for the next premiers'

meeting to be held in Halifax. In the meantime Hicks was given the blessing of his colleagues in his crusade to enlist Ottawa's support in solving the region's transportation difficulties.[73]

To keep up the momentum, APEC sponsored a three-day seminar on the Atlantic provinces' economy. Held at the University of New Brunswick from 13 to 15 September, the conference consisted of panel discussions on such issues as 'Government Policy in Relation to Economic Development' and 'Atlantic Regional Trade Problems.' Among the invited guests were representatives from the New England Council and the federal government.[74] Flemming attended many of the sessions; Hicks and Matheson made an appearance on the last day. In a background paper to the seminar, Professor W.S. MacNutt described the history of Atlantic grievances and caught the spirit of regional chauvinism that was quickly gaining ascendancy:

> To those polite protests of the experts at the interprovincial conferences who insist that money payments to the provinces must be on the basis of equalization we can say, rudely if necessary: Where is the equalization in the operation of tariff policy, in the apportionment of western lands, in the St. Lawrence Seaway, in the pipeline contract? Why has Ottawa permitted all the beneficial adjustments in the freight rates resulting from the Duncan Report to be frittered away in inflation? We can say that, since we started on fairly even terms in 1867, equalization as seen from Ottawa has had some curious results.[75]

Mischievously drawing upon his vast knowledge of Canadian history, MacNutt warned the St Laurent government against the 'spectacle of a third nation "warring in the bosom of a single state,"' and suggested that once the Atlantic premiers and their experts had produced their ideas, the prime minister, 'accustomed to think of the position of his own racial minority as the dominant Canadian problem, will have the opportunity to consider the place of a minority that has experienced economic rather than military conquest.' These were fighting words.

Late in October Robert Stanfield led his Progressive Conservative Party to victory in Nova Scotia. Like Flemming, Stanfield had little to lose in taking on the Liberal government in Ottawa. He was also a strong proponent of state initiative. 'Undoubtedly private enterprise has a most important part to play in the redevelopment of the Atlantic economy,' he proclaimed in a pre-election address, 'but the government too has an important role and heavy responsibility.'[76] The earnest and purposeful Stanfield set out immediately to get federal aid for Nova Scotia's ailing coal industry, stimulate investment through Industrial Estates Limited, and expand state-sponsored health services.[77]

In December the federal Progressive Conservatives held a leadership convention in which John Diefenbaker, the colourful western populist, emerged the victor. Flemming was close to Diefenbaker and moved his nomination. Stanfield, fresh from his victory in Nova Scotia, delivered the convention's keynote address. Both premiers co-operated with Reginald Bell, leader of the Progressive Conservative Party in Prince Edward Island, in presenting convention resolutions for 'National Adjustment Grants,' 'National Resource Development,' and, at P.E.I.'s insistence, 'Claims for the Maritimes in Lieu of Crown Lands.'[78]

The preliminary report of the Gordon Commission was released in January 1957. The Atlantic provinces were singled out by the commissioners as deserving of 'positive and comprehensive' attention. Included among the recommendations were a capital projects commission to co-ordinate public investment in the region, increased geological surveys, a land-use classification program, increased subventions on Nova Scotia coal, decentralization of government purchasing, and a commission to review the region's transportation problems. A suggestion to provide 'generous assistance' to those people who might wish to move to other parts of Canada where 'there may be greater opportunities' was met with scathing derision.[79] Obviously decades of out-migration had not served the region very well as a development strategy. Despite this lapse in judgment, the report sanctioned the interventionist thrust now supported by all Atlantic governments. Newspaper publisher, Michael Wardell, his sharp sense of timing as keen as ever, gave a peremptory command to the premiers to get on with their proposals to St Laurent.[80]

Before the premiers had time to act, Ottawa seized the initiative. In Walter Harris's pre-election budget he promised to introduce legislation to reduce the region's outbound freight rates to their 1945 level as a temporary expedient until a full-scale study of transportation problems could be undertaken. He also offered federal assistance for the construction of thermal power plants and transmission lines for the region. Although there were many Atlantic demands left unmet, Harris's 'Maritime budget' represented a major turning point in federal policy and was given grudging approval even by Flemming and Stanfield.[81] By this time Ottawa had also moved on Term 29. J.B. McNair, chief justice of New Brunswick, was appointed in February to chair the royal commission specified under Newfoundland's Confederation agreement.

APEC's new president, R.J. Rankin, and several APEC officials met with the prime minister on 20 March.[82] They urged immediate action on the other Gordon recommendations, reiterated their complete agreement with the Atlantic premiers on regional development, and suggested 'a closer liaison between the Atlantic Council and those departments of government concerned with future planning for the region.' On 8 May

'Persuasive sort of fellow, isn't he?' In this Robert Chambers cartoon (*Atlantic Advocate*, Sept. 1959), the Atlantic provinces display their solidarity, in this case with Newfoundland's demand for a royal commission to review its financial status under Term 29 of the 1949 union agreement.

Stanfield presided over a conference of Atlantic premiers in Halifax. Nothwithstanding the impending election, the two Liberal and two Progressive Conservative premiers came to an agreement on the seven items on their agenda.[83] Their 'wish list' included federal subventions on coal used in Maritime power plants, joint Atlantic regional offices in the United Kingdom and possibly in the United States and the West Indies, annual federal payments for capital projects in the region, compensation for northern territories allotted to other provinces, a Prince Edward Island causeway, and co-operation in expanding educational and similar institutions. A permanent four-man committee was established to maintain continuous contact among the four governments.[84]

Hard on the heels of the premiers' conference came the Atlantic Provinces Manifesto, the result of a meeting of the region's Progressive Conservative candidates in Moncton on 11 May. With the help of Flemming's able secretary, Kenneth Carson, Conservative Party organizer Dalton Camp tapped out the 'Atlantic Resolutions' in the quiet atmosphere of a room in the Brunswick Hotel while the politicians 'talked policy' downstairs. The manifesto released to the press urged remedial action to solve the region's economic problems. Concrete policy suggestions for federal initiatives included a national resource-development program, decentralization of industry, federal aid to power development, freight-rate adjustment, a capital-projects program, adjustment grants, and a Canadian coast guard.[85]

On 10 June the federal Progressive Conservatives squeaked to victory with a seven-seat margin over the Liberals. Twenty-one of the party's supporters were from Atlantic Canada, sixteen more than in 1953. Diefenbaker may not have been instrumental in drawing up the Atlantic Resolutions and he may, as Camp suggests,[86] have been coerced by Flemming into accepting them during the campaign, but he was sympathetic, as any prairie politician might be, to the spirit of the document. He appointed four cabinet ministers from the Atlantic region, more than at any time since the Second World War; and, for the first time since Confederation, the Atlantic and western ministers in the cabinet totalled more than ministers from Quebec and Ontario. The politics of regionalism at last seemed to be paying off.

The new federal government tried not to move too precipitately and was encouraged in its caution by officials in the Department of Finance.[87] The Atlantic pemiers, however, were in no mood to take the long view. With its minority position, the Progressive Conservative government might be relieved of its powers at any time. Flemming and Stanfield were quick to press their individual concerns on their new federal allies. At their September meeting, the Atlantic premiers polished their resolutions and added a few more to the list, including the use of Canadian ports for Canadian trade, a regional farm-credit policy, and a tariff on fluorspar to help create a market for the Newfoundland product.[88] Flemming also used the occasion to complain about the Bank of Canada's 'tight money' policy, which was causing added stress for a region where unemployment, not inflation, was the major economic problem. While the provincial ministers and their professional advisers struggled to coordinate the Atlantic program in such a way as to present a common front to Ottawa, Atlantic cabinet ministers kept up the pressure on their colleagues. Finally the dam broke. Before the people of Canada went to

'Throwing the switch at Beechwood, June 1955.' New Brunswick fought a long but eventually successful campaign for federal aid for electrical power development. Here Premier Hugh John Flemming throws the switch initiating construction of the Beechwood hydroelectric project.

the polls again in March 1958, several policies proposed in the Atlantic Resolutions had been implemented. They included a $29.5-million loan to Beechwood, subventions on coal, aid to the development of thermal plants and interconnecting transmission lines, and $25 million in Atlantic provinces adjustment grants. Although the Liberals under Lester Pearson jumped on the regional bandwagon in 1958, Atlantic Canadians, like other Canadians, contributed the majority of their seats – twenty-five out of thirty-one – to the Progressive Conservative landslide.

### THE LIMITS OF DEVELOPMENT

Even before the cheers from the election had died down, cracks began to appear in the Atlantic front. The McNair Commission handed down its report in May with a recommendation for an annual $8-million dollar grant under Term 29.[89] Smallwood was furious. Although he had managed to get Newfoundland included in the adjustment-grant formula, he felt that his province should have at least an additional $15 million annually in perpetuity. He resorted to his highly public methods of making his discontent known, much to the annoyance of Diefenbaker, who was also not pleased with the fact that Newfoundland had been the only province in Canada not to give him a majority of its seats in 1958. When Diefenbaker and Smallwood clashed over the woodworkers' strike in the winter of 1959, Diefenbaker not only refused to authorize sending the RCMP to Newfoundland, he also made a $36.5-million grant over a five-year period the 'final and irrevocable settlement' under Term 29. Smallwood summoned the forces of Newfoundland nativism to de-certify the International Woodworkers of America and crushed his op-position in a snap election. He was less confident that his Atlantic allies would stand by him in his 'finest hour.' At the Atlantic premiers' con-ference in 1959, Smallwood announced that he would not ask his col-leagues to take an official stand on Term 29. If they did not respond favourably to his invitation, he reasoned, he would no longer be able to associate with them. 'It would be a pity,' he concluded, 'if the Atlantic front were broken.'[90] Smallwood had always stood slightly aloof from the Atlantic front, hoping that the special status of his province as the youngest member of Confederation would serve him better than the politics of regionalism. It was now clear that Newfoundland would be obliged to share the identity that its geography and economic condition dictated.

While Smallwood's alienation from Diefenbaker did not interfere with regional co-operation, internal differences did. Prince Edward Island was unhappy with the division of the adjustment grant on a 30:30:30:10 ratio,[91] and was soon in conflict with New Brunswick over regional-development strategy. Spurred by expectations of massive government investment, business interests in New Brunswick, led by industrialist K.C. Irving and the indefatigable Michael Wardell, dreamed up a series of construction projects that would transform the region's economy. Dubbed the 'three Cs,' they consisted of the Chignecto canal, the Prince Edward Island causeway, and a corridor road through Maine to Quebec. As the federal government dithered on funding, anxious developers began pursuing their pet projects. Wardell threw caution to the winds in 1959 by stating that the canal took precedence over the causeway if the two were in conflict.[92] In 1960 the Island's new Progressive Con-servative premier, Walter Shaw, a former provincial deputy minister of agriculture and no stranger to the strategies of political posturing, took Flemming to task for promoting the Chignecto canal exclusively in a speech delivered in Montreal.[93] Word from Nova Scotia was also dis-couraging on the canal project, which would help Saint John at the expense of Halifax and the Strait of Canso. The fact that Flemming was

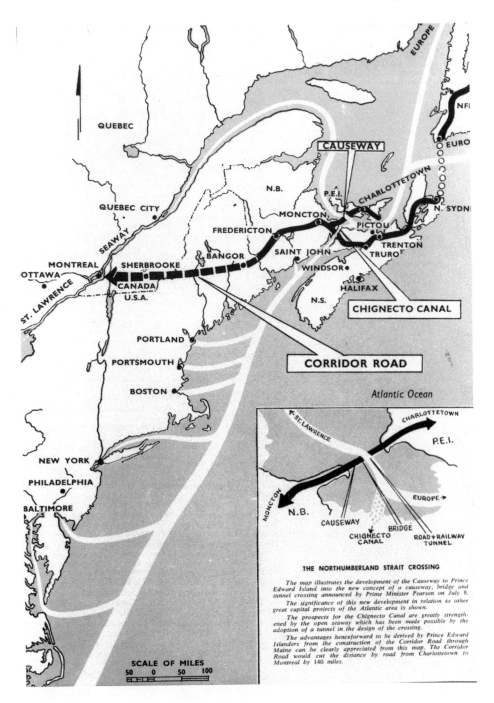

'The Three Cs,' 1965. Michael Wardell, editor of the *Atlantic Advocate*, advocated construction of a Chignecto canal, a corridor road through Maine to link the region to Montreal, and a Prince Edward Island causeway, all in order to shorten distances between Maritime producers and their markets.

chairman of the Chignecto canal committee and Wardell the honorary secretary only accentuated the narrow provincial interests of both men.

It soon became clear that the leading spokesman for the Atlantic Revolution was neither infallible nor invincible. In a hotly contested election in June 1960, Flemming suffered a crushing defeat at the hands of the youthful and equally purposeful Louis J. Robichaud. Two issues in the campaign, both indirectly tied to the decade's development strategy, were the province's puritan liquor laws and the premium levied to cover the provincial share of the hospital-insurance plan. There was also growing resentment in rural and francophone areas of New Brunswick that the benefits of the new era of co-operative federalism were not being equally distributed. Predictably, a change of regime in New Brunswick did not reduce the pressure on Ottawa for favourable regional policies. Robichaud continued to agitate for the Chignecto canal and to support his fellow premiers in promoting regional development.

The New Brunswick experience pointed to difficulties of another order on the Atlantic front. The rank and file of voters were often uninformed about the goals and strategies of the movement or out of sympathy altogether with the development thrust. Those still eking out a living in the marginal farming and fishing communities sometimes felt threatened by the bureaucratic apparatus and capitalist values invading their culture, while organized labour had misgivings about the rhetoric of development that assumed their compliance in plans to entice industry from 'high-cost labour regions.'[94] Moreover, the irresponsible behaviour of several high-profile promoters brought into the region to manage development projects did little to inspire confidence among the disaffected. The most notorious of these outside experts was undoubtedly Alfred Vladmanis, who was hired by Smallwood as an economic adviser to the government in 1951 and jailed for fraud three years later.[95] But even honest promoters were often resented, both for their superior airs and their inflated salaries.

Women, too, were marginal to the movement, though they made up half the potential electoral support. There were no women on the board of APEC when it was first constituted, and a Women's Atlantic Council, designed as an 'auxiliary' to the men's organization, failed to reach its intended audience.[96] Founded in 1957 under the direction of Saint John housewife Laura Foster, the women's council as late as 1960 had only 100 members and two branches, one in Saint John and the other in Moncton. Its name was conspicuously absent from a petition demanding equal pay for equal work, supported by twenty-two women's organizations in New Brunswick and presented to Flemming early in January 1960.[97] Nor was the issue taken up by any other organizations designed to solve the region's economic difficulties.

Ultimately the dreams of regional prosperity based on massive federal aid were shattered by a national financial crisis and opposition from other regions of Canada to the special status accorded the Atlantic provinces. As soon as Diefenbaker announced the Atlantic provinces adjustment grants, there were protests over what they meant for national policy. Douglas Campbell of Manitoba was annoyed because a general agreement on federal-provincial fiscal matters had been shelved so that the claims of the Atlantic provinces could be dealt with, and he complained that special grants for the Atlantic region reduced the amount available in the general pot. 'Let us not have narrow, patch work, regional settlements,' he urged. 'Let us have national plans embracing all parts of Canada.'[98] As the post-war boom began to slow down and unemployment became a pressing issue elsewhere than in the Atlantic region, a chorus of voices soon joined Campbell's.[99] Finance Minister Donald Fleming, the officials in his department and their counterparts in the Bank of Canada fought a rearguard action against the Atlantic assault on the federal coffers. Fleming told provincial treasurers at a meeting in 1959 that a regional monetary and fiscal policy was out of the question while James Coyne, governor of the Bank of Canada, continued to pursue a tight-money policy, much to the dismay of those hoping for a new era of flexible federalism.[100]

Under pressures from all sides, the Diefenbaker government began resorting to the policies of its predecessors. Royal commissions were appointed on transportation and coal, and projects such as the canal and causeway were buried under surveys and cost-benefit analyses. The Atlantic region's ministers were left to do the best they could to turn their portfolios to regional advantage. With Nowlan in National Revenue and on the Treasury Board, MacLean in Fisheries, and Flemming, after his defeat in the 1960 provincial election, in Forestry, the Maritime ministers were in a position to shape policy in key economic sectors. In 1960 Diefenbaker appointed Nowlan to chair the cabinet committee on economic policy. The committee included an Atlantic provinces development board and a national economic development board among its many recommendations. Donald Fleming's 1960 'baby budget' offered tax incentives for industries establishing in depressed areas, and in the following year adjustment grants were increased. But the Chignecto canal project was never seriously considered, a fate shared by the P.E.I. causeway. And neither the Atlantic nor the National Development Board was in place by the time Canadians went to the polls in 1962.

Leaders of the Atlantic Revolution refused to be daunted by such stalling tactics. At a joint meeting of the premiers and APEC in St John's in September 1958, the Atlantic Provinces Research Board was established to assist provincial organizations and act as a link between the

'The Order of Good Cheer – circa 1960.' The four Atlantic premiers were optimistic about the region's economic prospects, provided that Ottawa could be persuaded to support their demands for regional development.

premiers and APEC.[101] Among the issues to be investigated by the new body was a flexible monetary policy, transportation problems, and the effects of the St Lawrence Seaway on the region. The initiative of the premiers and APEC also inspired the establishment of Atlantic House in London in 1958, took APEC president Frank MacKinnon and his entourage in search of markets in the Canadian North in 1959, and stimulated imaginative thinking on regional development.[102]

In September 1960, the Atlantic Conference, combining the annual meeting of APEC, the premiers' conference, and the senators and MPs from the Atlantic region was held in Halifax.[103] The occasion marked a turning point in the Atlantic Revolution. While the principle of 'special status' based on fiscal need was now an integral part of national policy considerations, the presentation of two reports framed to coincide with the conference blunted the optimism characteristic of the early days of the revolution. Chief Justice Ivan Rand's royal commission report on the coal industry indicated that there were no easy solutions for the declining markets in coal. Several mines would have to be closed and the unemployed miners put to work on such projects as Cape Breton Highlands National Park and the restoration of Louisbourg.[104] The implication was that industrial Cape Breton would never recover its former glory. Another report came from Professor A.K. Cairncross, who had been spirited from the University of Glasgow by the Atlantic Provinces Research Board to study the effects of monetary and fiscal policy on the region's economy. After spending five weeks in the region during the summer of 1960 he presented an interim report *in camera* to the premiers while they were attending the Atlantic Conference. Organizers of the conference expected the Cairncross report to be the highlight of the event. Instead, it brought more unsettling news. Like Rand, Cairncross could offer no easy panaceas. Certainly monetary and fiscal policies alone would not bring prosperity to the region, any more than Canadian control over such policies could shield the nation from the adverse effects of American economic power.[105] In short, neither the interventionist state nor orthodox economics had the answer for underdeveloped regions like Atlantic Canada.

CONCLUSION

W.S. MacNutt warned in 1957 that while premiers might be united in action, 'unless the people of the Atlantic Provinces are united behind them the Atlantic Revolution would be one of the great mute, inglorious revolutions of history.'[106] The Atlantic Revolution of the 1950s was not mute, nor was it altogether inglorious, but it failed to move beyond the narrow business and bureaucratic circles in which the battles were fought. Nevertheless, the Atlantic Revolution left an important legacy. It established regional equality as a goal of Canadian national policy, created a bureaucratic apparatus to fight regional battles, and sanctioned the role of the interventionist state at both the provincial and federal levels in dealing with regional disparity. The Atlantic Revolution had another, more enduring impact. In defining a regional consensus based on the belief in a vigorous capitalist economy, an interventionist democratic state, and mass consumption, it also brought Atlantic Canada into line with the dominant currents of North American culture.[107]

Ten years later when the politician returned to visit Henry and his wife a week before election day, he did not find them on the front porch. Instead they were inside watching television. The politician did not have much time to stay and chat. He was on his way to the provincial capital where he would appear in a television interview. 'You don't mean to tell me that you're actually going to be on television!' Henry exclaimed, with a note of false wonderment in his voice. 'Why yes, he is,' reproved his wife. 'We've seen a lot of them political fellas on television lately – lawyers most!' Having settled this point for her husband she turned to their caller with a note of impatience in her voice: 'We haven't got a car yet but you needn't bother sending one for us on election day. Don and Mary will be out from the city driving for a friend of theirs. They'll see we get to the polls.'

# CHAPTER TWELVE

# The 1960s
## The Illusions and Realities of Progress

The 1960s was a pivotal decade. The growing importance of new technologies stimulated change throughout the western world. As part of a long period of economic growth, the decade saw substantial improvements in Canadian living standards. Faith in material progress was accompanied by an optimistic and egalitarian idealism that encouraged concern for the plight of minorities and the poor, the questioning of traditional values, and new attempts to define national goals and aspirations.

For the Atlantic provinces, perhaps the most significant developments of the decade were the profound changes in the financing and delivery of government services. Canada seemed finally to have found a solution to the incongruity of a national structure that hived the principal industrial and financial resources into two central provinces and yet expected the others to finance from within their borders the growing welfare and developmental costs of a modern industrial state. The changes, which began in the late 1950s and were expanded and consolidated in the 1960s, generally followed the principles outlined by the Rowell-Sirois Commission of two decades before. The commission had proposed that the federal government, with its ability to tax wealth wherever located, assume responsibility for some basic social programs, while transferring sufficient monies to the poorer provinces to ensure minimal standards in social and educational services throughout the country. By the 1970s the Atlantic governments were obtaining more than a third of their revenues from federal equalization payments, while comparable amounts were transferred into the regional economy through federal social and development programs.

The decade opened on an optimistic note as politicians, bureaucrats, economists, and businessmen confidently predicted the narrowing of the economic gap between the Atlantic provinces and the rest of the country. Much was accomplished. New highways, power plants, factories, and industrial parks sprouted throughout the region. Communities expanded into modern high-rises, subdivisions, shopping malls, and urban renewal programs. There were substantial improvements in income levels, employment opportunities, municipal services, education, health care, ethnic relations, and interprovincial co-operation. But rising expectations still came up short of fulfilment, and by the end of the decade disillusionment had once again begun to set in. Though the region's relative decline had been checked, statistically the gap between regional and national living standards narrowed only a little. As the end of the decade neared, accomplishments were taken for granted while hopes were tempered by industrial failures, continued unemployment, and the realization of an unprecedented dependency on federal assistance.

POLITICS AND REGIONAL DEVELOPMENT

The strategies of interprovincial co-operation in Atlantic Canada developed during the 1950s had begun to pay dividends in the context of federal-provincial relations. The region's call for special development assistance met a sympathetic response from the federal Conservative administration of John Diefenbaker – a response facilitated by Ontario's ending its traditional opposition to federal fiscal transfers. The new special grants and regional-development programs not only enabled the introduction of national social programs, but also, in a period of minority governments when Atlantic voters received unusual attention from federal politicians, were politically appealing. Thus, by the time of John Diefenbaker's defeat in 1963, the Liberals under Lester Pearson's leadership were already promising close attention to the problems of the region – a promise that materialized in expanding financial support for regional development and a close rapport between Prime Minister Pearson and provincial premiers Louis Robichaud and Robert Stanfield. The succession of Pierre Trudeau to the Liberal leadership in 1968 saw him in competition for the region's support with opposition leader Robert Stanfield, a former premier of Nova Scotia and an experienced proponent of regional development. Although personally less conversant with the Atlantic provinces, Trudeau's appointments of New Brunswick's Romeo LeBlanc and Nova Scotia's Allan MacEachen gave the region an effective voice at the cabinet level. He himself endorsed the attack on regional disparity as a national priority: 'If the underdevelopment of the Atlantic Provinces is not corrected – not by charity or subsidies but by helping them become areas of economic growth – the unity of the country is almost as surely destroyed as it would be by French-English confrontation.'[1]

Louis Robichaud discusses progress with workers. During Robichaud's tenure as premier, many hospitals, schools, and public buildings were built in New Brunswick, especially in the northern and eastern fringes of the province, which had been scantily provided with government services to that time.

Meanwhile the Atlantic leaders worked hard to consolidate their united front while pressing ahead with specific proposals. In particular, the Atlantic Provinces Economic Council (APEC) had been instrumental in promoting political and social co-operation within the region. Since the calling of the first Atlantic premiers' conference in 1956, APEC had worked closely with the political leaders to establish regional priorities and to formulate joint appeals to Ottawa about such matters as transportation costs, resource development, and fiscal policy. At the Atlantic premiers' conference of 1959, which welcomed the recently elected Prince Edward Island Tory premier Walter R. Shaw, the premiers considered joint projects such as the Prince Edward Island–New Brunswick causeway, the Chignecto canal, and harbour development. In September 1960, the Liberal premier of New Brunswick, Louis J. Robichaud, and his Conservative counterpart from Nova Scotia, Robert Stanfield, opened an interconnecting interprovincial power-grid system that was later expanded to include Prince Edward Island. Similarly, in 1960, Nova Scotia and New Brunswick agreed to establish a joint school for the deaf in Amherst.

The arrival of the young, aggressive Acadian Louis Robichaud at the premiers' table in 1960 strengthened interprovincial co-operation. Backed by a new breed of professional economic advisers such as Delbert Gallagher, Robichaud endorsed virtually all the major economic, political, educational, and social programs on the regional agenda, including the causeway and canal, the Association of Atlantic Universities, and a reconstruction of federal tax-concession and equalization programs.[2] In 1964, when it looked as though Quebec might seriously consider separating from Canada, leaving the Atlantic region in geographic if not economic limbo, Robichaud called on his fellow premiers to discuss the possibilities of a more formal rationalization of the region's economic and political structure.

While Prince Edward Island was sceptical and Newfoundland indifferent, Robichaud's revival of the century-old proposal for regional union attracted national attention. So, too, did Joey Smallwood's alternative suggestion that the island provinces should join together, since their island experience provided for greater common interests. Smallwood's plan received little support in the 'Garden of the Gulf,' and by 1965 Newfoundland was taking a less active part. Preferring to deal with Ottawa directly, Smallwood dropped out of the Atlantic premiers' conferences after 1965.

Fearful that interprovincial co-operation was disintegrating, Robichaud continued to push for Maritime union. In 1968 the three Maritime premiers, including the new Liberal premier of Prince Edward Island, Alexander Campbell, elected in 1966, asked Dr John J. Deutsch to chair a special study of Maritime union encompassing physical, economic, and other forms of regional co-ordination and co-operation. The commission reported in 1970 that it had encountered a 'Kaleidoscope of opinion,' but that it believed all efforts should be directed towards achieving eventual physical union.[3] The premiers were unwilling to support the ultimate recommendation, but they did agree that the region, including Newfoundland, must work towards greater integration of all regional concerns, from motor-vehicle licensing to industrial-development policy.[4] They also agreed that they must jointly support the principles of redistribution, equalization, and regional development in national policies and programs.

Increasingly, the Atlantic provinces turned directly to a responsive Ottawa for guidance and support in promoting Atlantic trade and industry. By the early 1960s the role of APEC as the guiding body behind the Council of Atlantic Premiers was decreasing. Part of this was due to the establishment in the late 1950s and early 1960s of provincially

"*At the steps of the church, the bride took over*"

New dreams of union, 1964. The centennial of the Charlottetown Conference prompted discussion of a union of the four Atlantic provinces.

administered development agencies – Nova Scotia's Industrial Estates Limited, Newfoundland's Newfoundland and Labrador Corporation, New Brunswick's Development Corporation, and Prince Edward Island's Industrial Enterprises Incorporated. More significant, however, was the creation in 1962 of a new federal agency, the Atlantic Development Board.

In the late 1950s, in addition to adjustment grants, the federal government had responded to the demands of APEC and the Atlantic premiers with several short-term development projects including 'Roads to Resources' and financial assistance for construction of thermal generating stations. But the first major regional program came in 1961 with passage of the Agricultural and Rural Development Act (ARDA). A fifty-fifty cost-sharing program, ARDA was aimed at improving economic conditions and potential in the poor, rural, agricultural areas of the country. While the Atlantic provinces readily responded to the available funds and projects, there was concern that ARDA did not address the problem of industrial underdevelopment. This concern was further underscored by the recommendations of A.K. Cairncross's report on the Atlantic region's economy (1960) and the report of the Gordon Royal Commission on Canada's Economic Prospects (1958) that the Atlantic provinces must make the transition from a seasonal, low-productivity economy to an industrial economy. Cairncross urged the provincial governments to offer tax incentives, market guarantees, freight subsidies, capital grants, and loan guarantees to prospective developers. He also stressed that Ottawa must assist by reimbursing the provinces for their incentive costs. APEC members agreed and urged the Atlantic premiers' conference to ask Ottawa to set up a federal agency empowered to deal specifically with co-ordinating and stimulating industrial growth in the Atlantic region.[5]

Ottawa responded to the demand for government-sponsored industrial stimulation and for a co-ordinating body. In 1962, John Diefenbaker announced the creation of the Atlantic Development Board (ADB). Initially comprising five private-sector members and possessing no project funds, this new research and advisory agency reported to the federal cabinet on the wishes of the Atlantic premiers and co-ordinated the efforts of all government bodies involved in Atlantic regional economic development.[6] APEC continued to conduct local research to formulate programs and to promote Atlantic trade, but its direct participation in the conferences of Atlantic premiers diminished. This was particularly true after April 1963 when Prime Minister Pearson changed the original nature of the ADB. Now placed under the secretary of state, its eleven members were authorized to award, from a fund of $100 million, grants for development projects according to set provincial ratios and 'to prepare an overall co-ordinated plan for the promotion of the economic growth of the Atlantic region.'[7] A more political body than APEC had envisaged, the ADB became the Atlantic premiers' key to the federal treasure chest. Meetings between APEC and the provincial authorities declined in number, while those between provincial cabinet ministers and bureaucrats and their federal counterparts increased markedly.

For several years the ADB handed out money to assist provinces in attracting industry. The main area of concentration was the development of modern infrastructure services – power, roads, industrial parks, bridges, wharves, and water-pollution controls. This priority was largely determined by a report released in 1964 by the Atlantic Research Board. In it Professor Thomas Wilson stressed the need for extensive infrastructure investment as the key to attracting developers and exploiting resources. Similarly, in 1961 the federal royal commission on transportation had reported that better highways and air and rail services were essential to bolster the Atlantic economy. Federal and provincial monies were therefore directed towards upgrading transportation facilities across the region. In New Brunswick alone the mileage of surfaced roads increased by 60 per cent over the decade.[8] The Trans-Canada in Newfoundland was completed in 1965. The 'Roads to Resources' program provided $30

"And when he comes to the door don't forget to sit up and beg like I taught you to."

Knocking on the door of opportunity, 1969. Mega-projects needed enormous subsidies from both provincial and federal governments. Deuterium of Canada's heavy-water plant at Glace Bay wasted hundreds of millions of taxpayers' dollars without producing any substantial product.

million per province to build new roads to areas of resource development potential. ADB provided funds, and special non-renewable grants were also available, including $6 million given to New Brunswick in 1968 to improve the highway along the north shore. Air service and terminals were expanded, starting with the opening of the Halifax International Airport in 1960. The ice-free harbours of Saint John and Canso were expanded as superports for bulk cargo, and Halifax unveiled its first container port for general cargo. While some entrepreneurs, such as K.C. Irving, also envisaged construction of the Chignecto canal and Northumberland Strait causeway as integral parts of the region's transportation system, Ottawa ultimately did not. Construction on the causeway approaches, begun in 1966, was halted in 1969. Instead, Ottawa provided new ferries and terminals.

Transportation was only one area given priority by Ottawa and the ADB. Another was electrical-power development. Recognizing that new industries would need reliable, cheap power the provinces set out, with federal help, to maximize their resource output. New Brunswick, Nova Scotia, and Newfoundland built new thermal plants during the decade. New Brunswick entered the nuclear age in 1970, agreeing to build a Candu reactor at Point Lepreau, and in 1966 the Atlantic Tidal Power Programming Board began feasibility studies of the tidal power potential of the Bay of Fundy. In New Brunswick, however, the highlight was the Mactaquac development on the Saint John River, which went into service in 1967, attracting Ste Anne–Nackawic Pulp and Paper to build a new mill on the dam's head pond. That same year Newfoundland's Bay d'Espoir project went on line, stimulating new manufacturing investment like Electrolytic Reduction Company (ERCO) of Canada along the province's south coast. Although production did not start until 1972, work also began in the mid 1960s on harnessing the magnificent Churchill Falls in Labrador.[9] The largest hydroelectric installation in the western world, while providing hundreds of jobs in the construction and supply sectors, did not mean cheap power for Newfoundland. Instead, in 1969 the province signed a forty-four-year contract selling virtually all power produced to Hydro-Québec.

By 1968, $188 million had been spent by the ADB, with amounts varying from $14.6 million in Prince Edward Island to $57.9 million in Newfoundland.[10] As the national economy prospered, the federal government became increasingly willing to support the underdeveloped regions. By mid-decade national industrial growth, extensive wheat sales, and dropping unemployment rates all meant enlarged private and public-sector capital industrial spending.[11] So, too, the Atlantic provinces began to experience stirrings of economic rejuvenation as production levels in mining, lumbering, and pulp and paper rose, new export markets opened, and the regional unemployment rate dropped to 5.5 per cent in 1967.[12] Although still well above the Canadian rate of 3.8 per cent, the fact remained that a generally buoyant national economy as well as the new federal investment had helped to restore confidence in the Atlantic region. Nova Scotia, for example, saw twenty new manufacturing firms go into production in 1965 alone. Average incomes rose by more than 40 per cent between 1956 and 1966, 7 percentage points higher than the Canadian average increase.[13]

For all its beneficence, however, the ADB did not and could not work a miracle. By late 1967 the country was entering another period of economic slowdown. Ever tied to the national condition, the eastern provinces experienced a similar decline in economic growth. Rising costs, failing markets, increasing unemployment, and burgeoning deficits combined with federal austerity policies to curtail the growth in living standards. It was clear that the ADB could not shield the region from the inevitable economic fluctuations. The premiers feared that Ottawa might succumb to the advice of those who argued that risk capital in have-not areas was a luxury only for good times. At the federal-provincial conference of 1969 the four Atlantic provinces, speaking as a single voice, demanded a review of the ADB and a constitutional guarantee that regional development and equalization would be a federal priority. Ottawa, although non-committal about constitutional guarantees, nevertheless did introduce, in 1969, the largest regional-disparity initiative of the decade. In an effort to rationalize the multitude of regional development agencies and programs, it created the federal Department of Regional Economic Expansion (DREE), which absorbed existing federal bodies, including ARDA and ADB. In order to ensure continued regional input the ADB was replaced by the Atlantic Development Council. Members were appointed by Ottawa after consultation with the provinces and were to advise DREE on regional concerns and needs.

The new umbrella agency, the first federal integrated approach to the problem of regional disparity, was to formulate a long-term comprehensive development plan for the Atlantic region, blending local and national objectives and priorities. It was empowered to provide incentives through cash grants for infrastructure projects and entrepreneurial location, expansion, and modernization in high-unemployment districts and designated 'growth centres.' This latter concept had been espoused and partially applied by ARDA and the ADB. Professor Wilson, in his report, had reiterated the idea of the 'growth centre' approach. He argued that geographical concentration of industry was far more efficient and profitable in the long run than helter-skelter developments determined more by political necessity and human sympathy than economic evaluation and practicality. Initially, DREE applied the 'growth centre' to the letter. However, as Michael Kirby noted 'the growth centre approach proved to be bad politics if not bad economics. It left too many people ... out of the infrastructure sweepstakes.'[14]

The creation of DREE did not lessen the link between the provincial and federal governments. The Atlantic region had become heavily dependent on the financial resources of Ottawa. The result was not always the economic boom promised. In fact, there were 'some spectacular industrial development failures,' which, it has been suggested, 'further increased the scepticism which many senior federal policy makers have about the possibility of any regional development program ever being successful.'[15] Losses were never fully recouped from the collapse of Nova Scotia's Clairtone Sound and Deuterium of Canada; New Brunswick's Fundy Chemical; Prince Edward Island's Gulf Garden Foods and

Bathurst Marine; and Newfoundland's Come by Chance refinery. To some such losses were luxuries that a region susceptible to market fluctuations and federal policy changes could ill afford.

ATTRACTING INDUSTRY

Industrial expansion and resource-development diversification were clearly regarded, by bureaucrats and economists alike, as the keys to revitalization in the Atlantic region. They placed great emphasis on attracting new industry, convinced it would reduce unemployment and out-migration rates. With a stronger taxable base there would be more money for the much-needed social services. While the provinces still concentrated on the traditional economic activities of the region – farming, fishing, and lumbering – they now turned their attention increasingly to tourism, mining, and secondary manufacturing.

Throughout the decade the Atlantic agricultural community experienced the same general trends as many other parts of the country – fewer and larger farms and fewer people dependent on agriculture for a living. While the western farmers benefited from newly negotiated grain deals with the U.S.S.R. and China, the Atlantic farmers felt neglected. Capital investment in agriculture increased between 1965–71, but the farm labour force in Atlantic Canada declined by 43 per cent.[16] In New Brunswick, the average farm size increased by 30 per cent over the decade. In Prince Edward Island the farm population fell from 33.2 per cent to 19.1 per cent over the same period. Similar trends existed throughout the region. By 1970, the remaining provinces recorded less than 4.3 per cent of their populations employed in farming.[17] Profit margins dropped on small farms, and many farmers joined the ranks of the unemployed or moved to urban jobs. By the end of the decade, even in Prince Edward Island, where agriculture continued to be the main economic activity, the government accepted the offerings of the federal Fund for Rural Economic Development (1966) and acknowledged the recommendations of the Task Force on Agriculture (1969) in discouraging small farm operations in favour of farm consolidation.[18]

Provincial governments supported diversification and capitalization, often in conjunction with ARDA programs. In order to help stimulate local production, the governments assisted in the establishment of agriculture-related industries, including fertilizer production and food processing. This was part of the rationale behind New Brunswick's Belledune and Fundy Chemical Fertilizer ventures and the expansion of the McCain french-fry and frozen-vegetable facilities. In Nova Scotia, freezing and canning capacities were increased by processors, including Scotian Gold, Canada Foods, and M.W. Graves. Food processors encouraged farmers

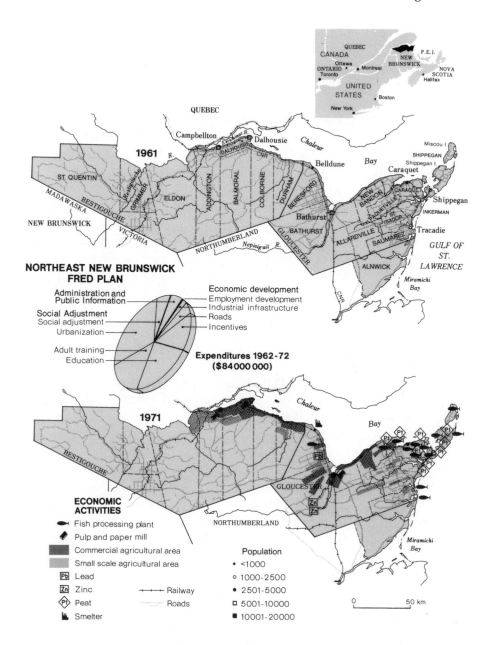

Figure 13 Regional development and planning in northeastern New Brunswick in the 1960s

to expand acreage, thereby making large consolidated farms more attractive. Greater variety and better quality were sought by Island producers like Seabrook Farms and Langley Fruit Packers, which opened in the sixties.

Like farming, fishing was undergoing structural changes in the 1960s. Decreasing catches among inshore fishermen, low incomes, and under-employment forced governments to re-examine their fisheries policies. In Newfoundland, where the decline in the inshore fishery most directly affected the majority of the population, the government set out to en-courage the surplus of inshore fisherman to shift to offshore fishing or to seek employment in other industries. Since 1953, the Newfoundland government had assisted, in a formal way, the depopulation of isolated, non-viable, outport fishing communities. Initiated by the requests of a few communities, the program became a matter of government policy in 1965 under the Fisheries Household Resettlement Program. Through a joint federal-provincial scheme under the 'growth centre' strategy of ARDA, residents were paid to relocate in one of the seventy designated areas where services and employment opportunities were supposedly better than in the outports. Ninety (later 80) per cent of the community had to agree to leave, but families could select the area they wished, subject to government approval.

For some, resettlement was seen as a conspiracy 'to wither the fish-eries,' while for others it was the only way 'to create viable new economic and social units' and to reduce the costs of public expenditures on welfare and outport servicing.[19] In the end, about 250 communities disappeared, affecting more than thirty thousand people.[20] Perhaps some did achieve a higher standard of living, but ultimately resettlement resulted in much dissatisfaction. The elderly often felt pressured to leave their homes and found it difficult to adapt to unfamiliar surroundings. 'Growth centres' like Burgeo, simply did not have the services or employment oppor-tunities necessary to meet the demands of such a population influx. Compensation for loss of business and house value was inadequate or non-existent. Only 14 per cent of those who moved actually settled in major, fisheries-oriented growth centres, and the offshore industry, itself in trouble by 1970, could not absorb the inshore surplus. Ironically, resettlement did little to reduce the exodus of Newfoundlanders to the mainland.[21]

In keeping with the large-scale development ethic of the decade, the state turned to the promotion and subsidization of the offshore fishery. Fish processors and shipbuilders were encouraged to expand. Compa-nies like National Sea Products and Birds Eye Fisheries added to their dragger and trawler fleets as well as their factory capacities. To promote modernization, governments financed such projects as construction of the region's first steel stern trawler in Bathurst in 1962. Processing plants, including a unique floating plant of Mersey Seafoods at Liverpool and the first North American plant to produce high-purity fish protein at Canso, sprang up across the region. All were heavily dependent on

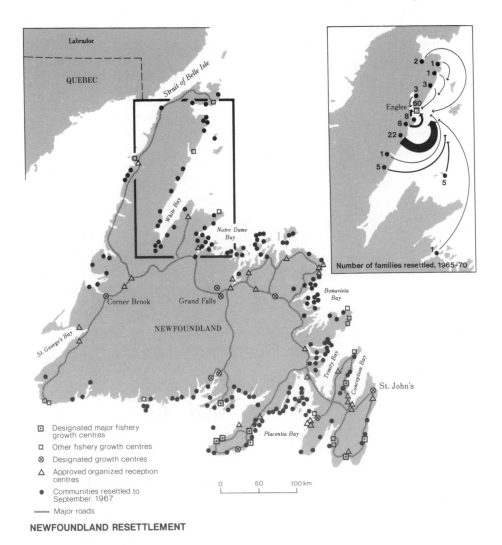

Number of families resettled, 1965-70

Designated major fishery growth centres

Other fishery growth centres

Designated growth centres

Approved organized reception centres

Communities resettled to September, 1967

Major roads

**NEWFOUNDLAND RESETTLEMENT**

Figure 14 The pattern and progress of Newfoundland resettlement to 1967

provincial government support and funds from ADB. Ottawa also encouraged research in fishing and fish-processing methods through its Fisheries Research Board, while Newfoundland's College of Fisheries, opened in 1964, trained a professional breed of fishermen to deal with modern technology in the industry.

Nevertheless, by the end of the decade the offshore fishery, like the inshore, was suffering from catch reductions, as stocks of cod and haddock declined. Foreign-exchange rates, excessive European production, and declining American markets resulted in the closure of several processing companies and shipyards, including Ross-Steers, Birds Eye Fisheries, Bathurst Marine, and Gulf Garden Foods. In 1968, Ottawa stepped in to help by guaranteeing a minimum price for frozen fish and the following year agreed to buy all unsold processed stock. Two years later the federal Saltfish Corporation set a guaranteed price for saltfish. Little wonder the fisherman and factory workers, concerned for their future survival, formed an industrial union in 1970, the Newfoundland Fishermen, Food and Allied Workers. The problem of supply would worsen in the seventies, forcing government action to protect fish stocks through quotas, licensing, and extension of the 1964 economic seaward terminal limit.

While the traditional primary products still attracted the greatest share of government incentive money, tourism emerged in the sixties as one of the region's major growth industries. Under ARDA, monies were available for new provincial parks and, in 1966 alone, Newfoundland used such funds to set up twelve parks. Ottawa also opened several new national parks, including Terra Nova in Newfoundland, Kejimkujik in Nova Scotia, and Kouchibouguac in New Brunswick. Federal funds began to pour into Cape Breton for the reconstruction of Fort Louisbourg, while provincial heritage projects, including New Brunswick's Kings Landing and Village Historique Acadien and Prince Edward Island's Acadian Pioneer Village, were also undertaken. At the community level, fairs, exhibitions and produce festivals proliferated, while folk festivals and Highland Games became increasingly popular. In Prince Edward Island tourism rose from the bottom of the list of revenues from major industries to second from the top in 1974. By the mid-seventies it placed third in net income in New Brunswick and Nova Scotia.[22] In Newfoundland, during the Come Home campaign of 1965–6, the gross value of tourism more than doubled.[23]

Federal financial incentives directed to the industrial development of the Atlantic region did much to attract new investors and encourage existing industries to expand. The most prominent beneficiaries of direct and indirect subsidies were mining and pulp and paper. Mineral production in New Brunswick outpaced in value all other sectors over the decade, and the output of forest-related products doubled.[24] In Newfoundland the value of mining multiplied more than three and a half times between 1965 and 1975.[25] Through long-term low-interest loans, tax concessions, and protection from expropriation and anti-pollution laws, provinces were able to attract foreign manufacturers like Volvo of Sweden, Toyota of Japan, South Nelson Forest Products of Italy, and Anil Canada Limited of India, as well as encouraging the activities of such local entrepreneurs as Irving, McCain, Joudry, and Sobey. Typical concessions included twenty-five years of low-cost power for Nova Scotia's ERCO Industries; land, buildings, financing, and municipal tax

Louisbourg reconstructed, 1969. As tourism flourished during the 1960s, historic sites were enthusiastically developed. Fortress Louisbourg was a project of the federal government.

concessions for Clairtone Sound; and $50 million in long-term loans for New Brunswick's Bay Steel. The companies came to set up shop, often with little risk to themselves.

As the economy began to falter towards the end of the decade and companies closed or sold out, people began to wonder if such 'forced growth' had been a good idea. Public discussion of failures and scandals overshadowed the successes. The long-term value of foreign investment was questioned. Did the investors come simply to exploit a resource-rich underdeveloped economy in order 'to supply needs of more developed economies?'[26] Many argued that the concessions had been excessive, often politically motivated, and detrimental to local control over development practices. Even politicians in the same party were split on the issue. In May 1968, John Crosbie and Clyde Wells left the Smallwood cabinet and crossed the floor to sit as independents because they opposed a $5-million interim-financing arrangement with New York promoter John Shaheen to continue building the Come by Chance refinery complex. In 1969, Robert Higgins, New Brunswick's minister of economic growth, refused to support Premier Robichaud's plans for a new particle-board plant in St George. Conservationists and environmentalists claimed that uncontrolled industrial expansion resulted in growing water and air pollution and the loss of valuable agricultural land. Traditionalists feared that manufacturing and commercialized tourism were threatening the social values and the landscape of the region.[27] Balancing the culture of the past with the aspirations of the future seemed to be well-nigh impossible.[28] By 1970 many might well have agreed with one contemporary that 'the Maritime provinces are the victims of industrial progress' because of their desire 'to become equal partners at the social and economic levels with the citizens of the other parts of Canada.'[29]

## A 'JUST SOCIETY'

The growing public awareness of social inequalities that swept North America in the 1960s touched the region most significantly through the extension of the social-welfare system. Poverty became a targeted concern of the period. More affordable and accessible social services in health care and education and more financial assistance for individuals formed the basis of the still-emerging faith in government-directed social and economic development. Atlantic Canadians were ready participants in federal, cost-sharing, social-welfare schemes, which more than doubled in cost during the decade. But federal largesse had penalties as well as benefits. By accepting federal programs and spending priorities, the provinces, especially the poorer Atlantic provinces, knowingly gave up more and more of their powers of self-determination.[30] The federal government's extension of its role, whereby it offered and financially facilitated expanded social services through new programs like the Canada Assistance Plan, the Old Age Security Guaranteed Income Supplement, and medicare, often aroused debate over constitutional jurisdiction. Nevertheless, Atlantic voters quickly came to expect and demand these services as their right.

Social reforms in the area of health care were perhaps the most dramatic and far-reaching of the 1960s. New kinds of treatment and services became available, contributing to a drop in the infant and mother mortality rate and a drop in the death rate generally. In 1964, because of an epidemic of gastro-enteritis in 1963 and evidence of infantile scurvy, Newfoundland henceforth required the mandatory addition of vitamin C to evaporated milk, which was commonly used in the largely non-agricultural province. By mid-decade, in all four provinces, widespread compulsory immunization programs for diphtheria, polio, measles, and mumps had brought those diseases under control. During the decade, existing hospitals and centres for the physically, hearing-, and sight-handicapped were expanded, and new ones were built. In 1964, Newfoundland opened the Dr Charles A. Janeway Health Centre, a children's hospital in St John's, and in Halifax in 1968 construction began on the new Izaak Walton Killam Hospital for Sick Children, designed to serve all the Maritime provinces. In an effort to rationalize and improve hospital services in New Brunswick, the Llewelyn-Davies Report on Health Services recommended in 1970 that the French and English hospitals in Moncton be merged, as well as St Joseph's and the General Hospital in Saint John. The report also suggested that several small rural hospitals be closed or turned into community health centres.

The Atlantic region could claim one first in the area of medical-care funding. In 1957 Newfoundland had introduced a medical plan to give children under sixteen free hospital and medical coverage. Smallwood resorted to this step because of the poor medical record of the province.[31] Then, in 1959, all four Atlantic provinces joined the national schemes for hospital assistance with the passage of Hospital Care Insurance acts in each province. They responded more slowly to the national Medical Care Insurance program announced by the federal government in 1967. The provincial governments were willing to participate, but, with financial constraints increasing as expenditures outstripped even bouyant revenues, Newfoundland and Nova Scotia delayed until 1969, Prince Edward Island until 1970, and New Brunswick until 1971. None of the four provinces opted for a premium system to help fund the program. It was not surprising that New Brunswick, which had defeated a Conservative government in 1960 over the issue of a hospital premium tax, would decide to fund the system through general revenues. Newfoundland, Prince Edward Island, and Nova Scotia also concluded that the imposition of a premium would be both politically unpopular and administratively burdensome. On the whole the scheme encountered little opposition in the region. As Frederick Rowe concluded, 'No part of Canada benefited more from this program than did Newfoundland with its large families and lowest per capita income in Canada.'[32] Much the same could be said of the Maritime provinces.

The considerable strain that the increasing 'baby boom' population was imposing on health and welfare structures was also being felt in the education system. While population increases were smaller in the Atlantic region than in other parts of Canada, they were none the less significant. The region also had some of the highest unemployment and illiteracy rates in the country. There was a pressing need for new facilities at all levels, not only because of increased enrolment and enforcement of compulsory school attendance, but also because of the need for trained professional and skilled workers. Education emerged as 'the major growth industry of the Sixties in Canada,' as the federal government increasingly supplemented municipal and provincial funding sources.[33] Seen as the keystone to immediate and future economic advancement, education was a political priority throughout the decade, becoming the single largest item in provincial budgets.[34]

Atlantic universities experienced very dramatic growth during the decade. Between 1960 and 1970 in Nova Scotia, enrolment rose from 5,811 to 15,820.[35] In Newfoundland, Memorial University saw its annual total of graduates multiply six times over the same period.[36] At the start of the decade, universities were generally poorly financed and inadequately equipped to meet such enrolment pressures. Crash programs of expansion in buildings, equipment, and staff were undertaken in all four provinces. Funds from private donors and government assistance were used to build new residences, science centres, libraries, and athletic facilities on the region's campuses. Dalhousie University and the University of New Brunswick built new law-school facilities. Memorial University added a medical school. Construction was completed on the Bedford Institute of Oceanography, which was affiliated with Dalhousie and which rapidly became one of the leading oceanographic research centres in the world.

In New Brunswick, changes in university structure followed the report of the 1962 provincial Royal Commission on Higher Education. The Deutsch Commission recommended long-term savings, greater efficiency, and increased offerings through a reduction in the number of universities from six to three, the establishment of a single degree-granting French-language university, the removal of St Thomas University from Chatham to the University of New Brunswick campus, and the opening of a branch of the University of New Brunswick in Saint John. The Liberal government responded. Robichaud owed much to the Acadian community, and in 1963 the Université de Moncton was opened, becoming a major symbol of a twentieth-century coming-of-age for nearly 300,000 French-speaking Maritimers.[37] In 1964 the Saint John Campus of the University of New Brunswick opened as a junior college offering first-year arts and science courses.

In Prince Edward Island the university debate of the decade centred on religious rivalries and the formation of a single, non-denominational, provincial university. In 1963, the secular Prince of Wales College reiterated its demands to be given full university status. Two years later the Royal Commission on University Education recommended the granting of that status, but urged St Dunstan's and Prince of Wales College to co-operate with a view to eventual federation. In 1965 the Prince of Wales College Act granting university status was proclaimed, and three years later, despite intense controversy, the single, public, non-denominational University of Prince Edward Island became a reality.

The major development in Newfoundland was the creation of a new campus for an existing university. By the late 1950s Memorial had outgrown its downtown facilities in St John's. Anxious to offer increased educational opportunities to Newfoundlanders, Smallwood pursued an extravagant, multi-phased relocation of the university near the new Confederation Building in the suburbs of the capital. Adopting an innovative lease-purchase arrangement with American investors, Newfoundland began development of a modern campus. In October 1961, the first five buildings were opened. Construction continued throughout the decade, culminating in 1969 with the opening of the Faculty of Medicine facilities, creation of which had been one of the recommendations of the 1966 Report of the Royal Commission on Education and Youth.

Efforts to rationalize universities in Nova Scotia also brought a few modest changes. In 1966, Mount Saint Vincent University provided for lay representation on its board of governors, and in 1970 control of Saint Mary's University passed from the Archdiocese of Halifax to a lay board. Acadia University, like Mount Allison in New Brunswick, ended denominational control of the university's governing body. Similarly, in an effort to improve resources without the expense of duplication, Mount Saint Vincent and the Nova Scotia Technical College set up linkages with Dalhousie for the use of libraries, equipment, and staff.

As in New Brunswick, the fate of French-language post-secondary education came under scrutiny. Debate on the future of the Collège Saint-Anne at Point d'Eglise drew many suggestions, including a recommendation for some kind of affiliation with the Université de Moncton. But nothing was resolved in the sixties. Moncton itself still suffered from growing pains and regional jealousies. In 1969, New Brunswick appointed the Commission de Planification Académique to study and make recommendations on the education needs of the francophones of New Brunswick. Released in 1972 and 1973, the recommendations formed the basis of the structural and curriculum reforms at the Université de Moncton during the seventies.

The financial burden of university expansion was shared by the federal and provincial governments. In 1960, the Nova Scotia government made its first regular contribution to the operating budgets of provincial universities. It also introduced a capital-assistance program paying up to 90 per cent of the cost of university buildings. In 1967, the minister of education in New Brunswick tabled a report of the Committee on the Financing of Higher Education in New Brunswick, which pointed out that increasing enrolments would necessitate an immediate doubling of financial aid to the province's universities and colleges. It also called for the formation of a permanent agency to advise the government on post-secondary educational needs. The Robichaud government, believing education to be a key aspect of a new reform program, which it called

Equal Opportunity, responded enthusiastically and allotted almost $20 million dollars for post-secondary education in 1967, an amazing contrast to the $3.5 million available in 1963.[38] The government also appointed an advisory committee under James F. O'Sullivan, known as the Higher Education Commission.

By the mid-sixties, provincial advisory and grants committees in all four provinces were calling for greater federal participation. Although education was a provincial responsibility, the federal government had agreed in 1951 to provide annual grants directly to universities in order to help with operating costs and capital investment. The agreed-upon formula increased over the years, but less rapidly than provincial demands and the apparent requirements of the universities. In 1965, the Royal Commission on Financing Higher Education in Canada recommended that federal grants to universities be more than doubled. The commission pinpointed research in science and technology as the areas most needing attention. Two years later, Ottawa passed the Federal-Provincial Fiscal Arrangements Act. As in other areas of federal assistance, there now was a shift from direct federal grants paid to the universities to unconditional grants paid to the provinces, which, in turn, would decide how best to spend them.

Meanwhile, rising tuition fees became a contentious issue. In 1965, the Newfoundland government initiated a program of paying the tuition fees of all students attending Memorial University. The other provinces did not follow suit, and eventually the Smallwood government was forced to limit the program to the financially needy.[39] In February 1968, Université de Moncton students boycotted classes for ten days to protest fee increases. Attracting the support of other students across the province, many with the blessing of their university presidents, on February 20 they marched on Fredericton demanding increased government grants and staged the first sit-in in a government building in the region's history. At another sit-in the following January, Université de Moncton students turned the funding issue into a French-English controversy by claiming that the English-language University of New Brunswick received more than the French-language university. The demonstration finally ended on 23 January, when the president, Adélard Savoie, announced that he had asked the province for a major increase in the university's budget allotment over the next five years. It was a delaying tactic that tempered criticism pending the report of the Commission de Planification.

Student militancy became part and parcel of the university scene across North America during the sixties. Influenced in part by the American civil-rights movement and the philosophy of social justice, Canadian student activists began to organize sit-ins and demonstrations. In the

The Strax affair, University of New Brunswick, 1969. UNB students symboli-
cally buried their board of governors over restrictions on individual liberties
during the international student movement of the turbulent sixties.

Atlantic provinces, conflict between university administrations and students arose over student demands for more democratic university government, including a say for students in the setting of tuition fees and
in the administration of the universities. Seeing themselves as the ca-
talysts of social change, student protesters in Atlantic universities embraced causes ranging from the non-renewal of a professor's contract to
university amalgamation. Generally protests were orderly. The most
controversial involved Norman Strax, an American-born professor at
the University of New Brunswick, who took up what he claimed was
the cause of individual freedom by refusing in November 1968 to use
an identification card that was required to remove books from the university library. Strax was suspended and ordered off the campus. The
student government's denunciation of the university administration found
support from the Canadian Association of University Teachers, which
investigated the case and censured the university. Strax was ultimately
deported, but for several months unrest and tension reigned in the university's hallowed halls.

Elementary and secondary educational systems also had to adapt to increased numbers and economic needs. Each of the provinces responded with policies of consolidation. Prince Edward Island realized the first stages of consolidation in 1960 with the completion of its first regional high school. By 1963 fifteen new consolidated units had been arranged. With the introduction of the Comprehensive Development Plan in 1969, the process of closing small schools and building large consolidated ones intensified. Eventually, more than a hundred local school boards were reduced to five rural and two urban boards that directed much of the administration and fiscal responsibilities of each district.

In Newfoundland, school reforms concentrated on costs, curriculum, and reorganization. A consolidation process begun in 1954 at the high-school level continued slowly throughout the sixties. Concern, however, for the high drop-out rate and the generally low level of educational attainment focused attention on the funding of the school system and the need for better elementary facilities. The provincial government, in the fall of 1965, announced its intention to provide $4 million to school boards for school construction, to cover 75 per cent of the cost of all textbooks, and to pay on a monthly basis $1.50 per child to parents to help defray school fees charged by school boards for the heating and maintenance of buildings.[40] Following the release of the report of the Royal Commission on Education and Youth in 1967, Newfoundland passed a new Education Act, embarking on a systematic reorganization of the Department of Education along functional rather than denominational lines. The province initiated an aggressive school-amalgamation program of reducing 300 boards to 36, abolishing fees, and establishing provincial-government responsibility for school maintenance costs. In keeping with the ecumenical movement that was gaining acceptance across the Christian community in Canada, in 1969 the Anglican, Salvation Army, and United churches agreed to full integration of their school systems.

In Nova Scotia the Liberal government of the early fifties had implemented a system of regional and vocational schools. The Stanfield administration continued the policy of school consolidation in rural areas, and in 1965 it introduced a comprehensive provincial school system uniting academic and vocational education into one system. In the late sixties the province called for voluntary school-board amalgamation, in hopes of reducing the existing 89 major boards and almost 700 boards of school trustees. The initial response was surprisingly positive, and in 1969 three amalgamated school boards were ready to come into existence.

For New Brunswickers there was nothing voluntary about school reform. Consolidation had begun in the 1950s, but a profound disparity in the financial resources of the municipalities meant that the reforms had been unevenly implemented. Meanwhile, high rates of illiteracy prevailed in the most economically depressed areas of the province. In 1965, following the recommendations of the Royal Commission on Finance and Municipal Taxation (the Byrne Commission), the province relieved the municipalities of their responsibilities by assuming full control over primary and secondary education. In 1966, a highly controversial Schools Act aimed to remedy some of the worst inequalities in the system. Through a drastic reduction in the number of school districts from 422 to 33, the government hoped to eliminate curricular disparities and create new opportunities for students. The Department of Education assumed responsibility for school finances, setting salary scales and creating a standard core curriculum and grading system. District boards were to prepare budgets for departmental approval, appoint all teachers, and administer programs. The New Brunswick Schools Act also dealt with the abolition of a separate Roman Catholic school system. Feelings ran high over secularization, but in the future only non-sectarian schools would receive provincial financial assistance.

Opponents claimed that consolidation would destroy community spirit and cost too much. Others denounced the new district boundaries and bus routes. In New Brunswick where the consolidation process was most rapid and highly centralized, opposition was particularly vocal. For example, in September 1968 the parents of Shippegan Island refused to send their children to schools on the mainland at Shippegan, ostensibly for reasons of safety. The eventual resolution of the dispute saw a junior high school for Lamèque on the island and a senior high school in Shippegan.

Throughout the decade all four provinces sought to improve teaching standards by raising salaries and requiring higher qualifications. Provincial departments of education expanded programs of teacher training, including subsidized summer schools, and in classification for salaries emphasized professional training and university graduation. In New Brunswick, the provincial English-language teacher's college was expanded and moved to the UNB campus, and in 1968 the primarily French-language Ecole Normale opened at the Université de Moncton.

One motive for educational reform was the retraining of the workforce for more advanced technology. In 1960 the federal Technical and Vocational Assistance Act provided provinces with money to construct, equip, and operate vocational-training schools and technical programs. So too did ARDA. All four provinces expanded high-school vocational offerings and built post-secondary facilities, including Holland College at Charlottetown, the Nova Scotia Technical College in Halifax, the Bathurst Trade School, and the Newfoundland College of Trades and

Technology in St John's. In spite of the attention to education throughout the sixties, the region's educational services continued to lag behind those of most other parts of Canada. A report of the federal Department of Regional Economic Expansion in 1969 drew attention to the region's lower teacher qualifications and salaries, higher illiteracy rates, lower expenditures on education per pupil, and lower numbers of students pursuing post-secondary education.[41] In 1971 the residents of the Atlantic provinces and Quebec had the lowest median levels of education in Canada. New Brunswick and Newfoundland, between 1961 and 1971, reported the lowest percentage of high-school graduation in the country. Yet such figures were a reflection of previous neglect and should not be used to obscure the very real progress then being made. In New Brunswick, for example, the magnitude of the change was reflected in the school-attendance figure for fourteen- to seventeen-year-olds, which went from 59.7 per cent in 1960 to 85.2 per cent in 1971.[42]

Fostering the intellectual welfare of the young was only one social concern of the decade. Caring for their physical well-being was another. Each of the provinces directed its attention to child-welfare reforms during the decade by amending or introducing new legislation to deal with such issues as child labour, legitimacy and adoption laws, social-worker qualifications, and minimum standards of care and facilities for foster homes and children's-aid agencies. Child-care also received attention, following the introduction in 1966 of the Canada Assistance Plan, which made funds available on an equal cost-sharing basis to provinces agreeing to provide day-care for children in families deemed to be in need. The plan also incorporated existing shared-cost programs for the aged, blind, and disabled and provided matching support for all mothers'-allowance schemes.

Trying to keep young people in their region was another concern of the decade. In 1960 Louis Robichaud appointed a new ministry of Youth and Welfare, inviting young New Brunswickers to help the government in setting policy and goals. In 1969, New Brunswick passed a Youth Allowance Act providing a small monthly allowance to students aged sixteen and seventeen as enticement to remain in school. The other provinces watched with interest, but preferred to direct their assistance to their youth through educational reforms and economic-development programs.

One result of the previous out-migration of youth was that the region was left to care for a greater percentage of the elderly. Here, too, the provinces in the region sought to provide expanded facilities and improved services.[43] Once the sole responsibility of private and religious groups, care of the elderly now came to involve direct government participation. In 1965 Newfoundland financed the Hope Home in St John's, and in 1966 Nova Scotia provided monies to build a model home at Eastern Passage, incorporating facilities for institutional care in a home-like atmosphere. By mid-decade all four provinces had legislation on homes for the aged. New Brunswick led the way in 1963 with the first regular inspection system under a provincial government supervisor. The terms of enforcement and standards varied considerably, however. The provincial governments also launched a number of home-care projects under the Canada Assistance Plan, including new homes for the aged and expanded hospital facilities for geriatric care.

URBANIZATION

The industrialization of the Atlantic provinces, which began in the 1950s and accelerated in the 1960s under the stimulation of government incentives, radically changed the physical and social character of the urban community. Between 1961 and 1971 the urban population in New Brunswick jumped from 46.5 per cent to 56.9 per cent.[44] By 1971, Newfoundland was technically the most urban Atlantic province at 57.2 per cent.[45] But the largest metropolitan area of Halifax-Dartmouth held 23.7 per cent of Nova Scotia's population.[46] Attracted by promises of employment in new industries and by access to education and to a modern technological life style, Atlantic Canadians followed the trend of North America, moving to the cities and towns.

The accelerated urbanization brought new burdens for municipal governments. Growing pains were intensified by outdated facilities, inefficient utilities, housing shortages, and traffic congestion. It was worse in some places than in others. While some communities, such as Bridgewater, took time to plan for industrial expansion with the arrival of Michelin Tire, others like Corner Brook and Port Hawkesbury did not. They grew too fast and suffered from haphazard construction, urban sprawl, and serious financial difficulties. As a dormitory town for the Point Tupper Industrial Park complex, Port Hawkesbury in the late 1960s simply could not cope with the physical demands placed on its services. Larger cities, such as Halifax, Saint John, and Moncton, experienced the same problems to varying degrees. Thus, municipal officials began to turn for help to such professional town planners and consultants as John Crispo and Thomas Plunkett. All major Atlantic cities hired professionals to plan for the construction of new services, urban renewal, slum removal, and land redevelopment. Their twenty-year plans set priorities to cope with future growth and recommended ways to raise monies for proposed developments, including tax incentives to commercial devel-

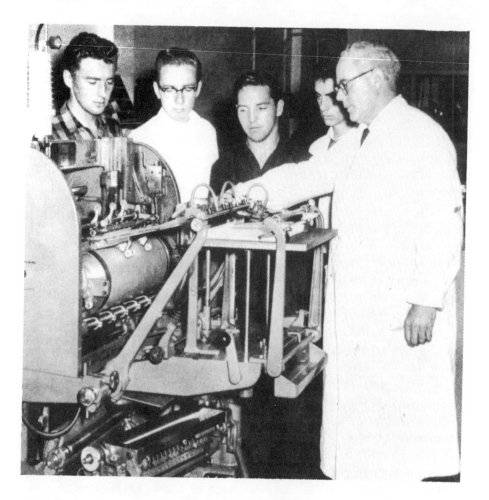

Newfoundland College of Trades and Technology. Technical education and
retraining were introduced at the post-secondary level as a means of meeting
the demands of 'modern industry.' In the end, students more often employed
their skills elsewhere in Canada, when the technical jobs did not materialize
at home.

opers, property taxes, and federal assistance such as that offered by the
Canada Mortgage and Housing Corporation. For instance, in 1962 St
John's obtained $13 million in federal help for port remodelling.[47]
   A massive construction boom accompanied the arrival of new industries and municipal-development programs. To accommodate the expanded population, new suburbs were created, such as the 200-acre
mixed housing project in Saint John's Huntington Valley. Luxury high-
rises like Halifax's Embassy Towers and Park Victoria rose on the horizon, and low-income rental units replaced old slums. Revitalization of

deteriorating city cores was realized in a variety of projects, including Halifax's Scotia Square complex in 1969, a development offering residential, retail, office, and recreational facilities. The outer limits of communities turned to shopping malls, like the Halifax Shopping Centre (1962) and the Avalon Mall (1967). New city halls in St John's and Dartmouth symbolized municipal vitality. With the cities' housing, shopping, and recreation needs met, city officials also planned for more efficient traffic circulation, bypasses, and bridges. Industries, too, encountered a sense of municipal order as they were placed in industrial parks, some, like that in Bridgewater, in order to protect a community, and others, like Westmorland Chemical Park near Dorchester, in order to help revive a depressed area.

All these developments cost money. Some was obtained from the increased tax base and the absorption of rural non-farm areas to help pay for costly municipal services. Amalgamations such as that of Saint John with three other communities in 1967 and Halifax's annexation of four suburbs in 1969 became common, as did municipal expropriations and incorporations. Another solution to financing lay in structural and administrative changes in municipal government. The issue of financing was most pressing in New Brunswick, where by the early 1960s some counties were on the verge of bankruptcy. Inequalities in services were extreme, owing to wide variations in taxable resources. Based on the recommendations of the Byrne Commission in 1964, assessment and municipalities acts swept away all previous municipal legislation and abolished the fifteen county councils. In their place were incorporated villages, towns, and cities, each with elected governments responsible for local services. Unincorporated areas, called local service districts, were to be administered directly by the Department of Municipal Affairs as of 1 January 1967.

The municipal inequalities in services and debt burdens so evident in New Brunswick may have been less pronounced in the other Atlantic provinces, but they too realized that reforms were needed to improve social services and ensure equal access. In 1969 Nova Scotia announced plans for municipal reform based on a report urging the province to assume greater responsibility for general services and to reduce the number of units of municipal government through annexation and amalgamation. That same year Premier Campbell received a municipal-study report calling for a more equitable provincially administered municipal system with a single real-property assessment rate. Newfoundland, too, financed a commission on municipal government, which reported in 1972 that the province needed a more rational and centralized municipal system to ensure the future viability of an increasingly urban province.

MINORITY RIGHTS

As elsewhere in North America, concern for ethnic equality and minority rights surfaced as political and social issues in the Atlantic region during the 1960s. In Canada this concern was partly demonstrated by the enactment of the Canadian Bill of Rights in 1960, a bill which, though not entrenched, recognized basic individual freedoms in matters under federal jurisdiction. The heightened awareness of minority rights and the multicultural nature of society resulted in a more formal organization of interest and lobby groups. In Atlantic Canada demands for equality of treatment and opportunity were voiced by Atlantic women and the francophone, aboriginal, and Black communities.

The 1960s and 1970s have been described as 'témoin d'un réveil sans précédent dans pratiquent tous les domains chez les Acadians.'[48] Like other parts of Canadian society, the francophone communities were being affected by secularization, urbanization, and industrialization.[49] In the midst of these social changes Acadians experienced a revitalization of their own collective identity.

The more than 70 per cent of Maritime francophones living in New Brunswick – 38.3 per cent of the population in 1960 – made the province a natural centre for Acadian nationalist sentiment.[50] The demands were motivated by concern for cultural and linguistic survival. Improved transportation and the availability of better education and television had contributed to an increased contact with the anglophone majority. As well, high unemployment, poor social services, and inadequate financial resources in northern and southeastern New Brunswick, where the majority of francophones lived, had resulted in increased out-migration, urbanization, and secularization. Assimilation rates had been climbing. Whereas in 1951, 93.7 per cent of those of French ethnic origin in New Brunswick had claimed French as their mother tongue, by 1960 that had fallen to 90.7 per cent. In Nova Scotia and Prince Edward Island only about 45 per cent of those of French ethnic origin spoke French as their mother tongue in 1961.[51]

One symbol of change came in the person of Louis J. Robichaud, who became the first elected Acadian premier in June 1960. The Liberal campaign for better economic conditions and social services and the abolition of the hospital premium tax attracted widespread support, especially in the poor, rural areas where the majority of francophones lived.[52] Robichaud's election raised Acadian expectations for increased participation in the cabinet and civil service. They were not disappointed. More than 50 per cent of the first cabinet was francophone, and it remained so for the decade. Similarly, the civil service saw a much greater hiring of francophones. Neither were francophone New Brunswickers disappointed with Robichaud's 'Program of Equal Opportunity' – designed 'to guarantee acceptable minimum standards of social, economic and cultural opportunity' – which was particularly beneficial to the depressed areas of northern and southeastern New Brunswick.[53] The province's assumption of municipal debts and centralization of education and health care were greeted with enthusiasm in predominantly Acadian areas.

Equality of opportunity was not a popular principle with everyone. Some anglophones saw it solely as an excuse to integrate the francophones more securely into the political, cultural, and economic life of the province at anglophone expense. They regarded the Equal Opportunity program as 'a manifestation of a French takeover.'[54] Even so, the pursuit of equal rights for Acadians in the public sphere was becoming a permanent feature of the political landscape, particularly in New Brunswick.

French-English relations experienced considerable stress during the sixties at the national level. French Canadians in Quebec were caught up in the growing controversy over Quebec's place in Confederation. Talk of 'maîtres chez nous,' sovereignty-association, and even separation left the future unity of the country in doubt. General Charles de Gaulle's outburst of support for an independent Quebec in Montreal in 1967 and Robichaud's subsequent refusal to dine with the French president augmented tensions. Within New Brunswick, the trip to Paris at the invitation of de Gaulle in 1968 of four leading Acadian spokesmen who returned with financial assistance for L'Evangéline, a French cultural centre, and the Université de Moncton, further incensed some anglophones. The pieces of legislation that most threatened French-English harmony nationally and provincially, however, were those regarding language.

In 1966–7 the federal Royal Commission on Bilingualism and Biculturalism called for the granting of equal status to French and English as official languages in Canada and increased bilingualism in the federal civil service. The federal government responded with legislation in 1969, as did the Province of New Brunswick. In April the Official Languages for New Brunswick Act gave both French and English equal status in a general sense. Initially, only seven sections of the act were operative, and guarantees were limited. However, the act did establish a policy of linguistic equality that later received practical expression.

In spite of heightened French-English tensions, the francophone community maintained its push for cultural equality. Acadian cultural organizations like the Société Saint Thomas d'Aquin (1919) and the Société Nationale des Acadiens (1957) increased their membership and activities. Realizing that they too needed a provincial nationalist organization, Nova Scotia Acadians formed the Fédération Acadienne de la Nouvelle-

Ecosse in 1967. In New Brunswick, the Société Historique Acadien (1960) set out to promote research and publication of Acadian history. Bodies like these heightened government awareness of past injustices and encouraged changes in policy and legislation. In 1968 the Prince Edward Island legislature became officially bilingual; by 1970 most school texts in New Brunswick were available in both languages. French newspapers flourished, French CBC radio and television were set up in Moncton, and French cultural programs were expanded. As Père Anselme Chiasson noted, by 1970 'l'Acadie n'est pas près de mourir mais est plus vivante que jamais.'[55] Many young Acadians began to question the approaches of the traditional nationalist organizations. The more militant university students, stimulated by a mixture of radical socialism and pan-Quebec nationalism, met in 1966 at the Ralliement de la Jeunesse Acadienne to espouse an ideology of neo-nationalism. They wanted to be masters of their own Acadian destiny in some kind of autonomous state. The political expression of this sentiment was the formation of the Parti Acadien in 1972.

Traditionally, the Native people of the region had lacked a common front from which to lobby for redress of grievances regarding land claims, treaty rights, and poor employment and educational opportunities. By mid-decade, however, some leaders had become more outspoken and aggressive in their criticism of the Indian Act. Atlantic Native groups began to challenge the system by insisting on their aboriginal rights to year-round hunting and fishing as guaranteed under seventeenth- and eighteenth-century treaties. In January 1968 in New Brunswick, a judicial decision to the effect that federal and provincial legislatures were not constitutionally bound by any pre-Confederation treaties only served to strengthen the resolve of Native groups. New Brunswick in 1968 and Nova Scotia in 1969 led the way with provincial umbrella organizations to speak out for Native interests. The release, in 1969, of the federal government's misguided White Paper on Indian Policy, recommending the replacement of the special-status provisions of the Indian Act with a new approach based on an equal-status philosophy, set the stage for a lengthy debate. Fear that Ottawa intended to pursue a policy of cultural assimilation made aboriginal peoples, including Atlantic Indians, more determined to see their special status receive constitutional recognition.

In the Black community, the influence of external forces such as the American civil-rights movement, race riots in the United States, and the Black Panther organization resulted in a more vocal and militant denunciation of racial prejudice and a more formalized demand for social change. Representing 1.6 per cent of the provincial population and concentrated in specific communities, the largest in the Halifax-Dartmouth

Seaview Baptist Church, Africville. A small enclave along Halifax's Bedford Basin, Africville had few urban amenities. Along with the rest of the community, this church was bulldozed to the ground in 1967. The memory of the community remains a focal point in Black Maritimers' consciousness.

area,[56] the Nova Scotia Blacks were the most influential lobby group. They were particularly provoked by the Halifax council's decision to destroy Africville, a Black community on the Bedford Basin. The city wanted to rid itself of what it perceived as an unsightly and dangerous health hazard, partly to facilitate a more rapid integration, or assimilation, of Blacks into the general community. An unstated motive may have been the freeing of potentially valuable waterfront property for a container port. Despite strong verbal protests, Africville families were relocated into low-cost housing projects within the city.

The following year Halifax's Black community welcomed several Black Panthers to the region, and the formation of the militant Black United Front (BUF) in 1969 gained the attention of the province, as Black leaders sought to instil a sense of identity and pride among their people as well as to publicize evidences of racism in the wider community.

Slowly governments responded to Black demands for the elimination of discrimination. Legislative reforms came federally between 1962 and 1967, as race and colour were removed as factors in determining immigrant selection. Starting with Nova Scotia in 1963, each of the provinces introduced its own human rights act and overseeing agency. Official segregation became a thing of the past. In 1965 Nova Scotia set up a fund to assist Black people to complete high school and enter postsecondary education. Ottawa awarded the BUF a four-year assistance grant to facilitate self-improvement projects such as a Black housing program in Beechville. Although informal discrimination continued and the socio-economic condition of Black Maritimers did not dramatically improve in the 1960s, public sensitivity to racial injustice and inequality was heightened, and governments did rectify some of the institutionalized injustices of the past.

Acadians, Micmacs and Blacks were not alone in their campaign for equality. As across North America, women of the Atlantic region became more vocal in their demands for equal treatment before the law and in the workplace. The women of the 1960s had experienced the rapid changes taking place in the lives of women since the Second World War. Higher levels of education and greater social, economic, and sexual freedom increased women's awareness of their subordinate status. Atlantic women, like others, formed feminist interest groups and began to enter the political arena. The National Council of Women and the Canadian Federation of Business and Professional Women's Clubs, whose members included New Brunswick's Muriel M. Fergusson, Canada's first woman speaker of the Senate (1972), pushed for a greater role for women in political and economic circles. During the decade, all three Maritime provinces elected their first female MLAs. Homemakers, too, made their mark. In 1966 a group of women in St John's, appalled by high food prices, boycotted local supermarkets. The result was the appointment of one of their number to head up a provincial Inquiry into the Price of Food and Drugs. Fears of the potential of an atomic war brought women like Halifax's Muriel Duckworth to the fore as activists for world peace through the Voice of Women (1961). The Committee on Equality for Women articulated the growing concern about the need for day-care, equal pay for equal work, and greater participation of women in nontraditional careers and forced the federal government in 1967 to set up a Royal Commission on the Status of Women. One of its members was Judge Doris Ogilvie of New Brunswick.

The movement still had far to go. In 1965 the governments of New Brunswick and Newfoundland did not send representatives to a federally sponsored conference on maternity leave because the issue was not a priority. Such attitudes frustrated militant women and resulted in the formation of women's liberation groups, including one in Halifax in 1969. The 1960s did witness a revitalization of the women's movement; but, as in the case of other disadvantaged groups, it would take more than a few new organizations and tentative legislative reforms to reverse generations of stereotyping and inequities.

## LABOUR

The most concrete evidence of the changing role of women was the sharp increase in their participation rates in the labour force. Economic and social factors, including rising inflation, increasing male unemployment, and growing divorce rates, contributed to this increase. Between 1967 and 1973 the Atlantic region experienced an annual growth rate of women in the labour force of 8.5 per cent, significantly above the Canadian rate of 8.1.[57]

Numbers alone did not ensure women greater respect or equality in the workplace. Women were still relegated to lower-paid jobs in the often non-unionized clerical, sales, and service sectors. For single female parent families in 1971 the average income in the Atlantic area was $4,112.25 compared to the Canadian average of $5,074.00.[58] Male-dominated unions, concerned with wages and job security, also were slow to take up such women's causes as pay equity. Women were left particularly dependent on modest increases provided for in the various provincial minimum-wage acts.

The growing shift to manufacturing, mining, construction, and public-service employment in the Atlantic region during the 1960s resulted in an increased number of unionized workers. While the Maritime Fishermen's Union and the National Farmers' Union represented more traditional rural employees, the largest concentration of union members by 1970 was found, predictably, in the urban centres. One of the biggest membership increases took place in the civil-service sector, where the modernization and expansion of provincial and municipal services produced a dramatic expansion in numbers of government employees, including teachers, nurses, and clerical staff. In Nova Scotia, for example, the number of government workers doubled between 1953 and 1966 and again between 1966 and 1976.[59] Similar increases took place in New Brunswick, Prince Edward Island, and Newfoundland, so that by 1971 approximately 50 per cent of personal income in the region was derived from government sources.[60] Meanwhile, owing to the phenomenal growth in the construction industry, the labour force there also mushroomed.[61] Comparable growth occurred in the booming mining and pulp-and-paper industries. In 1961, 1,460 persons were employed in New Brunswick mining; by 1966, thanks to base-metal-mining development by Cominco, Heath Steel, and Brunswick Mining and Smelting, the number had jumped to 4,850.[62]

As government employees grew in number, their associations demanded collective bargaining, the right to strike, and wage parity with the private sector. In Nova Scotia the Civil Service Association (1958) finally convinced the government in 1967 to set up a joint-council grievance procedure to conduct collective-bargaining negotiations. In New Brunswick, where the right to collective bargaining and the appointment of a joint council were granted in 1964, civil servants achieved a regional first four years later when they won, with a few emergency exceptions, the right to strike. In 1967–8, Nova Scotia nursing assistants and police also gained collective-bargaining rights. In Newfoundland, however, strikes and lockouts stopping hospital services were prohibited in 1963.

In the private sector, wages, worker safety, and job security in the face of new technology were the predominant issues in a scattering of labour stoppages through the decade.[63] In some cases the strikes achieved their ends. In New Brunswick, for instance, the average weekly wage rose by about 60 per cent over the decade.[64] Other actions never got off the ground, such as the Irving Pulp and Paper strike, which was called off because workers were 'afraid of the overwhelming bargaining power of K.C. Irving.'[65]

Perhaps the most significant gains for labour came in changes in the government's regulation of labour-management relations. Newfoundland modified the restrictive decertification clause in its Trade Union Act, while Prince Edward Island set up, under its Industrial Relations Act, an industrial-inquiries commission and increased the certification powers of the Labour Relations Board. Nova Scotia in 1962 initiated a system of tripartite bodies representing labour, management, and the state to resolve strikes and labour unrest through voluntary labour-management consultation. Governments were anxious to ensure industrial harmony in order to make the region attractive to investors. Labour, likewise, was in favour of a major role for government in industrial development.[66] The tripartite bodies were seen by industrial-relations specialists and labour lawyers as serving the interests of all concerned.

Growing government involvement in efforts to shape the economy of the region was also reflected in decisions by both federal and provincial governments to take control of the Maritime coal and steel industries. During the decade, the lives of coal miners and steelworkers were more tightly bound to public assistance than ever before. By 1960 coal mining was rapidly declining as oil and gas replaced coal in homes and industry. Stockpiles mounted in Minto and Cape Breton, and miners were laid off for increasing periods of time. In 1960, the Royal Commission on Coal defended continued investment in the industry, calling for larger federal subsidies. But the companies, particularly the Dominion Steel and Coal Company (DOSCO), claimed that subsidies did not cover market losses. They believed that the social costs of closing the mines in Cape

Breton were the responsibility of governments. DOSCO was concerned with profit margins. Thus, in 1967, the Cape Breton Development Corporation, a new federal Crown corporation, purchased DOSCO's mining operations and kept them open. The following year the New Brunswick government also took action. Backed with federal money under the Grand Lake Development Act, the province called in the leases, bought the mines, phased them out, and attempted to transfer and retrain displaced miners.

The fate of the steel industry was much the same. In 1967, DOSCO indicated that it could no longer profitably compete with central Canada's Algoma and Stelco. Reasons cited included the distance from markets, high freight rates, and high costs of modernization and diversification. As in the case of the coal industry, the social and political costs of closing the Sydney Steel complex prompted the Nova Scotia government to create a new Crown corporation, Sydney Steel, to buy the mill from DOSCO. Although the report of Metra Consulting Group Limited advised DREE in 1969 that the Atlantic industry would be better closed, production continued.[67] Dependent on public support, the coal and steel industries of Cape Breton limped into the 1970s.

CULTURAL EXPRESSION

Like other sectors in the sixties, the cultural community in the Atlantic region became increasingly dependent on federal-government subsidies during the sixties. This was particularly true of orchestras, theatres, and heritage projects. Federal monies bolstered private and provincial donations to build much-needed facilities, including the Arts and Culture Centre in St John's (1967), the Arts Centre at Dalhousie University (1970), and, the largest project of all, the Fathers of Confederation Building in Charlottetown (1964). With proper facilities it was much easier to attract a wide variety of travelling programs as well as to feature and encourage local visual artists, musicians, and dancers.

New facilities, federal grants, and greater financial potential enabled artists to develop at home while gaining a national reputation. Home-grown entertainers like Don Messer, writers like Ernest Buckler (*The Cruelest Month*, 1963, and *Ox Bells and Fireflies*, 1968), and craftspeople like the Roulstons and Deichmans brought national acclaim to the Atlantic region. The more radical experimental approach of the Nova Scotia School of Art and Design, in 1967 the only degree-granting art school in the country, attracted students from across Canada. Regional visual artists benefited too, among them sculptors Claude Rousell and Tom Taylor, marine artists like Jack Gray, Earl Bailly, and Joseph Purcell, and more contemporary painters like Miller Brittain, Jack Humphrey, Good-

'Parade of Concern,' Sydney, 19 November 1967. When London-based Hawker Siddeley announced the shut-down of its Sydney steel plant, 17,000 angry protesters demanded that the plant be nationalized. It was subsequently taken over by the provincial government.

ridge Roberts, Joseph Kashetsky, Fred Ross, and the three Mount Allison University art instructors Lauren P. Harris, Ted Pulford, and Alex Colville. It was this latter group that contributed to the training of the emerging realist painters Tom Forrestall and Mary and Christopher Pratt.

Atlantic Canada shared in the growing national interest in live theatre, as witnessed by the number of new professional theatre companies that emerged across Canada during the decade. On 1 July 1963, the doors opened in Halifax for the inaugural performance of the Neptune Theatre, Nova Scotia's first professional theatre company. In 1964 the Charlottetown Festival made its home in the Fathers of Confederation Building. Despite endemic financial worries, the summer theatre featuring Canadian musicals proved to be a major success and a wonderful drawing card for the Island's tourist industry. This was largely due to the initial hit performance of the musical *Anne of Green Gables*. Similarly, Theatre New Brunswick set up shop in 1968 at the newly built Playhouse in Fredericton. But the realities of touring and increasing production costs were such that, even with generous grants from the Canada Council as well as private, corporate, and government funds, financial disaster never seemed far away. In 1966, for example, the Neptune Theatre dropped its winter season to help reduce its debt.

Similar problems plagued the musical community. In 1962 the New Brunswick Symphony was established, with considerable help from the Canada Council. It hoped to conduct concerts throughout the province, but costs soon proved prohibitive. At the same time in Nova Scotia, lack of sufficient physical and financial resources threatened the survival of the only professional orchestra east of Montreal, the Halifax Symphony Orchestra. Officials of the two orchestras decided to try a dose of interprovincial, regional co-operation and consolidation. In 1968 the two merged to form the Atlantic Symphony Orchestra. Optimism reigned in the first three years, but in time the age-old problem of travel and production costs again raised doubts as to the viability of a fully professional symphony orchestra in the region.

Cultural activities of the decade included a new emphasis on oral traditions and activities of the past. The Centre d'Etudes Acadiennes (1968) set out to preserve Acadian historical and cultural documents and researchers like the Rev. Père Anselme Chiasson worked to preserve and revitalize Acadian legends, folklore, and customs. Helen Creighton, too, was collecting ghost stories and songs of the Maritime region, and the Newfoundland Folklore and Language Archives was researching such local outport customs as Christmas mumming.

DISILLUSIONMENT RETURNS

Although the poorer provinces had won a major accommodation to their needs through federal transfer payments and national social, developmental, and cultural programs, they were slow to achieve formal recognition for these changes in the constitutional discussions of the era. Canadians had yet to agree on a formula for constitutional change that did not involve an awkward appeal to the British Parliament. Constitutional conferences in 1960 and 1964, at which the four Atlantic premiers pushed for the recognition of the strong role now played by the federal government, failed to yield a consensus. The discussions were complicated by Quebec's 'Quiet Revolution.' Under the leadership of Jean Lesage, the Quebec government participated in those of the new national programs that worked to its advantage economically, but was unwilling formally to recognize any strengthening of the federal role that might interfere with its ability to foster all aspects of the French-Canadian culture. As regional rivalries and ethnic tensions increased, in 1967 the minister of justice, Pierre Trudeau, concluded that the immediate outlook for constitutional consensus was hopeless.

Despite pessimism in this area, confidence in the future of Canada peaked between 1964 and 1967. The Atlantic provinces enthusiastically joined in marking Canada's centennial celebrations. Royal visits, new buildings, cultural events, heritage restorations, community improvement projects, picnics, and parades all helped to reinforce the region's faith in the federation it had once so reluctantly joined. As George Rawlyk put it, 'Expo-euphoria, Centennial enthusiasm and the Queen's visit all helped to crystallize what might be called the Maritime sense of Canadianness.'[68] Most Atlantic residents seemed to agree with Premier Campbell's exclamation: 'we're Canadians before we're anything else.'[69] Confidence that basic economic and constitutional inequities were being addressed made it easier for regional residents whole-heartedly to identify with the nation of which they formed a part.

As the sixties drew to a close, however, there were signs that this confidence was already being eroded. True, in many ways things had never been so good. Road and power facilities had been greatly expanded. Capital investments in mining, forestry, and tourism had increased dramatically. New varieties of manufacturing had brought economic diversity. Social conditions and living standards had improved markedly. Larger transfer payments had allowed for expansion in education, health care, and welfare services. Special federal programs had fostered cultural and heritage initiatives. Yet in spite of these improvements, and partly because of them, old and new problems continued to plague the region. Economic and social disparities and inequalities continued. Average incomes stayed well below the Canadian average.[70] Unemployment rates remained higher.[71] And, while out-migration rates dropped, in all four provinces many in the most productive and skilled age group, fifteen- to thirty-four-year-olds, continued to leave.[72] Federal and provincial development policies, whatever their approach, may have alleviated but had not eliminated basic regional disparities. Still dependent on fishing, agriculture, forestry, and mining – and on a consumer goods-and-services import surplus – the regional economy was sensitive to fluctuating markets, foreign competition, rising transportation costs, and changing technology. Moreover, dependence on federal policy and finance in everything from cultural activities to social programs was more deeply rooted than ever before.

When the national economy began to falter and the inflation rate rose in the late sixties, the Atlantic region was bluntly reminded of its susceptibility to the political and bureaucratic whims of the federal government. Government advisers increasingly cautioned against investment in high-risk regions. They suggested that the policies of regional economic incentives based on the principle of equality of opportunity and service were economically irrational. While the bureaucrats criticized the very philosophies behind federal programs, the various interest groups in the region sniped at the programs themselves. They argued that the Atlantic Development Board had failed to formulate an integrated, long-term development plan. They claimed that both the ADB and DREE awarded grants more on the basis of political pressure than the availability of resources and markets.[73] They suggested that shared-cost programs had built-in discrepancies that tended to favour the wealthier provinces.[74] But critical though the Atlantic region might be, its leaders did not dare to complain too vociferously. Politicians, labour leaders, investors, and consumers alike all looked to Ottawa as the ultimate source for financial support and for essential, if imperfect, economic, social, and cultural programs.

Bearing witness to a continued faith in federally supported industrial development was the fifteen-year Comprehensive Development Plan that Premier Campbell signed with Ottawa in 1969 – a plan that would, he promised, assist Islanders to climb 'the economic ladder to a standard of living and quality of life equal to any Canadian.'[75]

By 1970 the national conviviality of centennial year seemed to be a thing of the past. Since Charles de Gaulle's undiplomatic outburst in 1967 and the formation in 1968 of the separatist Parti Québécois, espousing sovereignty-association, there had been much talk of what place the Atlantic provinces would have in a broken federation. When the federal government adopted the Official Languages Act and New Brunswick followed suit, cultural tension and uncertainty increased. Radical Acadian nationalists, calling for a separate Acadia, and reactionary members of the Maritime Loyalist Association, calling for an English-only country, fuelled the flames of fear based largely on misconception and ignorance. The murder of Pierre Laporte by members of the Front de Libération Québécois in October 1970 seemed a dark portent of future strife. Nevertheless, the people of the Atlantic provinces remained supportive of a united Canada. Neither annexation to the United States nor a separate Atlantic province were seen as serious alternatives.[76] The majority still believed in the viability of Canada and in the need for a strong central federal system.[77] It was, after all, the lesson of the sixties that national unity must be more than an illusion if the Atlantic region hoped to continue to develop socially and economically. Such unity required not only ethnic and cultural equality but a more equitable distribution of economic resources across the country.[78] The process had come far in the 1960s, although the Atlantic provinces still had a long way to go before they achieved the degree of equality in living conditions and opportunities to which their residents now aspired.

# CHAPTER THIRTEEN

# The 1970s

## Sharpening the Sceptical Edge

### PROSPECTS FOR CHANGE

As the Atlantic provinces entered the 1970s, at least one commentator detected 'a new feeling of optimism.'[1] Whether any such feeling was justified was debatable. During the later years of the previous decade the regional economy had faltered yet again, and in 1969 unemployment in the region stood at 7.5 per cent, compared to 4.7 per cent for Canada as a whole. The census year of 1971 would reveal per-capita personal incomes in Atlantic Canada ranging from $2,176 in Prince Edward Island to $2,661 in Nova Scotia, as compared to $4,019 in Ontario.[2] Not surprisingly, many Atlantic Canadians were not content to stay at home when better opportunities beckoned elsewhere. Between 1966 and 1971, New Brunswick suffered a net out-migration of 35,233, which represented almost half of the province's natural population increase for the same period. Newfoundland and Prince Edward Island were almost as badly off, and even Nova Scotia – the most successful of the four at retaining its population – experienced out-migration representing 12 per cent of its natural increase.[3] By some, this was seen as a healthy sign. One economist suggested in 1966 that a cheap one-way fare to Montreal would solve the region's economic problems.[4] The reality was better expressed in Don Shebib's award-winning 1970 film, *Goin' Down the Road*, which documented the aspirations of young Maritimers leaving for Toronto, and the personal price that could be exacted of them. Those who stayed behind, meanwhile, had to put up with being the butt of demeaning stereotypes. The general perception of New Brunswick in central Canada, remarked the province's director of cultural affairs, Robert Pichette, in the dying days of the 1960s was that of 'a cultural Sahara.'[5]

So why the optimism? For one thing, during the 1968 election campaign, Pierre Elliott Trudeau's successful Liberal Party had promised new action on regional development, and the Department of Regional Economic Expansion (DREE) had been established in 1969. Although sceptics could argue – rightly, as matters turned out – that the inauguration of this ministry with a Canada-wide mandate represented a move away from concentration on the specific problems of Atlantic Canada, DREE did offer the possibility of a much-needed rationalization of previous federal programs.[6] A second possible source of optimism was the forthcoming Maritime Union Study, which was seen in some quarters as a means of salvation. 'The political union of the Maritime Provinces,' argued the Atlantic Provinces Economic Council (APEC) in 1969, 'is the most effective ... way, that the region will be able to maximize its own economic and social development potentialities in a dynamic world and to contribute to the growth of the nation of which it is a part ...'[7] There was scepticism, too, but in the context of the overall economic growth of Canada in the 1960s, any argument that promised full participation for these provinces was an attractive one. Finally, there was a third consideration. Test drilling off the Atlantic coasts raised the intriguing possibility of commercial finds of oil and natural gas. As the 1970s began, rumours of such riches were proliferating.[8]

Certainly, the electorates of all four provinces were in the mood for change, whether economic or political. The year 1970 saw three general elections in the Maritimes, the first in Prince Edward Island in May. Although this was the only one of the three in which an existing government was returned to power, it was nevertheless a vote for change: for drastic change, if Premier Alex Campbell's Liberal campaign was to be believed. 'Our enemy,' declared Campbell immediately after his overwhelming victory over George Key's opposition forces, 'is not the Progressive Conservatives but regional disparity.'[9] The basis for Campbell's pronouncement, and the only major issue in the election campaign, was the Federal-Provincial Comprehensive Development Plan for Prince Edward Island signed in March 1969. The plan promised the investment of $725 million in economic development over a fifteen-year period, and included recommendations for the reorganization of the infrastructure of the provincial economy in areas such as education. The federal contribution would be $225 million. The specific objectives were diverse, but all were aimed at producing an expanded economic base through the attraction of new industries and the consolidation of the traditional ones, agriculture and fisheries.[10]

The development plan was controversial from the start. Initial criticism focused on the federal government's cancellation of an existing commitment to a fixed crossing of the Northumberland Strait. The cancellation was announced by Prime Minister Trudeau in the House of Commons two days before the signing of the plan, and cynics were quick to point out that the government had probably saved more by reneging on its promise than the entire amount that it was now committing to economic development. The plan also gave far-reaching powers to federal authorities in its complex administrative structure, and led a prominent Island political scientist to conclude that it represented 'in effect the loss of responsible government.'[11] The criticism that would gather the greatest force as time went on was a more general one: that the wholesale introduction of new industries and other economic developments such as the promotion of tourism, would irreparably damage the distinctive character of Prince Edward Island as a community and would have an especially harmful effect on agriculture. This point was made by the opposition during the 1970 campaign, but for the time being Premier Campbell's prediction of 'a great and wonderful future' had an irresistible appeal.[12]

Premiers G.I. Smith of Nova Scotia and Louis J. Robichaud of New Brunswick had no such dramatic measures to take to their respective electorates in October, and both went down to defeat in campaigns that were overshadowed by the gathering crisis in Quebec. The Nova Scotia campaign was uninspiring in any case, as the insipid pronouncements of both major party leaders brought journalist Harold Shea to accuse them of turning politics into a dull 'parlor game.' The result was the narrowest of victories for Gerald Regan's Liberals, who won twenty-three seats to the Conservatives' twenty-one, with two Cape Breton seats taken by the New Democrats.[13] The New Brunswick campaign was also low-key, but there were more complex undercurrents. Public debate centred on Liberal defences of the record of the Robichaud government, in the face of opposition charges that Equal Opportunity programs had been inefficiently administered and had led to unduly high taxation. On election night the Conservatives secured thirty-six seats to the Liberals' twenty-six, and in mid-November Richard Hatfield was sworn in as the new premier. The *Moncton Times* could find little to say about the whole affair, except that the campaign had been a clean one. *L'Evangéline*'s editorial comment was more penetrating. Two days after the election, the newspaper eulogized the achievements of the defeated Acadian premier, and on the following day it turned to the prospects for francophones under the new regime. Hatfield, after all, was a unilingual anglophone with only two francophones in his caucus. The editorial was careful to praise his personal record of opposing language discrimination, but went on to declare that 'nous n'avons pas la même certitude quant à tous ses députés.'[14] No matter how quiet the election campaign, New Brunswick had reached a crossroads where the linguistic policies – and the related social and economic policies – of the Robichaud government might be continued or a quite different direction taken.

The Maritime region as a whole had also reached a crossroads of sorts. Political leadership had changed in two of the provinces, and the average age of the Maritime premiers was now only thirty-nine years. It was this youthful group that had to confront the ancient question of Maritime union. The Deutsch Commission duly recommended political unification in November 1970. Yet by early 1973 even APEC, as a voluble advocate of the scheme, had to concede that there was 'a virtual public opinion void' on the matter.[15] Long before that time, in fact, the three provincial governments had been edging away from the notion of full political union, as their initially friendly reception of the Deutsch Commission's report had given way to the realization that it promised few political gains and many pitfalls. The inauguration of the Council of Maritime Premiers in May 1971 was a direct result of the Maritime Union Study, and other interprovincial agencies – such as the Maritime Provinces Higher Education Commission (MPHEC) – were to follow. But that would be all. The anticlimax came as a disappointment to some, and as early as February 1971 the *Ottawa Journal* was chiding the premiers for their caution. 'These,' the *Journal* loftily inquired, 'are the three bright young men of the East, the political Goliath-killers who are going to usher the Maritimes into a new era? The attitudes seem all too familiar, and disappointing.'[16] In reality, political expediency and a shrewd appreciation of the value of having three voices rather than just one in national discussions had combined to emasculate the proposal for Maritime union.

The three Goliath-killers were soon to be joined by another. In the summer of 1968, stung by Newfoundland Liberal reverses in the June federal election, J.R. Smallwood, at the age of sixty-seven, announced his impending retirement. As the 1969 leadership convention approached, however, Smallwood reversed his decision rather than risk being succeeded by his estranged former minister of health, John Crosbie. The convention provided a clear victory for Smallwood, but at the price of bitterly alienating Crosbie. A considerable minority supported Crosbie and joined him in 1970 in an independent 'Liberal Party Reform Group.'[17] By June 1971, Crosbie had moved all the way across to the Progressive Conservative Party, led since 1970 by Frank Moores. With Smallwood's mandate about to expire, the battle lines were drawn.

In the election campaign that followed in October 1971, Smallwood proved to have considerable remaining personal popularity in the rural areas, which had always supplied his political strength. Much of his rhetoric, however, sounded dated to an electorate that included, for the first time, a generation yet unborn in the spring of 1949. 'Apart from life itself,' the premier insisted on proclaiming, 'Confederation is the greatest blessing ever bestowed on the people of Newfoundland.'[18] When the ballots were counted – and some re-counted – the result was a virtual stalemate. Although the Conservatives were far ahead in the popular vote, they managed to win only twenty-one seats to the Liberals' twenty, with one seat going to the leader of the New Labrador Party, Tom Burgess. No fewer than five judicial re-counts were demanded. The *Evening Telegram* judged that the results constituted 'a major defeat' for Smallwood and predicted that 'the history books will note that, in truth, October 28 marked a watershed in modern Newfoundland politics.'[19] Frank Moores certainly thought so, as he drove into St John's in a triumphant motorcade two days after the election. Smallwood, however, thought otherwise, and refused to resign. Thus began a sad and degrading descent from office for a premier who could so easily have retired undefeated just two years before.

The series of defections from caucuses and promises made and broken that dominated the political headlines in Newfoundland during the winter of 1971–2 defy concise analysis. They were, in any case, essentially no more than a backdrop to events that had an air of inevitability, no matter that some of the leading protagonists refused to admit to the fact. Smallwood eventually announced that he would retire in the New Year, and on 7 February 1972 he was replaced as Liberal leader by his young protégé, and former minister of health, Ed Roberts. In the meantime, he had also resigned as premier. On 12 January, the provincial Supreme Court had awarded the disputed seat of St Barbe South to the Conservatives, and a week later Moores was sworn in with a seemingly clear majority in the House of Assembly. By 1 March, when the House opened, defections from the government ranks had produced the bizarre situation of a Liberal opposition with more members than the government. The following day, one of the Liberals suddenly and mysteriously resigned. With the parties now equal, Moores seized the chance to call for a dissolution, and a new general election was set for 24 March. 'What a screaming farce,' declared political columnist Ray Guy as the one-day legislative session ended. The result of the election, though, was never in serious doubt. Defeated thirty-three to nine, Roberts sounded relieved on election night that the whole thing was over. He was, he allowed, 'not surprised.' Smallwood went off to Florida to work on his memoirs. Moores, with Crosbie as his chief lieutenant, had a clear field at last.[20]

In certain respects, the Newfoundland election of 1972 proved to be less of an epoch-making event than it seemed at the time. The Moores government came to power committed to very little, other than the deposition of the Liberals and the investigation of alleged corruption under the Smallwood regime. A royal commission was duly appointed in March 1972 to look into leasing arrangements for the buildings used by the Newfoundland Liquor Commission, and it reported soon afterwards on serious conflicts of interest within the Smallwood government;

1971
cents

# *The* ATLANTIC ADVOCATE

## J·O·E·Y*

### *A Different Kind of Four Letter Word That Spells
## N·E·W·F·O·U·N·D·L·A·N·D

Joey resigns. Premier of Newfoundland for more than two decades,
J.R. Smallwood had pursued policies of development that by 1972 were
tarnished with controversy.

but the impetus for change soon weakened. 'Thereafter,' the *Evening
Telegram* wryly commented years later, 'the PC government went on to
outstrip its predecessor with its own crop of wrongdoing ...'[21] Nevertheless, the decisive defeat of the Liberals was profoundly significant in
Newfoundland's political history, effectively bringing to an end the immediate post-Confederation era. The election of the thirty-nine-year-old

Moores also confirmed the regional trend towards new and younger political leadership. A major turnover of power had taken place, and further general elections in the three Maritime provinces in 1974 and in Newfoundland in 1975 would produce few surprises – except for the reappearance of Smallwood in 1975 at the head of a Liberal Reform Party, which effectively split the Liberal vote – and no reversals. In effect, the political pattern was set until the late 1970s.

### DEVELOPMENT AND DISPARITY

It was one thing for new political leaders to assume power. A different question, and ultimately a more important one, was whether the change would make any difference to social and economic conditions in the region. The immediate past provided a mixed legacy. It was true that the general Canadian prosperity of the 1960s had led to expansion of social services. By 1 January 1971, for example, all four provinces had implemented medicare programs, with the help of transfer funds. Federal payments flowed into the region in a variety of other forms, with DREE functioning as a channel for federal investment directly aimed at reducing regional disparities. Powerful ministers, such as Donald Jamieson of Newfoundland and Allan J. MacEachen of Nova Scotia, put the region's case in the federal cabinet as the 1970s went on. Nevertheless, scepticism emerged. The Economic Council of Canada, in a major nation-wide 1977 study of regional disparity, cited evidence from Atlantic Canada indicating that DREE's subsidy programs had been 'far less successful than published estimates of job creation would imply.' The same report noted the persistent complaints from the Atlantic provinces that federal transportation policies worked against the cause of economic development. 'Is there no end to the succession of hammerblows inflicted on the Atlantic regional economy,' asked the Saint John *Telegraph-Journal* of its readers in early 1971, 'by railway freight rate increases?'[22] For a region that had to move its products a thousand miles or more to reach the major centres of population, industrial subsidies were of limited use as long as transportation costs hindered effective marketing.

The use of government subsidies to lure capital investment to the region also had other inherent problems, as Nova Scotia's costly embarrassments of the 1960s – the Deuterium heavy-water plant at Glace Bay and the Clairtone television factory in Stellarton – had already shown.[23] Newfoundland was well on its way to a similar unhappy experience with the linerboard mill being constructed at Stephenville. This $144-million dollar scheme had been initiated by the American entrepreneur John C. Doyle, and yet his company had put up only $29

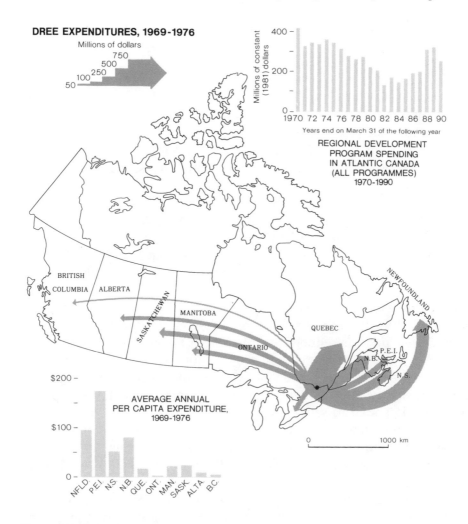

**DREE EXPENDITURES, 1969-1976**

Millions of dollars

REGIONAL DEVELOPMENT
PROGRAM SPENDING
IN ATLANTIC CANADA
(ALL PROGRAMMES)
1970-1990

AVERAGE ANNUAL
PER CAPITA EXPENDITURE,
1969-1976

Figure 15 Federal government expenditures for regional and industrial development in Atlantic Canada, c. 1970–90

million, the balance coming from federal grants, provincial loan guarantees, and further loan guarantees from the government of Great Britain. By the time the Moores government ejected Doyle from the project in 1972, the province's loan guarantees had swelled to $114 million, and the mill was not yet in production. It eventually struggled through a few unprofitable years before succumbing in 1977. The St John's *Evening Telegram*'s editorial comment in March 1972 was worth noting by all concerned. 'The loose and irresponsible handling of the linerboard deal,' the *Telegram* pointed out, 'and the slapdash way that money was thrown about shows that any government which is involved with promoters and speculators, invited or uninvited, in the development of its resources has to watch them with the cold and penetrating eyes of a hawk.'[24]

More disasters were to come. In 1971, construction of a 100,000-barrel-per-day oil refinery began at Come by Chance, at the head of Newfoundland's Placentia Bay. Again, heavy federal and provincial commitments were involved, though the real promoter and prospective owner of the plant was John Shaheen, yet another developer from the United States. The refinery was officially opened in October 1973, in a pretentious series of festivities adorned by the presence of the Cunard liner *Queen Elizabeth II*, chartered at a reported fee of $97,000 per day. The opening ceremony itself was brief: the speeches were kept to a minimum to allow the 4,000 guests to adjourn to a banquet table that measured a quarter of a mile in length. The spirit of the occasion was best expressed by the unnamed participant who was reported to have left the scene with a boiled lobster in each jacket pocket, and it was not only Ray Guy who realized that the 'porky pigs' were feasting at the expense of all Newfoundlanders.[25] Newfoundlanders were also left with the much larger bill – including $41 million directly owed to the provincial government – when the refinery went bankrupt twenty-nine months later. The 1973 OPEC oil embargo had been a major blow, but there were also numerous technical problems at the plant and over-optimistic projections on supply and marketing. Like the linerboard mill, the refinery had been intended to provide employment and – in combination with centralization programs – to contribute to the diversification of the Newfoundland economy. The pretence that it could fulfil either of these goals could not long be sustained, as the 500 laid-off workers knew best of all.

In New Brunswick, meanwhile, American entrepreneur Malcolm Bricklin was promising a profitable future for his proposed gull-wing sports car. The provincial government was duly convinced, and the $9-million project was announced in Saint John in June 1973. At first, all went well. Factories were established in Saint John and at Minto and, by the time of the provincial election in November 1974, some 300 Bricklins had been produced, one of which was used by Premier Hatfield during the campaign. As soon as the government was re-elected, Bricklin asked for and received more provincial funds to offset increasing costs. Not quite a year later, by September 1975, 'Malcolm Twist' – named by the *Telegraph-Journal* – had succeeded in involving the province to the amount of $19.7 million. That was the limit. On 19 September 1975, even the minister of economic growth, Lawrence Garvie, expressed doubts about the project's future in the wake of plant lay-offs. Five days later, reporters discovered Garvie and Hatfield entering a Saint John hotel, by the kitchen entrance, for a final meeting with Bricklin. The next day the

The Bricklin sports car, 1974. Richard Hatfield lost his gamble to industrialize his province with the Bricklin auto plant, a loss that cost the people of New Brunswick $19.7 million.

company went into receivership, and its factories were closed. Bricklin declared that it was only 'a temporary setback.' For him, it may have been. For the workers, and for the New Brunswickers whose tax dollars had been committed and lost, the results were more permanent. Once again an attempt to produce employment by feeding subsidies to an outside entrepreneur had produced disruption in the lives of individuals, families, and communities, and had led only to eventual disillusionment.[26]

Even more successful ventures raised difficult questions. In July 1969 the establishment of two tire-manufacturing plants in Nova Scotia by the Michelin company had been announced with great fanfare. In this case, there was no collapse. Michelin expeditiously built factories at Granton and Bridgewater, and in 1979 the company announced that a third would be added, at Waterville in Kings County. Large sums of public money were involved. Of the $150 million of projected investment in the original two plants it had been agreed that approximately two-thirds would come in one form or another from government sources.[27] A price was also paid in the form of the power that the Michelin company would henceforth exercise over successive provincial

Michelin tire plant, Granton, N.S. Nova Scotia backed a winner with Michelin, which eventually expanded into three large plants employing thousands of workers. Part of the cost has been some very controversial labour legislation.

governments. Employing some 3,500 Nova Scotians by the late 1970s, with the prospect of a further 2,000 employees at Waterville, and with even more jobs created in related industries and service sectors, the company could now exercise enormous influence in a province of high unemployment. This was reflected in the government's eagerness to act in the interests of Michelin's non-union policy. In 1973, the International Union of Operating Engineers held a successful sign-up campaign among skilled workers at Granton, only to see the rules for certification of craft unions changed by the Regan government in such a way as to block its application. Then in 1979, following a more general sign-up campaign by the United Rubber Workers, the Progressive Conservative government of the day prepared legislation – soon known as the 'Michelin bill' – to require that the prospective bargaining unit include all Michelin plants in the province, thus invalidating the union's efforts at Granton.

Despite bitter opposition from the Nova Scotia Federation of Labour and serious misgivings expressed by some business leaders, the bill found quick passage. The official Michelin view, announced on the same day as the plan for the third factory, was that the bill would provide 'the necessary background for increased stability, production, and development in Nova Scotia.'[28] Well it might, but in the meantime Nova Scotians were left to reflect on the raw political power apparently being wielded by a non-accountable corporation.

Large-scale, publicly funded economic-development initiatives were proving in the 1970s, therefore, to have a variety of drawbacks. There was a price to be paid for both success and failure. Prince Edward Island, in this sense, was more fortunate than its neighbours, for the 1970s brought neither spectacular success nor spectacular failure. What was clear by the end of the decade, however, was that the economic development plan would not live up to the high expectations of its founders. 'A decade old, it's still a big, fat flop,' was the succinct verdict of Island journalist Kennedy Wells in 1979.[29] The plan had unquestionably produced growth in certain areas: the provincial civil service had expanded rapidly, and so had the province's reliance on federal transfers of funds. The $279 million received in transfer payments in 1979 (including transfers to individuals and to the government) represented 38 per cent of Prince Edward Island's gross domestic product. Ten years earlier, the level had been 31 per cent. Personal incomes had risen, though the 1981 level of 67.4 per cent of the national average was the second-lowest in Canada, Newfoundland's 64.9 per cent being the lowest.[30] Progress had been made in health and education services. The retail sector had flourished, with the proliferation of shopping malls in Charlottetown and Summerside. Beyond that, the future was less encouraging. A series of new industrial parks had yielded no major disasters, but had also produced little significant diversification of the economy. Even tourism, though bringing a summer invasion that by 1980 amounted to some 600,000, or nearly five times the Island's population, had declined in its annual growth rate since 1975.[31] Through it all, the move away from the land continued unabated, as census data clearly showed. In 1971, some 21,000 Prince Edward Islanders lived on farms, or 18.9 per cent of the population; by 1981 it was only 12,000, representing 9.8 per cent. Unemployment, meanwhile, had risen substantially during the decade. On the tenth anniversary of the signing of the development plan, in March 1979, the seasonally adjusted rate stood at 12.2 per cent, well above the national average and again second only to Newfoundland.[32] The prosperity that had been so easy to predict in 1969 had thus proved elusive.

Nevertheless, there was one serious argument that could be made in favour of the plan, and in favour of other regional development efforts of the 1970s. It was concisely stated in 1979 by Tom Kent, former deputy minister of DREE: 'that regional policy has not produced the hoped-for improvements is not grounds for any sweeping condemnation of it as ill-conceived; the alternative in the 1970s would probably have been a period of major deterioration in Atlantic Canada.'[33] That this was a hypothetical argument was true, and yet it went far towards explaining the complex and sometimes contradictory attitudes towards regional-development programs that existed in the region during the decade. The same policies that produced scandalous and expensive débâcles could also prompt modest and unpublicized, though locally important, successes in establishing small enterprises that would not otherwise have been attempted. In Cape Breton, for example, employment in manufacturing industry was kept at a stable level throughout the late 1970s, despite lay-offs at Sydney Steel.[34] Nobody would have pretended that this represented a breakthrough for the island's troubled economy, but it reflected a holding operation of sorts. The awareness that matters could easily become worse was also a factor in the seeming addiction of provincial governments to the offering of lavish inducements to in-coming industries, an addiction that afflicted even those who had taken a different view while in opposition. The original occasion of John Crosbie's feud with Smallwood had been Crosbie's disapproval of the New-foundland government's generosity to Shaheen in the early stages of the Come by Chance negotiations in the late 1960s, and yet Crosbie was a prominent member of the later government that supported the project from 1972 onwards. Gerald Regan was a severe critic of indus-trial-development policies as opposition leader in the late 1960s, and was again on the opposition benches in 1979 when he condemned the Michelin bill as 'a dark act.'[35] In 1973, however, he had headed the government that imposed the 'Michelin regulation.' While it is tempting to attribute such conversions to political opportunism, and to dismiss the whole apparatus of regional development as a scheme for giving away the nation's – and the region's – wealth to bloated adventurers, the reality was more complex. Livelihoods were at stake, and the harsh fact was that the bargaining position of provincial governments was woefully weak in the context of high and rising unemployment. None of that excused the failures of the decade, but it made them more understandable.

It remained true that the easy optimism that had surrounded the development initiatives of the late 1960s had proved ill-founded. Worse still, the region suffered throughout the decade from damaging internal disputes and disparities. Quarrels between the provinces were, of course, nothing new, although the 1970s were distinguished by the bitterness of some such in-fighting. The perennial rivalry between the ports of Halifax and Saint John was intensified by the scramble to gain the upper hand in new container-port facilities. By decade's end, Halifax had successfully defended its position as the leading east-coast port, but not without much agitation about the 'growing threat' from its competitor.[36] Another contested matter in the mid-1970s was the location of the proposed veterinary college, claimed by both Nova Scotia and Prince Edward Island. The Council of Maritime Premiers provided a forum for the debate, but no solution would be found until Nova Scotia finally gave way in time to allow the college to open in Charlottetown in 1986.[37] More fundamental was the questioning in Newfoundland of the very concept of an Atlantic region. In 1975, the *Evening Telegram* noted that federal employment in Newfoundland had actually declined in the preceding decade, while it had increased substantially in the Maritimes. The newspaper complained of the federal tendency to assume 'that Newfoundland can be administered far better from somewhere like Halifax or Moncton than it can from Ottawa,' in the form of Atlantic regional offices of federal departments. 'Surely,' it concluded, 'we didn't join Canada to end up as a colony of Nova Scotia.'[38] Unity of interest within Atlantic Canada was hard to define and even harder to live by.

There were also divisions within the region that related not only to interprovincial rivalries, but to socio-economic disparity. Such prosperity as existed was unequally distributed, according to social class, ethnicity, gender, and – conspicuously in each of the provinces – according to rural or urban location. In general terms, the decade of the 1970s was much better for the major urban centres than for rural areas and the smaller towns. There were exceptions. The Canso Strait, for example, since the building of the causeway in 1955, had become the outstanding deep-water port in eastern Canada, and by 1973 Port Hawkesbury was being described by one writer as 'Nova Scotia's only certifiable boom town.'[39] It was true that Port Hawkesbury was already paying a social price for ill-planned growth arising out of rapid industrialization in which local residents were playing only a limited role, and also that it would later suffer the fate of most boom towns. Nevertheless, a form of economic growth did take place in the strait area that Halifax's *Chronicle-Herald* would have liked in 1969 to rename 'Novaport.'[40] Economic growth was much more securely accomplished in the Halifax-Dartmouth metropolitan area. In part, the reason for this was emblazoned in the banner headlines of the *Chronicle-Herald* on 5 October 1971. 'It's Oil,' the newspaper trumpeted, with an accompanying photograph of a smiling Gerald Regan holding up a tiny bottle to represent Mobile Oil's 'vast' discovery off Sable Island.[41] Sable Island oil, and even natural gas, would be a disappointment in terms of commercial exploitation, but the

Boom town on Chedabucto Bay, 1970. For a time after the causeway was built, Port Hawkesbury rivalled Sydney for dominance of Cape Breton's economy. Three mega-projects were attracted to the Strait area; the heavy-water plant, a Gulf Canada refinery, and the Stora Forest Industries pulp mill. Only the pulp mill continues to operate.

economic stimulus of offshore exploration continued throughout the decade and beyond.

The real origins of the economic growth of the Halifax-Dartmouth area went farther back, however. This part of Nova Scotia had been a prime beneficiary of the general expansion of the Canadian economy since the 1950s. The port was handling an increasing flow of imports and exports. Related functions of transportation and distribution were reflected in, for example, the establishment of major trucking companies. Increased government expenditures, made possible by expanding tax revenues across Canada, had direct results in the increasing number of government employees and in the construction of buildings to house their offices. Government funds were also responsible for the enormous expansion of education and health-care facilities, as anyone could gather from a short walk down Halifax's University Avenue from Dalhousie University to the Victoria General Hospital. If the walk were extended to the downtown bank towers, or if the walker got on a bus to one of the large shopping centres that had sprung up on the periphery as well as in the city centre, the impression of prosperity would be confirmed. To be sure, the wealth was unevenly distributed even within the city, and it was also true that a large proportion of it was controlled from far outside the region, whether in Ottawa offices or in corporate head-quarters; but wealth there was in Halifax and the surrounding districts in the 1970s. Very different was the situation in the industrialized towns of the province, towns that were still struggling to cope with the history of lay-offs and plant closures that had persisted since the 1920s. Centres such as Amherst, Truro, and New Glasgow did enjoy some of the continuing effects of the 1960s development in retail marketing and light industry, but others, such as Glace Bay and Springhill – its economy devastated by the mining disaster of 1958 – had no such comfort. Sydney, notwithstanding the events of 'Black Friday' in October 1967, was holding to its main industry, but large annual losses and frequent lay-offs gave uncomfortable evidence that Sydney Steel was not yet safe. Then again, there were areas of rural decline. 'The largest poverty group [in Nova Scotia] ...' argued the Dalhousie University Institute of Public Affairs in late 1969, in a brief to a Senate committee, 'is the rural non-farm population.'[42] From the sleek, high-rise office towers of Halifax to, say, the isolated areas of rural Kings County that tourists were not encouraged to visit was not a long drive. In terms of the material quality of life, the distance was much greater.

Similar disparities could be found in Prince Edward Island and Newfoundland. Such growth as the Prince Edward Island development plan was able to generate largely affected the central part of the Island. Charlottetown and Summerside grew substantially, and so did tourist areas within easy reach of the national park. King's County, still recovering from the ignominious collapse of the Georgetown Industries project in the mid-1960s, participated much less fully, and the western part of Prince County hardly at all. Whether or not the results of the new forms of development were desirable was an increasingly controversial matter, as the 1970s went on and the proliferation of Summerside shopping malls and Cavendish 'tourist traps' aroused critical comment. But there was no doubt that high incomes were being earned in Queen's County and east Prince, through opportunities that did not exist elsewhere.[43] In Newfoundland, as the 1970s opened, the west coast seemed to have a promising future. A national survey of eighty-nine selected cities, published in July 1969, showed Corner Brook to have the highest per-capita income in Atlantic Canada and placed it twenty-third in Canada.[44] At that time, too, it was still possible to hope for great things for the Stephenville linerboard mill. This latter illusion would not last long, and the early 1980s would see Corner Brook itself thrown into turmoil by the threatened closure of its one major industry, the Bowater paper mill. For the time being, though, the city enjoyed an apparent stability that was symbolized in 1975 by the establishment there of Sir Wilfred Grenfell College, a campus of Memorial University. St John's, meanwhile, began in the late 1970s to experience the rapid, if also speculative, urban development brought about by the Hibernia oilfield discoveries, which, unlike those off Sable Island, were quickly identified as commercially exploitable. Again, however, there were other areas of the province that presented a contrast. The desperation of once-prosperous mining towns such as Buchans and St Lawrence was reflected in strikes that placed small local work-forces in unequal battles with outside owners. Inshore fisheries, meanwhile, had to cope with a resource that was being grossly overfished by offshore foreign vessels. The declaration of the two hundred-mile limit in 1977 was greeted with optimism, but the ensuing over-investment and the disastrous rise in interest rates in the last years of the decade combined with stagnant markets to ensure that the fishery would continue in a state of crisis.[45] The socio-economic divide between the two major urban areas and the less prosperous rural areas of Newfoundland was a persistent problem.

Nowhere in Atlantic Canada was intra-provincial disparity more dramatically evident in the 1970s than in New Brunswick. For the main urban centres of southern New Brunswick this was a decade of expansion. Fredericton benefited especially from growth in the civil service and, in the earlier years of the decade, higher education. Saint John had its port activities, and the federally subsidized flourishing of shipbuilding at the Saint John Drydock, as well as a series of large construction projects including a major oil refinery. Greater Moncton's growth was evident in spectacular retail market development, notably in the town of Dieppe, and for the time being the city retained its status as an important railway centre. The recession of the late 1970s would take its toll on all three of these cities, but until then they had good reason to expect continued prosperity. Moncton and Saint John were helped by the 'growth-centre' philosophy that underlay much of DREE's develop-

Bowater pulp-and-paper mill, Corner Brook, Nfld. Pulp and paper has become the cornerstone of the regional forest industry, though the accompanying pollution has raised concerns about the long-term impact on the environment.

ment philosophy and had been designated 'special areas' for development assistance.[46] DREE, however, was not nearly so eager to assist the more isolated communities of northern New Brunswick, or the resource-extraction industries on which many of them relied. Mining communities, often one-industry towns, were chronically vulnerable to fluctuations in the world market and to the calculations of the outside-owned or transnational corporations that had control of their resources.[47] Mining activities had grown rapidly in the 1960s, bringing growth especially to the city of Bathurst. The early 1970s, however, saw the reverse side of the coin become visible, as retrenchments were made both in mining and in pulp and paper.

On 4 January 1972, Nigadoo Mines announced that its operations would be suspended immediately, with the loss of three hundred jobs in the tiny coastal community near Bathurst. This was only the latest in a series of economic blows to the area, and the angry popular reaction was enough to prompt the New Brunswick Federation of Labour to call for a 'Day of Concern' to be held in Bathurst on 16 January. Among those invited to participate were DREE minister Jean Marchand, Premier Hatfield, and the leaders of the federal and provincial opposition parties.[48] All of them did attend, a remarkable achievement in itself, and a testament to the genuineness of the crisis facing the northern part of the province. A few days before the event, Hatfield and Marchand jointly announced a new $10-million program to create three thousand temporary jobs, but the scheme did little to assuage aroused feelings.

The Day of Concern proved to be a dramatic day, and more conflict was to follow in the ensuing weeks. Some three thousand marchers made their way to the Bathurst College, where as many as possible crowded into the college gymnasium. Crowds amounting to as many as fifteen thousand were reported to have gathered in the general vicinity. Then the speeches began. Only Jean Marchand and union organizer Mathilde Blanchard – who castigated the politicians and called for nationalization of primary industries – were allowed an uninterrupted hearing. Significantly, both were speaking in French to the largely francophone audience. The inequalities within the province had been poignantly and very publicly made clear, and the point was reinforced on 14 February, when the Unemployment Insurance office in Bathurst was occupied by about one hundred of the unemployed. The intervention of police to clear the office was followed three days later by a peaceful demonstration by some thousand people in the streets of the city, and by a near-riot just over a week later. The *Moncton Times* worried editorially about 'agents provocateur[s]' and 'revolutionary fervour,' while *L'Evangéline* emphasized a different form of provocation arising from late UI payments from the Bathurst office.[49] In retrospect, the anger and violence of the winter of 1972 showed most graphically that unemployment and poverty coexisted, in the Atlantic Canada of the 1970s, with conspicuous prosperity elsewhere in the region. In this one case, the issue had boiled over, but the problem was by no means confined to northern New Brunswick.

SEIZING THE INITIATIVE

An essential element in the internal division of New Brunswick, of course, was the relationship between socio-economic disparity and language. It was not a simple relationship, for the early 1970s were years of deep social and political division among New Brunswick Acadians. For two decades leadership had been asserted by a middle-class élite, largely based in the southeastern part of the province, that had striven for reform by presenting Acadians as a hard-working, responsible population who wished only for full participation in every facet of provincial life. Now this approach was under attack: by nationalistic students, whether at the Université de Moncton or Bathurst College, who argued that only a radical political struggle could change the colonial status of the Acadians; and by the hard-pressed working class of the northeast, whose experience confirmed that 'equal opportunity' was still a long way from reality. The conflict was made intense by the politicization that had taken place in the northeast as a result of the controversies of the late 1960s over the role of the Conseil Régional d'Aménagement du Nord-Est (CRAN), and of the realization (soon to be confirmed by 1971 census returns) that the francophone proportion of the New Brunswick population had declined significantly during the 1960s.[50] The Bathurst outbreak in early 1972 was as much a threat to the established pattern of Acadian political influence as it was to the unity of New Brunswick, and the founding of the Parti Acadien in the midst of the turmoil – with Euclide Chiasson, a faculty member of Bathurst College, as president of the executive committee – greatly reinforced this point. Significantly, the new party – which, according to Chiasson, was aimed initially at politicizing Acadians rather than winning seats in the legislature – was not welcomed by established francophone political figures. Jean-Maurice Simard, minister of finance, dismissed the party as irrelevant to the needs of Acadians, while Louis J. Robichaud described it as a waste of time and effort.[51] Simard and Robichaud, as party politicians, were obviously not neutral observers, but their comments accurately reflected the incipient alarm of the Acadian political establishment that the Parti Acadien might succeed only in threatening the existing process of gradual reform in language matters. L'Evangéline, through its editor, Claude Bourque, took a more sympathetic view, though not minimizing the potential for Acadian disunity. Writing on 3 February, Bourque attributed the Parti Acadien's founding five days earlier to 'de nombreuses raisons mais l'une des principales est certes la montée du nationalisme chez la jeunesse acadienne.' The party would grow, he warned, 'dans la mesure où les autres partis politiques refuseront de reconnaître les légitimes aspirations des Acadiens.'[52]

Acadian unity, however, was strengthened by the rekindling of language-related conflicts in Moncton. The telecast of the National Film Board's L'Acadie, l'Acadie on 8 January 1972 reignited the feelings of some Université de Moncton students by starkly recalling the treatment given by Mayor Leonard Jones and the Moncton city council to the students of 1968. After the program had ended, some 200 students spontaneously marched through the streets, and a dozen or so later threw pieces of ice at Jones's house in the early hours of the morning.

The *Moncton Times* made light of the affair, but also called upon Jones to implement the promise he had made in 1968 to strike a committee to consider the issue of bilingualism in civic government. For one writer of a letter to the editor, however, the simple truth was that 'the French College in Moncton doesn't really want a bilingual city, they want a French City.'[53] There the matter might have rested, had it not been for a related series of events that had begun in the previous month. On 18 December 1971, the new Moncton city hall had been opened, in the Assumption Place complex. Built through Acadian enterprise – notably the Assumption Mutual Life Company and its president, Gilbert Finn – the project could be seen as a conspicuous symbol of the success of the Acadian élite's strategy of gradual expansion of Acadian economic and political participation, and thus as a repudiation of more radical measures. The opening ceremonies, however, represented anything but a celebration of Acadian achievements. As described editorially by Bourque, the opening was a 'triste spectacle,' a humiliation for those Acadians who attended. No Acadian flag was raised, even among the 'heritage' flags. The French language was used only minimally at the ceremony itself, and at the banquet that evening 'on ... réussit à ne pas parler un seul mot de français.'[54] The event had managed dramatically to snatch ill-will from the jaws of reconciliation.

More was to come. Early in the New Year, following from the city-hall débâcle, came renewed demands from francophones for bilingual services in Moncton. Not only *L'Evangéline* but also the *Moncton Times* called upon Jones to honour his commitment to form a committee to study the matter. On 15 February, however, the mayor used his deciding vote to pass a council resolution to do nothing. The meeting was a tense one, with numerous petitions presented from local organizations – most in favour of the bilingualism committee – and some two hundred Université de Moncton students attending as spectators, five of whom were arrested in subsequent demonstrations. Jones justified his – and thus the council's – decision on the ground that the rights of the unilingual majority must be safeguarded against those who wished Moncton to become a French city. His later election, in 1974, as independent MP for Moncton showed clearly that he represented a large body of anglophone opinion in the city. The council's decision, however, was strongly condemned, not only by *L'Evangéline* but also by the *Moncton Times*, which went on to praise the peaceful protest of three thousand demonstrators three days later as 'a credit to all concerned.'[55]

In the long term, the events of the turbulent weeks from December 1971 to February 1972 were crucially significant in forging Acadian unity and giving renewed impetus to the cause of bilingual services in New Brunswick. The attack by the city of Moncton authorities on even the most moderate of Acadian demands immediately defused any attempt to discredit Acadian nationalism by associating it exclusively with the violence of Bathurst or with student demonstrations. The result was to reinforce the legitimacy of Acadian aspirations and to prompt anglophones to grapple, as the *Moncton Times* had done, with questions of linguistic justice. The rejection of Jones as a Progressive Conservative candidate by federal party leader Robert Stanfield in 1974 was a dramatic signal of the change that was taking place. Less conspicuous, but of permanent importance, was the gradual implementation of reform by the Hatfield government throughout the decade, including proclamation of sections of the Official Languages Act dealing with educational and judicial matters. Even the city of Moncton was not immune. A small item on page 15 of the *Moncton Transcript* of 23 December 1977 noted that the city's switchboard was now fully bilingual and that the city was committed 'to increasing the use of French within the administration as the capabilities become available.'[56] That city-hall bilingualism should be relegated to an obscure part of the newspaper was in itself an indication of how far Moncton had travelled. Linguistic rivalries in southeastern New Brunswick were not yet dead, as controversies of the 1980s would show, and questions over the employability of unilingual persons in a bilingual province continued to be of concern to New Brunswickers who were very far from being open to charges of bigotry. Nevertheless, the events of early 1972 had led to an increasingly clear understanding that New Brunswick *was* a bilingual province, and that there was little to be achieved by pretending otherwise.

Another result was to check the possible splintering of Acadian movements that might easily have taken place in early 1972. On successive days in February, *L'Evangéline* printed editorials by Bourque headed, 'Trouble en Acadie.' Dealing respectively with the upheavals in Bathurst and in Moncton, Bourque's comments carried the message that the unemployed of the north shore and the advocates of bilingual services in Moncton were enlisted in the same struggle, even though they might be divided by geography, age, or social class.[57] Complete unity was, to be sure, an unrealistic goal. The tensions between Acadians in Moncton and in the northeast and northwest of the province flared up again in late 1975, when the Maritime Provinces Higher Education Commission recommended the integration of colleges at Edmundston and Shippegan into a reformed and highly centralized Université de Moncton, rather than accepting the findings of a study it had commissioned under Judge Louis Le Bel that had favoured a more decentralized structure. A citizens' committee in Bathurst described the MPHEC's action as 'une insulte faite à la population du Nord du N.B.,' and emergency negotiations took place in Fredericton in mid-December, under the pressure of demonstrations mounted by protesters from many northern communities. The result was a victory for decentralization. 'Les Acadiens du Nord-Est et Nord-Ouest ont mené une bataille héroïque pour sauver un foyer de culture important dans leur coin de pays,' commented L'Evangéline.[58]

More complex were the political choices facing Acadians. The Parti Acadien made only a limited impact on the New Brunswick general election of 1974, fielding thirteen candidates on a lacklustre platform and nowhere coming close to winning a seat.[59] By the time of the next election, in October 1978, the party had a clear proposal to offer to the voters: decentralization of government offices and the eventual creation of an Acadian province by the splitting of New Brunswick from northeast to southeast. The party also had more experienced candidates, and was expected to be a significant force in Acadian ridings. The eventual results were disappointing in the sense that the party failed to win a seat; but it did poll 12,901 or approximately 12 per cent of the Acadian vote.[60] Underlying the party's program, and the voting pattern that emerged, was the serious dilemma that faced all Acadians – not just those in New Brunswick – as a result of the 1976 Quebec general election. With the Parti Québécois government committed to supporting sovereignty-association in a forthcoming referendum campaign, eventually held in May 1980, three Acadian options could be defined simply enough. One was to maintain the status quo, though with a renewed drive towards bilingualism and, in New Brunswick, towards the overall equality of the two major language groups. Strongly advocated by the New Brunswick government, particularly through Jean-Maurice Simard, and favoured editorially by L'Evangéline, this possibility had strong attractions too for the francophones of the other three Atlantic provinces. As was made clear in 1978 by the publication of The Heirs of Lord Durham: Manifesto of a Vanishing People by the Fédération des Francophones hors Québec (FFHQ), these minority groups were facing high rates of assimilation. 'The federal government,' the manifesto declared, 'must prove the validity of the confederative system.' A second option, favoured by the author Michel Roy among others, was for the Acadians simply to throw in their lot with Quebec.[61] Finally, there was the possibility of an Acadian province.

The 1978 election was certainly less than a triumph for the Parti Acadien, but it was enough to carry the momentum of the party's supporters to the Convention d'Orientation Nationale des Acadiens in Edmundston in October 1979. Organized by the Société des Acadiens du Nouveau-Brunswick, the convention brought together more than a thousand delegates. Presented with options for the future, 800 of them voted: 53.3 per cent indicated that the Acadian province would be their ideal choice. In the days that followed, there was much debate on the significance of the vote, but dissatisfaction with the status quo had been clearly registered. Almost unnoticed amidst the excitement was the speech of Jean-Maurice Simard, promising to introduce a bill in the provincial legislature that would recognize explicitly the equality of the two official-language communities. A largely symbolic measure, perhaps. Yet it was on the basis of this proposal, carried into effect as Bill 88 in 1981, that the Progressive Conservative Party would succeed in taking over a large part of the Acadian vote in the general election of 1982.[62] In the process, the Hatfield government would not only defeat the Liberals, who had harshly opposed Simard's bill, but also virtually annihilate the Parti Acadien as an electoral force. Thus, the phase in the Acadian struggle that had begun in the turbulence of early 1972 was effectively brought to an end ten years later. The eclipse of the Parti Acadien was an obvious setback to Acadian political nationalism, and to the belief that only autonomous political structures could ensure the cultural and economic survival of Acadians. Nevertheless, it was also an indication of the extent to which advocates of the Acadian cause had succeeded in discrediting the status quo as it had existed in the early 1970s and in prompting the anglophone majority to accept – or at least to acquiesce in – the need for significant change.

Other groups also sought change. For Black Maritimers, especially but not exclusively in Nova Scotia, the 1970s saw the maturing of a strategic shift that had already been under way in the late 1960s. 'Inspired not only by their own experience,' writes the historian James Walker, 'but by the example of American blacks and the new assertiveness of many Canadian groups, blacks became much more confrontationist, insisting upon positive intervention to break the syndrome which kept them unequal.'[63] The late 1960s had seen such initiatives as the establishment of the Nova Scotia Human Rights Commission in 1967, and of the Black United Front in 1969. The tasks that faced these agencies were formidable. Although some significant victories had been won in the post-Second World War years in ending overt forms of discrimination such as segregation of movie theatres, Blacks continued to face high rates of unemployment, low incomes, and a lack of educational opportunity. The results were seen partly in the form of racial tensions in Halifax. Less conspicuous, but also damaging and intractable, were the problems of rural poverty. A 1969 study of poverty in Nova Scotia estimated that rural, non-farm residents, representing fully 42 per cent of the Black population, lived 'in "poverty pockets" hardly above the subsistence level.'[64]

The founding of the Black United Front (BUF), along with the increasing volume of grievances presented to the Nova Scotia Human Rights Commission, represented a major effort to seize the initiative in combating the problems faced by Nova Scotia's approximately 20,000 Black people. The organizational roots of BUF lay in the American United Baptist Association of Nova Scotia, although the new organization also indicated a move away from church leadership and towards more secular political action. BUF also drew in part on the lessons gained from the destruction of Africville between 1964 and 1967. 'Black people are bitter and hostile,' commented one leader in 1969, 'and a lot of Black communities now learned of the necessity for them to get together when the Man comes out and starts talking relocation.'[65] As well as direct advocacy of the Black cause, BUF had a further cultural mandate, discharged throughout the 1970s in forms as public as the major Black Cultural Conference held in Halifax in May 1976 or as inconspicuous as the organization of baseball games between teams from rural Black communities in different areas of the province.[66] Also cultural in approach was the effort throughout the decade to eliminate derogatory stereotypes of Black people from school textbooks. Other priorities included the measure taken by the Human Rights Commission to reveal continuing patterns of adverse employment conditions for young Blacks and to promote affirmative action programs as well as programs to enhance educational opportunities. Although no dramatic reversal of the situation of Black Nova Scotians had taken place by the end of the 1970s, and although by that time BUF itself was facing criticism from other Black leaders for growing aloof from its community roots, there was no doubt of the continuing importance of Black collective action.[67]

The shift towards a more activist approach was also clear in the development of Indian and other Native movements in the region. Again, an important impetus for change had become evident during the late 1960s, as shown by, for example, the founding of the Union of New Brunswick Indians in 1967 and the Union of Nova Scotia Indians in 1969. Also important for its stimulating effect was the Native peoples' struggle at the national level against the assimilationist thrust of the federal government's 1969 White Paper on Indian Policy. Native people in Atlantic Canada were not numerous, their 1981 total population of just over 18,000 representing 0.8 per cent of the overall population. In Newfoundland and Labrador, the majority were Indian and Inuit living in Labrador, far from the centres of power; while the Micmac of the island of Newfoundland were still engaged in a complex and not yet successful battle to be recognized as an indigenous Indian people. Even in that province, however, the late 1970s saw significant advances in organization, with the foundation of the general Native Association of Newfoundland Indians, which in 1979 was restructured as an island-wide Micmac government centred on the Conne River community.[68] Here as on the mainland, organizational changes were accompanied by

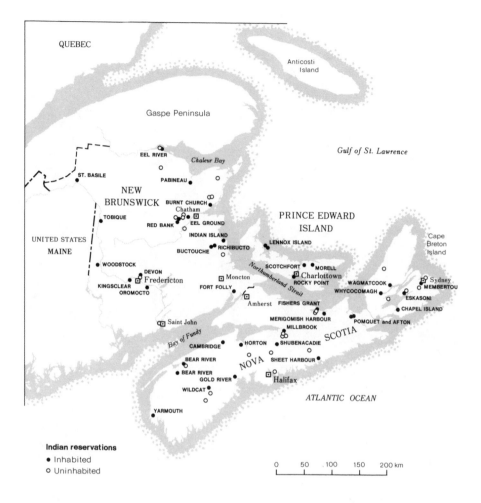

Figure 16 Indian reserves of the Maritime provinces, c. 1988

action on substantive questions. Major issues of the 1970s included education and land claims.

In 1972, the National Indian Brotherhood published its landmark policy paper, *Indian Control of Indian Education*. Its compelling argument that 'the present school system is culturally alien to native students' gave force to its call for curricula to reflect Indian values, for measures to combat high drop-out rates caused by cultural alienation, and for band control of schools. Federal policy changed accordingly, and by the end of the 1970s federal schools were beginning to be replaced by band-controlled institutions. The significance of the change was limited, as noted in the 1983 report of the Parliamentary Special Committee on Indian Self-Government, by continuing interventions in Indian educational affairs by all levels of government. Nevertheless, if fully realized,

Micmacs demand equality, 1968. Eskasoni Micmacs' demands for better
housing, sanitation, and medical services marked a new era of confrontation
in relations between the federal government and Native peoples. Like many
other groups, the Micmacs took their demands to the street in hopes of
strengthening their bargaining position.

Indian control of education offered the possibility of reversal not only
of the drop-out rates that remained high through the 1970s, but also of
the deeper trend towards and long-standing threat of cultural assimilation.[69] In the area of land ownership, major claims by the Indian and
Inuit peoples of Labrador were in the preliminary stages of negotiation
by the decade's end. Maritime Indian peoples, meanwhile, faced an
uphill battle throughout the 1970s, for reasons made explicit in a 1979
declaration of the minister of Indian affairs, Hugh Faulkner, that the
federal government would not entertain land claims in these provinces
because it considered them to have been 'superseded by law.'[70] This
was, as the 1983 parliamentary committed described it, 'a strange concept under which a law passed since the situation arose can be asserted
to have erased the government's lawful obligation.'[71] In the Maritime
context, it was essentially a legalistic form of words for the notion that
Native land loss had occurred so long ago that the government had no

intention of tracing the matter to its roots. By the end of the 1970s research by Native organizations – notably by the Métis and non-status Indian associations – had yielded specific historical and legal counter-arguments, based on such sources as the 1752 treaty of peace and friend-ship between the Micmac and the British, and the Royal Proclamation of 1763. As in the case of Black communities, continuing adverse socio-economic realities for Native people in the region forestalled any un-qualified celebration, but the 1970s had revealed the achievements that were possible even for peoples whose numbers were small, when efforts for self-determination were strongly pursued.[72]

Much larger in numbers, but also entering the 1970s with an increasing recognition of the need for collective organization, was 'the neglected majority,' so named in a book published during the decade. Women in Atlantic Canada, in fact, were just moving into a majority position during the 1970s: the censuses of 1971 and 1981 showed the female population growing from 49.5 to 50.2 per cent.[73] Nevertheless, as in Canada as a whole, women continued to be grossly underrepresented in non-tradi-tional areas of employment, and especially in senior positions, as well as in political life. The law, notably where it related to marital property, still reflected entrenched notions of women's subordination to men. Facilities that offered the potential to assist individual women to break free of traditional constraints – such as day-care, or women's counselling centres – were either lacking or underdeveloped. All these issues, and more, were addressed by the National Advisory Council on the Status of Women, created by the federal government in the spring of 1973 after intensive lobbying by women's groups and as part of the government's response to the 1970 report of the Royal Commission on the Status of Women in Canada.[74] Similar lobbying efforts followed in the Atlantic provinces, with mixed results. The New Brunswick experience showed clearly the obstacles posed not only by resistance but also by the sheer inertia of governments and others, although offering some evidence, too, of the rewards that could be gained by persistent pressure. In the fall of 1974, a province-wide conference entitled 'New Perspectives for New Brunswick Women' was held in Memramcook. Paramount among its many recommendations was one for the creation of a provincial advisory council on the status of women. At the end of the following year, amid the fanfares of International Women's Year, legislation was passed to create the council. Yet it took a further two years of intensive lobbying activity before the members were finally named and a chair appointed in the person of Madeleine Delaney-LeBlanc. Under her lead-ership, the council began its vigorous public advocacy.[75]

Results were not rapidly achieved. Although women began during the 1970s to appear in provincial cabinet positions, the numbers remained small. The Prince Edward Island Advisory Council on the Status of Women took out large newspaper advertisements during the election campaign of 1979 to remind Island women that they represented half the voting population and to suggest possible questions for candidates on matters of concern to women. One of the concerns was that, of the seventy candidates running for thirty-two seats, only four were women.[76] The National Advisory Council on the Status of Women reflected in 1979 on the continuing inequalities of employment and wage levels, as well as in other areas, that persisted despite nearly a decade of women's efforts to prompt implementation of the reforms recommended by the 1970 royal commission.[77] More optimistically, there was no doubt that the 1970s had seen an increasingly clear articulation of the disparities faced by women in both regional and national contexts. Although equality of opportunity in employment was still a distant goal, women's participation in education had increased perceptibly. By the year 1977–8, for example, women undergraduates at Maritime universities represented 46.5 per cent of total enrolment – more than two percentage points higher than the national average – where ten years before they had been only 33.9 per cent. In New Brunswick in 1981, 16.9 per cent of females had completed high school, compared with 11 per cent of males. At the same time, academic study of women's social roles was elaborating the details of the hitherto widely ignored truth that women's work was central to the social and economic functioning of regional society, and always had been. That in itself was a potent argument for a more just allocation of both status and wealth.[78]

To obtain that kind of justice was a major goal also in the struggles of east-coast fishers during the 1970s. The decade, which saw increasing unionization in the fishing industry, opened with a bitter strike in the Canso Strait area, beginning in March 1970. Union organization in the fisheries had to contend with the inherent complexities of an industry that encompassed many different forms of production, and with the tenacious notion of fishers as independent producers operating in a free market. To these difficulties, in the Canso strike, was added a conflict between unions. The United Fishermen and Allied Workers' Union (UFAWU), which began the strike in an effort to gain recognition from fish-processing companies in Canso, Mulgrave, and Petit-de-Grat, succeeded after eight months in gaining a 'memorandum of agreement' for improvements in fish prices and in berthing facilities, only to find itself under attack by the Canadian Food and Allied Workers' Union (CFAWU), which was attempting, with the blessing of the Canadian Labour Congress to establish itself as the representative of all Canadian fishers.[79] The resulting inter-union dispute effectively loosened the UFAWU's foot-

Equality for fishermen, 1975. The Fishermen, Food and Allied Workers' Union, first organized in 1971, represented inshore fishermen and offshore trawlermen employed by fish companies, as well as plant workers. Here workers picket in St John's during the 1974–5 strike for higher wages and benefits.

hold in Nova Scotia, but the Canso strike itself was a prelude to more successful efforts elsewhere. In 1971, the Newfoundland Fishermen, Food and Allied Workers' Union (NFFAWU) was launched, at first as an autonomous division of the CFAWU. Under the presidency of Richard Cashin, the new union secured its position of strength through two successful strikes: at Burgeo in 1971, and the widespread trawler-crew strike of 1974–5. The NFFAWU, however, was more than a conventional fishers' union. It also included shore workers, and sought to participate in a process of restructuring the industry that went beyond the mere launching and winning of strikes. Among its achievements in the mid-1970s was the abolition of the 'co-adventurer' system on Newfoundland trawlers, by which the owners had disclaimed responsibility for trawler crews as employees. Henceforth, the crews would be paid a daily wage as well as a piece rate for the fish caught.[80]

The NFFAWU had an advantage not enjoyed by any fishers' union in the Maritime provinces: the Newfoundland legislature, in the spring of 1971, became the first in Canada to enact legislation specifically granting collective-bargaining rights in the fishery. Not until 1982 did the Maritime Fishermen's Union succeed in gaining equivalent rights in New Brunswick. In the Maritimes, the MFU was emerging by the end of the 1970s as the most powerful advocate of the principle that inshore fishers were workers rather than operators of independent businesses. Thus, it came in conflict with the co-operative principles of the long-established United Maritime Fishermen, and of other smaller fishers' organizations in the region. Only the achievement of bargaining rights in New Brunswick would give the MFU a secure position from which to consolidate its membership throughout the Maritimes. With the NFFAWU extending its operations to Nova Scotia in the early 1980s, the two unions by that time would have emerged as the leading representatives of fishers in Atlantic Canada.[81]

The organizations representing Blacks, Native people, women, and fishers in Atlantic Canada in the 1970s were obviously diverse in their policies and their forms of organization. They were not necessarily in harmony with one another, as was shown in the later years of the decade by debates over the status of Native women. Sandra Lovelace, a Maliseet from the Tobique reserve in New Brunswick, returned there in 1977 after divorcing her non-Indian husband, to be denied housing on the grounds that she had lost her Indian status on her marriage. The resulting controversy pitted the human rights of women against the principle that Indian bands should determine their own membership. Vindication for Lovelace came only after a successful appeal to the Human Rights Committee of the United Nations.[82] Nevertheless, all these organizations were formed with the purpose of claiming justice for disempowered groups in regional society. All enjoyed some success in doing so, and thus in combating disparities based on ethnicity, gender, and social class, although all found as well that established power structures would not yield easily. All were political organizations, though outside the conventional partisan political process. Together, they provided clear evidence that, through collective action, the political initiative could be seized in specific areas by groups whose divisions had previously helped to keep them powerless.

ENVIRONMENT AND CULTURE

The same was true of a cluster of other issues that related to the relationship between human beings and the environment. Although the effects of pollutants had not gone entirely unnoticed during the previous two decades, it was the 1970s that saw the real ecological awakening of Atlantic Canada. As awakenings go, it was a rude one. On 3 February 1970, the Liberian oil tanker *Arrow* went aground in Chedabucto Bay, spreading its cargo over forty miles of coastline in the Canso Strait area. The disaster gave an unprecedented indication of the dangers of large-scale pollution in the region. In one sense, though, this was a simpler issue than those raised by other ecological dangers. Nobody could approve of oil spills, although there might be different opinions as to how best to prevent them in the future. More controversial were cases in which ecological arguments came into direct conflict with economic interests. In New Brunswick and in Cape Breton, campaigns were waged against the anti-spruce budworm spraying of the forests. The most determined phase of opposition in New Brunswick got under way in the spring of 1976, led by Betty Keddy, in the wake of medical studies that linked budworm spraying to the often-fatal children's disease Reye's Syndrome. The forest industry countered by asserting not only that the spray was safe but also that it was essential for the health of the province's economy. The *Moncton Times* had hard words for the protestors, describing their efforts as 'alarmist' and 'somewhat fanatical,' but even it could say nothing better of the spray program than that it was 'the lesser of two evils.'[83] The provincial government thought so too, and spraying was allowed to continue. The protests did result, however, in stricter regulation of the program and of the chemicals used.

Protesters against New Brunswick's entry into the nuclear industry also had mixed success. Protests against the possible building of a nuclear plant at any one of a number of possible sites on Chaleur Bay initially gained considerable attention in the press. After the provincial government announced in July 1974, however, that it had selected a different site near Saint John, at Point Lepreau, any local attempts to resist were easily overcome by the thought of the numerous construction jobs that would be created.[84] Another form of environmental issue was raised in Prince Edward Island by the Brothers and Sisters of Cornelius Howatt, in alliance with the National Farmers' Union (NFU). Since the inauguration of the development plan, the NFU had been predicting the decline of the family farm, and in 1971 farmers had protested by stalling tractors on the highway from Borden to Charlottetown to disrupt tourist traffic. The Brothers and Sisters, founded in response to the officially sponsored celebrations of the centennial of Prince Edward Island's 1873

Fishing in troubled waters, 1969. Towns and industries have allowed the tides to take care of the effluent they create, which often contains toxic wastes. The practice has had disastrous consequences for the marine life of the region and is also linked to high levels of cancer and other environmental diseases.

entry into Confederation, and named in honour of the leading anti-Confederate of that day, also pointed to the damage done to Island society by the excesses of tourism and the related decline of agriculture.[85]

Also environment-related were the controversies in all four provinces over proposed national or provincial parks. Plans for a provincial park on Nova Scotia's eastern shore, centred on Ship Harbour, and for a national park in King's county, P.E.I., aroused debate in 1973, and both were effectively scuttled by the protests of local residents who feared losing their homes and livelihoods.[86] Meanwhile, the Gros Morne National Park project, on the west coast of Newfoundland north of Corner Brook, went ahead despite an angry confrontation at the official opening in August 1973 between Jean Chrétien – the federal minister responsible – and members of local communities. Concessions were made, however, to prevent forced removals from the park area.[87] No such guarantees had been given in the case of Kouchibouguac National Park in New Brunswick, opened in 1969, and the treatment of those whose homes

'National Park Steam Roller Co. Ltd., 1973.' This cartoon appeared shortly after residents of Nova Scotia's Eastern Shore had demonstrated in Halifax against the provincial park proposed for that area of the province. This opposition and Jackie Vautour's battle to retain his land in Kouchibouguac National Park were among several incidents that forced park authorities to reassess their expropriation policies.

and lands had been expropriated became a recurring *cause célèbre* throughout the 1970s. Jackie Vautour and his family had their property expropriated in 1970, and were offered compensation of $20,760. Vautour, claiming that $150,000 would have been a more realistic figure, refused to leave until his home was bulldozed in November 1976. After staying in a Richibucto motel for the winter, the family was forcibly evicted in March 1977, and male family members were sent to face criminal charges arising out of their attempts to resist. *L'Evangéline*, while warning against exploitation of the issue for ideological purposes, condemned the entire handling of the Kouchibouguac affair as 'un crime contre la dignité humaine.'[88] Still unresolved by the decade's end, the dispute was essentially the result of a clumsy and high-handed procedure of a kind rendered indefensible in the 1970s by popular efforts in each of the provinces.

An even more widely publicized issue was the Newfoundland seal hunt. Protests against the hunt were heard throughout the decade, notably from the International Fund for Animal Welfare and its New Brunswick-based leader, Brian Davies. Not until the late 1970s, however, did the campaign reach a crescendo, as international publicity brought a heavy flow of funds from donors in the United States and Europe, and as the number of protesting organizations grew to include, among others, Greenpeace. The arguments against Newfoundland sealers came down to two essential claims: that the harp seal was an endangered species, and that the hunt was a barbaric and inhumane practice. The first claim was repeatedly contradicted by scientific evidence that quotas imposed by the federal Department of Fisheries in 1971 had been effective in reversing an earlier decline in the seal herd, and that the one to two million harp seals were in no danger of extinction.[89] It was the second charge that brought the real emotional heat into the debate. In the late winter of 1977, following demonstrations on the ice in 1976 by Greenpeace and others, a large advertising poster appeared near the Canadian High Commission in London showing a seal being clubbed and carrying the bold legend, 'Canada's Shame.' Then the theatrics began, and the rhetoric that posited baby seals pitted against brutal Neanderthals gathered force. The French film star Brigitte Bardot was the most eminent personage produced by Davies and his colleagues: although Bardot missed a helicopter trip to the sealing front on 16 March by lingering too long over lunch, she did visit the ice a few days later. On 22 March, a rump of the United States House of Representatives passed a motion condemning the hunt as 'a cruel practice,' and the damage could not be undone even by an all-party resolution in favour of the sealers, passed in Ottawa by the House of Commons two days later.[90]

The reality was that Newfoundlanders had few effective weapons with which to counteract the well-organized and well-funded anti-sealing campaign. Such spontaneous responses as the booing of Brian Davies as he arrived in St Anthony only gave further ammunition to those who wished to portray the local residents unfavourably. By early 1978, the province was better prepared. Premier Moores embarked in January on an international series of press conferences in which he and others put the case in favour of sealing.[91] What the tour ultimately proved, however, was that argument could not compete with the emotional effect of repeated images of white seal pups and blood on the ice. Anger and frustration in Newfoundland took a number of forms as 1978 went on. *Decks Awash*, the magazine of Memorial University's extension department, devoted an entire issue to the problem, declaring that Newfoundlanders 'don't hunt seals for sport.'[92] Yet, just as the anti-sealers had made effective use of theatrical tactics, so were the most effective rejoinders theatrical in nature. The Mummers Troupe, which had been producing successful alternative theatre in the province since 1972, toured Canada in 1978 with its production of *They Club Seals, Don't They?* Criticized by some for portraying the anti-sealers as red-nosed buffoons while the hunters were wholesome, hard-working pillars of their families, the Mummers were certainly no less even-handed than those they opposed. The same could be said in 1979 of Codpeace, a St John's-based group formed to satirize the seal-hunt protesters. Codpeace's well-publicized efforts to save its fictional protégé Cuddles the Cod from the cruel depredations of Heinrich Von Harp and other jagged-toothed seals probably made not a single convert in the earnest ranks of the protesters. None of the counter-efforts of the Newfoundlanders, in fact, could prevent the hunt's demise, as seal products were boycotted in Europe and the United States in the early 1980s. At least, though, there was some satisfaction in landing satirical barbs on those who had so successfully undermined a long-established part of Newfoundland's economy and besmirched the province's good name with such calm efficiency.[93]

That the theatre should have emerged in the seal-hunt debate as an effective proponent of a popular cause was no accident in the Atlantic Canada of the 1970s. In this decade cultural resources assumed great importance. Theatre was a clear example. In Newfoundland, the Mummers Troupe was only one of the collective theatre groups that flourished at various times during the decade. The other major ones were CODCO, from 1973 to 1978 and in occasional revivals thereafter, and Rising Tide Theatre, a splinter group from the Mummers formed in 1978. In Cape Breton, *The Rise and Follies of Cape Breton* quickly gained a popular following in 1977 for its satirical treatment of the island's efforts to cope with the buffeting of economic changes. The Mulgrave Road Theatre Co-operative, beginning in 1977 at Mulgrave and moving to Guysborough two years later, opened with its humorous *Mulgrave Road Show* and went on to a wide variety of collective productions later in the decade and in the 1980s. Mulgrave Road maintained a close connection with its Guysborough community base, but also toured extensively. The same could be said for the Théâtre Populaire d'Acadie, founded in Caraquet in 1976, a group that gave wide exposure throughout Acadian New Brunswick to plays by young Acadian authors.[94] What all these theatre endeavours had in common was that their productions were original to them, and thus to Atlantic Canada, and that they dealt with the people and the problems of the region as they were in the 1970s: whether through making audiences laugh at themselves, as in *The Rise and Follies*, or by sharp-edged commentary on specific issues, as in the

Mummers' *Gros Mourn* or *Buchans – A Mining Town*. Either way, the result was the popularization of theatre and the use of the stage to define the dilemmas and weaknesses – and also the strengths – of the communities of the region.

Other literary, performing, and visual arts served a similar purpose. The range of cultural production in Atlantic Canada during the 1970s was enough that no short treatment could hope to be comprehensive. Nevertheless, no reader of the novels of Antonine Maillet, David Adams Richards, or Percy Janes, or the short stories of Alistair MacLeod, or the poetry of Milton Acorn, Alden Nowlan, Rita Joe, Raymond LeBlanc, or Herménégilde Chiasson could fail to recognize the confidence with which Atlantic-Canadian writers were exploring the dark places of the region's past and present. Films such as Shebib's *Goin' Down the Road* and Pierre Perrault's *L'Acadie, l'Acadie* challenged the emotions of Maritime audiences, while Atlantic region productions of the National Film Board included several that dealt innovatively with the history and culture of the region. Academic study flourished as well, with the founding in Fredericton in 1971 of the journal *Acadiensis*, dedicated to scholarly articles on Atlantic-Canadian topics, and with the development of courses on regional history and society in universities. School textbooks, as Paul Robinson pointed out in 1979, offered a less encouraging picture, with most texts produced elsewhere and reflecting more or less alien cultural values.[95] Nevertheless, Atlantic Canadians enjoyed better access to their own history and cultural character in 1980, whether through theatre, film, or creative or scholarly writing, than they had ten years before.

Significantly, the cultural changes of the decade extended also to journalism. As the 1970s began, an unflattering portrait of Maritime journalism was emerging from the hearings of a special Senate Committee on the Mass Media. Chaired by Senator Keith Davey, the committee owed its existence partly to the actions of Senator Charles McElman of New Brunswick in March 1969. McElman, a veteran of the Robichaud government and of its disputes with K.C. Irving earlier in the 1960s, had publicly denounced Irving's acquisition of control of the Fredericton *Daily Gleaner* – discreetly carried out in 1968 to complete Irving's monopoly of English-language daily newspapers in the province – and had requested the Combines Branch of the Department of Consumers' Affairs to conduct an investigation. Within a week, that investigation was begun and the Davey committee created. The committee began its hearings late in the year, and on 16 December Irving himself appeared to testify. As well as taking the opportunity to attack McElman and the Robichaud government, Irving staunchly maintained under questioning that he played no role in the running of the newspapers he owned, least of all in their editorial policies, and that he did not even take profits from them.[96] The committee was unimpressed. Its eventual report, released in December 1970, was blunt in its condemnation of the Irving influence. The Irving newspapers, the committee found, were enormously profitable and yet – along with the Halifax dailies – had been instrumental in making New Brunswick and Nova Scotia 'journalistic disaster areas.'[97] It was a judgment that confirmed the critiques of the established daily newspapers that were already appearing in the alternative press in the region itself. The *Fourth Estate*, founded in Halifax in early 1969, consistently criticized the *Chronicle-Herald* for its lack of investigative reporting and for its editorial abdications even on issues as current and controversial as the troubles of the heavy-water plant at Glace Bay. In Fredericton, the *Mysterious East* appeared in November 1969 as a monthly published by an editorial board composed of 'people who are fed up, frustrated, angry with rotten journalism.' Offering detailed investigative reports on a wide range of provincial and regional topics, the magazine continued to reserve much of its harshest criticism for 'the Irving press' and its editorial shortcomings.[98]

Investigation of the Irving newspapers under the Combines Investigation Act resulted in 1972 in the conviction of the Irving group for contravening the act's monopoly provisions, and in an order to break up the ownership of the five newspapers owned by the group. Three years later, however, the conviction was overturned on appeal, and this decision was upheld by the Supreme Court of Canada in 1978. Thus, the newspapers continued under Irving ownership, as did the New Brunswick Broadcasting Company, the owner of the province's nearest approach to a CBC television station. Also by that time, the *Fourth Estate* and the *Mysterious East* had ceased publication, amid strong suggestions in the case of the *Fourth Estate* that the newspaper's demise in 1974 had been caused or hastened by an advertising boycott led by the Sobey's grocery chain in reaction to the paper's editorial policy.[99] Another alternative journal, the *Plain Dealer*, flourished briefly in Fredericton, and then was gone. The flurry of critical comment and the growth in alternative journalism of the early 1970s had little immediate impact on the major English-language dailies of the Maritimes, but changes did take place. Alternative newspapers, short-lived as they might be, had been staffed by a generation of relatively young writers whose careers did not end with the journals themselves. Furthermore, there were other journalistic opportunities. *L'Evangéline* took a consistently critical and independent editorial line throughout the decade. Weekly newspapers such as the *Eastern Graphic*, in Montague, Prince Edward Island, could provide more trenchant editorial comment than did, in this case, the Thomson-owned dailies in Charlottetown. In St John's, meanwhile, readers had the luxury of genuine competition between daily newspapers, and even the staid pages of the *Evening Telegram* frequently harboured satirical or analytical columns that were as biting as any in Canada. In magazine journalism, the founding of *Atlantic Insight* in 1979 was a significant departure, in that the new magazine promised that it would criticize as well as celebrate. As years went by, the promise was kept in varying degrees as the magazine's fortunes rose and fell. At its best, however, *Atlantic Insight* provided another outlet for the best in the new regional journalism that had developed during the 1970s.[100]

The most important and innovative general characteristic of changes in cultural production during the decade, therefore, was the widening of available knowledge of Atlantic Canada, past and present. Through education, creative arts, scholarly research, and independent journalism, hitherto unprobed areas of regional life were analysed, portrayed, and brought to the attention of the public. It was no accident that disempowered minorities made education a major concern, that popular theatre was drawn into environmental debates, or that academic research was shaking the foundations of long-standing conventional beliefs as to the origins of the region's economic difficulties. In all these respects, and more, knowledge was power. Knowledge and its control, up until the late 1960s, had been the preserve of a remarkably small group of political, business, and educational leaders. By the end of the 1970s, although there was still no reason for complacency, this was so no longer.

## THE SCEPTICAL EDGE

Yet surely political life was continuing to go on in its normal way, despite these supposed cultural changes? Aside from the Parti Acadien, the 1970s saw the emergence of no new political parties of any significance. The Liberal and Progressive Conservative parties continued to dominate, while the New Democratic Party (NDP) failed almost totally to make electoral inroads. Apart from the brief representation of the Newfoundland federal constituency of Humber–St George–St Barbe by a New Democrat from a 1978 by-election to the general election of 1980, the sole area of NDP strength was in Nova Scotia, and largely in Cape Breton at that. In the Nova Scotia provincial election of 1974, the NDP had gained some 17 per cent of the popular vote – though only three seats – and leader Jeremy Akerman had declared boldly that the party would be 'going for the jackpot' the next time around.[101] Akerman duly waged a strong campaign in 1978, but attained an increase only to four seats, all in industrial Cape Breton. Tensions existed between, on the one hand, Akerman and his long-standing colleague Paul MacEwan, and, on the other, those – including a strong group in Halifax – who believed that

Akerman and MacEwan were leading the party into a quest for power at the cost of principle. Certainly, Akerman's 1978 campaign had placed what was, for the NDP, an unusual emphasis on the need for fiscal responsibility as a precondition for effective economic planning.[102] Nobody could have predicted, however, how quickly and how spectacularly the party would descend into internecine quarrelling after the election. By 1980, Akerman had resigned to take a senior position in the provincial civil service, while MacEwan was expelled from the party on a variety of grounds relating to such issues as his allegations of Trotskyism among mainland New Democrats and his solicitation of corporate donations for party electoral funds. To make matters worse, Father Andy Hogan – NDP MP for Cape Breton – East Richmond since 1974 – met defeat in the federal election of February 1980. Eliminated from the House of Commons, and reduced to two members in the only provincial legislature where it held any seats at all, the NDP in the Atlantic provinces faced a formidable task for the 1980s.

Not so the Progressive Conservative Party, at least in electoral terms. In a nine-month period between September 1978 and June 1979, that party would win majorities in general elections in all four provinces, defeating existing Liberal governments in Nova Scotia and Prince Edward Island. The real beginning of this round of elections, however, was in April 1978 in Prince Edward Island. In a campaign described by the Charlottetown *Guardian* as 'about as exciting as a rag-pickers' reunion,' Alex Campbell's governing Liberals obtained only the barest of majorities over the Conservatives, whose new leader was the veteran MP for Queen's County, Angus MacLean.[103] Premier Campbell, after twelve years in office, resigned shortly afterwards and was succeeded by former education minister Bennett Campbell. A new election was then called for April 1979, and MacLean's Conservatives completed the task they had begun a year before. Even more in 1979 than in 1978, MacLean campaigned on a conservationist platform that reflected the earlier arguments of the Brothers and Sisters of Cornelius Howatt and the National Farmers' Union. MacLean promised a 'rural renaissance,' as opposed to the elaborate planning strategies of the now-moribund development plan. He also advocated controls on the proliferation of shopping malls and rejected the Liberal government's plan to buy nuclear-generated electricity from New Brunswick. The nuclear question emerged, in fact – especially as the campaign came soon after the much-publicized malfunction of the Three Mile Island plant in the United States – as the most important single issue; and on election day the voters gave a substantial majority to the Conservatives.[104]

In Nova Scotia, meanwhile, another Liberal government had already fallen. Fighting a losing battle against the public reaction to high power rates, as well as against opposition suggestions that a recently arranged subsidy program for domestic electricity reflected the political co-option of the Nova Scotia Power Corporation by a desperate government, Gerald Regan lost decisively on 19 September 1978 to John Buchanan's Progressive Conservatives.[105] Just over a month later, Richard Hatfield gained re-election in New Brunswick. Although the Conservative majority was reduced to only two seats, even that narrow victory represented a remarkable feat of survival by Canada's most durable premier of the day. The collapse of the Bricklin project in 1975 had provoked public cynicism and ridicule, coming as it did less than a year after Hatfield had used a gaudily coloured Bricklin as one of his main campaign props. Worse had followed in March 1977, when Liberal leader Robert Higgins had begun his response to the government's throne speech by warning that 'my participation [in the debate] will not be in the traditional sense,' and had gone on to reveal allegations of a 'kickback' scheme by which Progressive Conservative fund-raisers were extorting contributions from individuals and companies doing business with the government. Higgins' most damaging charges were that Hatfield himself had known of the scheme, and that the provincial department of justice had sought to interfere in the ongoing RCMP investigation. He concluded by calling for a royal commission to investigate the entire question of party funding. Hatfield's initial response was silence. Then, eight days after Higgins had spoken, the premier made a statement brusquely denying all knowledge of kickbacks, rejecting the notion of a royal commission, and promising only a judicial inquiry into the specific allegation that the RCMP had been impeded in its investigation. On that point, the government was vindicated by the report of Chief Justice C.J.A. Hughes, released on 25 January 1978. Three hours later, Higgins resigned as leader of the opposition. Hatfield's skilful footwork in limiting the scope of the inquiry had effectively wrested control of the issue away from the opposition.[106] Not until May 1978 did the Liberals elect Joe Daigle as their new leader, and the party's morale had little time for improvement before the government called the fall election. Even so, the Conservatives' success depended heavily on their continuing inroads in northern New Brunswick. With the Liberal vote challenged in the north by the Parti Acadien, with the Liberal Party damaged by suggestions that it was attempting to downplay the Acadianness of its leader in order to win votes in the south, and with a swing to the Conservatives in the city of Saint John, Hatfield was able to scrape home.[107]

The re-election of the Conservatives in Newfoundland in June 1979 was an altogether more decisive affair. Following the resignation of Frank Moores earlier in the year, to devote himself to business pursuits and political lobbying, Brian Peckford had been elected party leader –

and therefore premier – in March. Young, aggressive, and with a reputation gained by effective negotiation with the major oil companies while minister of mines and energy, Peckford wasted no time in calling a general election. Here, too, the Liberal Party was in disarray, under a leader – William Rowe – who had recently admitted to leaking a confidential police report to the press in an attempt to discredit a former minister in the Moores cabinet.[108] Soon after the election call, Rowe was thrust aside, as veteran former federal cabinet minister Don Jamieson suddenly arrived to take over the leadership with just two weeks to make good on Liberal expectations that he alone could provide serious competition for Peckford. Anti-climax followed. Jamieson was already tired from the demands of the recent federal election, which the Liberals had narrowly lost to Joe Clark's Progressive Conservatives in May. The Newfoundland campaign was fought on matters of style rather than substance, and Peckford's vigour was more than Jamieson could match. 'Don,' declaimed Peckford from the top of a flatbed truck in a Stephenville shopping-mall parking lot, 'things have changed, old man, and you're not the man for this day or tomorrow.'[109] Whether by nature or artifice, the thirty-six-year-old Peckford was campaigning with all the fire and arrogance that youth could muster. He represented the new Newfoundland in two senses. A former teacher with outport roots, he was a member of the new middle class that Confederation – and Memorial University – had created during the Smallwood years. In his aggressive advocacy of Newfoundland interests in energy matters, whether directed at the oil companies or at the resource-ownership claims of the federal government, Peckford also represented the newly found hope that Newfoundland would soon enter a new era as a 'have' rather than a 'have-not' province – and that it would do so not through federal subsidies and conventional development schemes but through its own shrewd management of its natural resources. There was also a cultural element in the new Conservatism of Peckford and his colleagues. Figgy Duff played 'lively, toe-tapping Newfoundland traditional music' at election rallies, and prominent government figures were seen much more often at the Longshoremen's Protective Union Hall now that it was the home of the Mummers Troupe than when it had been a union headquarters. The government, in 1979, was offering the voters a potent combination of cultural populism and the rhetoric of economic self-reliance, and it was duly rewarded on election day.[110]

Taken together, the political developments of the late 1970s yielded certain important clues to more general changes that had taken place in Atlantic Canada during the decade. One of these lay in the response of the English-speaking portions of the region to the approaching Quebec referendum on sovereignty-association. Events in Quebec, arising from the victory of the Parti Québécois in the general election of November 1976, caused urgent debate and some anguish among Acadians in all the provinces, and for good reason: members of francophone minorities, even the large minority in New Brunswick, had to weigh the merits of support for fellow francophones in Quebec against the possibility of isolation among the residual English-speaking majorities if Quebec took its own path.[111] Among anglophones, too, the issue was debated, and 'national unity' dutifully appeared on newspaper front pages, and in editorials, for three and a half years. There was, however, an undercurrent of weariness and cynicism that came at times to the surface. 'The unity circus,' wrote Ray Guy in 1979, 'strikes us here as being so heavy-handed it stinks of desperation.'[112] With the Quebec referendum campaign well into its final month, Michael Forrestall, Progressive Conservative member for Halifax East, charged in the House of Commons that the federal government was trying to buy off the Quebec voters by 'kicking Atlantic Canada in the ass.' The recent announcement that Quebec shipyards would be favoured in bidding for a forthcoming program for building naval frigates, he maintained, 'clearly indicates to the rest of Canada that it is the intention of this government to ignore regional disparity.'[113] This was, of course, an extension of the same arguments that the Atlantic premiers had been making a decade before, but now there was a more sceptical edge, an implied doubt as to whether federal action could ever lead to real improvements.

A second change that had occurred was shown in the texture of the general-election campaigns of the late 1970s in three of the four provinces. Each province had, throughout the decade, essentially a two-party system. The names of the two parties remained the same, and ostensibly political life went on at the end of the decade much in the same way as it had at the beginning. Appearances, however, were deceptive. The range of pressures on governments had widened. Pressure groups that were not partisan in the conventional sense played an increasing role in providing, at times, opposition to existing governments, and at other times the intellectual and ideological stimulus by which governments could renew themselves. In 1978, the Progressive Conservatives in New Brunswick survived in government largely because the party was on its way to becoming an important vehicle for the political aspirations of Acadians in the province. By the time of the next election in 1982, with Simard's Bill 88 safely passed, the party would be in control of most Acadian ridings. In 1979, the Progressive Conservatives of Prince Edward Island came to power on a platform largely inspired by the conservationist arguments of extra-parliamentary groups of the early 1970s, such as the Brothers and Sisters of Cornelius Howatt. Prompting a rural renaissance proved to be a difficult task once office had been attained, although the restriction of shopping malls and the repudiation of nuclear power were election promises quickly fulfilled.[114] The Peckford government in Newfoundland, meanwhile, had laid an effective political claim to the cultural legacy of the popular theatre and music of the 1970s, which it combined with a form of economic nationalism to produce a combination that would be electorally invincible far into the ensuing decade. In each case, the Progressive Conservative Party had embraced causes and movements that ten years earlier would have been alien to it, and had thereby gained momentum towards gaining or retaining office. Whether the party had a real moral right to the conversions it professed, or whether it was simply strip-mining attractive campaign issues, was a judgment that could not yet be made. But any notion that political discourse had remained as unchanging as the names of the major parties was clearly mistaken.

Some things had not changed in Atlantic Canada during the 1970s. Personal incomes in 1980 were still far below the national average, with the Atlantic provinces just as firmly in the four lowest places in the national table as they had been when the decade had opened. Even such income levels as were achieved – ranging in 1982 from 64 per cent of the national average in Newfoundland to 79.1 per cent in Nova Scotia – depended to an uncomfortable extent on federal transfers of one kind or another. Unemployment also remained high, and the onset of the economic recession of the early 1980s allowed little ground for hopes that it would fall significantly in the near future. Out-migration continued, though now the favoured destination was the 'oil patch' of Alberta.[115] None of the great hopes of 1970 had been fully realized. The future of DREE was in doubt, following the successive changes in federal government in 1979 and 1980. Furthermore, it had become clear that the department's substantial infusions of federal funding had failed to alter fundamentally the balance between regions. During the 1970s, DREE's share of the federal budget had fallen considerably, and the proportion of its expenditures allocated to the Atlantic region had fallen from 53 per cent to 36 per cent. Of this funding, much had been devoted to infrastructure rather than to direct stimulation of manufacturing industry, and large-scale industrial growth had not ensued.[116] Maritime union, meanwhile, had been a political non-starter almost from the day on which the Deutsch Commission's report had appeared in late 1970. Offshore energy development remained an enticing prospect, at least for Newfoundland and Nova Scotia, but its full effects for good or ill were yet to be seen.

Yet some changes had occurred, and some lessons had been learned. Whatever remaining faith Atlantic Canadians had had, in 1970, that economic disparities would be easily eliminated through government action was now gone. As with any other loss of faith, confusion and cynicism followed. The collapse of industrial-development projects and the worsening of disparities within the provinces led in the early 1970s to the unrest of which the Bathurst upheavals of early 1972 were one manifestation. Nevertheless, this particular faith had implied an acceptance of dependency on the federal government, and tolerance for the questionable, and often secret, dealing of the agencies and promoters who so often promised more from their development schemes than was ever delivered. The 1970s saw the growth of a new tendency towards self-direction, in the form of united action by those who faced disparities along the lines of geographical location, ethnicity, gender, and social class. Accompanied by public debate on issues affecting the human and physical environment, and by the diversification of popular culture, these movements had shown, by the later years of the decade, the ability to effect some changes in society itself and a considerable change in political discourse. By 1980, it was clear from the performance of the Canadian economy that difficult years still lay ahead for the Atlantic provinces. But at least the often-turbulent experiences of the 1970s provided a better preparation than the uncritical belief in ready progress that had innocently lingered in the region as it entered the decade.

# Epilogue
## The 1980s

Although closeness to events tends to undermine historical perspective, one can sketch the broad outlines of the region's experience in the past decade. In the 1980s the Atlantic provinces faced problems of adjustment as Canada began a fundamental shift in economic and constitutional orientation. The decade opened with a serious recession, confounding traditional economics with a stagnant economy accompanied by double-digit inflation and the highest interest rates ever. The victims of the recession included not only the traditionally vulnerable construction workers and unskilled labour but also the middle class, as corporations trimmed managerial staff in a drive to be more competitive. The upwardly mobile were often the ones losing their homes or savings as rising interest rates more than doubled mortgage payments and eventually burst real-estate bubbles in western cities. In the Atlantic provinces dreams of rapid offshore-oil development were dashed for Newfoundland and Nova Scotia, and promised manufacturing in New Brunswick failed to materialize. As economists revised their theories to account for the new conjunction in trends, British and American leaders Margaret Thatcher and Ronald Reagan trimmed social expenditures and encouraged efforts to make private industry more competitive – 'leaner and meaner' in the cliché of the period.[1] In Canada economists evolved a neo-conservative rhetoric, which, decrying government intervention in general and subsidies in particular, proclaimed the gospel of 'competition,' 'efficiency,' and 'privatization.' Closely associated with the new economics was the advocacy of a more decentralized federalism.

Such ideas had profound implications for the Atlantic provinces. It was by government intervention in the form of fiscal transfers that these provinces had, at least partially, solved their constitutional dilemma in a country that was 'national' for making money but 'provincial' for social spending and economic development. As the Rowell-Sirois Commission had recognized in 1939, only the federal government had the authority to redistribute to the poorer provinces the wealth drawn from the whole country but concentrated in the central metropolises. The 1950s, 1960s, and 1970s had seen the growth of payments to provincial governments, at least partly on the basis of need, and federal social and developmental programs that included direct payments to people and industry. Both of these represented net transfers of income from metropolises to hinterlands. They enhanced the standard of living in the Atlantic provinces, while the money returned to the metropolises through expanded purchases of goods and services. But the proponents of the new creed included these transfers in their negative critique of the federal interventionist state.[2]

In an effort to rationalize the needs of the Atlantic provinces with a more decentralized constitution, economist T.J. Courchene in 1979 revived the old 'equilibrium theory' to argue that aid for Canada's outlying regions was counter-productive, as it tended to discourage or delay 'economic adjustment.' If wages fell low enough in the Atlantic provinces the people would either leave, thus saving on welfare costs, or stay, thus providing a pool of cheap labour that would help to attract new industry. Economist William Y. Smith later noted in response that 'equilibrium theory never worked in the Maritimes,' and sociologist Ralph Matthews cited the 'extreme hardship' that acceptance of the new philosophy would mean for 'residents of poorer regions.' Historian David Alexander criticized the new economics and warned of the dangers for Canada as a whole from the proposed decentralization, particularly given the centrifugal pressures of French-Canadian nationalism. In spite of these warnings, however, Courchene's views were widely accepted.[3]

Decentralizing forces were in evidence at the constitutional conference of 1982. At the Victoria conference a decade earlier the provinces seemed disposed to give constitutional recognition to the fiscal transfers upon which the Atlantic provinces depended. But in 1982 Quebec refused to concede the federal government's right to continue direct payments to people and industry, though these probably represented about half of the total net transfers to the Atlantic region. Thus only equalization payments to provinces were mentioned in the new constitution, these to enable provinces to 'provide reasonably comparable levels of public service at reasonably comparable levels of taxation.'[4]

The clearest enunciation of the neo-conservative ideology came in the report of and studies for the Macdonald Commission. Before resigning as prime minister, Pierre Elliott Trudeau had appointed a royal commission to look into Canada's economic and constitutional needs in a changing world – the most comprehensive investigation since the Rowell-Sirois Commission. Just as the former found itself influenced heavily by Keynesian economics and ideas developed during the Depression, the latter drew on the new ideology emerging from the 'stagflation' experience and the demands of the business sectors in the United States and Great Britain. The Conservatives, who had stressed aspects of the neo-conservative rhetoric prior to the election of 1984, found no difficulty in continuing the investigation under the business-oriented Donald Macdonald when they came to power. Nor was there any shortage of like-minded economists to prepare studies along the lines suggested in the preliminary investigation.

These scholars advanced a more revolutionary agenda than that contemplated by any previous commission. They recommended the dismantling of the traditional 'National Policy' in tariffs and transportation in favour of a new free-trade arrangement with the United States. To meet the resulting competition, industry would require a lessening of the burden of the state. This they urged through a 'rationalization' of subsidies and social programs and changes designed to shift much of the tax load from manufacturing to the sale of goods and services. In their discussion of the Atlantic provinces, equilibrium theory appeared to dominate. Ken Norrie, Richard Simeon, and Mark Krasnick, for example, noted that the theory set out in Courchene's 1979 article had received little empirical testing. Nevertheless they found its logic 'compelling' in presenting it as part of the case for federal decentralization.[5]

Most conspicuous in the Macdonald Commission's report and its related studies was the omission of any discussion of metropolitan-hinterland relations. Sixty years earlier Sir Andrew Rae Duncan had noted how the centralization of industry and finance had upset the financial balance in the Canadian constitution. Before the Second World War the Rowell-Sirois Commission made a central issue of the need to use the federal government as a means of distributing revenues back to the hinterlands from the metropolises. The role of the metropolises was further explored by such mainstream academics as historian J.M.S. Careless and geographer Donald Kerr.[6] Yet the Macdonald Commission appeared oblivious to such scholarship. Thus, rare figures on interprovincial trade not available to other commissions were simply recorded with little attempt at analysis. These showed Ontario in 1979 to have a $7-billion annual surplus in the sale of goods and services within the country; the Atlantic provinces had a $3.5-billion deficit. The extent to which both surpluses and deficits were products of metropolitan-hinterland relations, the role of the transfer payments in facilitating such relations, and the potential impact of the commission's recommendations in undermining them simply went unexplored.

Although neo-conservative logic supplied the basic rationale for the report, its recommendations also contained a series of offsetting provisos based on fairness and humanitarian concern. Thus, existing transfers to

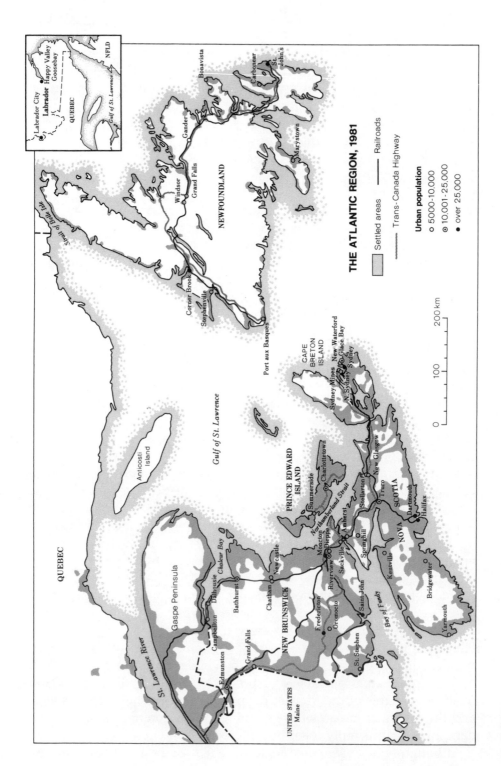

Figure 17 The Atlantic Canada region in 1981

individuals would be reduced only after a new 'Universal Income Security Programme' was in place; unemployment insurance would be cut
back only after an 'income stabilization' program had been implemented
for the fishermen; and the federal government would terminate regional
assistance to industry only after a new program was in place to distribute
industrial funds to the poorer provinces on essentially the same basis
as equalization payments and in addition to them. Such schemes, the
commissioners claimed, could be financed with money going to existing
programs and would exert no additional pressure on federal budgets.[7]
Unfortunately, none of these offsetting recommendations was implemented by the new Conservative government.

That government did move quickly to put in place the other major
recommendations of the report. Indeed, never have Canadians faced in
so short a time such a bewildering array of initiatives of fundamental
importance. Encouraged by the new ideology and by mounting budget
deficits, the government had already begun the reduction of subsidies
and social programs. The government in 1984 proposed and then backed
away from the elimination of universality in old-age pensions.[8] In the
same year it appointed the Erik Neilsen task force to review government
programs and identify those that might be reduced or eliminated. Here
the Atlantic provinces were vulnerable. Just as they had gained the most
from the growth of federal programs and services through the previous
three decades, they now had the most to lose through their dismem-
berment. When regional representatives expressed alarm at the super-
ficiality of the studies in the seventeen-volume report tabled in 1986
and asked for the opportunity to defend particular programs, they were
informed that the report did not represent the views of the government
and was not being implemented.[9] Yet the programs remained targeted
for the time when budgetary and other political considerations might
allow their elimination.

At a meeting of federal-provincial first ministers at the Meech Lake
conference centre in 1987, the prevalence of the new ideology made it
easier for the federal government to accept the constitutional revision
demanded by a Quebec government concerned to demonstrate its defence of provincial autonomy. The choice for Atlantic leaders was not
an easy one. On one hand, the special status proposed for Quebec, long
rejected under Trudeau, and the opting-out provisions in federal programs could impair the federal government's role in redistributing funds
to the poorer regions. But the separation of Quebec suggested an even
greater threat to that role. The one Liberal and three Conservative premiers from the region all accepted the accord.

The theoretical attack on federal subsidies most directly threatened
the Atlantic region in the area of transportation. At the beginning of the

decade, Transport Canada appeared sympathetic to the railways' desire to cut back unremunerative activities, including passenger services and branch lines. It funded studies critical of both the rates established by the Crow's Nest Pass Agreement in western Canada and the various rate subsidies in the Atlantic region. Negotiations with western leaders ultimately resulted, in 1984, in the termination of the Crow freight rates in return for payments of about $650 million a year and the protection of most railway lines on the Prairies – the so-called 'grain-bearing' lines. In the Atlantic region the subsidies to reduce regional rates under the Maritime Freight Rates Act of 1927, which had been extended to trucking under the Atlantic Provinces Freight Rates Assistance Act of 1969, appeared threatened when in 1983 the federal government hired a consulting firm to investigate the impact of their termination. Regional leaders breathed a sigh of relief when, J.F. Hickling's study having reported that up to 12,000 jobs were dependent on the subsidies, transportation minister Don Mazankowski promised their continuation.[10]

Nevertheless, with potential allies in the West largely neutralized by the 1984 Crow-rate settlement, the Atlantic provinces seemed to bear the brunt of new initiatives. In 1985 in a policy paper entitled 'Freedom to Move,' the federal government announced its conversion to 'deregulation.' Besides freeing railways from rate regulation, or even having to publish the rates charged, the new policies also released them from considerations of 'national interest' in the abandonment of branch lines and other services on which the railways were losing money. In the Atlantic region, CNR announced its plans to close its repair shops in Moncton – a policy not unrelated to the corporation's plans to terminate railway services in Newfoundland and Prince Edward Island, and to reduce road beds in New Brunswick and Nova Scotia by 45 and 39 per cent respectively. While such changes meant loss of service and potential rate inequities for regional producers, these appeared less serious in an age when most freight already moved by truck. Yet this reality in turn highlighted the problem of deteriorating highways and the diversion of transportation responsibilities to the provinces without any accompanying transfer in financial resources.[11]

The federal government continued to direct economic development funds into the Atlantic provinces, though the region's share of such funds appeared to decline. Ottawa did not implement the recommendation of the Macdonald Commission for the channelling of development money to the provinces on the basis of a 'need' formula similar to that of the equalization payments. It seemed to be taking a step in that direction in 1986 when it created the Atlantic Canada Opportunities Agency (ACOA) as a successor to the Department of Regional Industrial Expansion (DRIE), which in 1982 had replaced the Department of Regional Economic Expansion (DREE). Funded with half a billion dollars over five years, it was supposed to function from a regional headquarters and be in a position to respond quickly and sensitively to regional needs for development capital. But when the government established a similar agency for feeding federal development funds into western Canada, once again the line between 'need' and political expediency became sadly blurred.

The most important recommendation of the Macdonald Commission was not implemented until the end of 1987 when Canadian and American negotiators produced a free-trade agreement. In a rare exercise of its legislative power the Canadian Senate refused to sanction the treaty, thus forcing the government to seek public approval in a federal election. As the contest neared in the fall of 1988, the free-trade issue seemed to dwarf all others in the campaign. With a few notable exceptions, large corporations lined up with the Conservatives in support of the agreement. Proponents of the deal expressed a fear of looming protectionism in the United States and the need for a larger market in light of a trend towards large international trade blocs. Critics argued that too much had been surrendered and that resulting pressures to make business competitive would undermine programs for health, social welfare, and regional development. In the Atlantic provinces advocates of the agreement cited new opportunities for business and invoked the myth of historic trade ties with New England. Opponents talked of potential job losses, particularly in the primary manufacturing sector and of the threat to social programs and fiscal transfers.

To the extent that the election can be interpreted as a referendum on the free-trade agreement, Atlantic residents registered a decisive no. On election night the trends, which would end in the government's re-election, appeared only after the results began to filter in from time zones farther west. In the Atlantic region, though the 'anti' vote was divided between two opposition parties, the Conservatives won but twelve of thirty-two seats. They received 41 per cent of the popular vote compared with 46 for the Liberals and about 11 per cent for the NDP.[12]

With the election over and the free-trade agreement reaffirmed, the regional implications in the government's neo-conservative program became increasingly apparent. The session of 1989 saw cutbacks in unemployment insurance eligibility and the announcement that, despite the pre-election tax cuts, a deficit crisis would require draconian cutbacks in general expenditures. Trial balloons were floated to see which of the programs targeted for elimination could marshal the strongest defences. The Atlantic provinces were among the weakest politically, and here the cuts were the most severe. Four of their military bases were slated for reduction or elimination. Annual railway subsidies of $35 million to support flour and grain traffic through Halifax and Saint John were

cancelled. Passenger subsidies were cut in half, signalling sweeping reductions in future services. The principle of universality in social programs was finally breached through a tax-back provision in old-age
pensions. The negotiations of development agreements with provincial
governments were delayed, and these were substantially scaled down.
ACOA funding was reduced, although that of its western counterpart
remained unchanged. Meanwhile, the proposed tax reforms suggested
windfall profits for the centrally located manufacturing sector, while
hinterland residents braced for a new tax on the sale of goods and
services – a tax the impact of which was compounded by the higher
provincial sales taxes in the region. These strategic losses for the region
came in a period of boom. Their full impact would be realized only in
the downturn in the economic cycle that was still to come.

In retrospect, regional interests in the Atlantic provinces appeared to
be the victims of an economic philosophy that was international in origin
and difficult to resist in the Canadian context. But how well did Atlantic
leaders manoeuvre to limit the damage, to slow the process until their
interests could be protected, and to keep their needs and concerns force-
fully before planners and decision makers at the national level? Here,
compared with other periods in their history, they do not show well.
They had often been successful in the past in influencing national policies to their advantage. In the 1870s, 1880s, and 1890s Maritime representatives secured tariff protection for their products and a substantial
share in railway developments. In the 1920s they fought reverses by
mounting a conspicuous public agitation and by punishing politicians
who ignored their demands. Their own analyses of their constitutional
interests in the early 1930s enabled them to influence the Rowell-Sirois
Commission in its investigations. Thanks in part to the persistent efforts
of Atlantic politicians and bureaucrats, that commission's ideas came to
fruition in an evolving constitutional accommodation of the Atlantic
provinces in the 1950s, 1960s, and 1970s.

The one factor common to virtually all the region's past gains was
the provinces' ability to identify mutual interests and to co-operate in
their pursuit. The divisions among the four provinces have seldom been
more pronounced than they were in the 1980s. To Newfoundland's Brian
Peckford, who had succeeded Frank Moores as Conservative premier in
1979, the regional perspective offered few attractions. Thanks to the
Hibernia offshore gas and oil discoveries, the 200-mile limit with new
policies of fish-stock management, and soaring energy prices, Peckford
looked forward to the escape of his resource-rich province from the
region's 'have-not' status. Such expectations and the barriers in their
way seemed primarily provincial. It was Newfoundland alone that had
somehow to persuade Quebec to share its windfall profits from the

Churchill Falls contract or at least to allow further hydro development. It was Newfoundland that had to gain control over the potential royalties and other benefits from Hibernia. It was Newfoundland that had the most at stake in greater provincial control of the fisheries.[13] From this perspective it was easy to view the Maritime provinces as potential competitors in such matters as the allocation of fish stocks and the reaping of benefits from offshore oil. Even in the issue of transportation, the province's Sullivan Commission of 1978–9 seemed to find more threat to Newfoundland's transportation interests from its Maritime neighbours than from the railway corporation that was seeking to close its lines.[14]

Peckford was conspicuously absent from the public conference of 1981 hosted by Maritime premiers to discuss common constitutional concerns. With bursts of rhetoric he launched his province's own campaign to demand from the federal government access to the 'economic levers' in offshore oil and gas, hydro export, and fisheries. His campaign did not fare well. In 1983 provincial legislation intended to force Quebec back to the bargaining table on the Churchill Falls contract was overturned by the courts. A similar ruling met his province's claims to offshore oil and gas.[15] Meanwhile, the federal government was not disposed to surrender any of its power over the fisheries or to offend Quebec with the construction of an interprovincial power line. Peckford's only apparent success came in 1985 in an agreement with the newly elected federal Conservatives for the development of Hibernia – an agreement that claimed to 'recognize the right of Newfoundland and Labrador to be the principal beneficiary of the oil and gas resources off its shores.'[16]

Newfoundland not only confronted the *realpolitik* of traditional federal-provincial relations but also suffered disproportionately from forces beyond provincial or regional control. Most damaging was the failure of the cod and other fish stocks as federal management estimates proved over-optimistic. Thus the restructuring of the fisheries following the Kirby task force of 1983 involved a defensive downsizing of the industry through slashes in quotas, the concentration of capital, and the permanent closure of processing plants. Slumping oil prices, too, seemed to push offshore gas and oil developments ever farther into the future. The year 1983 also saw the European Economic Community respond to the emotional propaganda of environmentalists with a ban on the import of 'seal pup' skins, thus sounding the death knell of another traditional industry.[17]

By mid-decade the province undertook a reassessment of its goals through a Royal Commission on Employment and Unemployment. Eschewing previous dreams of quick fixes through oil, hydro, or fisheries, the commission's report offered suggestions as to how existing industries could be stabilized or improved. The report cited the flaws in previous economic studies, which ignored the importance of occupational pluralism and household production in the local economy. In recognizing the prominent role played by these elements, especially in conjunction with unemployment insurance and other transfers, the report offered an analysis capable of broad regional application. 'To an important degree, we *are* part of an Atlantic regional economy,' the commissioners wrote. Yet they were not prepared to recommend that the government depart from the previous policy of '"non-alignment" with the Maritime Provinces.' While the province 'should not isolate itself from those Atlantic Region initiatives from which it can benefit,' it was important that it maintain its identity as a 'distinct region' in its dealings with Ottawa.[18]

If Newfoundland continued to go its own way on the major issues facing the region, there was little evidence of much active policy coordination among the other three. There was, for example, no Maritime presentation before the Macdonald Commission. Rather than influencing ideas at their inception, the provinces seemed to react in a belated, ad hoc fashion. Thus the Liberal government of Joe Ghiz in Prince Edward Island supported the Meech Lake Accord, attacked the free-trade deal, and announced its intention of fighting the closure of its railways. Frank McKenna's Liberal government, newly elected in New Brunswick in 1986, delayed the implementation of Meech Lake, but supported the free-trade agreement, even against the opposition of the federal Liberal Party. McKenna had little to say about the railway closures, but waged an unsuccessful campaign for federal help in the upgrading of the Trans-Canada Highway through New Brunswick. Nova Scotia's Conservative premier, John Buchanan, supported free trade and Meech Lake, but gave little encouragement to those fighting the closure of his province's branch lines. Brian Peckford's Conservative administration in Newfoundland supported free trade and Meech Lake, and also secured a separate deal for the province by which the federal government's constitutional responsibility for the railway was exchanged for fifteen years of assistance with the Trans-Canada Highway. In 1988 Peckford's successor, Liberal Clyde Wells, threatened to rescind approval for Meech Lake as tending to undermine efforts to overcome regional disparity.

Provincial divisions were not the only ones weakening the region through this period. Cutbacks to Via Rail's passenger services in 1982 brought little protest from the Atlantic Provinces Transportation Commission, which seemed to identify its interests exclusively with those of the shippers. Labour – in other decades a prominent force in the defence of regional interest – and the individual municipalities were left to fight alone in defence of the Moncton repair shops. On the issue of passenger services they joined a national organization, Transportation 2000, which supported the retention of public transportation on environmental grounds. In the crises of the 1989 cutbacks, two transportation lobbies were to be found competing for public attention in the region; one defending Via Rail, the other the railway subsidies.

In rejecting the free-trade agreement in the election of 1988, a majority of Atlantic voters were continuing a tradition of seeking national integration, a goal that, as this study shows, they had supported surprisingly consistently over more than a century of Confederation. Many had imbibed the dream of nationhood in the 1860s and sought integration politically and economically in succeeding decades. Even the secession and protest traditions so prominent in the 1880s and 1920s were largely fuelled by frustration at inequities in the union. Maritimers wanted in, not out. They wanted to be full participants on the basis of equality, in a country with a constitutional framework and a financial base that would render this possible. Making Confederation equitable proved no easy task, as the growth of central metropolises steadily undermined initial financial agreements. Joined by Newfoundlanders, Maritimers pursued the goal of constitutional accommodation with considerable success, acquiring in the process an ever-greater vested interest in the preservation of a strong and united Canada.

After the rapid changes in their nation's constitutional and economic orientation during the 1980s, they now face a formidable challenge both in identifying and in defending the region's long-term interests. Here a starting point might be the reflection on past experiences, on those policies and strategies that worked and those that did not. These suggest that the region's past achievements in this area have rested primarily upon the ingenuity and persistence of the people of the Atlantic provinces.

# Election Data

New Brunswick general elections since Confederation

| Year | Liberals | Conservatives | Others |
|------|----------|---------------|--------|
| 1870* | 16 | 24 | 1 |
| 1874* | 5 | 35 | 1 |
| 1878* | 10 | 31 | 0 |
| 1882* | 22 | 18 | 0 |
| 1886* | 33 | 8 | 0 |
| 1890 | 26 | 15 | 0 |
| 1892 | 25 | 12 | 4 |
| 1895 | 34 | 9 | 3 |
| 1899 | 40 | 4 | 2 |
| 1903 | 33 | 10 | 3 |
| 1908 | 12 | 31 | 3 |
| 1912 | 2 | 44 | 2 |
| 1917 | 27 | 21 | 0 |
| 1920 | 24 | 13 | 11 |
| 1925 | 11 | 37 | 0 |
| 1930 | 17 | 31 | 0 |
| 1935 | 43 | 5 | 0 |
| 1939 | 29 | 19 | 0 |
| 1944 | 37 | 11 | 0 |
| 1948 | 47 | 5 | 0 |
| 1952 | 16 | 36 | 0 |
| 1956 | 15 | 37 | 0 |
| 1960 | 31 | 21 | 0 |
| 1963 | 32 | 20 | 0 |
| 1967 | 32 | 26 | 0 |
| 1970 | 26 | 32 | 0 |
| 1974 | 25 | 33 | 0 |
| 1978 | 28 | 30 | 0 |
| 1982 | 18 | 39 | 0 |
| 1987 | 58 | 0 | 0 |

SOURCES: Calvin A. Woodward, *The History of New Brunswick Provincial Election Cam-

*paigns and Platforms, 1866–1874* (Toronto 1976); Paul W. Fox (ed.), *Politics Canada*, 5th ed. (Toronto 1982); New Brunswick Legislative Library, *Elections in New Brunswick* (Fredericton 1984); Howard Scarrow, *Canada Votes: A Handbook of Federal and Provincial Election Data* (New Orleans 1962)

Others: 1870 (1 Independent); 1874 (1 Independent); 1892 (4 Independent); 1895 (3 Independent); 1899 (2 Independent); 1903 (3 Independent); 1908 (3 Independent); 1920 (9 United Farmer; 2 Labour)

*Denotes loose affiliation with the national party. Affiliation with the national parties was slow to develop in New Brunswick provincial politics. It was not until 1935 that the New Brunswick Liberals officially ran under the party banner, and not until 1943 that the Conservatives followed suit. By this time, however, close ties with the national parties had been a reality for decades. The early provincial elections tended to focus on particular issues; the election of 1874, for example, was fought almost exclusively over the question of sectarian or non-sectarian schools. During the period from 1870 to 1890, individual members of the Legislative Assembly tended to align themselves with the party that came closest to their own concerns and often changed parties when it was in their best interests. The characteristics of the modern party system emerged after Andrew Blair gained the premiership in 1883. Blair's government imposed party discipline on its supporters, instituted the nomination of candidates by party convention, and presented the first province-wide campaign platform in 1890.

Premiers of New Brunswick
(C – Conservative; L – Liberal; PC – Progressive Conservative)

| Premier | Term of Office | Party |
| --- | --- | --- |
| Andrew Wetmore | 1867–70 | C |
| George King | 1870–71 | C |
| George Hatheway | 1871–72 | C |
| George King | 1872–78 | C |
| James Fraser | 1878–82 | C |
| Daniel Hanington | 1882–83 | C |
| Andrew Blair | 1883–96 | L |
| James Mitchell | 1896–97 | L |
| Henry Emmerson | 1897–1900 | L |
| Lemuel Tweedie | 1900–7 | L |
| William Pugsley | 1907 | L |
| Clifford Robinson | 1907–8 | L |
| John D. Hazen | 1908–11 | C |
| James K. Flemming | 1911–14 | C |
| George Clarke | 1914–17 | C |
| James Murray | 1917 | C |
| Walter Foster | 1917–23 | L |
| Peter Veniot | 1923–25 | L |
| John Baxter | 1925–31 | C |
| Charles Richards | 1931–33 | C |
| Leonard Tilley | 1933–35 | C |
| Allison Dysart | 1935–40 | L |
| John McNair | 1940–52 | L |
| Hugh John Flemming | 1952–60 | PC |

Premiers of New Brunswick (cont'd)
(C – Conservative; L – Liberal; PC – Progressive Conservative)

| Premier | Term of Office | Party |
|---|---|---|
| Louis Robichaud | 1960–70 | L |
| Richard Hatfield | 1970–87 | PC |
| Francis McKenna | 1987– | L |

Nova Scotia general elections since Confederation

| Year | Liberals | Conservatives | Others |
|---|---|---|---|
| 1867 | 36 | 2 | 0 |
| 1871 | 24 | 14 | 0 |
| 1874 | 24 | 14 | 0 |
| 1878 | 8 | 30 | 0 |
| 1882 | 24 | 14 | 0 |
| 1886 | 29 | 8 | 1 |
| 1890 | 28 | 10 | 0 |
| 1894 | 25 | 13 | 0 |
| 1897 | 35 | 3 | 0 |
| 1901 | 36 | 2 | 0 |
| 1906 | 32 | 5 | 1 |
| 1911 | 27 | 11 | 0 |
| 1916 | 30 | 13 | 0 |
| 1920 | 29 | 3 | 11 |
| 1925 | 3 | 40 | 0 |
| 1928 | 20 | 23 | 0 |
| 1933 | 22 | 8 | 0 |
| 1937 | 25 | 5 | 0 |
| 1941 | 23 | 4 | 3 |
| 1945 | 28 | 0 | 2 |
| 1949 | 28 | 7 | 2 |
| 1953 | 23 | 12 | 2 |
| 1956 | 18 | 24 | 1 |
| 1960 | 15 | 27 | 1 |
| 1963 | 4 | 39 | 0 |
| 1967 | 6 | 40 | 0 |
| 1970 | 23 | 21 | 2 |
| 1974 | 31 | 12 | 3 |
| 1978 | 17 | 31 | 4 |
| 1981 | 13 | 37 | 2 |
| 1984 | 6 | 42 | 4 |
| 1988 | 21 | 28 | 3 |

SOURCE: J.M. Beck *Politics of Nova Scotia*, 2 vols (Tantallon, N.S. 1985, 1988); *Canadian Parliamentary Guide*.

Others: 1886 (1 Independent); 1906 (1 Independent); 1920 (7 Farmer; 4 Labour); 1941 (3 CCF); 1945 (2 CCF); 1949 (2 CCF); 1953 (2 CCF); 1956 (1 CCF); 1960 (1 CCF); 1970 (2 NDP); 1974 (3 NDP); 1978 (4 NDP); 1981 (2 NDP); 1984 (3 NDP; 1 Cape Breton Labour); 1988 (2 NDP; 1 Independent)

*Confederation provoked a realignment of politicians as pro- and anti-Confederates. The former were allied nationally with the Macdonald Conservatives, and the latter gradually allied themselves with his Liberal opponents.

Premiers of Nova Scotia
(Anti-Conf. – Anti-Confederate; Conf. – Confederate; C – Conservative; L – Liberal; PC – Progressive Conservative)

| Premier | Term of office | Party |
|---|---|---|
| Hiram Blanchard | 1867 | Conf. |
| William Annand | 1867–75 | Anti-Conf. |
| P.C. Hill | 1875–8 | L |
| Simon H. Holmes | 1878–82 | C |
| J.S.D. Thompson | 1882 | C |
| W.T. Pipes | 1882–4 | L |
| W.S. Fielding | 1884–96 | L |
| George H. Murray | 1896–1923 | L |
| Ernest H. Armstrong | 1923–5 | L |
| Edgar N. Rhodes | 1925–30 | C |
| Gordon S. Harrington | 1930–3 | C |
| Angus L. Macdonald | 1933–40, 1945–54 | L |
| Alexander S. MacMillan | 1940–5 | L |
| Harold J. Connolly | 1954 | L |
| Henry D. Hicks | 1954–6 | L |
| Robert L. Stanfield | 1956–67 | PC |
| George I. Smith | 1967–70 | PC |
| Gerald A. Regan | 1970–8 | L |
| John M. Buchanan | 1978–91 | PC |

Prince Edward Island general elections since Confederation

| Year | Liberals | Conservatives | Others |
|---|---|---|---|
| 1873* | 10 | 20 | 0 |
| 1876* | 19 (free school) | 11 (denominational) | 0 |
| 1879 | 4 | 24 | 2** |
| 1883 | 9 | 19 | 2** |
| 1886 | 12 | 18 | 0 |
| 1890 | 15 | 15 | 0 |
| 1893 | 32 | 7 | 0 |
| 1897 | 21 | 9 | 0 |
| 1900 | 21 | 9 | 0 |
| 1904 | 22 | 8 | 0 |
| 1908 | 16 | 14 | 0 |
| 1912 | 2 | 28 | 0 |
| 1915 | 13 | 17 | 0 |
| 1919 | 25 | 4 | 1 |
| 1923 | 5 | 25 | 0 |
| 1927 | 24 | 6 | 0 |

Prince Edward Island general elections since Confederation (cont'd)

| Year | Liberals | Conservatives | Others |
|------|----------|---------------|--------|
| 1931 | 12 | 18 | 0 |
| 1935 | 30 | 0 | 0 |
| 1939 | 27 | 3 | 0 |
| 1943 | 20 | 10 | 0 |
| 1947 | 24 | 6 | 0 |
| 1951 | 24 | 6 | 0 |
| 1955 | 27 | 3 | 0 |
| 1959 | 8 | 22 | 0 |
| 1962 | 11 | 19 | 0 |
| 1966 | 17 | 15 | 0 |
| 1970 | 27 | 5 | 0 |
| 1974 | 26 | 6 | 0 |
| 1978 | 17 | 15 | 0 |
| 1979 | 11 | 21 | 0 |
| 1982 | 11 | 21 | 0 |
| 1986 | 21 | 11 | 0 |
| 1989 | 30 | 2 | 0 |

SOURCES: Ian Ross Robertson, 'Religion, Politics and Education in Prince Edward Island', (MA thesis, McGill University 1968); *Canadian Parliamentary Guide*; Paul W. Fox (ed.), *Politics Canada*, 5th ed. (Toronto 1982); Howard Scarrow, *Canada Votes: A Handbook of Federal and Provincial Election Data* (New Orleans 1962); *Evening Patriot* (Charlottetown)

Others: 1919 (1 Independent)

*The development of the present party system in Prince Edward Island was inhibited in the 1870s by the 'School Question.' During the election of 1876, parties with a strong denominational element formed around the issue of free vs religious schools. The Liberal and Conservative parties re-emerged as distinct political entities in the 1880s, after W.W. Sullivan became premier in 1879.

**No party affiliation could be found for two successful candidates in the 1879 election: Donald Montgomery, 4th District, Queen's County; Lauchlin McDonald, 1st District, King's. No party affiliation could be found for two successful candidates in the 1883 election: A.D. MacMillan, 4th District, Queen's; J.E. Robertson, MD, 4th District, King's.

Premiers of Prince Edward Island
(Coal. – Coalition; C – Conservative; L – Liberal; PC – Progressive Conservative)

| Premier | Term of office | Party |
|---------|----------------|-------|
| J.C. Pope | 1873 | C |
| L.C. Owen | 1873–6 | C |
| L.H. Davies | 1876–9 | Coal. |
| W.W. Sullivan | 1879–89 | C |
| Neil Macleod | 1889–91 | C |
| Frederick Peters | 1891–7 | L |
| A.B. Warburton | 1897–8 | L |
| Donald Farquharson | 1898–1901 | L |
| Arthur Peters | 1901–8 | L |

Premiers of Prince Edward Island (cont'd)
(Coal. – Coalition; C – Conservative; L – Liberal; PC – Progressive Conservative)

| Premier | Term of office | Party |
|---|---|---|
| F.L. Haszard | 1908–11 | L |
| H. James Palmer | 1911 | L |
| John A Mathieson | 1911–17 | C |
| A.E. Arsenault | 1917–19 | C |
| J.H. Bell | 1919–23 | L |
| James D. Stewart | 1923–7 | C |
| Albert C. Saunders | 1927–30 | L |
| Walter M. Lea | 1930–1 | L |
| James D. Stewart | 1931–3 | C |
| Wm. J.P. MacMillan | 1933–5 | C |
| Walter M. Lea | 1935–6 | L |
| Thane A. Campbell | 1936–43 | L |
| J. Walter Jones | 1943–53 | L |
| A.W. Matheson | 1953–9 | L |
| Walter R. Shaw | 1959–66 | PC |
| Alexander B. Campbell | 1966–78 | L |
| W. Bennett Campbell | 1978–9 | L |
| J. Angus MacLean | 1979–81 | PC |
| James M. Lee | 1981–6 | PC |
| Joseph A. Ghiz | 1986– | L |

Newfoundland general elections since 1949

| Date | Liberal | Conservative | Other |
|---|---|---|---|
| 1949 | 22 | 5 | 1 |
| 1951 | 23 | 5 | 0 |
| 1956 | 32 | 4 | 0 |
| 1959 | 31 | 3 | 2 |
| 1962 | 34 | 7 | 1 |
| 1966 | 39 | 3 | 0 |
| 1971 | 21 | 20 | 1 |
| 1972 | 9 | 33 | 0 |
| 1975 | 16 | 30 | 5 |
| 1979 | 19 | 33 | 0 |
| 1982 | 8 | 44 | 0 |
| 1985 | 14 | 37 | 1 |
| 1988 | 31 | 21 | 0 |

SOURCES: *Encyclopedia of Newfoundland and Labrador*, 3 vols (St John's 1981) vol. 1; Paul W. Fox (ed.), *Politics Canada*, 5th ed. (Toronto 1982); *Canadian Parliamentary Guide*

Others: 1949 (1 Independent); 1959 (2 United Newfoundland Party); 1962 (1 Independent); 1971 (1 New Labrador Party); 1975 (4 Liberal Reform; 1 Independent Liberal); 1985 (1 NDP)

Premiers of Newfoundland
(L – Liberal; PC – Progressive Conservative)

| Premier | Term of office | Party |
|---|---|---|
| Joseph R. Smallwood | 1949–72 | L |
| Frank D. Moores | 1972–9 | PC |
| A. Brian Peckford | 1979–89 | PC |
| Thomas G. Rideout | 1989 | PC |
| Clyde K. Wells | 1989– | L |

Results of Canadian federal elections in the Atlantic provinces
(C – Conservative; L – Liberal; O – Other)

| Year | N.B. | | | N.S. | | | P.E.I. | | | Nfld | | |
|---|---|---|---|---|---|---|---|---|---|---|---|---|
| | L | C | O | L | C | O | L | C | O | L | C | O |
| 1867 | 7 | 8 | – | 18 | 1 | – | | | | | | |
| 1872 | 9 | 7 | – | 11 | 10 | – | | | | | | |
| 1874 | 11 | 5 | – | 18 | 3 | – | 6 | – | – | | | |
| 1878 | 11 | 5 | – | 7 | 14 | – | 5 | 1 | – | | | |
| 1882 | 7 | 9 | – | 7 | 14 | – | 4 | 2 | – | | | |
| 1887 | 6 | 10 | – | 7 | 14 | – | 6 | 0 | – | | | |
| 1891 | 3 | 13 | – | 5 | 16 | – | 4 | 2 | – | | | |
| 1896 | 5 | 9 | – | 10 | 10 | – | 2 | 3 | – | | | |
| 1900 | 9 | 5 | – | 15 | 5 | – | 3 | 2 | – | | | |
| 1904 | 7 | 6 | – | 18 | – | – | 1 | 3 | – | | | |
| 1908 | 11 | 2 | – | 12 | 6 | – | 3 | 1 | – | | | |
| 1911 | 8 | 5 | – | 9 | 9 | – | 2 | 2 | – | | | |
| 1917 | 4 | 7 | – | 4 | 12 | – | 2 | 2 | – | | | |
| 1921 | 5 | 5 | 1 | 16 | – | – | 4 | – | – | | | |
| 1925 | 1 | 10 | – | 3 | 11 | – | 2 | 2 | – | | | |
| 1926 | 4 | 7 | – | 2 | 12 | – | 3 | 1 | – | | | |
| 1930 | 1 | 10 | – | 4 | 10 | – | 1 | 3 | – | | | |
| 1935 | 9 | 1 | – | 12 | – | – | 4 | – | – | | | |
| 1940 | 5 | 5 | – | 10 | 1 | 1 | 4 | – | – | | | |
| 1945 | 7 | 3 | – | 9 | 2 | 1 | 3 | 1 | – | | | |
| 1949 | 8 | 2 | – | 10 | 2 | 1 | 3 | 1 | – | 5 | 2 | – |
| 1953 | 7 | 3 | – | 10 | 1 | 1 | 3 | 1 | – | 7 | – | – |
| 1957 | 5 | 5 | – | 2 | 10 | – | – | 4 | – | 5 | 2 | – |
| 1958 | 3 | 7 | – | – | 12 | – | – | 4 | – | 5 | 2 | – |
| 1962 | 6 | 4 | – | 2 | 9 | 1 | – | 4 | – | 6 | 1 | – |
| 1963 | 6 | 4 | – | 5 | 7 | – | 2 | 2 | – | 7 | – | – |
| 1965 | 6 | 4 | – | 2 | 10 | – | – | 4 | – | 7 | – | – |
| 1968 | 5 | 5 | – | 1 | 10 | – | – | 4 | – | 1 | 6 | – |
| 1972 | 5 | 5 | – | 1 | 10 | – | 1 | 3 | – | 3 | 4 | – |
| 1974 | 6 | 3 | 1 | 2 | 8 | 1 | 1 | 3 | – | 4 | 3 | – |
| 1979 | 6 | 4 | – | 2 | 8 | 1 | – | 4 | – | 4 | 2 | 1 |
| 1980 | 7 | 3 | – | 5 | 6 | – | 2 | 2 | – | 5 | 2 | – |
| 1984 | 1 | 9 | – | 2 | 9 | – | 1 | 3 | – | 3 | 4 | – |
| 1988 | 5 | 5 | – | 6 | 5 | – | 4 | – | – | 5 | 2 | – |

Others: 1921 N.B. (1 Progressive); 1940 N.S. (1 CCF); 1945 N.S. (1 CCF); 1949 N.S. (1 CCF); 1953 N.S. (1 CCF); 1962 N.S. (1 NDP); 1974 N.B. (1 Independent), N.S. (1 NDP); 1979 N.S. (1 NDP), Nfld (1 NDP)

Regional outcome of Canadian general elections

| Year | No. of seats | Liberal | Conservative | Other |
|------|-------------|---------|--------------|-------|
| 1867 | 34 | 25 | 9 | 0 |
| 1872 | 37 | 20 | 17 | 0 |
| 1874 | 43 | 35 | 8 | 0 |
| 1878 | 43 | 19 | 24 | 0 |
| 1882 | 43 | 18 | 25 | 0 |
| 1887 | 43 | 19 | 24 | 0 |
| 1891 | 43 | 12 | 31 | 0 |
| 1896 | 39 | 17 | 22 | 0 |
| 1900 | 39 | 27 | 12 | 0 |
| 1904 | 35 | 26 | 9 | 0 |
| 1908 | 35 | 26 | 9 | 0 |
| 1911 | 35 | 19 | 16 | 0 |
| 1917 | 31 | 10 | 21 | 0 |
| 1921 | 31 | 25 | 5 | 1 |
| 1925 | 29 | 6 | 23 | 0 |
| 1926 | 29 | 9 | 20 | 0 |
| 1930 | 29 | 6 | 23 | 0 |
| 1935 | 26 | 25 | 1 | 0 |
| 1940 | 26 | 19 | 6 | 1 |
| 1945 | 26 | 19 | 6 | 1 |
| 1949 | 34 | 26 | 7 | 1 |
| 1953 | 33 | 27 | 5 | 1 |
| 1957 | 33 | 12 | 21 | 0 |
| 1958 | 33 | 8 | 25 | 0 |
| 1962 | 33 | 14 | 18 | 1 |
| 1963 | 33 | 20 | 13 | 0 |
| 1965 | 33 | 15 | 18 | 0 |
| 1968 | 32 | 7 | 25 | 0 |
| 1972 | 32 | 10 | 22 | 0 |
| 1974 | 32 | 13 | 17 | 2 |
| 1979 | 32 | 12 | 18 | 2 |
| 1980 | 32 | 19 | 13 | 0 |
| 1984 | 32 | 7 | 25 | 0 |
| 1988 | 32 | 20 | 12 | 0 |

SOURCE: J.M. Beck, *Pendulum of Power: Canada's Federal Elections* (Scarborough 1968); *Canadian Parliamentary Guide*, 1988; *Herald* (Halifax), 1988

# Notes

ABBREVIATIONS

CAR   *Canadian Annual Review of Public Affairs*
CHAAR   Canadian Historical Association, *Annual Report*
CHAHP   Canadian Historical Association, *Historical Papers*
CHCD   Canada, House of Commons, *Debates*
CHR   *Canadian Historical Review*
Dal   Dalhousie University
DCB   *Dictionary of Canadian Biography*
DR   *Dalhousie Review*
Hs/SH   *Histoire sociale / Social History*
JCS   *Journal of Canadian Studies*
JHA   *Journals of House of Assembly*
L / Le t   *Labour / Le travailleur* (now *Labour / Le travail*)
NAC   National Archives of Canada
NBM   New Brunswick Museum
NS   *Newfoundland Studies*
NSHS   Nova Scotia Historical Society
PANB   Provincial Archives of New Brunswick
PANS   Public Archives of Nova Scotia
PAPEI   Provincial Archives of Prince Edward Island
QQ   *Queen's Quarterly*
SMU   Saint Mary's University
TRSC   *Transactions of the Royal Society of Canada*
UNB   University of New Brunswick
UWO   University of Western Ontario

## Preface

1 Among reviews of the trends in regional historical writing, see Gail G.

Campbell, 'Canadian Women's History: A View from Atlantic Canada,' *Acadiensis* 20:1 (Autumn 1990); Judith Fingard, 'Ideas on the Periphery or Peripheral Ideas?: The Intellectual and Cultural History of Atlantic Canada,' *JCS* 24:3 (Autumn 1989); Janine Brodie, 'The Political Economy of Regionalism,' in Wallace Clement and Glen Williams (eds), *Canadian Political Economy* (Montreal and Kingston 1989); Phillip A. Buckner, 'Limited Identities and Canadian Historical Scholarship: An Atlantic Provinces Perspective,' *JCS* 23:1–2 (Spring–Summer 1988); I.R. Robertson, 'Historical Writing on Prince Edward Island since 1975,' *Acadiensis* 18:1 (Autumn 1988); Eric W. Sager, 'Dependency, Underdevelopment and the Economic History of the Atlantic Provinces,' *Acadiensis*, 17:1 (Autumn 1987); John G. Reid, 'Towards the Elusive Synthesis: The Atlantic Provinces in Recent General Treatments of Canadian History,' *Acadiensis*, 16:2 (Spring 1987); Phillip A. Buckner (ed.), *Teaching Maritime Studies* (Fredericton 1986); Terrence Murphy, 'The Religious History of Atlantic Canada: The State of the Art,' *Acadiensis* 15:1 (Autumn 1985); W.G. Godfrey, '"A New Golden Age": Recent Historical Writing on the Maritimes,' *QQ*, 76:1 (Spring 1984); Peter Neary, 'The Writing of Newfoundland History: An Introductory Survey,' in Peter Neary and James K. Hiller (eds), *Newfoundland in the Nineteenth and Twentieth Centuries: Essays in Interpretation* (Toronto 1980); E.R. Forbes, 'In Search of a Post-Confederation Maritime Historiography,' *Acadiensis* 8:1 (Autumn 1978), reprinted in E.R. Forbes, *Challenging the Regional Stereotype: Essays on the 20th-Century Maritimes* (Fredericton 1989); Margaret Conrad, 'The Birth of Canada's Past: A Decade of Women's History,' *Acadiensis* 12:2 (Spring 1983).

## Prologue: The Atlantic Colonies before Confederation

1 Alan G. Macpherson (ed.), *The Atlantic Provinces* (Toronto 1972); John Warkentin, 'The Atlantic Colonies,' in John Warkentin and Cole Harris, *Canada before Confederation* (Toronto 1974); Graeme Wynn, 'The Maritimes: The Geography of Fragmentation and Underdevelopment,' and Michael Staveley, 'Newfoundland: Economy and Society at the Margin,' in L.D. McCann, *Heartland and Hinterland: A Geography of Canada* (Toronto 1987)

2 L.S.F. Upton, *Micmacs and Colonists: White-Indian Relations in the Maritime Provinces, 1712–1867* (Vancouver 1975); F.W. Rowe, *Extinction: The Beothuks of Newfoundland* (Toronto 1977); Ralph T. Pastore, 'The Collapse of the Beothuk World,' *Acadiensis* 19:1 (Autumn 1989); Ingeborg Marshall, 'Beothuks and Micmacs: Re-examining Relationships,' *Acadiensis* 17:2 (Spring 1988); H.F. McGee (ed.), *The Native Peoples of Atlantic Canada: A History of Ethnic Interaction* (Toronto 1974); and Ruth Holmes Whitehead, 'I Have Lived Here since the World Began: Atlantic Coast Artistic Tradi-

tions,' in *The Spirit Sings: Artistic Traditions of Canada's First Peoples* (Toronto 1987)

3 J.B. Brebner, *New England's Outpost: Acadia before the Conquest of Canada* (New York 1927); A.H. Clark, *Acadia: The Geography of Early Nova Scotia to 1760* (Toronto 1966); Jean Daigle, 'Acadia, 1604–1763: An Historical Synthesis' in Jean Daigle (ed.), *The Acadians of the Maritime: Thematic Studies* (Moncton 1982); N.E.S. Griffiths (ed.), *The Acadian Deportation: Deliberate Perfidy or Cruel Necessity?* (Toronto 1969); John G. Reid, *Acadia, Maine and New England: Marginal Colonies in the Seventeenth Century* (Toronto 1981); and George A. Rawlyk, *Nova Scotia's Massachusetts: A Study of Massachusetts–Nova Scotia Relations, 1630–1784* (Montreal and Kingston 1973)

4 Margaret Conrad (ed.), *They Planted Well: New England Planters in Maritime Canada* (Fredericton 1988); W.P. Bell, *The 'Foreign Protestants' and the Settlement of Nova Scotia*, 2nd ed. (Fredericton 1990); W.S. MacNutt, *The Making of the Maritime Provinces, 1713–1784* (Ottawa 1960)

5 J.B. Brebner, *The Neutral Yankees of Nova Scotia: A Marginal Colony during the Revolutionary Years* (Toronto 1969); Neil MacKinnon, *'This Unfriendly Soil': The Loyalist Experience in Nova Scotia, 1783–1791* (Kingston and Montreal 1984)

6 J.M. Bumstead, *The People's Clearances, 1770–1815: Highland Emigration to British North America* (Edinburgh 1982); R.A. MacLean and D. Campbell, *Beyond the Atlantic Roar: The Scots of Eastern Nova Scotia* (Toronto 1974)

7 J.M. Bumstead, *Land, Settlement, and Politics in Eighteenth-Century Prince Edward Island* (Kingston and Montreal 1987); A.H. Clark, *Three Centuries and the Island* (Toronto 1959)

8 Francis W.P. Bolger (ed.), *Canada's Smallest Province: A History of P.E.I.* (Charlottetown 1973)

9 C. Grant Head, *Eighteenth-Century Newfoundland: A Geographer's Perspective* (Toronto 1976); Keith Matthews, *Lectures on the History of Newfoundland, 1500–1830* (St John's 1988)

10 John Mannion (ed.), *The Peopling of Newfoundland: Essays in Historical Geography* (St John's 1977); and G.E. Gunn, *The Political History of Newfoundland, 1832–1864* (Toronto 1966); F.F. Thompson, *The French Shore Problem in Newfoundland: An Imperial Study* (Toronto 1961)

11 Phillip A. Buckner, *The Transition to Responsible Government in British North America* (Westport, Conn. 1985)

12 Eric W. Sager and Gerald E. Panting, *Maritime Capital: The Shipping Industry in Atlantic Canada, 1820–1914* (Kingston and Montreal 1990)

13 T.W. Acheson, 'The Great Merchant and Economic Development in Saint John, 1820–1850,' *Acadiensis* 8:12 (Spring 1979); David Sutherland, 'Halifax Merchants and the Pursuit of Development, 1783–1850,' *CHR* 59 (1978); Julian Gwynn, 'Golden Age or Bronze Movement? Wealth and

Poverty in Nova Scotia,' *Canadian Papers in Rural History* 8 (Kingston 1991)

## 1 The 1860s: Forging the Bonds of Union

1 Phillip A. Buckner, 'The Maritimes and Confederation: A Reassessment,' in Ged Martin (ed.), *The Causes of Canadian Confederation* (Fredericton 1990) 114–29 (also in *CHR* 71) [Mar. 1990]
2 Rosemarie Langhout, 'Public Enterprise: An Analysis of Public Finance in the Maritime Colonies during the Period of Responsible Government' (PhD thesis, UNB 1989); and her 'Developing Nova Scotia: Railways and Public Accounts, 1848–1867,' *Acadiensis* 14:2 (Spring 1985); Carl M. Wallace, 'Saint John Boosters and the Railroads in Mid-Nineteenth Century,' *Acadiensis* 6:1 (Autumn 1976); Carl M. Wallce, 'Sir Samuel Leonard Tilley,' *DCB* vol. 12; and his 'Charles Fisher,' *DCB* vol. 10.
3 Ian Ross Robertson (ed.), *The Prince Edward Island Land Commission of 1860* (Fredericton 1988); and Peter Neary, 'The French and American Shore Questions in Newfoundland History,' in J.K. Hiller and Peter Neary (eds) *Newfoundland in the Nineteenth and Twentieth Centuries: Essays in Interpretation* (Toronto 1980)
4 Jean Daigle (ed.), *The Acadians of the Maritimes: Thematic Studies* (Moncton 1982); N.E.S. Griffiths, *The Acadians: Creation of a People* (Toronto 1973).
5 T.W. Acheson, *Saint John: The Making of a Colonial Urban Community* (Toronto 1984); Thomas H. Raddall, *Halifax: Warden of the North* (Toronto 1948); Judith Fingard, *The Dark Side of Life in Victorian Halifax* (Porter's Lake, N.S. 1989); Douglas Baldwin and Thomas Spira (eds), *Gaslights, Epidemics and Vagabond Cows: Charlottetown in the Victorian Era* (Charlottetown 1988); P. O'Neil, *The Oldest City: The Story of St. John's*, 2 vols (Erin, Ont. 1975); L.D. McCann, 'The Mercantile-Industrial Transition in the Metals Towns of Pictou County, 1857–1931,' *Acadiensis* 10:2 (Spring 1981); and Gerald E. Panting, 'Cradle of Enterprise: Yarmouth Nova Scotia, 1840–1889,' in Lewis R. Fischer and Eric W. Sager (eds), *The Enterprising Canadians: Entrepreneurs and Economic Development in Eastern Canada, 1820–1914* (St John's 1979)
6 Ian Ross Robertson, 'The Bible Question in Prince Edward Island from 1856 to 1860,' *Acadiensis* 5:2 (Spring 1976); and his 'Party Politics and Religious Controversialism in Prince Edward Island from 1860 to 1863,' *Acadiensis* 7:2 (Spring 1978)
7 Ian McKay, 'The Crisis of Dependent Development: Class Conflict in the Nova Scotia Coal Fields, 1872–1876,' in Gregory S. Kealey (ed.), *Class, Gender and Region: Essays in Canadian Historical Sociology* (St John's 1988); Phyllis Blakley, 'Samuel Cunard,' *DCB* vol. 10

8  H.A. Innis, *The Cod Fishery: The History of an International Economy* (Toronto 1940); B.A. Balcom, *A History of the Lunenburg Fishing Industry* (Lunenburg 1977); Shannon Ryan, *Fish out of Water: The Newfoundland Saltfish Trade, 1814–1914* (St John's 1986); Steven Antler, 'The Capitalist Underdevelopment of Nineteenth-Century Newfoundland,' in Robert J. Brym and R. James Sacouman (eds), *Underdevelopment and Social Movements in Atlantic Canada* (Toronto 1979); and David A. MacDonald, ' "They Cannot Pay Us in Money": Newman and Company and the Supplying System in the Newfoundland Fishery, 1850–1884,' *Acadiensis* 19:1 (Autumn 1989); James E. Candow, *Of Men and Seals: A History of the Newfoundland Seal Hunt* (Ottawa 1989)

9  Eric W. Sager and Gerald E. Panting, *Maritime Capital: The Shipping Industry in Atlantic Canada, 1820–1914* (Kingston and Montreal 1990); David A. Sutherland, 'Halifax Merchants and the Pursuit of Development, 1783–1850,' *CHR* 59 (1978); T.W. Acheson, 'The Great Merchant and Economic Development in Saint John, 1820–1850,' *Acadiensis* 8:2 (Spring 1979); Rosemary E. Ommer (ed.), *Merchant Credit and Labour Strategies in Historical Perspective* (Fredericton 1990)

10  L.D. McCann, ' "Living a Double Life": Town and Country in the Industrialization of the Maritimes,' in Douglas Day (ed.), *Geographical Perspectives on the Maritime Provinces* (Halifax 1988); Graeme Wynn, *Timber Colony: A Historical Geography of Early Nineteenth Century New Brunswick* (Toronto 1981); Rusty Bitterman, 'Economic Stratification and Agrarian Settlement: Middle River in the Early Nineteenth Century,' in Kenneth Donovan (ed.), *The Island: New Perspectives on Cape Breton History, 1713–1990* (Sydney and Fredericton 1990)

11  H.A. Innis, *Cod Fishery*; Ryan, *Fish out of Water*; Peter Sinclair, *From Traps to Draggers: Domestic Commodity Production in Northwest Newfoundland, 1850–1982* (St John's 1985)

12  Rusty Bitterman, 'The Hierarchy of the Soil: Land and Labour in a 19th Century Cape Breton Community,' *Acadiensis* 18:1 (Autumn 1988)

13  Judith Fingard, 'The Decline of the Sailor as Ship Labourer in 19th Century Timber Ports,' *L / Le t* 3 (1977); Judith Fingard, *Jack in Port: Sailortowns of Eastern Canada* (Toronto 1982); Ian McKay, 'Class Struggle and Mercantile Capitalism: Craftsmen and Labourers on the Halifax Waterfront, 1850–1902,' in R.E. Ommer and Gerald E. Panting (eds), *Working Men Who Got Wet* (St John's 1980)

14  Joseph Greenough, *The Halifax Citadel, 1825–1860: A Narrative and Structural History* (Ottawa 1977); Susan Buggey, 'Building Halifax, 1841–1871,' *Acadiensis* 10:1 (Autumn 1980); Daniel Francis, 'The Development of the Lunatic Asylum in the Maritime Provinces,' *Acadiensis* 6:2 (Spring 1977)

15  Eric W. Sager, *Seafaring Labour: The Merchant Marine of Atlantic Canada, 1820–1914* (Montreal 1989); Fingard, *Jack in Port*; Ommer and Panting

(eds), *Working Men Who Got Wet*

16 J.S. Martell, 'Early Coal Mining in Nova Scotia,' *DR* (1945); James M. Cameron, *The Pictonian Colliers* (Halifax 1975); Marilyn Gerriets, 'The Impact of the General Mining Association on the Early Development of the Nova Scotia Coal Industry,' *Acadiensis* 21:1 (Autumn 1991); and D.A. Muise, 'The General Mining Association and Nova Scotia's Coal, 1828–1858,' *Bulletin of Canadian Studies* (1982)

17 Richard Rice, 'The Wrights of Saint John: A Study of Ship-building and Shipping in the Maritimes, 1839–1885,' in D.S. MacMillan (ed.), *Canadian Business History, Selected Studies: 1497 to the Present* (Toronto 1972); Greg Finley, 'The Morans of Saint Martins, N.B., 1850–1880: Toward an Understanding of Family Participation in Maritime Enterprise,' in Fischer and Sager (eds), *Enterprising Canadians*; and Sager and Panting, *Maritime Capital*

18 C.B. Fergusson, *The Labour Movement in Nova Scotia before Confederation* (Halifax 1964); Kenneth G. Pryke, 'Labour and Politics: Nova Scotia at Confederation,' *Hs/SH* 6 (Nov. 1970); Richard Rice, 'A History of Organized Labour in Saint John, New Brunswick 1813–1890' (MA thesis, UNB 1968)

19 Peter M. Toner (ed.), *New Ireland Remembered: Historical Essays on the Irish in New Brunswick* (Fredericton 1988)

20 Alison Prentice, Paula Bourne, Gail Cuthbert Brandt, Beth Light, Wendy Mitchinson, Naomi Black, *Canadian Women: A History* (Toronto 1988); and Marjorie Griffin-Cohen, *Women's Work: Markets and Economic Development in Ninetenth Century Ontario* (Toronto 1988)

21 Robert Sedgewick, *The Proper Sphere: The Influence of Women in Christian Society* (Halifax 1856)

22 *Essays on the Future Destiny of Nova Scotia, Improvement of Female Education and Peace* (Halifax 1946)

23 Marilyn Porter, '"She Was Skipper of the Shore Crew": Notes on the History of the Sexual Division of Labour in Newfoundland,' *L / Le t* 15 (Spring 1985)

24 T.W. Acheson, 'A Study in the Historical Demography of a Loyalist County [Charlotte County, N.B.],' *Hs/SH* (Apr. 1968); Bitterman, 'Hierarchy of the Soil'; Alan A. Brookes, 'Out-Migration from the Maritime Provinces, 1860–1900: Some Preliminary Considerations,' *Acadiensis* 5:2 (Spring 1976); Patricia A. Thornton, 'The Problem of Out-Migration from Atlantic Canada, 1871–1921: A New Look,' *Acadiensis* 15:1 (Autumn 1985); Graeme Wynn 'New England's Outpost in the Nineteenth Century,' in Stephen J. Hornsby, Victor A. Konrad, and James J. Herlan (eds), *The Northeastern Borderlands: Four Centuries of Interaction* (Fredericton 1989)

25 D.A. Muise, 'Confederation,' in Muise (ed.), *A Reader's Guide to Canadian History: I. Beginnings to Confederation* (Toronto 1982); see also Buckner,

'Maritimes and Confederation.'

26 Langhout, 'Public Enterprise'; S.A. Saunders, *The Economic History of the Maritime Provinces* (Fredericton 1984); and Ralph C. Nelson, Walter C. Sodurlund, Ronald H. Wagenberg, and E. Donald Briggs, 'Canadian Confederation as a Case Study in Community Formation,' in Martin (ed.), *The Causes of Canadian Confederation*

27 Alison Prentice, *The School Promoters: Education and Social Class in Mid-Nineteenth-Century Upper Canada* (Toronto 1977); and Alison Prentice and Susan Houston (eds), *Family, Schools and Society in Nineteenth-Century Canada* (Toronto 1985); Janet Guildford, 'Schools and Socio-economic Change: A Study of Halifax Society' (PhD thesis, Dal 1990)

28 Ian Ross Robertson, 'Reform, Literacy and the Lease: The Prince Edward Island Free Education Act of 1852,' *Acadiensis* 20:1 (Autumn 1990)

29 W.E. Hamilton, 'Saints and Schools in Nova Scotia,' in J.D. Wilson, R.M. Stamp, and L.P. Audet (eds), *Canadian Education: A History* (Scarborough, Ont. 1970); Katherine F.C. MacNaughton, *The Development of the Theory and Practice of Education in New Brunswick, 1784–1900: A Study in Historical Background* (Fredericton 1947)

30 F.W. Rowe, *The History of Education in Newfoundland* (Toronto 1952); Philip McCann, 'The Politics of Denominational Education in Newfoundland,' in W.A. McKim (ed.), *The Vexed Question: Denominational Education in a Secular Age* (St John's 1988); and David G. Alexander, 'Literacy and Economic Development in Nineteenth-Century Newfoundland,' in David G. Alexander, *Atlantic Canada and Confederation: Essays in Canadian Political Economy* (Toronto 1983)

31 J.K. Chapman, 'The Mid-Nineteenth Century Temperance Movement in New Brunswick and Maine,' *CHR* 35 (1954); Acheson, *Saint John*; E.I. Dick, 'From Temperance to Prohibition in 19th Century Nova Scotia,' *DR* 61 (Autumn 1981); Gail Campbell, 'Disfranchised but Not Quiescent: Women Petitioners in New Brunswick at Mid-19th Century,' *Acadiensis* 18:2 (Spring 1989); J.H. Morrison and J. Moreira (eds), *Tempered by Rum: Rum in the History of the Maritime Provinces* (Porter's Lake, N.S. 1988); Martin Hewitt, 'The Mechanics' Institute Movement in the Maritimes, 1831–1889' (MA thesis, UNB 1986)

32 W.L. Morton, *The Critical Years: The Union of British North America, 1857–1872* (Toronto 1964); Nelson et al., 'Canadian Confederation'

33 D.A. Muise, 'Parties and Elections: Federal Politics in Nova Scotia, 1867–1878' (PhD thesis, UWO 1971); Charles Tupper, *Recollections of Sixty Years in Politics* (London 1916); L.S.F. Upton, 'The Idea of Confederation, 1754–1858,' in W.L. Morton (ed.), *The Shield of Achilles: Aspects of Canada in the Victorian Age* (Toronto 1968)

34 J.M. Beck, *Joseph Howe*, 2 vols (Kingston and Montreal 1982–3), vol 2; and J.M. Beck, *The Politics of Nova Scotia*, 2 vols (Tantallon, N.S. 1985),

vol 1; W.S. MacNutt, *New Brunswick: A History, 1784–1867* (Toronto 1963); Gail Campbell, 'Smashers and Rummies: The Rise of Parties in Charlotte County, New Brunswick, 1846–1857,' *CHAHP* (1987)

35 Robertson, 'Party Politics and Religious Controversialism'; Ian Ross Robertson, 'Political Realignment in Pre-Confederation Prince Edward Island, 1863–1870,' *Acadiensis* 15:1 (Autumn 1985); G.E. Gunn, *The Political History of Newfoundland, 1832–1864* (Toronto 1966)

36 Robertson, 'Political Realignment'

37 P.B. Waite, *The Life and Times of Confederation, 1864–1867: Politics, Newspapers and the Union of British North America* (Toronto 1962); Morton, *The Critical Years*

38 D.G. Creighton, *The Road to Confederation: The Emergence of Canada* (Toronto 1964); and P.G. Cornell, *The Great Coalition* (Ottawa 1966); Morton, *The Critical Years*

39 P.B. Waite, *The Charlottetown Conference* (Ottawa 1963)

40 Kenneth G. Pryke, *Nova Scotia and Confederation, 1864–74* (Toronto 1979); W.M. Whitelaw, *The Quebec Conference* (Ottawa 1966)

41 Francis W.P. Bolger, *Prince Edward Island and Confederation, 1863–1873* (Charlottetown 1976); Harry Baglole and David Weale, *The Island and Confederation: The End of an Era* (Summerside 1973)

42 James K. Hiller, 'Confederation Defeated: The Newfoundland Election of 1869,' in Peter Neary and J.K. Hiller (eds.), *Newfoundland in the Nineteenth and Twentieth Centuries: Essays in Interpretation* (Toronto 1980)

43 Bolger, *The Island and Confederation*; and Hiller, 'Confederation Defeated'

44 Muise, 'Parties and Elections,' ch 2; P.B. Waite, 'Halifax Papers and the Federal Principle, 1864–5,' *DR* (1962)

45 Carl M. Wallace, 'Albert Smith, Confederation and Reaction in New Brunswick, 1852–1882,' *CHR* (1963); A.G. Bailey, 'The Basis and Persistence of Opposition to Confederation in New Brunswick,' and his 'The Railroads and Confederation in New Brunswick,' both in A.G. Bailey, *Culture and Nationality: Essays by A.G. Bailey* (Toronto 1972); and MacNutt, *New Brunswick*

46 J.K. Chapman, *The Career of Arthur Hamilton Gordon, First Lord Stanmore 1829–1912* (Toronto 1964); James A. Gibson, 'The Colonial Office View of Canadian Federation, 1856–1868,' *CHR* (1954); P.B. Waite, 'Edward Cardwell and Confederation,' *CHR* (1962)

47 Wallace, 'Albert Smith'; MacNutt, *New Brunswick*; W.M. Baker, *Timothy Warren Anglin, 1822–96: Irish Canadian Catholic* (Toronto 1977)

48 Pryke, *Nova Scotia and Confederation*, ch. 2; and D.A. Muise, 'The Federal Election of 1867 in Nova Scotia: An Economic Interpretation,' NSHS *Proceedings* (1968)

49 *Morning Chronicle* (Halifax), 7 Mar. 1866; see D.A. Muise, 'Some Other Poets of Confederation in Nova Scotia,' *DR* (1968).

50 J.M. Beck, 'Joseph Howe and Confederation: Myth and Fact,' *TRSC* (1964); and his *Joseph Howe: Anti-Confederate* (Ottawa 1965)

51 L.J. Burpee (ed.), 'Joseph Howe and the Anti-Confederation League,' *TRSC* (1916)

52 Wallace, 'Samuel Leonard Tilley'; and Carl M. Wallace, 'Sir Leonard Tilley: A Political Biography' (PhD thesis, University of Alberta 1972)

53 Kenneth G. Pryke, 'The Making of a Province: Nova Scotia and Confederation,' *CHAHP* (1968); and D.A. Muise, 'Parties and Elections'

54 P.B. Waite (ed.), *CHCD*, 1867–8 (Ottawa 1968)

55 Pryke, *Nova Scotia and Confederation*, ch. 6

56 D.A. Muise, 'Two Letters on the "Pacification" of Nova Scotia,' *Nova Scotia Historical Quarterly* 1 (Mar. 1971)

57 R.H. Campbell, 'The Repeal Agitation in Nova Scotia,' NSHS *Collections* (1942); and D.F. Warner, 'The Post-Confederation Annexation Movement in Nova Scotia,' in R.D. Francis and D.B. Smith (eds), *Readings in Canadian History, Post-Confederation* (Toronto 1986)

58 Beck, *Howe*, vol. 2; and Pryke, *Nova Scotia and Confederation*, ch. 6

59 Pryke, *Nova Scotia and Confederation*, ch. 7; Muise, 'Parties and Elections,' ch. 3

60 Baker, *Timothy Warren Anglin*; Ken Cruikshank, 'The People's Railway: The Intercolonial Railway and the Canadian Public Enterprise Experience,' *Acadiensis* 16:1 (Autumn 1986)

61 Muise, 'Parties and Elections,' ch. 4

62 R.S. Longley, 'The Fisheries in Nova Scotia Politics, 1865–1871,' NSHS *Collections* 25 (1942); R.S. Longley, 'Peter Mitchell: Guardian of the North Atlantic Fisheries, 1867–1871,' *CHR* (1941)

63 G. Smith, *The Treaty of Washington: A Study in Imperial History* (Ithaca, N.Y. 1941); Innis, *Cod Fishery*; and J.M. Beck, *Pendulum of Power: Canada's Federal Elections* (Scarborough, Ont. 1968), ch. 2

64 Bolger, *Prince Edward Island and Confederation*

65 Hiller, 'Confederation Defeated'

## 2 The 1870s: Political Integration

1 See Phillip A. Buckner, 'The Maritimes and Confederation: A Reassessment,' *CHR* 71:1 (Mar. 1990).

2 Carl M. Wallace, 'The Life and Times of Sir Albert James Smith' (MA thesis, UNB 1960), 302

3 Ibid., 114

4 Tilley to Macdonald, 22 May 1868, in Carl M. Wallace, 'Albert Smith, Confederation and Reaction in New Brunswick: 1852–1882,' *CHR* 44 (1963), 298–9

5 D.A. Muise, 'Parties and Elections: Federal Politics in Nova Scotia,

1867–1878' (PhD thesis, UWO 1971), 176–7

6 Kenneth G. Pryke, *Nova Scotia and Confederation, 1864–74* (Toronto 1979), 125

7 Quoted in Wallace, 'Albert Smith, Confederation and Reaction,' 299

8 Muise, 'Parties and Elections,' 186

9 *Daily Telegraph* (Saint John), 27 July 1872

10 See J.M. Bumsted, '"The Only Island There Is": The Writing of Prince Edward Island History,' in Verner Smitheram, David Milne, and Satadal Dasgupta (eds), *The Garden Transformed: Prince Edward Island, 1945–1980* (Charlottetown 1982), esp. 13.

11 Frank MacKinnon, *The Government of Prince Edward Island* (Toronto 1951), 132

12 See A.H. Clark, *Three Centuries and the Island* (Toronto 1959), 140–2.

13 Francis W.P. Bolger, *Prince Edward Island and Confederation 1863–1873* (Charlottetown 1964), 210

14 See Ian Ross Robertson, 'Political Realignment in Pre-Confederation Prince Edward Island, 1863–1870,' *Acadiensis* 15:1 (Autumn 1985), 35–58.

15 Bolger, *Prince Edward Island and Confederation*, 262

16 Muise, 'Parties and Elections,' 142–4

17 Quoted in Muise, ibid., 165

18 Mackenzie to Jones, 11 Mar. 1873, printed in the *Report of the Board of Trustees of the Public Archives of Nova Scotia* (Halifax 1952)

19 Wallace, 'Life and Times,' 144

20 Ibid., 155–6

21 Frank MacKinnon, 'David Laird of Prince Edward Island,' *DR* 27 (Winter 1947), 414

22 Mills to Mackenzie, 10 Oct. 1876, quoted in Sister Teresa Avila Burke, 'Mackenzie and His Cabinet, 1873–1878,' *CHR* 41 (1960), 144

23 The words quoted are Sister Burke's in ibid., 144

24 Mackenzie to Robert Mackenzie, 31 Jan. 1878, quoted in F.H. Underhill, 'The Development of National Parties in Canada,' *CHR* 16 (1935), 383–4

25 Muise, 'Parties and Elections,' 273

26 *Moncton Times*, 9 Nov. 1876, quoted in Wallace, 'Life and Times,' 168–9

27 Muise, 'Elections and Constituencies,' 275

28 See Ben Forster, *A Conjunction of Interests: Business, Politics, and Tariffs, 1825–1879* (Toronto 1986), 177.

29 See Carl M. Wallace, 'Sir Samuel Leonard Tilley,' *DCB*, vol. 2: 1057–8.

30 Gordon T. Stewart, *The Origins of Canadian Politics: A Comparative Approach* (Vancouver 1986), 87–9

31 There is abundant evidence of this in the patronage files of Tupper and Tilley in their papers in the NAC.

32 Additional grants of $80,000 and $70,000 were given to Ontario and Quebec at the same time.

33 See the *Daily Telegraph*, 20 Oct. and 6 Dec. 1871.

34 Wallace, 'Life and Times,' 140

35 The letters between Tilley and Fraser in the Tilley Papers in the NAC make very clear that Tilley was sympathetic to the needs of the provincial government but could not move because of opposition from the Canadian ministers.

36 Nancy Jean MacNeill, 'W.W. Sullivan and Provincial Finance in Prince Edward Island, 1879–1889' (MA thesis, UNB 1976)

37 Wilfrid Eggleston, *The Road to Nationhood: A Chronicle of Dominion-Provincial Relations* (Toronto 1946), 51

38 Ibid., 51–2

39 *Chronicle* (Halifax), quoted in *Daily Telegraph*, 21 Jan. 1872, quoted in Wallace, 'Life and Times,' 139

40 Hugh James Whalen, *The Development of Local Government in New Brunswick* (Fredericton 1963), 24

41 See S.A. Saunders, 'Forest Industries in the Maritime Provinces,' in A.R.M. Lower (ed.), *The North American Assault on the Canadian Forest* (Toronto 1938), 347–9.

42 Eric W. Sager and Gerald E. Panting, 'Staple Economies and the Rise and Decline of the Shipping Industry in Atlantic Canada, 1820–1914,' in Lewis R. Fischer and Gerald E. Panting (eds), *Change and Adaptation in Maritime History: The North Atlantic Fleets in the Nineteenth Century* (St John's 1985), 10–11

43 Eric W. Sager and Lewis R. Fischer, *Ships and Shipbuilding in Atlantic Canada* (Ottawa 1986), 1

44 Sager and Panting, 'Staple Economies,' 36

45 Donald McKay, in the *Maritime Trade Review* (Saint John), July 1875, quoted in Alan Gregg Finley, 'Shipbuilding in St. Martin's, 1840–1880: A Case Study of Family Enterprise on the Fundy Shore' (MA thesis, UNB 1979), 50

46 See Judith Fingard, *Jack in Port: Sailortowns of Eastern Canada* (Toronto 1982) and Eric W. Sager, *Seafaring Labour: The Merchant Marine of Atlantic Canada, 1820–1914* (Montreal 1989).

47 Daniel Hickey, 'Moncton, 1871–1913: le commerce et l'industrie d'un carrefour ferrovoire,' in Daniel Hickey (ed.), *Moncton: 1871–1929: changements socio-economique dans un ville ferrovoire* (Moncton 1990), 39–62

48 L.D. McCann, 'Staples and the New Industrialism in the Growth of Post-Confederation Halifax,' *Acadiensis* 8:2 (Spring 1979), 47–79

49 T.W. Acheson, *Saint John: The Making of a Colonial Urban Community* (Toronto 1984), 23

50 Ibid., 14–16

51 Gordon MacKay Haliburton, 'A History of Railways in Canada' (MA thesis, Dal 1955), 165

52 Elizabeth W. McGahan, *The Port of Saint John: Volume One: From Confederation to Nationalization* (Saint John 1982), 79

53 Acheson, *Saint John*, 24

54 Robert H. Babcock, 'Economic Development in Portland (ME) and Saint John (N.B.) during the Age of Iron and Steam, 1850–1914,' *American Review of Canadian Studies*, 9:1 (Spring 1979), 17

55 Quoted in John Alexander Watt, 'Uneven Regional Development in Canada: A Study of Saint John, N.B., 1880–1910' (PhD thesis, University of Waterloo 1981), 148

56 Ian McKay, 'Industry, Work and Community in the Cumberland Coalfields, 1848–1927' (PhD thesis, Dal 1983), 124

57 Ken Cruikshank, 'The People's Railway: The Intercolonial Railway and the Canadian Public Enterprise Experience,' *Acadiensis* 16:1 (Autumn 1986), 98

58 See ibid., 88.

59 See Wilfrid Harrison, 'The Maritime Bank of the Dominion of Canada 1872–1887' (MA thesis, UNB 1970), and Douglas O. Baldwin, 'The Growth and Decline of the Charlottetown Banks, 1854–1906,' *Acadiensis* 15:2 (Spring 1986), 28–52.

60 Kris Inwood and John Chamard, 'Regional Industrial Growth during the 1890s: The Case of the Missing Artisans,' *Acadiensis* 16:1 (Autumn 1986), 111–13

61 Alan A. Brookes, 'The Exodus: Migration from the Maritime Provinces to Boston during the Second Half of the Nineteenth Century' (PhD thesis, UNB 1978), 72–6

62 Patricia A. Thornton, 'The Problem of Out-Migration from Atlantic Canada, 1871–1921: A New Look,' *Acadiensis* 15:1 (Autumn 1985), 3–34

63 Martin Hewitt, 'The Mechanics' Institute Movement in the Maritimes, 1831–1889' (MA thesis, UNB 1986), 272–3

64 McGahan, *Port of Saint John*, 56–9; Kenneth G. Pryke, 'Labour and Politics: Nova Scotia at Confederation,' *Hs / SH* 6 (Nov. 1970), 40

65 Richard Rice, 'A History of Organized Labour in Saint John, New Brunswick, 1813–1890' (MA thesis, UNB 1968), ch. 3

66 Pryke, 'Labour and Politics,' 44–6

67 Ian McKay, '"By Wisdom, Wile or War": The Provincial Workmen's Association and the Struggle for Working-Class Independence in Nova Scotia, 1879–97,' *L / Le t* 18 (Fall 1986), 23–4

68 Hewitt, 'Mechanics' Institute Movement,' 279–80

69 Colin Howell, 'Reform and the Monopolistic Impulse: The Professionalization of Medicine in the Maritimes,' *Acadiensis* 11:1 (Autumn 1981), 15–17

70 Ruth Elizabeth Spence, *Prohibition in Canada* (Toronto 1919), esp. 117, 123–7

71 This term was originally used by J.S. Moir, in *Church and State in Canada West: Three Studies in the Relations of Denominationalism and Canadian Thought in the Victorian Era* (Montreal 1979); quoted in William Westfall, *Creating a Protestant Ontario: The Anglican Church and the Secular State,* Canada House Lecture No. 12 (London 1981), 4. See also Westfall's, *Two Worlds: The Protestant Culture of Nineteenth-Century Ontario* (Montreal 1989).

72 See D.G. Bell, 'The Persistence and Transformation of Allinism in 19th-Century New Brunswick: First Thoughts' (paper delivered to the Atlantic Canada Workshop, Fredericton, 27 Sept. 1986), 6–8.

73 George Edward Levy, *The Baptists of the Maritime Provinces* (Saint John 1946), 158

74 William B. Hamilton, 'Society and Schools in Nova Scotia,' in J.D. Wilson, R.M. Stamp, and L.P. Audet (eds), *Canadian Education: A History* (Scarborough, Ont. 1970), 101–5

75 C.B. Sissons, *Church and State in Canadian Education* (Toronto 1959), 362–5

76 Peter M. Toner, 'New Brunswick Schools and the Rise of Provincial Rights,' in Bruce W. Hodgins, Don Wright, and W.H. Heick (eds), *Federalism in Canada and Australia: The Early Years* (Waterloo Ont. 1978), 97, 100, 103–4

77 George F.G. Stanley, 'The Caraquet Riots of 1875,' *Acadiensis* 2:1 (Autumn 1972), 21–38

78 Regis Brun, *La ruée vers le hommard des Maritimes* (Moncton 1988)

79 Naomi Griffiths, 'Longfellow's *Evangeline*: The Birth and Acceptance of a Legend,' *Acadiensis* 14:1 (Autumn 1974), 28–41

80 Léon Thériault, 'Acadia, 1763–1978: An Historical Synthesis,' in Jean Daigle (ed.), *The Acadians of the Maritimes: Thematic Studies* (Moncton 1982), 63

81 Quoted in Della M.M. Stanley, *A Man for Two Peoples: Pierre-Amand Landry* (Fredericton 1988), 18

82 Ibid., 46

83 Thériault, 'Acadia, 1763–1978,' 68–9

84 Alexandre-J. Savoie, 'Education in Acadia: 1604–1970,' in Daigle (ed.), *Acadians of the Maritimes,* 408–9

85 James Douglas Leighton, 'The Development of Federal Indian Policy in Canada, 1840–1890' (PhD thesis, UWO 1975) 275

**3 The 1880s: Paradoxes of Progress**

1 Burton Glendenning, 'The Burchill Lumbering Firm 1850–1906: An Example of 19th Century New Brunswick Entrepreneurship' (MA thesis, Concordia University 1978)

2 T.W. Acheson, 'The National Policy and the Industrialization of the Maritimes, 1880–1910,' *Acadiensis* 1:2 (Spring 1972), 3–28

3 Ben Forster, *A Conjunction of Interests: Business, Politics, and Tariffs 1825–1879* (Toronto 1986)

4 Donald MacLeod, 'Practicality Ascendant: The Origins and Establishment of Technical Education in Nova Scotia,' *Acadiensis* 15:2 (Spring 1986), 53–92

5 Peter Delottinville, 'The St. Croix Cotton Manufacturing Company and Its Influence on the St. Croix Community, 1880–1892,' (MA thesis, Dal 1979), and his 'Trouble in the Hives of Industry: The Cotton Industry Comes to Milltown, New Brunswick, 1879–1892,' *CHAHP* (1980), 100–15

6 This analysis is based on the personal schedules of the 1891 census for Saint John and Halifax-Dartmouth. Female cotton operatives for the St Croix mill were not analysed because of the number of Americans who were included in that work-force.

7 Royal Commission on the Relations of Capital and Labour, *Evidence – Nova Scotia* (1889), *Evidence – New Brunswick* (1889); also abridged version of reports and evidence in Gregory S. Kealey (ed.), *Canada Investigates Industrialism* (Toronto 1973); D.A. Muise, 'The Industrial Context of Inequality: Female Participation in Nova Scotia's Paid Labour Force, 1871–1921,' *Acadiensis* 20:2 (Spring 1991), 3–31

8 Ian McKay, 'The Realm of Uncertainty: The Experience of Work in the Cumberland Coal Mines, 1873–1927,' *Acadiensis* 16:1 (Autumn 1986), 3–57; Robert McIntosh, 'The Boys in the Nova Scotian Coal Mines: 1873 to 1923,' *Acadiensis* 16:2 (Spring 1987), 35–50

9 Ian McKay, '"By Wisdom, Wile or War": The Provincial Workmen's Association and the Struggle for Working-Class Independence in Nova Scotia, 1879–97,' *L / Le t* 18 (Fall 1986), 39–40

10 Michael J. Troughton, 'From Nodes to Nodes: The Rise and Fall of Agricultural Activity in the Maritime Provinces,' in Douglas Day (ed.), *Geographical Perspectives on the Maritime Provinces* (Halifax 1988), 30–1

11 *Daily Sun* (Saint John), 2 Apr. 1887, quoting *The Times* (London)

12 P.B. Waite, *Canada 1874–1896: Arduous Destiny* (Toronto 1971), 202–5

13 B.A. Balcom, *History of the Lunenburg Fishing Industry* (Lunenburg 1977)

14 C.R. MacKay, 'Investors, Government and the CMTR: A Study of Entrepreneurial Failure,' *Acadiensis* 9:1 (Autumn 1979), 94

15 Dean Jobb, 'The Politics of the New Brunswick and Prince Edward Island Railway, 1872–1886,' *Acadiensis* 13:2 (Spring 1984), 90

16 *Daily Examiner* (Charlottetown), 31 Dec. 1884

17 Mary K. Cullen, 'The Transportation Issue, 1873–1973,' in Francis W.P. Bolger (ed.), *Canada's Smallest Province: A History of P.E.I.* ([Charlottetown] 1973), 232–44

18 David G. Alexander and Gerald E. Panting, 'The Mercantile Fleet and Its Owners: Yarmouth, Nova Scotia, 1840–1889,' *Acadiensis* 7:2 (Spring 1978), 3–28; Eric W. Sager and Lewis R. Fischer, 'Atlantic Canada and the Age of Sail Revisited,' *CHR* 63:2 (June 1982), 125–50; and their 'Patterns of Investment in the Shipping Industries of Atlantic Canada, 1820–1900,' *Acadiensis* 9:1 (Autumn 1979), 19–43; Eric W. Sager with Gerald E. Panting, *Maritime Capital: The Shipping Industry in Atlantic Canada, 1820–1914* (Montreal 1990)

19 Patricia A. Thornton, 'The Problem of Out-Migration from Atlantic Canada, 1871–1921: A New Look,' *Acadiensis* 15:1 (Autumn 1985), 16

20 Alan A. Brookes, 'Out-Migration from the Maritime Provinces, 1860–1900: Some Preliminary Considerations,' *Acadiensis* 5:2 (Spring 1976), 26–55

21 L.D. McCann, 'The Mercantile-Industrial Transition in the Metals Towns of Pictou County, 1857–1931,' *Acadiensis* 10:2 (Spring 1981), 34–5

22 Alan A. Brookes, 'The Golden Age and the Exodus: The Case of Canning, Kings County,' *Acadiensis* 11:1 (Autumn 1981), 57–82; Margaret Conrad, 'Myths and Realities for Maritime Canadians in the United States, 1870–1920,' in Stephen J. Hornsby, Victor A. Konrad, and James J. Herlan (eds), *The Northeastern Borderlands: Four Centuries of Interaction* (Fredericton 1989), 97–119

23 Douglas O. Baldwin, 'The Growth and Decline of the Charlottetown Banks, 1854–1906,' *Acadiensis* 15:2 (Spring 1986), 28–52

24 James D. Frost, 'The "Nationalization" of the Bank of Nova Scotia, 1880–1910,' *Acadiensis* 12:1 (Autumn 1982), 3–38

25 Colin Howell, 'W.S. Fielding and the Repeal Elections of 1886 and 1887 in Nova Scotia,' *Acadiensis* 8:2 (Spring 1979), 28–46

26 Nancy Jean MacNeill, 'W.W. Sullivan and Provincial Finance in Prince Edward Island, 1879–1889' (MA thesis, UNB 1976)

27 Michael Gordon, 'The Andrew G. Blair Administration and the Abolition of the Legislative Council of New Brunswick, 1882–1892' (MA thesis, UNB, 1964)

28 Judith Fingard, *The Dark Side of Life in Victorian Halifax* (Porters Lake, N.S. 1989), ch. 8

29 Judith Fingard, 'George Munro,' *DCB* vol. 12, 771–3

30 Judith Fingard, 'College, Career and Community: Dalhousie Coeds 1881–1921,' in Paul Axelrod and John G. Reid (eds), *Youth, University, and Canadian Society: Essays in the Social History of Higher Education* (Montreal 1989), 26–50; Lois K. Kernaghan, '"Someone wants the Doctor": Maria L. Angwin, M.D. (1849–1898),' *Collections of the Royal Nova Scotia Historical Society*, 43 (1991), 33–48

31 NBM, Minutes of the Haven and Rescue Work 1887–1893

32 Martin S. Spigelman, 'The Acadian Renaissance and the Development of

Acadien-Canadien Relations, 1864–1912: "Des frères trop longtemps séparés"' (PhD thesis, Dal 1975); Perry Biddiscombe, '"Le Tricolore et l'étoile": The Origin of the Acadian National Flag, 1867–1912,' *Acadiensis*, 20:1 (Autumn 1990), 120–47

33 *Daily Sun*, 17 Mar. 1884

34 *Morning Chronicle* (Halifax), 16 Jan. 1884

35 *Morning Chronicle*, 30 Oct. 1885

36 Robin W. Winks, 'Negro School Segregation in Ontario and Nova Scotia,' *CHR* 50:2 (June 1969), 164–91; Judith Fingard, 'Race and Respectability in Victorian Halifax,' *Journal of Imperial and Commonwealth History*, 20:2 (May 1992), 169–95

37 Brenda Lee Potter, 'Poor Relief in Nova Scotia in the 1880s' (Honours essay, Dal 1978), chs 1 and 3

38 Nova Scotia, *Journal of the Legislative Council*, 1886, App. 10: The Poor of Digby; P.B. Waite, *The Man from Halifax: Sir John Thompson, Prime Minister* (Toronto 1985), 92–5

39 *Critic* (Halifax), 8 Apr. 1887

40 Emma M. Stirling, *Our Children in Old Scotland and Nova Scotia* (London [1892])

41 *Census of Canada*, 1891, Personal Schedules, Halifax-Dartmouth and Saint John

42 *Daily Sun*, 19 Mar. 1887; Judith Fingard, '"A Great Big Rum Shop": The Drink Trade in Victorian Halifax,' in James H. Morrison and James Moreira (eds), *Tempered by Rum: Rum in the History of the Maritime Provinces* (Porters Lake, N.S. 1988), 89–101; Jacques Paul Couturier, 'Prohiber ou contrôler? L'application de l'Acte de témperance du Canada à Moncton, N.-B., 1881–1896,' *Acadiensis*, 17:2 (Spring 1988), 3–26

43 *Daily Sun*, 2 June 1887

44 John G. Reid, *Mount Allison University, Vol.1: 1843–1914* (Toronto 1984), ch 4

45 *Daily Sun*, 10 June 1887

46 *Daily Sun*, 17 Mar. 1887

47 *Daily Examiner*, 31 Dec. 1885

48 Desmond Pacey (ed.), *The Collected Poems of Sir Charles G.D. Roberts* (Wolfville 1985), 119

49 Murray Barkley, 'The Loyalist Tradition in New Brunswick,' *Acadiensis* 4:2 (Spring 1975), 3–45; Bonnie L. Huskins, 'Public Celebrations in Victorian Saint John and Halifax' (PhD thesis, Dal 1991)

50 *Daily Sun*, 10, 11, 13 June 1887

51 *Critic*, Jubilee Number, June 1887. For another analysis of the 1880s, see John G. Reid, *Six Crucial Decades: Times of Change in the History of the Maritimes* (Halifax 1987), 127–57.

## 4 The 1890s: Fragmentation and the New Social Order

The critical comments of Bill Godfrey, Naomi Griffiths, and George Rawlyk on earlier drafts of this chapter are gratefully acknowledged. Ian McKay kindly shared his research on the region's labour movement. Valuable research assistance was provided by Andrew Ferguson, Sharon Myers, Anne-Marie Smith, and Rhianna Watt.

1 J.M. Beck, *Pendulum of Power: Canada's Federal Elections* (Scarborough, Ont. 1968), 68
2 Discussion of the 1896 election and its impact in the Maritimes draws upon Beck, *Pendulum of Power*, 72–86, and J.M. Beck, *Politics of Nova Scotia*, 2 vols (Tantallon, N.S. 1985), 1:262–6; John I. Little, 'New Brunswick Reaction to the Manitoba Schools Question,' *Acadiensis* 1:2 (Spring 1972), 43–58; K.M. McLaughlin, 'W.S. Fielding and the Liberal Party in Nova Scotia,' *Acadiensis* 3:2 (Spring 1974), 65–79; and D.A. Muise, 'Parties and Constituencies: Federal Elections in Nova Scotia, 1867–1896,' *CHAAR* (1971).
3 *Herald* (Halifax), 15 June 1896, 4
4 Beck, *Pendulum of Power*, 71 and 86
5 Robert Craig Brown and Ramsay Cook, *Canada, 1896–1921: A Nation Transformed* (Toronto 1974)
6 See PANS, MGI, vol. 1300, 'Diary written by Maurice A. Harlow,' for this vision of a unified Canada.
7 PANB, MC259, 'Diary of Alvaretta Estabrooks'
8 E.R. Forbes, 'Misguided Symmetry: The Destruction of Regional Transportation Policy for the Maritimes,' in David Jay Bercuson (ed.), *Canada and the Burden of Unity* (Toronto 1977), 63
9 Graeme Wynn, 'Ethnic Migrations and Atlantic Canada: Geographical Perspectives,' *Canadian Ethnic Studies / Etudes Ethniques au Canada* 18 (1986), 1–15
10 L.D. McCann and Jill Burnett, 'Social Mobility and the Ironmasters of Late Nineteenth Century New Glasgow,' in L.D. McCann (ed.), *People and Place: Studies of Small Town Life in the Maritimes* (Fredericton 1987), 59–77; Muriel K. Roy, 'Settlement and Population Growth,' in Jean Daigle (ed.), *The Acadians of the Maritimes: Thematic Studies* (Moncton 1982), 180; and Martin S. Spigelman, 'Race et religion: les Acadiens et la hiérarchie catholique irlandaise du Nouveau-Brunswick,' *Revue d'histoire de l'Amérique française* 29:1 (June 1975), 69–87
11 T.W. Acheson, 'The National Policy and the Industrialization of the Maritimes, 1880–1910,' *Acadiensis* 1:2 (Spring 1972), 3–28
12 L.D. McCann, '"Living a Double Life": Town and Country in the Industrialization of the Maritimes,' in Douglas Day (ed.), *Geographical Perspec-*

*tives on the Maritimes* (Halifax 1988), 93–113; and Alan A. Brookes, 'Out-Migration from the Maritime Provinces, 1860–1900: Some Preliminary Considerations,' *Acadiensis* 5:2 (Spring 1976), 26–55

13 Ian McKay, '"By Wisdom, Wile or War": The Provincial Workmen's Association and the Struggle for Working-Class Independence in Nova Scotia, 1879–97,' *L / Le t* 18 (Fall 1986), 13–62

14 E.R. Forbes, *Aspects of Maritime Regionalism, 1867–1927* (Ottawa 1983), 7–11

15 Beck, *Politics of Nova Scotia*, 1:262

16 *Daily Telegraph* (Saint John), 18 Jan. 1890, 3

17 *Globe* (Saint John), 30 Sept. 1895, 2

18 Hugh G. Thorburn, *Politics in New Brunswick* (Toronto 1961), 49–51

19 Beck, *Politics of Nova Scotia*, 1:258–62

20 Kris Inwood and John Chamard, 'Regional Industrial Growth during the 1890s: The Case of the Missing Artisans,' *Acadiensis* 16:1 (Autumn 1986), 112

21 Acheson, 'National Policy and the Industrialization of the Maritimes'

22 Canada, Bureau of Statistics, *The Maritime Provinces since Confederation* (Ottawa 1927), 69

23 C.L. Cantley, 'A Sketch of the Development and Present Operations in the Iron and Steel Industry of Nova Scotia,' *Transactions of the Canadian Mining Institute* 16 (1913), 348

24 L.D. McCann, 'The Mercantile-Industrial Transition in the Metals Towns of Pictou County, 1857–1931,' *Acadiensis* 10:2 (Spring 1981), 29–64

25 PANS, MG2, vol. 1244, no. 12, 30, J.W. Carmichael, 'Pictou Presbyterianism – Its Political and Educational Influence'

26 See, for example, Acheson, 'National Policy and the Industrialization of the Maritimes,' 15–18; and Michael Hinton, 'The National Policy and the Growth of the Canadian Cotton Textile Industry' (paper delivered to the Conference on Quantitative Methods in Canadian Economic History, Wilfrid Laurier University, 1984).

27 Acheson, 'National Policy and the Industrialization of the Maritimes,' 16–17

28 L.D. McCann, 'Metropolitanism and Branch Businesses in the Maritimes, 1881–1931,' *Acadiensis* 13:1 (Autumn 1983), 111–25

29 David Frank, 'The Cape Breton Coal Industry and the Rise and Fall of the British Empire Steel Corporation,' *Acadiensis* 7:1 (Autumn 1977), 3–34; and Don MacGillivray, 'Henry Melville Whitney Comes to Cape Breton: The Saga of a Gilded Age Entrepreneur,' *Acadiensis* 9:1 (Autumn 1979), 44–70

30 MacGillivray, 'Henry Whitney,' 54

31 Frank, 'Cape Breton Coal Industry,' 11

32 *Canadian Mining Review*, Apr. 1902, 72, as quoted in MacGillivray, 'Henry

Whitney,' 57

33 The development of the Grand Lake coalfield is discussed in Allen Seager, 'Minto, New Brunswick: A Study in the Class Relations between the Wars,' L / Le t 5 (1980), 86–90.

34 David G. Alexander, 'Economic Growth in the Atlantic Region, 1880 to 1940,' Acadiensis 8:1 (Autumn 1978), 58

35 Canada, The Maritime Provinces, 'Agriculture – General Review,' 42–52; Margaret Conrad, 'Apple Blossom Time in the Annapolis Valley, 1880–1957,' Acadiensis 9:2 (Spring 1980), 14–39; and Michael Troughton, 'From Nodes to Nodes: The Rise and Fall of Agricultural Activity in the Maritime Provinces,' in Douglas Day (ed.), Geographical Perspectives on the Maritimes (Halifax 1988), 25–46

36 Dispatch (Woodstock), 15 Feb. 1899, 1

37 Ralph S. Johnson, Forests of Nova Scotia: A History (Halifax 1986), 108–10; and Paul H. Stehelin, The Electric City: The Stehelins of New France (Hantsport, N.S. 1983)

38 The Wood Industries of New Brunswick (London 1897)

39 Johnson, Forests of Nova Scotia, 101–15; Barbara R. Robertson, Saw-Power: Making Lumber in the Sawmills of Nova Scotia (Halifax 1986); and Canada, The Maritime Provinces, 'Forestry,' 59–63

40 Kennedy Wells, 'The Great Lobster Boom,' in his The Fishery of Prince Edward Island (Charlottetown 1986), 131–49

41 B.A. Balcom, History of the Lunenburg Fishing Industry (Lunenburg 1977), 25–34

42 Data discussed in this paragraph are compiled from the Census of Canada, 1871–1901.

43 Roy, 'Settlement and Population Growth,' 166–75

44 The relationships between immigrants and occupations are derived from extensive research on the nominal manuscript censuses for 1871, 1881, and 1891. The figure for immigrants who remained in the region is from Canada, The Maritime Provinces, 7.

45 Examination of these records as part of a research project on social and geographical mobility in several Maritime industrial towns facilitates tracing the various forms of transiency. Some of this evidence is reported in McCann and Burnett, 'Social Mobility,' 72–5; and McCann, '"Living a Double Life,"' 100–3.

46 Catherine A. Johnson, 'The Search for Industry in Newcastle, New Brunswick, 1899–1914,' Acadiensis 13:1 (Autumn 1983), 93–111

47 Union Advocate (Newcastle), 30 May 1899, as quoted in Johnson, 'Search for Industry,' 93

48 Michael Hatfield, 'H.H. Pitts and Race and Religion in New Brunswick,' Acadiensis 4:2 (Spring 1975), 46–65

49 Katherine F.C. MacNaughton, The Development of the Theory and Practice

*of Education in New Brunswick, 1784–1900: A Study in Historical Background* (Fredericton 1947), as quoted in Hatfield, 'H.H. Pitts,' 47

50 Hatfield, 'H.H. Pitts,' 57

51 Léon Thériault, 'The Acadianization of the Catholic Church in Acadia, 1763–1953,' in Daigle, (ed.), *Acadians of the Maritimes* 305–14

52 Ian McKay, 'Strikes in the Maritimes, 1901–1914,' *Acadiensis* 13:1 (Autumn 1983), 10

53 McKay, '"By Wisdom, Wile or War,"' 55

54 *Acadian Recorder* (Halifax), 13 July 1897, 3

55 *Acadian Recorder*, 3 Aug. 1897, 3

56 Acheson, 'National Policy and the Industrialization of the Maritimes'; and L.D. McCann, 'Staples and the New Industrialism in the Growth of Post-Confederation Halifax,' *Acadiensis* 8:2 (Spring 1979), 47–79

57 McCann, 'Metropolitanism'

58 James D. Frost, 'The "Nationalization" of the Bank of Nova Scotia, 1880–1910,' *Acadiensis* 12:1 (Autumn 1982), 3–38

59 Elizabeth W. McGahan, *The Port of Saint John: Volume One: From Confederation to Nationalization, 1867–1927* (Saint John 1982), 107–59

60 David A. Sutherland, 'The Personnel and Policies of the Halifax Board of Trade, 1890–1914,' in Lewis R. Fischer and Eric W. Sager (eds), *The Enterprising Canadians: Entrepreneurs and Economic Development in Eastern Canada* (St John's 1979), 95–110

61 McGahan, *Port of Saint John*, 249

62 'Inaugural Address of His Worship Mayor Alexander Stephen, Esq.,' *Annual Report of the City of Halifax, 1897–98* (Halifax 1898), 13–16

63 E.R. Forbes, 'Battles in Another War: Edith Archibald and the Halifax Feminist Movement,' in E.R. Forbes, *Challenging the Regional Stereotype: Essays on the 20th-Century Maritimes* (Fredericton 1989)

## 5 The 1900s: Industry, Urbanization, and Reform

1 *Herald* (Halifax), 1 Jan. 1900; Robert Page, *The Boer War and Canadian Imperialism* (Ottawa 1987)

2 Quoted in Michael J.E. Smith, 'Female Reformers in Victorian Nova Scotia' (MA thesis, SMU 1986) 6

3 Robert Wiebe, in *The Search for Order 1877–1920* (New York 1967), refers to these reformers as members of the 'new middle class.' See also Richard Hofstadter, *The Age of Reform* (New York 1955); Reginald Whitaker, 'The Liberal Corporatist Ideas of Mackenzie King' *L / Le t* 2 (1977) 137–69; T. Jackson Lears, *No Place of Grace: Anti-modernism and the Transformation of American Culture, 1880–1920* (New York 1981); Angus McLaren, *Our Own Master Race: Eugenics in Canada 1885–1945* (Toronto 1990); Mariana Valverde, *The Age of Light, Soap, and Water: Moral Reform in English Canada,*

*1885–1925* (Toronto 1991); Neil Sutherland, *Children in English-Canadian Society: Framing the Twentieth-Century Consensus* (Toronto 1976).

4 Ramsay Cook, *The Regenerators: Social Criticism in Late Victorian English Canada* (Toronto 1985)

5 Richard Allen, *The Social Passion: Religion and Social Reform in Canada 1914–1928* (Toronto 1971). For a discussion of progressivism as an alternative to populism and socialism, see James Weinstein, *The Corporate Ideal in the Liberal State: 1900–1918* (Boston 1968). This theme is pursued in Colin Howell, 'Economism, Ideology and the Teaching of Maritime History,' in Phillip A. Buckner (ed.), *Teaching Maritime Studies* (Fredericton 1986).

6 *Morning Chronicle* (Halifax), 20 Aug. 1908

7 Mary K. Cullen, 'The Transportation Issue, 1873–1973,' in Francis W.P. Bolger (ed.), *Canada's Smallest Province: A History of P.E.I.*, (Charlottetown 1973) 232–64. See also the *Watchman* (Charlottetown), 15 Mar., 2 Apr. 1902; *Patriot* (Charlottetown), 17 Mar. 1903.

8 James A. Maxwell, *Federal Subsidies to Provincial Governments in Canada* (Cambridge 1963), 113

9 E.R. Forbes, *Aspects of Maritime Regionalism, 1867– 1927* (Ottawa 1983) 13

10 Robert Craig Brown and Ramsay Cook, *Canada, 1896–1921: A Nation Transformed* (Toronto 1974), 18–19, 50–1

11 Robert Craig Brown, *Robert Laird Borden: A Biography, Volume I: 1854–1914* (Toronto 1975)

12 Brown and Cook, *Canada, 1896–1921*, 189–90

13 Quoted in John English, *Robert Borden* (Toronto 1977), 50

14 Ibid., 64–5. Deficits increased sharply after Blair's resignation. See Ken Cruikshank, 'The People's Railway: The Intercolonial Railway and the Canadian Public Enterprise Experience,' *Acadiensis* 16:1, (Autumn 1986), 91.

15 Brown and Cook, *Canada, 1896–1921*, 152–3

16 *The Case of the Province of New Brunswick re the taking over of the Valley Railway by the Federal Government* (Fredericton 1927), 2–3. This brief, written by W.C. Keirstead, was intended to substantiate claims to the Duncan Commission during the 1920s, and to amplify the summary comments that appeared in the Duncan Commission Report.

17 Ibid., App. 2, 6–7

18 J.M. Beck, *The History of Maritime Union: A Study in Frustration* (Fredericton 1969); Reginald Harris, 'The Union of the Maritime Provinces,' *Acadiensis* 6 (1906), 172–84; 247–59; *Herald* (Halifax), 27 Aug. 1909

19 T.W. Acheson, 'The National Policy and the Industrialization of the Maritimes, 1880–1910,' *Acadiensis* 1:2 (Spring 1972), 3–28

20 L.D. McCann, 'Metropolitanism and Branch Businesses in the Maritimes, 1881–1931,' *Acadiensis* 13:1 (Autumn 1983), 114

21 James D. Frost, 'The "Nationalization" of the Bank of Nova Scotia, 1880–

1910,' *Acadiensis* 12:1 (Autumn 1982), 3–38

22 *Census of Canada*, 1911; D.A. Muise, '"The Great Transformation": Changing the Urban Face of Nova Scotia, 1871–1921,' *Nova Scotia Historical Review* 11:2 (1991), 1–42

23 *Census of Canada*, 1911

24 Craig Heron, 'The Great War and Nova Scotia Steelworkers,' *Acadiensis* 16:2 (Spring 1987), 4

25 Ron Crawley, 'Off to Sydney: Newfoundlanders Emigrate to Industrial Cape Breton, 1890–1914,' *Acadiensis* 17:2 (Spring 1988), 27–51

26 *Sydney Post*, 1 June 1901

27 See Catherine A. Johnson, 'The Search for Industry in Newcastle, New Brunswick, 1899–1914' *Acadiensis* 13:1 (Autumn 1983), 93–111; *Watchman*, 20 Mar., 1 May, 29 May 1903; *Patriot*, 19 Mar. 1903.

28 Ian McKay, 'Strikes in the Maritimes, 1901–1914,' *Acadiensis* 13:1 (Autumn 1983), 29

29 *Daily Sun* (Saint John), 10 July 1901

30 On the idea of 'civic populism' see Christopher Armstrong and H.V. Nelles, *Monopoly's Moment: The Organization and Regulation of Canadian Utilities, 1830–1930* (Philadelphia 1986; Toronto 1988).

31 David Frank and Nolan Reilly, 'The Emergence of the Socialist Movement in the Maritimes, 1899–1916,' *L / Le t* 4:4 (1979), 85–113

32 Robert H. Babcock, *Gompers in Canada: A Study in American Continentalism before the First World War* (Toronto 1974), 38–9, 46, 82, 119–123

33 *Watchman*, 10 Jan., 21 Feb. 1902

34 Ian McKay '"By Wisdom, Wile or War:" The Provincial Workmen's Association and the Struggle for Working-Class Independence in Nova Scotia, 1879–97,' *L / Le t* 18 (Fall 1986), 12–62

35 *Herald* (Halifax), 4 July 1909

36 Ibid., 6 July 1909

37 Ibid., 8 July 1909

38 Ibid., 23 June 1909

39 See, e.g., *Cotton's Weekly*, 12 Aug., 2 June 1909, 30 June 1910.

40 *Herald* (Halifax), 18 Aug. 1909

41 Province of Nova Scotia, *Report of the Royal Commission on Hours of Work* (Halifax 1910), 10–15

42 Ibid., 75–8

43 *Annual Report of the Superintendent of the Public Schools of Nova Scotia, 1906–1907* (Halifax 1907), xvi

44 *Census of Canada*, 1911

45 Margaret Conrad, 'Apple Blossom Time in the Annapolis Valley, 1880–1957,' *Acadiensis* 9:2 (Spring 1980), 14–39

46 *Census of Canada*, 1911, vol. 4, table 90

47 James Bickerton, *Nova Scotia, Ottawa, and the Politics of Regional Develop-*

*ment* (Toronto 1990), 41; L. Gene Barrett, 'Underdevelopment and Social Movements in the Nova Scotia Fishing Industry to 1938,' in Robert J. Brym and R. James Sacouman (eds), *Underdevelopment and Social Movements in Atlantic Canada* (Toronto 1979), 133–4; John J. Cowie, 'The Atlantic Fisheries of Canada,' in Adam Shortt and Arthur G. Doughty (eds), *Canada and Its Provinces*, 14, sec. 7, pt 2 (Toronto 1914), 589

48 B.E. Fernow, C.D. Howe, and H.H. White, *Forest Conditions of Nova Scotia* (Ottawa 1912); R.B. Miller, 'Forest Resources of the Maritime Provinces,' in Shortt and Doughty (eds), *Canada and Its Provinces*, 612–24; L. Anders Sandberg, 'Forest Policy in Nova Scotia: The Big Lease, Cape Breton Island, 1899–1960,' *Acadiensis* 20:2 (Spring 1991)

49 *Patriot*, 26 Mar. 1903

50 *Census of Canada*, 1911. For an interesting treatment of rural decline in a single county see Tim F. Archibald, 'A Question of Staying or Leaving: Rural Decline in Guysborough County' (MA thesis, SMU 1987).

51 Raymond Malhot, 'Prise de conscience collectiv acadien au Nouveaux Brunswick, 1860–1891' (PhD thesis, University of Montreal 1973), 436

52 Ibid., 459

53 Forbes, *Aspects of Maritime Regionalism*, 11; Pierre Biddiscombe, '"Le tricolore et l'étoile"; The Origin of the Acadian National Flag, 1867–1912,' *Acadiensis* 20:1 (Autumn 1990), 120–47

54 Léon Thériault, 'The Acadianization of the Catholic Church in Acadia, 1763–1953,' in Jean Daigle (ed.), *The Acadians of the Maritimes: Thematic Studies*, (Moncton 1982), 304; Philip Doucet, 'Politics and the Acadians,' in ibid., 252; Richard Wilbur, *The Rise of French New Brunswick* (Halifax 1989), 64–78

55 Graeme Wynn, '"Images of the Acadian Valley": The Photographs of Amos Lawson Hardy,' *Acadiensis* 15:1 (Autumn 1985), 59–83; Carrie MacMillan, 'Seaward Vision and Sense of Place: The Maritime Novel, 1880–1920,' *Studies in Canadian Literature* (Spring 1986), 19–37

56 Graeme Wynn, 'W.F. Ganong, A.H. Clark and the Historical Geography of Maritime Canada,' *Acadiensis* 10:2 (Spring 1981), 5–28

57 *Proceedings and Transactions of the Nova Scotia Institute of Science* 10 (1899–1900), 2, xxxvii

58 Ibid. (1900–1), 3, vii

59 *Patriot*, 29 July 1908; Lorne C. Callbeck, 'Economic and Social Development since Confederation,' in Bolger (ed.), *Canada's Smallest Province*, 350

60 See *Report of City Health Officer, Annual Reports, City of Charlottetown*, App. G (1893–1903); Colin Howell, 'Reform and the Monopolistic Impulse: The Professionalization of Medicine in the Maritimes,' *Acadiensis* 11:1 (Autumn 1981), 9; Douglas O. Baldwin and Thomas Spira (eds), *Gaslights, Epidemics and Vagabond Cows: Charlottetown in the Victorian Era* (Charlottetown 1988).

61 New Brunswick, *JHA*, 1910, '23rd Annual Report of the Provincial Board of Health for the year 1909'

62 Ibid., 1907, '20th Annual Report of the Provincial Board of Health for the year 1906'

63 Dr Edward Farrell, 'President's Address,' *Maritime Medical News* 7:8 (Aug. 1895), 116

64 J.B. Black, 'Race Suicide with Suggestions of Some Remedies,' *Maritime Medical News* 19:7 (July 1907) 247–54

65 A.B. Atherton, 'Presidential Address to the Maritime Medical Association,' *Maritime Medical News* 19:8 (August 1907) 292–6; Angus McLaren, '"The Creation of a Haven for Human Thoroughbreds": The Sterilization of the Feeble-Minded and the Mentally Ill in British Columbia,' *CHR* 67:2 (June 1986), 127–50

66 J. Edward Chamberlain and Sandra Gilman (eds), *Degeneration. The Dark Side of Progress* (New York 1985)

67 *Patriot*, 21 Mar. 1903; David Howell and Peter Lindsay, 'Social Gospel and the Young Boy Problem, 1895–1925,' in Morris Mott (ed.), *Sports in Canada: Historical Readings* (Toronto 1989), 220–34

68 Michael Smith, 'Graceful Athleticism or Robust Womanhood: The Sporting Culture of Women in Victorian Nova Scotia, 1870–1914,' *JCS* 23:1 (Spring 1988) 120–37; Helen Lenskyj, *Out of Bounds: Women, Sport and Sexuality* (Toronto 1986)

69 *Globe* (Saint John), 25 June 1901

70 Colin Howell, 'Baseball, Class and Community in the Maritime Provinces, 1870–1910,' *Hs/SH* 22:44 (Nov. 1989), 265–86

71 Quoted in *Herald*, 10 Jan. 1910

72 PANS, vol. 112, 1904, Power Scrapbook

73 *Herald*, 7 Jan. 1910

74 Ibid., 7 Jan., 7 July 1910

75 W.H. Hattie, 'The Prevention of Insanity,' *Maritime Medical News* 16:2, (Feb. 1904), 41–8

76 W.H. Hattie, 'The Care of the Adolescent,' *Maritime Medical News* 18:12 (Dec. 1906), 456; n.a., 'The Proper Housing of the Labouring Classes,' ibid., 18:4 (Apr. 1906), 128–30; George W.T. Irving, 'The Residuum,' ibid., 17:4 (Apr. 1905), 127–30; n.a., 'The Housing of the Working Classes,' *Canada Lancet* 10 (June 1906), 921

77 'The Province's Penal Institutions,' *Acadian Recorder*, 25 Feb. 1903

78 'Institution for the Feeble Minded,' *Acadian Recorder*, 18 Mar. 1903. See also ibid., 21 July 1903.

79 *Acadian Recorder*, 25 Feb. 1903

80 See the debate between Dr A.P. Reid and an anti-vaccinationist in the *Herald*, 21, 22 May 1909.

81 Jay Cassell, *The Secret Plague: Venereal Disease in Canada 1838–1939*

(Toronto 1987)

82 *Herald*, 6 July 1909

83 George H. Cox and John W. MacLeod, *Consumption: Its Cause, Prevention and Cure* (London 1912), estimated $3 million as the yearly economic loss to Nova Scotia alone through consumption. See also *Patriot*, 30 June 1908.

84 Sheila Penney, 'Tuberculosis in Nova Scotia, 1882–1914' (MA thesis, Dal 1985)

85 *CAR* (1909), 452

86 Marlene Russell Clark, 'Island Politics,' in Bolger (ed.), *Canada's Smallest Province*, 320–2

87 E.R. Forbes, *Challenging the Regional Stereotype: Essays on the 20th-Century Maritimes* (Fredericton 1989), 27

88 Henry Roper, 'The Halifax Board of Control: The Failure of Municipal Reform, 1906–1919,' *Acadiensis* 14:2 (Spring 1985), 46–65

89 Quoted in *CAR* (1908), 410; E.R. Forbes, 'The Ideas of Carol Bacchi and the Suffragists of Halifax,' *Atlantis* 10:2 (Spring 1985), 119–26

90 Smith, 'Female Reformers'

91 Ibid.

92 Carlotta Hacker, *The Indomitable Lady Doctors* (Toronto 1974), 77, 95–7; Judith Fingard, 'College, Career and Community: Dalhousie Coeds, 1881–1921,' in Paul Axelrod and John G. Reid (eds), *Youth University and Canadian Society: Essays in the Social History of Higher Education* (Kingston 1989), 26–50; E.R. Forbes, 'Battles in Another War: Edith Archibald and the Halifax Feminist Movement,' in his *Challenging the Regional Stereotype*, 67–90

93 Elspeth Tulloch, *We the Undersigned: A Historical Overview of New Brunswick Women's Political and Legal Status, 1784–1984*, (Moncton 1985), 51

94 Quoted in ibid., 48. See also Mary Clark, 'The Saint John Women's Enfranchisement Association' (MA thesis, UNB 1979).

## 6 The 1910s: The Stillborn Triumph of Progressive Reform

1 Saint John *Standard*, 7 June–1 July 1914; Robert H. Babcock, 'The Saint John Street Railwaymen's Strike and Riot, 1914,' *Acadiensis* 11:2 (Spring 1982), 3–27, citation at 3

2 E.R. Forbes, *Maritime Rights: The Maritime Rights Movement, 1919–1927; A Study in Canadian Regionalism* (Montreal 1979), 17–22

3 See, for example, Colin McKay, 'The Other Side of the Labour Question,' *Busy East*, Feb. 1914, 11–12.

4 For Halifax, see Henry Roper, 'The Halifax Board of Control: The Failure of Municipal Reform, 1906–1919,' *Acadiensis* 14:2 (Spring 1985), 50; the women's movement is discussed by E.R. Forbes, 'Battles in Another War: Edith Archibald and the Halifax Feminist Movement,' in E.R. Forbes,

*Challenging the Regional Stereotype: Essays on the 20th Century Maritimes* (Fredericton 1989), 67–89; on the Social Gospel, see Michael Boudreau, 'The Emergence of the Social Gospel in Nova Scotia: The Presbyterian, Methodist and Baptist Churches and the Working Class 1800–1914' (MA thesis, Queen's University 1991); on the Council of Women see PANS, MG20, vol. 204, Records of the Halifax Local Council of Women.

5 *CAR* (1911), 533

6 *Busy East*, July 1910

7 David G. Alexander, 'Economic Growth in the Atlantic Region, 1880–1940,' in Phillip A. Buckner and David Frank, eds. *Atlantic Canada after Confederation* (Fredericton 1985), 157

8 *Busy East*, Sept. 1910

9 Forbes, *Maritime Rights*, 3

10 *Herald* (Halifax), 31 Dec. 1910

11 *Herald*, 22 Jan. 1915; see also 17 Mar. 1913.

12 David Schwartzman, 'Mergers in the Nova Scotia Coal Fields: A History of the Dominion Coal Company, 1893–1940' (PhD thesis, University of California 1953); David Frank, 'The Cape Breton Coal Industry and the Rise and Fall of the British Empire Steel Corporation,' in Buckner and Frank, eds. *Atlantic Canada after Confederation*, 299–330

13 Kris Inwood, 'Local Control, Resources and the Nova Scotia Steel and Coal Company,' *CHAHP* (1986), 254–82

14 E.R. Forbes, 'Misguided Symmetry: The Destruction of Regional Transportation Policy for the Maritimes,' in David Jay Bercuson (ed.), *Canada and the Burden of Unity* (Toronto 1977), 60–86

15 Department of Labour, *Report on Labour Organizations in Canada*, 1911, 1914

16 For the exclusivity of trade unions *vis-à-vis* Acadians, see Peter Latta, 'A Labour Aristocracy in Amherst, Nova Scotia, 1890–1914' (MA thesis, SMU 1991).

17 See Kirby Abbott, 'The Coal Miners and the Law in Nova Scotia: From the 1864 Combination of Workmen Act to the 1947 Trade Union Act,' in Michael Earle, ed., *Workers and the State in Twentieth Century Nova Scotia* (Fredericton 1989), 24–46.

18 See James Robert Allum, 'Science, Government and Politics in the Abolition of the Commission of Conservation, 1909–1921' (MA thesis, Trent University 1988).

19 See J.M. Beck, *Politics of Nova Scotia*, 2 vols; *vol. 2, Murray-Buchanan, 1896–1988* (Tantallon, N.S. 1988), chs 1–3.

20 Christopher Armstrong and H.V. Nelles, 'The Great Fight for Clean Government,' *Urban History Review* 2 (Oct. 1976), 50–66; Roper, 'Board of Control,' 52; Christopher Armstrong and H.V. Nelles, 'Getting Your Way in Nova Scotia: Tweaking Halifax, 1909–1917,' *Acadiensis* 5:2 (Spring

1976), 105–31

21 D.A. Muise, 'The Industrial Context of Inequality: Female Participation in Nova Scotia's Paid Labour Force, 1871–1921,' *Acadiensis* 20:2 (Spring 1991), 3–31

22 James Snell, 'Marital Cruelty: Women and the Nova Scotia Divorce Court, 1900–1939,' *Acadiensis* 18:1 (Autumn 1988), 3–32

23 Cited in Elspeth Tulloch, *We, the Undersigned: A Historical Overview of New Brunswick Women's Political and Legal Status, 1784–1984* (Moncton 1985), 47–8

24 Forbes, 'Battles in Another War,' 67–9

25 *Herald*, 31 Dec. 1912

26 Ibid.

27 *Standard* (Saint John), 31 July 1914; *Herald*, 1 Aug. 1914

28 *CAR* (1915), 589; Peter G. Rogers (ed.), *Gunner Ferguson's Diary: The Diary of Gunner Frank Ferguson 1st Canadian Expeditionary Force 1915–1918* (Hantsport, N.S. 1985), 17

29 *Shelburne Gazette and Coast Guard*, 22 Feb. 1917

30 *CAR* (1914), 544, 567, 571; *Herald*, 1 Sept. 1915; 9 Dec. 1914; 21 May 1915; 6 Sept. 1915

31 *Busy East*, Dec. 1914; *Herald*, 31 Dec. 1914; *Busy East*, Sept. 1915

32 William Kilbourn, *The Elements Combined: A History of the Steel Company of Canada* (Toronto 1960), 100–1; *Financial Times* (Montreal), 22 Jan. 1916

33 *Busy East*, Apr. 1916; *Herald*, 6 Jan, 12 May, 11 Sept. 1915

34 *Herald*, 27 Dec. 1915

35 Craig Heron, 'The Great War and Nova Scotia Steelworkers,' *Acadiensis* 16:2 (Spring 1987), 14; NAC, RG27, vol. 304, f.15 (28); for the later strike, NAC, RG27, vol. 304, f.15 (42); *Herald*, 23 Aug. 1915

36 *CAR* (1915), 347; *Herald*, 26 Dec. 1914; 8, 30 Nov. 1914; 25 Apr. 1916; 31 Dec. 1915

37 Barry M. Moody, 'Acadia and the Great War,' in Paul Axelrod and John Reid (eds), *Youth, University and Canadian Society: Essays in the Social History of Higher Education* (Kingston and Montreal 1989), 145

38 *Herald*, 5 Aug. 1915; *Busy East*, Apr. 1916

39 *CAR* (1916), 303; (1915), 589; (1916), 617 gives Nova Scotia recruitment at the end of 1915 and in August, over which period the percentage of men in the relevant age group increased from 21.1 to 21.8 per cent; *A Short History and Photographic Record of the Nova Scotia Overseas Highland Brigade C.E.F.* (np 1916), 2; *CAR* (1918), 656; *Herald*, 9 Sept. 1915; *CAR* (1916), 638. For additional evidence of a gap between Prince Edward Island and Nova Scotia on the one hand, and New Brunswick on the other, see Christopher A. Sharpe, 'The Great War,' in Donald Kerr and Deryck Holdsworth (eds), *Historical Atlas of Canada*, 3 vols; vol. 3, *Addressing the Twentieth Century* (Toronto 1990), pl. 26.

40 *Herald*, 26 July 1914; 26 Mar. 1918; 31 July 1915

41 *Herald*, 25 Jan. 1916; the brigade was to be composed of the already re-cruited 85th Battalion, Nova Scotia Highlanders, and three additional bat-talions: the 185th from Cape Breton, the 193rd from mainland Nova Scotia's eastern counties, and the 219th from western Nova Scotia. On the 'Highland' theme and recruiting, see Paul Maroney, 'Recruiting the Canadian Expeditionary Force in Ontario, 1914–1917' (MA thesis, Queen's University 1991), ch. 3; for Nova Scotia's military experience in general, see M. Stuart Hunt, *Nova Scotia's Part in the Great War* (Halifax 1920).

42 *Herald*, 9 Sept. 1915

43 *CAR* (1916), 639

44 W.R. Young, 'Conscription, Rural Depopulation, and the Farmers of On-tario, 1917–19,' *CHR* 53 (Sept. 1972), 289–320

45 *Herald*, 3 Dec, 1915; 25 Aug. 1915; see also *Herald*, 2 Oct. 1915, for an article singling out Springhill's war contribution; 'Cape Bretoners and the First World War,' *Cape Breton's Magazine* 33 (nd); *Herald*, 2, 29 Nov. 1917; *CAR* (1914), 546.

46 E.R. Forbes, 'Prohibition and the Social Gospel in Nova Scotia,' in Forbes, *Challenging the Regional Stereotype*, 28–9

47 *CAR* (1916), 634; (1918), 668; *Herald*, 23 June 1916

48 Forbes, 'Battles in Another War,' 67

49 *Herald*, 3 Dec. 1917; 1 Nov. 1917

50 *Herald*, 15 Aug. 1914

51 On Micmacs in the war, see *Herald*, 6 Nov. 1918.

52 James W. St G. Walker, 'Race and Recruitment in World War I: Enlistment of Visible Minorities in the Canadian Expeditionary Force,' *CHR* 70: 1 (Mar. 1989), 1–26; Calvin W. Buck, *Canada's Black Battalion: No. 2 Con-struction 1916–1920* (Halifax 1986); *Herald*, 13 July 1916; 11 Mar. 1918 (ar-rests); 16 Aug. 1915 (Washington); 26 Apr. 1916 (*Atlantic Advocate*); 9, 26 July 1919 (Orphans' Home); 21 Mar. 1916 (protest against the film); 30 Sept., 5, 16 Nov. 1919 (racial disturbances); 25 Mar. 1919 (campaign to keep the Home for Colored Children in a Black area); 6 Apr., 20 May 1921 (aggressively racist cartoons)

53 Andrew Merkel (ed.), *Letters from the Front* (Halifax nd), 29–30

54 PANS, unpublished typescript, micro, Robert N. Clements, 'Merry Hell: The Way I Saw It: The Story of the 25th Nova Scotia Regiment C.E.F. 1914–1919'

55 *Herald*, 18 May 1915. For an appraisal of Salisbury Plain confirming Crowell's impressions, see G.W.L. Nicolson, CD, *Canadian Expeditionary Force, 1914–1919* (Ottawa 1962), 35–8.

56 *Bridgewater Bulletin*, 7 Aug. 1917

57 *CAR* (1918), 667; *Herald*, 15 Sept. 1915; *Progress-Enterprise* (Lunenburg), 18 Sept. 1918

58 *Progress-Enterprise*, 7, 21 Aug. 1918

59 *Herald*, 12 Apr. 1918 (memories of P. Raymond Jackson)

60 *Herald*, 29 Dec. 1917

61 *Herald*, 7 Aug. 1914; see also Robert Craig Brown and Ramsay Cook, *Canada, 1896–1921: A Nation Transformed* (Toronto 1974), 238–9; *Busy East*, Dec. 1917.

62 *Herald*, 4 July 1918

63 *Berwick Register*, 1 May 1918 (advertisement of the Canada Food Board)

64 *Herald*, 18 May 1916; *Herald*, 16 Dec. 1916 (on Nova Scotia's unusually high cost of living, based on provincial estimates by Sir Herbert Ames); *CAR* (1914), 531; *Herald*, 14 Aug. 1914; 8 Jan. 1918

65 *Herald*, 20 Feb. 1915; 21 Dec. 1914; 2 June 1915; 8 Apr., 7 May, 31 July, 27, 28 Aug. 1915; Arthur T. Doyle, *Front Benches and Back Rooms* (Toronto 1976), 38–207

66 Doyle, *Front Benches*, 184. There were 1,250 deaths from influenza in Nova Scotia alone in the last three months of 1918. *CAR* (1919), 698

67 *CAR* (1918), 651; Suzanne Morton, 'The Halifax Relief Commission and Labour Relations during the Reconstruction of Halifax, 1917–1919,' in Earle, ed., *Workers and the State*, 47–67

68 Brown and Cook, *Canada, 1896-1921*, ch. 12, 249

69 *Halifax Chronicle*, cited in *News* (New Glasgow), 14 June 1918; *Herald*, 15 June 1918

70 NAC, RG27, vol. 307, f.18 (26)

71 *Herald*, 30 July; 1, 17 Aug. 1918

72 *Standard*, 2 Oct. 1918

73 New Glasgow *News*, 15 Dec. 1917; NAC, RG27, vol. 306, f.17(71), M.A. Doak, Assistant Secretary, Eastern Car, memorandum to Department of Labour; *Herald*, 14 Dec. 1917

74 David Frank, 'Class Conflict in the Coal Industry: Cape Breton 1922,' in Gregory S. Kealey and Peter Warrian (eds), *Essays in Canadian Working-Class History* (Toronto 1976), 162–4

75 Heron, 'Steelworkers,' 23

76 *Standard*, 21 Apr. 1917; *Herald*, 10 Aug. 1917; Armstrong and Nelles, 'Great Fight for Clean Government'; *Herald*, 27 Apr. 1918; NAC RG27, vol. 307, f.18 (9), J.B. McLachlan to F.A. Acland, 28 Apr. 1918 (copy of telegram); *Amherst Daily News*, 19 Apr. 1918

77 *CAR* (1917), 640–2

78 *CAR* (1917), 606; J.M. Beck, *Pendulum of Power: Canada's Federal Elections* (Scarborough, Ont. 1968); *Daily Post* (Sydney), 14 Dec. 1917; for labour in Cape Breton in the election, see A.A. MacKenzie, 'The Rise and Fall of the Farmer-Labour Party in Nova Scotia' (MA thesis, Dal 1969), 35–9; *Herald*, 15 June 1917; 18, 28 June, 6, 18 Aug. 1917.

79 Doyle, *Front Benches*, 149; *Berwick Register*, 27 Feb. 1918; CHCD (19 Apr.

1918), 959, 969; James M. Cameron, *Pictonians in Arms: A Military History of Pictou County, Nova Scotia* (Fredericton 1969), 101

80 *Herald*, 22 Apr. 1918; 18 Feb., 18 June 1918; *Progress-Enterprise*, 19 June 1918

81 For discussion of the Acadians and the war, see Philippe Doucet, 'Politics and the Acadians,' in Jean Daigle (ed.), *The Acadians of the Maritimes: Thematic Studies* (Moncton 1982), 252–7; Doyle, *Front Benches*, 134–6; 'Veterans de la Première Guerre Mondiale 1914–1918,' *La revue d'histoire de la société historique Nicolas-Denys* 14:2 (Apr.-July 1986); *CAR* (1916), 350, 352. Without making hazardous assumptions about the 'nationalities' represented by various surnames, any effort to compare the pattern of Acadian enlistment with that of other groups would seem difficult.

82 Martin S. Spigelman, 'Les Acadiens et les Canadiens en temps de guerre: le jeu des alliances,' *Les cahiers de la société historique acadienne* 8:1 (Mar. 1977), 6, 10; *L'Evangéline*, 27 Apr. 1916; *CAR* (1916), 630; *Le moniteur acadien*, 22 Mar. 1917

83 *Herald*, 21 May 1918; *Le moniteur acadien*, 30 May 1918

84 *Herald*, 11 July 1918; *Bridgewater Bulletin*, 7 Aug. 1917; *Progress-Enterprise*, 29 May 1918; *Herald*, 28 May 1918

85 *Herald*, 31 May 1918; 27, 28 May 1918; 20, 21, 24 Feb. 1919; 28 Mar. 1919

86 *Herald*, 12 Apr. 1918

87 *Labour Gazette* (Ottawa), Jan. 1919, 98; *Herald*, 9 June 1920

88 See Thomas Adams, 'Planning and Development of Land in the Maritime Provinces,' *Busy East*, Sept. 1917, for a précis of his progressive views on planning.

89 *Herald*, 27 June 1919

90 Mrs Donald Shaw in *Herald*, 8 May 1920

91 *CAR* (1919), 715; (1920), 676–7, 698; (1919), 713; John Weaver, 'Reconstruction of the Richmond District in Halifax: A Canadian Episode in Public Housing and Town Planning, 1918–1921,' *Plan Canada* 6:1 (Mar. 1976), 36–47; Samuel Henry Prince, *Catastrophe and Social Change Based upon a Sociological Study of the Halifax Disaster* (New York 1920); *CAR* (1918), 345; (1919), 703, 724; Suzanne Morton, 'Labourism and Independent Labour Politics in Halifax, 1919–1926' (MA thesis, Dal 1986), 52

92 For discussions of workers' control in the daily press, see *Herald*, 10 Apr., 21 May 1919; for new union structures, see Nolan Reilly, 'The General Strike in Amherst, Nova Scotia, 1919,' *Acadiensis* 9:2 (Spring 1980); Heron, 'Steelworkers,' and Ian McKay, *The Craft Transformed: An Essay on the Carpenters of Halifax, 1885–1985* (Halifax 1985), ch. 3; estimates of union strength are from Forbes, *Maritime Rights*, 40. For Sydney policemen: *Herald*, 24 Nov. 1919; P.E.I. mail carriers: *Herald*, 19 Nov. 1919; P.E.I. teachers, *CAR* (1919), 725. On the Halifax labour council, see Mor-

ton, 'Labourism,' 1; on mass negotiations, *Herald*, 21 Feb. 1919.

93 NAC, RG27, vol. 317, f.19 (315), Oscar Downey of Curryville to Department of Labour, nd; *Moncton Times*, 21 Aug. 1919

94 *Amherst Daily News*, 25 June 1920; NAC, RG27, vol. 321, f.20 (198)

95 Forbes, 'Prohibition and the Social Gospel in Nova Scotia,' in *Challenging the Regional Stereotype*, 13–40; Janet Guildford, 'Coping with De-industrialization: The Nova Scotia Department of Technical Education, 1907–1930,' *Acadiensis* 16:2 (Spring 1987), 69–84; Kathryn M. McPherson, 'Nurses and Nursing in Early Twentieth-Century Halifax' (MA thesis, Dal 1982); Tulloch, *We, the Undersigned*, 61; Forbes, 'Battles in Another War,' 88–9

96 *Citizen* (Halifax), 23 Jan. 1920

## 7 The 1920s: Class and Region, Resistance and Accommodation

1 See NAC, RG76, vol. 498, f.775789, pt 2, Immigration Branch Records.

2 S.A. Saunders, *Economic History of the Maritime Provinces* (Fredericton 1984 [1939]), 37–44

3 Patricia A. Thornton, 'The Problem of Out-Migration from Atlantic Canada, 1871–1921: A New Look,' *Acadiensis* 15:1 (Autumn 1985), 3–34

4 For examples of critiques based on older approaches, see Frank Underhill, 'Conception of a National Interest,' in his *In Search of Canadian Liberalism* (Toronto 1960), and W.L. Morton, 'Clio in Canada: The Interpretation of Canadian History,' *University of Toronto Quarterly* 15:3 (Apr. 1946). Recent approaches are introduced by David Frank, 'The Nine Myths of Regional Disparity,' and Ian McKay, Gregory S. Kealey, and Nolan Reilly, 'Canada's Eastern Question,' *Canadian Dimension* 13:2 (July 1978).

5 Frank H. Underhill, *The Image of Confederation* (Toronto 1964), 62–4

6 A.A. MacKenzie, 'The Rise and Fall of the Farmer-Labour Party in Nova Scotia' (MA thesis, Dal 1969); Allan M. Trueman, 'New Brunswick and the 1921 Federal Election' (MA thesis, UNB 1975); Andrew Robb, 'Third Party Experience on the Island,' in Verner Smitheram, David Milne, and Satadal Dasgupta (eds), *The Garden Transformed: Prince Edward Island: 1945–1980* (Charlottetown 1982), 84–6

7 Saunders, *Economic History*, 61–7; Tom Murphy, 'The Structural Transformation of New Brunswick Agriculture' (MA thesis, UNB 1983)

8 Trueman, 'New Brunswick and the 1921 Federal Election,' ch. 6, provides the most detailed study of the UFNB. Political platforms are reproduced in Trueman's Appendices A and B.

9 Anthony Mardiros, *William Irvine: The Life of a Prairie Radical* (Toronto 1979), 82

10 F. Waldo Walsh, *We Fought for the Little Man: My Sixty Years in Agriculture* (Moncton 1978), 34–49

11 *Report of the Royal Commission on Maritime Claims* (Ottawa 1926), 38–40 (hereafter Duncan Report)

12 L. Gene Barrett, 'Underdevelopment and Social Movements in the Nova Scotia Fishing Industry to 1938,' in Robert J. Brym and R. James Sacouman (eds), *Underdevelopment and Social Movements in Atlantic Canada* (Toronto 1979), 133–7

13 Errol Sharpe, *A People's History of Prince Edward Island* (Toronto 1976), 142, 177; *Gloucester Northern Light*, 11 Apr. 1929; Dale Briggs, 'Gloucester Fishermen's Association: Fishermen's Movement or Government Program?' (unpublished paper 1981); Alvin Donovan, '"Sharing the Catch": The Origins and Development of the United Maritime Fishermen to 1938' (MA thesis, UNB 1989). See also George Boyle, *Father Tompkins of Nova Scotia* (Toronto 1953), and Wallace Clement, *The Struggle To Organize: Resistance in Canada's Fishery* (Toronto 1986).

14 *Report of the Royal Commission Investigating the Fisheries of the Maritime Provinces and the Magdalen Islands* (Ottawa 1928)

15 Saunders, *Economic History*, 55, 77; Saunders, 'Forest Industries in the Maritime Provinces,' in A.R.M. Lower (ed.), *The North American Assault on the Canadian Forest* (Toronto 1938), 368–9

16 See Nancy Jon Colpitts, 'Alma, New Brunswick, and the Twentieth Century Crisis of Readjustment: Sawmilling Community to National Park' (MA thesis, Dal 1983). I am also grateful for the use of unpublished materials by Peter deMarsh and William Parenteau.

17 David Frank (ed.), 'The Economic Gospel of J.B. McLachlan,' *New Maritimes* (Dec. 1983–Jan. 1984)

18 David Frank, 'The Cape Breton Coal Industry and the Rise and Fall of the British Empire Steel Corporation,' *Acadiensis* 7:1 (Autumn 1977) 3–34

19 David Frank, 'Company Town / Labour Town: Local Government in the Cape Breton Coal Towns, 1917–1926,' *Hs / SH* 14:27 (May 1981), 177–96, and David Frank, 'Contested Terrain: Workers' Control in the Cape Breton Coal Mines in the 1920s,' in Craig Heron and Robert Storey (eds), *On the Job: Confronting the Labour Process in Canada* (Montreal 1986), 102–23

20 For these events see David Frank, 'Class Conflict in the Coal Industry: Cape Breton 1922,' in Gregory S. Kealey and Peter Warrian (eds), *Essays in Canadian Working-Class History* (Toronto 1976), and David Frank, 'The Trial of J.B. McLachlan,' *CHAHP* (1983). See also C.B. Wade, 'History of District 26, UMWA' (unpublished ms 1950), and Paul MacEwan, *Miners and Steelworkers: Labour in Cape Breton* (Toronto 1976).

21 Don Macgillivray, 'Military Aid to the Civil Power: The Cape Breton Experience in the 1920s,' *Acadiensis* 3:2 (Spring 1974), 45–64

22 David Frank, 'Working-Class Politics: The Elections of J.B. McLachlan, 1916–1935,' in Kenneth Donovan (ed.), *The Island: New Perspectives on*

*Cape Breton History, 1713–1990* (Sydney and Fredericton 1990)

23 *Report of Provincial Royal Commission on Coal Mining Industry in Nova Scotia* (Halifax 1926); NAC, R.L. Borden Papers, Hume Cronyn to R.L. Borden, 14 Feb. 1926

24 PANS, E.N. Rhodes Papers, R.S. Gordon to E.N. Rhodes, memorandum, 16 June 1926, Hector McInnes to Rhodes, 13 July 1926

25 Ian McKay, *The Craft Transformed: An Essay on the Carpenters of Halifax, 1885–1985* (Halifax 1985), ch. 3

26 Allen Seager, 'Minto, New Brunswick: A Study in Class Relations between the Wars,' *L / Le t* 5 (Spring 1980), 81–132; Fred Winsor, '"Solving a Problem": Privatizing Workers' Compensation for Nova Scotia's Offshore Fishermen, 1926–1928,' in Michael J. Earle, (ed.), *Workers and the State in Twentieth Century Nova Scotia* (Fredericton 1989)

27 Marianne Grey Otty, *Fifty Years of Women's Institutes in New Brunswick* (np 1961); *Maritime Labor Herald*, 17 Dec. 1921; Carrie Best, *That Lonesome Road: The Autobiography of Carrie M. Best* (New Glasgow 1977), 44; Veronica Strong-Boag, 'The Girl of the New Day: Canadian Working Women in the 1920s,' *L / Le t* 4 (1979), 131–64

28 William Young Smith, Jr, 'Axis of Administration: Saint John Reformers and Bureaucratic Centralization in New Brunswick, 1911–1925' (MA thesis, UNB 1984), 47–71; Margaret E. McCallum, 'Keeping Women in their Place: The Minimum Wage in Canada, 1910–1925,' *L / Le t* 17 (Spring 1986), 29–33; Michael J. Earle and Ian McKay, 'Introduction: Industrial Legality in Nova Scotia,' in Earle (ed.), *Workers and the State*

29 The standard source on the history of Maritime Rights is E.R. Forbes, *Maritime Rights: The Maritime Rights Movement, 1919–1927; A Study in Canadian Regionalism* (Montreal 1979), and the following discussion relies heavily on its evidence. A more critical brief portrait is given by George A. Rawlyk in 'Nova Scotia Regional Protest, 1867–1967,' *QQ* 80:1 (Spring 1968), 105–23.

30 J. Nolan Reilly, 'The Emergence of Class Consciousness in Industrial Nova Scotia: A Study of Amherst, 1891–1925' (PhD thesis, Dal 1983), 277–86

31 L.D. McCann, 'Metropolitanism and Branch Businesses in the Maritimes, 1881–1931,' *Acadiensis* 13:1 (Autumn 1983), 124

32 James D. Frost, 'The "Nationalization" of the Bank of Nova Scotia, 1880–1910,' *Acadiensis* 12:1 (Autumn 1982), 3–38

33 *Maritime Labor Herald*, 1 Nov. 1924, 7 Mar. 1925

34 Mimeographed prefatory letter, 23 Sept. 1926, included in the Nova Scotia document, *A Submission of Its Claims with Respect to Maritime Disabilities within Confederation as Presented to the Royal Commission* (Halifax 1926), copy at Harriet Irving Library, UNB

35 Duncan Report, 9–11

36 Duncan Report, 28–9
37 Duncan Report, 38–40
38 *CAR* (1927–8), 436
39 E.R. Forbes (ed.), 'P.E.I. Opts Out,' *Acadiensis* 6:1 (Autumn 1976), 113–14
40 'Complementary Report of Dr. H.A. Innis,' *Report of the Royal Commission – Provincial Economic Inquiry* (Halifax 1934). On the impact of subsidized freight rates after 1927, see A.W. Currie, *Canadian Transportation Economics* (Toronto 1967), 113–21.
41 Antonine Maillet, *Mariaàgélas* (Toronto 1986 [1973]), 22 *et passim*
42 For an introduction to the literature on the prohibition era, see C. Mark Davis, 'Atlantic Canada's Rum Running Tradition,' *Acadiensis* 14:2 (Spring 1985), 147–56. See also Geoff and Dorothy Robinson, *The Nellie J. Banks* (Summerside 1972); Don Miller, *I Was a Rum Runner* (Yarmouth 1979); E.R. Forbes and A.A. MacKenzie, (eds), *Four Years with the Demon Rum, 1925–1929: The Autobiography and Diary of Temperance Inspector Clifford Rose* (Fredericton 1980); B.J. Grant, *When Rum Was King: The Story of the Prohibition Era in New Brunswick* (Fredericton 1984).
43 John G. Reid, 'Mount Allison College: The Reluctant University,' *Acadiensis* 10:1 (Autumn 1980), 35–66; John G. Reid, 'Health, Education, Economy: Philanthropic Foundations in the Atlantic Region in the 1920s and 1930s,' *Acadiensis* 14:1 (Autumn 1984), 64–83
44 Douglas F. Campbell, 'A Group, a Network and the Winning of Church Union in Canada: A Case Study in Leadership,' *Canadian Review of Sociology and Anthropology* 25:1 (1988), 41–66; Twila F. Buttimer, '"Great Expectations": The Maritime Methodist Church and Church Union, 1925' (MA thesis, UNB 1980); Richard Allen, *The Social Passion: Religion and Social Reform in Canada, 1914–1928* (Toronto 1971); N.K. Clifford, *The Resistance to Church Union in Canada, 1904–1939* (Vancouver 1985)
45 Charles Allain, 'The Impact of the Automobile on the Government of New Brunswick, 1897–1932' (MA thesis, UNB 1987); Russell Hunt and Robert Campbell, *K.C. Irving: The Art of the Industrialist* (Toronto 1973)
46 Peter Morris, *Embattled Shadows: A History of Canadian Cinema, 1895–1939* (Montreal 1978), 120; Gwendolyn Davies, 'The Song Fishermen: A Regional Poetry Celebration,' in L.D. McCann (ed.), *People and Place: Studies of Small Town Life in the Maritimes* (Fredericton 1987); Dawn Fraser, *Echoes from Labor's War: Industrial Cape Breton in the 1920s* (Toronto 1976)
47 See Claude Darrach, *Race to Fame: The Inside Story of the 'Bluenose'* (Hantsport 1985).
48 Jean Daigle (ed.), *The Acadians of the Maritimes: Thematic Studies* (Moncton 1982); Arthur T. Doyle, *Front Benches and Back Rooms* (Toronto 1976), ch. 13; Allain, 'Impact of the Automobile'; Irène Landry, 'Saint-Quentin et le retour à la terre: analyse socio-économique, 1910–1960,' *Revue de la société historique du Madawaska* 14:4 (Oct.-Dec. 1986); Régis Brun, *De*

*Grand-Pré à Kouchibougouac* (Moncton 1982), 161–3

49 James Overton, 'Coming Home: Nostalgia and Tourism in Newfoundland,' *Acadiensis* 14:1 (Autumn 1984), 84–97; A.J.B. Johnston, 'Preserving History: The Commemoration of 18th Century Louisbourg, 1895–1940,' *Acadiensis* 12:2 (Spring 1983), 53–80; Ian McKay, 'Among the Fisherfolk: J.F.B. Livesay and the Invention of Peggy's Cove,' *JCS* 23:1/2 (Spring/ Summer 1988), 23–45

50 Neil Hooper, 'A History of the Caledonia Amateur Athletic Club, Glace Bay, Nova Scotia' (MPhE thesis, UNB 1987). See also Ronald Lappage, 'Sport as an Expression of Western and Maritime Discontent between the Wars,' *Canadian Journal of History of Sport and Physical Education* (1977), 50–71.

51 Alexander J. Young, 'Maritime Attitudes toward Women in Sport, 1920–30s,' *Proceedings, 5th Canadian Symposium on the History of Sport and Physical Education* (Toronto 1982), 227–31

52 Catherine L. Cleverdon, *The Woman Suffrage Movement in Canada* (Toronto 1974 [1950]), ch. 6; Elspeth Tulloch, *We, the Undersigned: A Historical Overview of New Brunswick Women's Political and Legal Status, 1784–1984* (Moncton 1985), 52, 70–1; Joanne Reid, 'Muriel McQueen Fergusson: A Study of Interwave Feminism in New Brunswick' (MA report, UNB 1988)

53 For research on Miss Canada 1923, I am indebted to an unpublished paper by David Barrett, prepared for a course at UNB in 1981. Dawn Fraser's poem appears in Fraser's *Narrative Verse and Other Comments* (Glace Bay 1944[?]), 244–5.

## 8 The 1930s: Depression and Retrenchment

1 K.G. Jones, 'Response to Regional Disparity in the Maritime Provinces, 1926–1942: A Study in Intergovernmental Relations' (MA thesis, UNB 1980), 45–7, and E.R. Forbes, *Maritime Rights: The Maritime Rights Movement, 1919–1927; A Study in Canadian Regionalism* (Montreal 1979), 180

2 Canada, Dominion Bureau of Statistics (hereafter DBS), *The Maritime Provinces in Their Relation to the National Economy of Canada* (Ottawa 1948), 59–94

3 Canada, DBS, *National Accounts Income and Expenditure, 1926–1956* (Ottawa 1958), 64

4 *Canada Yearbook* (1933), 778; Carol Ann Ferguson, 'Responses to the Unemployment Problem in Saint John, New Brunswick, 1929–1933' (MA thesis, UNB 1984), 28–30

5 Nova Scotia, Assembly, 'Report of the Royal Commission on Coal,' *JHA* (1932), App. 31, 22.

6 See Parzival Copes, 'Fisheries Management on Canada's Atlantic Coast: Economic Factors and Socio-Political Constraints,' *The Canadian Journal of*

*Regional Science* 6:1 (Spring 1983), 1–32, and Canada, DBS, *Maritime Provinces*, 44–5.

7 James Struthers, *No Fault of Their Own: Unemployment and the Welfare State, 1914–41* (Toronto 1983), 6

8 *CHCD* (3 Apr. 1930), 1225–8

9 NAC, RG27, vol. 213, Department of Labour Papers, 'Dominion Unemployment Relief since 1930' (Jan. 1940), 39

10 E.R. Forbes, 'Cutting the Pie into Smaller Pieces: Matching Grants and Relief in the Maritime Provinces during the 1930s,' *Acadiensis* 17:1 (Autumn 1987), 43–5

11 PANB, Minutes of the Municipal Council of Northumberland, 17 and 18 Jan. 1934

12 J.M. Beck, *The Evolution of Municipal Government in Nova Scotia, 1749–1973* (Halifax 1973), 32–3, and Peter Johnson, 'Relations between the Government of Nova Scotia and the Union of Nova Scotia Municipalities, 1906–1966' (MA thesis, Dal 1968), 70–4

13 Royal Commission on Dominion-Provincial Relations, Public Accounts Inquiry, *Dominion of Canada and Provincial Governments: Comparative Statistics of Public Finance* (Ottawa 1939), 95

14 NAC, RG27, vol. 213, Department of Labour Papers, 'Dominion Unemployment Relief'

15 NAC, RG27, vol. 2096, f.Y 40–0, monthly 'Direct Relief Reports' from Nova Scotia to the minister of labour. These are complete from Apr. 1933 to Mar. 1934 and largely complete from Oct. 1932 until the end of the decade.

16 *Proceedings of the Union of Nova Scotia Municipalities* (1934), 143

17 David Frank and Don MacGillivray (eds), *George MacEachern: An Autobiography. The Story of a Cape Breton Radical* (Sydney 1987), 44

18 NAC, RG27, vol. 2096, f.Y 40, Department of Labour Papers; calculated from J.K. Houston, 'An Appreciation of Relief as Related to Economic and Employment Tendencies in Canada,' 31 Oct. 1936

19 L.J. Cusack, 'The Prince Edward Island People and the Great Depression, 1930–1935' (MA thesis, UNB 1972), 51–3

20 Frank and MacGillivray, (eds), *George MacEachern*, 43

21 Cusack, 'Prince Edward Island People and the Great Depression,' 71–3, and 'Report of the Baptist Missions in the Canadian West,' *Baptist Yearbook of the Maritime Provinces of Canada* (1937), 139

22 Ferguson, 'Responses to the Unemployment Problem in Saint John,' 73, 77, 80

23 See also James Struthers, 'A Profession in Crisis: Charlotte Whitton and Canadian Social Work in the 1930s,' *CHR* 62:2 (June 1981), 169–85.

24 Ferguson, 'Responses to the Unemployment Problem in Saint John,' 206

25 PANB, New Brunswick Cabinet Papers, J.W. Farth to J.B. McNair, 20 Aug.

1935 and A.W. Bennett to A.J. Leger, 13 Mar. 1931

26 Royal Commission on Dominion-Provincial Relations, 'Report of Proceedings,' 23 May 1938, 9085

27 PAPEI, Premiers' Office Papers, A.C. Saunders to Rev. T. Constable, 26 Nov. 1928

28 PANB, Minutes of the Municipality of Gloucester, 24 Jan. 1936

29 *Light* (Yarmouth), 3 July 1930 (clipping in NAC, MG27, III, vol. 15, J.R. Ralston Papers). See also E.N. Rhodes's speech in Moncton in the *Moncton Times*, 21 July 1930.

30 *CAR* (1934), 268, and Kenneth Bryden, *Old Age Pensions and Policy-Making in Canada* (Montreal 1974), 84–97, 101

31 *CAR* (1937–8), 265–6

32 E.M. Poirier, 'The Founding of Allardville Settlement' (MA Report, UNB 1973), 21; New Brunswick, *Report of Department of Lands and Mines* (1939), 120

33 M.C. Urquhart and K.A.H. Buckley, *Historical Statistics of Canada* (Ottawa 1983), 875–81

34 A. Gosselin and G.P. Boucher, *Settlement Problems in Northern New Brunswick* (Ottawa 1944), Canada, Department of Agriculture Publication No. 764, 24–9

35 PANB, RG10, RS106, Box 42, 're Reconstruction,' Department of Lands and Mines, 'A Discussion of Land Settlement in New Brunswick'

36 L.L. Patterson, 'Indian Affairs and the Nova Scotia Centralization Policy' (MA thesis, Dal 1985), 33

37 PANS, RG7, vol. 225, f.9, Provincial Secretary-Treasurer's Papers, J.A. Fulton to E.H. Blois, in Fulton to John Doull, 4 Apr. 1931

38 Patterson, 'Indian Affairs,' 19

39 Robin W. Winks, *The Blacks in Canada: A History* (Montreal 1971), 419–20

40 Calixte F. Savoie, *Mémoires d'un nationaliste acadien* (Moncton 1979), 281

41 Ibid., ch. 41

42 *Report of the Royal Commission on Education for the Province of New Brunswick, Canada* (Fredericton 1932), 19–21, 25–6, 38

43 *Savoie, Mémoires*, ch. 48, and Paul Surette, 'Les acadiens et la campagne électorale provinciale de 1935 au Nouveau-Brunswick,' *Le société historique acadienne, 45 ième cahier* 5:5 (Oct., Nov., Dec. 1974), 205

44 Léon Thériault, 'L'acadianisation de l'Eglise catholique en Acadie, 1763–1953' in Jean Daigle (ed.), *Les Acadiens des Maritimes* (Moncton 1980), 359

45 A.J. Savoie, 'L'enseignement en Acadie de 1604 à 1970,' in Daigle (ed.), *Les Acadiens des Maritimes*

46 *Annual Report of the Chief Superintendent of the Province of Prince Edward Island for the Fiscal Year Ended December 31, 1935*, pt IV, 42; Georges Arsenault, *Les acadiens de l'Ile, 1720–1980* (Moncton 1987), 177–8

47 George A. Rawlyk and Ruth Haftner, *Acadian Education in Nova Scotia: An Historical Survey to 1965*, Studies of the Royal Commission on Bilingualism and Biculturalism, 11 (Ottawa 1970), 72
48 Michael J. Earle, 'The Rise and Fall of a Red Union: The Amalgamated Mine Workers of Nova Scotia, 1932–36' (MA thesis, Dal 1985), 20–35
49 P.S. Mifflen, 'A History of Trade Unionism in the Coal Mines of Nova Scotia' (MA thesis, Catholic University of America 1951), 76
50 Bruce Randall, 'Plant Council Labour Struggles at the New Brunswick International Paper Company, Dalhousie, N.B. 1933–37' (thesis in progress, UNB).
51 Frank and MacGillivray (eds), *George MacEachern*, 61–2
52 Allen Seager, 'Minto, New Brunswick: A Study in Canadian Class Relations between the Wars,' *L/Le t* 5 (Spring 1980), 114–23
53 P.H. Burden, 'The New Brunswick Farmer-Labour Union, 1937–1941' (MA thesis, UNB 1983), 64–5
54 Frank and MacGillivray (eds.), *George MacEachern*, 77–80
55 Ron Stang, 'Community, Industry and Workers along Nova Scotia's North Shore: The Malagash Salt Miners' (Honours thesis, Dal 1980), 53
56 See for example, 'Report of the Social Service Board,' *United Baptist Yearbook of the Maritime Provinces of Canada* (1938), 138–45; Church of England, 'Report of the Council for Social Service,' *Diocesan Yearbook* (1934), 133–8; and United Church of Canada, *Minutes of the Ninth Maritime Conference* (Sackville, June 1933), 45–6.
57 George A. Rawlyk, 'Fundamentalism, Modernism and the Maritime Baptists in the 1920s and 1930s,' *Acadiensis* 17:1 (Autumn 1987), 18–31
58 NAC, MG27, III, vol. 27, Ralston Papers, 'The Work of the Oxford Group in Canada,' 7, 25, 28
59 M.M. Coady, *Masters of Their Own Destiny: The Story of the Antigonish Movement of Adult Education through Economic Cooperation* (New York 1963)
60 D.W. MacInnes, 'Clerics, Fishermen, Farmers and Workers: Antigonish Movement and Identity in Eastern Nova Scotia, 1928–39' (PhD thesis, MacMaster University 1978), 178–92, 218
61 Ibid., 223
62 Quoted in F.J. Mifflen, 'The Antigonish Movement: A Summary Analysis of Its Development, Principles and Goals,' *Canadian Journal of Public and Comparative Economy* 10 (Jan.-Dec. 1977), 88
63 United Church of Canada, *Minutes of the Thirteenth Maritime Conference* (Sackville, June 1937), 46, and Ian MacPherson, *Each for All: A History of the Co-operative Movement in English Canada, 1900–1945* (Ottawa 1979), 123
64 MacInnes, 'Clerics, Fishermen, Farmers and Workers,' 242
65 Alvin Donovan, '"Sharing the Catch": The Origins and Development of

the United Maritime Fishermen to 1938' (MA thesis, UNB 1989), ch. 4

66 *Report of the Royal Commission on Price Spreads* (Ottawa 1937), 184–5

67 Donovan, '"Sharing the Catch,"' 102

68 NAC, MG27, III, B11, vol. 22, Ralston Papers, R.P. Bell to J.L. Ralston, 25 Oct. 1934

69 Donovan, '"Sharing the Catch,"' 185–8

70 J.T. Croteau, *Cradled in the Waves: The Story of a People's Co-operative Achievement in Economic Betterment on Prince Edward Island* (Toronto 1951), 5, 12–19, and G.E. Macdonald, '"And Christ Dwelt in the Heart of His House": A History of St. Dunstan's University, 1855–1955' (PhD thesis, Queen's University 1984), 436–40

71 Jean Daigle, *Une force qui nous appartient: la fédération des caisses populaires acadiennes, 1936–86* (Moncton 1990), 52

72 MacPherson, *Each for All*, 170

73 Earle, 'Rise and Fall of a Red Union,' 194

74 Burden, 'New Brunswick Farmer-Labour Union,' 118

75 L. Gene Barrett, 'Development and Underdevelopment, and the Rise of Trade Unionism in the Fishing Industry of Nova Scotia, 1900–1950' (MA thesis Dal 1976), 152–89

76 J.C. Webster, *The Distressed Maritimes* (Toronto 1926)

77 George F.G. Stanley, 'John Clarence Webster: The Laird of Shediac,' *Acadiensis* 3:1 (Autumn 1973), 59–61

78 Gary Hughes, 'The Maritime Art Association, 1935–43: Regionalism and the National Response' (paper read before the annual meeting of the Universities Art Association of Canada, University of Victoria 1986); Alfred Pinsky, 'Painting in New Brunswick, 1880–1946,' in R.A. Tweedie, Fred Cogswell, and W.S. MacNutt (eds), *Arts in New Brunswick* (Fredericton 1967), 149–61

79 Ferguson, 'Responses to the Unemployment Problem,' 1

80 Veronica Strong-Boag, *The New Day Recalled: Lives of Girls and Women in English Canada, 1919–1939* (Toronto 1988), 137–8

81 Ferguson, 'Responses to the Unemployment Problem,' 24

82 P.D. Lambly, '"Towards a Living Wage": The Minimum-Wage Campaign for Women in Nova Scotia, 1920–35' (Honours Essay, Dal 1977), 78–89

83 Joanne Reid, 'Muriel McQueen Fergusson: A Study of Interwave Feminism in New Brunswick' (MA report, UNB 1988)

84 See PANB, RS9, Cabinet Papers, Francis Fish to C.D. Tilley, 14 May 1934 and biographical sketch of Fish 14 July 1934.

85 Earle, 'Rise and Fall of a Red Union,' 161

86 MacInnes, 'Clerics, Fishermen, Farmers and Workers,' 237

87 F. Waldo Walsh, *We Fought for the Little Man: My Sixty Years in Agriculture* (Moncton 1978), 51–2

88 Ibid.

89 E.R. Forbes, 'Rise and Fall of the Conservative Party in the Provincial Politics of Nova Scotia' (MA thesis, Dal 1967), ch. 6

90 Ibid.

91 J.M. Beck, *The Government of Nova Scotia* (Toronto 1957), 340–1

92 Jones, 'Response to Regional Disparity in the Maritime Provinces,' 59–60

93 Carmen Carroll, 'The Influence of H.H. Stevens and the Reconstruction Party in Nova Scotia, 1934–35' (MA thesis, UNB 1972), 193

94 J.R. Rowell, 'An Intellectual in Politics: Norman Rogers as an Intellectual and Minister of Labour, 1929–40' (MA thesis, Queen's University 1978), 143–4

95 W.J. White, 'Left-Wing Politics and Community: A Study of Glace Bay 1930–1940' (MA thesis, Dal 1978), 93, 121, 136, and Michael J. Earle and H. Gamberg, 'The United Mine Workers and the Coming of the CCF to Cape Breton,' *Acadiensis* 19:1 (Autumn 1989), 17–21

96 See A.P. Paterson, *The Problems of the Maritime Provinces within Confederation* (Saint John 1930).

97 K.H. LeBlanc, 'A.P. Paterson and New Brunswick's Response to Constitutional Change, 1935–9' (MA Report, UNB 1989)

98 Struthers, *No Fault of Their Own,* 140

99 R.A. Tweedie, *On with the Dance: A New Brunswick Memoir, 1935–1960* (Fredericton 1986), 56

100 New Brunswick, Assembly, *Debates* (1939), 199

101 Cusack, 'Prince Edward Island People and the Great Depression,' 15–19

102 Wayne E. MacKinnon, *The Life of the Party: A History of the Liberal Party in Prince Edward Island* (Summerside 1973)

103 Hartwell Daley, *'Volunteers in Action': The Prince Edward Island Division of the Red Cross Society, 1907–1979* (Summerside 1981), 80–6

104 A.E. Grauer, *Public Health* (Ottawa 1939), 35, 75

**9 The 1940s: War and Rehabilitation**

1 Harriet Parsons, 'Sunshine and Shadow in the Maritime Economy,' *Maritime Advocate and Busy East,* Nov. 1948, 5

2 C.P. Stacey, *Arms Men and Governments: The War Policies of Canada, 1939–1945* (Ottawa 1980), 33

3 Eugene A. Forsey, 'Labour and the Constitution in Atlantic Canada,' in his *Perspectives on the Atlantic Canada Labour Movement and the Working Class Experience* (Sackville 1985), 11

4 Elizabeth Ewing, *History of Twentieth Century Fashion* (London 1973)

5 J.H. Thompson, 'Cartoons, Humorous,' *The Canadian Encyclopedia,* 3 vols (Edmonton 1988) 1:374–5

6 Ronald H. Sherwood, 'Miracle Men of the Maritimes,' *Maritime Advocate,* Feb.-Mar. 1948

7 William R. Young, 'Academics and Social Scientists versus the Press: The Policies of the Bureau of Public Information and the Wartime Information Board, 1939 to 1945,' *Historical Papers* (1978), 217–40

8 Ottawa, Wartime Information Service Board (WISB), *Canada at War* 4 (1945), 24. For a discussion of the role of women, see Ruth Roach Pierson, '"Jill Canuck": CWAC of All Trades but No "Pistol Packing Mamma,"' *Historical Papers* (1978), 106–33; Ruth Roach Pierson, *'They're Still Women After All': The Second World War and Canadian Women* (Toronto 1986).

9 Stacey, *Arms, Men and Governments*, 344–5

10 Marc Milner, *North Atlantic Run: The Royal Canadian Navy and the Battle for the Convoys* (Toronto, 1985)

11 Peter Moogk, 'From Fortress Louisbourg to Fortress Sydney,' in Kenneth Donovan (ed.), *Cape Breton at 200: Historical Essays in Honour of the Island's Bicentennial, 1785–1985* (Sydney 1985); R.B. Mitchell, 'Sydney Harbour – The War Years,' in R.J. Morgan (ed.), *More Essays in Cape Breton History* (Windsor 1977); Thomas H. Raddall, *Halifax: Warden of the North* (Toronto 1948), 313; Kay Piersdorff, 'Anyone Here from the West?' *Nova Scotia Historical Review* 5:1 (1985)

12 Canada, House of Commons, *Debates* 3 (1941), 2579

13 WISB, *Canada at War*, 102

14 Ibid., 87

15 E.R. Forbes, 'Consolidating Disparity: The Maritimes and the Industrialization of Canada during the Second World War,' *Acadiensis* 15:2 (Spring 1986), 4

16 Ibid., 19

17 Raddall, *Halifax*, 313

18 Forbes, 'Consolidating Disparity,' 18 and 10

19 Douglas G. Cruikshank, 'Dominion Wartime Labour Policy and the Politics of Unionism, 1939–1945: The Experience of the Canadian Congress of Labour's Eastern Canadian Shipyard Unions' (MA thesis, Dal 1983), 26

20 Stacey, *Arms, Men and Governments*, 72

21 Forbes, 'Consolidating Disparity,' 15–16

22 *Census of Canada*, 1951, Table 12

23 B.S. Kierstead, *The Economic Effects of the War on the Maritime Provinces* (Halifax 1944), 111–12

24 M.C. Urquhart and K.A.H. Buckley, *Historical Statistics of Canada* (Toronto 1965), 84–6

25 Miriam Chapin, *Atlantic Canada* (Toronto 1956), 79; Piersdorff, 'Anyone Here from the West?'; Jean Bruce, *Back The Attack* (Toronto 1985); Aida McAnn, 'Maritime Women at Work in War and Peace,' *Public Affairs* 7:2 (Winter 1943)

26 Ian McKay, *The Craft Transformed: An Essay on the Carpenters of Halifax,*

*1885–1985* (Halifax 1985), 97–8

27 Kierstead, *Economic Effects*, 211

28 PAPEI, Premiers' Papers, Walter Jones Papers, P.E.I. Command to Jones, 23 Mar. 1945

29 Kierstead, *Economic Effects*, 211

30 Saint John Board of Trade, *Minutes*, 27 Apr. 1939

31 Kierstead, *Economic Effects*, 211

32 Halifax Junior Board of Trade, *The Scope of the Housing Problem in Halifax* (Halifax 1943), 13

33 Raddall, *Halifax*, 318–19

34 Halifax Junior Board of Trade, *Scope of the Housing Problem*, 11–13; see also John Bacher, 'From Study to Reality: The Establishment of Public Housing in Halifax, 1930–1955,' *Acadiensis* 18:1 (Autumn 1988), 120–35. For a good description of the national housing situation, see John Bland, *Housing and Community Planning* (Montreal 1944).

35 Raddall, *Halifax*, 310

36 James F.E. White, 'The Ajax Affair: Citizens and Sailors in Wartime Halifax, 1939–1945' (MA thesis, Dal 1984), 10; see also Graham Metson, *An East Coast Port: Halifax at War, 1939–1945* (Scarborough, Ont. 1981); Christina Simmons, 'Helping the Poorer Sisters: The women of the Jost Mission, Halifax, 1905–1945,' *Acadiensis* 14:1 (Autumn 1984), 26.

37 R.L. Kellock, *Report on the Halifax Disorders* (Ottawa 1945), 10

38 United States Maritime Commission, A.J. Sullivan to E.S. Land, 30 Mar. 1942

39 Raddall, *Halifax*, 311

40 Bacher, 'From Study to Reality,' 130–1

41 For a fuller discussion of the riot see Kellock, *Report on the Halifax Disorders*; Stanley Redman, *Open Gangway: The (Real) Story of the Halifax Navy Riot* (Hantsport, N.S. 1981); Cyril Robinson, 'Report on Riots,' *Canadian Business* 18 (Nov. 1945); Frank Flaherty, 'Halifax Has Seen It Happen Before,' *Canadian Business* 19 (May 1946).

42 P.B. Waite, *Lord of Point Grey, Larry MacKenzie of UBC* (Vancouver 1987)

43 *Report of the New Brunswick Committee on Reconstruction* (Fredericton, 23 June 1944), 23; G.A. McAllister, 'War's Impact on the Maritime Provinces: A Review,' *Public Affairs* 8;1 (Autumn 1944)

44 PAPEI, Jones Papers, Jones to J.J. Carrier, 16 Aug. 1944; Jones to Owen McCabe, 6 Mar. 1944

45 Ibid., Jones to W.L.M. King, 14 Dec. 1944

46 J.R. Petrie, 'The Regional Economy of New Brunswick,' App. A, *Report of the New Brunswick Committee on Reconstruction* (Fredericton 1944), 419–26

47 *Interim Report of the Prince Edward Island Advisory Reconstruction Committee* (Charlottetown, 20 July 1945), 59

48 Margaret Conrad, 'Apple Blossom Time in the Annapolis Valley, 1880–

1957,' *Acadiensis* 9:2 (Spring 1980), 26–34, and Margaret Conrad, *George Nowlan: Maritime Conservative in National Politics* (Toronto 1986), 92

49 *Census of Canada*, 1951, Table 4, Agriculture

50 Parsons, 'Sunshine and Shadow,' 78

51 Forbes, 'Consolidating Disparity,' 13ff

52 John Hawkins, *The Life and Times of Angus L.* (Hantsport, N.S. 1969)

53 Neil Jourdrey, *The Public Life of A.S. MacMillan* (MA thesis, Dal 1966)

54 Chapin, *Atlantic Canada*, 125; see also Verner Smitheram, David Milne, and Satadal Dasgupta (eds), *The Garden Transformed: Prince Edward Island, 1945–1980* (Charlottetown 1982), 42.

55 See R.A. Tweedie, *On with the Dance: A New Brunswick Memoir 1935–1960* (Fredericton 1986)

56 See Douglas Owram, *The Government Generation: Canadian Intellectuals and the State, 1900–1945* (Toronto 1986), 236; J.L. Granatstein, *The Ottawa Men: The Civil Service Mandarins, 1935–1957* (Toronto 1981), 273; R.O. Macfarlane, 'Canada: One Country or Nine Provinces,' *DR* 18 (1938–9), 15.

57 Saint John Board of Trade, *Minutes*, 17 Oct. 1940; Nova Scotia, *Report of the Royal Commission on Provincial Development and Rehabilitation* (Halifax 1944), 10

58 NBM, A.P. Paterson Papers, *Preliminary Report* by W.P. Jones on Royal Commission, 23 May 1940

59 See Leonard Marsh, *Report on Social Security for Canada 1943* (Toronto 1975)

60 PAPEI, Jones Papers, L.G. Dewar to Jones (Ottawa nd)

61 Nova Scotia, *Report of the Royal Commission on Provincial Development*, 54–5, 87–9

62 *Report of the New Brunswick Committee on Reconstruction*, 43

63 Dale C. Thomson, *Louis St. Laurent, Canadian* (Toronto 1967), 169

64 Ibid., 171

65 *Canada Year Book* (1959), 408–11

66 Nova Scotia, *Report of the Royal Commission on Provincial Development*, 49

67 *Report of the New Brunswick Committee on Reconstruction*, 58

68 *Interim Report of the Prince Edward Island Advisory Reconstruction Committee*, 44

69 Marian Fox, 'New Brunswick's King Midas,' *Maritime Advocate* (Oct. 1948)

70 John G. Reid, 'Health, Education, Economy: Philanthropic Foundations in the Atlantic Region in the 1920s and 1930s,' in L.D. McCann (ed.), *People and Place: Studies of Small Town Life in the Maritimes* (Fredericton 1987), 101–22

71 PAPEI, Jones Papers, Jones to L.W. Shaw, 10 May 1944

72 *Interim Report of the Prince Edward Island Advisory Reconstruction Committee*, 69

73  Ida Delaney, *By Their Own Hands* (Hansport, N.S. 1985), 62

74  John F. Graham, *Fiscal Adjustment and Economic Development: A Case Study of Nova Scotia* (Toronto 1963), 91

75  Ibid., 52n

76  P.E.I. *Gazette*, 22 Feb. 1949

77  *Report of the New Brunswick Committee on Reconstruction*, 23

78  NBM, A.P. Paterson Papers, Rotary Address, 9 Dec. 1940

79  Saint John Board of Trade, *Council Minutes*, 19 Oct., 1944

80  Ibid., 3 Apr. 1944

81  For example, Kierstead, *Economic Effects*, 222; he called for regional boards to deal with forest and fisheries management, similar to those advocated by W.A. Robson for the United Kingdom.

82  Chapin, *Atlantic Canada*, 32

83  Robert A. Young, '"And the People Will Sink into Despair": Reconstruction in New Brunswick, 1942–52,' *CHR* (June 1988), 127–66

84  *Guardian* (Charlottetown), 9 July 1947; see also the very personal account in Lee Zink, *The Rooster Crows at Dawn: My Eighty Years in the Nova Scotia Village of Blandford* (Hantsport, N.S. 1987), 94–9.

85  Young, 'And the People,' 149

86  Dalton Camp, Gentlemen, *Players and Politicians* (Toronto 1970), 3–7

87  *Maritime Advocate*, June 1949, 4, cited in Margaret Conrad, 'The Atlantic Revolution of the 1950s,' in Berkeley Fleming (ed.), *Beyond Anger and Longing: Community and Development in Atlantic Canada* (Fredericton 1988)

88  Halifax and Dartmouth, *Day by Day*, 28 June to 4 July 1948

89  Ibid., Apr. 1948

90  J.W. Pickersgill and D.F. Forster, *The MacKenzie King Record*, 4 vols (Toronto 1970), 4:237–8

91  Colin Howell, 'Baseball and the Decline of Community in the Maritimes,' *New Maritimes* 3:3 (Nov. 1984)

92  George Peabody, Carolyn MacGregor, and Richard Thorne, *The Maritimes: Tradition, Challenge and Change* (Halifax 1987), 78

93  *Maritime Advocate*, Jan. 1948

94  Peabody, et al., *The Maritimes*, 70

95  PAPEI, Jones Papers, Jones to C.D. Howe, 11 Sept. 1945; 12 Sept. 1945; Jones to Ralston, 26 July 1944

96  *Maritime Advocate*, Nov. 1948

97  Saint John Board of Trade, *Minutes*, 8 Dec. 1940; 19 Oct. 1944

98  PAPEI, Jones Papers, Jones to Ian MacKenzie, 1 Sept. 1945

99  Ibid., Herbert Jones to J. Walter Jones, 28 Feb. 1945

100  Ibid., Jones to W.L.M. King, 1 Feb. 1945; Vaughan to Jones, 6 Apr. 1944; W.E. Robinson to Jones, 15 Feb. 1950

101  Intraregional rivalry even divided the Maritime CCF; see Ian McKay, 'The Maritime C.C.F.,' *New Maritimes* (July-Aug. 1984), 8.

102 Saint John Board of Trade, *Minutes*, 19 Oct. 1944
103 Terrance D. MacLean, 'The Co-operative Commonwealth Federation in Nova Scotia, 1938–56,' in Morgan (ed.), *More Essays*, 37
104 Michael J. Earle and H. Gamberg, 'The United Mine Workers and the Coming of the CCF to Cape Breton,' *Acadiensis* 19:1 (Autumn 1989), 3–26; Chapin, *Atlantic Canada*, 48
105 McKay, 'Maritime C.C.F,' 8. See also Paul MacEwan, *Miners and Steelworkers: Labour in Cape Breton* (Toronto 1976), ch. 19.
106 *Maritime Advocate*, Nov. 1948, 28
107 Quoted in Michael J. Earle, 'Down with Hitler and Silby Barrett: The Cape Breton Miners' Slowdown Strike of 1941,' *Acadiensis* 18:1 (Autumn 1988), 56
108 Stuart Jamieson, *Time of Trouble: Labour Unrest and Industrial Conflict in Canada* 1900–1966 (Ottawa 1968), 304
109 *Canada Year Book* (1950), 666
110 Jamieson, *Time of Trouble*, 305; Smitheram, et al. (eds), *Garden Transformed*, 44; Forsey, 'Labour and the Constitution,' 12–15; *Canada Year Book* (1950), 666; P.E.I. *Gazette*, 2 Mar. 1946
111 Forsey, 'Labour and the Constitution,' 15
112 John De Mont, 'A Combative Billionaire,' *Maclean's*, 6 Feb. 1989, 40
113 Robert Rumilly, *Histoire des acadiens*, 2 vols (Montreal 1955) vol. 2; Ronald Labelle, 'In the Shadow of Quebec: Toward an Understanding of the Ideology of the Acadian Leadership 1914–1945' (Student essay, UNB 1988); Anselme Chiasson, 'Le clergé et le reveil acadien 1864–1960,' *Revue de l'université de Moncton* 11:1 (Feb. 1978); Marguerite Maillet, 'La littérature acadienne de 1874 à 1960,' *Revue de l'université de Moncton* 11:2 (May 1978); Guy R. Michaud, *La paroisse de l'immaculée-conception Edmundston, N.B. 1880–1980* (Saint-Basille 1980)
114 McKay, 'Maritime C.C.F.,' 7
115 Conrad, 'Atlantic Revolution,' 7
116 W.P. Oliver, 'Cultural Progress and the Negro in Nova Scotia,' *DR* (1949); see also Bridglae Pachai, *Dr. William Pearley Oliver and the Search for Black Identity in Nova Scotia*, Occasional Paper No. 3, Studies in national and International Issues, SMU International Education Centre (Halifax 1979).
117 Aubrey Fullerton, 'Micmacs Look Back and Ahead,' *Maritime Advocate*, Aug. 1948; Lisa Lynne Patterson, 'Indian Affairs and the Nova Scotia Centralization Policy' (MA thesis, Dal 1985)

**10 Newfoundland Confronts Canada, 1867–1949**

1 Richard Gwyn, *Smallwood: The Unlikely Revolutionary*, rev. ed. (Toronto 1972), 121–2; *Evening Telegram* (St. John's), 1 Apr. 1949

2 Typescript of speech in Bradley papers (private collection)

3 *Daily News* (St. John's), 31 Mar. 1949. Printed in F. Hollohan and M. Baker, *A Clear Head in Tempestuous Times. Albert B. Perlin: The Wayfarer* (St John's 1986), 157–60

4 Patrick O'Flaherty, *The Rock Observed: Studies in the Literature of Newfoundland* (Toronto 1979), 49–59; Keith Matthews, 'The Class of '32: St. John's Reformers on the Eve of Representative Government,' *Acadiensis Reader* 2 vols, 1:212–26

5 *Census of Newfoundland*, 1874

6 David G. Alexander, 'Newfoundland's Traditional Economy and Development to 1934,' in James K. Hiller and Peter F. Neary (eds.), *Newfoundland in the Nineteenth and Twentieth Centuries: Essays in Interpretation* (Toronto 1980), 28, Table 4

7 Average for the period 1870–4

8 J.D. Rogers, *A Historical Geography of Newfoundland*, 2nd ed. (1911; Oxford 1931), 159, 190

9 Averages for the period 1870–4

10 James K. Hiller, 'The Newfoundland Credit System: An Interpretation,' in Rosemary E. Ommer (ed.), *Merchant Credit and Labour Strategies in Historical Perspective* (Fredericton 1990), 86–101. On the codfishery in general, see Shannon Ryan, *Fish out of Water: The Newfoundland Saltfish Trade, 1814–1914* (St. John's 1986).

11 J.K. Hiller, 'The Newfoundland Seal Fishery: An Historical Introduction,' *Bulletin of Canadian Studies* 7:2 (Winter-Spring 1983–4), 49–72

12 David G. Alexander, 'Literacy and Economic Development in Nineteenth Century Newfoundland,' in David G. Alexander, *Atlantic Canada and Confederation: Essays in Canadian Political Economy* (Toronto 1983), 115

13 Ibid., 136–7

14 C. Grant Head, *Eighteenth-Century Newfoundland: A Geographer's Perspective* (Toronto 1976); John Mannion (ed.), *The Peopling of Newfoundland: Essays in Historical Geography* (St John's 1977); R.J. Lahey, 'Religion and Politics in Newfoundland: The Antecedents of the General Election of 1832' (unpublished lecture to Newfoundland Historical Society 1979).

15 F.F. Thompson, *The French Shore Problem in Newfoundland: An Imperial Study* (Toronto 1961); Peter F. Neary, 'The French and American Shore Questions as Factors in Newfoundland History,' in Hiller and Neary (eds), *Newfoundland in the Nineteenth and Twentieth Centuries*, 95–122

16 Public Record Office (PRO), CO 194/212, Minute by Herbert, 21 Jan. 1890, 625

17 Report of the joint select committee on the railway, Newfoundland, *JHA* (1880), 125

18 James K. Hiller, 'The Railway and Local Politics in Newfoundland, 1870–1901,' in Hiller and Neary (eds), *Newfoundland in the Nineteenth and*

*Twentieth Centuries*, 123–47

19 M. Harvey, 'This Land of Ours' (lecture to the St John's Athenaeum, 11 Feb. 1878), in Harvey's *Newfoundland as It Is in 1899* (London 1899), 81

20 James Murray, *The Commercial Crisis in Newfoundland. Cause, Consequences and Cure* (St John's 1895), 13

21 Alexander, 'Newfoundland's Traditional Economy', 24–5

22 J.K. Hiller, 'A History of Newfoundland, 1874–1901' (PhD thesis, Cambridge University 1971), ch. 4

23 R.E. Ommer, 'What's Wrong with Canadian Fish?' *JCS*, 20:3 (1985), 130

24 Such constraints are considered in W.G. Reeves, 'Alexander's Conundrum Reconsidered: The American Dimension in Newfoundland Resource Development, 1898–1910,' *Newfoundland Studies* 5:1 (Spring 1989), 1–38.

25 Eric W. Sager, 'The Merchants of Water Street and Capital Investment in Newfoundland's Traditional Economy,' in Lewis R. Fischer and Eric W. Sager (eds.), *The Enterprising Canadians: Entrepreneurs and Economic Development in Eastern Canada, 1820–1914* (St John's 1979), 92

26 For a general account of this period, see Hiller, 'A History,' chs 5, 6 and 7.

27 Hiller, 'A History,' 302–8; H. Mitchell, 'Canada's Negotiations with Newfoundland, 1887–1895,' *CHR*, 40 (1959), 277–93

28 Hiller, 'A History,' 341–67; and Hiller, 'Railway and Local Politics,' 138–41

29 Morris in the House of Assembly, 24 Feb. 1898, reported in the *Evening Herald* (St John's), 28 Feb. 1898

30 Bond in the House of Assembly, 25 Feb. 1898, reported in the *Evening Telegram* (St John's), 1 Mar. 1898

31 Under the 1901 agreement Reid surrendered the right to the ownership of the railway and the telegraph system. He also gave up a large amount of land.

32 J.K. Hiller, 'The Origins of the Pulp and Paper Industry in Newfoundland,' *Acadiensis* 11:2 (Spring 1982), 52–64

33 On economic developments in this period, see Reeves, 'Alexander's Conundrum Reconsidered.'

34 S.J.R. Noel, *Politics in Newfoundland* (Toronto 1971), 36–76

35 W.F. Coaker, in *The Fishermen's Advocate*, 29 Oct. 1910. For the FPU in general, see: I.D.H. McDonald, 'To Each His Own': William Coaker and the Fishermen's Protective Union in Newfoundland Politics, 1908–1925, ed. J.K. Hiller (St John's 1987); McDonald, 'W.F. Coaker and the Balance of Power Strategy: The Fishermen's Protective Union in Newfoundland Politics,' in Hiller and Neary (eds.), *Newfoundland in the Nineteenth and Twentieth Centuries*, 148–80; and W.F. Coaker, *Twenty Years of the Fishermen's Protective Union of Newfoundland* (St John's 1930; repr. 1984).

36 P.R. O'Brien, 'The Newfoundland Patriotic Association: The Administra-

tion of the War Effort, 1914–1919' (MA thesis, Memorial University 1981)

37 C.A. Sharpe, 'The "Race of Honour": An Analysis of Enlistments and Casualties in the Armed Forces of Newfoundland, 1914–1918,' *Newfoundland Studies* 4:1 (1988), 27–55

38 Morris adopted the title 'prime minister' rather than 'premier' in 1909, and his example was followed by his successors. Newfoundland began to call itself a 'dominion' after 1918.

39 This account of the collapse of the National Government and the election of Squires follows the narrative in McDonald, *'To Each His Own'*, ch. 5.

40 The fullest account of the Coaker Regulations is given by McDonald, *'To Each His Own'*, ch. 6; David G. Alexander, *The Decay of Trade: An Economic History of the Newfoundland Saltfish Trade, 1935–1965* (St John's 1977), 19–28

41 Alexander, *Decay of Trade*, 29

42 David G. Alexander, 'Economic Growth in the Atlantic Region, 1880 to 1940,' in his *Atlantic Canada and Confederation*, 66. In the Maritimes, the contraction was 1 per cent per year, or 8.5 per cent overall.

43 R.A. McKay (ed.), *Newfoundland: Economic, Diplomatic and Strategic Studies* (Toronto 1948), App. A, 511

44 J.K. Hiller, 'The Politics of Newsprint: The Newfoundland Pulp and Paper Industry, 1915–1939,' *Acadiensis* 19:2 (Spring 1990), 3–39

45 R.M. Elliott, 'Newfoundland Politics in the 1920s: The Genesis and Significance of the Hollis Walker Enquiry,' in Hiller and Neary (eds.), *Newfoundland in the Nineteenth and Twentieth Centuries*, 181–204; Noel, *Politics in Newfoundland*, 149–79

46 Noel, *Politics in Newfoundland*, 179–85

47 Jim Overton, 'Economic Crisis and the End of Democracy: Politics in Newfoundland during the Great Depression,' *L / Le t* 26 (Fall 1990), 85–124

48 Noel, *Politics in Newfoundland*, 186–203

49 The best account of these events is to be found in Peter F. Neary, *Newfoundland in the North Atlantic World, 1929–1949* (Kingston and Montreal 1988), 12–43.

50 *Newfoundland Royal Commission, 1933. Report*, Cmnd 4480 (London 1933)

51 Alderdice in the House of Assembly, 28 Nov. 1933, printed in Peter F. Neary (ed.), *The Political Economy of Newfoundland, 1929–1972* (Toronto 1973), 41

52 Alexander, 'Newfoundland's Traditional Economy,' 35

53 J.A. Thomas in House of Commons 12 Dec. 1933, printed in Neary (ed.), *Political Economy*, 55

54 Noel, *Politics in Newfoundland*, 221–43; Neary (ed.), *Political Economy*, 66–98; T. Lodge, *Dictatorship in Newfoundland* (London 1939). For a sympathetic account of the Commission's stewardship, see Neary, *Newfound-*

land in the North Atlantic World.

55 Malcolm MacLeod, *Peace of the Continent: The Impact of Canadian and American Bases in Newfoundland* (St John's 1986); Dominions Office, *Report on the Financial and Economic Position of Newfoundland* (Cmd 6849, 1946)

56 D. MacKenzie, *Inside the North Atlantic Triangle: Canada and the Entrance of Newfoundland into Confederation, 1939–1949* (Toronto 1986); P. Bridle, *Documents on Relations between Canada and Newfoundland. Volume 1, Defence, Civil Aviation and Economic Affairs, 1935–1949; Volume 2, 1940–1949, Confederation* (Ottawa 1984)

57 Peter F. Neary, 'Great Britain and the Future of Newfoundland, 1939–1945,' *Newfoundland Studies* 1:1 (Spring 1985), 29–56; Neary, 'Newfoundland's Union with Canada, 1949: Conspiracy or Choice?' *Acadiensis Reader* 2:377–86; Neary, *Newfoundland in the North Atlantic World*, 214–345

58 See Gwyn, *Smallwood*; Harold Horwood, *Joey* (Toronto 1989); and J.K. Hiller, 'The Career of Gordon F. Bradley,' *Newfoundland Studies* 4:2 (Fall 1988), 163–80. Another useful source is Don Jamieson, *No Place for Fools: The Political Memoirs of Don Jamieson* (St John's 1989).

59 Noel, *Politics in Newfoundland*, 244–55; Neary, *Political Economy*, 103–30; MacKenzie, *Inside the North Atlantic Triangle*, ch. 8; J. Webb, 'Newfoundland's National Convention, 1940–48' (MA thesis, Memorial University 1987)

60 'An Appeal,' from the Confederate, 31 May 1948, in Neary (ed.), *Political Economy*, 142

61 Jeff A. Webb, 'The Responsible Government League and the Confederation Campaigns of 1948,' *Newfoundland Studies* 5:2 (Fall 1989), 203–20

62 *Monitor*, Nov. 1947, in Neary (ed.), *Political Economy*, 131

63 Malcolm MacLeod, *Nearer than Neighbours* (St John's 1982); his 'Subsidized Steamers to a Foreign Country: Canada and Newfoundland, 1892–1949,' *Acadiensis* 14:2 (Spring 1985), 66–92; and his 'Students Abroad: Preconfederation Educational Links between Newfoundland and the Mainland of Canada,' *Historical Papers* (1985), 172–92

64 The terms of union are printed in Noel, *Politics in Newfoundland*, App. C.

65 For accounts of the campaigns, see Noel, *Politics in Newfoundland*, 255–61; Neary (ed.), *Political Economy*, 130–73; MacKenzie, *Inside the North Atlantic Triangle*, 196–204; Gwyn, *Smallwood*, 96–123; J.R. Smallwood (ed.), *The Book of Newfoundland*, 6 vols (St John's 1967), 3:4–130.

66 R.B. Blake, 'New Beginnings: Political Organization in Post-Confederation Newfoundland, 1949–1951' (paper presented to the Atlantic Canada Studies Conference 1988). Peter F. Neary, 'Party Politics in Newfoundland, 1949–1971: A Survey and Analysis,' in Hiller and Neary (eds.), *Newfoundland in the Nineteenth and Twentieth Centuries*, 205–9; Noel, *Politics in*

*Newfoundland,* ch. 17

67 Peter F. Neary, '"A More than Usual ... Interest": Sir P.A. Clutterbuck's Newfoundland Impressions, 1950,' *Newfoundland Studies* 3:2 (Fall 1987), 258

68 Bradley papers, Bradley to George Sellars, 3 Apr. 1952

## 11 The 1950s: The Decade of Development

Portions of this chapter have appeared previously in my 'The Atlantic Revolution of the 1950s,' in Berkeley Fleming (ed.), *Beyond Anger and Longing: Community and Development in Atlantic Canada* (Fredericton 1988), 55–96.

1 *Maritime Advocate and Busy East,* Sept. 1949, 15
2 Although there is no comprehensive analysis of economic and social change in post-war Atlantic Canada, two studies outline the broad trends for Prince Edward Island and New Brunswick: Verner Smitheram, David Milne, and Satadal Dasgupta (eds), *The Garden Transformed: Prince Edward Island, 1945–1980* (Charlottetown 1982); Robert A. Young, 'Development, Planning and Participation in New Brunswick, 1945–1975' (D.Phil thesis, Linacre College 1979). See also, Donald Savoie (ed.), *The Canadian Economy: A Regional Perspective* (Toronto 1986); George A. Rawlyk, *The Atlantic Provinces and the Problems of Confederation* (St John's 1979); T.W. Acheson, 'The Maritimes and "Empire Canada"' in David Jay Bercuson, (ed.), *Canada and the Burden of Unity* (Toronto 1977), 87–114.
3 Robert Bothwell, Ian Drummond, and John English, *Canada since 1945: Power, Politics, and Provincialism* (Toronto 1981)
4 Warren Susman with Edward Griffin, 'Did Success Spoil the United States? Dual Representations in Postwar America,' in Lary May (ed.), *Recasting America: Culture and Politics in the Age of the Cold War* (Chicago 1989), 19–37
5 Elon Salmon, 'Pugwash Has Helped Halt the Nuclear Threat,' *Chronicle-Herald* (Halifax), 3 Mar. 1989
6 T.N. Brewis, *Regional Economic Policies in Canada* (Toronto 1969), 166–7; APEC, *First Annual Review: The Atlantic Economy* (Oct. 1967), 51
7 APEC, *Defence Expenditures and the Economy of the Atlantic Provinces* Pamphlet No. 9 (Dec. 1965)
8 Noel Iverson and D. Ralph Matthews, *Communities in Decline: An Examination of Household Resettlement in Newfoundland,* Newfoundland Social and Economic Studies, No. 6 (St John's 1968). For a different interpretation of the process, see F.W. Rowe, *The Smallwood Era* (Toronto 1985), 107–28.
9 Ian McKay, 'Springhill 1958,' *New Maritimes,* 2:4 (Dec.-Jan. 1983–4)
10 Alan Story, 'Old Wounds: Reopening the Mines of St. Lawrence,' *New*

*Maritimes* 4:6 (Feb. 1986), 6–7

11 Miriam Chapin, *Atlantic Canada* (Toronto 1956), 115–16; Rachel Carson, *Silent Spring* (New York 1962), ch. 9

12 Elspeth Tulloch, *We, the Undersigned: A Historical Overview of New Brunswick Women's Political and Legal Status, 1784–1984* (Moncton 1985), 108

13 For a discussion of this process in the potato industry see Tom Murphy, 'The McCain's Revolution: The New Capitalism in New Brunswick Potato Farming,' *New Maritimes* 5:6 (Feb. 1987), 7–11.

14 *Women's Institute of Nova Scotia, Through the Years, The Women's Institute Story: A History of WINS, 1913–1979* (Truro 1979), 29

15 Tulloch, *We, the Undersigned*, 72

16 Muriel Duckworth and Peggy Hope-Simpson, 'Voice of Women Dialogue,' *Atlantis* 6:2 (Spring 1981), 168–76

17 H. Landon Ladd, 'The Newfoundland Loggers' Strike of 1959,' in W.J.C. Cherwinski and Gregory S. Kealey (eds), *Lectures in Canadian Labour and Working-Class History* (St John's-Toronto 1985), 152, 163–4

18 APEC, *Collective Bargaining and Regional Development*, Pamphlet No. 18 (May 1973), 7

19 Margaret Conrad, *George Nowlan: Maritime Conservative in National Politics* (Toronto 1986), 231–50

20 Ian McKay, *The Craft Transformed: An Essay on the Carpenters of Halifax, 1885–1985* (Halifax 1985), chs 4, 5

21 C.H.J. Gilson and A.M. Wadden, 'The Windsor Gypsum Strike and the Formation of the Joint Labour/Management Study Committee: Conflict and Accommodation in the Nova Scotia Labour Movement,' in Michael Earle (ed.), *Workers and the State in Twentieth-Century Nova Scotia* (Fredericton 1989), 191–216

22 *Labour Gazette* 57 (1957), 1274–5

23 Anthony Thompson, 'The Nova Scotia Civil Service Association, 1956–1967,' *Acadiensis* 12:2 (Spring 1983), 81–105

24 Canadian Welfare Council, *Public Welfare Services in New Brunswick* (Fredericton 1949); Patricia T. Rooke and R.L. Schnell, *Discarding the Asylum: From Child Rescue to the Welfare State in English Canada (1800–1950)* (Latham, Md 1983), 366–74

25 Nova Scotia, *JHA* (1957), vol. 2, 'Report of the Inspector of Humane Institutions'

26 Rowe, *Smallwood Era*, 87–105

27 Peter F. Neary, '"Traditional" and "Modern" Elements in the Social and Economic History of Belle Island and Conception Bay,' *CHAHP* (1973), 105–36

28 Cited in (Ian McKay), '"You Love Their Simple and Honest Ways": Nova Scotians as Pleasing Peasant Folk,' *New Maritimes* 5:11–12 (July-Aug. 1987), 10

29 Jim Lotz, *Head, Heart and Hands: Craftspeople in Nova Scotia* (Halifax 1968), 23

30 The studies were published as *The Sterling County Study of Psychiatric Disorder and Sociocultural Environment*: vol. 1, Alexander Hamilton Leighton, *My Name Is Legion: Foundations for a Theory of Man in Relation to Culture* (New York 1959); vol. 2, Charles Campbell Hughes, *People of Cove and Woodlot: Communities from the Viewpoint of Social Psychiatry* (New York 1960); vol. 3, Dorothy Leighton, *The Character of Danger: Psychiatric Symptoms in Selected Communities* (New York 1963).

31 Chapin, *Atlantic Canada*, 158

32 Patrick O'Flaherty, *The Rock Observed: Studies in the Literature of Newfoundland* (Toronto 1979), 144–83: Marguerite Maillet, *Histoire de la littérature acadienne: de rêve en rêve* (Moncton 1983)

33 Chapin, *Atlantic Canada*, 129

34 Helen Creighton, *A Life in Folklore* (Toronto 1975), 159

35 Frank Peers, *The Public Eye: Television and the Politics of Broadcasting, 1952–1968* (Toronto 1979)

36 Donald Wetmore, 'Television Drama Festival in St. John's,' *Journal of Education* (Apr.-June 1959), 79–80

37 Colin Howell, 'Baseball and the Decline of Community in the Maritimes,' *New Maritimes* 3:3 (Nov. 1984), 13–14

38 Ray Fraser, *The Fighting Fisherman: The Life of Yvon Durelle* (Halifax 1983)

39 Léon Thériault, 'Acadia, 1763–1978: An Historical Synthesis,' in Jean Daigle (ed.), *The Acadians of the Maritimes: Thematic Studies* (Moncton 1982), 82

40 Jean-Paul Hautecoeur, *L'Acadie du discours* (Quebec 1975), 197–8. Cited in Céleste Thibodeau-Stacey, 'Prelude to the Parti Acadien' (Transcript, Acadia University 1988)

41 Muriel K. Roy, 'Settlement and Population Growth in Acadia,' in Daigle (ed.), *Acadians of the Maritimes*, 186; see also, Georges Arsenault, *The Island Acadians, 1720–1980* (Charlottetown 1989), 227–55

42 W.A. Spray, *The Blacks in New Brunswick* (Fredericton 1972), 66

43 F.H. Leacy (ed.), *Historical Statistics of Canada*, 2nd ed. (Ottawa 1982), Series W94–149, and *Annual Reports* for the provincial departments of education provide statistics for enrolments and expenditures for education.

44 John G. Reid, *Mount Allison University, Vol. II: 1914–1963*, 2 vols (Toronto 1984), ch. 12

45 Rowe, *Smallwood Era*, 82

46 *Journal of Education* (Feb. 1952), 11

47 Guy Henson, 'Looking Ahead in the Atlantic Provinces,' *Journal of Education* (Dec. 1956), 5–21

48 W.S. MacNutt, 'The Atlantic Revolution,' *Atlantic Advocate*, June 1957, 11–13

49 Royal Commission on Canada's Economic Prospects, *Final Report* (Nov. 1957), 403; Brewis, *Regional Economic Policies*, 17

50 Donald Patterson, 'Regional Aspects of the Canadian Economy' (paper presented to the Meeting of the Minister of Finance of Canada and Ministers of Finance and Treasurers of the Provinces, Fredericton, Oct. 1959), 3, 7

51 *Maritime Advocate and Busy East*, June 1949, 4

52 Canada, Senate, *Debates*, 13 Feb. 1951, 71–7

53 J.R. Smallwood, *I Chose Canada: The Memoirs of the Honourable Joseph R. 'Joey' Smallwood*, 2 vols, vol. 2, *The Premiership* (Scarborough, Ont. 1973), 26

54 *Ottawa Journal*, 21 June 1955

55 Robert A. Young, 'Planning for Power: The New Brunswick Electric Power Commission in the 1950s,' *Acadiensis* 12:1 (Autumn 1982), 73–99; James Lawrence Kenny, 'Politics and Persistence: New Brunswick's Hugh John Flemming and the "Atlantic Revolution," 1952–1960' (MA thesis, UNB 1988)

56 Wayne E. MacKinnon, *The Life of the Party: A History of the Liberal Party in Prince Edward Island* (Summerside 1973), 127–8

57 'Invasion of Hungary Secured Springhill Aid,' *Globe and Mail* (Toronto), 21 Jan. 1987

58 Peter Stursberg, *Diefenbaker: Leadership Gained, 1956–1962* (Toronto 1975), 79

59 L.W. Simms, 'The Maritimes Transportation Commission,' *Maritime Advocate and Busy East*, Jan. 1952, 37–42; E.R. Forbes, 'Misguided Symmetry: The Destruction of Regional Transportation Policy for the Maritimes,' in Bercuson (ed.) *Canada and the Burden of Unity*, 60–86

60 'Industrial Development of the Atlantic Provinces,' *Maritime Advocate and Busy East*, Jan. 1952, 29–36

61 C.H. Blakeny, 'Proposal for Survey of Economic Conditions of the Atlantic Provinces,' *Maritime Advocate and Busy East*, Jan. 1953, 23–6

62 A.T. Parkes, 'Report of MPBT-Premiers' Meeting in Moncton on September 14, 1953,' *Maritime Advocate and Busy East*, Jan. 1954, 37

63 *Maritime Advocate and Busy East*, Sept. 1954, 31

64 A.T. Parkes, 'Atlantic Provinces Economic Council Is Now an Established Fact,' *Maritime Advocate and Busy East*, Oct. 1954, 11; APEC, *The APEC Story* (np, nd)

65 Arthur Johnson, 'Newfoundland,' *Atlantic Advocate*, Apr. 1960, 35–7. Newfoundland became a full member of APEC in 1960 with Arthur Johnson as the first Newfoundland president of APEC.

66 R.D. Howland, seconded to the Gordon Commission from the Nova Scotia Department of Trade and Industry, produced a study entitled *Some Regional Aspects of Canada's Economic Development* (Ottawa 1958), which

provided useful evidence for those seeking aid on the basis of economic need.

67 NAC, RG19, vol. 4151, N–15, Department of Finance, 'Speech by Hugh John Flemming to the Federal Provincial Conference, 1955'

68 'The Fredericton Conference of Atlantic Premiers,' *Atlantic Advocate*, Sept. 1956, 28

69 PANB, RS415, C9b, Hugh John Flemming Papers

70 PANB, RS415, C9b, Hugh John Flemming Papers, R. Whidden Ganong to Hugh John Flemming, 1 May 1956

71 'Fredericton Conference,' 28–48

72 PANB, RS415, box 9, C9b/2, Hugh John Flemming Papers, William Smith to Hugh John Flemming, 20 June 1956

73 *Atlantic Advocate*, Sept. 1956, 49

74 R. Whidden Ganong, 'APEC – Its Beginning and Meaning,' *Atlantic Advocate*, Sept. 1956, 15–19

75 W.S. MacNutt, 'The Fredericton Conference: A Look Backward and a Look Forward,' *Atlantic Advocate*, Sept. 1956, 11–13

76 'Partial Text of a Speech by R.L. Stanfield at the Progressive Conservative Convention in Inverness,' 20 June 1956

77 Geoffrey Stevens, *Stanfield* (Toronto 1973); Roy E. George, *The Life and Times of Industrial Estates* (Halifax 1974)

78 PANB, RS415, box 8, C8c(2), Hugh John Flemming Papers, R.R. Bell to Hugh John Flemming, 28 Nov. 1956; Robert Stanfield to Hugh John Flemming, 1 December 1956; Hugh John Flemming to Robert Stanfield, 4 Dec. 1956

79 For a compilation of several editorials see *Atlantic Advocate*, Mar. 1957, 90.

80 *Atlantic Advocate*, Mar. 1957, 93

81 *Chronicle-Herald*, 15 Mar. 1956

82 'Atlantic Provinces Economic Council Visits the Prime Minister,' *Atlantic Advocate*, May 1957, 57, 101–2

83 PANB, RS415, box 9, C9b/2, Hugh John Flemming Papers, Minutes of Atlantic Provinces Premiers' Conference, Halifax, 8 May 1957

84 Published in the *Atlantic Advocate*, June 1957, 11; see also 'The Atlantic Revolution: A Commentary on the Atlantic Premiers' Conference,' in the same issue, 11–13.

85 *Atlantic Advocate*, July 1957, 11

86 Dalton Camp, *Gentlemen, Players and Politicians* (Toronto 1970), 337

87 NAC, RG19, 4151, N–15, Department of Finance, Kenneth Taylor to Donald Flemming, 15 Aug. 1957. See also *Atlantic Advocate*, Dec. 1957, 9.

88 *Atlantic Advocate*, Oct. 1957, 11

89 Peter Neary, 'Party Politics in Newfoundland, 1949–71: A Survey and Analysis,' in James K. Hiller and Peter F. Neary (eds), *Newfoundland in the Nineteenth and Twentieth Centuries: Essays in Interpretation* (Toronto

1980), 219–26

90 *Atlantic Advocate*, Oct. 1959, 28

91 NAC, RG19, vol. 4128, f.20/1, Department of Finance; *Guardian* (Charlottetown), 12, 14 Apr. 1958

92 *Atlantic Advocate*, Mar. 1959, 12

93 PANB, RS415, box 8, C8e, Hugh John Flemming Papers, Walter Shaw to Hugh John Flemming, 15 Mar. 1960; Hugh John Flemming to Walter Shaw, 18 Mar. 1960

94 See *Atlantic Advocate*, June 1961, 17, for an interesting 'new charter of liberty' for labour.

95 Rowe, *Smallwood Era*, 19

96 Charles Brown, 'The Women's Atlantic Council,' *Atlantic Advocate*, Sept. 1958, 37–40

97 PANB, RS415, box 5, A7, Hugh John Flemming Papers. For an insight into the difficulties faced by the Women's Council see a letter from Laura Foster to Hugh John Flemming, 30 Jan. 1960.

98 PANB, RS415, box 9, C9a(3), Hugh John Flemming Papers, Douglas Campbell to John Diefenbaker, 15 Dec. 1957

99 Conrad, *George Nowlan*, 249

100 Acadia University Archives, George Nowlan Papers, Press Release Files, seech by Donald Flemming to Halifax Tax Conference, Oct. 1959

101 *Atlantic Advocate*, Jan. 1959, 14

102 *Atlantic Advocate*, July 1958, Oct. 1958, May 1959, Sept. 1960

103 *Atlantic Advocate*, Sept. 1960, 22–3

104 I.C. Rand, *Report of the Royal Commission on Coal* (Ottawa 1960)

105 A.K. Cairncross, *Economic Development and the Atlantic Provinces* (Fredericton 1961); 'Atlantic Conference,' *Atlantic Advocate*, Oct. 1960, 12–13

106 MacNutt, 'Atlantic Revolution,' 13

107 May (ed.) *Recasting America*

**12 The 1960s: The Illusions and Realities of Progress**

1 Michael J.L. Kirby, 'Federalism and Regional Economic Development,' in Abraham Rotstein (ed.), *Walter L. Gordon Lecture Series, 1978–79* 5 vols (Toronto 1979) 3:55. For further comment on regional development see Tom Kent, 'The Brief Rise and Early Decline of Regional Development,' *Acadiensis* 9:1 (Autumn 1979), 120–5.

2 Paul H. Evans, *Report on Atlantic/Maritime Interprovincial Co-operation between 1950 and 1971* (Halifax 1985), 94

3 *Canadian News Facts*, 1–15 Sept. 1969; Maritime Union Study, *The Report on Maritime Union Commissioned by the Governments of Nova Scotia, New Brunswick and Prince Edward Island* (Fredericton 1970)

4 In 1968 the premiers agreed that 'co-operation rather than union is the

key.' Evans, *Report*, 126

5 Ibid., 81

6 'Atlantic Development Board Act: A Summary of Speeches in Parliament,' *Atlantic Advocate*, Jan. 1963, 14–20, 77–87; David F. Symington, 'Generator of Atlantic Growth,' *Canadian Business*, June 1966, 68–74; Evans, *Report*, 89

7 Evans, *Report*, 97

8 *New Brunswick Today* (Fall 1970), 21

9 Robert H. Winters, 'The Hamilton Falls Project,' *Canadian Geographical Journal* 70 (1965); F.W. Rowe, *The Smallwood Era* (Toronto 1985), 27–39; Philip Mathias, *Forced Growth* (Toronto 1971), 43–4, 77–80

10 T.N. Brewis, *Regional Economic Policies in Canada* (Toronto 1969), 185–6

11 *CAR* (1964), 249

12 Ibid. (1967), 301

13 John Braddock, 'How Goes the Gap,' *Atlantic Advocate*, Jan. 1966, 13–15

14 Kirby, 'Federalism and Regional Economic Development,' 60. For a particular view of regional economic disparity, see Ralph R. Krueger and John Koegler, *Regional Development in Northeast New Brunswick* (Toronto 1975).

15 Ibid., 61. Also see D. Ralph Matthews, *The Creation of Regional Dependency* (Toronto 1983).

16 Henry Veltmeyer, 'The Capitalist Underdevelopment of Atlantic Canada,' in Robert J. Brym and R. James Sacouman (eds), *Underdevelopment and Social Movements in Atlantic Canada* (Toronto 1979), 20

17 APEC, *Atlantic Canada Today* (Halifax 1977), 75

18 William Janssen, 'Agriculture in Transition,' in Verner Smitheram, David Milne, and Satadal Dasgupta (eds), *The Garden Transformed Prince Edward Island: 1945–1980* (Charlottetown 1982), 116; Daniel Kubat and David Thornton, *A Statistical Profile of Canadian Society* (Toronto 1974), 17

19 Farley Mowat, Parzival Copes, Noel Iverson, and D. Ralph Matthews, 'The Fate of the Outport Newfoundlander: Four Views of Resettlement,' in Peter F. Neary (ed.), *The Political Economy of Newfoundland, 1929–1972* (Toronto 1973), 224. Also see Parzival Copes, *The Resettlement of Fishing Communities in Newfoundland* (Ottawa 1972).

20 D. Ralph Matthews, 'The Outport Breakup,' *The Collection of Horizon Canada* 102 (Apr. 1987), 2438

21 Mowat et al., 'Fate of the Outport Newfoundlander,' 144. Also see D. Ralph Matthews, 'The Smallwood Legacy: The Development of Underdevelopment in Newfoundland, 1949–1972, *JCS* 13:4 (Winter 1978–9), 89–108.

22 APEC, *Atlantic Canada Today* , 80. Also see William M. Baker, *The Foundations of Tourism and Recreation Travel in the Maritime Provinces* (Ottawa 1972).

23 Rowe, *Smallwood Era*, 144

24 APEC, *Atlantic Canada Today*, 80

25 Ibid., 82

26 Mowat et al., 'Fate of the Outport Newfoundland,' 231

27 Judith Adler, 'Tourism and Pastoral: A Decade of Debate,' in Smitheram, et al. (eds), *Garden Transformed*, 135

28 Wayne E. MacKinnon, *The Life of the Party: A History of the Liberal Party in Prince Edward Island*, (Summerside 1973), 153

29 Pierre-Yves Pépin, *Life and Poverty in the Maritimes* (Ottawa 1968), 227

30 Robert Bothwell, Ian Drummond, and John English, *Canada since 1945: Power, Politics, and Provincialism* (Toronto 1981), 312

31 Kubat and Thornton, *Statistical Profile*, 50

32 F.W. Rowe, *A History of Newfoundland and Labrador* (Toronto 1980), 519

33 Richard Edsall, 'Education: The Boom that Never Goes Bust,' *Canadian Business*, Oct. 1963, 56

34 John J. Deutsch, 'Education for National Growth,' *Atlantic Advocate*, May 1965, 15. Also see Douglas Myers, *The Failure of Education Reform in Canada* (Toronto 1973), 36.

35 *Report of the Royal Commission on Post-Secondary Education in the Province of Nova Scotia* (Halifax 1985), 13

36 James Overton, 'Towards a Critical Analysis of Neo-Nationalism in Newfoundland,' in Brym and Sacouman (eds), *Underdevelopment and Social Movements*, 238

37 Della M.M. Stanley, *Louis Robichaud: A Decade of Power* (Halifax 1984), 89

38 Ibid., 192

39 Lord Taylor, 'Memorial Moves Up,' *Atlantic Advocate*, May 1968, 13–19

40 Rowe, *Smallwood Era*, 71–8, 84–6; *CAR* (1965), 192

41 *Canadian News Facts*, 16–31 Aug. 1969. Also see Jean-C. Vernex, *Les acadiens* (Paris 1979).

42 Statistics Canada, *Profile Studies: Education Attainment: Canada* (Ottawa 1977), 14; and Kubat and Thornton, *Statistical Profile*, 119

43 Albert Rose, 'Social Services,' in Robert Craig Brown (ed.), *The Canadians: 1867–1967* (Toronto 1967), 738

44 Kubat and Thornton, *Statistical Profile*, 12

45 Ibid.

46 APEC, *Atlantic Canada Today*, 58

47 *Atlantic Advocate*, June 1962, 20–4

48 Clarence-J. d'Entremont, Jean Daigle, Léon Thériault, and Anselme Chiasson, *Petit manuel d'histoire d'Acadie des débuts à 1976* (Moncton 1976), 36

49 Léon Thériault, 'Acadiens et anglophones des Maritimes ou les ambiguités d'une co-existence,' in E.L. Austin (ed.), *Crossroads Canada: An Exploration of English-Acadian Relations* (Amherst, N.S. 1978), 13

50 Muriel K. Roy, 'Settlement and Population Growth in Acadia,' in Jean Daigle (ed.), *The Acadians of the Maritimes: Thematic Studies* (Moncton 1982), 186

51 Ibid.

52 Ibid., 172. Also see Victor Raiche, (La population du Nord et de l'Est' (MA thesis, Université d'Ottawa 1962).

53 *White Paper on the Responsibilities of Government* (Fredericton, 4 Mar. 1965), 1

54 Patrick J. Fitzpatrick, 'New Brunswick: Politics of Pragmatism,' in Martin Robin (ed.), *Canadian Provincial Politics: The Party Systems of Ten Provinces* (Scarborough, Ont. 1972), 124. Also see Léon Thériault, *La question du pouvoir en Acadie* (Moncton 1982).

55 d'Entremont et al., 'Petit manuel d'histoire d'Acadie,' 38

56 Alan G. Macpherson, 'People in Transition: The Broken Mosaic,' in Alan G. Macpherson (ed.), *Studies in Canadian Geography: The Atlantic Provinces* (Toronto 1972), 59

57 Statistics Canada, *Perspectives Canada II* (Ottawa 1977), 23

58 For income rates see Statistics Canada, *Perspectives*, 26. Also, for union participation see Veltmeyer, 'Capitalist Underdevelopment,' 30.

59 Anthony Thomson, 'The Nova Scotia Civil Service Association, 1956–1967,' *Acadiensis* 12:2 (Spring 1983), 82

60 APEC, *Atlantic Canada Today*, 101; Stanley, *Louis Robichaud*, 91; Overton, 'Towards a Critical Analysis,' 238

61 Ian McKay, *The Craft Transformed: An Essay on the Carpenters of Halifax, 1885–1985* (Halifax 1985), 119

62 Roger Guimond, *The New New Brunswick*, reprinted from *Mining in Canada*, June 1966, 7

63 McKay, *Craft Transformed*, 128

64 *New Brunswick Today*, Fall 1970, 18

65 *Labour Gazette*, Feb. 1969, 77. Also see Russell Hunt and Robert Campbell, *K.C. Irving: The Art of the Industrialist* (Toronto 1973) and John DeMont, *Citizens Irving: K.C. Irving and His Legacy. The Story of Canada's Wealthiest Family* (Toronto 1991).

66 Ibid., Oct. 1962, 119

67 *Canadian News Facts*, 1–15 May 1969

68 George A. Rawlyk (ed.), *The Atlantic Provinces and the Problems of Confederation* (St John's 1979), 88

69 Ibid., 41, 88

70 Ibid. Also see Tim J. O'Neill, *A Comparative Study of Income and Wage Differentials, Prince Edward Island, New Brunswick, Nova Scotia, and Canada* (Charlottetown 1972).

71 APEC, *Atlantic Canada Today*, 126

72 Veltmeyer, 'Capitalist Underdevelopment,' 21, 23

73 Rawlyk (ed.), *Atlantic Provinces*, 212–13, 265; R.D.S. MacDonald, 'Fishermen's Incomes and Inputs and Outputs in the Fisheries Sector: The P.E.I. Case,' in Rowland Lorimer and Stanley E. McMullin (eds), *Canadian Is-*

sues: *Canada and the Sea* (Spring 1980), 98

74 Kent, 'Brief Rise,' 123

75 Adler, 'Tourism and Pastoral,' 205

76 Rawlyk (ed.), *Atlantic Provinces*, 95–7

77 Ibid., 97–8, 175

78 Ibid., 90, 92, 110–11, 120, 127

## 13 The 1970s: Sharpening the Sceptical Edge

1 Frank Fillmore, in *Fourth Estate* (Halifax), 15 Jan. 1970

2 F.H. Leacy (ed.), *Historical Statistics of Canada*, 2nd ed. (Ottawa 1983), Series A2–A6, D491–D492, F91–F96. For definition of 'personal income,' see ibid., notes to Series F76-F102.

3 Ibid., Series A339–49

4 Colin Howell, 'Economism, Ideology, and the Teaching of Maritime History,' in Phillip Buckner (ed.), *Teaching Maritime Studies* (Fredericton 1986), 18

5 Quoted in *Telegraph-Journal* (Saint John), 31 Dec. 1969

6 See D. Ralph Matthews, *'There's No Better Place than Here': Social Change in Three Newfoundland Communities* (Toronto 1976), 122–8; Margaret Conrad, 'The "Atlantic Revolution" of the 1950s,' in Berkeley Fleming (ed.), *Beyond Anger and Longing: Community and Development in Atlantic Canada* (Fredericton 1988), 55–96; Conrad, 'The 1950s,' in this volume; and Della M.M. Stanley, 'The 1960s,' also in this volume.

7 *APEC Newsletter* 13:3 (Apr. 1969), 3

8 *Fourth Estate*, 15 Jan. 1970

9 *Guardian* (Charlottetown), 12 May 1970

10 Department of Regional Economic Expansion (DREE), *Development Plan for Prince Edward Island* (Ottawa 1970)

11 *Guardian*, 6, 8 Mar. 1969; Frank MacKinnon, 'Prince Edward Island,' in John Saywell (ed.), *CAR* (1969), 153–4

12 *Guardian*, 8 Mar. 1969

13 *Chronicle-Herald* (Halifax), 10, 15, 17 Oct. 1970. See also J.M. Beck, *Politics of Nova Scotia*, 2 vols (Tantallon, N.S. 1985–8), 2:314–17.

14 *Moncton Daily Times*, 28 Oct. 1970; *Le progrès l'Evangéline* (Moncton), 28, 29 Oct. 1970. See also Richard Starr, *Richard Hatfield: The Seventeen-Year Saga* (Halifax 1987), 50; and Michel Cormier and Achille Michaud, *Richard Hatfield: un dernier train pour Hartland* (Moncton and Montreal 1991), 62–5.

15 Maritime Union Study, *The Report on Maritime Union Commissioned by the Governments of Nova Scotia, New Brunswick and Prince Edward Island* (Fredericton 1970), 121–2; *APEC Newsletter* 17:3 (Mar. 1973), 1

16 *Ottawa Journal*, 1 Feb. 1971

17 Peter F. Neary, 'Party Politics in Newfoundland, 1949–71: A Survey and Analysis,' in James K. Hiller and Peter F. Neary, (eds), *Newfoundland in the Nineteenth and Twentieth Centuries: Essays in Interpretation* (Toronto 1980), 232–5

18 *Evening Telegram* (St.John's), 28 Oct. 1971

19 Ibid., 29 Oct. 1971

20 Ibid., 1, 2, 25 Mar. 1972

21 Ibid., 9 June 1979; see also Leslie Harris, 'Newfoundland,' in John Saywell (ed.), *CAR* (1972), 235.

22 Economic Council of Canada (ECC), *Living Together: A Study of Regional Disparities* (Ottawa 1977), 191, 215; *Telegraph-Journal*, 1 Feb. 1971; for a detailed discussion of regional-development policies, and an appraisal of the significance of these efforts in Atlantic Canada, see Donald J. Savoie, *Regional Economic Development: Canada's Search for Solutions*, 2nd ed. (Toronto 1992), *passim*.

23 See Roy E. George, *The Life and Times of Industrial Estates Limited* (Halifax 1974), 77–90.

24 *Evening Telegram*, 21 Mar. 1972; ECC, *Newfoundland: From Dependency to Self-Reliance* (Ottawa 1980), 9

25 *Evening Telegram*, 11 Oct. 1973; ECC, *Newfoundland*, 11

26 *Telegraph-Journal*, 22 June 1973; 16, 17, 22, 23, 25, 26, 27 Sept. 1975; *Moncton Times*, 8, 21, 22 Nov. 1974. See also H.A. Fredericks with Allan Chambers, *Bricklin* (Fredericton 1977), *passim*.

27 George, *Life and Times of Industrial Estates*, 91–2

28 *The Regulations of Nova Scotia Tabled at the 1973 (2nd Session) of the Legislature* (Halifax 1973), 159–62; *Statutes of Nova Scotia*, 28 Elizabeth II c. 78; *Chronicle-Herald*, 21, 22 June 1973, 5 Dec. 1979. See also Ralph Surette, 'Michelin Whistles. Cabinet Rolls Over,' *Atlantic Insight* 1:4 (July 1979), 11–12; Ken Clare, 'Michelin – the Fortress that Didn't Fall,' *New Maritimes* 4:11–12 (July-Aug. 1986), 4–8.

29 Kennedy Wells, '"The Plan": A Decade Old, It's Still a Big, Fat Flop,' *Atlantic Insight* 1:7 (Oct. 1979), 16–17

30 Statistics Canada, *Provincial Economic Accounts, Experimental Data, 1965–1980* (Ottawa 1982), 6–7, 134–5, 160–1. See also Donald Nemetz, 'Managing Development,' in Verner Smitheram, David Milne, and Satadal Dasgupta (eds), *The Garden Transformed: Prince Edward Island, 1945–1980* (Charlottetown 1982), 155–75; Savoie, *Regional Economic Development*, 191.

31 Kennedy Wells, 'The Garden of the Gulf Becomes Asphalt Jungle,' *Atlantic Insight* 1:4 (July 1979), 10; 'Industrial Parks: Good Deals That May Be Just Too Good,' ibid., 1:1 (Apr. 1979), 15; *Guardian*, 5 Apr. 1978. Judith Adler, 'Tourism and Pastoral: A Decade of Debate,' in Smitheram et al. (eds), *Garden Transformed*, 143, 150

32 *Census of Canada*, 1971, vol. 1, bulletin 1.1–9, 10–2; ibid., 1981, vol. 1, catalogue 92–901, 7–2; Statistics Canada, *Canadian Statistical Review, April 1979* (Ottawa 1979), 47

33 Tom Kent, 'The Brief Rise and Early Decline of Regional Development,' *Acadiensis* 9:1 (Autumn 1979), 121

34 *Industrial Cape Breton Fact Book*, 4th ed. (Halifax 1986), 40

35 *Chronicle-Herald*, 29 Dec. 1979; George, *Life and Times of Industrial Estates*, 61–2

36 *Chronicle-Herald*, 3 Sept. 1976

37 Ibid., 4 Sept. 1976

38 *Evening Telegram*, 20 Mar. 1975. See also Savoie, *Regional Economic Development*, 173–6.

39 Donald Cameron, in *Fourth Estate*, 4 Jan. 1973

40 *Chronicle-Herald*, 21 July 1969; see also Raymond L. Foote, *The Case of Port Hawkesbury: Rapid Industrialization and Social Unrest in a Nova Scotia Community* (Toronto 1979).

41 *Chronicle-Herald*, 5 Oct. 1971

42 Institute of Public Affairs, *Poverty in Nova Scotia: Brief for Special Committee on Poverty, November 1969* (Halifax 1969), 3

43 See Satadal Dasgupta, 'The Island in Transition: A Statistical Overview,' in Smitheram et al. (eds), *Garden Transformed*, 249.

44 *Chronicle-Herald*, 15 July 1969

45 See Task Force on Atlantic Fisheries, *Navigating Troubled Waters: A New Policy for Atlantic Fisheries* (Ottawa 1985), 19–23, 31–2; Wallace Clement, *The Struggle to Organize: Resistance in Canada's Fishery* (Toronto 1986), 27, 34, 54; Rick Williams, 'The Poor Man's Machiavelli: Michael Kirby and the Atlantic Fisheries,' in Gary Burrill and Ian McKay (eds), *People, Resources, and Power: Critical Perspectives on Underdevelopment and Primary Industries in the Atlantic Region* (Fredericton 1987), 67–73. On Buchans and St Lawrence, see [J. Ralph Dale], 'Buchans,' in Joseph R. Smallwood (ed.), *Encyclopedia of Newfoundland and Labrador*, 3 vols to date (St John's 1981–[1991]), 1:282–3; Alan Story, 'Old Wounds: Reopening the Mines of St. Lawrence,' in Burrill and McKay, *People, Resources, and Power*, 186–91.

46 See the editorial comments in *Telegraph-Journal*, 1 Jan. 1970; see also APEC, *Fifth Annual Review*, 26–8, and APEC, *Sixth Annual Review: The Atlantic Economy* ([Halifax] 1972), 7–9.

47 See Ralph R. Krueger and John Koegler, *Regional Development in Northeast New Brunswick* (Toronto 1975), 15–16.

48 *Moncton Times*, 5 Jan. 1972

49 Ibid., 17 Jan., 26 Feb. 1972; *L'Evangéline* (Moncton), 15, 16, 17, 18, 25 Feb. 1972. See also Richard Wilbur, *The Rise of French New Brunswick* (Halifax 1989), 246–7; and, on the general question of intraprovincial disparities, Savoie, *Regional Economic Development*, 192–7.

50 See Richard Wilbur, 'New Brunswick's Francophones: A Self-Inflicted Genocide,' *Mysterious East* (Fredericton), Mar.-Apr. 1971, 4–11; also Jean-Paul Hautecoeur, *L'Acadie du discours: pour une sociologie de la culture acadienne* (Quebec 1975), chs 3, 4, 5. On the CRAN question, see Stanley, 'The 1960s,' in this volume; also Della M.M. Stanley, *Louis Robichaud: A Decade of Power* (Halifax 1984), 114, 205. The proportion of New Brunswickers whose mother tongue was French stood at 35.2 per cent in 1961 and at 34.0 per cent in 1971. *Historical Statistics of New Brunswick* (Ottawa 1984), 15; see also Muriel K. Roy, 'Settlement and Population Growth in Acadia,' in Jean Daigle (ed.), *The Acadians of the Maritimes: Thematic Studies* (Moncton 1982), 169–89.

51 *L'Evangéline*, 2, 8, 9 Feb. 1972

52 Ibid., 3 Feb. 1972

53 *Moncton Times*, 10 Jan. 1972

54 *L'Evangéline*, 22 Dec. 1971

55 Ibid., 16, 17 Feb. 1972; *Moncton Times*, 16, 17, 19, 25 Feb. 1972

56 *Moncton Transcript*, 23 Dec. 1977. See also Michel Bastarache, 'Acadian Language and Cultural Rights from 1713 to the Present Day,' in Daigle (ed.), *Acadians of the Maritimes*, 370–6.

57 *L'Evangéline*, 17, 18 Feb. 1972

58 Ibid., 9, 10, 11, 15, 16, 17, 18 Dec. 1975

59 *Moncton Times*, 4, 12 Nov. 1974

60 *L'Evangéline*, 24 Oct. 1978; Léon Thériault, *La question du pouvoir en Acadie* (Moncton 1982), 95

61 Fédération des francophones hors Quebec (FFHQ), *The Heirs of Lord Durham: Manifesto of a Vanishing People* (Ottawa 1978), 17; George A. Rawlyk and Terry Campbell, 'The New Brunswick Acadian Response to the Problems of Confederation: *L'Evangéline*, Quebec and the Francophone Problem, 1967 to 1978,' in George A. Rawlyk (ed.), *The Atlantic Provinces and the Problems of Confederation* (St John's 1979), 264–80; Michel Roy, *L'Acadie perdue* (Montreal 1978)

62 Thériault, *La question du pouvoir*, 108–13; *L'Evangéline*, 9 Oct. 1979

63 James W. St G. Walker, 'Black History in the Maritimes: Major Themes and Teaching Strategies,' in Buckner (ed.), *Teaching Maritime Studies*, 101–2

64 *Fourth Estate*, 29 May 1969; Walker, 'Black History in the Maritimes,' 100–2; and Donald H. Clairmont and Fred Wien, 'Blacks and Whites: The Nova Scotia Race Relations Experience,' in Douglas F. Campbell (ed.), *Banked Fires: The Ethnics of Nova Scotia* (Port Credit, Ont. 1978), 164–76; Institute of Public Affairs, *Poverty in Nova Scotia*, 94

65 Quoted in Donald H. Clairmont and Dennis W. Magill, *Africville Relocation Report* (Halifax 1971), 362. The figure of 20,000 for the black population of Nova Scotia is an estimate, in the absence of satisfactory census

data. See Clairmont and Wien, 'Blacks and Whites,' 177.

66 *Mail-Star* (Halifax), 26 May 1976; *Chronicle-Herald*, 31 May 1976; National Film Board, *Seven Shades of Pale*, directed by Les Rose (1975)

67 Clairmont and Wien, 'Blacks and Whites,' 175–80; see also George Elliott Clarke (ed.), 'Rocky Jones: The Politics of Passion,' *New Maritimes* 5:9 (May 1987), 4–7.

68 Dorothy C. Anger, 'The MicMacs of Newfoundland: A Resurgent Culture,' *Culture* 1 (1981), 78–81; see also Statistics Canada, *Canada's Native People* (Ottawa 1984).

69 National Indian Brotherhood, *Indian Control of Indian Education* (Ottawa 1972), 9 and *passim*; *Indian Self-Government in Canada: Report of the Special Committee* (Ottawa 1983), 27–31; Marie Battiste, 'Micmac Literary and Cognitive Assimilation,' in Jean Barman, Yvonne Hébert, and Don Mc-Caskill (eds), *Indian Education in Canada, Volume I: The Legacy* (Vancouver 1986), 38-9

70 Quoted in G.P. Gould and A.J. Semple, *Our Land: The Maritimes* (Fredericton 1980), 111; see also Indian and Northern Affairs Canada, *In All Fairness: A Native Claims Policy* (Ottawa 1981), 7–30.

71 *Indian Self-Government in Canada*, 114

72 Ibid., 114–15; Gould and Semple, *Our Land*, *passim*. See also Fred Wien, *Socioeconomic Characteristics of the Micmac in Nova Scotia* (Halifax 1983); and A.J. Siggner, D. Perley, and D. Young, *An Overview of Demographic, Social and Economic Conditions among New Brunswick's Registered Indian Population* (Ottawa 1982).

73 Susan Mann Trofimenkoff and Alison Prentice (eds), *The Neglected Majority: Essays in Canadian Women's History* (Toronto 1977); *Census of Canada, 1971*, vol. 1, bulletin 1.1–9, 10–1; ibid., 1981, vol. 1, catalogue 92–901, 1–1

74 *Report of the Royal Commission on the Status of Women in Canada* (Ottawa 1970); *Annual Report of Advisory Council on the Status of Women, 1973–4*

75 Elspeth Tulloch, *We, the Undersigned: A Historical Overview of New Brunswick Women's Political and Legal Status, 1784–1984* (Moncton 1985), 69–70

76 *Guardian*, 12, 18 Apr. 1979; on the New Brunswick experience, see Robert E. Garland and L. Gregory Machum, *Promises, Promises ... An Almanac of New Brunswick Elections, 1870–1980* (Saint John 1979), 55–6

77 Canadian Advisory Council on the Status of Women, *Ten Years Later* (Ottawa 1979), *passim*

78 Maritime Provinces Higher Education Commission, *Statistical Compendium* (Fredericton 1986), 20; Sheva Medjuck, 'Discovering Maritime Women: New Developments in the Social Sciences,' in Buckner (ed.), *Teaching Maritime Studies*, 130–5, 133; Martha MacDonald, 'Studying Maritime Women's Work: Underpaid, Unpaid, Invisible, Invaluable,' in *ibid.*, 119–29; Margaret Conrad, 'Out of the Kitchen and into the Curriculum:

Women's Studies in Maritime Canada,' in *ibid.*, 108–18

79 Silver Donald Cameron, *The Education of Everett Richardson: The Nova Scotia Fishermen's Strike, 1970–71* (Toronto 1977); Clement, *Struggle to Organize*, 105–7

80 Clement, *Struggle to Organize*, 112–17. See also Richard Cashin, 'Fisheries Policy,' *The Canadian Encyclopedia*, 3 vols (Edmonton 1985) 1:644–5; Gordon Inglis, *More Than Just a Union: The Story of the NFFAWU* (St John's 1985).

81 Sue Calhoun, *A Word to Say: The Story of the Maritime Fishermen's Union* (Halifax 1991), 150–9 and *passim*; Clement, *Struggle to Organize*, 113, 126–30, 146–52; Rick Williams, 'Inshore Fishermen, Unionisation, and the Struggle Against Underdevelopment Today,' in Robert J. Brym and R. James Sacouman (eds), *Underdevelopment and Social Movements in Atlantic Canada* (Toronto 1979), 171–2; *Statutes of Newfoundland*, 1971, Act 53, 197–225

82 Tulloch, *We, the Undersigned*, 117–22

83 *Moncton Times*, 18 May 1976. On the more successful Cape Breton protest, see Elizabeth May, *Budworm Battles: The Fight to Stop the Aerial Insecticide Spraying of the Forests of Eastern Canada* (np 1982). For an earlier exposition of environmental questions raised by budworm spraying, see also Rachel Carson, *Silent Spring* (Boston 1962), 129–35.

84 See Richard Wilbur, 'New Brunswick,' in Saywell (ed.), *CAR* (1974), 209–10; also *Moncton Times*, 31 May 1974.

85 Harry Baglole and David Weale (eds), *Cornelius Howatt: Superstar!* (Belfast, P.E.I. 1974); on the farmers' demonstrations, see Frank MacKinnon, 'Prince Edward Island,' in Saywell (ed.), *CAR* (1971), 194.

86 Adler, 'Tourism and Pastoral,' 140; *Chronicle-Herald*, 20 Mar. 1973; Duncan Fraser, 'Nova Scotia,' in Saywell (ed.), *CAR* (1973), 142

87 *Evening Telegram*, 14 Aug. 1973; see also Chris Brookes, *A Public Nuisance: A History of the Mummers Troupe* (St John's 1988), 88–9.

88 *L'Evangéline*, 22, 30 Mar. 1977; see also *Moncton Transcript*, 25, 31 Mar. 1977.

89 K. Ronald and J.L. Dougan, 'Sealing,' *Canadian Encyclopedia* 3:1668–9; see also Briton Cooper Busch, *The War against the Seals: A History of the North American Seal Fishery* (Kingston and Montreal 1985), 246–58.

90 *Evening Telegram*, 3, 17, 26 Mar. 1977; *Moncton Transcript*, 17, 21, 25 Mar. 1977. For fuller discussion of the anti-sealing campaign and its rhetoric, see Calvin Coish, *Seasons of the Seal: The International Storm over Canada's Seal Hunt* (St John's 1979); and James K. Hiller, 'Whales and Seals,' *Acadiensis* 15:2 (Spring 1986), 161–8.

91 *Moncton Transcript*, 7 Jan. 1978

92 *Decks Awash* 7:1 (Feb. 1978), 61

93 Renate Usmiani, *Second Stage: The Alternative Theatre Movement in Can-*

*ada* (Vancouver 1983), 105–6; Brookes, *Public Nuisance*, 194–206; Susan Sherk, 'Nearer My Cod to Thee,' *Atlantic Insight* 1:1 (Apr. 1979), 11. For more detailed discussion of the seal hunt issue in the 1970s and 1980s, see James E. Candow, *Of Men and Seals: A History of the Newfoundland Seal Hunt* (Ottawa 1989), 116–38.

94 Usmiani, *Second Stage*, 90–107; Brookes, *Public Nuisance*, 43–77, 78–96, 111–27; Gwendolyn Davies, 'Digressions on the K-Mart Bus: Teaching Maritime Literature,' in Buckner (ed.), *Teaching Maritime Studies*, 209–11; Richard Paul Knowles, 'Mulgrave Road: A Co-op Theatre and Its County,' *New Maritimes*, 3:10 (Aug. 1985), 4–6, and Knowles, 'Guysborough, Mulgrave, and the Mulgrave Road Co-op Theatre Company,' in L.D. McCann (ed.), *People and Place: Studies of Small Town Life in the Maritimes* (Fredericton and Sackville 1987), 227–44

95 Paul Robinson, *Where Our Survival Lies: Students and Textbooks in Atlantic Canada* (Halifax 1979)

96 *Telegraph-Journal*, 17 Dec. 1969; see also Russell Hunt and Robert Campbell, *K.C. Irving: The Art of the Industrialist* (Toronto 1973), 155–70.

97 *The Uncertain Mirror: Report of the Special Senate Committee on Mass Media*, 3 vols (Ottawa 1970) 1:70, 84, 85, 88–90

98 *Fourth Estate*, 12 Feb. 1970; *Mysterious East*, Nov. 1969, 2

99 See *Fourth Estate*, 4 July 1974; also Eleanor O'Donnell MacLean, *Leading the Way: An Unauthorized Guide to the Sobey Empire* (Halifax [1985]), 69.

100 *Atlantic Insight* 1:1 (Apr. 1979), 3

101 *Chronicle-Herald*, 3 Apr. 1974

102 *Chronicle-Herald*, 1 Sept. 1978; see also Paul MacEwan, *The Akerman Years: Jeremy Akerman and the Nova Scotia NDP, 1965–1980* (Antigonish 1980); and Patrick Jamieson, '"The Only Honest Politician": Paul MacEwan and the Strange World of Fourth Party Politics in Cape Breton,' *New Maritimes* 5:2 (Oct. 1986), 5.

103 *Guardian*, 8 Apr. 1978

104 Ibid., 17, 24 Apr. 1979; see also David Milne, 'Politics in a Beleaguered Garden,' in Smitheram et al. (eds), *Garden Transformed*, 51.

105 *Chronicle-Herald*, 1, 20 Sept. 1978. See also Beck, *Politics of Nova Scotia*, 2:342–5; Peter Kavanagh, *John Buchanan: The Art of Political Survival* (Halifax 1988), 52–3.

106 *Moncton Transcript*, 4, 12 Mar. 1977, 25, 26 Jan. 1978; Starr, *Hatfield*, 105–17; Cormier and Michaud, *Richard Hatfield*, 87–118

107 *L'Evangéline*, 13, 23 Oct. 1978; see also Garland and Machum, *Promises, Promises*, 46–8.

108 See Bob Wakeham, 'Has Bill Rowe Blown His Chances for Good?' *Atlantic Insight* 1:3 (June 1979), 14.

109 *Evening Telegram*, 5 June 1979

110 Ibid., 11, 19, 20 June 1979; see also James Overton, 'A Newfoundland

Culture?' *JCS* 23 (1988), 5–22.

111 See FFHQ, *Heirs of Lord Durham*, 17, 19–20.

112 Ray Guy, 'Unity Garbage Is Canadian Garbage,' *Atlantic Insight* 1:4 (July 1979), 64

113 *Moncton Transcript*, 30 Apr. 1980. For more detailed discussion of Atlantic Canadian attitudes to the national unity question, see Rawlyk, *Atlantic Provinces and the Problems of Confederation*, chs 4–8.

114 See Milne, 'Politics in a Beleaguered Garden,' 52.

115 Mario Polèse, 'Regional Economics,' *Canadian Encyclopedia*, 3:1559–61

116 See Ralph Matthews, *The Creation of Regional Dependency* (Toronto 1983) 109–10; 'Regional Economic Development: Third Time Lucky?' *APEC Newsletter* 26:8 (1982), 2–3; William Y. Smith, *An Overview of Economic Development Policies and Programs for Atlantic Canada* (Halifax 1976); Frank T. Walton, 'Canada's Atlantic Region: Recent Policy for Economic Development,' *Canadian Journal of Regional Science* 1:2 (1978), 35–51.

## Epilogue: The 1980s

1 Peter Perkins, *Mrs. Thatcher's Revolution: The Ending of the Socialist Era* (Cambridge 1987); and Sidney Weintraub and Marvin Goodstein, *Reaganomics in the Stagflation Economy* (Philadelphia 1983)

2 E.R. Forbes, *Challenging the Regional Stereotype: Essays on the 20th Century Maritimes* (Fredericton 1989) 200–17

3 T.J. Courchene, *Regional Adjustment, the Transfer System and Canadian Federalism*, Research Paper, Department of Economics, UWO (London 1979); Ralph Matthews, *The Creation of Regional Dependency* (Toronto 1983), 58–68; David G. Alexander, 'New Notions of Happiness: Nationalism, Regionalism, and Atlantic Canada' (1980) in his *Atlantic Canada and Confederation: Essays in Canadian Political Economy* (Toronto 1983), 87

4 Richard Simeon, *Federal-Provincial Diplomacy: The Making of Recent Policy in Canada* (Toronto 1972), 119; Roy Romanow, John Whyte, and Howard Lesson, *Canada Notwithstanding: The Making of the Constitution, 1967–1982* (Toronto 1984), 83–4

5 Kenneth Norrie, Richard Simeon, and Mark Krasnick, *Federalism and the Economic Union in Canada*, vol. 59 of report of the Royal Commission on the Economic Union and Development Prospects for Canada (Toronto 1986), 278–9

6 J.W. Warnock, *Free Trade and the New Right Agenda* (Vancouver 1988), 145–8; D.P. Kerr, 'Metropolitan Dominance in Canada,' in John Warkentin (ed.), *Canada: A Geographical Interpretation* (Toronto 1968), 531–5; J.M.S. Careless, 'Aspects of Metropolitanism in Atlantic Canada,' in Mason Wade (ed.), *Regionalism in the Canadian Community* (Toronto 1969),

117–29. See also T.W. Acheson, 'The Maritimes and "Empire Canada,"'
in David Jay Bercuson (ed.), *Canada and the Burden of Unity* (Toronto
1977), 87–114; L.D. McCann, 'Metropolitanism and Branch Businesses in
the Maritimes, 1881–1931,' *Acadiensis* 13:1 (Autumn 1983), 111–25.

7 *Report: Royal Commission on the Economic Union and Development Prospects
for Canada* 3 vols (Ottawa 1985) 2:459, 815–16, 824–6, 3:395–6

8 Robert Bothwell, Ian Drummond, and John English, *Canada since 1945:
Power, Politics and Provincialism* (Toronto 1989), 458

9 Atlantic Provinces Transportation Commission (APTC), *Transportation Review and Annual Report, 1986–87*, 37

10 M.J. Laslovich, *Changing the Crow Rate: State-Societal Interaction*, Depart-
ment of Political Science, Carleton University, Occasional Paper No. 11
(Ottawa 1985), 27; James F. Hickling Management Consultants Ltd, *The
Impact of Freight Transportation Subsidies under the Maritime Freight Rates
Act and the Atlantic Region Freight Assistance Act* (Ottawa 1983), 13, 20

11 *Freedom to Move: A Framework for Transportation Reform* (Ottawa 1985);
APTC, *Impact of Future Changes in Railway Services in the Maritime Provinces* (Moncton 1987), 26; Forbes, *Challenging the Regional Stereotype*,
136–47

12 Canada, *Thirty-Fourth General Election Report of the Chief Electoral Officer:
Appendix A* (Ottawa 1989), 19

13 *Managing All Our Resources: A Development Plan for Newfoundland and Labrador, 1980–85* (St John's 1980), xii, xiii

14 Canada, *Report of the Royal Commission Inquiry into Newfoundland Transportation*, 2 vols (St John's 1978), vol 1

15 *CAR* (1983), 309–13, and *CAR* (1984), 303

16 Quoted in IDP Consultants Ltd, *Newfoundland's Offshore Oil and Gas Industry: An Analysis of the Variables Affecting Present and Future Involvement of Local Business*, Royal Commission on Employment and Unemployment, Newfoundland and Labrador (St John's 1986), 36

17 *CAR* (1983), 313

18 *Building on Our Strengths: Report of the Royal Commission on Employment
and Unemployment* (St John's 1986), 441

# Illustration Credits

Acadia University Archives: page 75 (painting by Mrs. Eva Scott, reproduced by permission of Acadia Divinity College), 253 (McRitchie Collection, 8 December 1925, Row 1 #4); 265

*Atlantic Advocate*: 378, 379, 397, 399, 408, 415, 435, 441, 446, 465, 477, 486, 489

Beaton Institute for Cape Breton Studies, Sydney: 91, 165 (77-620–75Y), 247, 250, 341, 456

Black Cultural Centre, Dartmouth: 17, 451

Chambers Collection, Acadia University Archives, courtesy of Robert Chambers and *The Chronicle-Herald* and *The Mail Star*: xi, 278, 308, 309, 323, 334, 411, 418, 425, 427, 492, 493

Charles P. deVolpi Collection, Special Collections Department, Dalhousie University Library: 18, 20, 23, 51, 60, 64, 66, 68, 71, 78, 94, 107, 144

Coady International Institute, Antigonish: 292

Maritime Museum of the Atlantic, Halifax: 24 (N-16,766), 62 (N-10,988); 313 (N-14,433); 368 (N-12,963)

National Archives of Canada: 33 (C733); 215 (PA22744); 320 (top PA122582, bottom PA168014); 331 (C45315); 387 (PA115449)

New Brunswick Museum: 193 (X12493)

Nova Scotia Information Service: 385 (35263), 406 (9680), 470 (26904), 474 (26004)

Prince Edward Island Public Archives and Records Office: 35 (268415); 122 (Acc. 2320, Item 42/8); 138 (Acc. 2689, Item 62); 213 (Acc. 2767/107); 237 (Acc. 3466, Item 73-129-25); 240 (P.E.I. Heritage Foundation Collection, Acc. 3466, Item 78-95-19); 335 (Acc. 2320, Item 41-11)

Provincial Archives of New Brunswick, Fredericton: 25 (P5-170); 30 (Tupper P61-351, Tilley P37-40); 72 (P37-402); 85 (P11-87); 113 (P13-51); 128 (cotton mill P5-318A, Gibson P37-488-2); 134 (P5-330); 147 (P18-216); 168 (P11-105); 177 (P38-204); 181 (P5-181); 185 (P123-5); 188 (P145-61); 204 (P61-405); 217 (P107-1); 227 (P98-43); 243 (P11-73); 273 (P28-8); 279 (P37-

# Contributors

PHIL BUCKNER holds degrees from the universities of Toronto and London. A member of the history department at the University of New Brunswick, he was the founding editor of *Acadiensis: Journal of the History of the Atlantic Region*. His publications include *The Transition to Responsible Government in British North America, Eastern and Western Perspectives*, and *Teaching Maritime Studies*.

MARGARET CONRAD holds degrees from Acadia University and the University of Toronto. She teaches at Acadia University and is a former co-editor of *Atlantis: A Women's Studies Journal*. Her publications include *George Nowlan: Maritime Conservative in National Politics*, (co-editor) *No Place Like Home: Diaries and Letters of Nova Scotia Women 1771–1938*, and (editor) *They Planted Well: New England Planters in Maritime Canada*.

JUDITH FINGARD holds degrees from Dalhousie University and the University of London. She is a faculty member at Dalhousie University. Her publications include *The Anglican Design in Loyalist Nova Scotia, Jack in Port: Sailortowns of Eastern Canada*, and *The Dark Side of Life in Victorian Halifax*.

ERNIE FORBES holds degrees from Mount Allison, Dalhousie, and Queen's universities. He teaches at the University of New Brunswick. His publications include *The Maritime Rights Movement, 1919–1927: A Study in Canadian Regionalism* and *Challenging the Regional Stereotype: Essays on the 20th Century Maritimes*.

DAVID FRANK holds degrees from the University of Toronto and Dalhousie University. He teaches at the University of New Brunswick, where he edits *Acadiensis*. His publications include *Echoes from Labor's War, Industrialization and Underdevelopment in the Maritimes, The New Brunswick Worker*, and *George MacEachern: An Autobiography*.

JAMES K. HILLER holds degrees from Cambridge University. He teaches at

Memorial University. His publications, which reflect his interests in economic and political history, include *Newfoundland in the Nineteenth and Twentieth Centuries: Essays in Interpretation*.

COLIN HOWELL holds degrees from Dalhousie University and the University of Cincinnati. A founder of the Gorsebrook Institute and former co-editor of the *Canadian Historical Review*, he teaches at Saint Mary's University. His publications include *A Century of Care: A History of the Victoria General Hospital in Halifax, 1887–1987* and (co-editor) *Jack Tar in History: Essays in the History of Maritime Life and Labour*.

LARRY McCANN holds degrees from the universities of Victoria and Alberta. Director and Davidson Professor of Canadian Studies at Mount Allison University from 1987 to 1992, he currently teaches in the geography department at the University of Victoria. His publications include *Heartland and Hinterland: A Geography of Canada* and *People and Place: Studies of Small Town Life in the Maritimes*.

IAN McKAY holds degrees from Warwick and Dalhousie universities. He teaches at Queen's University. His publications include *The Craft Transformed: An Essay on the Carpenters of Halifax, 1885–1985* and (co-edited) *People, Resources and Power: Critical Perspectives on Underdevelopment and Primary Industries in the Atlantic Region*. He is an editor of *New Maritimes*, published in Halifax.

CARMAN MILLER holds degrees from Acadia and Dalhousie universities and Kings College, University of London. He teaches at McGill University. His publications include *The Fourth Earl of Minto: The Education of a Viceroy* and *Painting the Map Red: Canada and the South African War*.

DEL MUISE holds degrees from St Francis Xavier and the University of Western Ontario. Formerly at the National Museum he now teaches at Carleton University. His publications, which reflect his interests in the confederation era and industrialization, include *A Reader's Guide to Canadian History* and *Coal-mining in Nova Scotia to 1925*.

JOHN REID holds degrees from Memorial University and the University of New Brunswick. He teaches at Saint Mary's University. His publications include *Acadia, Maine and New Scotland: Marginal Colonies in the Seventeenth Century*, *Mount Allison University: A History, Volumes 1 and 2*, and *Six Crucial Decades: Times of Change in the History of the Maritimes*.

DELLA STANLEY holds degrees from Mount Allison University and the University of New Brunswick. She teaches at Mount Saint Vincent University, where she is Co-ordinator of Canadian Studies. Her publications include *Pierre-Armand Landry: Au Service de deux Peuples* and *Louis Robichaud: A Decade of Power.*

# Index